LIDIA'S
MASTERING THE ART OF
ITALIAN CUISINE

LIDIA'S
MASTERING THE ART OF
ITALIAN CUISINE

Everything You Need to Know to Be a Great Italian Cook

Lidia Matticchio Bastianich
with
Tanya Bastianich Manuali

Alfred A. Knopf
New York
2015

**THIS IS A BORZOI BOOK
PUBLISHED BY ALFRED A. KNOPF**

Copyright © 2015 by Tutti a Tavola, LLC

All rights reserved. Published in the United States by Alfred A. Knopf, a division of
Penguin Random House LLC, New York, and in Canada by Appetite by Random House,
a division of Penguin Random House Canada, Ltd., Toronto.

www.aaknopf.com

Knopf, Borzoi Books, and the colophon are registered trademarks of
Penguin Random House LLC.

Library of Congress Cataloging-in-Publication Data
Bastianich, Lidia.
Lidia's mastering the art of Italian cuisine : everything you need to know to be a
great Italian cook / by Lidia Matticchio Bastianich, with Tanya Bastianich Manuali.—
First edition.
pages cm
ISBN 978-0-385-34946-8 (hardcover) —ISBN 978-0-385-34947-5 (eBook)
1. Cooking, Italian. I. Manuali, Tanya Bastianich. II. Title.
III. Title: Mastering the art of italian cuisine.
TX723.B3227 2015
641.5945—dc23 2015001871

Jacket illustration by Anthony Volpe
Jacket design by Kelly Blair

Manufactured in the United States of America
First Edition

TO ALL THE PASSIONATE COOKS IN THE WORLD:

For those of you who have invited me and my recipes into your kitchen, thank you.
Let's continue to create more delicious and easy Italian dishes together.

For those who are new to my recipes and guidance,
I look forward to being part of your kitchen as I share with you
my passion for and knowledge of Italian food.

LET'S GET COOKING!

Tutti a tavola a mangiare!

CONTENTS

ACKNOWLEDGMENTS

MY INFINITE GRATITUDE for my first experiences in the kitchen, which are the foundation and the basis for my passion and love of cooking today, belongs to my maternal grandmother Rosa, who nurtured me, inspired me, and taught me much about food and about life in that small courtyard, more than sixty years ago. An equal amount of gratitude I have for my mother, Erminia, who has always encouraged me and been by my side helping me and sharing with me the raising of my family, so that I could pursue my passion and my profession, cooking. Much love and gratitude also to my coauthor and daughter, Tanya Bastianich Manuali. Without her brilliant organizational, research, and writing skills this book might never have happened. Her loving support, encouragement, and collaboration give me the strength and desire to write ever more recipes and carry on with her our culinary traditions.

Such a comprehensive book can only be a collaboration of many. Deep appreciation goes to Amy Stevenson, who is always by my side as we cook, measure, and create: she is a true gem and I am honored to be her friend. A big thank-you to Peter Gethers and Christina Malach, whose ideas, tweaking, and input made this a better book. Thank you to Jenna Brickley for not letting any of the details escape us. Thank you to Paul Bogaards for our many years of working together and for his friendship. To the Knopf promotional team of Sara Eagle and Erin McGrath, much thanks for getting the word out there and supporting this book. It is always a pleasure to work with Kristen Bearse and, in addition, her keen eye and sense of design are incomparable. Kelly Blair, thank you for making the cover look wonderful and knowing what we want to put our best foot forward. For the wonderful drawings, I give heartfelt thanks to Anthony Volpe, who really worked *con passione.*

Thank you to my restaurant and office staff; only with their support am I able to find the time to write my books. Thank you to the American Public Television team for always doing a stellar job distributing my show. And thanks to the wonderful team at my presenting station, WGBH in Boston—Laurie Donnelly, Anne Adams, Bara Levin, and Matthew Midura. Their enthusiasm is contagious and their professionalism is exemplary. My show would not be possible without my sponsors: Cento and Il Consorzio del Grana Padano, and thanks to the wonderful showroom consultants at Clarke who, along with Sub-Zero Refrigeration and Wolf, have provided me with my beautiful new kitchen.

INTRODUCTION

SOMEHOW FOOD HAS always been a very big part of my life, not only for breakfast, lunch, and dinner, but as part of my existence, part of my growing up, and ultimately my life's dedication. I grew up in Istria, a small peninsula in the Adriatic. It was once the northeast corner of Italy; then after World War II, it was given to Yugoslavia, a newly formed communist country, and it is now part of Croatia. Life was meager in my formative years under the communist regime, but I was blessed with my rich heritage and a loving family, in which Grandma Rosa and Grandpa Giovanni grew, produced, cured, and dried most of the food that we needed. Our house was set in the center of a courtyard, with the animals' pens on the outside of the courtyard. This was on an unpaved street in a small town called Busoler, with our planting fields standing next to the courtyard and other homes. I was Grandma Rosa's little assistant, and I loved it. Milking the goats and helping to make ricotta, collecting the still-warm eggs and helping to make fresh pasta, collecting clover to feed the bunnies—these were all my jobs. I would tag along for the harvest of the grapes when it was time for Grandpa to make the wine, and would climb up the olive trees in November to harvest the hard-to-reach olives for Grandma. November was also the season for the slaughter; one of my jobs was to hold the casing while Grandma filled the sausages; another was to bring the salt to Grandpa so he could rub it into the hind legs of the pig, which he would cure and then slice into delicious thin slices of prosciutto by late summer. The plowing and planting of the earth started in February and March, and I would be in charge of bringing the *merenda,* a midafternoon snack, to Grandpa in the fields. As the vegetables and fruits grew, I had my little basket ready for the harvest. The summer was glorious with all the delicious fruits. First the strawberries and cherries, then the apricots, peaches, plums, figs, and grapes; in the fall, we had pears, apples, almonds, and walnuts. The process of saving the extra summer bounty for the long cold winter months was a lot of work: shelling the dry beans, braiding the garlic, canning the tomatoes, and laying the figs and prunes in the summer sun to dry to be enjoyed in the holiday desserts. Those flavors, aromas, and sentiments are still part of me, of my passion, and who I am today as a chef.

When my mother and father decided to escape communism and bring my brother and me back to Italy, it was a difficult transition. The family was happy to be in Italy and free but economically under stress. In the aftermath of the war, jobs were hard to find and my parents decided to stay in a political-refugee camp, the Risiera di San Sabba, on the outskirts of Trieste, and await the chance to emigrate to the United States. After two years, in 1958, we received our visa approval and came to New York with the assistance of Catholic Relief Services. It was a very difficult adjustment for me. I felt my umbilical cord of contentment and security severed. I missed Grandma Rosa and Grandpa Giovanni so very much, and the memories of that time and of that food remained my connecting link; it has been my passion ever since. When I cook, the aromas and flavors I recall bring me back to that courtyard in Busoler, and I want to share my passion and my memories ever more with the world through my restaurants, my TV shows, and my books.

Over the past forty-six years, I have proudly shared with America the richness, deliciousness, and beauty of Italian food. I was fortunate to have been born into such a fecund culture and have had the privilege of being able to communicate my traditions to my adopted home, America. My passion is now to share and to teach, and this book provides the forum for me to collect everything I want to communicate to you in one place, in one big book, my master class. Here I have gathered my life's memories, my philosophy, my passion, my art. These are the ingredients I love to cook with, and the cooking techniques I have learned and developed through my forty-plus years in the kitchen. I have dedicated forty-six years of my life to that early passion, and continue to do so with enthusiasm, but there are milestones along the way that make you reflect, make you feel the need to put down on paper all you have collected and deemed important along the way. This book is one of those milestones, a milestone of nearly half a century of experience that I want to share with you. I will share with you tips for buying and storing food, the delight of cooking and eating with the seasons, the traditional foods of Italy that bring the flavors of my homeland to your home and table, all included in the more than four hundred recipes on these pages. Italian food is always about authentic ingredients, intense flavors, and the enjoyment that comes when family and friends get together. I want you to beckon your family to the table with good food cooked with love. And I want to impart every bit of wisdom I have, so you can feel confident in the kitchen and spend more time enjoying your family and friends at the table.

All of the above might seem difficult to achieve, but I like to keep it simple in the kitchen, because Italian food at its best is simple. That means being straightforward in my explanations as well as creating recipes that lead to easy, successful cooking. One of the most important parts of the cooking process is understanding the ingredients, and then the tools and techniques needed to elevate them. The first portion of this book includes a comprehensive guide to the ingredients I love and use most often. From vegetables to pastas, cheeses, other proteins, and more, I clearly explain the cooking techniques that you must master to use these ingredients with ease. I explain to you in detail the tools that are most important to me and that help make those tasty dishes. There are short explanations about each region of Italy, and a discussion about olive oils, cheeses, and wines. In the appendix, there are even some phrases you can use when traveling and dining in Italy or at your local Italian restaurant. And at the back of the book you'll find a full glossary of the Italian words most often used when referring to food.

Within the section on ingredients, I share with you how to buy, store, and prepare vegetables. Maybe you are put off by artichokes because you think they are difficult to clean and cook, but they are one of my favorite ingredients, and I will teach you how to clean them in a jiffy. My tip for poached eggplant will help you use this delicious ingredient in several different recipes based on this simple technique, rather than always serving it fried. Crushing tomatoes properly, baking radicchio, and storing strawberries and cherries are all skills that I know will become your own. If you are not familiar with the deliciousness and intensity of flavor in tomato paste, I will share with you how and when to use it. Also, I will pass along nutritional tips, which I am learning more and more about as we become more aware of the effects of food on our overall health. How do you store truffles and preserve their intoxicating aroma? What is the right consistency for pasta dough? These and many more questions are all answered in this book. In writing the book, I have wanted to enter your kitchen and be by your side when you ask yourself, What do I do next? I want your kitchen to be your comfort zone.

I love a kitchen that is full of aromas; herbs and spices are important to me when I cook. They can make all the difference in a dish, and I want you to use them and establish an ease in handling and adding them to your recipes. So I will teach you how to buy, store, and use them with conviction. You'll come away from this book knowing how to cut up a chicken, how to fillet a fish, and what pasta shapes are best paired with which sauce. I share with you my favorite cooking techniques: how to roast, steam, grill, braise, broil, sauté, and many others. Cleaning calamari or cooking a whole fish becomes a simple task, and before even getting to the cooking, I will talk you through what to look for at the market to buy the freshest fish. I'm often asked what are the essential cooking tools that each person should have in the kitchen, so I've included it. No meal would be complete without some wine, so I will walk you through making wine and beverage choices that you can best enjoy with your Italian meal.

My teachers have been my traditions, my family, Grandma Rosa, and all the grandmothers and mothers I met along the way in my yearly returns to Italy, who openheartedly shared their family recipes with me. I also thank all the professionals who took me into their kitchens, and the food artisans who shared their passion with me. I feel gratitude for all of them, and a need to continue to share the tips I learned from them. You have invited me into your homes with my books and on the television screen, and you have visited me in my restaurants. You have cooked my pasta, dressed it with my sauce, and enjoyed it with a sip of my wines. I love the connection we have, and I want it to continue. I offer this book to you, a book in which I have collected the results of my many years as an Italian cook-chef. This book is very sentimental to me and I share it with you like a dowry a mother gives her young bride. It's all in this book, everything you need to know to cook Italian food. *Lidia's Mastering the Art of Italian Cuisine* is my most comprehensive book on Italian cooking so far. Make it your own, for knowledge is power, and this book will give you the tools and know-how to be the master of Italian cooking in your kitchen.

INGREDIENTS
AND TECHNIQUES

INGREDIENTS

Dalla mia cucina alla vostra.
—Lidia Bastianich

From my kitchen to yours.

IN ITALY AND ELSEWHERE IN EUROPE, there are abbreviations on food-product labels that might be confusing but provide a guarantee; when buying Italian products, look for them.

These marks protect the Italian product and guarantee it as being made in Italy. Some Italian sellers and many non-Italian producers make products in the Italian style that are not grown or made in Italy. The designations guarantee that your purchase is authentically Italian.

DOP, or Denominazione di Origine Protetta, is a mark endorsed by the European Community to promote and guarantee that the food or agricultural product you are about to buy is consistent in its authenticity and artisan characteristics, and that it represents the designated geographical area for that product.

IGP, Indicazione Geografica Protetta, applies to agricultural products and foods whose qualities derive from the growth and transformation of a specific area.

DOCG, Denominazione di Origine Controllata e Garantita, applies to wine-production zones and determines specific wine-growing zones, ensuring that a specific wine is produced from officially prescribed grapes or blend of grapes.

Fruits and Vegetables

Vegetables are the protagonists and excel in Italian cuisine. Pasta might hold the title as the most popular category, but as far as I am concerned, vegetables and legumes are the silent winners. Italy has a year-round growing season and is one big garden; vegetables are not only side dishes but are at the base of most Italian main dishes, from meats to fish to pasta. The freshness, flavors, and colors of Italian cuisine are due to the vegetables. Unlike in many other cultures, where proteins reign, in Italy a meal might be 60 to 70 percent vegetables and legumes.

Italians like to cook with fruit. The natural sugar in fruit is favored in Italian desserts, which tend to be less sweet. Many desserts have fruit baked right in them. Berries are used when in season to top ice cream or dolci al cucchiaio or other desserts eaten with a spoon. Often fruits are poached or baked and served warm. Fruit renders best in cooking and is its sweetest when perfectly ripe, just before it begins to decay. Of course, fruits should be used and eaten in season.

Always wash your produce, and use all your senses when buying it. For example, artichokes should squeak, so use your ears. Do not prep produce far in advance of when you will be cooking with it—it can oxidize and become discolored and lose some of its aromas, nutrients, and freshness. Store produce properly: Onions and potatoes must stay in a cool, dark place. Refrigerate items such as broccoli or spinach, and try not to refrigerate items such as tomatoes. Fresh herbs should be stored in a damp towel, or in a vase with water, like flowers. Allow fruit to ripen naturally at room temperature, or in a brown paper bag, which speeds up the process. You can revive leafy greens in a bath of cold water in the sink; this not only washes the produce, but also freshens it up.

ALMONDS

Some of the best almonds grow in Sicily, a region known for its extensive repertoire of almond dishes. Blooming almond trees, which are fruit trees, are a beautiful sight, like white clouds dotting the landscape in spring, especially around the towns of Noto and Avola. One of the most traditional and well-known Sicilian desserts is pasta reale, the almond paste that so many Sicilian desserts are made with, such as little white lamb-shaped treats sold around Easter, cassata, and the beautiful fruit macaroons. Almond trees were brought to Sicily from Asia by the Greeks in the fifth century B.C. and grew throughout the island in profusion. Crushing fresh almonds in water to make almond milk is a tradition among Sicilians; they allow the mixture to steep for a day or two, strain it, and then drink the liquid. One could compare it to coconut milk. Almond milk is a refreshing drink, and is delicious poured over ice on a hot summer day. In the warmer months, ice cream and sorbet are made with this natural almond water. In Italy, the almond drink known as orzata is available at bars and stores all over the country.

APPLES

The apple is one of the most widely cultivated fruits. There are more than seven thousand different varieties. Originating in China, it has been grown in Asia and Europe for thousands of years, and was brought to North America by the colonists. The United States is now the second-largest producer of apples, but Italy does its share of growing and using apples, especially in the Val di Non in the Trentino–Alto Adige region. Besides eating apples as a fruit and using them in desserts, I find apples delicious in salads, paired with roasted or cooked vegetables, and baked or sautéed with meats, especially pork, game, and fowl. Applesauce is a great fat substitute for low-fat baking. Simply substitute half as much apple-sauce as the fat that is called for.

ARTICHOKES

Artichokes are one of my favorite vegetables. People shy away from cooking with them because of the seemingly laborious process for cleaning and prepping them, but I love their taste, their look, and their versatility. They can be stuffed, baked, fried whole, thinly sliced for a salad, or used in a pasta sauce or a grand risotto. The part of the artichoke plant we eat is actually a thistle flower prior to blooming. If the thistle is left on the plant, it will turn into a flower with a beautiful purple center. The artichoke is easier to handle and to eat when it is small and young; a larger artichoke, though still delicious, needs to have its tough outer leaves plucked off, its stem cleaned, and its beard in the center cleaned out prior to being used in cooking. Artichokes come in seven or more sizes, so make sure you buy the best size for the recipe. They should be firm, almost squeaky when pressed, and vibrant green, sometimes with tinges of purple. Brownish streaks in the leaves indicate that the artichoke is old. Look for and always ask for ones with the stems attached: the stem acts as a reserve food supply for the vegetable and will keep it fresh longer. Springtime is the best season for artichokes, usually around April and May. If you are in Rome, the Italian capital of artichoke eating, every single restaurant menu will have artichokes prepared several ways—braised, fried, sautéed, with pasta, with meat, artichokes every way. In May, the artichokes are big enough to yield good portions, but they have not developed the inside beard, so they are tender and can be eaten whole. The soft inner heart part is the prized section of the artichoke, although I do enjoy very much scraping the pulp off the inner leaves and sucking out the juice when I braise or bake them—a little messy but loads of fun. The cardoon, the artichoke variety that is indigenous to the Mediterranean Basin, was known to be used in cookery in ancient Greece and Rome. Today Italy is the top country in artichoke cultivation and production in the world—all varieties of artichoke. Artichokes come in different color varieties; most are green, but in Italy the large purple artichoke, Romanesco, is particularly prized. In the United States, Castroville, California, is the epicenter of artichoke production. During their off-season, there are always artichoke hearts jarred in oil or vinegar, which are good for antipasto, and can be added to sauces, battered and fried, or added to salads.

CLEANING ARTICHOKES Fill a bowl with cold water, and add the juice of one lemon plus the squeezed-out lemon halves. Peel and trim the stem of an artichoke. Pluck off any tough outer leaves and discard. Using a paring knife, trim away any tough parts around the base and stem of the artichoke. With a serrated knife, cut off the top third of the artichoke petals and discard.

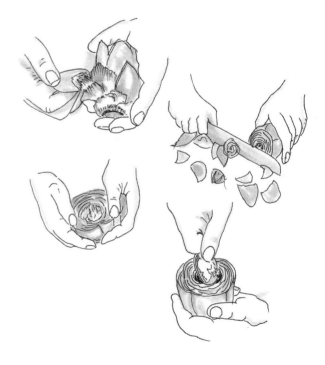

Now push the leaves out gently to expose the fuzzy purple choke. With a small spoon, scrape out all of the choke to expose the heart at the bottom of the artichoke. Put the prepared artichoke in the bowl of water with the lemon juice, to keep it from oxidizing (turning brown), and finish cleaning the remaining artichokes. If you are particular about your hands, wear gloves during cleaning: artichokes will also leave a dark brown stain on your hands, and sometimes the outer leaves are sharp and will pinch.

ARUGULA

Arugula is an aromatic, peppery salad green of the mustard family that is very popular in Italian cuisine and grows wild all over the Mediterranean. There are several varieties of domesticated and wild arugula on the market, different in the shape of their leaves and in the intensity of flavor. Usually, the thinner and spikier the leaves, the more peppery the taste. When buying any arugula, look for fresh, firm, vibrant green leaves. They should not be wilted, yellowing, or slimy. When buying packaged arugula, make sure the bag contains no excess water, because moisture can cause arugula to rot quickly. It should be stored in the refrigerator and kept dry. Arugula is delicious in salads, as a sandwich stuffer, sautéed and cooked in soups or frittatas, made into a pesto, or combined with garlic to make a sauce for pasta.

ASPARAGUS

This popular vegetable is best when it's in season, from February through June. Although green is the most common, white and purple asparagus are good options as well. White asparagus is grown slightly covered by mulch or plastic, which prevents photosynthesis, resulting in its white color. As with green asparagus, the tips of the white asparagus are tasty and sweet, but the stem can be woody and must be discarded. On the other hand, purple asparagus is more like the green, but it loses its purple coloring during cooking. Once the stems are peeled and trimmed, they become more tender. When buying asparagus, look for firm, bright green stalks with tight tips. I recommend buying them on the day you'd like to prepare them. If you do need to store them, wrap them in a damp paper towel and set them, stems down, in a container with an inch of water; they should remain fresh for three to four days in the refrigerator. When preparing asparagus, peel the lower two-thirds of each stem with a potato peeler. Then cut off the tough bottom of the stem, usually about an inch. Asparagus is great blanched, steamed, roasted, grilled, or pan-sautéed. When I find myself in Italy in the spring, I love to go foraging for wild asparagus; the stalks of wild asparagus are much thinner than regular asparagus, and have a more pronounced bitter taste, which I love. Through my travels in America, I have looked for wild asparagus but have not yet found any.

BEETS

Look for medium-sized beets that are firm and have a smooth skin. There are many different varieties besides the more common red beet, such as yellow, orange, and Chioggia red-and-white beets. Try to use beets from March to October, when they are at their best. When they are young and the leaves are small, green, and crisp, try slicing them thin or grating them raw and tossing them in a salad. One of my favorite ways to use beets is to make beet risotto, which has great flavor and color. When cooking with beets, you should boil or bake them first and then peel them. At that point you can use them in salads, soups, or risottos, and feel free to experiment. Beets with hairy root tips tend to be tougher. Make sure you use the greens. When they are smaller, and blanched, they are delicious tossed in a salad; boil the larger ones and serve them as a delicious vegetable, dressed with olive oil and vinegar. Too often these nutritious and delicious leaves are discarded.

BELL PEPPERS

The pepper family is a large group of vegetables with flavors ranging from sweet to extremely spicy. Italian cooking most often uses the sweet bell pepper. It can vary in color from green to yellow, red, brown, purple, or orange. The color does not make a major difference to the taste, although the red ones are more ripe than green, and in general, the more brightly colored the peppers, the sweeter the flavor.

When choosing peppers always look for firm, taut skin. A pepper that has a bright green stem and feels heavy when picked up is also good. Avoid shriveled peppers with soft or brown spots. Store unwashed, uncut peppers in the vegetable compartment of your refrigerator, and they can keep well for up to ten days.

Peppers are a very rich source of antioxidants and vitamin C. They are indigenous to Mexico and northern South America and were brought to Europe by Columbus.

They are easy to prepare by simply cutting them in half, removing the seeds and inner membrane, and cutting out the stems, then proceeding to cut as per the recipe instructions.

TWO WAYS TO ROAST PEPPERS Roasting peppers imparts a subtle flavor to them, softens their texture, and makes it easy to remove the skin, which some people find hard to digest. Here are two ways to roast a pepper. Whether you are roasting green, red, or yellow peppers, choose thick-fleshed peppers that are boxy in shape—they will char more evenly and be easier to peel.

Turn the gas burners on high and, working with a pair of long-handled tongs, place the peppers on the grates, directly over the flames. Roast the peppers, turning them as necessary, until evenly blackened on all sides, about eight minutes. Remove the peppers, place them in a bowl, and cover tightly with plastic wrap. Let stand until they are cool enough to handle.

Or place a rack in the uppermost position and preheat the oven to 475 degrees Fahrenheit. Put the peppers on a baking sheet and roast them, turning as necessary, until all sides are evenly blackened, about twelve minutes. Remove the peppers to a bowl and cover tightly with plastic wrap. Again, let them stand until they are cool enough to handle.

To peel the peppers: Pull out the stems and hold the peppers upside down, letting the seeds and juices flow out. Cut the peppers in half lengthwise and, using a short knife, scrape away the blacked skin, ribs, and remaining seeds. If there are still some seeds and skin, rinse the peppers under running cold water, quickly so as not to lose too many flavorful juices.

BROCCOLI

Broccoli, found year-round, is part of the cabbage family and is closely related to cauliflower. In Italian, *broccoli* means "cabbage sprout." Because of its different components, broccoli provides a variety of tastes and textures, ranging from soft and flowery to fibrous and crunchy. The most popular broccoli sold in the United States is known as Italian green, or Calabrese, named after the Italian province of Calabria, where it first grew. When buying broccoli, look for firm stalks with tightly closed florets. The florets should be a blue-green or purplish-green color. Small yellow buds mean the broccoli has passed its prime. When storing broccoli, refrigerate it in a loosely sealed plastic bag for up to three days. To cook broccoli, separate the stalks from the florets and wash thoroughly. But do not throw away the stalks; I peel them like potatoes, then cut them into strips and cook them with the florets.

ROMANESCO BROCCOLI is green and strikingly pointed; it is a favorite in the area around Rome and is best served steamed whole and topped with grated pecorino.

BROCCOLI RABE

Found from the fall to the spring, broccoli rabe is popular in Italy and is cooked in many fashions. Also called rapini in Italy, it is in the mustard family and has a slightly bitter finish. It resembles broccoli in that it grows like a small bouquet of tender green leaves with small florets. When preparing broccoli rabe, you want to make sure you remove the lower leaves, which are tough and have a pungent, bitter flavor. The slender green florets are the best part. Clip off about a third of the lower part of the stems, remove the tough larger leaves, and, if the remaining stems are tough, peel them with a standard potato peeler. Wash in plenty of cold water, and drain. If using for pasta sauce cut them crosswise in shorter pieces. You can blanch it, braise it, or steam it; it is especially good with sausage, garlic, and oil, and also delicious cooked with bacon or anchovies. It makes a great vegetable side, appetizer, or pasta dressing, and the leftovers make great sandwiches.

BRUSSELS SPROUTS

Brussels sprouts are not everyone's vegetable of choice, because if they are cooked as whole florets the center can be quite strong-tasting. To make Brussels sprouts delicious, cut them in half and peel off all tough outer leaves, then proceed to cook them your favorite way. I usually pan-cook them with olive oil and a little garlic, and at the end I add a touch of red wine vinegar. With their strong, nutty flavor, Brussels sprouts go well with any rich meat, including ham, duck, and game. When buying, you should look for firm sprouts that are compact and heavy and have a bright green color. Brussels sprouts are best between the months of September and February.

CABBAGE

Green, savoy, red, bok choy, Brussels sprouts, kale, and cavolo nero are all part of the cabbage family. Vegetables in the cruciferous family are rich in nutrients but also quite accessible and affordable. In Italy, cabbage is used mostly in the winter months, when it is in season and at its best. The green cabbage is great for salads, stuffed, or fermented into sauerkraut, but I like to cook with savoy cabbage as a vegetable, and with some pancetta it makes a great pasta sauce. Cavolo nero is also a favorite in Tuscany, to make ribollita soup or, once braised, piled on a grilled piece of bread to make a bruschetta. Cabbage is quite resilient and keeps well longer then other vegetables; in the refrigerator, it can keep up to a month. This makes it a good vegetable to have in the house when you don't shop daily.

CAPERS

Caper berries are the fruit of the caper plant, after the flower has blossomed. You can find them packed in a briny vinegar solution. Caper berries, the seed-containing fruit, are crunchy, acidic, and flavorful—much like a pickle— with some hint of the caper's nuttiness. Caper berries are good served as a part of an antipasto, or tossed into salads, or used in a buttery pan sauce. Capers, on the other hand, are the buds before they bloom. The caper plant is a crawling plant, usually found hanging from walls, predominantly in southern Italy. If not picked, the bud of the plant will grow into a white flower with purple stems. To harvest capers, the buds of the plant are picked and preserved by dry-packing them in salt or by bottling them in brine. I prefer the ones in brine, which you should drain before using; if you choose salt-packed capers, make sure you wash them well, and salt any dishes you are preparing with them lightly.

CARDOONS

Cardoons are not well known in the United States, but they are much loved in Italy. They are grown in California and appear in our supermarkets in the winter months. The large heads are gray-green and resemble a cross between artichokes and giant heads of celery. They won't be crisp like celery, but should look fresh and feel heavy and moist. A rough rule of thumb is to buy one pound of cardoons for each two portions. To minimize discard, try to buy several lighter cardoon heads, 2½ pounds or under, rather than one big head, so you'll get a greater proportion of slender, inner stalks. In any case, you'll need to trim the stalks and cook them, leaving them a bit firm, before breading and frying them, or baking them in the oven topped with some cheese. Cardoons may seem to require a lot of work, but they are unique in taste and delicious, so do give them a try.

CARROTS

Carrots are root vegetables, usually large and orange in color and used in Italian cooking for soups or boiled as a side dish. But in today's market, especially in the spring, there is a selection of carrots that are smaller and come in a rainbow of colors. These heirloom carrots are delicious and make a great addition to the plate. Sometimes I feel that carrots are an underappreciated standby: we tend to use them for everything, but we rarely highlight them. I also love making carrot purée with a touch of nutmeg, and sometimes I add a potato or two to give the dish extra body. Whether you eat them raw, boiled, fried, or puréed, always get the best you can. Buying organic and crispy carrots with fresh greens still attached to them will ensure they stay fresh longer. Carrots are at the base of many dishes, from soups to roasts to braised meats. In Italian food, the mixture of finely diced carrots, celery, and onion is called a *soffritto,* and it is at the base of many braised recipes.

CAULIFLOWER

Cauliflower is a wonderful winter vegetable that is great served raw in salads. You can also cook cauliflower by blanching, steaming, baking, or sautéing it. Choose firm, compact heads. The attached leaves should have a bright green color. Avoid cauliflower that has spots, an aging yellowish color, or spreading florets—all strong indications that the cauliflower is getting a little old. But do experiment with different colors of cauliflower; yellow, green, purple, and the traditional white are all delicious. The yellow cauliflower seems to be nutritionally more beneficial, but once it's cooked there is not much difference in the flavor.

CELERY

Celery is a delicious vegetable, and yet it tends to be under-used. It is found most often in soups or chopped in a tuna or chicken salad. I love celery. It is always available, and it is very economical. I like it braised with tomato and olives, I like it baked in the oven topped with grated cheese, and I love making a salad with the celery leaves and shavings of Grana Padano cheese. There is not much work in cleaning celery: just peel the strings that run along the ribs, which can be annoying to eat. To remove them, I take a peeler and lightly run it along the back of the celery rib. Another method: When you are trimming the base or the top of the stalk, don't just chop away; hold the stalk in your hands and cut toward you from the inside of the stalk to the outside without cutting all the way through. Then, before finishing the cut, pull the knife toward you, with your thumb holding the uncut celery strings. The strings should peel off down the length of the stalk.

DRESS UP YOUR CELERY Celery goes extremely well with cheeses like Grana Padano, Parmigiano-Reggiano, or Gorgonzola. Take the smaller but tender ribs from a washed head of celery and fill the cavity, up into the leaves, with room-temperature sweet Gorgonzola. You can serve these stuffed celery ribs as an appetizer or a snack. Another way to enjoy the combination of celery and Gorgonzola cheese is to serve them together warm. Trim and cut the celery ribs in thirds. Cook the cut stalks in lightly salted water for ten minutes, then drain them well. Press each one lightly with the side of a knife to flatten, and set them, side by side, in a buttered baking pan. Sprinkle plenty of crumbled Gorgonzola or grated Grana Padano over them, and bake in a 425-degree oven until the cheese is melted, about five to ten minutes.

CELERY ROOT

Celery root, also known as celeriac, is a bulb in the celery family, harvested when it reaches two to three inches. The taste is similar to that of the celery stalks we are familiar with. You can buy just the bulb, but look for a bulb with the stalks attached, and use the stalks as well as the root for soups. Celery root, once peeled, is delicious in salads, stews, or roasted or boiled in the skin, then peeled and dressed. I love it mashed with potatoes. When buying celery root, look for firm and crispy bulbs. They will keep up to three months when wrapped loosely in a plastic bag and kept in the coolest part of the refrigerator.

CHERRIES

Cherries, the first stone fruit of the warm-weather season, are usually best between May and June. When buying or picking cherries, choose ones that are plump and have a deep uniform color. Fresh cherries should be clean, bright, and shiny with no blemishes. They should also be firm, although sour cherries are a bit softer. Try to avoid cherries with cuts, bruises, or stale, dry stems. Cherries are one of my favorite fruits; I recall as a child climbing the cherry tree in our backyard and not coming down until I'd had my fill. They are nutritionally very sound, full of vitamins and anti-inflammatory properties. I love the big black Bing cherries the best, but cherries come in many different shades and intensities of sweetness and color. The darker the color, the sweeter the cherry. Eating fresh cherries is my favorite, but I also love them poached with some honey, to eat in the morning with yogurt, or to add to a cherry vanilla sundae. Store cherries unwashed in a plastic bag in the refrigerator, and wash just before eating.

CHICKPEAS

Chickpeas, also called garbanzo beans, are common throughout all of Italy, but they thrive best in a warm climate and hence grow primarily in the southern regions of Italy. Chickpeas—ceci in Italian—have been a staple in Mediterranean cooking for hundreds of years and are both versatile and delicious. They are delicious in pasta sauces, as a side dish, and in soups. They are sometimes made into flour for pastas, breads, and such specialties as panelle, Sicilian chickpea fritters. They are also delicious puréed, flavored with garlicky pesto, and used as a bread spread or dip. I love them when they are fresh in the spring and the green garbanzo can be eaten directly out of the pod or tossed into a salad. In most cases, though, they are available dried, usually packaged in plastic bags, cooked and canned, or cooked and frozen. The cooked canned or frozen chickpeas can be used immediately; just rinse and use. Dried chickpeas need to soak six to eight hours in cold water, and then to boil for forty minutes before being added to a recipe. Chickpeas are nutritionally sound, not expensive, and have a nutlike taste and buttery texture.

CRANBERRIES

Cranberries are just beginning to appear in Italian markets. They are not traditionally grown in Italy, but I love cooking with them. I make chutney with them to serve with cheese or roasted meats. I love them as an ingredient in jam, for breakfast or desserts; orange-and-cranberry jam, for instance, is delicious. I add them to an apple strudel, and I toss them into roasted butternut squash. Dried cranberries are very versatile; you can substitute them almost anywhere you would use raisins, in savory or sweet dishes.

EDIBLE FLOWERS

Chefs must be careful that all the ingredients used in their dishes are safe for their guests. Often when a chef decides to use edible flowers as a garnish, they are returned to the kitchen uneaten: patrons are unsure if they can really eat the violets surrounding the salad. But think of the number of foods we categorize as vegetables when they're really flowers, such as artichokes. Violets can be found in savory dishes as well as desserts, where they are often candied. The flowers of herbs, such as basil, mint, or rosemary, will lend a flavor similar to that of the leaves. However, when cooking with flowers or including edible flowers in our food, we must pair carefully, so as not to overpower the delicate flavor of the flower. Eating flowers is a long-standing practice, dating back to Roman times, when it was also popular in the East. It's important that you make absolutely sure the flower you want to use is edible. The best scenario would be if you grew these flowers on your own, without using chemicals or pesticides in the soil. For maximum flavor, the flowers should be hand-picked early in the morning, at their peak of fullness, and used as quickly as possible. You should introduce edible flowers to your diet slowly, to check for any allergic reactions. Always rinse the flowers before use, and store in a damp paper towel in the refrigerator.

EGGPLANT

Eggplants come in many different shapes and various colors. The most common has a dark purple skin and is elongated, and plump at the bottom end. The Italian is dark purple as well, but evenly elongated. The Sicilian is a smaller version of the common eggplant but has a lighter purple coloring with white streaks. The Chinese is long and conical, with even purple coloring. There is also the white eggplant, but I find that species tough and with a lot of seeds. These are just some types you will find while shopping. Whatever kind you buy, choose eggplants that have smooth skin, shiny and free of blemishes. The body should be firm to the touch, the stem long and as green as possible. A green stem is an indication that the eggplant has been harvested recently—something that is true for all vegetables with stems, so look for stems on the vegetables you buy. I like the Italian or the Chinese eggplant best; long and conical, without the potbelly, these varieties have fewer seeds, and it is the seeds that make eggplants bitter. When you cut into an eggplant, the seeds should be fresh and white; if they are dark, the eggplant has been around for a while, and it will be more bitter. To remove some of the bitterness, slice the eggplant and layer it in a colander, sprinkling each layer with coarse salt. Put some weight on the slices, and allow them to drain for an hour. The salt will extract liquid from the eggplant, and with it some of the bitterness. Rinse the eggplant, pat dry, and proceed with the recipe. To clean the eggplant, cut off the stem and peel it. If the skin is fresh and shiny, I take off the eggplant skin in alternating strips, like a zebra, leaving about half of the skin on.

POACHED EGGPLANT Eggplants are a much-loved vegetable, particularly by Italians, and the most common way of preparing them is to fry them. Today everybody is ever more health-conscious, and frying is not the cooking technique of choice; blanching eggplant is another very good option. Medium eggplants are best for poaching. Cut in sections lengthwise, and poach in liquid that is three parts water and one part red wine vinegar. Season with salt to taste, and then marinate in olive oil, sliced garlic, and a few leaves of mint. You can enjoy poached eggplant in many ways. It is great as an antipasto—as a crostini topping, chopped into small bits with slices of prosciutto. It is also great with tuna in olive oil, marinated mackerel, or tomato sauce for pasta.

ESCAROLE

Escarole is in the endive family and is best in the cold months. The center leaves, light green in color and tender, are great for salads; the outer, tougher leaves are delicious sautéed or braised with oil and garlic, or added to some beans and made into a great soup. Typical of the endive family, there is a slight bitterness to the taste, and when escarole is fresh the leaves have a crisp texture. It is readily available and easy to clean. If you have any braised escarole left over, add it to sandwiches. Blanched escarole leaves can be filled with a bread-and-sausage stuffing, tied into small packets, and baked.

FAVA BEANS

Fava beans grow side by side in dull to bright green insulated pods that can reach a foot in length. When you buy fava beans, look for sound pods with little discoloration, and feel free to make sure they are filled with firm, fully developed beans. Empty or partially filled pods, or pods that contain tiny beans, mean a lot of wasted labor, and you may find yourself with fewer beans than you need for a specific recipe. Before you begin to shell the beans, bring a large saucepan of water to a boil. Snap the stem of each pod and use it to pull off the string that runs the length of the pod along the seam. Open the pod along this seam, and brush the beans into a bowl.

Add the beans to the boiling water, and cook them just until you can see a dark spot in the center of the bean's skin, about three minutes. Drain the beans, and refresh them with cold water until they are cool enough to handle. Drain them well. With a paring knife, pull off the dark, crescent-shaped marking at one end of each bean. Squeeze the bean out through this opening. Discard the shell. The favas are now ready to eat, or to use in a recipe. It takes about 1¼ pounds of fresh favas in the pod to yield a half-pound shelled. Sometimes you will find shelled fava beans in the market. They are just as good, but might be a bit more expensive. You will still need to blanch the beans and peel the skin off.

FENNEL

Fennel is a deliciously unique vegetable, crunchy when raw and mellow and sweet when braised or roasted. It has been used for thousands of years as an herb, a vegetable, and a spice. Fennel has a sweet licorice flavor when raw, which mellows out as it's cooked. When shopping for fennel, look for crispy, compact white bulbs and fresh green fronds. I love it braised slowly with some onions and capers, but you can also sauté, grill, steam, and bake it. Toss the fronds into a salad, or add them to soups, or use them like chopped parsley, to add color and flavor.

FIDDLEHEAD FERNS

Fiddlehead ferns are the young, unfurled shoots of actual ferns; once they mature, they are tough and inedible. They are only available for three weeks in May, and they are foraged almost anywhere in the United States—in the wild, not farmed. Despite their sci-fi looks, they taste like asparagus and artichoke. Look for bright, tightly coiled ferns, and remove any dirt by swishing them in a bowl with cold water and rubbing off excess dirt with your fingers. Cook them immediately (they'll only keep for a few days in the fridge). Blanching them will take away some of the bitterness, then use them as you would asparagus, in pesto, in risotto, tossed with buttered linguine, or sautéed with other spring goodies, like morels.

FRESH BEANS

Dried beans are a great source of vegetable proteins; they are tasty and economical. But when spring comes around and there are fresh beans to be had—such as favas, limas, or borlotti beans— make sure you indulge in some. These fresh beans are sweet and delicious and, of course, don't have to be soaked, and the cooking time is much less. They usually come in pods and need to be shelled—sometimes twice, like the favas. They make great additions to quick pasta sauces, and great soups, and they sing of spring when brought to the table on their own or as a vegetable side dish.

GARLIC

Yes, we Italians use garlic in our cooking, but it is in Italian American cooking that garlic became such a dominant seasoning. There are basically three garlic varieties in the United States: the very strong and white-skinned American garlic, Mexican garlic, and Italian garlic, which is milder and has a mauve-colored skin. Garlic is basically sold by the head; the dried heads, with their stems, may be braided and hung for storage. When buying garlic, look for a tight and compact head of cloves covered by a tight parchmentlike membrane. Avoid garlic that is soft, whose covering membrane is peeling off, or whose cloves are breaking apart. Garlic will keep up to two months when stored in a dark, cool place. Once the cloves are broken from the head, they will last one to two weeks.

A KINDER, GENTLER GARLIC Garlic's flavor is released when the cell walls are broken and the enzymes react with the flavor molecules, so the technique you use to prepare garlic affects the flavor. The more you chop garlic, the more intense the flavor and aroma; if you want a milder flavor, either slice the garlic or crush the clove and add it to your recipe. The garlic will release its aromas and still remain identifiable, so it can be removed from the dish before serving. On the other hand, if garlic is thoroughly cooked or baked, it loses its pungency. When garlic cloves are completely cooked, the enzymes responsible for the release of their harsh bite are neutralized, leaving the garlic mild-flavored. Roasted garlic can be made into a delicious purée, which melts into hot soup, lending it a lovely undertone of garlic with a velvety texture. Use roasted or poached purée of garlic to flavor sauces, dressings, roasts, and braises.

GREEN BEANS

There are more than 130 different varieties of green beans. They can be green, yellow, red, streaked, or purple, and their shapes may be thin, round, long, or flat (known as Romano). Green beans are easy to clean; just cut the stem attachment and the pointy tip. Some green beans do have a string running along the length of the pod, and that is best removed by pulling the string off when cutting the stem. Green beans are delicious and readily available, but they can be boring. So give them some complexity and flavor by melting a little Gorgonzola or some other soft, flavorful cheese into the beans. They can be a great appetizer or side dish that goes perfectly with grilled or roasted meats.

KALE

Kale—cavolo nero in Italian, also known as dinosaur kale or lacinato kale—is a delicious winter vegetable, highly nutritious, with powerful antioxidant and anti-inflammatory properties. Though black-leaf kale appears in the markets in November and continues through spring, it's best when the leaves have felt the sting of frost.

The traditional ribollita soup of Tuscany is made with black kale, stale bread, and beans; braised kale served with beans is a popular accompaniment for steak in Tuscany. Young kale cut into shreds is delicious in salads. Recently kale has reached a peak of popularity in U.S. chefs' kitchens and has segued into American homes. It is easy to prepare, whether braised or in soups, or as a vegetable, or as a pasta condiment. It is delicious and considered to be one of the most nutritious green vegetables.

LEEKS

Leeks are a member of the onion family, with a sweeter and more mellow flavor than yellow or Spanish onions. If you've never cooked with leeks before, I'd recommend substituting them for onions in a favorite recipe, to become familiar with the taste. Because leeks grow in sandy soil, you will find grit deep between the leaves. To clean them, pick away any tough outer leaves, slice from the root all the way through the leek lengthwise, then cut in half around the stalks, submerge, wash in plenty of water, let rest for ten minutes, then fish out with a spider or hand strainer, leaving the grit on the bottom. The outer, tougher green leaves are great to flavor stock, and the white and yellowish or pale green parts can be used wherever you would use onions in your recipes. I love leeks also served as a side dish or an appetizer. They can easily be steamed, dressed with olive oil and red wine vinegar, and topped with some walnuts.

LEMONS

There are endless uses for the lemon. The juice is high in acidity and is used for cocktails and lemonade, as well as in marinades for fish, as a tenderizer for meats, and as a flavoring agent for grilled fish and meat. Because of its acidity, lemon juice is also used as a preservative for fish, meats, and fruits. The rind and zest are used for their aromatic oils and flavor in baking and cooking, such as in osso buco or roast chicken, and for making chutney and preserves. The aromatic

lemon of choice in the States is the Meyer lemon; in Italy, the Sorrento lemon is a favorite, from which good limoncello is made. When buying lemons, always look for a specimen that is plump, full of juice, and not soft or shriveled. In cooking with the lemon zest, try to avoid the white pithy part, which is bitter.

LENTILS

Lentils are dried seeds, which range in size and color from tiny and nearly black to large and yellow, green, or reddish brown. Though they are usually sold in the shell, some types are shelled. Shelled lentils, which you can spot by their bright orange-pink color, will take much less time to cook and in most cases will dissolve in the cooking liquid. To prepare lentils, wash them under cold water, and plunge them into a soup or boiling water, where they should take thirty to forty minutes to cook, depending on the size. Lentils are great in soups, salads, as a side dish, and in a pasta sauce. They can also be made into a great purée to spread on bread.

MUSHROOMS/WILD MUSHROOMS

When buying mushrooms, make sure they are firm, dry, and fresh, with caps tight to the stem. Preparing mushrooms is not complicated. Trim away any tough parts—with odd-shaped mushrooms, just feel them to determine what needs trimming. And don't soak mushrooms in water when cleaning: quickly toss them in and fish them out if they're very dirty, but otherwise wipe them with a damp paper towel to remove any grit or dirt. My favorite fresh mushroom mixes have some of the amazing wild mushrooms we usually serve at Felidia: fresh porcini, chanterelles, morels, and even wilder varieties. If any of these are available, you should certainly include them with ordinary cultivated mushrooms in any of my recipes—even a few will add special flavor. All of my recipes, however, will be delicious with the domestic cultivated mushroom types available in the supermarket: common (white) mushrooms and cremini.

MORELS Morels can be found growing all over the world, in a wide variety of habitats, every spring. Their rich and complex flavor goes well with almost any food. Morels should be eaten fresh in the spring, but are delicious dried the rest of the year. The fresh morels have a slightly chewy honeycomb texture and a rich, smoky flavor. They are very popular in cream sauces, with grilled or roasted meats, or even plain, as a side dish. I love them sautéed with ramps and made into a pasta sauce or used in a frittata. Dried morels are usually added to soups, stuffings, and stews, because the flavor of the mushroom is intensified by the drying and will be brought out by the slow cooking. You can find dried morels in most stores, and the fresh ones, in the spring, in many specialty stores or farmers' markets.

PORCINI Porcini are one of the most prized varieties of wild mushrooms. In Italy, they are in season from early summer into fall. They are recognized by their batlike stipe, their smooth brown cap, and, instead of gills, a spongelike textured underlining. The tight, small ones are much appreciated raw in a salad or sliced and sautéed, whereas the larger caps and sliced stipes are great for grilling. Porcini have the flavor of meat; all you need is a drizzle of olive oil and a pinch of salt. When buying porcini, look for a firm stipe and cap, and dry, not wet or slimy. Porcini can vary in color from light cream to brown. To store them, spread the porcini on a tray lined with paper towels and cover with a slightly damp paper towel; they should keep for four or five days.

DRIED PORCINI I always have dried porcini in my cupboard. They deliver a wallop of flavor to soups, pasta sauces, or braised and grilled meats. Dried porcini can be made into porcini powder, to season meats before grilling, or to use in stuffing and breading. Make sure the porcini are crackling dry; sometimes they absorb moisture and are soft and hard to pulverize. If so, toast them lightly under the broiler, and let cool. To make a tablespoon or so of the powder, break up a quarter cup of dried porcini into pieces, put them in a spice grinder, a clean coffee grinder, or a powerful mini-chopper, and pulverize them as fine as possible. Sift the ground powder through a fine sieve. (Keep the larger pieces for another use; for instance, throw them into a sauce or stew without even hydrating them, to add loads of flavor.) Store the powder or the dried porcini for a few months sealed in a glass jar, in a dry place.

NETTLES

Admittedly, it's a chore to get nettles into the kitchen (remember to use gloves!). However, the chemicals and tiny needlelike hairs that give the stinging nettle its name and reputation are neutralized when it's cooked. Though it might sound like a hassle, cooked nettles are well worth the effort. In addition to having a beautiful deep green color and mild flavor, they're packed with nutrients. Prepare them as you would any other leafy green—steam or sauté them for dressing or stuffing pasta, add them to soups, use them to top bruschetta, or serve them as a clean and simple side dish. Nettles are just one example of the growing popularity of foraged foods; this back-to-basics trend is as good for our wallets as it is for our bodies.

ONIONS

The onion, one of the oldest cultivated vegetables, is used in cuisines around the world. Yellow onions, which are the most commonly used, have an intense flavor and caramelize when cooked, giving your dish a complex flavor. Caramelized onions are used in bases for soups and sauces; they disintegrate and make the dish richer. White onions are lighter and sweeter. I like using them for risottos, pasta sauces, and fried onion rings. The purple onion (also called red onion) has a great crunch and great color; it is best added to salads, grilled and chopped finely, or served next to grilled meats. When buying onions, make sure they are firm and tight. They should feel heavy in your hand. Onions keep well for two or three months when stored properly. Take them out of the plastic bag and spread them out in a cool, dark, well-ventilated place.

SLICING ONIONS WITHOUT TEARS When I have lots of onions to slice up, here's a simple tip I use to avoid crying my eyes out. Peel the onions, cut them in half, and wet the two pieces with cold water—I just hold them for a moment under the faucet. Shake off excess water, and cut the halves into thin slices or dice while they're still damp. The film of water that clings to the surface of the onions will prevent—or at least reduce—the dispersion of the onion vapors that cause tearing. It may not work perfectly all the time, but at least you'll be sniffling instead of bawling.

ORANGES

The orange tree is one of the most widely cultivated trees in the world. Every part of the orange can be used in the kitchen, including the juice for drinking, baking, cooking, making marinades, and mixing into dressings. When you're cooking with oranges, it is important to note the characteristics you want most for each recipe. Do you want their sweetness, acidity, or aroma? Choose the variety accordingly. The bitter orange makes a great marmalade, a favorite with our English ancestors, and the Italians love their blood orange. It seems that blood oranges, known as sanguinella, were first cultivated in Sicily around the fifteenth century. Blood-orange juice is my favorite morning drink.

PEAS

Peas are best in the spring, but can be found into summer. There is, among some cooks, a phobia about overcooking peas. To many people, peas must stay bright green and intact, little bullets running around the plate as you chase after them with a fork. Well, I love my fresh peas "smothered" until they are just about olive-green in color, when their sweetness and flavors have really concentrated and they begin to break down and cling together. I do not mean peas that are overcooked in lots of water, or steamed till they are gray-green, watery, and tasting of tobacco. Peas are delicious in just about any dish, such as various pasta dishes and soups or with fish, and also when mixed with other vegetables as a side. I also love a purée made of fresh peas; with some olive oil, it makes a great spread for bread instead of butter. Buy fresh peas in their pods, and make sure the pods are full and plump. After you shell them, they keep for a week in the refrigerator; if you freeze them raw, they are delicious when defrosted.

SNAP PEAS Snap peas, also known as sugar snap peas, differ from snow peas in that their pods are round rather than flat. The pods are juicy, crisp, sweet, and crunchy, and are delicious fresh and uncooked, right from the garden. When buying snap peas, look for a bright green color and pods that feel crisp. Snap peas are often steamed or sautéed. In addition to the pea pods, you can also harvest and enjoy eating the flower blossoms and leafy plant tips or pea shoots. In the past they were found only in the springtime, but they can now be bought year-round.

POTATOES

It's incredibly important to know the distinction between mealy and waxy potatoes before you purchase potatoes for a specific dish. Mealy potatoes, such as Idaho and russet, are also known as bakers—obviously, because they bake so well. They have a high starch content and a thick skin. These are the best potatoes for deep-frying and puréeing, as well as for making gnocchi and mashed potatoes. Waxy potatoes are a more creamy potato, such as Yukon gold and red bliss, and are best for boiling, soups, salads, and roasting with meats.

NEW POTATOES New potatoes, sometimes called creamers or fingerlings, are a younger version of other varieties of potatoes. Because of their small size, they stand up well to roasting with meats and boiling. Buy these potatoes as you need them; because of their thin skin, they can spoil quickly. Keep them in a paper bag (never plastic) in a cool, dark place, such as your pantry or basement, for up to a week. Before cooking, make sure they're well scrubbed, have smooth skin, and no visible sprouts or green spots. You can peel them before cooking, but I just scrub them well under running water and then cook them in their skins. These potatoes are delicious in potato salads and as a side dish along with braised meats and roasts.

STORING POTATOES Potatoes should be stored in a dark and cool place. Light triggers the production of chlorophyll, which makes potatoes green and bitter. You should also never wash your potatoes until you're ready to use them: they will spoil quicker. If you have leftover peeled potatoes, keep them submerged in water until you're ready to use them. Properly stored, fresh potatoes should last for two months. Potatoes shrivel because they have lost moisture when kept a long time, but do not discard them—they are still good.

PRUNES

Prunes—dried plums—are used in cooking both savory and sweet dishes. Italians are big consumers of dried prunes. They stew them with apples, quince, and other winter fruit to make a compote, from which the fruit is eaten but also the stewing liquid is drunk as a tea, especially in northern Italy in the winter months. You can have prune ice cream, prune Danish, or prune strudel, and prunes poached in bourbon are delicious over vanilla ice cream. I love to stuff a pork roast with prunes soaked in bourbon, and throw a few into the accompanying vegetables to sweeten and enhance the flavors. After opening a package of prunes, store them in a sealed jar in the refrigerator or a cool storage place.

RADICCHIO

Although it is great in a salad, sweet and bitter at the same time, in the cold winter months I like radicchio trevisano better when it has been cooked, braised, or baked, savoring its taste and texture— it is sweet, bitter, and crunchy. Radicchio makes a great risotto, or a great sauce for pasta. When buying radicchio to bake with, look for the long, thin radicchio trevisano, also known as spadone. The small round heads called Chioggia (the kind most often found in the supermarket) and trevisano (the variety with long but wide leaves, resembling purple romaine lettuce) are both great when tossed in a salad, which can be served as an antipasto or a vegetable course.

RAISINS

Raisins, which are basically dehydrated or dried grapes, are used all over the world. Besides the basic raisin, dried from large dark-colored grapes, there are the blond or sultana raisins and the smaller currants, dried from small black Corinth grapes. All three are interchangeable in cooking, baking, or brewing a beverage. In the Italian traditions, raisins are used a lot in baking and desserts, but also in stuffings, marinades, and the braising of meat or fish. They are best when they are moist, although the natural sugars tend to crystallize and make them a bit grainy. Store in a tight plastic bag in a cool place. If they do dry out, they are easy to reconstitute for cooking by soaking them in warm water. For baking, soak them in a liquor of your choice; I prefer rum.

RAMPS

Ramps, sometimes called wild leeks, resemble scallions but with broader leaves, and have a garlicky, sweet flavor. Their appearance is a sign that spring is finally here. Take advantage of their bounty when they are around. I have them for breakfast in a frittata, for lunch with pasta, and for dinner with grilled meats or fish. The season is too short to let it pass by. When buying ramps, you should choose those that are firm with bright-colored greens. Ramps can be used both raw and cooked. The bulbs and white stems need about twice as long to cook as the leaves. Ramps are great in stuffings, risottos, frittatas, or soups, or pickled, on their own and as a side. You can store ramps by wrapping them tightly in plastic and refrigerating for up to one week.

RHUBARB

Rhubarb is a springtime fruit, often considered a vegetable. It grows in low, bushy plants that look very similar to celery but instead of being a tight head, the stalk and leaves are spread out. The stalks are pinkish green or sometimes magenta. Though it is tougher, it has the crisp texture of celery; its flavor is more vegetal and tart. It is ideal for making chutneys or sweet dishes like crisps, compotes, and pies. Rhubarb also lends a puckery-tart fruitiness to savory dishes, and pairs very nicely with pork and poultry.

ROMAINE LETTUCE

Romaine lettuce is not used all that much in Italy. It gained its popularity with the onset of the Caesar Salad (page 127), which was invented in America. This long-leaf tight-head lettuce is both crispy and tender; it keeps well when fresh and wrapped in the refrigerator. It is easy to use—just wash, cut, and toss. If the outer leaves are too green and tough, save them for a risotto or a soup.

ANOTHER WAY TO CUT ROMAINE

Instead of cutting it across, in chunks, another way of serving it is to cut it in long sections. Start by trimming away the tough outer leaves and damaged tips. Then, with a sharp knife, cut it in wedges by splitting the head lengthwise in six or eight sections, depending on the size of the head. You can now set the wedges of the romaine on the plate to be served, and drizzle the dressing over the sections.

SCALLIONS

Scallions, also called green onions or spring onions, are part of the onion family. They do not develop a bulb like the onion, but do have similar hollow, long leaves. The flavor is much milder and less pungent than that of the onion, and they are delicious eaten raw, tossed in a salad, or grilled, boiled, or braised. I like adding them to soups, risottos, and pasta sauce, and I love making a scallion frittata. To clean the scallions, cut off the hairy roots, peel off any tough outer skin, and wash well. I like using the white part as well as two-thirds of the green leaves, discarding only the tips, which may be tougher. Store in the vegetable section of the refrigerator, wrapped in a paper towel and then placed in a plastic bag.

STRAWBERRIES

Strawberries are tastiest, most plentiful, and most affordable when they are in season, June and early July—the best and most economical way to eat is to eat locally and seasonally. One thing to keep in mind as you shop is that, contrary to popular belief, bigger is not always better. Smaller berries often contain less water, giving them a more concentrated sweetness. At the market, look for firm berries with a strong scent. Strawberries don't keep in the refrigerator for too long; if you won't finish them in more than a couple of days, opt for the freezer instead. Try puréeing them before freezing or spreading them out on a tray and allowing them to freeze separately; when they're frozen, you can store them together. For a delicious summer treat, drizzle some balsamic vinegar on your ripe strawberries, let them macerate for twenty to thirty minutes, then spoon them over vanilla ice cream. If you have a very sweet tooth, you might want to add a teaspoon or two of powdered sugar per pint of berries.

SWISS CHARD

Chard is a leafy green vegetable resembling spinach, but it grows much larger and taller. It has large, wide leaves on long stalks. The stalks take longer to cook than the leaves and are cooked separately, or they are thrown in the pot before the leaves, and when they are semi-cooked the leaves are added. It is nutritionally very rich, and is common in the cuisines of the Mediterranean Basin. Chard may have a white stalk and green or red leaves, or a yellow stalk with green leaves. The color does not change the taste much. At the market, chard is usually found in tied bundles of stalks with leaves. Look for crispy stalks, bright in color, and firm leaves, bright and green, with no blemishes or dry spots. To clean the chard, untie and wash it twice in abundant water. Sometimes the chard will have sandy soil, so make sure it has all washed off. Then remove the green, leafy part from the stalks. Cut the stalks in half-inch pieces and add to boiling water, then cut the leaves in shreds and, after twenty minutes, add to the cooking stalks. Cook everything together an additional twenty minutes, drain, and sauté or dress as a salad. When adding chard to a soup or sautéing the chard, use the same two-step process: first the stalks, then the leaves. Chard is delicious in stuffings, to make crostatas, or to dress pasta.

TOMATOES

When most people think of Italian food, tomato sauce comes to mind; however, the tomato was not indigenous to Italy and was actually brought to Europe from America with the returning Spanish colonizers. A fruit, the tomato is quite versatile and is eaten raw— tossed in a salad or sliced for a caprese—cooked down in a sauce, made into a soup, stuffed and baked in the oven, as pizza topping, and juiced for drinks.

In Italy, the first written record of a tomato dates back to the sixteenth century, in the Medici household records; after that, it really caught on. The volcanic soil surrounding Vesuvius is particularly conducive to growing pulpy tomatoes with fewer seeds, perfect for making tomato sauce. It Italy, tomatoes are usually named for the region or area where they are grown—for example, the Pomodorino del Piennolo del Vesuvio, the hanging tomato of Vesuvius. Similar eponymous tomatoes are Roma, San Marzano, and the Costoluto Genovese. There are some DOP tomatoes in Italy, which means they need to be grown in a specific geographic area, such as Pomodoro di Pachino, from Sicily. Today small cherry tomatoes are particularly popular, and in our restaurants heirloom tomatoes are a favorite during the hot summer months. Many different varieties are plentiful in neighborhood markets. The beefsteak tomato is good sliced in a sandwich or for a salad. Grape tomatoes are small and elongated, like grapes, and great as a snack, in a salad, or to make bruschetta. Campari tomatoes, a little larger than cherry tomatoes, sweet and juicy, are also good eaten raw. Plum tomatoes are common in local markets; they are similar in shape to San Marzano, have a lot of pulp and few seeds, and are good for making sauce or tomato paste.

CRUSHED TOMATOES For cooking Italian sauces, especially in the winter months, the canned whole peeled tomato in its juices is the best way to go. Short of having perfectly ripe plum tomatoes in the summer, canned tomatoes make the best sauce. The San Marzano imports, or the San Marzano or plum varieties grown here in the States, are the best canned varieties to buy. They are meaty and sweet to the taste, with fewer seeds. Crush them with your hands or in a vegetable mill, and then proceed to make the sauce. I

do not like the pre-crushed or diced tomatoes in the purée to make sauces, since you don't know which tomatoes you are getting. Get in the habit of tasting the tomatoes as soon as you open the can and you will be able to tell which ones you like best; then stick to that brand. Keep in mind that tomatoes are packed seasonally and may vary from year to year, even from the same brand.

TOMATO PASTE Tomato paste is made by dehydrating ripe, cored, and seeded tomatoes, either by simmering them for a long time or—as it is done in southern Italy—by spreading a very smooth purée of cooked tomatoes on a wooden board to dry in the sun. The mixture is turned and spread like spackle several times a day for several days, until it dries into a paste. In both cases, the result is a very dense purée with an intense tomato flavor, low acidity, and a high sugar content. American tomato paste is usually found in six-ounce cans, whereas Italian imports come in tubes like toothpaste. I prefer the toothpaste packaging, because it's easier to store. Remember to keep either type in the refrigerator after opening, and to transfer the leftover canned variety to a nonmetal container and top with some olive oil. Tomato paste is used in cooking to bring that extra tomato flavor to the finished dish. I use it in soups, and it is especially good when making sauces with game meat such as venison, pheasant, quail, or boar. Remember that tomato paste is best when cooked for longer periods of time in the preparation—thirty minutes or more—it is not an ingredient that you can add at the last minute! Tomato paste, so important to the cooking of the north of Italy, where my roots are, is always a staple in my kitchen. Whenever I add tomato paste, I drop it directly onto the pan bottom—in what I call a hot spot—and cook it for a minute before stirring it in with other ingredients. The brief toasting, or caramelizing, deepens the taste and layers additional flavor into the paste.

TRUFFLES

White truffles, rare bulbs found attached to the base of oak, hazel, beech, and linden trees in the fall, tend to be expensive—they can range from $1,500 to $3,000 a pound or more. But if you decide to splurge, you won't be disappointed. The white truffle (*Tuber magnatum*) is mostly found in the northern part of Italy, although it is also found in Molise and Abruzzo, and in Istria, Croatia. The best do come from the Langhe area in Piedmont, in the countryside around Alba and Asti. The clusters of truffles form a symbiotic relationship with the roots of trees in clayey but well-drained soil. October and November are the best months for truffles, which are harvested by a *triffolaio* and his sniffing dog. The search usually happens at night, so no competitors see the spot, since truffles do grow on the same tree each year. The prized quality of the truffle is the distinct aroma; it has a pale cream or brown flesh with white marbling. When you are buying a truffle, its size is of some importance, but freshness and pungency are key. A fresh truffle should be hard and crisp and as near to egg-shaped as possible. It should emit a pungent garlic-and-mushroom odor, which you should smell well before you open the package. Truffles can be kept for up to ten days if buried in rice and refrigerated in an airtight container. The truffle will impart great flavor to the rice, so be sure to use the rice for a wonderful dish (perhaps a risotto). Or wrap the truffle in a paper towel and store it in a sealed plastic container. Brush truffles clean with a vegetable brush or with a moist paper towel. I like to shave raw truffle over basic pasta, risotto, or scrambled eggs. When you are using truffles with meat, they are best shaved over mild-flavored preparations of veal, fowl, or filet mignon. The black truffle, or black Périgord truffle (*Tuber melanosporum*), is the second-most commercially valuable species of truffle. It derives its name from Périgord, France, but is also found in Umbria, Italy, around Norcia, and is known as the Norcino truffle in Italy. It can also be found in Spain and China. The black truffle, too, has a symbiotic relationship with oak, birch, and hazelnut trees. It is harvested from early summer well into winter. It is much less aromatic than the white, and whereas the white truffle is shaved on delicate foods, such as pasta and risotto, the black truffle is used in stuffings, or to flavor sauces and soups; in Norcia, they make a walnut Norcia-truffle pesto to dress pasta. It is much less expensive than the white truffle; depending on the year, it can range from $250 to over $600 a pound. To clean it, brush it well with a vegetable brush under cold running water, dry well with a paper towel, and conserve in the refrigerator, wrapped in a paper towel. It can keep for a week.

TURNIPS

A member of the cabbage family, turnips are similar in appearance to such root vegetables as rutabagas or swedes (originally Swedish turnips). Turnips play an important role in Friulian cuisine, especially as brovada, turnips that have fermented for several months as a way to preserve them and to develop a pronounced and appetizing acidity. Turnips can also be kept in a vinegar and water solution for a few weeks and will develop a crispy acidity. Brovada is incorporated into many dishes; it can be grated and braised with sausages and other meats, added to soups, or just served as a tangy and healthful vegetable. The turnip is a great vegetable, especially in the winter months. Young and crispy turnips are good to eat as a crudité or shaved into a salad; the larger ones are excellent in stews, roasted with other root vegetables as an accompaniment to festive roasts, or braised with the addition of some vinegar for a tangy side dish.

WINTER SQUASH

Squash is slowly inching up into the popular-vegetable list, but I have always loved it and have always cooked with it. It is nutritious, versatile, and delicious. Northern Italy consumes more zucca (winter squash) than southern Italy, especially in the areas near Modena, in Emilia-Romagna, and Padova, in the Veneto. It makes a great filling for pasta, and it is great roasted with a drizzle of balsamic vinegar, as a side dish or an

appetizer. You can fry it, marinate it, grill, or boil it. In central Italy, they make savory and sweet chutneys with squash and serve them alongside meat roasts. There are so many varieties—acorn, butternut, pumpkin, and kabocha, to name a few—and they vary in color, size, and taste; all are rather easily grown. Acorn squash is shaped like an acorn with lengthwise ridges and can be deep green, orange, or beige, with a bright orange interior pulp. Butternut squash is long with a plump bottom, beige in color on the outside, with bright orange pulp, similar in flavor to the nutty, rich taste of pumpkin. Pumpkin squash are round with longitudinal ridges, and orange in color. Pumpkins, like other squash, are native to North America. Kabocha squash is an Asian variety of squash that is round in shape but slightly flattened, with a striped deep green outer skin and orange pulp.

ZUCCHINI

Zucchini are ubiquitous in the States. They are economical, easy to find, and available all year long, although their best growing season is the summer. My garden produces an abundance of zucchini; some are small, some somewhat round, some striped, and others large in size. In the squash family, zucchini are usually green in color, although there are some fancy yellow zucchini as well. Though used as a vegetable, it is actually a fruit; the zucchini flower is also delicious to cook with, stuffed and baked or battered and fried. When purchasing, you should look for firm, bright green zucchini with no bruises. The possibilities for cooking with zucchini are endless. I use them cubed in a vegetable soup, pasta dishes, or risottos, sliced for a frittata, grilled as a side or as a sandwich stuffer; they are also delicious when stuffed lengthwise and baked in the oven or sautéed with other vegetables in a caponata. Zucchini are an easy vegetable to grow in your garden. They need space to grow and crawl, but otherwise require little attention. If you grow the plant in your garden and it has gone wild and crawls all over the place, pick the young shoots, known as tendrils; they are great in a pasta sauce, and wonderful added to soups.

PREPARING VEGETABLES

Vegetables are among the most important ingredients in Italian cooking, and knowing how to shop for them, clean them, and store them is essential for best results in cooking them. Seasonal vegetables are the premier choice for Italians and will give you the best-tasting results, best value, and more nutrition. So buy vegetables in season, and as fresh as you can; buying locally grown produce will help. When buying vegetables, use your senses. Feel and smell the produce; it should be firm to the touch, with bright and crispy leaves. Vegetables should have roots, stems, and leaves attached, as much as possible, ensuring continued freshness. Once you have chosen your vegetables, knowing what to do with them and how to handle them is just as important. When you are making a vegetable soup, cutting the vegetables into perfect-sized cubes will produce a dish that has some viscosity in the liquid and some good bite-sized pieces that are not overly chunky. Knowing the right length of time to cook different-sized cubed or sliced vegetables is also important, particularly if the dish you are making is a mixture of vegetables. Cleaning a vegetable according to the needs of each recipe is essential, and one of the reasons recipes exist, to help you along. Knowing how much to clean off, not wasting good produce, and knowing what to discard all add up to having a properly cleaned vegetable and perfect finished dish. Knowing how to handle, clean, and cook vegetables to highlight their natural flavor and goodness and conserve good nutrients is part of the vegetable-cooking task.

BLANCHING VEGETABLES

Blanching vegetables means quickly boiling them, then draining them and tossing them into ice water. This technique keeps the vegetables bright in color, vibrant in taste, and crispy in texture, and helps them retain nutrients. One would think to blanch vegetables in salted water, but I like blanching them in plain water and salting them after they are cooked. I toss them immediately after draining with medium-coarse salt, while they are still steaming hot. Does it make that much difference? Indeed it does. Instead of making a saline solution out of the boiling water that permeates the vegetable throughout, salting later allows the vegetable to retain its pure vegetable flavor, and then the sprinkled salt adds another dimension of flavor by seeping in gently while still hot. The timing of the vegetables is important: cooking them too long causes them to become mushy. You can also place them in an ice bath after boiling, which quickly cools the vegetables and also halts them from cooking further. The vegetables that best respond to this method are string beans, broccoli, and zucchini, but I also like to blanch cabbage, beets, chard, and other greens.

GRILLING VEGETABLES

I love cooking vegetables in all different ways, but once the summer hits, nothing is better than to grill them. If you are thinking of grilling your vegetables, be sure to follow these simple steps to ensure that they are at their best. First make sure your vegetables are cut in consistent-sized pieces, so they finish grilling at the same time. Harder vegetables, such as potatoes or yams, need to be in smaller and thinner pieces; softer vegetables, such as tomatoes, grill nicely when sliced in half, and zucchini is fine in thicker slices. Make sure the grill surface is clean and lightly coated with oil to avoid sticking. Brush your vegetables with garlic-flavored olive oil, and season with salt and pepper. Vegetables also grill or roast well when wrapped in heavy-duty foil, in which you can include the garlic pieces and herbs with the olive oil. The vegetables should be removed before they are soft: they will continue cooking wrapped in the hot foil once they are removed from the grill. Vegetables are heat-sensitive, so be sure to keep an eye on them while they're grilling.

ROASTING VEGETABLES

Hearty vegetables, such as winter root vegetables, squashes, peppers, tomatoes, eggplants, and many more, roast very well on their own, without the help of a roasted meat to add flavor. Roasting vegetables brings out the sweetness and intensifies flavor. Seasoned roasted vegetables can be mixed with pasta, added to sandwiches, eggs, potatoes, and rice, or tossed into a salad. They are especially delicious as a pizza or focaccia topping, or served by themselves. Roasting vegetables is simple. Preheat the oven to 400 degrees. Slice the vegetables into halves or quarters, depending on what you prefer. Line a baking sheet with parchment paper, and place the vegetables on the sheet. Season them with salt and pepper, oil, and any spices or herbs you choose. Sage goes great with onion, rosemary with potatoes, and thyme with parsnips; sweet potatoes and winter squashes are great with brown sugar or honey. Toss the vegetables, and spread them apart on the parchment paper so they will brown quickly. Roast in the oven until the vegetables are soft, somewhat shriveled, and nicely caramelized on all sides.

SAUTÉING VEGETABLES

Vegetables can be blanched and then sautéed, or they can be sautéed directly in a pan, what the Italians call *strascinati*, which means to be set in a pan with oil and garlic and dragged around the pan. I like to sauté my vegetables directly in the pan with some garlic and olive oil. I let them sweat first with a cover on, tossing them gently now and then. Then I spice them up with a little crushed red pepper, uncover them, and let them finish cooking. Before sautéing your vegetables, you want to make sure that they are all cut in uniform sizes, to ensure even cooking. All vegetables—squashes, peppers, Brussels sprouts, green beans, broccoli, cauliflower, broccoli rabe, and spinach—are good pan-sautéed.

Herbs, Spices, and Seasonings

Fresh herbs are simply wonderful to cook with, and they should be ever-present in your kitchen. Some herbs are better to cook with, others better to add at the end, to finish a dish. For example, rosemary, bay leaves, and thyme are mostly used in long cooking, during which their oils are extracted slowly. Sage, oregano, and marjoram need very little cooking time. And herbs such as basil, parsley, and mint are great to toss in at the end—just enough to release their refreshing aromas. If you have small children, a wonderful way to introduce them to these aromas is to crush the herbs gently in your hands and let them smell them. I always did this with my children and grandchildren when they were very small, to get them excited about the world of herbs and food at an early age.

Whereas herbs grow in temperate zones, spices are from the tropical belt, and are usually made from dried fruit (like nutmeg and mace), seeds, leaves, barks, or roots. They are usually sold as whole or ground seeds, bark, or root. They impart a lot of flavor to a recipe, while some spices are also appreciated for their color, such as saffron or turmeric. Different cultures use spices for preserving food. Spices lose their intensity and flavor if kept for long periods, so buy small amounts as you use them, or mill them yourself for fresher flavor. For example, I prefer to have a pepper mill on the table, rather than a pepper shaker, because you get the full effect of the aroma from the just-milled peppercorns. Keep spices in sealed containers in a cool, dark place. Freezing spices like cinnamon prolongs the intensity and aroma.

I love some herbs more than others, and I use these more often. Cilantro, tarragon, and dill are among my least favorites. Chives do not appear much in my recipes, because I prefer scallions, which are in the same family, and which you will find in many of my recipes, but I do particularly like and use the flowers of the chive plant, an oniony-tasting cluster of small purple flowers, which I pluck and sprinkle in a salad or over a finished dish for decoration.

BASIL

There are so many different varieties of basil: Thai, Italian, deep purple basil, mint basil, and more. Tear a leaf off of each kind and see what you think. Let your palate be the guide, and use whichever kind you prefer. Fresh basil, with its enticing aroma, should be part of your everyday cooking, especially during the summer months. Use it in salads, especially with tomatoes, in sandwiches, sauces, soups, pasta, fish, and chicken. Adding basil enhances and refreshes any dish. Basil leaves are best when plucked off the plant, but if you buy basil on the branch, it will keep well in a vase with some water, or wrapped in a damp paper towel and then in a plastic bag for four or five days in the refrigerator. When basil is in season and you have too much, one of the best ways to save it is to make pesto in portion-sized contain-

ers and freeze them. Make sure you seal the top of the pesto with a thin film of olive oil, so the pesto does not oxidize and turn black. On the other hand, you can also freeze whole basil leaves when you have too much. Stuff small plastic containers with washed basil leaves, fill the containers with water until all the leaves are submerged, seal, and freeze. The leaves will remain bright green embedded in the ice. To use, allow the basil to defrost, or just pop the ice cube with the basil leaves directly into the sauce.

If you're using it so often, why not grow your own fresh basil? A small pot on a windowsill will provide you with great flavor for so many dishes, especially if you snip back the new shoots before they begin to flower so that the leaves retain their strength. Just keep the plant from flowering and you can harvest the leaves for months. Garden centers and specialty seed companies sell more varieties of Italian basil, but an ordinary sweet-basil plant like the ones I see in the supermarket will grow easily with a bit of attention. Once you have mastered basil growing, other herbs will be a snap.

BAY LEAVES

Bay leaves lend a complex herbal flavor to dishes. They are pungent and very aromatic when fresh. The fragrance of dried bay leaves is more mellow and somewhat similar to that of dried oregano and thyme. Use bay leaves in soups, stews, and long-cooked dishes, but be sure to take them out once your dish is finished cooking. Store fresh bay leaves in the refrigerator, wrapped in a paper towel in a plastic bag. Fresh bay leaves have a shelf life of about two weeks. Dried bay leaves should be stored in an airtight container in a cool, dry place, and replaced after twelve months, before they become stale and dull.

CINNAMON

Cinnamon, a good antioxidant, is a spice made from the inner bark of the cinnamomum tree. It is treated in seawater and then dried, after which it begins to release its essential oils. You can buy cinnamon milled into a powder or as cinnamon sticks. The sticks are excellent to use in braising savory dishes, or steeping and making teas and infusions. The powdered version is best when baking and making pies and strudels. Cinnamon needs to be used within a relatively short time span (do not store for years). Store in a tightly sealed plastic bag; for even longer storage, freeze it.

CLOVES

Cloves are seeds that are very aromatic with a pronounced flavor. They are best when added to long cooking techniques or in marinades. I like using them when braising beef, lamb, or game, and they are delicious in curing and roasting ham. You can buy them whole or powdered, but, whichever you choose, keep in mind that cloves are a strong spice, and a little will go a long way. If using whole cloves, tie them in cheesecloth and remove when you are finished cooking; the flavor and texture do not make them palatable in a dish. The best way to keep cloves is wrapped tight in plastic, in the freezer.

MARJORAM

Marjoram, an herb that resembles oregano, is in the mint family. It has a refreshing aroma—minty, green, and citric at the same time. You can buy marjoram dried, but I prefer it fresh. It has small leaves and is a hardy plant that grows well on a windowsill. I use it in stuffings, soups, and braises, and I love tossing a few leaves into my scrambled eggs.

MINT

Mint is a delicious herb that pops up during the spring season but lasts all summer long. Although dried mint is available, as with most herbs, choose the fresh form; it delivers so much more intensity in flavor and freshness. When buying fresh mint, look for leaves with a vibrant bright green color, with no dark spots or yellowing. To store fresh mint leaves, wrap them in a damp paper towel and place inside a loosely closed plastic bag. Store

in the refrigerator, where they should keep fresh for several days. Mint is delicious as a garnish, in salads, in drinks, and great in some types of pasta dishes. For a different touch to your tomato sauce, add a few leaves of fresh mint. Or, when making a marinade for fish, use a few leaves of mint with the chopped parsley. In the summer, make fresh mint tea and serve it iced.

NUTMEG

Nutmeg is a very aromatic tropical spice. The pronounced flavor is a combination of nuts, anise, and other spices. Even though it is not an indigenous Italian spice, it is loved by the Italians and used often in Italian cuisine, especially in pasta fillings, gnocchi dough, and mashed potatoes. Use a light hand when seasoning with nutmeg: its flavor becomes even more pronounced after cooking. You can buy nutmeg whole or ground. But since you need such small amounts at a time, I always recommend buying a whole seed and then grating it as needed. Although there are special graters made just for nutmeg, the smallest teeth of a box grater or a Microplane will work fine. Grate only as much as you need at the time, and keep the rest of the nutmeg sealed tightly in plastic wrap in the freezer.

OREGANO

Italians love using fresh herbs, but oregano intensifies when it is dried and imparts a lot of complex flavor. It accentuates the flavor of tomato in particular and is also great to use throughout the year, when the colder climate does not allow for fresh herbs. Oregano has been known since ancient times; it was popular in the cuisine of ancient Greece and Rome, in salads and rubbed on grilled meat and fish. I often buy a fillet of flounder for my grandchildren and bake it with oregano that has been tossed with some bread crumbs and olive oil on top; I serve this instead of fried fish sticks. The word "oregano" is derived from Greek, meaning "joy of the mountain," and, truthfully, its strong flavor makes it a joy to use in the kitchen. I recommend buying dried oregano on the branch, rather than the crushed leaves in jars. In my market, bouquets of dried oregano stalks, usually from Sicily, are packed in cellophane. To use in recipes, pull out one branch and, over a piece of parchment or wax paper, rub it lightly between your palms. Gather up the fallen leaves and measure; keep rubbing until you have the amount called for. The branches will last until you use the final leaf if kept in a dry place. You can also dry your own oregano for the winter months if you grow it fresh. Take branches of fresh oregano and leave them spread out in the sun to dry, turning them occasionally, until they are completely dry. Then tie together six to eight branches as you would a bouquet of flowers, with a regular piece of kitchen twine. Save the bouquets in a paper bag in a dry place, being careful not to crush them. Use as needed.

PARSLEY

Parsley is one of the most common and available herbs in the Mediterranean. Often used chopped to decorate finished dishes, it is also used in cooking soups, in stuffings, and in chopped-meat mixes like meatballs. In Italy, it is used to make certain pestos and for salsa verde. There are two varieties: the flat-leaf parsley, known as "Italian parsley," and the curly-leaf parsley. Parsley is best fresh and usually sold in a tied bunch. To store the parsley, put it in a cup with water, like flowers, and keep in the refrigerator; when it turns yellow, discard it.

PEPERONCINO/CRUSHED RED PEPPER

The hot pepper most commonly used in Italian cuisine is the diavolillo. It is the same species as the cayenne pepper that came from Central and South America, and in its dried, crushed form is known simply as peperoncino or, in English, as red pepper flakes. It is available either whole or as crushed flakes. The crushed form, which is the most typically used, contains both the flesh of the dried pepper and its seeds, which are the major source of piquancy. A pinch of peperoncino goes a long way when added to sautéing vegetables or a pot of soup. Whole dried peperoncini are sometimes simmered in vegetable dishes, pasta sauces, or soups, and removed before serving. Peperoncino is found as well milled into a fine powder, which, in the United States, is called cayenne. Peperoncino—either whole, crushed, or milled into cayenne—should be bright red; a brownish color indicates that it has been sitting around for a while.

PEPPERCORNS

Peppercorns come in many different varieties, colors, and flavors. Besides the common black, there are white, red, pink, and green peppercorns, which I use quite often. The white is milder, the green grassier, and the pink and red sweeter and more aromatic. Use freshly ground pepper. Do not cook the ground pepper, but always add it at the end; the flavor will be more intense. Pepper is a seed and has tannins that get bitter when cooked, so grind fresh pepper on finished food. I like to have a peppermill at the table for my guests' discretion as well. In long cooking techniques, such as broths and stocks, use whole peppercorns and strain them out. To prepare braised meat dishes, tie peppercorns in cheesecloth and discard when you are finished cooking.

ROSEMARY

Buy fresh rosemary sprigs whenever you can; they have a wonderful fragrance of pine and mint, which is somewhat lost when the herb is dried. Rosemary is great in stews and marinades, with roasted potatoes, and when grilling steaks and other meats. I especially love using it with roast lamb, but it goes well with all roasted meats. When using it in stews and roasts, I usually cut a sprig in half and add it to the pot; the leaves will cook off, and they can be strained out or left in, but do remove the twig. I also strip the leaves from the stem when I toss it with roasted potatoes and marinades. Try stuffing the cavity of a chicken or a whole fish with sprigs of rosemary and garlic cloves before grilling or roasting. Fresh rosemary sprigs will keep in the refrigerator, wrapped in a damp paper towel and placed in a plastic bag, for a week or more. To freeze, submerge the fresh rosemary leaves in a small container in water, and freeze. Defrost and use.

SAFFRON

Saffron is a spice derived from the saffron crocus flower. When the flower is in bloom, it is picked, and the stigmas of the flowers are collected and dried. Saffron is used to flavor and color many dishes in various cuisines, especially in Southwest Asia and in the Mediterranean Basin, particularly in Greece, Italy, and Spain. It has the aroma of hay and brings a beautiful golden color to foods; it really stands out in rice dishes, such as risotto and paella. You can buy dried saffron powder or dried saffron threads (stigmas). The dried stigmas are usually a better choice. Saffron is one of the most expensive spices, and a little goes a long way. Steep the saffron in a bit of hot water, soup, or tea, and add to the intended dish toward the last quarter of the cooking time. To store the saffron, seal it tightly in an airtight, preferably glass container and keep in a cool, dark place. Saffron will last for a year or more, but it will lose flavor and intensity along the way.

TOAST YOUR SAFFRON I learned this little trick to enhance the flavor of saffron from the elders in Navelli, a town on the high plains in Abruzzo known for its saffron, who cook with the saffron that they harvest. Carefully drop the saffron strands (as much as the recipe calls for) into a metal spoon. Hold the spoon over a low open flame for just a few seconds, toasting the threads very gently—the perfume will tell you it's working! Before they overheat, spill the threads out of the spoon into a bowl filled with hot water or stock for steeping or grinding, as called for in the recipe. This holds true for most of the other dried spices as well—toasting them in a skillet before using them will enhance their flavor.

SAGE

Sage has velvety green leaves, which are very aromatic, combining the flavor of leeks, basil, and mint. Always buy fresh sage in little branches with leaves about 1 to 1½ inches long. I do not like dried sage, as it loses flavor. Sage goes great in butter sauces for pasta and gnocchi, but it is also very good when cooking chicken, veal, pork, and rabbit. I cook the whole leaves in the sauce, or sometimes I throw in the whole branch and remove it when the sauce is done. To flavor stuffings, add some chopped sage leaves, but not too much: the taste is very pronounced. Its intense flavor mellows when the whole leaves are fried to a crisp, however. Fried in batter, they make great snacks or hors d'oeuvres. Sage leaves will keep, wrapped in a damp paper towel and placed in a plastic bag, for a week. They might seem wilted after a few days, but they will still have their aroma and flavor.

SALT

I prefer to use natural sea salt that is made by evaporation from seawater or mined from large deposits—usually a remnant of a salt lake. Sea salt comes in different grades of coarseness. Grains of fine-crystal sea salt, which are the size of fine bread crumbs, are good in dishes that require very little cooking time or in cold dishes. I also use them to dress salads, to season meats and poultry when grilling or sautéing, or when I need to add that last pinch of salt to a dish. For preparations that require a long cooking time—such as boiling pasta and making soups or sauces, large meat cuts, and whole birds that roast or braise for a long time—I prefer the coarse-crystal sea salt or rock sea salt, which is grayish in color; it has a much more pronounced flavor of the sea. I also use coarse or rock sea salt to cure meats or marinate meats or vegetables.

Use kosher and sea salt according to your preference, but do experiment with the many different pink, gray, and black sea salts available. Sea salt has more potassium, magnesium, zinc, and other nutrients than table salt. The different colors reflect where the salt was harvested, and there are nuances of flavor as well. These gourmet salts are usually more expensive. There are also salt flakes called "sel de mer," larger sea salt crystals formed naturally in coastal flats; they are more flavorful and usually more expensive.

SALTING WHEN COOKING I find that I like to salt progressively while cooking. That is, I season with salt as I add each major ingredient to the pot. I suggest that, for each recipe you are about to cook, you measure out the total amount of salt called for, and then use a little bit of the measured salt to add at different stages of cooking, rationing it so that you have a little left to adjust to taste when the recipe is finished. The salt adjustment at the end is especially important if you are using ingredients that you did not make yourself, such as broth or butter, which can contain a lot of sodium.

SUGAR

I do not have much of a sweet tooth; in fact, I prefer fruit desserts with a bit of acidity. However, sugar is an important ingredient in the kitchen, not only in sweets. I often include a little sugar in a meat rub, because as it heats up it tends to caramelize the meat a bit more and adds a bit of finger-licking goodness. "Sugar" may mean white sugar, brown sugar, cane sugar, confectioners' sugar, or many other types. It is found in many plants, but the sugar we use in our food is derived from sugarcane or sugar beets, which are both very highly concentrated. I prefer to use unrefined sugar in my cooking, simply because it has

undergone less processing and is more natural. Used since ancient times, sugar is a carbohydrate composed of carbon, hydrogen, and oxygen. If you store sugar in tightly closed containers in a cool, dark place, it will last for over a year, providing it does not get any humidity, which will cause the sugar to solidify and lump. If it does solidify, you can break it down; it's still usable and good to eat.

ZUCCHERO DI CANNA I play around when I'm making *dolci*, desserts, as I always do in the kitchen, using different and less refined sweetening agents. Recently, I've enjoyed baking with the pale-gold cane sugars, called *zucchero di canna* in Italy, that I've found in the supermarkets in New York. These crystallized sugars are less processed and refined than ordinary table sugar; some brands are also from organically grown sugarcane (in Florida and Hawaii, I was glad to learn). The tint of the sugar, like its hint of deep flavor, comes from a very slight amount of molasses naturally retained by the crystals—not added during processing, as is the case with conventional brown sugars.

THYME

Thyme grows easily in a pot on a windowsill as well as in most sunny parts of the garden, but it is also readily available in sprigs at most supermarkets. Thyme goes especially well with fish and chicken, and adds a green freshness to soups, braised meats, and stuffing. In braising and roasting, I use the whole sprig, removing the stem before serving. For stuffing and seasonings, I strip the little leaves off the stem, chop them like parsley, and add them. Thyme will keep for about a week, wrapped in a damp paper towel and plastic bag and refrigerated.

Olive Oil, Vinegar, and Condiments

For millennia, olive trees and wine grapes have grown side by side throughout Italy. They produce two of the most essential food elements of the Italian table, olive oil and vinegar, as well as wine. In Italy the quality of olive oil and vinegar is of utmost importance, because they are used in their natural state, uncooked, especially in salads and as a raw dressing. At the base of traditional Italian cuisine are traditional Italian products, and olive oil and vinegar are the foremost. Every region of Italy produces olive oil, vinegar, and wines. There are hundreds of different varieties of the olive species, and hence different flavors of Italian oils. The same is true of wines. Getting to taste and know the different regional Italian oils can be rewarding and fun. Of all the Italian vinegars, the star is the Aceto Balsamico Tradizionale, an extraordinary traditional product, limited in production since it is produced only in and around Modena, in the region of Emilia-Romagna. But good wine vinegars are produced in every region of Italy, so getting to know them, and how to use them, is essential.

OLIVE OIL

The grade of olive oil—extra-virgin, virgin, etc.—that appears on each bottle's label is based on the residual oleic acid. The less acidic an olive oil is, the higher its quality.

EXTRA-VIRGIN OLIVE OIL has no more than 1 percent oleic acid.

VIRGIN OLIVE OIL contains from 1 to 3.3 percent oleic acid.

PLAIN OLIVE OIL has an acidity level higher than 3.3 percent.

OLIVE POMACE OIL is the oil extracted from olive pomace (crushed olives and pits) with the help of solvents; this oil is then purified and blended with virgin olive oil.

OLIO NOVELLO is newly pressed olive oil, usually less than two months old. It is vibrant green in color, very vegetal, fresh in flavor, and sometimes a bit murky, with small particles of pulp.

The International Olive Oil Council is responsible for setting and monitoring these grades. All olive oil is best when used within a year after pressing, because as olive oil ages, it loses its flavor. All olive oil is best when cold-pressed. When storing olive oil, to prevent oxidation or rancidity, store in full, small bottles, tightly shut, in a dark, cool place.

Here are some of my favorite regional olive oils.

Olive oil from Lombardy is very gentle and has a mild herbal aroma with a nutty finish. It is best used as a condiment for steamed vegetables, or for dressing salads.

Ligurian olive oil is gentle but herbaceous and aromatic, with a mild sweetness. It's a natural fit for making pesto, and great for fish and salads.

Tuscan olive oil is hearty and packed with flavor, and has a peppery finish. It's excellent with beans, thick soups, roasts, and grilled bread.

Umbrian olive oil is very herbal, with a buttery, nutty finish. It's perfect for risotto and braised meats.

Olive oil from Puglia is intense in its flavor, since the olives there ripen in the intense summer sun. I use it for basic cooking, such as braising, preparing vegetables, and soups.

Sicilian olive oil is similar to the oil from Puglia. It is great for Sicilian dishes rich with seafood and vegetables.

HOW TO USE OLIVE OIL

Olive oil is an essential staple in my home and in my restaurants. It is a great antioxidant. Extra-virgin olive oil is best when used raw, right out of the bottle, to drizzle on salads and before serving a bowl of soup or pasta. You get maximum olive-oil flavor this way. Do not use olive oil for frying—canola or vegetable oil is best—but you can add a little olive oil to the pan for flavor. You can use olive oil for other kinds of cooking and sautéing, but it is best when you are cooking at a lower temperature.

TASTING OLIVE OIL

Many people are familiar with wine tasting, but what about olive oil? To make a decision about which olive oil you should buy, taste four or five different ones first. When tasting an olive oil, examine the color before taking a sip. The riper the olives, the more yellow the oil; younger olives make for greener hues and usually more flavor. Freshly pressed olive oil can be shocking in its greenness, but as the oil ages, it mellows in color and taste. Next, take in the oil's aroma. Does it smell of grass? How about tomato leaf or almond? Finally, sip the olive oil while sucking in air and exhaling from your nose. High-quality olive oil should have flavors to match its aroma and should not feel heavy or greasy in the mouth; it should not be musty or oxidized. The different flavors of olive oil are determined by the varieties of olives used in making the oil.

GARLIC-INFUSED OIL

Garlic-infused olive oil is very handy to have in the kitchen. To make garlic-infused olive oil, add three thickly sliced cloves of garlic to each cup of extra-virgin olive oil. Let steep for two to three hours. Strain the oil, and discard the garlic if you're not using it immediately. Keep the oil in a sealed bottle in the refrigerator.

You must be careful, though: if any uncooked garlic is left to steep for too long, it can be a breeding ground for botulism, a rare but possible occurrence. If you are concerned, infuse the oil with blanched or roasted garlic.

SPICY "HOLY OIL"

I love the cooking of Abruzzo, mostly because of their use of peperoncino. Lavish spiciness is typical of southern-Italian cuisines, and although I am from the north, I can't get enough of it. The Abruzzesi often steep peperoncini in olive oil, creating a spicy-hot condiment called *olio santo* or "holy oil." If you love heat, a drizzle of this makes a good dish heavenly. To make your own *olio santo,* pour a cup of good-quality extra-virgin olive oil into a glass jar, and drop in a teaspoon of kosher salt and two tablespoons of small, whole dried peperoncini, about ten little peppers. Cover tightly, and let the oil infuse at room temperature for at least two days. Give it a good shake, and use. Store in a sealed jar, in a cool place, for a month or more.

UNCOOKED OLIVE OIL SAUCE

The resourceful cooks of Abruzzo are never at a loss for a quick and delicious way to dress fresh maccheroni or excellent dried pastas. Just take whatever is on hand, good-quality olive oil, a few cloves of garlic, hot pepper, a cluster of fresh herbs, or a handful of nuts, and you can produce a wonderful uncooked sauce with a mortar and pestle in minutes. The foundation of a simple sauce is the olive oil. Authentic olive oils from Abruzzo will always taste best, but any top-quality Italian extra-virgin olive oil will make a delicious sauce, too. These sauces are not only delicious on pasta; they are also marvelously versatile condiments for meats, fish, poultry, and vegetables. Choose your favorite herbs and nuts; they need only a whirl in the food processor and they are ready to dress your pasta. No cooking needed.

VINEGAR

There are many kinds of vinegar; it can be made from fruits, vegetables, wine, beer, dates, or rice, depending on the culture. In Italy the vinegars of choice are red and white wine, apple, balsamic, and Saba vinegar. I like red wine vinegar because it has a pronounced flavor and character of the wine grape it was made from. I use it to dress salads and panzanella, and to cook chicken and rabbit. White wine vinegar or champagne vinegar is milder, but still has the complexity of wine, and I like using it to pickle vegetables, to make my sour sauces, and in marinades for light meats like chicken. Apple vinegar is also good in marinades, as well as for making light sauces when cooking fish, chicken, or turkey; for roasting pork and pork chops; and for dressing salads with fruits in them. Balsamic vinegar and Saba are regional specialty vinegars in Italy. For these vinegars, the juice of the grape is cooked down or aged, yielding a complex taste. They are used for drizzling on cheeses, desserts, and cooking roasted meats. They bring a wallop of flavor.

ACETO BALSAMICO TRADIZIONALE
When shopping for balsamic vinegar, look for the legendary Aceto Balsamico Tradizionale, a product of the traditional method of production, which involves seven years in wooden barrels of different sizes and types of woods. The vinegar so labeled is far superior and is, accordingly, expensive. Its characteristics are a molasseslike consistency, a lively brown color, a mildly acidic "nose," and a smooth, subtle interplay of sweet and sour flavors. It is packaged and sold only in small bottles with a bulb bottom and a long neck. Aceto Balsamico Tradizionale is best when used without cooking; drizzle it on grilled steaks, salads, cheeses, fruit, and even ice cream.

ACETO BALSAMICO COMMERCIALE
On the other hand, Aceto Balsamico Commerciale is a blend of vinegar that is fermented in big barrels and aged for varying numbers of years in large oak casks with the addition, in different proportions, of some of the Tradizionale. It varies in taste, depending on the blend, and it is the balsamic vinegar that is best to cook with. When it is reduced, it concentrates and becomes syrupy and mellow. It is good in braising meats, roasting, making glazes, and tossing into salads. The bottles come in all different sizes and shapes. It is much cheaper than the Tradizionale.

CHUTNEY

Chutney is similar in consistency to jelly, salsa, or relish, and is used as a sweet-and-sour condiment. Usually made fresh, chutney contains fruit and sugar to give it a sweet taste, and almost all chutney contains vinegar and perhaps onions to give it a corresponding sour flavor. The ingredients are mixed together and then simmered slowly. There can be many variations of spices, often giving chutney a hot and spicy flavor. I love chutneys for both their concentrated flavor and the convenience. You make them and store them, and whenever you want that special treat, you can just pull them from the fridge or pantry. All you need is a spoonful to enjoy the concentrated essence of whatever ingredients you put into them. They are great served with roasted, grilled, or boiled meats, and with cheeses.

HONEY

Miele in Italian, honey is an underrated pantry staple. Popular in almost every region of Italy, the production of honey is often regarded with as much respect as that of olive oil or cheese. The regions of Sicily, Sardinia, Tuscany, and Piedmont are producing some of the finest honey in Italy. The flavor and aroma of honey are determined by the type of blossom from which the bees gather the nectar, and also, like wine or olive oil, by the climate, soil composition, and time of harvest. You can find honey made from acacia, thyme, sage, chestnut, and lavender, just to name a few. In addition to being a sweet treat, honey contains powerful antioxidants; darker varieties can even contain large quantities of the same agent found in red grapes that has been credited with reducing instances of heart disease among wine drinkers. Try drizzling acacia honey on your oatmeal in the morning, chestnut honey over your fruit or cheese, or simply spread the popular Italian *millefiore* ("a thousand flowers") honey on toast. Look for these unique flavors of honey at health-food stores and gourmet shops.

MOSTARDA

Mostarda, a condiment made of candied fruits and mustard-flavored syrup, has been part of the Italian culinary repertoire for centuries, originally as a way of preserving vegetables and fruits such as squash, apples, and pears for the winter months. Cooked in sweet syrup with dry, hot mustard added, mostarde were enjoyed as a crisp and fresh-tasting condiment when there was no fresh produce. The epicenter of the Italian mostarda culture is in and around Modena, but every region of Italy has some form of it. It is a great condiment for boiled meats, or grilled or poached poultry. I love it served with celery and a good ripe cheese, as well as with fresh sheep's-milk ricotta. And, suspended in its sweet syrup, it is also delicious on ice cream! It keeps in the refrigerator for months.

Cheese

Cheese making has a four-thousand-plus-year history; while the origin of cheese production seems to have been in Mesopotamia, in Italy cheese making dates back more than two thousand years. During the Roman Empire, the houses even had a separate room off the kitchen called a *caseale,* exclusively for cheese making and aging. Now there are more than 460 types of cheese made in Italy, and one could argue that Italian cheeses are some of the most loved in the United States. The United States is the largest consumer of cheeses, and mozzarella and ricotta constitute almost half of the cheese consumed. An unusual feature of the Italian cheese culture is that Italians include cheese in their cooking, whether it is Taleggio to stuff a veal chop, Gorgonzola to dress a plate of gnocchi, pecorino to mix in a stuffing, mozzarella to put on some dough or for pizza, or ricotta to make a cheesecake. To Italians, cheese is a necessary product for cooking and garnishing soups, pasta, and pizza; it's not just to enjoy with some fruit as a finale to a meal. Here I share with you some of my favorite Italian cheeses, including those I love to cook with.

ASIAGO

This is named after the Asiago plateau in the Veneto foothills, where it originated. It is a mild

cheese and has a slightly sweet flavor when young, whereas it becomes more flavorful and sharper when aged. It is matured for different durations: *mezzano* for three months, *vecchio* for about nine months, and *stravecchio* for up to two years. This DOP cow's-milk cheese, now produced anywhere from the Po Valley to the mountains of Trentino, is best served in salads, pasta, and soups or cut fresh as an antipasto or for a panino.

BEL PAESE

A mild, white creamy cheese made from cow's milk. Originally produced in Melzo, a small town near Milan, in the Lombardy region, it is now made in both Italy and the United States. Its buttery flavor is popular to pair with fruity wines. It is excellent as a snack or dessert cheese and melts easily for use on pizzas or in casseroles. It can be used as a substitute for mozzarella.

BURRATA

This cheese is usually made from cow's milk and is produced traditionally in Puglia, the region that makes up the heel of Italy's boot. It is sometimes made from *bufala* milk, especially when produced in Lazio, near Rome. The outer casing of burrata is solid mozzarella, but the inside contains both mozzarella and cream, giving it a distinctly creamy texture that earns its name: *burrata* is Italian for "buttered." The rich texture and delicate flavor of burrata make it a great companion to prosciutto crudo, sautéed broccoli rabe, nice crusty bread, or fresh tomatoes and olive oil. You can find this artisanal cheese at import and gourmet stores. Burrata has a very short shelf life and must be eaten within days after it is made.

CACIOCAVALLO

A stretched-curd cheese, this is most often made in southern Italy and can range from mild to

sharp, depending on how long it is aged. It can be made from sheep's or cow's milk and has a hard edible rind. These cheeses are usually hung with string to age in pairs.

CAPRINO

Caprino fresco is a rindless goat's-milk cheese that has a milky texture and usually has a sharp tang. It is delicious served with or crumbled into salad, and is also tasty when included in a pasta stuffing. Caprino that is aged longer develops a rind.

CASTELMAGNO

Castelmagno is a prized cheese from Piedmont that is usually made from unpasteurized milk of cows that graze at higher altitudes, with the addition of a little sheep and/or goat milk. It begins as a flaky cheese with a mild but complex milky taste, and as it ages it develops a crumbly texture with more complexity in flavor. Castelmagno has a round form and can range from ten to twenty pounds; its smooth rind is pale reddish yellow when it's young and thickens, hardens, wrinkles, and turns somewhat brown with age.

FONTINA

A cow's-milk cheese that has a superb flavor and melting ability, Fontina is produced in northern Italy, in the Valle d'Aosta region, but several types of Fontina cheese are also made in the United States, Switzerland, and France. The rinds of Italian Fontina are thin and rigid, and range from yellow-gold to reddish brown. The cheese has a distinct, sweet, buttery taste with some nutty

notes. Many people wonder what cheese makes the best fondue, and I like to recommend using genuine Fontina. It is unsurpassed in dishes that have that melted-cheese element. Who doesn't love dunking bread, crackers, and crudités in a pot of warm melted cheese? Imported authentic Fontina is widely available in U.S. markets with good cheese departments, and from gourmet Internet vendors. Be sure that you are buying DOP Fontina, with the distinctive imprint of an Alpine peak on the wheel. Though more expensive than other semisoft cheeses, it is well worth the cost. If DOP is not available, a less distinctive but similar cheese called Fontal, also imported from Italy, is a good substitute. This goes great on all kinds of food, from poached chicken or turkey breast to different steamed vegetables. It is also delicious poured over a bowl of hot polenta or gnocchi.

GORGONZOLA

This blue-veined cheese from Lombardy is made from 100 percent cow's milk that has not been skimmed. It can range from sweet, soft, and buttery (*dolce*) to firm, crumbly, quite salty, and *piccante,* with a "bite" from its blue veining.

GRANA PADANO

One of the most popular cheeses of Italy, its name comes from the noun *grana* ("grain"), which refers to the crumbly, grainy quality of the cheese. *Padano* refers to the lush valley around the river Po. Grana Padano is a hard cheese that is cooked and aged slowly (for up to eighteen months). Made in the regions of Piedmont, Lombardy, and Veneto, and in the province of Trento, it comes in rounds weighing around forty to fifty pounds with a pale yellow rind. The triangular logo of the Grana Padano seal is embossed on the rind. It is a delicious cheese to eat in chunks with fruit or bread, but is also grated for pasta fillings and for dressing soups and pasta; it makes a great tasty, crunchy top for baked vegetable and pasta dishes. In Italy, it holds a special place for children, who love its flavor. Every crumb of this cheese is useful—even the rinds, if washed and scrubbed, add lots of flavor when tossed into a perking minestra or other soup.

MASCARPONE

This Italian creamy cheese, made from 100 percent cow's milk, is a cousin of American cream cheese but without the acidity. Milky-white in color, it spreads easily and is a primary ingredient in the making of tiramisù. Mascarpone originated in the area between Lodi and Abbiategrasso, Italy, southwest of Milan, probably in the late sixteenth or early seventeenth century, and is still going strong as a traditional Italian product. It's one of my favorite cheeses, for its versatility in both sweet and savory dishes. It also has a wonderful flavor on its own, served with fresh fruit.

MONTASIO

This cheese originated in the region of Friuli–Venezia Giulia. Situated in the northeast corner of Italy, this region lies at the foothills of the Alps. Made in large wheels of twelve to fourteen pounds, Montasio is made from cow's milk and is available in three varieties. Montasio Fresco, or fresh, is at least two months old and has a mild flavor with a creamy consistency. Montasio Mezzano has been aged from five to ten months; the flavor deepens as it becomes firmer and its color turns golden. Montasio Stagionato (also called Montasio Stravecchio) is aged for more than ten months and is delicious grated on pasta or in soups. Montasio can be used as an appetizer, in cooking, or with fruit as a snack or after a meal. It is the traditional Italian cheese used for making frico, a fried-cheese dish, and makes a flavorful fondue. You can pick some Montasio up at your local gourmet or import shop.

MOZZARELLA

I have a hard time finding any domestic mozzarella that compares to the mozzarella di bufala that I find in Italy. When you are buying imported mozzarella di bufala, a reputable producer and distributor are very important. Look for a mozzarella that has been packaged in its own whey and is sealed tightly in plastic. When you open the package, the cheese should be firm and moist, not falling apart or very soft, and it should have sweet overtones.

Mozzarella is a fresh cheese made from "pasta filata," pulled or stretched curds, a method that gives the cheese its chewy texture and fresh flavor. The word *mozzare* means "to cut off," so the cheese's name refers to the cutting technique with which it's made. It can be formed in a medium-sized round ball, small round pieces known as bocconcini (small bites), braided (known as treccia), or in knots (nodini). Campania, the region in Italy that claims Naples for its capital, is the epicenter of Italian mozzarella making. Much of the mozzarella made in Campania starts with water-buffalo milk, which gives the cheese a special tang and complexity of flavor. According to the people of Campania, mozzarella di bufala should be eaten within three hours after it's made, a luxury not available to us in the States. Fortunately, we do have excellent mozzarella di bufala flown in almost daily.

Cow's-milk mozzarella is also made here in the States, and it is quite good. We make it continuously during the day at our Eataly markets and our Becco restaurant, as do many other Italian specialty shops and restaurants. It is best to use mozzarella quickly once the package is opened, but you can keep it for a day. I like to eat mozzarella at room temperature.

PARMIGIANO-REGGIANO

This is a grana, or a hard, granular Italian cheese, cooked but not pressed, named after the producing areas of Parma and Reggio Emilia, in Emilia-Romagna. "Parmigiano" is simply the Italian adjective form of "Parma." The term "Parmesan" is also loosely used as a common term for this cheese, but the truly Italian product carries the name Parmigiano-Reggiano, embossed over the whole rind of the cheese. It is aromatic, with full, fruity, and fragrant tones that intensify as it ages. Formed into wheels of fifty pounds and more, its rind is hard and slightly oily and straw-yellow in color, the interior flaky, grainy, and a rich yellow. It is a very versatile cheese, delicious when eaten as is, in chunks, with fruit and bread, or grated and used in pasta, soups, or stuffings, and to form delicious crusts on vegetables.

PECORINO

A sheep's-milk cheese and the cheese of choice from Tuscany down the Italian peninsula, pecorino has been made for over two and a half thousand years. Pecorino cheese can be aged anywhere from three months to two or three years. It is usually aged in a temperature-controlled environment but can also be aged wrapped in chestnut leaves, in hay, or nestled in grape must and stacked in underground rock stairways called *fosse*. Pecorino is a round cheese that ranges between two and six pounds; it has a hard rind that is smooth and pale yellow, and an interior that is soft and yellow but gets firmer and crumblier as it ages. During aging, the cheese becomes very aromatic and can sometimes be a bit salty. Pecorino from different regions has different characteristics:

PECORINO SARDO, usually 100 percent sheep's-milk cheese, comes to the market in both fresh and aged varieties. It is sweet, milky, and slightly acidic when young, becoming harder and a bit tangy with age. It is formed into wheels, with a thin, smooth, pale yellow rind in younger cheeses that hardens and darkens as it matures. The interior is white to pale yellow, with a few holes, called "eyes."

PECORINO SICILIANO is a sheep's-milk cheese with a hard, typically pale yellow rind, and a flaky interior ranging in color from ivory to pale yellow, with very few eyes. Sometimes you'll find black peppercorns embedded in the interior as well. It is salty, fruity, and sharp, intensifying as it matures.

PECORINO ROMANO is the pecorino most often found in markets. Made in the Lazio area, it is the favorite cheese in Rome, surpassing the grana cheeses, which tend to be more popular in the rest of the Italy. This cheese has ancient Roman roots; it was first made around the countryside of Rome and later was taken to different areas of Italy when shepherds immigrated. You can buy it fresh (in this form it is popular to eat with fava beans) or hard, which is often grated over local pasta dishes. Pecorino Romano is quite salty and is aged from five months to eight months or longer for a grating cheese.

PECORINO TOSCANO is a sheep's-milk cheese hailing from Tuscany, and comes in soft and semihard versions. It is formed into wheels. The rind is pale yellow to dark yellow, the interior white, ivory, or pale yellow, depending on age. The younger version is milder and a bit tangy; the mature version is sharper and has a nuttier flavor.

PROVOLONE

Provolone originated in Campania, near Vesuvius, and is a semihard cheese made from full-fat cow's milk. It is a pulled cheese, like mozzarella, that is formed in a pear shape, has a smooth skin, and is usually coated with some wax and hung to age. The taste of provolone may vary greatly. The provolone piccante—piquant, aged for a minimum of four months—has a sharp taste; provolone dolce is sweet with a very mild taste; and there are other varieties, including a smoked provolone, which is often used in cooking.

PROVOLA, a milder version of provolone, is mainly produced in the Veneto and the Po Valley, with cow's milk. This cheese has a conical or pear shape. It is semihard, and is often smoked as well.

RICOTTA

"Twice-cooked" is the literal translation of *ricotta*, and that is exactly what this cheese is. After cheese is made, the remaining whey is recooked, and soft curds are formed. Ricotta can also be made from whole milk by heating it to approximately ninety-six degrees, then adding some acidity such as lemon juice, to coagulate the milk and make soft curds. Ricotta, whether freshly made or bought in stores, is a delicious and soft, milky curd, adding flavor and texture to so many dishes in Italian cuisine. It shows up in a great variety of recipes, from appetizers and pasta sauces to pasta fillings and desserts. It represents an Italian *gusto,* or taste. I use it often in my desserts—in making a cheesecake and filling my cannoli. I especially like it in my ravioli and manicotti stuffing. If you do use ricotta in your recipes, it is essential that it be fresh. If it is watery, drain it for one hour; if compact and dry, use as is.

SCAMORZA

Similar to mozzarella, this is a cow's-milk cheese made by stretching the milk curd; it is formed round and hung with a string to age, which slightly elongates the shape. It can easily substi-tute for mozzarella in any baked dish and can be smoked and braided or made into *bocconcini,* small bite-sized pieces.

TALEGGIO

Taleggio is a semisoft cow's-milk cheese that hails from the Taleggio Valley, in Lombardy. It is square in form, about four to six pounds, and generally aged twenty-five to fifty days. The rind is thin and wrinkly, and can range in color from yellow to pink, depending on the mold. The interior is pale yellow. It is creamy, and has a strong, pungent aroma, with a mild, sweet, nutty flavor. It becomes rich, full-flavored, and tangier, with mushroom notes, as it ages. It melts smoothly and is great in meat dishes or just with some ripe pears or figs.

USING CHEESE

CHEESE RINDS

The rind of a cheese can tell you much about that cheese. You should buy cheese with a natural rind, not in wax or paraffin. Save your Grana Padano and Parmigiano-Reggiano rinds! When added to long-cooking soups and sauces, they add a subtle richness. I keep a zippered plastic bag of any sizable pieces of grating-cheese rind in a drawer in the refrigerator. Stored airtight, they will last indefinitely, or you can plop them in the freezer. Before adding them to a dish, rinse the rind pieces well, scrubbing or scraping off any mold residue or markings, and then drop the rind in the cooking soup or sauce. When the sauce or soup is finished, remove the rind piece (it will be soft and chewy), or cut it up in little cubes and throw it back in the soup as a surprise for some lucky person at your table.

GRATING CHEESE

Whether it's Grana Padano, Parmigiano-Reggiano, or Pecorino Romano, always buy the cheeses in chunks rather than already grated. You should grate your own cooking and serving cheese; simply put, it is fresher, and you know exactly what you are getting. Grate your cheese as close as possible to use. Pregrated cheese oxidizes and loses flavor. Any extra grated cheese you have should be stored in a tightly sealed container in the refrigerator. Grated cheese should be added at the end of the cooking process, with the flame turned off.

SHREDDED CHEESE When you are shredding softer cheeses, such as mozzarella or Fontina, the shreds can stick together because of their consistency and become more difficult to handle, especially if you are trying to distribute them evenly over dishes like lasagna and pizza. To avoid this, mix in some finely grated Parmigiano-Reggiano or Grana Padano cheese with the softer shredded cheese; that will loosen it up so you can proceed with the sprinkling.

PASTA AND GRATED CHEESE There is a natural affinity between pasta and cheese, but it's not as indiscriminate as one might think. In Italy, cheese is used with pasta very selectively and judiciously, and careful attention is paid to timing. It is always added when the pasta is ready to be plated, with additional grated cheese at the table. It is never served with seafood pasta, except in Sicily. When you are preparing pasta with game or with hot pepper, since the flavors are already intense, grated cheese is optional. So when does one use Grana Padano and when pecorino cheese? Grated Grana Padano, made from cow's milk, comes from the north of Italy; it is milkier and milder and goes well with milder sauces from the north of Italy. Grated pecorino, a sheep's-milk cheese, is more intense in flavor, and predominantly made and used in southern Italy, to accompany sauces with more pronounced flavor.

STORING CHEESE

Natural cheese is a living organism, with enzymes and bacteria that need air and moisture to survive. Cheese should be served at room temperature but stored in a cool place. Once you have opened a cheese, rewrap it in parchment or wax paper, then set in an individual plastic box or bag to create a microenvironment. However, do not leave cheese in the same wrappings for extended periods of time; change them every four or five days. Keep cheeses at the bottom of the vegetable and fruit bin, so their aromas do not permeate other foods and they do not pick up flavors. Firm cheeses can be kept for several weeks. Fresh and soft cheeses have a much shorter life-span and should be used within a week. You can freeze some cheeses to keep them longer, but I don't recommend it. Freezing will make the cheese mealy and ruin the wonderful texture of each particular cheese. For optimal flavor, bring cheese to room temperature before serving.

Pasta

Pasta is the most important and extensive chapter in any respectable Italian cookbook, and in every region of Italy there is some kind of pasta on the family table. Pasta seems to be such an all-encompassing term, and for Italians it is an extensive subject indeed. The main divisions of the Italian pasta universe are fresh and dried. Fresh pasta is somewhat wet and soft, usually made from different flours, with or without eggs, with or without olive oil, with water and/or milk. Dried pasta is made of durum-wheat flour and water, and then completely dried. Both categories come in different shapes, which are best suited for or paired with different sauces. Today these two categories are used across the whole Italian peninsula, but sixty or seventy years ago the peninsula was divided, with fresh pasta in the north and dried pasta in the south.

I often get asked which pasta I prefer, fresh or dried; for me, they are two different experiences, with their own cooking techniques, equally delicious in their results. It is evident that making fresh pasta is a bit more time-consuming and labor-intensive, but the results are extraordinary, and it is a labor in which every member of the family can take part. Choose which fresh pasta you will make according to the ingredients you have and love, the time you have to spend in making the pasta, and your family favorites, but sometimes do attempt a new fresh-pasta-making experience, and let me be your guide. On the other hand, when using a dried pasta the focus should be on what sauce you will make or what sauce you have the ingredients for. Once you have decided on the sauce, the shape of the pasta you choose can make a real difference. A flat, long pasta, such as spaghetti, is great with thick tomato and meat sauces; a tubular pasta will collect the flavorful morsels of your sauce in its nooks and crannies; ridges on your pasta will create a great mouth feel. For example, some pastas with crevices and nooks and crannies, like elbow or pipette, are good shapes for a sauce with peas, so they can hide in the crevices and pop in the mouth, adding texture and an element of surprise. Short shapes are usually more appropriate for chunky sauces. Next time you pass by the dried-pasta shelves, stop and check out the different shapes. Because pasta is such an extensive chapter in Italian cuisine, I am sharing with you many tips for you to keep in mind no matter which pasta recipe you are preparing.

FRESH PASTA

DOUGH CONSISTENCY

When making fresh pasta dough, you can use either a hand method or the food-processor method. However, if you are using a mixed-flour dough for the first time, I suggest you use the food processor. With nonwheat flours, some doughs will start out quite sticky or quite dry, and the processor blade can knead them to a workable consistency in seconds. Remember that any dough, whether hand- or machine-mixed, has to rest for thirty minutes before you roll it. After that you can roll, shape, and cut the pasta into the desired shape and cook it right away, without further delay.

EGGS AND HOMEMADE PASTA

The number of eggs one adds to pasta dough is a reflection of Italian cultural differences in the preparation of pasta over the centuries. The rich man can have his cook make pasta moistened entirely with fat-laden, tasty egg yolks. In frugal times a family might make their Sunday pasta with one precious egg, water, and a bit of oil; and sometimes fresh pasta can be made with just water and oil. So the ratio of ingredients in homemade pasta—eggs, flour, oil, and water—varies tremendously. The richest, all-egg-yolk fresh pasta is not necessarily the best. I like mine in the middle of the road, made with flour, two whole eggs, some extra-virgin olive oil, and water. I find this quite rich and delicious. Part of the fun is in mixing and matching the right pasta with the most compatible sauce; challenge yourself, and try making your own pairings, and have fun trying different ratios of ingredients in making fresh pasta. Some fresh pasta recipes use only flour and water.

FRESH PASTA WITH NUTS

Ground nuts can be incorporated into pasta doughs with great success—such as walnuts in buckwheat dough, hazelnuts in chickpea dough—and you can experiment with other combinations, using almonds and pecans, too. Follow these guidelines whenever you are adding nuts: For a one-pound batch of dough, start with a generous half cup of whole nuts (or halves) to get to a third of a cup of ground nuts. First, toast the whole nuts lightly in a dry pan to bring out the flavor. After they have cooled, pulse them in a food processor into tiny bits, smaller than an eighth of an inch. This will take only one or two seconds—don't grind them into a powder. Pick out any remaining larger pieces; crush them smaller, or eat them. Mix the dough by hand or in a food processor, as usual. When you turn the dough out for final kneading, spread it into a small rectangle and sprinkle the nut bits on top. Fold the dough over the nuts, and knead as you would normally, distributing the nuts well, until the dough is smooth and shiny; then let it rest. To roll a dough with nuts using a pasta machine: Divide the dough in quarters, and roll each piece slowly, at the widest setting, twelve times, folding and turning between rolls. Then roll through the narrower machine settings. If you see any nut pieces that are causing the dough to tear, remove them. If a strip does tear, fold it over and reroll at a wider setting to repair it. Roll the dough as thin as possible (it will never be as thin as plain dough, however). Cut dough with nuts by hand, crosswise, into *lacci,* or shoestrings, or fold the strips and cut lengthwise to form pappardelle.

GRAIN PASTA

Almost any milled grain—and finely ground seeds, nuts, and dried beans—can be mixed with all-purpose wheat flour to create pasta doughs. Some of these are traditional: whole-wheat, buckwheat, chestnut, and semolina flours, among others, have long been incorporated into pasta by Italian cooks, offering a diversity of flavors, textures, and (not least important) nutritional qualities. These days, there's an amazing variety of flours available, meeting a growing demand for healthful and flavorful whole foods.

SEMOLINA PASTA Semolina, the ground form of durum wheat, is mixed in a one-to-one ratio with all-purpose flour when making fresh pasta, creating a pasta that is nutty and resilient to the bite.

WHOLE-WHEAT PASTA Some of the first pastas in Italy, made by the Etruscans and later the Romans, were made out of barley and chickpea flour. When wheat came on the scene, it was milled as whole wheat and used for pasta. I find 100 percent whole-wheat pasta a bit dense and hard to digest, so I use equal proportions of white and whole-wheat to make a light, fast-cooking pasta with a distinctive taste.

BUCKWHEAT PASTA I love buckwheat pasta for the earthy, gritty character it brings to many dishes. Flour made from the buckwheat seed is used in Japanese soba noodles and is traditional in Italian pasta, too. In the Valtellina, they make a dish called *pizzoccheri,* buckwheat papparadelle dressed with cabbage, bacon, and Fontina. A spoonful of chopped walnuts lends marvelous texture and flavor to buckwheat pasta.

FLAXSEED PASTA If you are at all interested in eating healthfully with "whole foods," you have probably learned about flaxseed, hailed as a great source of fiber, with beneficial fatty acids and an abundance of micronutrients. But did you know that it makes a really tasty fresh pasta, too? Note that you need ground flaxseed meal—available in food-conscious markets.

CORNMEAL PASTA This pasta dough is made with a one-to-one ratio of all-purpose flour and instant polenta flour. The cornmeal gives the pasta great texture, flavor, and color.

BARLEY PASTA This is one of the oldest pasta doughs in Italy. The Romans would call it *lasagnum,* wide strips of pasta dressed with honey, cheese, and herbs.

CECI FLOUR PASTA Flour from dried ceci—the Italian name for garbanzo beans or chickpeas—is one of a number of bean flours with which one can make pasta. Like the others, this yields a good pasta with a different nuance of flavor—complex, buttery, with a tinge of sweetness from the bean. It's a great carrier for vegetable, game, or nut sauces. It's also gluten-free.

CHESTNUT PASTA Italians enjoy many traditional foods made with farina di castagne—chestnut flour—especially cakes and sweets. Pasta made partly with chestnut flour is delicious, too, as I hope you will discover. Imported farina di castagne is widely available in specialty markets.

POTATO FLOUR PASTA Potato flour, not to be confused with potato starch, makes pasta that has a delicious and distinctly potato-ey flavor. The dough will feel stiff when just mixed, but after resting it gets soft and easy to roll and cut.

SPINACH DOUGH PASTA Spinach pasta is made from regular pasta dough with the addition of cooked and puréed spinach. It is usually moister than other fresh pastas and will cook more quickly. Frozen chopped spinach works well with all-purpose flour.

HOW TO STORE FRESH PASTA

Ideally, you should cook fresh pasta the same day it is made, but it does keep well frozen. It is important that fresh pasta is tossed with coarse semolina flour or fine corn meal after it is cut and shaped so it does not stick. Long cuts of fresh pasta (such as fettuccine, trenette, or maccheroni) are best wound into a single-serving-size portion, set on a floured baking sheet, and frozen as individual mounds. Once frozen, several of them can be placed in a plastic sealed bag, then placed in a box so they don't get crushed in the freezer. Smaller shapes of homemade pasta (such as garganelli, gnocchi, and orecchiette) should be spread out and frozen on a sheet pan. Once frozen, they can be collected in single-portion amounts and frozen in sealed plastic bags. When you are ready to use the frozen pasta, shake off the excess flour and throw the frozen pasta directly into the boiling water; stir immediately so it does not stick.

STORING FRESHLY MADE RAVIOLI The great thing about making fresh ravioli is that they can be cooked within an hour or two of being made or they can be frozen, which allows them to last for a few weeks. If you have made fresh ravioli, just arrange them on a tray (so they are not touching) and keep them covered with a towel; if you will be cooking them immediately, leave them at room temperature. On the other hand, if you want to freeze uncooked ravioli, set the tray of fresh ravioli in the freezer; they should be frozen within two or three hours. Once they're frozen, set them in portion-sized ziplock bags and stack them securely in a plastic container, keeping in mind that frozen ravioli are very sensitive and chip easily. When cooking frozen ravioli, boil more water than you would for cooking fresh ravioli. This way, the water returns to a boil quickly after the chilly ravioli are added, and the ravioli

will not stick together. Once you have dropped them into the boiling water, stir gently with a wooden spoon, cover the pot, and return to the boiling point as soon as possible. Drain when cooked, and proceed to sauce.

FRESH PASTA SHAPES

BIGOLI A unique regional pasta, the signature of the Veneto region. Fresh bigoli are usually made of whole-wheat flour; they are thick and have a chewy texture. Bigoli are made by extruding the pasta dough through a torchio (a pasta press). Dried bigoli are now available in the pasta department of specialty food stores and online, or you can make it by using an electric pasta-extruder, or a meat grinder without the blade. I like to serve my bigoli the traditional way, with a gutsy chicken-liver sauce, or with an onion-and-anchovy sauce.

CAVATELLI Cylinders made with durum flour, rolled, then dragged across a wooden board to leave an indentation.

FREGNACCE Made in Lazio and Abruzzo, an egg-pasta dough rolled thin and cut into lozenge shapes.

FREGOLA Made by sprinkling water a bit at a time over flour and mixing the dough around by hand until small kernels of wet flour form; they are strained and then allowed to dry. Usually cooked in broth as a type of pastina.

GARGANELLI Made of fresh dough that is rolled into a thin sheet, then cut into diamonds; two ends are then folded into the middle onto each other, and pinched together. This is known as fusi istriani as well.

MACCHERONI ALLA CHITARRA An egg-dough pasta from Abruzzo, rolled into thin sheets and then pressed against the taut strings of a special "chitarra," a wooden box with strings like a guitar, and rolled over with a small rolling pin, so the dough falls apart into long strands. This cutting method is not just a charming old custom. The chitarra makes pasta strands that, when cooked, have wonderfully satisfying texture and substance. In my opinion, this sensation of mouth feel is one of the greatest gustatory pleasures, and maccheroni alla chitarra provides it in every bite. So get yourself a chitarra for making maccheroni. (More about this on page 81.)

MACCHERONI AL TORCHIO A durum-flour pasta extruded through a hand press, varying in shape and size depending on the die used in the press.

MALTAGLIATI Literally meaning "poorly or badly cut"; long sheets of dough are rolled out, and irregular lozenge shapes are cut from the dough.

ORECCHIETTE The name literally means "little ears." Durum-wheat pasta dough is mixed and kneaded, and then small pieces are pinched off the dough and rolled into long cylinders resembling pencils. Small pieces are cut from these strands of rolled dough, which are then pushed down against a wooden board and slightly dragged with a blunt knife. One side has a textured surface from the wooden board, and the other side has a small indentation as the dough slightly rolls up from being dragged along the board.

PAPPARDELLE Fresh egg dough rolled out into thin sheets, then cut into long ribbons, about 1½ inches in width.

PASSATELLI A thick spaghetti-like pasta made from bread crumbs, eggs, cheese, lemon, nutmeg, and parsley. It is delicious, and usually cooked and served in chicken broth. Once cooked, it

is also served with braised or roasted meats to absorb the sauce. This is another delicious way to use leftover bread. In Italy, traditional strands of passatelli are shaped with a special tool somewhat like a potato masher, with a heavy-duty perforated sheet that is pressed into the dough. Given enough pressure, the dough is forced through the holes and forms spaghetti-like pieces. It is important that the density of the dough be neither too hard nor too soft. A good alternative is to use an electric meat grinder, or the meat-grinder attachment of a food processor. Set it up as usual, with a disk of medium or large holes, but without the rotary cutting blade. The machine will now act as an extruder rather than a grinder: you drop the dough into the hopper and the auger will do the work, pushing it out the holes in a continuous stream of perfect passatelli. Let them fall onto a tray or plate and break naturally into pieces. Often served in cooked broth.

PICI Small pieces of fresh pasta dough individually rolled by hand into four-to-five-inch spaghetti-like shapes.

PIZZOCCHERI Made using buckwheat flour mixed with wheat flour and water. Thick, flat noodles about a quarter-inch wide and three inches long.

SCIALATIELLI Fresh dough is rolled out into a thick sheet, and long noodles are cut and then rolled around a metal stick the size of pencil, to form curly strands of pasta of which small pieces are pinched off, about six inches long.

SFOGLIA Literally translated as "a sheet." Rolled-out pasta-dough sheets, usually made with wheat, eggs, and water.

SPAETZLE Made with flour, water, and some milk. The shape is made by a utensil that looks like a cheese grater and pushes the dough through, directly into the boiling soup or water.

STRASCINATI Fresh dough pieces are pinched off and rolled by hand into cylindrical strands, which are then cut into short pieces, about an inch and a half long. These smaller pieces of dough are dragged across a wooden board, by finger or with a utensil, so they form a piece of dough two to three inches long, with an indentation.

STROZZAPRETI Literally "priest chokers." Fresh pasta rolled and formed into an elongated, twisted form of cavatelli.

TACCONI Made with corn flour, wheat flour, and water. The dough is rolled out, and strips about one inch wide are cut, and then cut again into a rhombus shape.

TROFIE Wheat-flour pasta dough often mixed with riced potato or chestnut flour. Pieces about an inch and a half long are pinched off the dough and rolled between the hands, giving a little twist to the dough.

STUFFED FRESH PASTA SHAPES

AGNOLOTTI A rectangular, ridged-edge shape; usually stuffed with mixed meat filling.

ANOLINI A pasta round folded in half on itself to make a semicircle, usually stuffed with a meat-and-grana-cheese filling.

CADUNSEI Round dough disks folded in half, usually filled with chicken giblets and herbs.

CANNELLONI Sheets of pasta boiled and then rolled around stuffing—usually meat, fish, or cheese—and then baked.

CAPPELLACCI Shaped like an ugly, slightly conical hat, formed by folding the dough square into a triangle, with the stuffing in the middle, pinching the two ends together, and then folding down the two corners sticking up. It can be stuffed with vegetables, such as squash, or meat-and-cheese fillings.

CAPPELLETTI Small hat-shaped pasta formed by folding a round disk of pasta dough in half, bringing the two corners together to meet, and pinching them together. Stuffed with a mixed meat filling or a cheese filling, and most often cooked in broth.

CARAMELLE Pasta stuffed with meats and cheese and twisted at both ends, like a candy wrapper.

CASONCELLI (CALZONCELLI) Rough dough disks about two inches in diameter. May be one disk folded in half, or two disks placed one on top of the other with the filling in between. Usually stuffed with a filling of ricotta, ground meat, and eggs.

CASONSEI Round disks of dough with serrated edges, folded in half and stuffed differently from region to region in Italy.

CJALSONS Stuffed round disks with serrated edges, sometimes half a circle and sometimes a full round circle of dough, stuffed with swiss chard, ricotta, smoked ricotta, and raisins. Made in Friuli–Venezia Giulia.

KRAFI A festive Istrian stuffed pasta. Fresh-dough ravioli with a filling of cheese, raisins, and spices such as nutmeg and cinnamon. The shape can be either a half-moon, in which the dough is folded onto itself, or two round disks with the filling placed in between and the edges pressed down so the stuffed pasta is sealed.

RAVIOLI Often a general term for stuffed fresh pasta, usually made of an egg-based dough that is cut into squares, rounds, half-moons, or triangles, and stuffed. The filling may be based on meat, cheese, vegetables, or even fish.

SCHIAFFETTONI A Sicilian type of cannelloni, dough is rolled out into a thin sheet, and four-inch squares are cut and stuffed with a filling of meat and cured meats. The dough is rolled around the filling, and the edges are tightly sealed and baked. There is also a dried pasta called schiaffoni, long and tubular, which is cooked, stuffed, and baked.

TORTELLI Fresh stuffed pasta squares or rounds. The fillings vary in different regions of Italy. There are also potato tortelli and squash tortelli. Tortelli maremmani are filled with spinach or nettles; tortelli romagnoli, from Romagna, are usually filled with greens and ricotta. Fillings can also be of mortadella, prosciutto, various meats, *grana* cheese, and spices. The dough is rolled out and cut into squares about one inch in size; some filling is put on top, and covered by a pasta square of the same size. The two dough pieces are pushed together along the edges to seal the filling in.

GNOCCHI

I love the feeling of working gnocchi dough with my hands, but gnocchi dough can be tricky, so it is important that, once the potatoes have been cooked and peeled, they are riced and set aside to cool completely. I do recommend buying a potato ricer if you don't already have one; it's a great tool to have on hand in the kitchen. Once the potatoes have cooled and started to dry, you can begin to form the dough mixture. Be sure not to overwork the dough or add too much flour, and you'll end up with perfect gnocchi—ready to plop into your favorite pot of perking sauce. Make sure you have abundant boiling water to cook your gnocchi in, 50 percent more than when boiling pasta. Fresh gnocchi contain extra flour and need space to roll in the water as they are cooking; otherwise, they will stick together.

COOKING FROZEN GNOCCHI When you are making gnocchi, you should either cook them as soon as they are made, or freeze them for later. To freeze fresh gnocchi, spread the gnocchi out, not touching, on a lightly floured baking pan, and set to freeze. When they are hard, in about two hours, gather them together, shake off any excess flour, and store them in sealed plastic bags, by portions, for future use. They will keep in the freezer for up to six weeks. To cook frozen gnocchi, make sure you have double the amount of cooking water that you would use to cook fresh gnocchi or pasta, because throwing in the frozen gnocchi will reduce the temperature of the boiling water. If there are too many frozen gnocchi and not enough boiling water, the gnocchi will disintegrate before the water returns to a boil and gives them get a chance to cook. It is imperative to get the water back to the boiling point as quickly as possible after you drop the frozen gnocchi into it and get them cooking.

CANEDERLI Made from stale bread instead of potatoes, with flour, milk, eggs, prosciutto, parsley, and grana cheese all rolled into balls a bit bigger than usual gnocchi, then boiled and served in sauce or in soup. Also known as Knödel or gnocchi di pane.

GNOCCHI ALLA ROMANI Made with semolina flour, salt, eggs, milk, butter, and grana cheese, all cooked together, poured out, and allowed to cool. Rounds are then cut and usually cooked in a baking pan, slightly overlapping, sprinkled with grated cheese, and baked.

POTATO GNOCCHI Made with flour and riced potato. The dough is rolled into long strands, about two centimeters (.79 inch) in diameter, which are then cut into small spheres about one inch in diameter. These small dumplings are gently rolled over the tines of a fork, creating indentations with lines on the outside and a small cranny where the finger had been placed to push the dumpling against the tines of the fork. Cooked in boiling water, and removed when they float to the surface.

SQUASH GNOCCHI Made with flour, squash, and eggs, and shaped the same way as potato gnocchi.

GNOCCHI SARDI (MALLOREDDUS) A traditional Sardinian pasta or gnocco (dumpling) made from semolina dough sometimes imbued with saffron. The shape is formed by pinching off small pieces of dough and rolling them between the hands to form strands the thickness of pencils. Small pieces about a half-inch long are cut from the strands. These small pieces are quickly and gently pushed with the thumb into a small wicker basket, perforated grater, or some other appropriate utensil, to create a texture on one side while the thumb creates an indentation on the other side.

This flicking motion creates a short oval shell with a hollow inside and a textured outer surface, perfect for picking up a dressing or sauce. And the hard-wheat dough gives each piece a wonderful chewy texture. In short, malloreddus is a little pasta with a big mouth feel. Dress it with sausage tomato sauce and top with grated pecorino cheese.

GNUDI Ricotta dumplings made with some spinach or other greens, kneaded together with some flour, then boiled in water and removed when they float to the surface.

DRIED PASTA

BUYING DRIED PASTA

When you buy *pasta asciutta* (dried pasta), look for these qualities: It should be made of 100 percent semolina flour; the higher the protein in the semolina, the better—17 percent is a good amount. The pasta should have a rough finish. It should be opaque, and should not be shiny or blotchy or have white specks, nor should it be cracked or broken. Imported Italian pasta is more likely to possess these characteristics. When buying pasta, look for different shapes, lengths, nooks and cranies, and ridges; they all add an extra element of texture and palate stimulation, and the sauces lodge better in the pastas with nooks and crannies.

DRIED PASTA SHAPES

With 320 officially recorded shapes of pasta, there is so much choice, so here I have included some of my favorites. Regional shapes are certainly paired well with regional sauces; pasta with nooks and crannies in which the sauce and vegetables can lodge, such as shells, cavatappi, and rigatoni, work well with a chunky sauce. Long and flat pastas, like spaghetti, linguine, and fettuccine, carry buttery and homogenized sauces such as clam, tomato, or garlic-and-oil sauce particularly well. However in many cases, a variety of different pasta shapes go well with a variety of sauces.

ACINI DI PEPE Small, round specks of pasta, like peppercorns but a bit smaller, served in broth.

ANELLI Shaped like tiny rings.

BAVETTE Thinner, convex tagliatelle.

BUCATINI Long pasta, like spaghetti but thicker, hollow in the middle. Also known as perciatelli.

CALAMARATA Shaped like the ring of a cut calamaro.

CAMPANELLE About an inch and a half in length, twisted to form a flower- or bell-like shape, with ruffled edges.

CANESTRINI Small bow-tie pasta often used in soups.

CAPELLINI Thin spaghetti.

CASARECCE Various shapes of flat, square, or rectangular pasta, cut differently from region to region.

CAVATAPPI A short corkscrew-shaped pasta.

CONCHIGLIE Shell-shaped pasta that comes in different sizes, often stuffed with ricotta and baked, but also boiled and served with sauce, depending on the size of the shell, usually with a ridged outside.

DITALINI Small tubular pasta, shaped like a thimble or *ditale,* but a bit smaller. Often used in minestre.

FARFALLE A bow-tie- or butterfly-shaped pasta. The pasta square, with smooth edges or serrated, is pinched in the middle to form the shape.

FIDELINI Also known as capelli di angelo. Very thin spaghetti, like hair.

FUSILLI A short cut of pasta that is shaped in a tight spiral, about two inches long.

FUSILLI LUNGHI A long, loose twisted spiral, about six inches long.

GALLETTI Shaped like a cock's comb, about an inch in length, slightly bent and tubular.

GEMELLI About one and a half inches in length. Looks like two strands of pasta twisted together. Literally, the name means "twins."

GRAMIGNA A kind of pastina created by grating the pasta dough on a grater with a large holed die. Factory-made versions look like squiggly worms.

LUMACHE Elbow-shaped pasta that can vary in dimensions. It has a ridged outside and is tubular and rounded, like a half-circle.

MACCHERONI Often used as a general term for pasta, but also a specific shape, about one inch in length, with a slight curl and indentations or lines down its length.

MAFALDE A flat, long pasta with curly edges, about half an inch in width and ten inches long.

ORZO Shaped like barley grains, and used most often in soups.

PACCHERI Wide tubes about two inches in length, the outside either ridged or smooth. Also known as "maniche rigate" (ridged sleeves). Mezzi paccheri are about two-thirds the size.

PASTINA Small, variously shaped pasta, served in broth.

PENNE A tubular pasta that can be smooth or ridged on the outside, with the ends cut on an angle. Mezze penne are about two-thirds the size.

PIPE RIGATE Shaped like conchiglie, although often a bit smaller in size.

RADIATORI A dry pasta about three-quarters of an inch in length, shaped like an old cast-iron radiator, with loads of nooks and crannies.

RIGATONI A thick tubular pasta with ridges, also known as maniche. Mezze maniche, also known as mezzi rigatoni, are about two-thirds the size.

RISI Small rice-shaped pasta similar to pastina but a bit rounder. Served in broth.

RUOTE Round pasta with ridges on the outside, shaped liked spoked wheels, about one inch in diameter.

SEDANI Tubular pasta, slightly curved, with ridges outside; about three inches long.

SPAGHETTI Dough rolled out and cut into long strips. Originally it was rolled by hand, but is now extruded through a die. About eleven inches long.

SPAGHETTINI A thinner version of spaghetti, about half its diameter.

STELLINE Tiny star-shaped pasta, sometimes with a small hole in the middle, cooked in broth.

TORTIGLIONI Tubular pasta with ridges on the outside that twist around the tube; about one and a half inches in length.

TRENETTE Long like spaghetti—thin, flat ribbons.

TUBETTI Small tubular pasta, about a quarter-inch in diameter and half-inch in length, either smooth or ridged outer texture.

VERMICELLI Long, thin strands of pasta, like spaghetti but thinner, made in various thicknesses.

ZITI Tubular pasta with a smooth outside, about a quarter-inch in diameter and one and a half inches in length.

EGG PASTA

Making egg pasta at home is one of the oldest Italian traditions. The number of eggs used in a recipe varies from region to region in Italy, and often the number of yolks used is greater than whole eggs. The more numerous the yolks, the more golden the egg pasta. Egg pasta can be served fresh, or dried and used later. The dough should feel silky smooth and not sticky or rough.

HOMEMADE EGG PASTA SHAPES

CAPELLI D'ANGELO (ANGEL-HAIR PASTA) Made by cutting thin sheets of egg pasta into very thin strands.

FETTUCCINE Long sheets of pasta, usually loosely rolled and then cut into strands about twelve inches long and two centimeters (.79 inch) wide. They can be made fresh or in a factory, with egg pasta or durum wheat. Usually allowed to dry in *nidi,* or nest shapes.

GARGANELLI Made at home with an egg-pasta dough, but also made commercially with durum wheat; a lozenge-shaped pasta with two ends brought together but not pinched down, creating a tube. Usually made on a ridged wooden board so that the outside of the pasta retains the ridge of the board.

LASAGNA Sheets of pasta, usually with egg-based dough if made at home or durum if commercially made, boiled and then used to create a layered pasta dish in a casserole baking dish, alternating with layers of cheese and sauce.

PAGLIA E FIENO A mixture of egg-pasta strands and green spinach-pasta strands, literally translated as "straw and hay."

QUADRUCCI Small pastina, usually with a pinch of nutmeg in the dough, cut into quarter-inch squares, and typically used in broth soups. It can be homemade or bought commercially.

STRANGOZZI Also known as stringozzi. Fresh dough is rolled out into a sheet of pasta, not too thick or thin, and long strips are cut, about an eighth of an inch wide and eight inches long. These long strips are then rolled between the hands, or on a surface, to make long wormlike pasta.

TAGLIATELLE Egg pasta rolled out into a thin sheet and then cut into ten-inch-long strips about a quarter-inch in width. The more eggs used, the yellower the pasta.

TAGLIOLINI Thinner tagliatelle.

TAJARIN Made mostly in Piedmont. Egg pasta rolled very thin, then cut in long, thin strings of square spaghetti.

TONNARELLI Thick, hand-rolled spaghetti.

PREPARING, SAUCING, AND SERVING PASTA

COOKING PASTA

Always season the pasta water with sea salt. Oil should never be added to the cooking water; it coats the pasta and makes it slippery, so the sauce won't adhere properly to the pasta. An exception to this is cooking wide fresh pasta such as lasagna, so it does not stick together, and the lasagna will have time to absorb sauce while baking. To test when pasta is done, bite into a strand to determine whether or not it has the al dente texture you desire. As soon as the pasta is done, drain immediately, shaking off all the excess water. Pasta should never be rinsed, unless you are making cold pasta dishes or baked pasta dishes such as lasagna or manicotti. Always sauce the pasta immediately, while it is still hot. After you have drained the pasta, return it to the cooking pot, immediately add a few tablespoons of sauce, and toss, or add drained pasta to a skillet with sauce and toss well to dress the pasta.

USING PASTA WATER IN YOUR SAUCE

Using the water in which the pasta was cooked is an essential component of skillet-sautéed pastas, both in the sauce-making stage and in finishing the dish. After you have cooked all your seasonings and sauce ingredients, add water from the pasta pot as a medium to extract and blend their flavors. There is no need to add stock, wine, or butter. In a large skillet, the water will evaporate quickly, so replenish the moisture with more pasta water whenever needed. If your sauce is complete but must wait awhile for the pasta to cook, it may thicken, so add pasta-cooking water. If there is not enough sauce to coat the pasta when you're tossing it in the skillet, add some pasta water. Remember that the cooking water is salty and has starchy qualities, which adds seasoning and body as you finish the pasta with the sauce. So, next time you are draining your cooked pasta, always save a cup or two of the cooking water.

MARINARA AND TOMATO SAUCE

Marinara sauce is a quick sauce, seasoned only with garlic, crushed red pepper, and basil. It is best when made with whole San Marzano or plum tomatoes, coarsely crushed by hand or passed through a food mill. Marinara can be left chunky; the texture of the finished sauce is fairly loose, and the taste is that of fresh tomatoes. Tomato sauce, on the other hand, is a more complex affair, starting with pureed tomatoes seasoned with onion, carrot, celery, and bay leaf, and left to simmer until thickened and rich in flavor. Sometimes a piece of fresh pork meat is added for additional flavor. The taste is sweeter and more complex.

SAUCE OR GRAVY?

In America, Italian-food enthusiasts will fight to the end for what they call their precious pasta topping. Is it sauce or is it gravy? The fact is, in Italy, sauce and gravy are different things. "Sauce" translates to *salsa*; it has a light, fresh flavor, often involving oil, garlic, and tomato, with a short cooking time, closer to marinara. Gravy, on the other hand, called *sugo* in Italian, takes much longer to cook and has a denser consistency and more complex flavor, closer to tomato sauce; it often contains meat and is darker in color.

HOW MUCH SAUCE DOES YOUR PASTA NEED?

In Italian, the verb we use to describe the final dressing of the pasta with sauce is *condire*, which means "to season, to flavor." And the phrase *condire la pasta* reminds us that the sauce should be considered a condiment, an enhancement to the pasta. I like to think of pasta, especially fresh egg pastas, as playing the leading role in the dish. So why drown the main character before the drama has started? Keep these ideas in mind when you bring your pasta and sauce together. If you see that the quantity of sauce is disproportionate to the pasta, spoon some of the pasta out (and save it for reheating, of course) before tossing and finishing the dish. If you see that the sauce is soupy and collects in the bottom of the skillet, raise the heat while tossing the pasta actively, evaporating the excess water and thickening the sauce so it adheres to the pasta. A properly dressed pasta should glide in the sauce, not drown in it or stick in lumps. When you are finished eating a bowl of pasta, basically no sauce should be left at the bottom of the bowl.

SERVING PASTA

Pasta should always be served in hot plates, as soon as it is cooked and sauced. For family meals, I serve it in a large, heated bowl, or I bring the skillet to the table and serve portions directly onto warm plates. For more formal occasions, I dish the pasta up into warm bowls in the kitchen and bring them quickly to the table. The shorter the trek from the hot skillet to the individual bowl, the better. Be sure to pass a bowl of freshly grated cheese around the table with the pasta.

LEFTOVER PASTA

Leftover pasta is delicious reheated the next day. The texture changes—it is not as resilient as it was when first cooked—but it takes on a new dimension, since it has absorbed some of the sauce. To heat leftover pasta, you can add any remaining sauce, chicken stock, or just plain water. Heat the pasta over low heat in a nonstick pan, stirring regularly. I love it when reheated pasta begins to form a crust and becomes a bit crunchy. Leftover pasta is also great to make a frittata with.

Rice, Seeds, Grains, and Bread

Every culture has a staple grain used in the cuisine as a medium to support or be the main player among vegetables and proteins. Italy is incredibly varied and quite prolific in its use of base staple carbohydrates. Pasta is the obvious first choice, but in Lombardy rice reigns supreme, just as in the northeast corner of Italy, polenta is the favorite. A beloved pasta from the Valtellina region is made from buckwheat, and Sicily loves to use sesame seeds in its sweet and savory food. Rice, seeds, and grains play an important part in Italian cuisine, and their many variations add much richness and nutritional value.

BARLEY

Barley is a wonderfully versatile cereal grain with a rich nutlike flavor and an appealing chewy, pastalike consistency. In appearance it resembles wheat berries, although it is slightly lighter in color. Americans might think of barley first for its role in the brewing of beer, but Italians have a fascinating history with barley, dating back centuries. Barley has even been used as currency at times. Today you'll find barley mostly in soups— I find it especially nice in mushroom and vegetable soups. It is also delicious when used as a risotto. I like serving it alongside braised meats and in stews, so it mops up the sauce, and it works great in a salad. It is even good as a dessert, tossed with honey and dried fruits and nuts. When cooking barley, be mindful that its texture will range from soft to chewy, depending on how long and with how much water it's cooked. You can generally find barley in its pearled, hulled, and flaked form. It is available packaged as well as in bulk containers. When buying in bulk, make sure the bins containing the barley are covered, with no evidence of moisture, to ensure its maximal freshness. Store the barley in a tightly covered container in a cool, dry place.

BREAD

I cannot imagine an Italian meal without bread on the table. *Pane quotidiano,* daily bread, is even part of a prayer. So, when some bread is left behind and not consumed, it is an act of due respect to use it in cooking somehow, never to throw it away. There are so many uses for day-old bread, in both sweet and savory recipes. For example, cut your leftover bread into cubes, spread them out on a tray, and let them dry out, either in an open space in the kitchen or in an oven with the pilot light on, for a day or two. Process those dry pieces in the food processor to create homemade bread crumbs. Day-old bread is also perfect for making panzanella salad (page 127), or tossed in any salad when made into croutons. Use your leftover bread for desserts such as bread pudding, chocolate pudding, and a chocolate-almond parfait of layers of old bread soaked in melted chocolate then layered with toasted almonds and whipped cream. Leftover bread is even great when tossed with ripe summer berries that have been macerated in honey and lemon juice. Let them steep together, then top with some whipped cream.

FARRO

Farro is one of the oldest grains, and I urge you to try it, especially if you are not familiar with it. You will quickly come to love it. An ancient form of wheat (also called emmer), farro cooks like pearl barley or rice, with no soaking. It has a wonderful nutty flavor and is quite nutritious.

Since it is now sold in many specialty markets and easily ordered online, it is easy to procure; it also stores well. I hope it becomes a staple in your pantry. It is great in soups, made into a salad with vegetables added, or tossed like a risotto with butter and cheese.

FETTE BISCOTTATE

Melba toast has an Italian cousin, and its name is "fette biscottate" (or, singular, "fetta biscottata"). These dry, toastlike crackers come in loaves and bear a striking resemblance in both taste and appearance to the infamous melba toast. In Italy, this snack food is commonly eaten as part of the early-morning breakfast, with a sweet spread such as Nutella, marmalade, or honey. Biscottate, plain or with a spread, are also nice dipped in coffee or tea. You can buy them in Italian-import stores, or you can make your own Italian breakfast (*colazione*) with whatever your local version of this classic cracker is. Look for the whole-grain and whole-wheat variety (*integrale*); I enjoy their nutty taste.

PINE NUTS

Pinoli nuts (often spelled "pignoli" in English) are the edible seeds found inside certain species of pinecones. Once the pine nut is removed from the cone, the shell is cracked to reveal a soft, ivory-colored nut. When mature, the pinecone releases the pine nuts naturally, but sometimes the cone has to be heated to remove all the nuts; this labor-intensive process is what makes pinoli so expensive.

These nuts have become so popular over time that the pine tree is in danger of depletion: we eat the seeds, and each tree needs quite a few years to mature and produce the pinecones that hold them. In Italian cuisine, pinoli are most often used in pesto, baking, and in savory dishes, especially in Sicily, where pine nuts are paired with raisins and used in fish and vegetable preparations. In the Italian American tradition, pinoli call to mind soft almond cookies covered in pine nuts. After purchasing pinoli, keep in mind that they turn rancid quickly and should be stored in an airtight plastic bag in the refrigerator for up to three months. If you freeze your pine nuts, they are good for up to nine months.

POLENTA

Polenta is unbelievably versatile. I could give you a thousand ways to enjoy it, because that's how many ways we ate it when I was growing up. It is delicious poured into a bowl and served as is, or you can allow it to chill and slice it, then grill or fry it for the next day's meal. You can even make a "mosaic" by folding diced cooked vegetables into the soft polenta, packing it into a loaf pan while it is still warm, and then chilling the vegetable-studded polenta. When you cut the chilled polenta loaf into slices, the vegetables will form a mosaic, beautiful to serve, delicious to eat.

Polenta can be runny or dense; it can be served as a side dish or as an accompaniment to braised meat or fish stews to mop up the sauce. I view polenta similarly to how I view pasta. Both serve as a means to carry so many flavors. But don't think that polenta has to be bland to showcase the accompanying tastes. When you make polenta at home, you can be very free with your choice of flavors. Try substituting milk for half of the water. Butter or oil can be added, as well as bay leaves, garlic, and rosemary (just be sure to remove these before serving). Grated or shredded cheese can be added during the last ten minutes of cooking. And feel free to experiment with sausage or vegetables in your polenta.

RICE, ITALIAN VARIETIES

Rice is a food product that feeds the largest number of people on this planet, with about forty thousand different varieties, each having its unique flavor and cooking properties. Rice reached Italy in the eighth century from the Orient, via Sicily; by the thirteenth century, rice had reached the Val Padana, the valley of the Po River. Italy today is the largest producer of rice in Europe. The Italian varieties are Arborio, Carnaroli, and Vialone Nano, all short-grain rice, which in the process of cooking releases its starch and yields a perfectly creamy risotto.

Rice's nuances of flavor and suitability for different dishes can be a matter of great debate in an Italian kitchen, but here are some guidelines: (1) The Lomellina area of Lombardy is particularly renowned for its *superfino* (large) varieties, especially Carnaroli (perhaps the favorite of chefs these days). (2) The Vialone Nano—a shorter, *semifino* rice that grows around Mantova, in Lombardy, and farther east, in the Veneto—is excellent for soups and desserts. Despite its smaller size, it also makes fine risotto. (3) Arborio is the best-known of the Italian rices, and the most readily available in the United States. Perhaps not as fashionable with cognoscenti as Carnaroli, Arborio is an excellent rice for most cooking procedures. Fortunately, all of these great rices are imported here, and all are delicious in traditional Italian recipes.

When you are buying rice for risotto dishes, Carnaroli, Arborio, and Vialone Nano are the varieties to look for. Look for shiny kernels of uniform pearly color, with no blotchiness, and a smooth surface that doesn't feel floury to the touch. The best cooking vessel for risotto is a wide, heavy, nonreactive skillet that evenly disperses heat and allows evaporation to occur uniformly. The ratio of rice to cooking liquid is one cup of rice for every 3½ cups of liquid. One cup of uncooked rice will yield two cups of cooked risotto. The essential technique for making a perfect risotto is to use boiling stock to add to the cooking risotto, and to make sure to stir it constantly. It's important that risotto be served and eaten immediately.

WHEAT BERRIES

The term "wheat berry" refers to the entire wheat kernel, not including the hull. Wheat berries are usually tan to reddish brown in color and are available either hard, when they are packaged dried, or soft and usually partially cooked, when they are packaged in a can as a processed grain. Wheat berries provide dietary fiber and vitamins B_1 and B_3. Look for them at your local health-food store or in the natural-foods section of your local supermarket. If they're dried, soak the wheat berries in water for five to six hours, then drain and cook in salted boiling water like other grains until soft, about forty-five minutes. Add drained cooked wheat berries to soups, or serve them hot as a side dish. Wheat berries have a nutty flavor, so they are great with fresh vegetables, or with honey and dried fruits as a dessert. They are often added to salads, or baked into a bread, to add a crunchy texture as a whole grain.

Fish and Seafood

I was born in Pula, an Adriatic seaside city, now in Istria, Croatia. The sea was an immeasurable source of food for my family and neighbors, and the sea is still the biggest source of food and nourishment for humanity. But as the earth we live on is slowly being depleted of its minerals, so are the oceans being depleted of fish. The need to raise our consciousness about preserving our environment, our source of food, is ever more urgent. We must respect and use all of the species with which the sea gifts us—not just the lobsters, shrimps, and big fish steaks—and keep those oceans ecologically sound, so the flora and fauna of those depths will continue to flower and the fish to thrive.

My uncle Emilio was an electrician by profession but a great, passionate fisherman in his spare time; sometimes he would take me on his small boat to help him. My chores were to get the bait ready, to untangle the fishing thread (because he had no fishing reels), and ultimately to collect the fish as he pulled it onto the boat and then sort it into the right bins. I recall trolling white strips of ripped old sheets so the calamari would come to the top to investigate and he could snarl them. I helped him pick up the rocks from the sandy shores so he could catch the worms that lurked underneath for bait; those wiggly worms were nasty and could pinch you if they got near your fingers. Of course, the fun was bringing the catch home. The big fish were sold to the local restaurants and markets. The smaller and less prized fish were divided among the family for a meal.

I love "blue fish"—sardines, mackerel, and other deepwater fish that live far from the coast—but they required different fishing techniques: netting for sardines, and trolling with multiple hooks for the mackerel. For crabs and lobster, we would drop the baited cages before fishing and return the next day to pull them up. It was so exciting, hanging off the side of the boat, waiting to see if a cage had a lobster or crab caught in it. Of course, a multiple catch meant a celebration. I cleaned the fish alongside my uncle, for all good fishermen gutted and scaled their fish in the ocean, and I learned to cook fish with him. Here in this section you will find most of my favorite fish that I would catch and cook, and many more I have gotten to know during my professional career. Short of going fishing, I will share with you what to look for in a fish when buying, how to clean it, how to store it, and ultimately how to cook it.

Learn what type of fish cooks well in the recipe you have chosen. Learn the different types of fish and the texture of the meat they have, flaky or meaty, oily or not. Also learn how to buy fresh fish. It should not smell bad, but should smell like fresh seawater. It is better to buy fish whole and ask the fishmonger to clean it for you if you need a fillet.

ANCHOVIES, THE ITALIAN JOLT OF FLAVOR IN COOKING

Anchovies add an unmistakable subtle flavor to all kinds of dishes, from hot to cold, raw to cooked, and simple to elaborate. There are two main types of anchovies available. Most people are familiar with the fillets that are packed flat in oil in little cans. If you can find anchovies packed in pure olive oil, stock up—they will have a richer flavor. Anchovies are also sold packed in salt, without oil, usually from huge cans kept on the counters of Italian, Greek, and Spanish specialty stores. Salt-packed anchovies have a firmer texture and a more pronounced flavor. They also will need some preparation before you can eat them or cook with them, because they still have skin, scales, and bones. To clean anchovies packed in salt, wash them well under cool running water and pat them dry. On a cutting board, hold the anchovies by the tail and scrape off most of the skin and any scales from both sides, with a paring knife. Separate the fish from its backbone into fillets with the tip of the paring knife by prying the fillets apart through the stomach opening. Pull or scrape out the backbone, cut off the tail, and cut the anchovy fillets depending on the type of recipe you are making. Both kinds of anchovies are delicious to cook with, add to salads, dressings, sauces, stuffing, roasts, or to eat as is.

BACCALÀ

Baccalà is dried salted codfish. Originally a product of the Nordic countries, it was a commodity during the era of ship trade and would travel well on long journeys. Baccalà has become a staple in many parts of the world, in particular the Mediterranean, Portugal, the Caribbean, and South America. Today it is an Italian delicacy, served particularly around the Christmas holiday. To prepare salted cod, rinse the cod and soak it in water for about ten to twelve hours to remove some of the saltiness, changing the water periodically. It can then be cooked in milk, in a tomato sauce, or whipped with olive oil and served as a spread on bread, which is my favorite way to enjoy it.

CALAMARI (SQUID)

Calamari are mollusks whose bodies are a tubular mantle with two wings, out of which the head protrudes, along with eight arms and two tentacles that have small suction cups. In the center of the head there is a hard plastic beak, resembling that of a parrot; this is the mouth. Two large eyes are set behind the tentacles and the whole body is covered by a thin skin with spots of pink-purple pigmentation. Calamari camouflage themselves and seem to disappear as a line of defense. All the digestive parts are in the tubular body, as is the ink sac, from which they squirt ink against predators and give themselves the time to escape. Every part of the calamari is edible except the inner digestive sacs, the beak, the plasticlike backbone, and the eyes. Calamari are very easy to clean: remove all the digestive and reproductive organs from the tubular body, cut out the eyes, remove the beak, pull out the backbone, and you are done. If the skin is nice and fresh, I leave it on; if the calamari has been handled a lot or frozen and the skin is a dark pink-purple, just peel it off. The flesh of calamari is firm and sweet, but be careful not to overcook it. Quick, high-heat cooking techniques are best, such as frying, searing, grilling, and quick poaching. The calamari can also be stuffed, roasted, or poached in a sauce; such dishes, requiring a longer cooking time, are more about the flavor that the calamari releases than the calamari meat itself. The long, braising method focuses more on the flavor of the sauce, by extracting the flavor of the calamari into the sauce, and is preferable if you want to make calamari sauce to dress pasta, risotto, or polenta. The whole cleaned tube of the calamari can be grilled or seared, including the head and tentacles, or stuffed and cooked, or the calamari can be cut in rounds and fried, seared, and poached for a salad. The size of the calamari can range from one inch to a foot or more, but I like them best when their bodies are four to six inches long.

CLAMS

Clams are officially bivalve mollusks, with two shells, and they usually live in sandy or muddy seawater. They range in species and size but most often when shopping you will find the smaller littleneck clams, about eight to ten per pound. They are delicious raw, stuffed, baked, or in a wine sauce. The cherrystone clam, about six to ten per pound, is a little larger and just as delicious as the littlenecks, but also delicious when chopped and baked and stuffed. They make a very good dressing for pasta as well. The top neck, about four clams per pound, and the chowder clam, three clams per pound, are best when chopped to make sauce for pasta as well as chowder and other soups. Now we find Manila clams on the market. They are usually smaller than littleneck clams and are delicious when braised in wine sauce, added in the shell to a sauce for pasta, and in fish soups. Clams are filter feeders, so sometimes they do have sand inside the shell. To clean clams, first discard any broken ones. Then check if any are opened; if so, tap the open-shell clam lightly on a surface; it should clam up if it is alive. If it does not close, discard the clam, because it is not fresh. Set the clams in a container with enough cold water to cover and let them sit for thirty minutes in the refrigerator; they should spit the sand out.

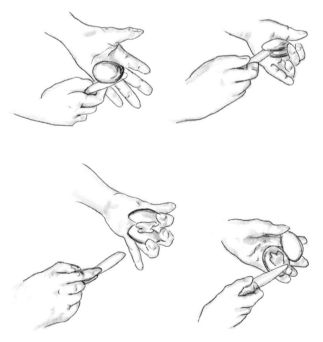

To open clams, you need a clam-shucking knife. If you try to use a paring knife or any other knife, you'll risk ruining your knife and injuring yourself. Prior to shucking the clams, set them on a baking sheet and put them in the freezer for thirty minutes. This freezes the clam muscles and allows for easier opening. When you are ready to shuck the clam, you'll notice that one side is evenly rounded and one side has a pronounced protrusion. Place the clam in the palm of your hand. Insert the blade of the shucking knife between the two shells, against the little protrusion, and, while applying firm pressure, wiggle the blade between the shells. Once the halves of the shell are pried apart, work the blade along the top of the top shell until the clam is released into the bottom shell. Simply twist off the top shell and discard it, then run the knife under the clam to release it from the bottom shell. Give the clam a quick rinse under cold running water to remove any sand or chipped shell. You can leave the clam in the shell and proceed to cook it that way, or scrape the clam out of the shell and chop for clam sauce or other sauces.

Keep in mind to reserve as much as you can of the clam juice while shucking. Let it rest, so the sand and shell particles settle to the bottom, and then strain through cheesecloth, leaving the solid particles behind.

Clams are delicious raw or slightly cooked. Take care not to overcook them, because they will be tough. During the cooking process, as the shell opens, the clam is cooked. The clams eaten most frequently in Italy are the vongola, the cozza, and the tellina. The tellina is the smallest in size, about as big as a thumbnail, and used shell and all, in making white clam sauce in Italy; the shells are discarded while eating.

LOBSTER

Lobster was not always the luxurious commodity it is today: during the Pilgrims' time and even later, it was given to prisoners and slaves to eat. The tables have turned, and lobster is considered a treat today. Lobster is graded by its size and by the hardness of its shell. Lobsters of 1 to 1¼ pounds are called "chicks"; they are cheaper, because the ratio of meat to shell is low. "Quarters," from 1¼ to 1½ pounds, make a good one-lobster-per-person portion. "Halves" are 1½ to 2 pounds; they are good split and served as half a lobster per portion. The "heavy" or "jumbo" is from 2 to 3 pounds and over; I find these too big, the meat too tough. When you are buying a lobster, look for a live lobster that when picked up raises its claws and flips its tail. Buy a lobster with a hard shell and long antennas—and one that is fresh from the ocean and that has not been in a tank long. Lobsters consume their own meat if left in a tank too long, and when cooked, the meat is mushy, not firm and resilient. Hard-shelled lobsters have more meat and better texture. The lobster should feel heavy for its size, and the shell, when pressed with the fingers, should be hard and firm, and not buckle under your pressure. Soft-shell lobsters are cheaper to buy; the meat is not as firm but it is sweet. When I intend to use the lobster to make sauce, I look for females with the roe. If you unfurl the back tail, you can see if it is a female with eggs: the sacs with eggs will be attached under the tail. Use lobster as soon as possible after buying, but if you are planning to save it for another time, wrap the live lobster tightly in plastic wrap, and freeze it whole as soon as you bring it home. To cook a frozen lobster, just add some time to the cooking.

Lobsters are best when cooked alive, but it seems many people have problems handling a live lobster. To avoid this, set a live lobster in the freezer half an hour before prepping and cooking it, then proceed to cook it or cut it. To make a sauce, or to bake a lobster in a half-shell, cut the claws off at the joints with scissors, and detach. Place the lobster on a cutting board, parallel to your body, with the tail held firmly in your left hand. Firmly insert the kitchen knife with its blade facing the tip of the head, at the joint where the head section is attached with the tail section. Once the knife is inserted, cut the lobster's head in half lengthwise, and bring the knife down the head in a swift motion; cut all the way down to the board, then turn the lobster around and cut the same way through the tail. The lobster should be split open now. Cut off the antennas and eyes with the shears, and clean out the digestive sac, right beneath the eyes. Note the dark mass of tomalley and perhaps roe in the body cavity; both are excellent to eat. The lobster halves are ready to cook now.

MONKFISH—A GREAT COOKING FISH

Monkfish is an easy fish to find, especially in Greek, Italian, and Mediterranean fish markets. It is an ugly fish with a big head but a delicious tail, and that is what is sold. The tail has one central bone. The skin is removed, and monkfish is sold either as fillets deboned off the central bone, or cut across the bone so that it looks like an osso buco. Fillets of monkfish not only cook well but won't fall apart on you. Monkfish is dubbed the poor man's lobster, because it is also sweet and firm and has a similar flavor. I would recommend a simple Livornese sauce for monkfish: cook some chopped onions and garlic in olive oil until wilted; add some crushed canned San Marzano tomatoes, salt, red pepper flakes, a few capers, and a few olives; and bring to a boil. In the meantime, salt and flour your fish fillet. In a separate pan, sauté the fish in olive oil until golden on both sides. Drain the oil, and add the fish to the bubbling tomato sauce; cook all together for ten minutes, and you will have yourself a delicious dish to enjoy! I like to serve it with some piping-hot polenta. Monkfish is also good just floured and fried and served in onions and a wine-vinegar sauce.

OCTOPUS

When buying octopus, ask your fishmonger for tenderized octopus. Otherwise, it will most likely be tough and chewy. When you are ready to cook it, place the octopus in a pot of cold water with some bay leaves. A special secret ingredient you'll also want to throw in the water, according to my grandmother, is a wine cork (one of the new synthetic corks won't do the trick); it seems that the enzymes in the cork help tenderize the octopus. I know of no scientific documentation for why this works, but it does. Cook the octopus until the tines of a fork penetrate the thickest part of the octopus easily; be careful not to overcook it, because it will get tough. Cooking freshly caught octopus can sometimes be difficult. I remember that the fishermen, including my uncle Emilio, would beat the octopus with a wooden mallet or against the sea rocks to render them tender. The defrosted octopus you buy at the fishmonger's, however, has most likely been tenderized, and will also be tenderized by the freezing process. Some of the best octopus I have found in the market comes from Puglia and Mexico. I like it when it is large, about two pounds. At this size, octopus is meaty and tender.

RAZOR CLAMS

Razor clams look exactly the way the name suggests, with a long shell, brownish in color, usually three to six inches long. They come from the Northeastern Coast of America as well as the West Coast; some of the best are from the Washington State coastline. Like regular clams, they nestle deep in wet, muddy sand, and they are usually dug out. Their shell is a bit thinner than that of regular clams, and breaks easily. When shopping for razor clams, you will usually find them tied in little bundles; the shells will be slightly opened, with the clam sliding out a bit. If they are fresh, the clam will retreat into its shell quickly when tapped. To clean razor clams, wash all the sand off, then line them up in a colander and pour boiling water over them just long enough for the shells to pop open. Immediately place the clams in cold water and remove the meat from the shell. The next step is to remove with scissors the gills and the digestive tract, the dark part of the clam. Now you are ready to cook. Whichever way you cook them, it must be quick, a maximum of one or two minutes; they are very sensitive and will overcook and become tough quickly. Sauté them or make a sauce. Another way to cook them is searing them in the shell. Once the shell has opened, remove as much of the digestive tract as you can, then season with some olive oil, parsley, and a sprinkle of peperoncino, and flip onto the griddle with the clam (open) side down. Put some pressure on them—one or two minutes and they're done.

SCALLOPS

Scallops are mollusks; the white scallop, as we know it, is the muscle attached to the shell, holding it together. The muscle opens and closes the mollusk and is responsible for the scallop's movement on the ocean floor. You can buy a scallop in its shell, or just the white muscle, sometimes with the orange roe attached, too, or you can buy scallops out of their shells. These may be graded as dry scallops, which have no additives and are my preference, or as wet scallops, which are treated with sodium tripolyphosphate to preserve them longer and allow them to freeze better. Scallops are delicious prepared in many ways, but I love to bake the scallop in its shell with some bread crumbs, herbs, and butter.

SCUNGILLI

The technical name for these whelks, a kind of sea snail, is *Bolinus brandaris,* and they can grow to around nine centimeters (3½ inches) in length. In Italian they're called scungilli, and I love them. They have such a wonderful texture, and a delicious sweet flavor. When cooked, removed from their shell, and sliced thin, they make a great salad, with the addition of some celery, olives, olive oil, and vinegar. They also go great with pasta when cooked in some spicy marinara sauce. Scungilli are very much a part of the Italian American table. They can be found fresh in their shells in Italian fish markets, or, in many seafood stores, removed from their shells and frozen. They are good both ways, although I prefer the frozen ones: the freezing process tenderizes them.

SHRIMP

Shrimp have become one of the most popular crustaceans in the United States. They come in a variety of colors, from pink and gray to brown, depending on the species and their diet. But when shrimp are cooked, the color turns to an opaque cream or pink. There are over three hundred different species of shrimp worldwide. In the United States, the most common type is the deep-water shrimp, or the pink shrimp. Most of the shrimp sold today are frozen, with heads removed; the shrimp are defrosted by the fishmongers to sell. Freezing the shrimp immediately when caught and still on the boat guarantees freshness. When you are buying shrimp, it is best to purchase from a local fish market that sells large quantities. Fresh shrimp with their heads on are also available when in season, but they are more expensive and sensitive to travel time. Fresh shrimp should have firm bodies still attached to their shells, with a slight saltwater smell. Shrimp is sold by size; the smaller the size, the cheaper the price, in most cases. Use shrimp within one to two days after buying. You can also freeze shrimp by placing them in a plastic bag and putting them in the coldest part of the freezer, but keep in mind that most likely they have been frozen once already. The use of shrimp in the kitchen is endless—appetizers, soups, salads, tossed with pasta, and as a main course. Just be careful not to overcook shrimp; they become tough.

Small shrimp make a lovely addition to skillet sauces, because they cook quickly—barely two minutes in the skillet. Before you cook, devein the shrimp by making a shallow cut along the curved back of the shrimp and extracting the black or gray vein that runs the length of the shrimp. The smaller the shrimp, the sweeter and less expensive it is. Again, just make sure that you don't overcook the shrimp. Start cooking your pasta before the sauce, so they finish at the same time. But if your pasta isn't ready when the shrimp and sauce are, just take the skillet with the sauce off the heat, and add to the pasta once the pasta is cooked and drained.

SKATE

Skate is a flat ocean-bottom creature in the ray family, with wings on either side that move it through the water. The fan-shaped wings, which weigh one to two pounds each, are the parts of the skate that get to the market, and you will find them already removed from the cartilage and filleted. You will see the narrow ridges and grooves where the branches of cartilage were attached. Skate fillets are fine to use, but if you have a fish market that gets the whole wings, I recommend that you have the fishmonger remove only the skin and leave the skate meat on the cartilage. Freshness is more critical with skate than with other fish, because the flesh begins to deteriorate and gives off an ammonia smell within a day or two after the wing has been skinned—even faster when it has been filleted. Fresh skate should smell like the clean sea. It is delicious just floured and pan-fried, sautéed in a lemon-and-caper sauce, or grilled.

SOFT-SHELL CRAB

Soft-shell crabs are crustaceans, and belong to a larger group of arthropods that includes sixty-seven thousand different species. What is unique about soft-shell crabs is that they are caught as they molt and shed their old shell to grow a new larger shell. In the United States, from April to September, the hard-shell blue-claw crab molts to grow, and it is in those periods that the crab is gastronomically known as soft-shell crab. Although hard-shell crabs make delicious sauces and salads, one has to work hard to dig the sweet meat from the hard shell. During the molting stage, all of the crab can be eaten with the exception of the gills and the stomach-mouth and eye parts. You should handle soft-shell crabs gently, and with scissors cut off the mouth and eye parts, then lift the back flap from the right, cut out the gills, and repeat on the other side. Rinse slightly under running water, pat dry, and cook. Soft-shell crabs do not need a long cooking time; they are delicious dipped in a batter and fried crisp. When buying soft-shell crabs, select them individually; when you pass your fingers over them, they should move slightly. They usually come in small, medium, and large sizes, and vary in cost according to size. The jumbo are usually the most sought-after, but I like them medium to small. Remember that, once it is cooked, you eat every morsel of the crab. In Venice, the traditional soft crab is called *moleca*. It is a mouthful, nice and crisp. We ate them like cherries—one after another.

SWORDFISH

Swordfish is usually available boneless, sold in portions or in a piece that you can portion at home. It is a migratory fish of the big open oceans with warmer currents. It will often grow to be from two to three hundred pounds, and can even reach over a thousand pounds. The flesh of the swordfish when fresh is light pink, with the blood veins, where it was attached to the bone, bright and red, not a dark brick color. The best piece is a cut from the center fillet, but the belly flap, known as *ventresca* in Italy, is also very tasty, thanks to its higher fat content. That is the part fishermen prize. As with most fish, do not overcook it, and season it well. It holds up well to most cooking techniques, including grilling, baking, and searing. If you have some trimmings left over, sauté with some garlic and tomatoes and you will have a great pasta sauce.

TUNA

Fresh tuna is related to the mackerel family. There are more than fifteen different species of tuna. The smaller tuna are about four pounds and up; the big tuna can reach up to fifteen hundred pounds and navigate the larger bodies of water. Tuna is much in vogue and sought-after these days, particularly high-grade sushi tuna. The much-loved yellowfin tuna is close to being extinct. The big tuna is sold boneless and sometimes skinless, although do buy it with the skin on if you can—this keeps it fresher for longer. Look for a bright red color in the meat, and avoid dark red or brown blood lines, which are an indication that the tuna has been around for a while. Buying a whole piece is better than slices, because it will keep longer. You should keep tuna in the refrigerator, at a low temperature. Do not overcook tuna, which becomes dry. Try grilling it or searing it only on one side and leaving the top uncooked; you can monitor the temperature of the cooking tuna by the rising white line on its side on the fire.

PRESERVED TUNA *Tonno* in Italian, canned tuna is a staple in any Italian pantry. This isn't your typical tuna for mayonnaise-soaked tuna-salad sandwiches—it's much, much better. Packed in olive oil, Mediterranean tuna, also called bluefin tuna (tonno rosso) is darker, richer, and very good for you. Italian tuna packed in olive oil has become readily available in American markets. Stock your shelves with it, and add it to your spread next time you make antipasto or just need a quick, healthy snack! Drain the olive oil before using the tuna. My grandmother would always find uses for that oil; sometimes she fed it to the cats, who loved it and licked their whiskers.

WHOLE INDIVIDUAL PORTION FISH: SNAPPER, BRANZINO, STRIPED BASS, BLACK BASS, ETC.

Today everybody wants a fillet of fish, a steak of fish, or boneless, skinless fish. I believe that some of the best morsels of meat in a fish are next to the bone, by the tail, behind the eyes and the cheeks, and I recommend that when you go fish shopping next time you look for a whole fish. There are many types of whole fish available, especially in more ethnic neighborhoods. Make sure the eyes are glossy and looking at you, the skin is shiny, the gills are bright red, and the flesh is firm. Have the fishmonger clean and scale the fish for you; then go home and season it with some salt, pepper, and olive oil, and fill the fish cavity with some garlic and thyme. Preheat the grill to very hot, and set the fish on that hot grill; don't move it until it has formed a crust on the bottom, after about fifteen minutes. Flip the fish with a long spatula, and leave it on the grill for another ten minutes; you will have a fabulous fish, Mediterranean-style.

USING FISH AND SEAFOOD

BUYING FISH

When you are buying fresh tuna, swordfish, or any large cut of fish, always look for the blood lines located centrally by the main bone. Make sure they are bright red and not a brick color or brown. Bright red in the blood lines is an indication of freshness. If you are buying a smaller whole fish, look at the eyes—they should be clear and bulging. If they are cloudy and sunk into the head cavity, the fish is old. Also, take a look at the gills. If they are bright red, like the blood line, they are fresh; dark red or brown is an indication that the fish is not fresh. The flesh of a fresh fish is firm to the touch and has a sheen. But your best tool to identify freshness in fish is your olfactory sense—your nose. If it smells of the sea, buy it; if it is fishy, move on.

SCALING FISH

Scaling a fish is a necessary process, and fortunately an easy one. All you'll need is a fish scaler or the back nonsharp side of a knife. To scale a fish, place it in your sink, grab it by its tail, and, under slowly running cold water, begin scraping the scales off, working from the tail toward the head. Scrape the scales with the scaler or the back of the knife, pressing along the body of the fish, and the scales should start popping off. Be careful not to damage the flesh of the fish by pushing too hard. Flip the fish over, and scale the other side. Once all the scales are removed, rinse the fish under cool water.

STORING FISH

Fish can go bad very quickly, and that is why it is so important to store it properly. The most important aspect of storing fish is temperature. The ideal range is between thirty and thirty-four degrees. If you choose to store it in your refrigerator (usually around forty-one degrees), you'll cut the shelf life of the fish in half. Therefore, you should store your fish on a bed of crushed ice, but make sure the fish does not touch the ice—protect it with plastic wrap. You can use ice cubes but keep the fish in a plastic bag, and be sure to keep your fish out of pools of melted ice water.

BAKING A WHOLE FISH

Fish cooked whole—on the bone, with the head and tail attached—I think is the best way to eat it. The meat around the bones is always sweeter

and tastier. I especially like the cheeks and the tail meat of the fish. A good fish to cook whole is the American striped bass. Like its Mediterranean counterpart, branzino, it is a rockfish, thriving near shores. The texture of the meat of striped bass is juicy, flaky, tasty, and very delicate. With a drizzle of good extra-virgin olive oil and lemon, it is sublime in its simplicity. If no striped bass can be found, black bass, red snapper, and other fish yield delicious results. The best size of a whole fish for two portions is around 1½ to 2 pounds. Toss the whole fish with some salt, drizzle it with olive oil, stuff the belly cavity with a few slices of lemon, set it on a lightly oiled sheet pan, and bake in a 475-degree oven for twenty minutes.

GRILLING WHOLE FISH

Set the fish on a hot grill, but do not touch the fish until it has formed a crust underneath, about fifteen minutes, then flip with a long spatula and cook for an additional ten minutes without touching. Serve with a sprinkle of coarse sea salt and a drizzle of the best extra-virgin olive oil you have.

POACHING FISH

To poach in the traditional way, it's important to make a good poaching liquid. Start with two quarts of water. Add a chopped small onion, a stalk of celery, and a chopped carrot, along with three ounces of vinegar, an ounce of lemon juice, a couple of bay leaves, a half-teaspoon of peppercorns, a handful of parsley stems, and a pinch of thyme. Let this simmer for forty-five minutes and you will have a great poaching liquid. Just strain the poaching liquid and then poach your fish in it.

GRILLING SEAFOOD

Grilling is a great method of cooking, especially in the warm summer months, especially shellfish, like shrimp and lobster, which is a quick fix and usually a family favorite. Be sure that your grill is clean by scraping the rack well. Just marinate your seafood in garlic and oil, and toss in some fresh herbs. Let your seafood marinate for about an hour before putting it on the grill. When you are ready to start cooking, make sure you coat the hot grill rack with an oiled paper towel before putting on the food. Set the food on the hot grill, and let it be. Grill the seafood without turning until it is deeply marked by the grill, anywhere from two to five minutes or more, depending on the type and size of the fish or shellfish. This will prevent the fish from sticking. Grill on the other side for a few minutes less than on the first side. Keep garlic oil handy, and drizzle or brush it on seafood sparingly while grilling, usually when turning the pieces. Try to avoid spilling any oil onto the lava rocks or coals, because this will cause flare-ups.

Meat

My meat training did not start with putting a filet mignon on the grill, or slicing a steak. It began with running after a chicken in my grandma's courtyard. She was on one side, and I was on the other, chasing the chicken that was going to be dinner that Sunday. Pouring the hot water over the chicken while Grandma plucked the feathers off, rotating it over the fire to burn off any remaining fine feathers—that was all part of my first meat-cooking experience. Cleaning the liver, the heart, the stomach, and collecting all the unlaid eggs in a container to save for a frittata for *merenda,* also my job. Then the head, wings, and feet were all cleaned and added to a pot with celery, carrots, onions, and herbs to make the soup. The remaining chicken pieces went into a delicious guazzetto, perfect for dressing the gnocchi at Sunday dinner. The next Sunday, we were chasing a rabbit or skinning a deer Grandpa had brought home from the hunt. Handling and cooking with meat was a special event at Grandma's house: it was scarce and considered precious. In that setting, I learned to appreciate and respect every morsel of the animal that provided us with nourishment. You will find that I share with you those memories, techniques, flavorings, and marinades, from my childhood as well as from my professional life as a chef. The world of my childhood was not complicated. The recipes were simple but delicious, and in harmony with that place and time. I have taken those values and applied them to the modified recipes of today, so let's cook.

BEEF

Beef is not as prominent in the Italian recipe repertoire as it is in the States. But along the way, being an adopted American daughter for fifty years plus, I have come to enjoy and love a good steak, a good prime rib, and a good hamburger, and to have fun cooking them. However, when I cook beef my way, it is most likely a secondary cut, such as oxtails, chuck made into a guazzetto, a meatloaf with some ricotta in it, or a nice piece of a flat-iron braised in Barolo wine until it melts.

Cooking beef means understanding the nature of the cut, the piece you have in front of you, and understanding the seasoning, technique, and method of cooking you will use. Herbs and spices can make a big difference in the outcome of the dish, as can marinades and rubs. But sometimes it is fun to go off-track from the recipe and try out spices that you love and herb flavorings that you have at home even if they are not mentioned in the recipe you are following.

BOAR MEAT

Home cooks tend to shy away from boar meat, but don't you do that! It is wonderful to cook with, full of flavor, nutritionally sound, and low in fat. Most boar meat available at your butcher is from a young animal with a mellow game flavor, but still possessing enough of the richness that one expects from game meat. When I braise boar meat to dress pasta or gnocchi, I use Barolo wine, which adds fruitiness and complexity, but any good full-bodied red wine will do. Remember that the end product is the sum of all its parts—the better the wine you use, the better the sauce will be.

CHICKEN

I heard somewhere that "chicken" was the most Googled recipe ingredient, and this makes sense to me, because I think it is the most often cooked meat. I love to eat chicken, and I love to cook it. The one thing that I am a stickler about with regard to chicken is that what I cook and eat be a naturally raised animal, free-range, scratching and feeding off the ground, and that it be free of hormones. I am then a happy camper. I also like every part of the chicken. I enjoy the liver, the thighs, the drumsticks, and I think that the neck, wings, and feet make the best soup. The breast is the easiest to prepare and tasty, but do give the other parts a shot. They are delicious, and using them keeps nature in balance: the whole animal is consumed, not just prime cuts. The secret to golden brown chicken pieces is to leave them be as they cook. They will brown better if you're not constantly turning them or checking on their progress.

DUCK AND QUAIL

Duck and quail are not on everyone's dinner menu, and yet in our restaurants they prevail, and people order and enjoy them. This leads me to believe that the preparation and the cooking of duck and quail might intimidate some home cooks. There is nothing easier to make and more delicious than a roast duck. Season it well, inside and out, then roast it until all the fat has dripped down and the skin is crispy and delicious and the meat falls off the bones. I like it this way. Restaurant menus often serve duck-leg confit, while the duck breast is seared rare. This is not all that difficult if you separate the two parts of the duck and cook them separately—a bit more work, but it can be done. There are also braised duck and duck guazzetto, and for these dishes just the duck legs will do; they are more economical and better-tasting. Quail, on the other hand, seem to be challenging because they are small birds; however, they are quite manageable and tasty. Now one can buy boneless quail, which, after seasoning, can be flattened in a hot pan and seared with a weight on them, or stuffed and roasted in the oven, or braised on top of the stove, or butterflied, seasoned, and thrown on a hot grill.

EGGS

They should be tested for freshness, and you should buy organic free-range eggs. If you crack an egg on a plate, it should maintain a domed shape. When you crack an egg, you can also look inside the shell, where a small membrane remains. The smaller the membrane, the fresher the egg. To separate an egg: with clean hands, crack the egg and let the albumen pass through your fingers into a bowl, retaining the yolk in your palm.

CONCERNED ABOUT THOSE EGGS If you are at all concerned about the risks of eating eggs that are not fully cooked when dressing your pasta, I have a few alternatives. One thing you can do is poach egg yolks in a small sieve. Slip the yolks into a small sieve and place it in a pot of simmering water to coddle for a minute, and then add it to the pasta. You can also search out pasteurized egg yolks, available in the dairy case of some supermarkets.

LAMB

Italians enjoy and often consume lamb, especially in the southern part of Italy from Tuscany on down. Because of the Apennines, the mountain chain that cuts across a good portion of the lower half of the boot of Italy, there are fewer pastures for cows, but sheep and goats are quite agile and easily climb the rocky slopes to find food. Southern Italy is a sheep-meat-and-cheese culture. Rome is known for its *abbacchio,* or young sheep, and the Abruzzo region for its spezzatino di abbacchio, whereas Tuscans much appreciate the scottadito, "finger-burning" lamb chops, taken by the bone hot off the grill and eaten. People in the northeastern part of Italy love to have goat and lamb served every Easter for dinner. The most tender and best lamb is spring lamb, less than six months old and still milk-fed. If you can find it at your butcher, lamb at that age does not contain any hormones or antibiotics. The meat is not as red as regular lamb, and there is less meat mass on the chops and other cuts, but it is tender and delicious. You will find grass-fed lamb specifically labeled as such in stores; it is usually six months to one year old. Having been fed just grass, it will not contain hormones or antibiotics. The meat is red, and there is more meat mass on the cuts. Grain-fed lamb, the most available lamb in stores, may be labeled as free of hormones and antibiotics only if it has been fed organically grown grain. Some of the best U.S. lamb comes from Colorado, and if you find it, I would suggest buying it. Big exporters of lamb to the States are New Zealand and Australia, both good-quality. Leg of lamb for roasts and lamb chops are popular cuts, but I would suggest also trying the shoulder lamb chops, shoulder lamb roast, lamb hamburgers, lamb tongue, and lamb kidneys, which are all delicious and more economical alternatives.

OFFAL

Offal—organ meats—are the internal organs of a butchered animal. Different cultures have varying attitudes toward offal. Some offal are eaten for special occasions, whereas others are an everyday economical food. When an animal is butchered, the offal are the first parts to be cooked. When my grandma butchered a chicken, the liver, intestines, and heart were the first; after a good cleaning, they were made into a frittata. Then the rest of the chicken was cooked in a soup or sauce. At the butchering of the pig in November, the blood was immediately made into a blood sausage, sangui-naccio, while the liver and the lungs were the first meal, sautéed with lots of onions and bay leaves. The kidneys, heart, and tripe came next; then the curing process started. The legs were salted and cured into prosciutto, the belly fat was then made into bacon, the ribs smoked, and so on down the line, until all the small pieces of meat were seasoned and made into sausage. Capuzzelle, the roasted head of a lamb with the brain, was a delicacy, as were veal sweetbreads. The butchers saved them for themselves when they butchered a whole calf. I love to cook and eat, in moderation, calf's liver alla veneziana with polenta, veal kidneys in a mustard sauce, tomato-braised tripe alla triestina with pieces of potatoes and lots of grated Grana Padano cheese. My mother from time to time puts in a request for crispy chicken livers with onions and a splash of vinegar, and I gladly prepare it for her and join her in enjoying it. It is important that you buy your offal from a reliable source and that it be fresh, but do enjoy it from time to time.

PORK

Pork, of all the meats we use, has undergone the greatest resurgence in use. Pigs need to be raised and fed the right way if the meat is to be delicious, tender, and healthy. So do look for a reliable supplier. Some of the varieties of heritage pork to look for are Berkshire, Red Wattle, Large Black, and Gloucestershire Old Spot. These will give you delicious pork flavor and some guarantee that the animal was raised in a humane and proper way. I say often about all products that good food is all in the quality of the fundamental ingredients, and this is absolutely true for pork meat.

PROSCIUTTO

Americans have become very fond of the thin, flavorful, air-cured delicacy known as prosciutto. Prosciutto is cured throughout the Italian peninsula; the two main types of prosciutto produced in Italy are Prosciutto di Parma, made in Emilia-Romagna, and Prosciutto di San Daniele, made in Friuli–Venezia Giulia. Prosciutto is the hind leg and thigh of a pig, although there is also boar pro-

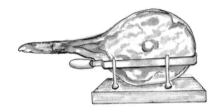

sciutto; the meat has been cleaned, salted, and left for two months, during which the leg is pressed to remove any blood that is left, and washed and salted several times. The leg is then hung to air-dry in a dark, well-ventilated area, with particular flavor-imparting molds, for eighteen months or more. There is a chunk of dense and flavorful meat (with a layer of flavorful fat) at the hoof end of a prosciutto, all that's left after the rest of the ham has been sliced paper-thin, in the traditional manner. The next time you are in an Italian deli or grocery, ask if they have one to sell you; it's a useful piece of meat to have on hand, and much less expensive than regular prosciutto. With the skin on, it will keep for a long time in your refrigerator or freezer, and you can use small amounts of the salt-cured meat to add flavor to sauces, soups, and pastas wherever you would use bacon. Remove the skin before cutting the prosciutto. You can use the layer of fat underneath to lend flavor to dishes. Just run the fat over the frying pan or the surface of a grill to apply a thin film; this will enhance whatever you cook or grill on it.

RABBIT

Rabbit is one of my favorite meats; it is light, it is tasty, and it is healthy, lower in fat, and easy to cook. It is not a terribly expensive meat, and environmentally it makes sense. My grandma had three or four pens full of rabbits. They were a source of fun—we played with them—and also a source of nourishment. Delicious and nutritionally sound, and with lots of flavor, rabbits multiply quickly and consume relatively little to reach their mature cooking weight, in about six months. Rabbit meat is similar to chicken meat—anything you can do to cook a chicken, you can do to a rabbit. The best parts are the meaty hind legs and the rabbit loin. You can cut up the whole rabbit like a chicken, and I prefer it alla cacciatora, braised with tomatoes, peppers, and mushrooms, or as rabbit stew. Rabbit is also delicious slowly braised with garlic and rosemary and a splash of vinegar.

SPECK

Speck, a smoked piece of the hind leg of the pig that is cured in salt like prosciutto, is a prominent ingredient in the Alto Adige region of Italy. This meat is seasoned with salt and spices that include pepper and juniper berries before it cures for a month. It is then smoked and aged for several months, to produce the smoky and flavorful product. Speck is often sliced thin and served like prosciutto, or diced and tossed into a salad, but it can also be used in cooking, easily replacing bacon as a smoky alternative. You can find speck at specialty food stores.

SQUAB AND PHEASANT

Squab and pheasant are a bit more challenging because of the cooking time and technique, and their delicious gamy flavors need to be managed. The pheasant is a glorified chicken, but the meat has more fiber and requires longer cooking, and needs the addition of more complex and rich flavors, such as dried porcini, juniper berries, truffles, or foie gras, as well as some good sherry or Cognac to splash on while cooking. The squab, on the other hand, is smaller but gamier, and richer in flavor than the pheasant. To season squab, think of deep, rich spices such as cloves, juniper berries, black truffles, porcini mushrooms, and rosemary. Keep in mind that the legs should be thoroughly cooked while the breast should remain rare. Separating the two and cooking them separately is a good idea, although I love a squab guazzetto, where the whole squab is cooked, and then the meat is pulled off the bones and returned to the sauce, perfect to dress my homemade pappardelle.

VEAL

A young calf yields delicious cuts of meat. The best veal meat is from a milk-fed calf. The meat is white and tender, even if the meat mass on the bone is smaller, much like lamb. Cuts of grass-fed veal, on the other hand, have more meat, and the meat has more color, from the iron in the grass. The largest veal is grain-fed veal, which contains more fat. The difficulty with veal is knowing whether the husbandry has been done in a humane and organic manner. Read the labels. I have researched the USDA (United States Department of Agriculture) site for Food Safety and Inspection Service, and here are their guidelines:

There are five grades for veal/calf: prime, choice, good, standard, and utility. Prime and choice grades are juicier and more flavorful than the lower grades. Because of the young age of the animals, the meat will be a light grayish-pink to light pink, fairly firm, and velvety. The bones are small, soft, and quite red. Cuts such as chops can be cooked by the dry-heat methods of roasting, grilling, or broiling.

VENISON

There were times when the climate and topography of where you lived determined how much game meat you ate. Today that is not the case, so I would suggest that you make your way through the Internet to a game-meat supplier and enjoy cooking and eating such game meat as venison and boar. Venison especially is great. Its anatomy resembles that of a calf, so the cuts of meat are basically the same: the chops, the loin, the rump, and muscle meat, which is cubed and great for braising. When getting ready to cook venison, think of how you would cook the same cut of beef and chances are that that will work well. Think of the venison meat as being gamier in taste, therefore marinating it overnight will work well, and covering it with a well-seasoned rub will improve it. The choice of seasoning is very important. Strong and pronounced flavors go well with the flavors of game, such as juniper berries, blueberries, cloves, dried porcini mushrooms, bay leaves, rosemary, and peppercorns—all intense flavors you would find in the wild. As a cooking liquid for venison think of full-bodied red wines like Barolo, Brunello, Primitivo, sherries, and bourbon. It is all sounding pretty flavorful and it is, so get cooking some venison.

GRINDING YOUR OWN MEAT

Grabbing a package of ground meat from the supermarket case is a convenience that all of us are accustomed to. However, I always prefer to grind my own meat, or ask the butcher to grind a selected piece of meat (or whole pieces of different kinds for a blend). I recommend this for several reasons. First, buying whole meat allows you to determine its freshness and quality, which is difficult when the meat has been ground and sealed in plastic. Second, because illness-causing contamination spreads easily in ground meat— especially during bulk commercial processing— you can minimize the health risks by grinding a small, selected batch yourself. Further, you can choose meat cuts that have the percentage of fat you want in your dish and grind them to the ideal texture—a great advantage since most supermarket meat is ground to the same size.

USING A DRY SPICE RUB

Rubs for meats are very important and will add much to the flavor and enhance the appearance of your cooked meats. You can buy prepared dry rubs as well as wet rubs or marinades, but they are usually very easy to make. The basic ingredients are salt and sugar, and the rest is finely ground spices and herbs. Usually a big component of dry rubs is pepper milled from peppercorns or spices milled from dry peppers, such as chili peppers or paprika. A rub reflects local culture. Italian rubs usually include dried porcini powder, and other cultures have their own favorites, such as turmeric, ginger, lemongrass, cinnamon, cloves, and so on. It is easy and fun to make your own rub. A dry rub is usually applied by sprinkling it on the meat and rubbing it in with your hands, or setting the protein, or pieces of a protein like chicken, in a plastic bag large enough to tumble the meat; add the dry rub to the plastic bag, and toss and turn until all of the meat is covered with the rub. The rubbed meat should rest in the refrigerator for a few hours, so the flavors can permeate the meat. A dry rub can easily be turned into a wet rub, or marinade, just by adding liquid to it. Olive oil or vegetable oil is good, turning the dry ingredients into a paste that can then be spread on the protein. Vinegar, lemon juice, orange juice, or pineapple juice can also be added to a dry rub. Add just enough of the liquid to make it a paste. If you add a lot of liquid like wine, vegetable juices, or fruit juices, you will turn your rub into a marinade.

MARINATING

Marinating is a great way of gently adding flavor to meats and fish when you feel they do not have enough intrinsic flavoring. Consider marinating your fish or meat even if the recipe does not call for it. To a marinade with plenty of liquid, chopped vegetables such as carrots, onions, and garlic are usually added, as well as such fresh herbs as basil, rosemary, and sage. The meat is set in a bowl or a plastic bag to which the marinade is added, tossed well, then allowed to steep for a few hours or overnight. When you are roasting meat that has been in a marinade, the marinade can be added to the cooking pot where it will become part of the sauce. To marinate properly, you must give the ingredients enough time to exchange flavors. Marinating is also a good way to introduce new flavors to your family, especially children. Strong flavors, such as garlic, rosemary, bay leaves, and ginger, can be difficult for a finicky eater to taste directly, but in marinades they come through in manageable levels. This is how I developed and trained my grandchildren's palates.

COOKING SECONDARY CUTS OF MEAT

Filet mignon, prime steak, thick veal chops, rack of lamb, and pork loin are considered prime cuts of meat and are part of every grand chef's menu. They are delicious cuts, and pricey as well. But I find the secondary cuts of meat, such as veal shoulder, beef flank, flat-iron steaks, pork and lamb shanks, oxtails, and short ribs, much more delicious, exciting, and economical to cook. You can elicit real flavor from these cuts by taking the time to cook and braise them slowly, adding aromas and spices to the braising liquid. Their meat will indeed be finger-sticking good.

WHAT ABOUT THE SHOULDER CUT? Everybody is familiar with lamb chops or leg of veal, but how about the shoulder? When is that used? The shoulder is my favorite roasting cut of veal or lamb. The meat is sweeter on the blade bone, and, with lots of cartilage to melt during roasting, the end result is finger-sticking good. The shoulder can be roasted or braised whole or cut into two inch pieces on the bone, then roasted or braised.

COOKING MUSCLE MEAT Find real flavor in your meat by taking the time to cook slowly and braise the tougher cuts, like veal shank. Used in the classic Italian dish osso buco, the veal shank provides the bone, marrow, and muscle. A lamb shank is also delicious when braised on the bone. When this connective tissue is cooked for a long period of time at a low temperature, the meat is absolutely delicious, and it becomes so tender, it just falls off the bone.

Dessert

Sweets are a big part of the Italian culinary tradition, but the enjoyment of sweets in Italy spreads out through the day—it is not just an after-meal affair. A cornetto or sweet croissant, a biscotto or cookie, a torta di frutta di marmellata or fruit tart, a piece of panettone or pandoro are all part of an Italian breakfast, served with a good caffè latte, cappuccino, or just a shot of espresso. After daily shopping at the market, the ladies meet for a cappuccino or caffè and a little dolce, and out come the more elaborate fruit tarts and cream-filled pastries, like torta della nonna, bomboloni or sugared doughnuts, and seasonal strudels. Lunch is a late event, and if all goes *all'italiana,* dessert or fruits would be served, followed by an espresso around 3:00 p.m. In the afternoon, people gather for a cup of tea or espresso and now leisurely enjoy a full piece of cake, a fruit tart, or a gelato while people-watching in the café. When you are visiting someone, a tray of beautifully packaged miniature pastry is the usual visiting card and always includes a diverse assortment. Dinner at home is usually followed by a dolce al cucchiaio, a spoon dessert, such as tiramisù, zabaglione with fruit, or slices of panettone soaked with grappa and topped with some custard or whipped cream. In elegant restaurants, the pastry chef is now as important as the chef, creating the "wow" effect of an elaborate dessert as a grand finale.

BISCUIT TORTONI is an ice cream, usually vanilla, made with eggs and cream, topped with a maraschino cherry and chopped almonds. This dessert was ubiquitous on Italian menus in the 1970s, served in soft paper cups.

CANNOLI, known in Italy as "cannoli siciliani," are very popular in the States. A tube-shaped, fried pastry dough is filled with sweet ricotta cream, sometimes with candied fruits or chocolate chips mixed in.

CASSATA is a Sicilian dessert, originally from around Palermo, made of sponge cake soaked in rum or fruit juices layered with ricotta-cream filling containing candied fruits, all covered by a thick layer of marzipan and colorful sugar icing.

CROSTATA, my favorite Italian dessert, simply refers to a tart; the filling can be fruit, ricotta, chocolate, or other ingredients. The dough can be almond paste or flaky pastry dough. The word *crostata* simply means it has a crust; the rest can be left up to the cook!

GELATO is a favorite among tourists in Italy; though it is similar to ice cream, it tends to be lighter. Gelato in Italy must have a minimum of 3.5 percent butterfat and has less air in it than regular ice cream, as well as a very smooth texture.

GRANITA is a Sicilian favorite: a semi-frozen slushy made from sugar, water, and various flavors, some favorites being lemon, orange, coffee, and mint.

ITALIAN ICE is more Italian American than it is Italian, made by adding fruit purées or juices to shredded ice. It has no eggs or dairy and is similar to sorbet. Some favorite flavors are cherry, blue raspberry, rainbow, and lemon.

MARZIPAN, *marzapane* in Italian, is an art form in Sicily, where sugar, honey, and almond paste are formed into fruit-shaped sweets in brilliant colors, known as frutta martorana, to be eaten particularly during the Christmas holiday season.

PANDORO, golden bread, is yeast bread served with confectioners' sugar during the Christmas holiday season as dessert, and often enjoyed with coffee for breakfast as well. I will often serve it with some zabaglione drizzled over it, and fresh macerated berries.

PANETTONE, a sweet yeast bread studded with candied fruits and raisins served during the Christmas holidays in Italy, is a favorite in our house. I like to use it to make a bread pudding as a special dessert on Christmas Day. It originated in Milan; legend has it that it was invented in the court of the Sforza dukes by the chef Toni—*pane di Toni,* or Toni's bread, becoming *panettone.* The bread has a round dome shape and usually weighs about two pounds.

PANFORTE, first made in thirteenth-century Siena, is similar to a fruitcake. Literally translated, the word means "strong bread," because of the large quantity of spices in it. Sugar and honey are heated together, and dried fruits, nuts, and spices are mixed in with some flour, all baked in a pan and sprinkled with confectioners' sugar when done.

PANNA COTTA is a creamy dessert made by blending cream, egg whites, and gelatin. The mixture is cooked at a very low temperature in the oven in a bain-marie (a hot water bath; the container with the mixture is set in a vessel containing water, which heats the cream gently). Panna cotta, literally "cooked cream," can be served as is, with some macerated berries, with a chocolate drizzle, or with caramel sauce.

PASTIERA NAPOLETANA is a ricotta cake from Naples that, according to legend, was first eaten during pagan celebrations of springtime; soft spring ricotta cheese would be used, mixed with wheat berries. The nuns of the convent of San Gregorio Armeno are credited with the modern pastiera; they added some candied citron, spring fragrances, and eggs as a symbol of the Resurrection, making it the perfect Easter cake. It needs to be cooked some days in advance, to allow the mixture to achieve the perfect flavor and fragrance.

PIZZELLE are Italian waffle cookies, originally from Abruzzo. They are made from flour, eggs, and butter or vegetable oil, flavored with orange, vanilla, lemon, or anise. In many an Italian American home, a pizzelle maker can be found, to create cookies that look like snowflakes.

RICCIARELLI are almond cookies covered with confectioners' sugar. They originated in Siena in the fourteenth century. They are oval in shape and typically served at Christmas.

SEMIFREDDO is a semifrozen dessert that can range from ice cream to mousse, usually a combination of ice cream and whipped cream. It can be made in different flavors, like ice cream, and toasted nuts and candied fruits can be added.

SFOGLIATELLE, originally from Naples, and often called lobster tails in the States, are shell-shaped flaky pastries filled with sweet ricotta.

SPUMONI is an Italian ice cream, usually made with three flavors of ice cream—strawberry, pistachio, and chocolate—all with some nuts and chopped cherries mixed in. Sometimes the chocolate ice cream is replaced by vanilla, simulating the Italian flag in ice cream.

STRUDEL is a Central European dessert, but strudels are common in Italy as well, especially in the regions of Trentino–Alto Adige and Friuli–Venezia Giulia, where I grew up. In both of these areas, the crossing of cultures has blended flavors, languages, and traditions, and making strudel is as common as making a plate of pasta. Strudel is a very thin and elastic simple dough filled with fresh or dried fruits, rolled, and baked. Wherever it's made, strudel is a delicious dessert; I especially love it when it is served warm with vanilla-cinnamon ice cream.

STRUFFOLI is a Neapolitan dessert of fried dough balls that are mixed with honey and usually stacked in a conical shape and topped with sprinkles.

TIRAMISÙ, meaning "pick me up," is a dolce al cucchiaio, a dessert eaten with a spoon. Ladyfingers (savoiardi) are soaked in espresso and layered, topped with a whipped mixture of mascarpone cheese, eggs, and sugar; the whole dessert is covered with powdered cocoa.

TORTA in Italian literally means "cake," but it is not only a dessert cake; it can be served at any meal. The name gives the indication that something good is encased in some form of dough. In Italian, there is torta salata, savory tart, or torta dolce—sweet tart. The savory tortas are usually filled with cheeses of all kinds but especially ricotta, braised vegetables in season, and often cured meats such as prosciutto, salami, mortadella, and sausages are added. Eggs are almost always included as a binding element as well as for flavor and nutrition. The sweet torta is usually filled with fresh fruit of the season or jams and nuts. Baking is usually the cooking method for a torta. Just like a cake, tart, or pie, it is cut in pieces and served either hot or at room temperature.

ZABAGLIONE, made from egg yolks, sugar, and Marsala wine, is whipped warm in a bronze bowl over a low flame, until very light and fluffy. It can be eaten on its own, but is usually served over a cake dessert or fresh berries.

ZEPPOLE, deep-fried dough balls topped with powdered sugar, are a staple of most street fairs and town celebrations in Italy. They can also be filled with custard cream. In Italy, they are served primarily in Rome and Naples. They are used to celebrate the Italian Father's Day, the feast of Saint Joseph, and are known as the bignè di San Giuseppe or sfinge.

ZUCCOTTO, a molded dessert made with sponge cake and ice cream, originated in Florence. It has a domed shape and is made by lining the mold with strips of sponge cake, then filling the center with ice cream. Once set, the cake is removed from the mold, turned to look like a dome, and covered in dark chocolate. *Zuccotto* means "little pumpkin" in Italian, and the cake is meant to look like a small half-pumpkin.

ZUPPA INGLESE is believed to have been invented at the court of Ferrara, where cooks were asked to replicate an English trifle that the dukes had tried at the Elizabethan court in the late nineteenth century. Ladyfingers or sponge cake is dipped in Alchermes and then covered with a layer of egg custard, and can be topped with chocolate, meringue, or cream.

Wine, Beer, and Other Drinks

Wine making and beer brewing have long traditions on the Italian peninsula and have evolved to the point that some of the best wines and beers in the world are produced there. *Vitis vinifera*, the common wine grape, was introduced to Italy from the Greek empire. There is evidence that wine has been made in Italy since the Etruscan times, while alcohol distillation, also a Greek invention, began in Italy around the twelfth century. Liquors and amaros (distilled alcohol flavored with infusions of fruit, herbs, spices, roots, and/or barks) had their beginnings in Italy in the thirteenth century, usually made by monks in monasteries.

Just as food products and pasta shapes in Italian cuisine are native to particular areas, so too are beverages. I find that, when in doubt, it is best to pair wines or beers with food from the same region. In Italy wine is considered an integral part of a meal; as bread is served at every Italian table, so is wine. Alcoholic beverages in Italy are mainly used to complement the meal. I certainly enjoy a good Barolo with some tajarin and truffles, or a crisp Greco di Tufo with Neapolitan spaghetti and clams—and of course a wonderful Italian-brewed beer with my pizza.

WINE

READING ITALIAN WINE LABELS: DOCG AND DOC

Have you ever wondered what DOC and DOCG mean on Italian wine labels?

DOC indicates wine that is "Vino a Denominazione di Origine Controllata," which is the Italian answer to the French certification AOC. In other words, DOC wines are produced in well-defined regions according to very particular rules that were designed to preserve traditional wine-making practices in that region.

"Vino a Denominazione di Origine Controllata e Garantita," or DOCG, is a similar but even more highly regulated certification system that represents only a handful of Italian wines. DOCG wines must pass a taste test, and growers are restricted in the amount of wine they may produce.

These labels safeguard the authenticity of the wine inside the bottle and are generally a good guide when you shop, but keep an eye out for the great wines that can sneak in under the radar. Some are not DOC or DOCG, but still excellent.

PAIRING FOOD AND WINE

Italians consider wine an integral part of eating. It usually appears on the table with every meal and is an essential part of Italian life. When I was young, there were no sodas to drink with a meal. There was water, and if we were lucky we got some wine added to that water; that was our drink. It was called a bevanda, and to this day I sometimes make it for myself, when I come to the table very thirsty and need something quenching.

Italy has twenty regions, and every region produces wine, and every region has regional varietals growing along with the international varietals. The most welcome gift one can bring to friends and family is home-baked goodies, wine, and local cheese. The wine tradition seems to go way back in the Italian history—some twenty-five hundred years ago, to the Etruscans, who seem to have brought the art of wine making to France. Wine adds multiple levels of flavors and experiences when paired with food.

When you are choosing wine to pair with your meal, simple rules apply. Drink what you like, and what you know and have tasted before. The time to learn and explore new wine is not with your dinner guests seated at the table, so start planning ahead. After you have planned your menu and are familiar with the tastes of that menu, you can begin choosing the wine. What fun!

Identify some main characteristics of the meal: Is it light or full of bold flavors? Is it acidic or rich? Is it fatty or lean? Is it spicy? Once you have identified these qualities, your goal is to choose a wine that will keep the flavors in balance and enhance the key ingredients. Consider cooking with the same wine you will be serving, for continuity of flavors. Acidity is usually higher in white wine, and tannins are higher in red wines. Pair mild wines with mild food, acidic wines with lighter flavors, like fish, and fatty food. On the other hand, bold-flavored foods, like steak and braised beef, pair well with big-flavored wines, such as Barolo, Zinfandel, and so on. If a food is rich and complex, try to match it with a big and rich wine; buttery sauces go well with chardonnay, for instance. If you are having an acidic dish, with lemon or vinegar, think of high-acid wines, or a wine with some sweetness. If you are having a spicy meal, a wine with a tinge of sweetness will also go well, to calm the spices; consider Riesling or Gewürztraminer. If you are ever unsure about how to pair a wine geographically when serving Italian food, serve the wines from the same region

as the food. This is a good rule of thumb no matter what cuisine you're making.

On the other hand, if you choose the food pairings to highlight a great wine that you have in your cellar, and the object of your occasion is to enjoy some wonderful, rare wine, you certainly don't want to overshadow the wine with assertively flavorful, aromatic, highly acidic, or intensely spiced foods. On such occasions, spicy tomato-based sauces are usually not recommended, nor are vegetables like artichokes, fennel, and asparagus—all high in mineral content. Keep the food delicious and complex, but not challenging to the wine.

And if you want to highlight delicate dishes and the food is the focus, the accompanying wine should be submissive. For example, if you serve a risotto with white truffles, or a wonderful foie gras, the character of the food should take precedence, and the wine you serve should be playing a supporting role. The wine should be of the finest quality but of a character that doesn't upstage the meal's starring players. Wines strong in tannins, acidity, bouquet, or fruitiness contend for dominance. As a general rule, one powerful palatal or olfactory sensation should be clearly experienced, not obscured by another, but exalted and harmonized.

CHOOSING THE RIGHT WINE WITH PASTA

When choosing wines to serve with pasta dishes, the main consideration should be the fat content of the sauce. If the sauce contains a high quantity of oil, cream, or butter, serve a wine with high acidity, such as Gavi, Friulano, Soave, Pinot Grigio, or spumante. Also, pay attention to the intensity of the sauce's flavor. Medium-intensity and tomato-based sauces go well with a Chianti. A more full-bodied wine like Barolo or Brunello would be appropriate for meat and mushroom sauces.

COOKING WITH WINE

When cooking with wine, do not to use any that are labeled "cooking wine," most of which contain added salt and flavorings. Cook with a good wine, a wine that you would drink. Save those unfinished bottles of wine, or those bottles you bought on sale, for cooking. Remember, what you get from wine in cooking is its acidity, tannins, and flavor; the better the wine, the better the flavor in your food.

Wine is good for marinades as well: the acidity in wine helps to tenderize meat, and it imparts flavor to whatever you are marinating. An important element to consider when choosing wine for cooking is whether you want dry wine or sweet wine.

You want to keep the wine's flavors in your dish but you want the alcohol to dissipate, so do not add any other liquid until the wine has cooked for a few minutes and the alcohol has had a chance to evaporate.

Should you cook with white wine or red? There is no set rule, but usually white wine goes well with lighter preparations, such as fish and chicken, and when you want a sauce to be light in color, whereas red wine is great for braising red meats and game. Red wine is also good in making a reduction for grilled or seared red meat, such as steaks, chops, and filet mignon.

Wine is also an excellent low-fat alternative in cooking. Instead of adding oil or butter, substitute wine for part of the fat; it will add the desired moisture and flavor. Wine is great in baking as well; substituting wine for fat in some cake recipes will lighten the cake and add flavor, too. Instead of adding all of the butter or oil to a dessert recipe, cut the fat in half and substitute a flavorful wine.

Wine should be added at the beginning of the cooking process, giving the alcohol time to evaporate. Simmer to reduce the wine and dissipate the alcohol.

BEER

Italy is synonymous with wine, but let us not forget the simple joy of cold beer on a hot day. Even though wine will always maintain top billing as Italy's drink of choice, the craft-brew scene is making up for lost time, bringing high-quality beer to the tables of haute-cuisine restaurants. This little revolution started about fifteen years ago, with a handful of small producers located primarily in the northern regions of Piedmont, Trentino–Alto Adige, and Friuli–Venezia Giulia, and has since grown to include producers in every region of the country, totaling upward of 250 microbreweries. Why not have some fun pairing artisanal beer with your favorite Italian dishes this summer? You can also get creative and try basting your roast chicken with beer. We are brewing some delicious ones in our Birreria, on the rooftop at Eataly, Twenty-third Street and Fifth Avenue in New York. (www.eataly.com).

COOKING WITH BEER

Like wine, beer can be an important element in cooking a dish, from soups to roasts, stews, and even desserts. In my recipes, I leave the choice of beer to you, but you want to use a premium-quality, flavorful beer in the dishes you cook. Keep in mind that the flavor of beer intensifies in the cooking process; start with the lighter ones and then graduate. The caramel maltiness of a dark lager will lend sweetness to a roast chicken or turkey; the bitterness of India pale ale will be imparted to the beef and braising sauce; the wheat beers are mild and fruity and good with fish. The effervescence of beer makes it an excellent addition to batters for frying, producing a lighter crust, and it is great when making biscuits as well. The quantity of beer added to the recipe also makes a difference: too much beer can make a dish unpleasantly bitter, so dilute it by adding stock or water, and start with small quantities, then increase. Beer is as good as wine in marinades and goes well with sweet vegetables, such as carrots, onions, and corn.

COFFEE

Of course, in Italy or America it is incredibly easy these days to find a coffee shop or a bar with a good barista and espresso on hand. But if you are making an espresso at home—and in Italy they still do, with the Mofea or Napoletana machine—the following rules apply.

It is said in Italy that to make a good cup of espresso you need the three "m"s:

1. *Miscela*—the right mix and toasting of the beans
2. *Macinatura*—the right ground of coffee
3. *Mano*—the hand; in other words, knowing the art of making coffee

So, to make a good cup of espresso, be sure to choose a good-quality espresso mix that has been properly toasted. Store the beans in a well-sealed glass or opaque container. It is often recommended not to buy very dark-colored beans or those that are excessively shiny. Try to grind the beans just before using them. Using bottled water is always better, because it is more of a constant; tap water may have more or less calcium or other minerals. The water temperature should reach just below the boiling point—200 degrees—and you should serve the coffee in warm cups. Italians enjoy espresso at different hours of the day—sometimes at breakfast, after other meals, and in the afternoon as a pick-me-up. Coffee with milk, such as cappuccino or caffè latte, is only consumed in the morning hours in Italy, and never after a meal.

ITALIAN NONALCOHOLIC BEVERAGES

CEDRATA is a sweet drink made from cedro, or citron, a citrus brought to Italy from the Middle East in the tenth century. Made mostly in Calabria and usually served over ice, it is a bubbly drink composed of water, natural brown sugar, lemon juice, carbon dioxide, and an infusion of the citron.

CHINOTTO is produced from the fruit of the myrtle-leaved orange tree and served as a soft drink. The dark color is similar to that of cola, but the bittersweet taste is distinct. It can also be used in cocktails and one particularly refreshing way is over ice with gin, lime juice, and basil leaves.

CRODINO is a favorite in Italy as a nonalcoholic aperitif, mostly served on ice with an orange or lemon peel. It has a slight bitter taste, but is sweet at the same time, produced from herbal extracts and sugar. The aperitif gets its name from Crodo, an area in northwest Piedmont. It is also used as a mixer to make several cocktails with alcohol.

LIMONATA would directly translate as "lemonade," but the Italian version is usually a bit more acidic than most lemonades of today, and made with sparkling water.

As the summer begins, I look for thirst-quenching natural drinks. Water is always a good choice, but if you want an extra kick, try some good old-fashioned lemonade, with an Italian twist, of course. I like my lemonade with all the pulp of the lemon squeezed in, served in a tall glass half full of ice. Not too sweet for me—just a touch of sugar. I top it off with a few leaves of either basil or mint from my garden, add a long straw, and drink up! When I was a child, lemons were not readily available in the summer, so my grandmother would substitute wine vinegar for the lemon juice, keeping the rest of the recipe the same. This is another healthy and delicious thirst-quencher.

ORZATA was originally a syrup made from a barley-almond blend, with a strong almond taste.

It is used in mixed drinks, and in Italy served in hot and cold beverages as an almond flavoring. Most orzata syrups also contain sugar, rose water, and orange-flower water. It is a refreshing sweet almond drink served over ice in a tall glass with club soda or sparkling water.

ITALIAN APÉRITIFS, DIGESTIFS, AND LIQUORS

AMARETTO, an Italian liqueur derived from the Italian word *amaro,* or "bitter," has bitter almond as a base. However, now sweeteners are often added.

AMARO, used in mixed drinks and as an after-dinner digestif, is an Italian herbal liqueur with a bittersweet flavor. It is made by macerating herbs and spices (perhaps mint, sage, thyme, or ginger), roots, citrus peels, bark, and flowers in alcohol. Fernet Branca, Cynar, and Amaro Averna are popular brands. Amaro can be made in different styles—for example, Fernet is very bitter, carciofo amaro is made with artichokes, and there is even rhubarb amaro.

ANISETTA is an Italian anise-flavored liqueur, made by distilling aniseed with sugar syrup.

APEROL, used in Italian apéritifs, is sweet-bitter and orange in color. It is made from bitter orange, gentian, rhubarb, and cinchona and has a low alcohol content, only 11 percent.

BELLINI, originating in Venice—invented by Giuseppe Cipriani, the founder of Harry's Bar—is a cocktail of prosecco and fruit purée (usually white peach) served in a flute glass. The pink color of the drink was similar to pinks used by the artist Giovanni Bellini—hence the name. The prosecco can be replaced by champagne, and other fruit purées can be used.

BRACHETTO, a slightly sweet, sparkling red wine, is often served in Italy as a dessert wine.

CAMPARI, an Italian apéritif with a highly recognizable red color, is used in many cocktails. It ranges in alcohol content from 20 to 28 percent. Gaspare Campari worked out the recipe over 150 years ago, and it is a highly guarded secret combination of herbs, aromatic plants, and fruit infused in alcohol and water. The dominant flavor in Campari is of bitter orange. It is most often served in the drinks Americano (Campari, vermouth, and club soda), Negroni (Campari, sweet vermouth, and gin), and Campari and soda.

CENTERBE, translated as "one hundred herbs," is a light green Italian liqueur made with medicinal herbs and alcohol, often used as a digestif. It has a high alcohol content, usually anywhere between 60 and 150 proof. Homemade centerbe may include sage, rosemary, marjoram, mint, and rue.

FRANGELICO is a sweet hazelnut liqueur with a bottle shaped like a Franciscan friar.

GRAPPA is a traditional distilled spirit in Italy, distilled from the pomace of the grapes after the juice has been pressed for wine making. It is a clear spirit, with the flavors and aromas of the grape varietal distilled. Grappa at its best is smooth and aromatic, leaving the flavors of the grape lingering on the palate. Fruits have been macerated in grappa for centuries. Dried figs macerate especially well in grappa, turning it into a cordial. Fill half a quart-sized glass jar with dried figs, and add grappa to fill the jar. Leave the jar in a cool place, loosely covered, for one week. Seal tightly, and allow to steep for two months, away from light. Serve the grappa and the fruit together in a brandy snifter as an after-dinner cordial. Grappa is usually enjoyed as a digestif with a cup of steaming espresso, and sometimes a tablespoon or so of grappa is added to the cup of hot espresso and the new drink is called "caffè corretto," corrected coffee.

LIMONCELLO is a lemon liqueur made mostly in the south of Italy. Lemon zests, without the pith, are soaked in alcohol until the oils are released from the rinds. This flavored alcohol is then mixed with simple syrup.

MOSCATO D'ASTI, a sparkling wine produced in the province of Asti in Piedmont, is a sweet wine, low in alcohol, served mostly with dessert.

PROSECCO, a sparkling Italian white wine, is made mainly in the Veneto and Friuli–Venezia Giulia; it is named for the small village of Prosecco, near Trieste. Often used in Italy as an aperitivo on its own, or mixed with fruit purée to create a Bellini cocktail.

SAMBUCA is a colorless anise-flavored Italian liqueur, usually served after dinner with a few coffee beans. It is made from anise, star anise, licorice, elderflowers, and other spices, with sweet syrup, in alcohol.

SPRITZ, German for "splash" or "sparkling," in Italy is a wine-based aperitivo (apéritif) commonly served in the Veneto region, in the northeast of the country. The spritz originated in Italy when northeastern Italy was part of the Austrian Empire; a common drink, the Austrian Spritz, was equal parts white wine and soda water. Today this refreshing drink may also be made by adding a splash of a bitter liquor, such as Campari or Aperol, to white wine or prosecco (Italian sparkling wine) and topping it off with a bit of sparkling mineral water. Experiment with the recipe and find a balance that is to your liking. Be sure to decorate your glass with a twist or slice of lemon or orange.

STREGA, meaning "witch," is an Italian herbal liqueur made from about seventy herbal ingredients, including mint and fennel; it is often used as a digestif.

VERMOUTH is a fortified wine served most often in cocktails used as apéritifs; it includes as aromatics bark, flowers, seeds, herbs, and spices. There are two types of vermouth, sweet and dry.

TECHNIQUES

Dura di più una pentola fessa che una nuova.
—Italian proverb

A cracked pot lasts longer than a new one.

General Tips

Use the best and freshest seasonal ingredients, use healthy cooking techniques, cook the food with awareness, make it tasty and visually appealing, and diversify what you cook and eat. These are the principles I keep in mind when I cook for my family, my guests, and myself. Eating should be pleasurable and approached with a positive state of mind and anticipation. There should be no guilt in eating; when we eat, we are nourishing our bodies, our minds, our souls. And we do it best in a context with others, be they family, friends, or strangers.

COOKING BASICS

Taste as you go. Learn and know the flavors, and understand how to pair them. Know your water; even that will influence the flavor of coffee or pasta, for instance. Water from different places has a different taste.

Think of the texture of the food, visually and tactilely (in the mouth). Cooking foods that belong together, hailing from the same cuisine and region, usually works. When plating a dish, think about how it will look. Food is an experience of the senses—the eyes and nose first, then texture and taste in the mouth.

If you are cooking and you taste something that needs adjusting, do it. You can correct too much salt by adding water to some dishes, or, in soups or when braising by adding one or two whole peeled potatoes. They will absorb some of the extra salt. You can add flavor with salt, pepper, and herbs. You can mellow out too much seasoning with dairy or butter. You can add sweetness if something is too acidic. You can add flavor with lemon, vinegar, salt, pepper, olive oil, butter, and sugar. Honey will also balance spices.

SHOPPING FOR FOOD

Buying seasonal and local is best. The food tastes better, it is more economical, and the food has traveled less, so it is less altered for preservation during traveling.

Respect the seasons and the authentic taste of the products you have chosen to use. Items eaten in season taste better, are more economical, and offer more nutrition. Shopping and cooking seasonally will make your cooking taste better—good cooking is primarily based on the quality of the ingredients.

In these days of convenience, we often don't pick our own produce and ingredients. But you must pick your own ingredients, and not just by appearance. Besides looking closely, you must feel and smell what you are buying.

Be tactile with food—especially vegetables, fruits, fish, and meats—when you are buying them, and also when you have brought them home and are ready to cook them. I have been asked many a time why I feel the ingredients when I cook. I understand the ingredients much better when I touch and feel them. I can tell much about the texture, and how I should cook it. Is the meat stringy and tough? I can tell how fresh fish is by the firmness of the flesh, and I can tell the ripeness of an avocado by the slightest pressure of my fingers. I can tell that vegetables are fresh when they are firm and crisp—an artichoke squeaks under my fingers, string beans snap when I bend them, the pepper squirts when I break it open, and an eggplant is shiny and firm to the touch.

EXPENSIVE INGREDIENTS The better, and not necessarily the more expensive, the ingredients you cook with, the better the final outcome will be. Just because an ingredient is more expensive does not mean it is better. To understand ingredients better, you should do comparative tastings, when possible, and read reviews and customer ratings of the product.

STORING FOOD

It is much better to store items in glass than in plastic or metal containers. Allow hot foods to cool down before storing them. Whether they are put in the cupboard, fridge, or freezer, be sure to date and label your food items so you know when you stored them.

ROTATE YOUR REFRIGERATOR Don't forget to look all the way in the back of the fridge, and use and rotate ingredients that you find there.

RAW AND COOKED Always store raw and cooked items apart. Store raw food in the lower parts of your refrigerator, in case they leak fluid.

FREEZING Instead of freezing chicken or fish, for example, in one big lump, freeze portions individually on a sheet pan; once they are frozen, place them in a bag in the freezer.

DEFROSTING It is better to defrost meats and fish in the refrigerator, in a bowl to catch liquid, allowing them to keep at a safe temperature. When in doubt, especially if something doesn't smell right, throw it out.

PREPARING THE KITCHEN TO COOK

It is important to have all ingredients and equipment ready and prepped before you begin cooking. Julia Child would say that the hands were one of the best tools in the kitchen, so use them.

CUTTING BOARD I prefer plastic or wood. These two materials are also easier on the blade of the knife than are marble, stainless steel, and granite. On the other hand, if I am making bread, kneading dough for pasta, or making dough for desserts, I like marble or granite. Be sure to wash your cutting board after you finish with each ingredient, especially after raw proteins, to avoid cross-contamination. Keep your kitchen cleaning cloth in a bowl of water to which some bleach has been added; it is also a disinfectant for your hands.

WORK SURFACE Place a wet paper towel or damp cloth under your cutting board, to prevent it from slipping.

SANITATION Do not use your hands or the same utensil to taste; keep a cup with plastic spoons near the stove, or use the proper utensil and wash it before using it again.

AROMA The aroma in your kitchen while you're cooking should be that of the food. Do not cook with scented candles burning or while wearing heavy perfume.

WASTE

Do not waste food. Save even the smallest amount of leftovers and leave for another meal, or freeze and reuse in another recipe. Before buying new ingredients, check what is in the house. Try making recipes using what you have in the house; it is interesting and fun to see what you can cook up with what you have. If you have lots of vegetables, a soup should come to mind, or a great pasta sauce or risotto.

TEMPERATURE

The heat applied in cooking is important and can make all the difference between overcooking, undercooking, or serving food quite simply at the wrong temperature. The temperature affects the amount of moisture extracted or left in the food. Control your heat, whether it's in the oven, or on the range or the grill; watch that temperature to get the desired results: crisp, charred, moist, soft, crunchy viscous, dry, and soupy textures are all determined by heat. When baking, always preheat the oven and check the temperature with an oven thermometer—some run hotter, others a bit cooler than what the dial indicates.

Be sure you have an oven mitt or a kitchen towel on handles of cooking instruments that you have just pulled out of the oven or off the stove, so people are aware and do not grab the hot handles. Never grab a hot handle with a wet cloth—the moisture conducts the heat much faster, and you will get burned.

An oven is always better to cook in than a microwave, which is fine for defrosting or reheating.

KEEPING ALL THOSE DISHES HOT FOR A FESTIVE MEAL Preparing and bringing all the dishes to the festive table nice and hot, and perfectly cooked, is a challenge we face at the restaurants every night, and is a challenge when cooking at home for a larger group or a holiday. All it takes is a bit of planning. One good option to keep in mind is to use the oven as much as you can. While the oven is still hot from the turkey or ham, use it to finish the vegetable dishes. Prepare the vegetables beforehand—parboil, steam, or sauté them. Then set them in a gratin dish and top them with bread crumbs seasoned with olive oil, butter, grated cheese, some chopped thyme, or other favorite herbs. Set the dish in the hot oven while you are carving the turkey or ham; the vegetables will be bubbling hot and crispy, which everyone loves. You can do this with potatoes, yams, string beans, or any vegetable of your choice.

BUTTER AND OIL

Add oil to a hot pan; it will heat immediately. If it smokes, throw it out, because it becomes toxic. Add butter to a cold pan, so the butter and pan heat together; otherwise, the butter sizzles and easily burns.

The flavor of olive oil or butter in finished dishes is something we all love, and we usually begin cooking with oil or butter. But to maximize that flavor and minimize the amount of butter or olive oil used, add most of it at the end of the cooking process. The heat and time of the cooking process dissipate the flavor and aroma of butter and olive oil; by adding them in the finishing steps of the recipe—whether sauce, soup, pasta, rice, or vegetables—you retain the maximum flavor.

One factor in choosing your cooking fats and oils is their smoking temperature: butter and olive oil have the lowest, canola oil the highest, with vegetable oils in between.

SERVING

It is usually a good idea to allow whole birds, meat roasts, and baked pasta dishes to rest before cutting, carving, or serving. When serving your food, keep it elegant and simple. Do not add any herbs just to garnish; use the same herbs you have used to cook in the presentation. What will work is something that complements the dish; for example, with fish, a wedge of lemon is appropriate. Use simple plates, especially if the food is complicated or dark in color. I always like a white plate. Before serving, be sure to use a clean kitchen towel to wipe around the rim of the plate, to remove smeared ingredients or fingerprints.

Tools

To excel in any métier or profession requires the proper tools, and nowhere is this truer than in the kitchen. When cooking, you need tools, vessels, surfaces to prepare, implements for serving, as well as cooking. The kitchen has to be efficient and functional. A well-equipped kitchen with a great collection of tools takes time and money to assemble, and as the skills of the chef grow, so does the need for new tools. There are different categories of kitchen tools: cutlery knives; cooking utensils, such as wooden spoons, spatulas, and whisks; cookware, such as pots, pans, skillets, and frying pans. Kitchen gadgets are necessary, and have become a favorite of people passionate about cooking—mandoline slicer, pasta roller, cutting surfaces, cutting boards, technical and mechanical gadgets, such as the food processor, mixer, and microwave.

There are some basics that every kitchen should have. Everyone needs a large stockpot for making soups. Soups made in a large quantity can be frozen and then easily made into a meal during the week, when time is precious. Heavy saucepans or Dutch ovens are great for roasts and braises, and I love a cast-iron skillet for high-temperature searing and delicious stovetop roasting, and it will last you a lifetime. Pasta lovers must have a good wide colander, and a fourteen-inch-diameter skillet so they can toss the pasta with the sauce just before serving. Such a pan is also perfect for quick-cooking meats and skillet-braising vegetables Italian-style. I find a potato ricer essential for preparing cooked potatoes for gnocchi and for making mashed potatoes. I also like the precision and consistency of slicing that a mandoline provides, and a Microplane grater is so smooth and easy to use that I even use it to grate my cheese. Obviously, every kitchen should have a good vegetable peeler to prep fruits and vegetables for cooking, and I certainly could not be without a food processor, which takes away an incredible amount of work in mixing and chopping.

CHITARRA FOR MACCHERONI

How do you use a chitarra in the kitchen? No, not the musical instrument, but the stringed pasta-maker. If you travel to Abruzzo, or have an Abruzzese family as your neighbors—and many immigrants from Abruzzo came to America—you most likely have heard of and/or tasted maccheroni alla chitarra. A chitarra is a rectangular pasta-cutting instrument with a wooden frame and metal strings on both sides. The freshly rolled pasta sheets are cut into maccheroni by being draped over the strings of the chitarra, then rolled and pressed back and forth with a rolling pin. You and your family will find it great fun to cut pasta dough through a chitarra and then enjoy the pleasures that only fresh homemade maccheroni's distinctive textural character can give. This instrument is now readily available in the United States. I recommend a traditional chitarra, with two sets of strings, one on each side of the frame, which allow you to cut very thin pasta strands (especially nice for cooking in soups) as well as a perfect thick maccheroni. And remember, just as a guitar needs to be tuned before playing, so does the maccheroni chitarra. Before each use, pluck on the strings and make sure they are taut and properly set in their notches on the chitarra frame. Most chitarras come with instructions for tightening the strings, usually a simple matter of turning the knobs that hold them.

KNIVES

The knife is the most important tool in the kitchen, and, like any good artisan, you do not loan your personal tools to anyone. Always bring your own knives when invited to someone's kitchen to cook. Use the right tool for the right job—in the kitchen this means having different knives for different tasks, but usually three or four knives suffice. Your chef's knife, the big knife, though capable of doing most jobs, shouldn't be relied on for everything. In a knife collection you should have a chef's knife, a paring knife, a boning knife, and a fillet knife. Others, such as a serrated knife and a slicer, are also very useful. A knife must be sharp, so be sure to steel your knives before every use, and get them sharpened whenever necessary. Even to serve cheese, the appropriate knife is important. A chisel-like knife works well on aged cheese, such as Grana Padano, whereas a slicing knife with holes is best for soft, creamy cheeses, such as Taleggio, so the cheese does not stick to it.

MANDOLINE SLICER

At one time, mandolines were found only in professional kitchens, but today many home cooks can find the much simpler version in stores for under $20. The mandoline is the perfect tool for creating cooking sensations quickly and easily. These slicers are great at cutting a wide variety of vegetables and fruits. Many mandolines also have attachments to cut things into julienne strips or other sizes. I recommend that every home cook have one, but please be very careful and be sure to always use the guard.

MORTAR AND PESTLE

The mortar and pestle have been around since the dawn of civilization. Using this ancient tool to grind spices and herbs yields a much more flavorful version of what you find packaged in the supermarket. It is also preferable to a food processor, because it provides a more gentle process of releasing the oils that give the spices their flavor. Simply press the batlike pestle down into the bowl in a circular motion, grinding the contents as finely as needed. Once you've mastered the mortar and pestle, you can skip the middleman and grab whole spices instead of ground at the supermarket! You can find this handy tool in many home- and kitchen-supply stores; it can be made of wood, marble, or volcanic stone—it is all a question of preference—but a good one is always rough on the inside of the mortar bowl so that the impact of the pestle creates traction and the spices or herbs are pulverized more effectively.

PIZZA STONE

A pizza stone, as it's called, is usually a rectangular tablet made of stone or terra-cotta that you place in your oven. It helps make good crusty pizza and focaccia because it heats to a high temperature and disperses the heat evenly over the bottom of the pizza, cooking it evenly and crisp. A pizza stone should not be washed, since it is porous; you just scrape and brush off any remaining debris. If you do not have a stone, baking the pizza on a baking sheet or in a cast-iron skillet will work as well.

POTATO RICER

The potato ricer is an essential tool in my kitchen. I mostly use it to rice the potatoes I am going to use to make gnocchi dough. I boil starchy potatoes such as Idahos or russets, with the skin on. When the potatoes are cooked soft, easily pierced with a fork, I drain them and let them cool a bit. While they're still warm, I peel them, set them in the barrel of the ricer, and gently press with the top cover and handle until all of the cooked potato is extruded through the small holes. I spread the riced potatoes on a kneading board or some other clean surface, lightly salt them, and, when they are cool, begin to make my gnocchi dough. The riced potatoes give gnocchi a smooth consistency. The technique is also excellent for making mashed potatoes, which will be smooth, not lumpy.

Cooking Methods

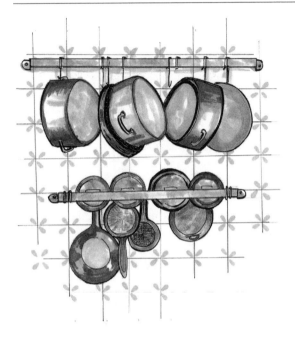

Knowledge is power, and it gives you confidence and certainty that you know what you are doing. This is especially true in the kitchen. Here I have assembled some of the basic methods of cooking. What does it really mean when a recipe tells you to boil, braise, poach, or roast? When you have decided on a recipe, this reference section will help clarify the how-to's of that recipe.

BAKING

The method that uses prolonged dry heat, acting by convection rather than by thermal radiation to cook food; it is normally done in an oven, but may also be done in hot ashes or on hot stones. The most common baked item is bread, and a great many other types of foods are, and can be, baked. Heat is gradually transferred from the surface of cakes, cookies, and breads to their center. As heat travels through, it gives batters and dough a firm, dry crust and a softer center.

BRAISING

A cooking method that combines both moist and dry heat. Most braises follow the same basic steps. The food to be braised (meat, poultry, or vegetables) is first seared at a high temperature to caramelize its surface and enhance its flavor. Then flavorful liquids, such as wine, stock, beer, vinegar, and juice, as well as herbs and spices, are added and the pot is covered, to develop and enhance the flavor of the protein and the sauce as it is braising. The liquid and the flavors permeate the meat, poultry, or vegetable, creating a distinct flavor for each dish.

BROILING

Cooking by exposing food to direct radiant heat, either on a grill over live coals or below a gas burner or electric coil. Broiling is an excellent technique for poultry, steaks, and meats in general. It differs from roasting or baking in that the food is turned during the process to cook both sides, and the crispy, caramelized outer surface of the protein being broiled keeps most of the juices inside the protein.

BRINING

This process is similar to marinating. The meat or poultry is soaked in brine (a flavored saline solution) for a period of time before being cooked. Equal parts sugar and salt are added to cold water in a container, in which the meat is usually soaked six to twelve hours, the time depending on the size of the meat.

FRYING

This is cooking food in an oil or other fats, such as lard, vegetable oil, grapeseed oil, or olive oil. A variety of foods can be fried, ranging from meats and fish to vegetables. There are several forms of frying, from deep-frying, in which the food is completely immersed in hot oil, to sautéing, in which food is cooked in a frying pan with only a thin coating of oil. Despite using liquid oil, frying is considered to be a dry cooking method, because water is not used in the cooking process and, ideally, the cooking oil will not be absorbed by the food. The frying temperature is extremely important, as is keeping that temperature constant during the frying process. If the temperature is too high, it will burn the outside, rendering it bitter and leaving the inside raw; having too low a temperature will allow the oil to be absorbed by the food, not a good thing. Frying is a wonderful option in the kitchen. The high temperature locks in flavor and keeps foods moist, while giving the food a delicious crispy coating. Some people like to stay away from frying because of the fat content, but if you fry correctly (and don't do it all the time) you don't have to worry about this.

DEEP-FRYING Get yourself a deep-frying thermometer; they are inexpensive and really the only way to judge the temperature of the oil accurately. Keep an eye on the thermometer when frying. If the oil becomes too hot, adjust the heat source. When the oil becomes too hot or is kept heated for a long time, it becomes difficult to digest and unpleasant to taste. When you are done with the oil, let it cool in the same cooking vessel; after the oil is completely cooled, you can discard it.

GRILLING

This consists of applying dry heat to the surface of food, either from above or from below. Grilling involves a significant amount of direct radiant heat, and tends to be used for cooking meat quickly. For best results, since grilling is a rather quick process, the food should be seasoned, marinated, or infused with a rub beforehand. When food is grilled on an open grill, the heat transfer is primarily via thermal radiation. When food is cooked on a griddle or grill pan, heat transfer is by direct conduction.

MARINATING

The process of soaking foods in a seasoned, often acidic liquid before cooking. The liquid,

or the "marinade," can be either acidic (made with ingredients such as vinegar, lemon juice, or wine) or enzymatic (made with ingredients such as pineapple or papaya juices, which help break down the proteins). In addition to these ingredients, a marinade often contains oils, herbs, and spices to add flavor to the food items. Besides flavoring foods, a marinade is also commonly used to tenderize tougher cuts of meat. The marinating process may last minutes or days, depending on the proteins to be marinated. Different marinades are used in different cuisines, reflecting the spices, herbs, and acidic liquids the culture uses.

POACHING

The process of gently simmering food in liquids such as milk, stock, wine, tomato sauce, vegetable sauce, or juices. Poaching is particularly suitable for delicate foods, such as eggs, poultry, fish, and fruit, which might easily fall apart or dry out. A much-used liquid in poaching fish is court bouillon. A classic court bouillon consists of an acid (wine, lemon juice) and aromatics (bouquet garni and mirepoix), which are boiled with water to flavor the court bouillon. After about thirty minutes, the protein is added to poach. It is important that the court bouillon have a low boil when poaching, so the fish does not fall apart.

ROASTING

This cooking method uses dry heat, whether an open flame, a wood-burning oven, or a gas or electric oven. Roasting enhances the flavor of meat, fish, or vegetables through caramelization—the Maillard reaction browns the natural sugars and proteins on the surface of the food. Meats and most root and bulb vegetables can be roasted with delightful results. A large piece of meat, on or off the bone, especially red meat, that has been cooked in this fashion is often called a roast. Roasting time is in direct correlation with the size of the cut and the species of the meat. A roast to feed a family can take one, two, or three hours to cook. The result of roasting usually leaves the outside crisp and the inside of the proteins tender and juicy, as well as developing a sauce or gravy from the drippings, juices, vegetables, and seasonings added.

SAUTÉING

This method uses a small amount of animal fat, oil, or butter over relatively high heat, usually in a shallow vessel. Ingredients are cut into pieces or thinly sliced to facilitate fast cooking. Food that is sautéed is usually browned first, to preserve its texture, then lightly braised to add moisture and flavor. For best results, make sure you leave enough room in the pan to cook everything you put in; do not overcrowd. The little bits left over in the pan by sautéing are often the best part. Deglaze the pan with some wine, water, or stock, and use this to make the sauce.

STEAMING

This easy and healthy cooking technique uses boiling water to vaporize into steam; the steam penetrates the meat, fish, or vegetables and cooks the food. The food needs to be kept separate from the boiling water but must have direct contact with the steam, which will cook the food while leaving it moist, and preserving more nutrients and flavors than boiling does.

Recipe Techniques

Here I have collected general tips, tools, and knowledge that I think can be useful and that I would certainly want to teach you if I were teaching a class. Much of this information I have accumulated over the years with experience in commercial kitchens, cooking for my family at home, and while working on my books and public television show. Learn the techniques because sometimes they make the recipe. Some techniques are quick and you can apply them to all your cooking, and some are very specific to a product or recipe. Make this information your own and use it to better your cooking. These techniques can serve as a base for creativity in your kitchen— use them as a springboard for creating your own recipes.

BACON CHIPS

Bacon chips are a great garnish that add flavor and texture to salads, vegetables, pastas, and especially soups. Cut bacon (about one slice per serving or a little less) crosswise into quarter-inch-wide strips. Cook in a heavy skillet over medium heat, turning frequently, until all the fat has rendered out and the strips are dark brown and crisp. Or crisp the bacon strips in a microwave. Remove with a slotted spoon, spread them out, and cover with paper towels to blot off the fat. When the strips cool, break them into chips.

BREAD CRUMBS

Bread crumbs are so easy to make; just give your dried-out old bread a whirl in the food processor, or gently grate it on a box grater, and—presto— you have a very versatile and usable product in your kitchen. At my house, we always save old bread and allow it to dry out. If you are in a hurry, you can dry the bread in your oven a bit. Store bread crumbs in an airtight container. Not only will these be some of the best crumbs you can find, but you also won't waste food. Bread crumbs can be used for frying, thrown into a sauce to add density if needed, added to roasting meat in the oven to make the gravy creamier, tossed into a stuffing, or even used at the bottom of a sweet pie, on top of the crust, to absorb any extra juices. I often use a mixture of bread crumbs and grated Grana Padano cheese on the poultry cutlets I prepare for my grandchildren, but instead of frying, I allow them to bake until crispy in the oven. The kids like the extra kick of flavor of the cheese added to the bread crumbs.

When I make my bread crumbs, I do not pre-season them; I add fresh herbs or spices as I am cooking the dish they will be used for.

SEASONED BREAD CRUMBS When a recipe calls for seasoned bread crumbs, add some grated Grana Padano, chopped parsley, lemon zest, dried oregano, and olive oil for moisture. Mix all the ingredients well in a bowl. These flavored bread crumbs work especially well in baking shrimp, chicken breasts, or fillets of fish. Season the protein with salt and pepper and toss with some olive oil, then dunk it in the bread crumbs to coat lightly. Set on a lightly oiled baking sheet, top with some more flavored bread crumbs, and bake at 375 degrees until crisp.

TOASTED BREAD CRUMBS As a substitute for grated cheese—for those who are lactose-intolerant, for example—golden-brown bread crumbs make a nice finishing touch on pasta dishes, a light counterpoint of texture, taste, and color. Start with ordinary dried crumbs that have some larger bits in them, rather than crumbs that have been ground and sieved into a fine powder. To toast, put the crumbs you need (a half-cup or so is right for most pasta dishes serving six to eight) in a small dry skillet with or without two tablespoons of extra-virgin olive oil, and set over medium heat. Keep tossing or stirring the crumbs; in a minute or so, they will start to color. Lower the heat if they're browning too fast, and keep tossing until the crumbs are getting fairly close to the color you want. Remove the skillet from the heat, and toss while the residual heat turns the crumbs the deep-golden color you like. Then turn them out of the pan. If you toast them completely and leave them in the skillet, they will get too dark, or even burn.

CACIO E PEPE

Cacio e pepe means "cheese and pepper," one of the simplest and yet tastiest pasta dishes in my repertoire; it requires no skillet for making the sauce. This old recipe was made by the shepherd community in the hills surrounding Rome and in Abruzzo, long before the tomato was even introduced to Italy after the discovery of America.

Pasta without a skillet sauce? That's right! Drain one pound of cooked pasta; then, in a warm bowl, simply toss the pasta with coarsely grated pecorino cheese and a few tablespoons of the pasta-cooking water, drizzle over it some extra-virgin olive oil, and sprinkle plenty of coarsely grated black pepper—I mean plenty! Serve it piping hot. This is an easy, satisfying dish that you can make on days when you need simplicity in your life but still want a wallop of flavor.

CRESPELLE FOR ANY MEAL

Crespelle are crêpes. Almost every culture has some form of crêpes in its cuisine. The fried flavored batter may be sweet or savory, and can be made by mixing different-grain flour. In Italy, we use crespelle in soups, to make manicotti, to layer lasagna, and, of course, to eat for dessert. As a child, I loved them most as dessert and ate them often, topped with sugar or sometimes just filled with marmalade. Rose-hip marmalade was my favorite. On special occasions, we filled warm crêpes with chocolate and topped them with toasted walnuts. Two or three of these crespelle and a glass of goat's milk was my supper on many an evening.

DICING VEGETABLES AND MEATS

When dicing vegetables, it is important always to be precise in the cuts you are making. Since vegetables come in different sizes, and smaller vegetables will cook faster than larger ones, it is important to cut your vegetables to a uniform size. The same rule goes for meats and other proteins. This will ensure that your vegetables or meats will be uniformly cooked, and no pieces will wind up under- or overcooked.

EGGPLANT PARMIGIANA ALTERNATIVES

I love that Italian American classic, too, but there are many more great eggplant dishes I've encountered in my travels through Italy that I want to share. In Sardinia, I was delighted to find a tradition of baked eggplant dishes with ingredients, tastes, and textures that I knew would appeal and are delicious. Here are two: baked sliced eggplant layered with onions and fresh tomatoes, and sliced eggplant baked in savory tomato sauce. Top with grated pecorino and/or chunks of young pecorino (or mozzarella), cover them with foil, and bake at 375 degrees until the eggplant is tender. In these preparations, the eggplant slices don't need frying (as they do in most eggplant-parmigiana recipes), which saturates them with more olive oil than necessary. No frying, and great flavor.

FETTUNTA

For a quick hunger fix or a great party appetizer, you can always count on fettunta, which translates as "oiled slice," referring simply to an oiled slice of bread. I always have oil, garlic, and salt in my cupboard, and most of the time I can find some day-old bread. Grill the bread, then rub it with crushed garlic cloves and brush with extra-virgin olive oil. The recipe works best with country-type bread, but any bread will do. If you want, you can elaborate on this dish by adding chopped tomatoes (with some onion and basil)— you now have bruschetta.

FRITTATAS: A GREAT ANYTIME RECIPE

An herb-and-vegetable frittata is wonderful as an appetizer, cut in wedges and served at room temperature, or served as a nice one-person lunch dish. The technique can be used with the full spectrum of seasonable vegetables, too. We always thought frittatas were best made in the springtime, when nettles, fennel fronds, young shoots of wild asparagus, or ramps could be gathered in the fields, but winter offers a nice bounty of shredded cabbage, shredded squash, and leaves of bitter greens, such as kale, which are all delicious when added to a frittata. You can also infuse the eggs with fresh thyme leaves, parsley, and chives, which you can get year-round.

GARLIC BUTTER: A LITTLE DOSE GOES A LONG WAY

To make garlic butter: Heat some extra-virgin olive oil in a pan. Add a little finely chopped garlic and a few chopped shallots. Cook these together over low heat for two or three minutes. Pour in some white wine and a little lemon juice, and boil until almost evaporated. Let this cool completely while two sticks of unsalted butter are softening at room temperature. Then blend well the softened butter, the cooled garlic-onion mixture, and some chopped fresh parsley. The flavored butter will keep in the refrigerator for a week or more— just roll it tightly in cellophane wrap. With this butter you can make quickly seared shrimp or scallops, or just toss with pieces of chicken breast and sauté. It's delicious, and a beautiful dish!

GREAT GRATINS

In order to produce a great gratin, as you are topping it with grated or shredded cheese you should let the cheese fall sparingly and evenly on the surface. If you're using a lot of cheese, let it build up in a fluffy layer so the oven's heat penetrates the granules, baking them into a crisp and generously colored crust. Resist the temptation to pat or press the cheese down, or it will turn into a gummy slab when it bakes. Often cooks remove their lasagna or manicotti when they see the first streaks of gold, afraid that it will burn in another minute. When the cheese has been applied with a light touch, it will darken gradually for a long time without burning. Not only will a longer baking produce a more spectacular-looking dish, but the deeper caramelization creates more flavors, too. For me, a great gratin must be dark and deep in color.

NUTS—TOASTED

Toasting any nuts brings out their oils and flavors, so always toast them just before using. Here are two quick options: Spread the nuts on a baking sheet and toast in a 325-degree preheated oven, shaking the pan once or twice as they bake, until lightly and evenly browned, about six minutes. Or toast pine nuts in a small skillet over medium heat, shaking the pan continuously, until they turn golden brown, about six minutes.

OLIVES DRESSED UP

To brighten up the flavor of cured olives you've bought, try some citrus. Prepare lemon zest, using a zester or a vegetable peeler and then cutting the zest into thin strips. Toss large, meaty green olives, such as Cerignolas, with the strips of lemon zest, a little lemon juice, some dried oregano, and a generous drizzle of olive oil. Or you can toss thin strips of orange zest with oil-cured Gaeta olives and a little squeeze of juice from the orange. Add some crushed hot red pepper, and let it steep for an hour before serving.

PESTO

When I say the word "pesto" to people in America (or anywhere outside Italy), they are most likely thinking of pesto alla Genovese, with its lush green color and intense perfume of fresh basil leaves. However, since "pesto" is a generic term for anything made by pounding, there are countless other kinds of pesto, and every region of Italy has its own rendition of pesto.

Pestare literally means "to trample," which is exactly what happens when making a pestata or a pesto. I like a pestata of garlic and pancetta, either smashed together with a mortar and pestle or chopped together in a mini-blender, and I use it when braising meats. A pestata of onions, carrots, and celery is a perfect base for soups and sauces. Pesto is classically from Liguria and consists of basil, olive oil, and pine nuts, which is great for dressing pasta, but every region has its own version of pesto. Pesto trapanese, made with basil, almonds, and fresh tomatoes, is a quick and easy way to dress pasta (see page 246). I also enjoy a pesto of walnuts and basil.

Whether you grow it or buy it, I highly recommend that, in late summer and fall (or whenever fresh basil is abundant in your area), you make a big batch of basil pesto to be stored in the freezer for those dreary winter days. In a food processor, combine fresh basil leaves, garlic, pine nuts, some fresh parsley leaves, and extra-virgin olive oil, and process until a nice even paste forms. Pour the pesto into ice-cube trays or small plastic containers, and freeze. Once it is frozen, pop the frozen pesto out, wrap the pieces individually in plastic, then seal the batch in giant zip-lock bags. Protected from freezer burn, your basil cubes will provide bursts of fresh flavor in soups, tomato sauces, and vegetable pasta sauces all winter long! Or you can freeze the remaining pesto in larger, portion-sized larger plastic containers, pour a thin film of olive oil over the top, and seal tight. The film of oil will protect the pesto from oxidizing. Thaw in refrigerator before using.

PIZZA THE TRUE NEAPOLITAN WAY

According to one of my good friends, a born Neapolitan, pizza in Naples should have a puffy, almost blistered cornice or rim, and a very thin center. The puffy cornice should be well toasted and should have the taste of the wood oven. The mozzarella should be made from water-buffalo milk and should be in distinctive pieces (not one big oozing, stringy mess). The tomato sauce should be the uncooked pulp of San Marzano tomatoes, passed through a mill, and there should not be too much of it on the pizza. When you cut into a pizza in Naples, it will be fairly contained and not ooze all over the plate. A few pieces of fresh basil scattered on top, and that is it. A minimalist approach to pizza making. What is paramount to a Neapolitan in eating pizza is the nuances of flavor in the dough.

RICOTTA: A SIMPLE AND DELICIOUS DESSERT

Think of this simple, yet wonderful dessert the next time you find fresh, large-curd ricotta cheese. Spoon the cheese into a fine sieve or a colander lined with a basket-type coffee filter. Set the sieve over a bowl, and let the ricotta drain in the refrigerator overnight. Spoon the drained cheese into a loaf pan lined with plastic wrap. Chill it until firm, and then invert it onto a serving platter. Cut the loaf into three-quarter-inch slices, and drizzle each slice with honey. A quick alternative is to spoon the drained ricotta onto a plate, forming quenelles, and drizzle the honey over them. Another option is to top it with toasted, chopped almonds, walnuts, or hazelnuts. Sweet ricotta is one of my favorite desserts—slightly sweet and fresh, but rich in flavor.

RISOTTO

Risotto is a northern Italian traditional recipe. It is specifically made with short-grain rice such as Carnaroli, Arborio, or Vialone Nano. As the rice is cooked a savory hot broth is added continuously and the mixture stirred often until the rice is al dente in a creamy sauce. Risotto can be made with any combination of vegetables, seafood, mushrooms, or meats; it can have deeply complex flavors or can be as simple as *alla Parmigiana,* made with onions and grated cheese.

THE NATURE OF THE LIQUID Some people are surprised to learn that you can make risotto with plain water. Of course you can, since the chemical processes are the same whatever liquid you use. If you have broth of any kind, and you want its particular flavor in your dish, use it. If you are adding a long-cooking sauce for flavor (especially if you use two cups), water is a good choice and better than a broth that might interfere with the sauce.

THE AMOUNT OF LIQUID There's no set amount of liquid to use in risotto—here's an instance where you are really in control. A general guideline for liquid is three and a half times the amount of rice; you should have this amount of very hot liquid on hand. But you may need far less. For one thing, it will evaporate at different rates in different pans and with different intensities of heat, and the amount of liquid it takes to produce a given consistency will therefore vary. Most important, you should add liquid until you have produced risotto with the texture you like.

THE AROMATICS Onions, cooked properly, provide a fine sweet base of flavor for simple risotto, but greater and more complex flavors will come if you add chopped leeks, shallots, or scallions. Shallots have a strong flavor (don't use more

than a half cup), but they mellow during cooking and they completely disappear in the risotto. Leek pieces will not disappear but add lovely flavor, as do scallions. You can add up to two cups of leeks and scallions to the pan, after the onions have started to sweat and wilt. But all moisture must be cooked out of the aromatics before toasting the rice. With each one cup increase of aromatics, add one tablespoon of olive oil.

OLIVE OIL OR BUTTER? This is a fascinating question with no single answer. It is important to understand that both olive oil and butter have an amalgamating property—bringing everything together texturally—that is always used to "finish" risotto (referred to as *mantecare* in Italian). Many people mistakenly think that butter—and lots of it—is always required as the finish, to make risotto creamy. (And some chefs whip in butter to give risotto creaminess when it wasn't developed through proper cooking.) But my basic recipe (page 203) shows you how to develop the creaminess by the slow release of starch and proper cooking.

Olive oil at the end adds a nice complexity that does not alter the essential flavor of the risotto: it is, in my opinion, a cleaner finish. I like using olive oil as a finish with fish risotto and some vegetable risottos, because it leaves the pristine flavors of the fish and vegetables clear and vibrant.

Butter, on the other hand, is a marvelous amalgamator: it makes the risotto even creamier and, obviously, buttery. I use it with all meat, all mushroom, and some vegetable risottos. The butter makes it rich and creamy, magnifies and to some extent alters the flavor. This can be desirable and there are many risotti where I love to use it. For instance, butter has the effect in tomato sauces of balancing the acidity—but it changes the taste in a way that olive oil does not.

FINISHING IT OFF When you are cooking risotto and the rice has cooked the amount of time suggested by the recipe, take a taste. If the rice is perfectly chewy and creamy, turn off the heat, and incorporate the finishing ingredients, chunks of room-temperature butter, and grated

Grana Padano cheese. Prepared this way, the risotto is called *mantecato*. If it is too al dente or a bit loose, cook for a couple more minutes, stirring. If the rice seems dry and undercooked, stir in a half-cup hot water or stock, or more if necessary, to loosen the rice, and cook over low heat for several more minutes, then taste again. On the other hand, if the rice seems soupy—and the rice grains seem fully cooked—you want to evaporate excess liquid quickly by keeping the lid off, raising the heat to high, and cooking the rice, stirring constantly, until it thickens.

SALAD

MAKING A PERFECTLY CRISP SALAD Washing salads will not only remove any dirt and grit, but will also revive your greens. About two hours before you are ready to make the salad, clean the greens and wash them twice in the sink with plenty of cold water. The first time, toss the greens in the sink filled with water, gently, then let them rest so all the dirt falls to the bottom. With a spider or a slotted ladle, fish the greens out in a colander. Drain the water, wash the sink well, and refill with cold water. Spread the greens out and let them steep for twenty to thirty minutes; then drain the salad greens well, and run them in a salad spinner. Set the salad in a bowl, cover with a slightly moist paper towel, and let sit in the refrigerator for one hour before dressing. The salad will be crisp and ready to dress.

DRESSING YOUR SALAD Always drain your salad well or spin-dry it before dressing it; otherwise, the dressing will dilute with the remaining water, lose flavor, and end up in a pool at the bottom of the bowl. Dress your salad as close to serving time as possible. Do not overdress it, or it will become heavy and soggy. Choose your dressing according to the texture of the salad: if the salad is silky and tender, use light liquid dressing; if the greens are resilient, use creamy and heavier dressings. If you are using olive oil and red wine vinegar, the ratio is usually one-third vinegar to two-thirds olive oil. Whisk the oil and vinegar first, add some salt, and then dress the salad. To give it some garlic flavor, add a few heads of crushed garlic to the oil-and-vinegar mixture. Let it steep for fifteen minutes, remove the garlic and toss the salad with the flavored dressing.

FREEZING SAUCE

The great thing about making a homemade sauce is that it can be frozen and used whenever you need it. The best way to freeze sauce is to let it cool once it is cooked, set a zip-lock bag in the pot, hold it open, and use a ladle to fill it up with the sauce. Zip it tight, lay it flat on a tray, and freeze it until you're ready to use it.

POACHING SWEET CORN IN SUMMER TOMATO SAUCE Next time you're making a tomato sauce in the summer, try this delicious tip. Shuck and rinse fresh corn, and drop a few ears into a pot full of perking tomato sauce. Cover the saucepan so it quickly returns to a gentle boil, and cook the ears for about eight minutes, until the kernels are tender. The corn will look beautiful covered in fresh tomato sauce, and you won't need to add butter to give the corn flavor. Plus, the corn will lend a delicious, slightly sweet flavor to the sauce!

SEADAS

If you travel to Sardinia, this is the dish to have. And if you want a taste of Sardinia at home, this is the dish to make (see page 109). Seadas resemble large ravioli, stuffed with sliced provolone. They're not cooked like pasta, but are fried until crisp, with oozing melted cheese inside. They're like grilled cheese sandwiches—kids love them. In fact, everybody does. Seadas make a great appetizer, flanked by some tossed salad or sliced tomatoes. For a more elaborate and substantial turnover, add some blanched asparagus or broccoli, or prosciutto or ham, to the stuffing; just cut down a bit on the cheese to make room. And if you make them half-sized, they're a terrific hors d'oeuvre to pass at a cocktail party. They are traditionally served drizzled with honey for flavor, but are delicious plain. For convenience, make and fill seadas in advance, but fry them when your guests arrive. If necessary, you can fry them up to thirty minutes ahead of time and keep them warm in the oven.

SOUPS

SERVING SOUP Sharing soup is a wonderful ritual of family meals, especially during the winter months. Though the soup itself may be simple, or just one of many courses, I like to give it the attention (and the garnishes) it deserves. I have one rule for serving soup, whether it's for a formal occasion or for an everyday supper—hot soup and warm bowls. If possible, I like to bring the soup to the table in a terrine or the cooking pot, have the warm bowls stacked up, and ladle out and garnish each serving when everyone is seated. Dress the soup with a drizzle of extra-virgin olive oil and some grated Grana Padano. I love the moment when there's a steaming bowl of hot soup in front of us, and we're all enjoying its warmth, its aromas—and one another's company.

GARNISHING MINESTRA AND OTHER SOUPS Adding flavor to any soup is simple and easy. One sure way is to drizzle some of the best extra-virgin olive oil you have over a bowl of minestra just before serving it. Freshly grated cheese always delivers extra flavor, or you can pass a nice chunk of Grana Padano or Pecorino Romano with a small grater around the table, so people can grate their own. I do both, and add some freshly ground pepper as well, for extra spice. Some crumbled bacon chips are delicious sprinkled over some soup. A plateful of grilled country bread brushed with garlic and olive oil, or of crispy croutons, is always a great accompaniment.

SOUPS AS SIDES A hearty, chunky soup is fantastic in cold weather, but it can also be an incredible accompaniment to other dishes as a side, a topping, or a base. To turn your favorite soup into a denser version for a side dish, try making the recipe with less water or stock. You'll end up with something that has a much thicker consistency but still all of the great flavor of your soup. Try a thickened apple soup as a base for a grilled pork chop, or a thickened bean soup as a side for grilled rib eye.

SOUP FOR MEAT LOVERS I often add cuts of meat to a big pot of soup I am cooking. Not only does the meat add flavor, but when it is done I remove it and serve it as a second course. In fact,

if your pot is big enough, you should be able to drop in a pound or more of meat, such as a piece of flat-iron beef or chuck. Country-style ribs, Italian sausages, and smoked pork butt are also delicious this way. Add the meat at the beginning. Simply wash the meat well with hot water before you add it to the pot, and continue cooking. When the meat is cooked, remove it from the soup, keep it warm until ready to serve, and then slice and serve alongside the soup, or as a second course sprinkled with some coarse salt, or with freshly grated horseradish and mustard, or your favorite chutney on the side.

MUSHROOM SOUP In making a mushroom soup, you'll get the best results when the soup has been made with several varieties of fresh wild mushrooms. Porcini, shiitake, chanterelle, and hen-of-the-woods are some great examples of mushrooms to look for. Be sure that they have been cleaned and trimmed. If you're using dried mushrooms, you'll want to rehydrate them for about twenty minutes. Fish out the soaked mushrooms and chop them to add to your soup. Use the soaking liquid as well—just make sure you strain it first, to avoid adding the grit that has settled on the bottom.

COOKING SOUPS WITH DRIED BEANS Beans and legumes are the best base for tasty, velvety soups. In most cases, one begins by soaking the beans. An overnight soak is the easiest way to rehydrate dried beans before cooking. Put the beans in a large bowl or pot with cold water, covering them by four inches or more. Most beans are sufficiently soaked in eight hours; old beans take longer but you can soak them up to twenty-four hours, until plump and not wrinkled. Skim off any floating particles, and then drain well before adding to soups to cook.

STOCK Stock is delicious, nutritious, versatile, and necessary to have on hand when cooking at home. It is easy to make, whether vegetable, fish, or meat stock. Though it is available in most food markets, I suggest that you cook up a batch of stock periodically and keep it in reserve. When straining stock, reserve the meats to eat and press the vegetables to get the most out of them and into the stock you have made. It stores well and can be concentrated (reduced) so that it takes up even less space. I like freezing stock in ice-cube trays and, once they're frozen, keeping them in a plastic bag, so I can just grab one or two quickly when I need them and plop them into whatever I am cooking.

MAKING CHICKEN STOCK There is always chicken stock at our house, whether perking on the stove or stashed in the freezer, waiting to be used. Fresh vegetables are essential when making chicken soup. Carrots, celery, parsley, parsnips, and leeks are the ones I use, and of course a free-range chicken will always make a superior stock. Do not use the breast and the legs for soup—save them for another meal. Use the bones, wings, neck, and, yes, if you have the feet, throw them in the pot, too. I also like the richness that turkey wings add to a chicken stock, so I use them as well if I have them. You can accumulate the chicken parts you need for stock in a resealable bag or container in the freezer. Or perhaps your butcher can sell you those lesser parts, which make the best soup and are cheaper. Be sure to remove the livers from the giblet bag before making stock—livers will add a bitter flavor—but use all the other giblets.

LEFTOVER SOUPS Many soup recipes make more than four or six servings, because most hearty soups cook better in large quantities, giving them a chance to percolate and the flavors to mellow. When you make a big batch of Pasta e Fagioli (page 156)—or any soup, for that matter—it is nice to freeze it and have some left over for another meal. Just remember, do not add pasta or rice to a soup until you're ready to serve it. Most soups taste better when they have rested and are reheated. Defrost the soup, add some water (about a quarter of the original volume), and bring all back to a boil, then add pasta or rice and cook until done. Drizzle with some olive oil and some grated Grana Padano, and serve.

RECIPES

ABOUT RECIPES

RECIPES ARE IMPORTANT in cooking, but, as in every profession, practice makes the difference. Use the recipe as a guideline, but use your senses when cooking: tasting, smelling, touching, looking, listening. The messages you collect from your senses will help you understand better what and how you are cooking, and will lead to better cooking. Your repeated experiences with food and cooking will make you a better cook.

When I identify a recipe that my family and I like, I find it interesting and helpful to read a few different versions of the same recipe. I learn from them all, and notice the differences between the recipes; sometimes I pick elements from each to create a new version, as well as make modifications along the way that reflect my personal preferences.

Timing is important in a recipe, but do not expect it to work perfectly every time; you should stay alert, when cooking, to look for the final desired result, and recognize it when it happens. If a recipe says to brown the onions for ten minutes, but after the ten minutes indicated in the recipe they are not brown, keep on cooking them, and so on.

Every time you try the same recipe over again, you are one step closer to perfecting it. But do keep in mind that there is slight variation each time you make the recipe, no matter how many times you do it.

Your input in the recipe (how you mix, how many times you mix, how fast or slowly you work, how you diced the ingredients) all somewhat affect the recipe.

Do not try to master everything, but work within your strengths. Getting a core mastery of the basics is essential; then you can build upon these. Each dish you make should excel in various aspects, not just one. It should be tasty, full of aroma, flavorful, interesting, well plated, beautiful, unique, balanced, and served at the right temperature, among other things.

Learn from cooking mistakes—don't be hindered by them. Most of them are correctable and acceptable, unless you burn the pot.

APPETIZERS

Mangiando viene l'appetico.
—Italian proverb

Appetite comes with eating.

Fava and Sesame Dip

Crema di Fave e Sesamo
SERVES 4 TO 6

¾ teaspoon kosher salt, plus more for the pot
4 pounds fresh fava beans (3 to 3½ cups),
   shelled
½ cup sesame seeds, lightly toasted
¼ cup freshly squeezed lemon juice
1 garlic clove, crushed and peeled
⅔ cup extra-virgin olive oil
Flatbread or bread sticks, for serving

Bring a large pot of salted water to a boil. Add the shelled favas, and blanch until bright green and tender, about 5 to 7 minutes, depending on their size. Cool in a bowl of ice water. Peel off the skins and discard. You should have about 2 cups peeled favas.

In a food processor, combine the favas, sesame seeds (reserving 1 tablespoon for garnish), lemon juice, garlic, and salt. With the machine running, add the olive oil in a stream to make a thick, chunky paste. With the machine still running, add warm water, a few tablespoons at a time (up to ⅓ cup), to thin the dip to your liking. It should be about the consistency of hummus.

Transfer the dip to a serving bowl. Garnish with remaining sesame seeds, and serve with flatbread or bread sticks for dipping.

Celery Stalks Stuffed with Gorgonzola and Apples

Coste di Sedano Farcite al Gorgonzola e Mele
SERVES 4 TO 6

4 ounces Gorgonzola Dolce, at room temperature
¾ cup mascarpone, at room temperature
½ Granny Smith apple, with skin, finely diced
6 inner celery stalks, trimmed and cut into
   3 pieces each
½ cup inner celery leaves, for garnish

In a medium bowl, mash together the Gorgonzola and mascarpone until smooth. Stir in the diced apple, and mix well.

Use a teaspoon to stuff the mixture into the celery stalks. Chill for an hour before serving, and serve garnished with the celery leaves.

Whipped Salt Cod Spread

Baccalà Mantecato
MAKES ABOUT 4 CUPS

1 pound boneless baccalà (salt cod)
1 medium russet potato (about ½ pound)
2 garlic cloves, finely minced
1 cup extra-virgin olive oil
½ cup half-and-half or light cream
½ cup poaching water from cooking the baccalà
Freshly ground black pepper to taste

Forty-eight hours before you want to prepare the baccalà, place it in a large bowl and cover it with cold water by several inches. Let it soak in the fridge to remove the salt, changing the water completely every 8 to 10 hours. When it is sufficiently soaked, drain and pat dry.

Cut the baccalà into smaller pieces—6 inches or so—and put them in a saucepan or deep skillet with at least an inch of water to cover. Bring to a boil, set the cover ajar (rest it on a wooden spoon set on the rim of the pan), and cook at a steady bubbling boil for about 20 minutes, until the cod is easy to flake but still has body and shape. Lift the baccalà out of the cooking water, and let it drain and cool in a colander. Reserve ½ cup of the cooking water.

Meanwhile, rinse the potato but leave it whole and unpeeled. Put it in a small pot and cover with cold water. Bring to the boil, and cook steadily until you can easily pierce the potato with a knife blade, 25 to 30 minutes. Let it cool, and peel it.

Set up the electric mixer, and flake all the fish into its bowl. Beat with the paddle at low speed to break the fish up more; drop in the minced garlic and the cooked and peeled potato, and beat at medium speed while you pour in half the olive oil very gradually. Raise the speed to high, then add the rest of the oil and whip the fish to lighten it. Reduce the speed to medium and incorporate the half-and-half gradually; then whip at high speed again. At this point, the whipped cod should be smooth and fluffy, almost like mashed potatoes but with texture. If it is very dense, thin it with the cooking water (but be careful: too much water will make it too salty). Finally, season with pepper and beat it in to blend.

🌿 If you use a food processor instead of a mixer, follow the same order of additions, and process as needed to form a light, smooth spread. Put the spread in containers and store sealed in the refrigerator for up to a week. You can also freeze baccalà mantecato; the texture will not be as creamy, but it will have good flavor and make a delicious pasta sauce.

Roasted Pepper Rolls Stuffed with Tuna

Peperoni Farciti con Tonno ed Acciughe
MAKES ABOUT 15 SMALL ROLLS, SERVING 6 AS
AN HORS D'OEUVRE

3 or 4 sweet red or assorted-color peppers (about 1½ pounds total)
⅓ cup extra-virgin olive oil, plus more as needed
1 teaspoon kosher salt
Two 6-ounce cans tuna in olive oil (preferably imported from Italy)
2 small anchovy fillets, drained and finely chopped
2 tablespoons small drained capers, finely chopped
1 tablespoon apple-cider vinegar
1 tablespoon Dijon mustard

⅓ cup mayonnaise
1 tablespoon chopped fresh Italian parsley

Preheat the oven to 350 degreees. Rub the peppers all over with 2 tablespoons olive oil, season with ½ teaspoon salt, and place on a parchment-lined baking sheet. Roast for 30 minutes or so, turning the peppers occasionally, until their skins are wrinkled and slightly charred.

Let the peppers cool completely. Slice in half (through the stem end), discard the stem and seeds, peel off the skin, and slice the halves lengthwise into strips 2 inches wide. Scrape any remaining seeds from the strips, quickly rinse the strips under cold water, and lay them in a sieve to drain and dry.

To make the stuffing: Drain the tuna, and break it into flakes in a medium-sized bowl. Mix the chopped anchovies, capers, vinegar, mustard, mayonnaise, parsley, 2 tablespoons olive oil, and about ½ teaspoon salt into the tuna with a fork. Stir vigorously, breaking up lumps of fish, until the stuffing is soft and fairly smooth.

Drop a scant tablespoon of stuffing at one end of each roasted pepper strip, and roll it up snugly, creating a neat cylinder. Press the pepper as you wrap, so it adheres to itself and stays closed.

To serve: arrange all the rolls on a platter, drizzle a bit more olive oil all over, and sprinkle lightly with coarse salt.

Swordfish-Stuffed Peppers

Peperoni Farciti con Pesce Spada
SERVES 6 AS AN APPETIZER OR LIGHT MAIN
COURSE

6 small red, yellow, or orange bell peppers
6 tablespoons extra-virgin olive oil
1 teaspoon kosher salt
6 cups crustless day-old bread cubes
1¼ pounds skinless swordfish steaks, coarsely chopped

1 teaspoon kosher salt
4 garlic cloves, finely chopped
1½ cups frozen peas
1 teaspoon chopped fresh thyme
½ cup dry white wine
2 bunches scallions, trimmed and coarsely
    chopped (about 2 cups)
¼ cup chopped fresh Italian parsley

Preheat the oven to 400 degrees. Cut each pepper into thirds lengthwise, along the natural folds. Remove the seeds to make 18 pepper "boats." On a rimmed baking sheet, toss the peppers with 2 tablespoons of the olive oil, and season with ½ teaspoon of the salt.

Put the bread cubes in a large bowl, cover them with water, and let them soak while you make the stuffing.

To a large skillet over medium-high heat, add the remaining olive oil. When the oil is hot, add the swordfish, and season with the remaining ½ teaspoon salt. Stir to coat the swordfish in the oil, then add the garlic. Once everything is sizzling, stir in the peas and thyme. Add the wine, and simmer until it has evaporated, about 5 minutes.

Add the scallions, and cook until they are wilted, about 3 minutes. Stir in the parsley. Scrape the mixture into a large bowl. Squeeze all of the water out of the soaked bread, and crumble the bread into the swordfish mixture. Mix well, and stuff the filling into the pepper boats. Cover with foil, and bake until set, about 20 minutes. Uncover, and bake until the top of the filling is golden brown, about 20 minutes more. Serve hot or at room temperature.

🌿 This preparation is also good with other sturdy fish, and is a good use for fish scraps like ventresca or belly flap, or if you have leftovers from cleaning whole fish.

Egg-Battered Zucchini Roll-Ups

Involtini di Zucchine Fritte
SERVES 10 AS AN HORS D'OEUVRE OR 6 AS A
SIDE DISH

2 pounds (5 or 6) small zucchini
2 cups all-purpose flour, for dredging
5 large eggs
¾ teaspoon salt
Freshly ground black pepper to taste
Canola or vegetable oil, for frying (2 cups or
    more, depending on skillet size)
1 or 2 tablespoons drained tiny capers in brine
Juice of ½ lemon, freshly squeezed

Rinse and dry the zucchini, and trim off the stem and blossom ends. Use a sharp knife to slice the squash lengthwise into strips about ⅛ inch thick, flexible but not paper-thin. (You should get five or six strips from each small zucchini.)

Dump the flour into a wide bowl or shallow dish. Beat the eggs well in another wide bowl, stirring in ½ teaspoon of the salt and some grinds of pepper. Set a wide colander on a plate, to drain the battered strips before frying. Tumble five or six zucchini strips at a time in the flour, coating them well on both sides.

Shake off the loose flour, and slide the strips into the beaten eggs. Turn and separate the strips with a fork so they're covered with batter; pick them up one at a time, letting the excess egg drip back into the bowl; lay the strips in the colander. Dredge and batter all the zucchini strips this way, and let them drain. Return the egg drippings collected under the colander to the batter, if you need more.

Pour an inch of oil into a deep skillet, and set it over medium-high heat. Cover a baking sheet or large platter with paper towels. When the oil is very hot but not smoking, test it by dropping in half a strip of battered zucchini. It should sizzle actively and begin to crisp around the edges, but not smoke or darken.

Fry the zucchini strips in batches, and when they are golden on both sides, remove them and set on the paper towels to drain, about 4 to 5 minutes per batch. Sprinkle with remaining salt.

To form the roll-ups: Place a fried strip on your worktable, with the wider end facing you. Place three or four capers on that end, then vertically roll the strip tightly, enclosing the capers in the center. Weave a toothpick all the way through the roll-up, so it stays together. Roll up all the strips. Just before serving, stand the roll-ups on end and squeeze drops of lemon juice all over the spiral tops. Arrange them on a serving platter. (If you like capers as much as I do, scatter another teaspoon or so of drained capers all over.)

Zucchini Fritters

Frittelle di Zucchine
SERVES 6

Vegetable oil, for frying
2 medium zucchini (8 ounces), washed and trimmed
3 large eggs
3 tablespoons chopped fresh Italian parsley
Grated zest of 1 lemon
⅔ cup all-purpose flour
½ teaspoon baking powder
½ teaspoon kosher salt, plus more for seasoning
Lemon wedges, for serving

In a straight-sided skillet, heat 1 inch of vegetable oil to 360 degrees. Grate the zucchini on the medium holes of a box grater onto a kitchen towel. Tightly wrap the zucchini in the towel, and wring out as much liquid as possible. Beat the eggs in a large bowl. Stir in the zucchini, breaking up any clumps with a fork. Stir in the parsley and lemon zest.

Sift together the flour, baking powder, and salt. Stir into the egg mixture until just combined—don't overmix.

Brush a soup spoon with vegetable oil, and

with it drop dollops of batter into the oil, patting the fritters lightly with the back of a spatula to flatten slightly. Fry, turning once, until golden on both sides and cooked through, about 2 minutes per side. Fry them in batches. The fritters are cooked when a fork inserted in the center comes out clean. Drain cooked fritters on paper towels, and season lightly with salt. Serve fritters right away, with lemon wedges.

Stuffed Zucchini Blossoms

Fiori di Zucchine Ripieni
SERVES 6

BLOSSOMS
24 zucchini blossoms
1 cup fresh ricotta
¼ cup freshly grated Grana Padano
Grated zest of 1 small lemon
Kosher salt and freshly ground black pepper

BATTER
1½ cups all-purpose flour
1 teaspoon baking powder
1 teaspoon kosher salt
One 12-ounce bottle amber beer, or 1½ cups seltzer

Vegetable oil, for frying

Gently pry open the zucchini blossoms, pull out the small yellow stamen from inside each, and discard. In a small bowl, stir together the ricotta, grated cheese, and lemon zest, and season with salt and pepper.

To stuff the blossoms, open the flowers and stuff with about 2 teaspoons or so of the ricotta mixture (an iced-tea spoon or other small spoon works well for this). Fold over the ends to close and seal the filling in the blossoms.

For the batter: In a medium bowl, whisk

together the flour, baking powder, and salt. Whisk in the beer to make a smooth batter; let rest 5 minutes.

Meanwhile, in a deep pot, heat 2 inches of vegetable oil to 360 degrees. Once the batter has rested, dip the blossoms in the batter one at a time, letting the excess drip back into the bowl. Fry in two or three batches, depending on the size of your pot, until the batter is crisp and golden, about 3 to 4 minutes per batch, turning to brown both sides. Drain on paper towels, season with salt while hot, and repeat with the remaining blossoms and batter.

Serve alone or atop a thin layer of hot marinara sauce.

Tomato Fritters

Frittelle di Pomodori
SERVES 6

Vegetable oil, for frying
6 medium under-ripened tomatoes
½ teaspoon kosher salt, plus more for seasoning
¼ cup fresh whole basil leaves
1 cup all-purpose flour, plus more for dredging
½ teaspoon baking powder
1 large egg, lightly beaten

In a deep pot or Dutch oven, heat several inches of oil to 365 degrees. Slice the tomatoes crosswise into ½-inch-thick slices, season with salt, and drain well on paper towels, flipping once, while you make the batter. Chop the basil leaves.

In a large bowl, whisk together the flour, baking powder, and ½ teaspoon salt. Whisk in the egg and ¾ cup water to make a smooth batter. Whisk in the chopped basil just enough to distribute it in the batter.

Spread about a cup of flour on a plate. Pat tomatoes dry once more, then lightly dredge them in the flour, on both sides. Dip in the batter (make sure the tomatoes are completely coated, or their juices will drip into the oil and create splatters), and fry, in batches, until the batter is puffed and dark golden, about 2 minutes per side. Drain on fresh paper towels, and season lightly with salt. Serve hot.

Eggplant Rollatini

Involtini di Melanzane
SERVES 6 AS A MAIN COURSE OR 12 AS A FIRST COURSE OR BUFFET SERVING

1½ pounds fresh ricotta, or 3 cups whole-milk ricotta
3 cups Tomato Sauce (page 161)
2 medium eggplants (about 2 pounds total)
Kosher salt
½ cup extra-virgin olive oil, or as needed
½ cup vegetable oil, or as needed
3 large eggs
All-purpose flour
1 cup freshly grated Grana Padano
3 tablespoons chopped fresh Italian parsley
Freshly ground black pepper
8 ounces fresh mozzarella, cut into ¼-by-¼-inch sticks
8 fresh basil leaves

Spoon the ricotta into a large fine-mesh sieve, or a colander lined with a double thickness of cheesecloth. Set the sieve over a bowl, and cover the ricotta well with plastic wrap. Drain the ricotta in the refrigerator at least overnight, or up to 24 hours. Discard the liquid in the bottom of the bowl.

Preheat the oven to 375 degrees. Warm the tomato sauce in a small saucepan. Trim the stems and ends from the eggplants. Remove alternating strips of peel about 1 inch wide from the eggplants, leaving about half the peel intact. Cut the eggplants lengthwise into ¼-inch-thick slices, and place them in a colander. Sprinkle generously with the kosher salt, tossing to expose all slices, and let drain for 1 hour. Rinse the eggplant under cool running water, drain thoroughly, and pat dry.

Pour ½ cup each of the olive and vegetable oils into a medium skillet over medium-high heat. While the oil is heating, whisk two of the eggs and 1 teaspoon salt together in a wide, shallow bowl. Spread about 1 cup flour in another wide, shallow bowl. Dredge the eggplant slices in flour, shaking off the excess. Dip the floured eggplant into the egg mixture, turning well to coat both sides evenly. Let excess egg drip back into the bowl.

When a corner of a coated eggplant slice gives off a lively sizzle when dipped into the hot oil, the oil is ready for frying. Add as many of the coated eggplant slices as fit without touching, and cook, turning once, until golden on both sides, about 4 minutes. Remove the eggplant to a sheet pan lined with paper towels and repeat with the remaining eggplant slices. Adjust the heat as the eggplant cooks, to prevent the egg coating from cooking too fast or overbrowning or the oil temperature from dropping. Add oil to the pan as necessary during cooking to keep the level more or less the same. Allow the new oil to heat before adding more eggplant slices.

Stir the drained ricotta, ⅔ cup of the grated cheese, and the parsley together in a mixing bowl. Taste, and season with salt and pepper. Beat the remaining egg and stir it into the ricotta mixture. Pour 1 cup of the tomato sauce over the bottom of a 10-by-15-inch baking dish. Sprinkle lightly with 2 tablespoons of the remaining grated cheese.

Lay one of the fried eggplant slices in front of you, with the short end toward you. Spoon about 2 tablespoons of the ricotta filling over the narrow end of the slice, and top it with a mozzarella stick. Roll, and place, seam side down, in the prepared baking dish. Repeat with the remaining eggplant slices and filling, placing the rolls side by side.

Ladle the remaining tomato sauce over the eggplant rolls to coat them evenly. Sprinkle the remaining grated cheese over the top of the eggplant, and tear the basil leaves over the cheese. Cover the dish loosely with foil, and bake until bubbling and the filling is heated through, about 30 minutes. Let rest 10 minutes before serving.

Stuffed Mushrooms

Funghi Ripieni
SERVES 6

24 white or cremini mushrooms, each about 1½ inches in diameter
2 tablespoons extra-virgin olive oil, plus more for drizzling
½ cup finely chopped scallions
½ cup finely chopped red bell pepper
½ cup coarse bread crumbs
½ cup freshly grated Grana Padano
¼ cup finely chopped fresh Italian parsley
Kosher salt and freshly ground black pepper
4 tablespoons unsalted butter
½ cup Chicken Stock (page 143) or Vegetable Stock (page 143)
¼ cup dry white wine

Preheat the oven to 425 degrees. Remove the stems from the mushrooms, and finely chop the stems. Heat 2 tablespoons of the olive oil in a medium pan over medium heat. Add the scallions, and cook until wilted, about 1 minute. Stir in the red pepper and chopped mushroom stems, and cook, stirring, until tender, about 3 minutes. Remove to a bowl and let cool.

Toss the bread crumbs, grated cheese, 2 tablespoons of the parsley, and the cooled sautéed vegetables until thoroughly blended. Season to taste with salt and pepper. Stuff the cavity of each mushroom with the filling, pressing it in with a teaspoon until even with the sides of the mushroom.

Using 2 tablespoons of the butter, grease a baking pan. Arrange the mushrooms side by side in the pan and, using the remaining 2 tablespoons butter, dot the top of each mushroom with about ¼ teaspoon butter. Add the stock, wine, and remaining parsley to the pan. Drizzle the tops of the mushrooms with olive oil. Bake until the mushrooms are cooked through and the bread crumbs are golden brown, about 20 minutes. Serve the mushrooms on a warmed platter, or divide them among warmed plates. Pour the pan juices into a small saucepan, and bring to a boil on top of the stove. Reduce until lightly thickened, to the consistency of gravy, 1 to 2 minutes. Spoon the juices over the mushrooms, and serve.

Stuffed Olives Ascolane

Olive Ascolane Ripiene
SERVES 6

STUFFING
1 tablespoon extra-virgin olive oil
8 ounces sweet Italian sausage without fennel seeds
½ cup dry white wine
1 large egg, beaten
¼ cup freshly grated Grana Padano
¼ cup fine dried bread crumbs

OLIVES
Vegetable oil, for frying
3 cups large green pitted olives, such as Ascolane
1 cup all-purpose flour
2 large eggs
2 cups fine dried bread crumbs
Kosher salt

For the stuffing: In a medium skillet, heat the olive oil over medium-high heat. Add the sausage. Cook and crumble with a wooden spoon until cooked through, about 5 minutes. Increase heat to high, add the white wine, and cook until

absorbed, about 3 minutes. Scrape into a medium bowl, and crumble sausage with a fork until very fine and crumbly. Let cool completely.

To the sausage, add one egg, the grated cheese, and bread crumbs. Mix well.

For the olives: In a deep pot, heat 2 inches of vegetable oil to 365 degrees. Line a sheet pan with parchment.

Press the stuffing into the cavities in the olives, filling all the way to the top and packing the stuffing tightly. Put the flour, two eggs, and bread crumbs into three separate shallow bowls. Dredge the olives in flour, and then in the whisked eggs, letting the excess drip back into the bowl. Roll to coat them in the bread crumbs, and rest on the sheet pan while you bread the remaining olives.

When all of the olives are breaded, fry, in three batches, until the breading is crisp and golden, about 3 to 4 minutes per batch. Drain on paper towels, and season lightly with salt—the olives are already salty.

Stuffed Artichokes

Carciofi Ripieni
SERVES 6

Grated zest from 1 lemon (save lemon for juicing)
Juice of 2 lemons, freshly squeezed
6 large artichokes
1½ cups fine dried bread crumbs
½ cup freshly grated Grana Padano
½ cup pine nuts, toasted and coarsely chopped
½ cup plus 2 tablespoons chopped fresh Italian parsley
½ cup plus 3 tablespoons extra-virgin olive oil
2 large hard-boiled eggs, finely chopped
¾ teaspoon kosher salt
1 cup dry white wine
⅛ teaspoon crushed red pepper flakes

Preheat the oven to 400 degrees. To clean and prepare the artichokes, fill a bowl with about a quart of cold water, and add the juice of one lemon, plus the squeezed-out lemon halves. Peel and trim the stem of the first artichoke, reserve the stem, and put artichoke and stem in the lemon water. Pull off any tough outer leaves and discard. Using a paring knife, trim away any tough parts around the base and stem of the artichoke. With a serrated knife, cut off the top third of the artichoke and discard. Push the leaves out to expose the fuzzy purple choke. With a small spoon, scrape out the choke to expose the heart. Put the prepared artichoke in the bowl of water and lemon juice to keep it from oxidizing. Repeat with remaining artichokes.

For the stuffing: In a medium bowl, mix together the bread crumbs, grated cheese, and chopped pine nuts. Stir in ½ cup of the parsley, ½ cup of the olive oil, the eggs, ¼ teaspoon salt, and the reserved lemon zest. Toss with a fork until the crumbs are moistened with the olive oil.

Remove the cleaned artichokes from the water, and drain them upside down on a kitchen towel. Spread the leaves of an artichoke open, by lightly prying with your fingers, and fill the center with the stuffing. Continue to work outward, sprinkling and packing stuffing into the rows of leaves as you separate them. When it is stuffed, set the artichoke in a baking dish that will hold all six snugly. Repeat with the remaining artichokes.

Pour the wine and 1 cup water around the artichokes, and add the remaining lemon juice and artichoke stems. Season the liquid with the remaining salt and the crushed red pepper flakes. Drizzle the remaining 3 tablespoons of olive oil over the artichokes. Tent the dish with foil, and bake for about 30 minutes. Uncover, and bake until the artichokes are tender all the way through and the crumbs are browned and crusty, about 20 to 30 minutes more. If the cooking juices are too thin, set the baking pan with artichokes on the stove and boil for a few minutes to reduce the sauce to your liking. Stir in the remaining 2 tablespoons of chopped parsley. Serve the artichokes in shallow soup plates, surrounded with the cooking juices.

Rice Balls

Arancini di Riso
MAKES ABOUT 24

5 cups Chicken Stock (page 143)
3 tablespoons extra-virgin olive oil
1 medium onion, chopped
1 cup finely diced ham or prosciutto (about 3 ounces)
2 cups Arborio rice
1 cup dry white wine
½ teaspoon kosher salt, plus more for seasoning
1 cup frozen peas, thawed
1 cup freshly grated Grana Padano
10 basil leaves, chopped
4 ounces fresh mozzarella, cut into 24 cubes
1 cup all-purpose flour
2 cups fine dried bread crumbs
2 large eggs
Vegetable oil, for frying

In a small pot, warm chicken stock over low heat. In a medium saucepan, heat the olive oil. When the oil is hot, add the onion and cook until it begins to soften, about 3 to 4 minutes. Add the ham or prosciutto, and cook a few minutes, until it begins to render its fat. Add the rice, and cook to coat it in the oil and fat. Pour in the wine, bring to a simmer, and cook until the wine is almost reduced away. Add 3 cups of the hot chicken stock and the salt. Cover, and simmer until the chicken stock is absorbed by the rice, about 7 to 8 minutes. Add the remaining 2 cups stock, and cover again. Cook until rice is al dente, about 6 to 7 minutes more. Uncover; if any liquid remains, increase heat and cook until all of the liquid is absorbed, another minute or two. Stir in peas, and spread rice on a rimmed sheet pan to cool.

When the rice is cool, put in a bowl and stir in grated cheese and chopped basil. Scoop out about ⅓ cup rice, and put a cube of mozzarella in the center, forming a tight ball around the cheese. You should get about twenty-four arancini.

Spread the flour and bread crumbs on two rimmed plates. Beat the eggs in a shallow bowl.

Dredge the arancini in the flour, tapping off the excess. Dip them in the beaten egg, letting the excess drip back into the bowl. Roll in bread crumbs to coat thoroughly.

In a large straight-sided skillet, heat 1 inch vegetable oil over medium heat until the tip of an arancino sizzles on contact. Fry arancini in batches, taking care not to crowd the skillet, turning on all sides, until golden, about 3 minutes per batch. Drain on paper towels, and season with salt while still warm.

Provolone Turnovers

Seadas
MAKES 12

3 cups durum-wheat flour
½ teaspoon kosher salt
2 tablespoons extra-virgin olive oil
3 tablespoons unsalted butter, at room temperature, cut into small chunks
9 ounces provolone, in 12 slices
Vegetable oil, for frying
Honey, for drizzling (optional)

Put the flour, salt, olive oil, and butter chunks in a food-processor bowl. Process until the fat has been incorporated and the mixture has a sandy texture. With the processor running, pour 1 cup minus 2 tablespoons water through the feed tube, and process just until a dough forms and gathers on the blade and cleans the sides of the bowl. If the dough is too sticky, add another tablespoon or two of flour; if too dry, add 2 tablespoons water. Process briefly, until the dough comes together; turn it out on a lightly floured surface, and knead by hand a few times, until it's smooth and soft. Press dough into a disk, wrap well in plastic wrap, and let rest at room temperature for at least ½ hour.

To make the seadas: Cut the rested dough in half. On a lightly floured surface, roll each piece out to a rectangular sheet about 12 by 16 inches; the dough should be about ¼ inch thick. Press a 3-inch round cookie cutter lightly on one sheet of dough but do not cut through it, making twelve marks. Break each provolone slice into three or four pieces, and arrange them, overlapping, to fit inside one of the traced circles, leaving space around the edges. (If the cheese slices are large or thick, or weigh an ounce or more, don't try to fit them all inside the dough circle. Each seada should have about ¾ ounce cheese.)

Roll the other half of the dough to roughly the same size as the first. Pick it up and drape it over the bottom dough, covering all the rounds of sliced cheese. Gently press the top sheet around the cheese layers so the edges are distinct. Dip the cookie cutter in flour, center it over one portion of cheese, and cut through both layers of dough, to the work surface, cutting out one seada. Cut all of them the same way, then pull away the excess dough between them. Pinch the edges of each seada, sealing the cheese inside.

Pour vegetable oil into the big skillet to a depth of ½ inch, and set it over medium heat. Let the oil heat gradually until a piece of dough starts to sizzle when dipped in but does not darken immediately. Carefully slide as many of the seadas into the pan as fit comfortably, with some space between them. Fry until crisp and golden, about 2 to 3 minutes per side. If the cheese begins to leak out during frying, flip the seadas to the other side. Drain the seadas on paper towels, and keep them warm in a low oven. Serve immediately, drizzled with honey if you like.

Frico with Montasio Cheese and Potatoes

Frico con Patate
SERVES 6

1 medium baking potato (about 8 ounces)
2 tablespoons extra-virgin olive oil
1 small onion, sliced
½ cup thinly sliced scallions
¼ teaspoon kosher salt
Freshly ground black pepper to taste
8 ounces Montasio cheese, shredded

Cook the potato in a pan of gently boiling water just until it is easily pierced with a sharp knife all the way through, but still intact and not mushy. Drain and cool the potato, remove the skin, and slice it into neat ¼-inch-thick rounds.

Pour the olive oil into a medium nonstick skillet, set over medium heat, and scatter in the sliced onion and scallions. Cook for a minute, then scatter the potato rounds in the pan. Gently toss the potatoes with the onion and scallions, and season with the salt and grinds of black pepper. Cook, tossing frequently, until the potato rounds are lightly crisped and golden, about 5 minutes.

Pile the shredded Montasio on top of the vegetables. Slide a metal spatula under some of the potatoes and flip them over, incorporating some of the cheese. Turn all the slices over and over this way, until the cheese shreds are well distributed. With the spatula, clean the sides of the skillet, and smooth the vegetables and cheese into a neat pancakelike disk, filling the pan bottom.

Lower the heat, and let the frico cook, undisturbed, as the cheese melts and crisps, until the bottom is very brown and nicely crusted, about 5 minutes. Shake the pan to loosen the disk, put a large plate on top, and invert, dropping the frico onto the plate, then slide it back into the skillet, top side down. Cook until the second side is crisp and brown, about 5 minutes more.

Slide (or invert) the frico onto the plate, and blot up excess oil from the cheese with a paper towel. Slice into six wedges, and serve immediately.

Frico with Montasio Cheese and Apples

Frico con le Mele
SERVES 6

2 small Golden Delicious or other firm apples
    (about 12 ounces)
1 tablespoon extra-virgin olive oil
8 ounces Montasio cheese, shredded

Peel and core the apples, and slice into wedges about ½ inch thick. Heat the olive oil in a medium nonstick skillet over medium heat. Scatter the apple wedges in the pan, and toss to coat with oil. Cook and caramelize the apples for about 8 minutes, tossing frequently, until tinged with brown and softened but not mushy. Scrape the caramelized apples onto a plate.

Sprinkle half of the shredded Montasio in an even layer over the bottom of the skillet. Return the apples to the pan, spreading them evenly on top of the cheese, then sprinkle the remainder of the shredded cheese over the apples.

Lower the heat, and let the frico cook, undisturbed, until the bottom is very brown and crisped, about 10 minutes. If the cheese releases a lot of fat in the pan, blot it up with paper towels. Shake the pan to loosen the disk, put a large plate on top, and invert, dropping the frico onto the plate, then slide it back into the skillet, top side down. Cook until the second side is crisp and brown, about 7 minutes more. Slide (or invert) the frico onto the plate, blot up oil, and slice into six wedges. Serve hot.

Cheese Baked in a Crust

Formaggio in Crosta
SERVES 6

4 ounces Gorgonzola, at room temperature,
    or 6 ounces Taleggio (because rind will be
    removed)
2 tablespoons heavy cream
1 sheet frozen puff pastry, thawed according to
    package directions
1 large egg, beaten
12 cups mixed baby greens
Red wine vinegar and extra-virgin olive oil, for
    dressing the greens
Kosher salt and freshly ground black pepper

Preheat the oven to 425 degrees. Crumble the Gorgonzola into a medium bowl, and mash with the cream. Lightly shape into six balls; they should just hold together, not be compacted. Chill while you roll the pastry.

On a floured work surface, roll out the pastry sheet to slightly thicker than ⅛ inch. Using a bowl with a 5-inch diameter as your guide, cut six rounds from the pastry.

Put the rounds on a parchment-lined baking sheet, and chill in the refrigerator for 10 minutes.

Remove rounds from the refrigerator, and put a cheese ball in the center of each. Brush the edges with the egg, and fold each into a half-moon. Press or crimp with a fork to seal. Brush the tops with more egg. Bake until puffed, browned, and crisp, about 12 minutes. Let cool 10 minutes before serving. When ready to serve, toss the greens lightly with vinegar and olive oil in a large bowl, and season with salt and pepper. Serve the baked cheese puffs on plates with a side of dressed greens.

Scrambled Eggs and Asparagus

Frittata di Asparagi e Uova
SERVES 4

1 pound pencil-thin asparagus
2 tablespoons extra-virgin olive oil
Kosher salt and freshly ground black pepper
8 large eggs

Remove and discard the tough lower ends of the asparagus. Cut the spears into 2-inch lengths. In a large nonstick skillet, sauté the asparagus spears in olive oil, sprinkling them lightly with salt. Cover the pan and cook over medium heat, stirring occasionally, until asparagus is tender but still firm, about 5 minutes.

Beat the eggs lightly in a bowl with salt and pepper. Add the eggs to the asparagus, scrambling the mixture lightly with a fork. Cook 2 minutes or less, depending on the texture desired, and serve immediately.

Ricotta Frittata

Frittata con Ricotta
SERVES 4 TO 6

3 tablespoons extra-virgin olive oil
1 large onion, sliced ¼ inch thick
1 large ripe tomato, sliced ½ inch thick
8 large eggs
½ teaspoon kosher salt
8 large basil leaves, shredded
½ cup freshly grated Grana Padano
6 tablespoons fresh ricotta

Preheat the oven to 375 degrees. Heat the oil in a 10-inch nonstick skillet over medium heat. Add onion and cook until softened, about 5 to 6 minutes. Push onion slices to one side of the skillet, and lay the tomato slices in one layer in the cleared space. Sear the tomato, turning once, until the slices soften just at the edges, about 30 seconds per side. Remove tomatoes to a plate, and let onions continue to cook while you prepare the eggs.

In a bowl, beat the eggs with the salt. Stir in the basil and ¼ cup of the grated cheese until well mixed. Spread the onion slices in an even layer in the bottom of the skillet, and pour the eggs on top. Reduce heat to medium low, and let cook until the eggs begin to set around the edges of the pan, about 2 to 3 minutes. Arrange tomato slices on top of the frittata, and drop tablespoons of the ricotta between the tomato slices. Sprinkle all over with the remaining grated cheese. Bake frittata until it is set all the way through and the top is golden, about 18 minutes.

Let rest for a few minutes; then run a knife around the edge of the skillet, and invert frittata onto a plate or cutting board. Serve in wedges, warm or at room temperature.

until no longer pink, about 3 to 4 minutes. Add the scallions, season with ¼ teaspoon salt, and cook, stirring, until the scallions begin to wilt, about 2 to 3 minutes. Add bell pepper and cook, stirring, until wilted but not completely limp, about 8 to 10 minutes.

Meanwhile, in a bowl, beat eggs with the milk and remaining salt. Let the bread cubes soak in the egg-milk mixture until moistened, about 2 to 3 minutes. Reduce heat under skillet to medium low, then pour in the egg mixture and the bread, and let cook until the eggs begin to set around the edges of the pan, about 2 to 3 minutes.

Sprinkle all over with the grated cheese. Put the skillet in the oven, and bake until the frittata is set all the way through and the top is golden, about 18 minutes. Let rest for a few minutes, then run a knife around the edge of the skillet and invert frittata onto a plate or cutting board. Serve in wedges, warm or at room temperature.

Sausage, Bread, and Pepper Frittata

Frittata con Salsiccia e Peperoni
SERVES 4 TO 6

3 tablespoons extra-virgin olive oil
8 ounces sweet Italian sausage, removed from casings (about 2 links)
1 large bunch scallions, trimmed and cut into ½-inch pieces
½ teaspoon kosher salt
1 red bell pepper, cut in ½-inch strips
8 large eggs
¼ cup milk
1½ cups ½-inch cubes from day-old loaf of country bread
¼ cup freshly grated Grana Padano

Preheat the oven to 375 degrees. Heat a medium (10-inch) nonstick skillet over medium heat. Add the olive oil. When the oil is hot, cook the sausage, crumbling with the back of a wooden spoon

Artichoke and Mint Frittata

Frittata di Carciofi con Menta
SERVES 4 TO 6

¼ cup extra-virgin olive oil
8 small artichokes, trimmed and cleaned, chokes removed (see page 6), halved and sliced ¼ inch thick
1¼ teaspoons kosher salt
1 bunch scallions, trimmed and cut into ½-inch pieces
8 large eggs
2 tablespoons chopped fresh mint

Heat a medium (10-inch) nonstick skillet over medium heat. Add the oil. When the oil is hot, add the artichokes and 1 teaspoon of the salt. Toss to coat the artichokes in the oil, then cover and cook until tender, stirring once or twice, about 15 minutes.

Uncover, add the scallions, and cook until wilted, about 3 to 4 minutes more. Meanwhile, in a large bowl, beat the eggs with the remaining ¼ teaspoon salt and the mint. Pour the eggs into the skillet and cover. Reduce heat to medium low, and cook until just set, about 10 minutes.

Invert onto a plate, and slide back into the skillet to brown the other side, about 5 minutes more. Slide onto a cutting board, and let cool at least 5 minutes before cutting into wedges to serve. Can be served warm or at room temperature.

Eggs Scrambled in Tomato Sauce

Uova Strapazzate al Pomodoro
SERVES 6

5 tablespoons extra-virgin olive oil
4 garlic cloves, thinly sliced
¼ teaspoon crushed red pepper flakes
One 28-ounce can Italian plum tomatoes, preferably San Marzano, passed through a food mill
¾ teaspoon kosher salt
½ teaspoon dried oregano, preferably Sicilian on the branch
6 large eggs
¼ cup freshly grated Grana Padano
¼ cup fresh basil leaves, coarsely shredded
6 slices grilled country bread, for serving

To a large skillet over medium heat, add the olive oil. When the oil is hot, add the garlic. Once the garlic is sizzling, in about 1 minute, add the red pepper flakes. Pour in the tomatoes and 1 cup water used to rinse out the tomato can. Bring to a simmer. Season with ½ teaspoon salt and dried oregano. Simmer until thickened, about 20 minutes. The sauce is sufficiently thickened when you can see the bottom of the skillet when you drag a wooden spoon through.

In a medium bowl, beat the eggs with the grated cheese and remaining ¼ teaspoon salt. Whisk the eggs into the simmering sauce with a fork, stirring to make raggedy pieces or *stracciatella,* until eggs are cooked, about 3 minutes. Stir in the basil, and serve in shallow bowls with the grilled bread.

Eggs Poached in Tomato Sauce

Uova Affogate in Salsa di Pomodoro
SERVES 6

5 tablespoons extra-virgin olive oil
4 garlic cloves, thinly sliced
¼ teaspoon crushed red pepper flakes
One 28-ounce can Italian plum tomatoes, preferably San Marzano, passed through a food mill
¾ teaspoon kosher salt
½ teaspoon dried oregano, preferably Sicilian on the branch
6 large eggs
6 slices grilled country bread, for serving

To a large skillet over medium heat, add the olive oil. When the oil is hot, add the garlic. Once the garlic is sizzling, in about 1 minute, add the red pepper flakes. Pour in the tomatoes and 1 cup water used to rinse out the tomato can. Bring to a simmer. Season with ½ teaspoon salt and dried oregano. Simmer until thickened, about 20 minutes. The sauce is sufficiently thickened when you can see the bottom of the skillet as you drag a wooden spoon on the base of the skillet.

Break one egg into a ramekin or small bowl. Gently slide the egg into the simmering sauce. Repeat with the remaining eggs, spacing them evenly in the sauce. Season the eggs with the remaining ¼ teaspoon salt. Baste the eggs with a little sauce, cover, and cook until done, about 5 minutes for set whites with still-runny yolks. Serve in shallow bowls, with some sauce and grilled bread.

Baked Eggplant and Eggs

Melanzane e Uova al Forno
SERVES 6

3 Italian eggplants (about 1¼ pounds total)
1 teaspoon kosher salt, plus more for salting the
   eggplant
6 tablespoons extra-virgin olive oil, plus more
   for brushing the gratin dishes
3 garlic cloves, sliced
One 28-ounce can Italian plum tomatoes,
   preferably San Marzano, crushed by hand
¼ teaspoon crushed red pepper flakes
2 sprigs fresh basil, plus 6 large leaves
All-purpose flour, for dredging
1 cup freshly grated Grana Padano
6 large eggs
1 teaspoon dried oregano, preferably Sicilian
   on the branch

With a vegetable peeler, peel strips lengthwise down the eggplant, leaving alternate stripes of peel. Cut off stems, and slice eggplant lengthwise into ¼-inch-thick slices. Line a large colander with the eggplant, overlapping if necessary; salt liberally on both sides, and let drain in the sink for 30 minutes. Rinse, drain, and dry the eggplant well.

Preheat the oven to 350 degrees. Meanwhile, to a large skillet over medium-high heat, add 3 tablespoons of the olive oil. When the oil is hot, add the garlic. Let the garlic sizzle until golden, about 1 minute, then pour in the tomatoes. Rinse the tomato can with 1 cup water, and add that as well. Season with 1 teaspoon kosher salt and the crushed red pepper flakes. Stick the basil sprigs in the sauce. Let the sauce simmer until slightly thickened, about 15 minutes. Remove basil sprigs.

Spread the flour on a plate. Lightly dredge the dried eggplant in flour, tapping off the excess. Heat the remaining 3 tablespoons olive oil in a large skillet over medium-high heat. When the oil is hot, brown the eggplant in batches, about 2 minutes per side. Remove the slices as they brown, and drain on a paper-towel-lined sheet pan.

Once the sauce and eggplant are ready, brush six individual gratin dishes with olive oil. Spread a scant ¼ cup of sauce in the bottom of each dish. Fold the eggplant slices to line and fit the gratin dishes in an even layer. Spread another scant ¼ cup of sauce over the eggplant. Sprinkle sauce with about ¾ cup cheese. Lay a basil leaf over the cheese, and crack an egg into each dish. Sprinkle with the remaining grated cheese and the dried oregano.

Place dishes on a baking sheet, and cover with foil. Bake until sauce is bubbly, about 15 minutes. Uncover, and bake until cheese is browned and eggs are done to your liking, about 5 minutes more for almost set yolks.

Baked Eggs with White Truffles

Uova con Tartufo Bianco
SERVES 6

1 white truffle about the size of a walnut
Six ½-inch-thick slices country bread
4 tablespoons unsalted butter, softened
6 tablespoons milk
6 tablespoons heavy cream
6 large eggs
Kosher salt and freshly ground black pepper

Preheat the oven to 325 degrees. Clean the white truffle (or truffles, if you're feeling especially extravagant) of all loose soil with a vegetable brush, and gently remove any dirt that is embedded in the edges with a paring knife.

Cut the bread into sticks about the width of your finger, and toast in the oven on a sheet pan until crispy, about 10 minutes. Let cool.

Brush six ramekins (3 inches in diameter) with 1 tablespoon of the softened butter. Pour 1 tablespoon milk and 1 tablespoon heavy cream into each of the ramekins. Cut the remaining 3 tablespoons butter into six pieces, and add a piece to each ramekin. Carefully break an egg into each ramekin, taking care not to break the yolk. Season with salt and pepper. Use a truffle slicer or Microplane grater to shave the rough edges on the outside of the truffle over the eggs, reserving the white inside of the truffle to add after baking.

Put the ramekins in a deep baking pan, and add hot water to come halfway up the sides. Bake about 10 to 12 minutes for cooked whites with still-runny yolks. Remove ramekins to plates, and shave over the eggs the remaining truffle. Serve with the toast sticks for dipping.

Mussels in Spicy Tomato Sauce

Cozze al Pomodoro Piccante
SERVES 4 TO 6

6 tablespoons extra-virgin olive oil
8 garlic cloves, sliced
One 28-ounce can Italian plum tomatoes, preferably San Marzano, crushed by hand or a food mill
½ teaspoon dried oregano, preferably Sicilian on the branch
½ teaspoon kosher salt
½ teaspoon peperoncino flakes
3 pounds mussels, scrubbed, debearded, and drained
10 large fresh basil leaves, shredded

Heat 5 tablespoons olive oil in a large Dutch oven over medium-high heat. Add the sliced garlic, and cook until the garlic sizzles and turns just golden around the edges, about 2 minutes. Add the tomatoes, slosh out the can with ¼ cup water, and add that to the pot. Season with the oregano, salt, and peperoncino. Bring to a boil, and simmer until slightly thickened, about 10 minutes.

Once the sauce has thickened, add the mussels, stir, and adjust the heat so the sauce is simmering. Cover, and simmer until the mussels open, about 5 minutes.

Once the mussels have opened (discard any

that have not), stir in the basil, and drizzle with the remaining tablespoon of olive oil. Transfer the mussels to a serving bowl, and pour juices over them. Serve immediately.

Steamed Mussels in Savory Wine Sauce

Cozze al Vino Bianco
SERVES 6

6 tablespoons extra-virgin olive oil
4 garlic cloves, crushed and peeled
1 large onion, sliced ½ inch thick
4 fresh bay leaves
½ teaspoon kosher salt
½ teaspoon peperoncino, or to taste
½ cup dry white wine
3 pounds mussels, scrubbed, debearded, and drained
¼ to ½ cup dried bread crumbs, or as needed
3 tablespoons chopped fresh Italian parsley

Pour 4 tablespoons olive oil into a large saucepan, drop in the crushed garlic, and set over medium heat. When the garlic is fragrant and sizzling, stir in the onion slices, bay leaves, salt, and peperoncino. Cook for a couple of minutes, tossing and stirring, just until the onion begins to wilt but still has some crunch. Pour in the wine, and bring to a boil. Immediately dump all the mussels into the pan, tumble them over quickly, cover tightly, and turn the heat up. Steam the mussels for 3 minutes, frequently shaking the covered pan, then toss them over, with a wire spider or wide slotted spoon. If the mussel shells have already opened (or almost all are open), leave the pan uncovered—otherwise, replace the cover and steam a bit longer.

As soon as the mussels have steamed open, sprinkle ¼ cup bread crumbs all over the pan. Quickly tumble the mussels over and over, still over high heat, so their liquor and the crumbs fall into the bubbling pan juices and create a sauce. (If the pan sauce is still thin after a minute of bubbling, sprinkle in more bread crumbs.) Remove bay leaves and garlic cloves.

Finally, drizzle remaining 2 tablespoons olive oil and sprinkle the chopped parsley on top, and toss briefly to distribute the seasonings. Turn off the heat, set the pan in the center of the table, and let people scoop mussels and sauce into their own warm soup bowls. (And remember to put out extra bowls for the shells.)

Clams Casino

Vongole al Forno con Pancetta
SERVES 6 AS AN APPETIZER

36 littleneck clams on the half-shell
2 red or yellow bell peppers, roasted (see page 24), peeled, and cut into 1-inch squares
6 ounces thinly sliced bacon, cut into 1-inch squares
3 tablespoons unsalted butter
3 tablespoons chopped fresh Italian parsley
Dry white wine, as needed

Preheat the oven to 450 degrees. Place clams on a rimmed baking sheet in one even layer. Top each clam in the shell with a pepper square and a bacon square (bacon on top). Top with a dab of butter, using all 3 tablespoons evenly. Sprinkle with chopped parsley.

Pour the reserved shucking juices into a 2-cup measure. Add enough white wine to make 1½ cups liquid, and pour into the bottom of the baking sheet. Bake the clams, uncovered, until the bacon is crispy and the clams are cooked all the way through, about 20 to 25 minutes. Serve on a platter, drizzled with the baking juices.

🍃 Have the fishmonger shuck the clams, reserving the clams and their juices and giving you thirty-six shells, into which you will reinsert the clam meat to bake. If you are shucking the clams yourself, reserve the clam juice as you shuck and leave each clam in its half-shell for baking.

Baked Clams Oreganata

Vongole Ripiene al Forno
SERVES 6

36 littleneck clams, shucked, juices reserved
1½ cups fine dried bread crumbs
½ cup finely chopped red bell pepper
¼ cup finely chopped fresh Italian parsley
1 teaspoon dried oregano, preferably Sicilian on the branch
½ teaspoon kosher salt
6 tablespoons extra-virgin olive oil
½ cup dry white wine
Lemon wedges, for serving (optional)

Preheat the oven to 425 degrees. As you shuck the clams, set them aside and reserve and strain their juices. Coarsely chop the shucked clams, and put in a large bowl. Add the bread crumbs, bell pepper, 2 tablespoons parsley, the oregano, and salt. Drizzle with 2 tablespoons olive oil, and toss with a fork to combine.

Stuff the clamshells with the filling, and place on a rimmed baking sheet; pour any extra juice, along with the white wine, into the bottom of the pan. Drizzle the clams with 3 tablespoons olive oil, and drizzle the remaining tablespoon oil and remaining 2 tablespoons chopped parsley into the bottom of the pan. Bake until the clam stuffing is browned and crispy, about 15 minutes. To serve: set the clams on a plate with remaining sauce and fresh lemon wedges for squeezing (if using).

Lentil Crostini

Crostini con Lenticchie
SERVES 6

1 cup small lentils, preferably lenticchie di
    Castelluccio
2 medium celery stalks, with leaves, finely
    chopped (about 1 cup)
2 fresh bay leaves
6 tablespoons extra-virgin olive oil, plus more for
    drizzling
2 plump garlic cloves, sliced
1 cup chopped onion
¼ teaspoon crushed red pepper flakes, or to taste
2 cups canned Italian plum tomatoes, preferably
    San Marzano, crushed by hand
2 teaspoons kosher salt
12 slices Italian bread

Rinse the lentils, and put them in a large saucepan
with the celery, bay leaves, and 3 cups cold water.
Bring to a boil, cover the pan, and adjust the heat
to maintain a gentle, steady simmer. Cook until
the lentils are almost tender, about 20 minutes (or
longer, depending on size).

Meanwhile, pour 4 tablespoons of the olive
oil into a medium skillet, and set it over medium
heat. Stir in the garlic and onion, and cook for
5 minutes or more, until the onion is soft and
glistening. Drop the red pepper flakes into a hot
spot in the pan, and let it toast for a minute; then
stir in the crushed tomatoes, season with a teaspoon of the salt, and bring the sauce to a simmer. Let it bubble gently about 5 minutes, until
slightly thickened.

When the lentils are just slightly undercooked,
pour the tomato sauce into the saucepan and stir
into the lentils. Return the sauce to a simmer, and
cook, partially covered, until the lentils are fully
cooked and tender, about 10 minutes. Remove
the cover, fish out bay leaves, stir in the remaining teaspoon salt, and let the lentils cook slowly,
stirring frequently, until they're very thick and
starting to fall apart, another 10 minutes or so.

Remove the pan from the heat, and stir in the
remaining 2 tablespoons olive oil.

🦋 I prefer the lentils hot or warm as a crostini
topping or side dish, but they are very good at
room temperature, too. For crostini, grill or toast
the bread slices, spoon a mound of lentils on each
crostino, and drizzle on a bit of fine olive oil.

Prosciutto and Fig Bruschetta

Bruschetta di Prosciutto e Fichi
SERVES 6

10 to 12 ripe fresh green or black figs
6 slices grilled country bread
6 long, thin slices Prosciutto di San Daniele or
    Prosciutto di Parma, or as needed
Freshly ground black pepper
Aceto Balsamico Tradizionale, for drizzling
    (optional)

Wipe the figs clean with a damp cloth or paper
towel. Slice the figs crosswise into ⅛-inch-thick
rounds.

Cover the grilled bread with overlapping fig
slices. Drape the prosciutto to cover the figs.
Grind some black pepper over the prosciutto,
drizzle with the balsamic if desired, and serve
immediately.

Baked Mushroom Crostini

Crostini di Funghi al Forno
SERVES 4

¼ cup extra-virgin olive oil
3 garlic cloves, crushed and peeled
1 pound mixed fresh mushrooms, sliced
    (cremini, button, shiitake, oyster, chanterelle)

4 fresh sage leaves, chopped
½ teaspoon kosher salt
2 tablespoons chopped fresh Italian parsley
8 slices country bread, very lightly toasted
1 cup grated Italian Fontina
½ cup freshly grated Grana Padano

Preheat the oven to 400 degrees. To a large skillet over medium-high heat, add 2 tablespoons of the olive oil. When the oil is hot, add the garlic cloves. Once the garlic is sizzling, add the mushrooms and sage, and cook, without stirring, until browned on one side, about 2 to 3 minutes. Stir, and brown the other side. Season with the salt, cover, and cook until tender, about 5 minutes. Uncover, remove the garlic, stir in the parsley, and set aside.

On a baking sheet, brush the lightly toasted bread on both sides with the remaining 2 tablespoons olive oil. In a medium bowl, toss together the grated cheeses. Stir half of the cheese mixture into the mushrooms.

Spread the mushroom mixture on the toasts, and sprinkle with the remaining grated-cheese mixture. Bake until the tops are browned and the cheese is bubbly, about 10 to 12 minutes. Serve hot.

Chicken Liver Crostini

Crostini di Fegatini di Pollo
MAKES ABOUT 12 CROSTINI, SERVING 6

3 tablespoons extra-virgin olive oil
1 cup finely chopped shallots
3 tablespoons drained tiny capers in brine
6 fresh sage leaves, chopped
12 ounces chicken livers, trimmed of fat and membranes, halved
½ cup dry Marsala
¼ teaspoon kosher salt
2 tablespoons unsalted butter
12 slices Italian baguette, grilled or toasted

To a large skillet over low heat, add the olive oil and the shallots, and cook, stirring occasionally, until the shallots are softened but not browned, about 5 minutes.

Increase heat to medium high, and add the capers and sage. Once they begin sizzling, add the chicken livers. Toss and cook until browned, about 3 to 4 minutes; then add the Marsala. Season with the salt, and cook until the Marsala is reduced by half, about 3 to 4 minutes. Whisk in the butter, remove from heat, and let cool.

When the chicken livers have cooled, purée the mixture in a food processor until almost smooth (a few chunks are okay). Spread on the grilled or toasted bread, and serve.

Sausage Crostini

Crostini con Salsicce
MAKES 8, SERVING 4

2 tablespoons extra-virgin olive oil
3 sweet Italian sausages, removed from casings (about 12 ounces)
1 cup diced celery
½ cup dry white wine
4 ounces shredded Taleggio or Fontina, plus 2 ounces thinly sliced
¼ cup freshly shredded Grana Padano
¼ teaspoon ground fennel seeds
Four ½-inch-thick slices day-old country bread, about 4 by 6 inches, halved

Preheat the oven to 400 degrees. To a large skillet over medium heat, add the olive oil. When the oil is hot, add the sausage and celery, and cook until browned, about 4 minutes.

Add the white wine, and adjust the heat so it simmers rapidly. Cook until wine has reduced away, about 2 minutes. Scrape into a medium bowl and let cool completely.

When it is cooled, add the shredded Taleggio, the grated Grana Padano, and the ground fennel, and toss well. Arrange the sliced bread on a baking sheet, and top with the sausage mixture. Top that with the sliced Taleggio. Bake until edges of the bread are toasted and the cheese is browned, about 7 minutes. Serve hot.

Rosemary and Lemon Foccacia

Focaccia al Rosmarino e Limone
SERVES 8

1 package active dry yeast
Pinch of sugar
5 tablespoons extra-virgin olive oil, plus more for brushing
5 cups all-purpose flour, plus more as needed
2¼ teaspoons kosher salt
Zest of 1 lemon
Leaves of 2 sprigs fresh rosemary, half chopped, half left whole
½ lemon, cut into quarters and thinly sliced

Dissolve yeast and sugar in ½ cup warm water (about 100 degrees) until slightly bubbly, about 5 minutes. Once the yeast is bubbly, add 3 tablespoons olive oil and 1½ cups room-temperature water.

In the bowl of a mixer fitted with the paddle attachment, put the 5 cups flour and 2 teaspoons salt. Pour in the yeast mixture, and add the lemon zest and chopped rosemary. Mix at low speed until combined. Switch to the dough hook, and knead at medium speed until the dough gathers on the hook and is smooth and springy, about 6 minutes, adding a little more flour or water if necessary. Transfer the dough to an oiled bowl, cover, and let rise at room temperature until doubled, about 1½ hours.

Punch the dough down. Brush a rimmed half-sheet pan with olive oil, and press the dough into the pan all the way to the edges. Cover loosely with plastic wrap, and let rise until doubled, about 45 minutes.

Preheat the oven to 450 degrees. In a small bowl, toss the lemon pieces, reserved whole rosemary leaves, remaining ¼ teaspoon salt, and remaining 2 tablespoons olive oil together. Press dimples all over the focaccia with your finger. Scatter the oil-rosemary mixture evenly over the risen dough. Bake on the bottom rack of the oven until the focaccia is cooked through and golden brown on the bottom, about 20 to 25 minutes. Remove from the pan, and cool on a rack.

Focaccia Filled with Soppressata and Provolone

Focaccia Farcita con Soppressata e Provola
SERVES 8

1 recipe focaccia dough from preceding recipe, made without lemon and rosemary
2 tablespoons extra-virgin olive oil
4 ounces soppressata, thinly sliced
4 ounces sliced provolone
4 large hard-boiled eggs, sliced

After the first rise (see preceding recipe), brush a 9-by-13-inch baking dish with 1 tablespoon olive oil. Punch the dough down, and divide it in half. Press half of the dough into the oiled dish, all the way to the edges, with an edge of about ½ inch pressed up the sides. Layer the soppressata, almost but not quite to the edges. Layer the cheese in the same manner over the soppressata, and layer the sliced egg over the cheese.

Roll or press the remaining dough to about 9 by 13 inches, and layer on top of the provolone. Press all around the edges to seal. Poke holes in the dough in five or six places with a paring knife. Lightly brush focaccia with remaining olive oil.

Cover with plastic wrap, and let rise 30 minutes. Preheat the oven to 375 degrees. After the second rise, remove plastic, cover the dish with foil, and bake until dough is puffed but not yet colored, about 20 minutes.

Uncover, and bake until dough is cooked through and golden on the top and bottom, about 20 to 25 minutes. Let cool in the baking dish on a rack at least 15 minutes before cutting into squares and serving, either warm or at room temperature.

Focaccia Filled with Speck and Fontina

Focaccia con Speck e Fontina
SERVES 8

1 recipe focaccia dough, made without lemon and rosemary (see page 119)
2 tablespoons extra-virgin olive oil
4 ounces speck, sliced
4 large hard-boiled eggs, sliced (optional)
4 ounces Italian Fontina, sliced

After the first rise, brush a 9-by-13-inch baking dish with 1 tablespoon olive oil. Punch the dough down, and divide it in half. Press half of the dough down into the oiled dish, all the way to the edges, with an edge of about ½ inch pressed up the sides. Layer the speck, almost but not quite to the edges. Layer the egg slices, if using, on top. Layer the cheese in the same manner over the speck.

Roll or press the remaining dough to about 9 by 13 inches, and layer on top of the Fontina. Press all around the edges to seal. Poke holes in the dough in five or six places with a paring knife. Lightly brush the focaccia with remaining olive oil.

Cover with plastic wrap, and let rise 30 minutes. Preheat the oven to 375 degrees. After the second rise, remove plastic, cover the dish with foil, and bake until dough is puffed but not yet colored, about 20 minutes.

Uncover, and bake until dough is cooked through and golden on the top and bottom,

about 20 to 25 minutes. Let cool in the baking dish on a rack at least 15 minutes before cutting into squares and serving, either warm or at room temperature.

Swiss Chard and Potato Crostata

Crostata con Bietole e Patate
SERVES 8 TO 12

DOUGH
2 cups all-purpose flour, plus more for rolling the dough
½ teaspoon kosher salt
½ cup extra-virgin olive oil
⅓ cup cold water, plus more as needed

FILLING
1 bunch Swiss chard, including stems, about 1½ pounds, washed and drained
2 potatoes, about 1½ pounds total
1 cup heavy cream
3 tablespoons extra-virgin olive oil
4 large eggs
2 teaspoons kosher salt
2 cups grated low-moisture mozzarella
1 cup freshly grated Grana Padano

For the dough: In a food processor, combine the flour and salt, and pulse. Mix the oil and water together, and with the machine running, add oil and water mixture, and process to make a smooth, soft dough, about 30 seconds. Add more flour or water if necessary, until the dough pulls off the sides of the food processor and forms a ball around the blade. The dough should be soft and slightly sticky to the touch.

Dump the dough onto a lightly floured work surface, and knead until very smooth, about 1 minute, sprinkling just enough flour so you can roll the dough into a smooth ball. Wrap the dough in plastic wrap, and let rest at room temperature for 30 minutes. (Dough can also be made a day ahead and refrigerated; let come to room temperature before rolling.)

For the filling: Bring a large pot of salted water to a boil. Cut the leaves from the stems of the chard and cut into 1-inch strips. Cut the stems into ½-inch pieces and keep separate. When the water boils, add the stems and boil for 10 minutes, then add the leaves, and boil until both are tender, about 15 minutes more. Drain, let cool, then squeeze in your hands until most of the water is out. Chop, and set aside.

Meanwhile, put the potatoes in another pot with water to cover, and simmer for about 30 minutes until tender when pierced with a fork. Drain. When they are cool enough to handle, peel the potatoes, return them to the pot, and mash, adding the cream and olive oil. Add the chopped Swiss chard and mix well. Beat the eggs and salt together, and mix into the potato-chard mixture. Fold in the mozzarella and Grana Padano, and set aside.

Preheat the oven to 375 degrees. On a floured surface, roll the dough to fit a rimmed half sheet pan with about 3 inches extra on all sides, trimming if necessary. Butter the pan. Fit the dough into the sheet pan, with the extra dough hanging off the sides, and spread the filling evenly over the dough. Fold the overlap of the dough over to form a 2-inch crust around the pan over the filling, leaving the center without crust. Bake until filling is set and crust is golden, about 40 to 45 minutes. Cool on a rack. Serve slightly warm or at room temperature.

Rice and Zucchini Crostata

Crostata di Riso e Zucchine

MAKES 15 OR MORE APPETIZER SLICES OR SEVERAL DOZEN HORS D'OEUVRES

FOR THE DOUGH

2 cups all-purpose flour, plus more for rolling out the dough
1 teaspoon kosher salt
½ cup extra-virgin olive oil
⅓ cup cold water, plus more as needed

FOR THE FILLING

1 pound small zucchini
½ cup Italian short-grain rice, such as Arborio, Carnaroli, or Vialone Nano
2 cups ricotta, preferably fresh, drained overnight
1 cup freshly grated Grana Padano
2 bunches scallions, trimmed and finely chopped (about 2 cups)
3 large eggs, lightly beaten
2 cups milk
2 teaspoons kosher salt
Unsalted butter, for the baking pan

To make the dough: Pour the flour and salt into a food processor fitted with the metal blade. Pulse a few seconds to aerate the dough. Mix the oil and water together and, with the processor running, pour the liquid through the feed tube and mix for about 30 seconds, until a soft dough forms and gathers on the blade. If it doesn't form, the dough is probably too dry, so add more water in small amounts until you have a smooth, very soft dough.

Turn the dough out onto a lightly floured surface, and knead by hand for a minute. Pat into a rectangle, and wrap loosely in plastic wrap. Let rest at room temperature for 30 minutes.

To make the filling: Shred the zucchini on the coarse holes of a box grater into a large bowl. Toss the rice and shredded zucchini together, and let sit for 30 minutes to an hour, until the grains have absorbed the vegetable liquid. Fold in the ricotta (breaking up any lumps), then the grated cheese, scallions, beaten eggs, milk, and salt, stirring thoroughly until mixed.

Preheat the oven to 375 degrees. Spread the butter on the bottom and sides of a 12-by-18-inch rimmed sheet pan.

On a lightly floured surface, roll the dough to a rectangle at least 4 inches longer and wider than the baking sheet. Transfer the dough to the pan, either by folding it in quarters and lifting it onto the sheet, or by rolling it up around the floured rolling pin and then unfurling it over the baking sheet. When the dough is centered over the pan, gently press its center flat against the bottom, and rim the pan, leaving even flaps of overhanging dough on all sides. (If the dough tears as you are moving it, patch it with a bit of dough from the edges.)

Scrape the filling into the dough-lined pan, and spread it to fill the crust in an even layer. Fold the dough flaps over the top of the filling, pleating the corners, to form a top-crust border that looks like a picture frame, with the filling exposed in the middle.

Set the pan in the oven, and bake until the crust is deep golden brown and the filling is set, 45 minutes to an hour. About halfway through the baking time, turn the pan in the oven, back to front, for even color and cooking. Cool the crostata on a wire rack for at least 30 minutes to set the filling before slicing. The crostata can be served warm or at room temperature, cut into pieces in any shape you like.

Lettuce and Bread Quiches

Tortini Salati di Lattuga e Pane
MAKES 10

Unsalted butter, softened, for lining the muffin tins
¼ cup bread crumbs
3 tablespoons extra-virgin olive oil
1 bunch scallions, trimmed and chopped (about 1 cup)
1 tablespoon fresh thyme leaves, chopped
¾ teaspoon kosher salt
Outer leaves from 1 head romaine lettuce, coarsely chopped (about 3 cups) (save the heart for salad)
5 large eggs
½ cup milk
Pinch of freshly grated nutmeg
½ cup freshly grated Grana Padano
1½ cups ½-inch bread cubes

Preheat the oven to 350 degrees. Brush ten cups of a standard muffin tin with softened butter. Sprinkle with the bread crumbs to coat all around, and tap out the excess.

To a large skillet over medium-high heat, add the olive oil. When the oil is hot, add the scallions and thyme. Season with ½ teaspoon salt. Cook and stir until scallions are wilted, about 4 minutes. Add the lettuce, cover, and cook until wilted, about 3 minutes. Uncover, increase heat to high, and cook away any excess liquid in the pan, about 1 minute. Remove from heat when the lettuce still has a little bite to it. Scrape into a bowl, and let cool.

In a large bowl, whisk together the eggs, milk, nutmeg, ¼ cup grated cheese, and remaining ¼ teaspoon salt. Stir in the bread cubes and the cooled lettuce mixture, and let soak 5 minutes.

Spoon solids into the lined muffin cups to distribute evenly, then pour in the egg mixture. Sprinkle the tops with the grated cheese. Bake until golden on top and set throughout, about 20 minutes. Cool on a rack for 5 to 10 minutes, then loosen the sides with a paring knife and serve. These are good warm or at room temperature.

❧ Use the crusts from the bread you use for cubes to make the bread crumbs to line the muffin tin. If they are very soft, dry them out in a 350-degree oven for 5 to 10 minutes.

Calf's Brain in a Lemon Sauce

Cervella di Vitello al Limone
SERVES 4 TO 6

1 pound calf's brain
½ cup white wine vinegar
½ teaspoon kosher salt, plus more for the pot
6 tablespoons extra-virgin olive oil
Juice of 1 lemon, freshly squeezed
Freshly ground black pepper
2 tablespoons chopped fresh Italian parsley
2 tablespoons drained tiny capers in brine
8 cups mixed greens

Trim the brain of all surface membranes and blood lines (or ask your butcher to do this for you). In a large glass or ceramic bowl, combine 1 quart water and the vinegar. Add the brain, and weight it with a plate to keep it submerged. Refrigerate 2 hours.

Bring a large pot of salted water to a boil. Drain and rinse the brain well. Add the brain to the boiling water, and simmer until cooked through, about 15 minutes. Drain, rinse, and pat dry. Salt lightly. Let cool to room temperature, then refrigerate until completely chilled, at least 2 hours.

Trim away any stray membranes, and thinly slice the brain. Arrange the brains on a bed of the greens on chilled serving plates. In a medium bowl, whisk together the olive oil and lemon juice. Whisk in the remaining salt and season with pepper. Whisk in the parsley and capers. Drizzle the dressing over the plated brains and greens, and serve immediately.

SALADS

A tavola non s'invecchia.
—Italian proverb

At the table one is always young.

Caesar Salad

Insalata alla Caesar
SERVES 6

2 cups country-bread cubes, about ½-inch pieces
4 tablespoons red wine vinegar
Yolks of 2 large hard-boiled eggs
3 garlic cloves
4 anchovy fillets
1 tablespoon Dijon mustard
⅓ cup extra-virgin olive oil
½ teaspoon kosher salt
Freshly ground black pepper
3 heads romaine hearts, cut into 1-inch pieces
    crosswise
½ cup freshly grated Grana Padano

Preheat the oven to 350 degrees. Scatter bread cubes on a baking sheet, and toast until crisp throughout, about 8 to 10 minutes. Set aside to cool.

In a mini–food processor, combine the vinegar, egg yolks, garlic, anchovies, and mustard. Process until smooth, scraping down the sides of the work bowl as needed. With the processor running, pour the oil through the feed tube to make a smooth dressing. Season with the salt and pepper.

Put the romaine and croutons in a large serving bowl. Drizzle with the dressing and toss well. Sprinkle with the grated cheese and toss again. Serve immediately.

Tomato and Bread Salad

Panzanella
SERVES 6

1 pound two-day-old country-style bread,
    crusts removed, cut into ½-inch cubes (about
    8 cups)
2 pounds ripe tomatoes at room temperature,

cored, seeded, and cut into ½-inch cubes
    (about 4 cups)
1 cup coarsely diced red onion
12 fresh basil leaves, shredded, plus a few extra
    sprigs for garnish
5 tablespoons extra-virgin olive oil
3 tablespoons red wine vinegar
Kosher salt and freshly ground black pepper

Toss the bread, tomatoes, onion, and shredded basil leaves in a large bowl until well mixed. Drizzle the olive oil and vinegar over the salad, and toss to mix thoroughly. (If bread is overly dry and hard, sprinkle with warm water and let it steep for 15 minutes; then make the salad.)

Season to taste with salt and pepper, and let stand 10 minutes before serving. Decorate with sprigs of fresh basil.

Scallion and Asparagus Salad

Insalata di Scalogna e Asparagi
SERVES 6

1 large bunch fresh asparagus (about 12 ounces)
1 bunch scallions
1 teaspoon kosher salt
3½ tablespoons extra-virgin olive oil
1½ tablespoons red wine vinegar
Freshly ground black pepper
3 hard-boiled eggs

Using a vegetable peeler, shave off the skin from the bottom 3 inches or so of each asparagus stalk, so they cook evenly. Snap off the hard stubs at the bottom—they'll break naturally at the right point as you bend the bottom of the asparagus. To prepare the scallions: Trim the roots and the wilted ends of the green leaves. Peel off the loose layers at the white end, so the scallions are all trim.

Bring 1 quart water (or enough to cover the vegetables) to a boil in a wide, deep skillet, and add the asparagus and scallions. Adjust the heat to maintain a bubbling boil, and poach the vegetables, uncovered, for about 6 minutes or more, until they are tender but not falling apart, cooked through but not mushy. To check doneness, pick up an asparagus spear by its middle with tongs: it should be a little droopy, but not collapsing.

As soon as they are done, lift out the vegetables with tongs and lay them in a colander. Hold the colander under cold running water to stop the cooking. Drain briefly, then spread on kitchen towels, pat dry, and sprinkle ½ teaspoon salt over them.

Cut the asparagus and the scallions into 1-inch lengths, and pile them loosely in a mixing bowl. Drizzle the oil and vinegar over the top, and sprinkle on the remaining salt and several grinds of black pepper. Toss well. Quarter the eggs into wedges, and slice each wedge into two or three pieces; scatter these in the bowl, and fold in with the vegetables. Taste, and adjust the dressing. Serve at room temperature, or chill the salad briefly; arrange it on a serving platter or on salad plates.

into fine strips (2 by ¼ inches) and let sit in ice water for 2 hours.

Meanwhile, drain the soaked beans and transfer them to a large saucepan. Pour in enough cold water to cover the beans generously. Bring to a boil, adjust the heat to a simmer, and cook until the beans are tender, about 40 minutes.

When all is cooked and cooled, whisk together the oil, vinegar, salt, and pepper in a medium bowl. Cut the boiled green leaves into pieces, and place them in a medium-sized bowl. Add the cooked beans and half of the dressing. Toss well. Add anchovies to remaining dressing and mix, toss in drained puntarelle center and tips, and toss well.

To serve: set the dressed cooked puntarelle and beans on a plate, and top with uncooked dressed puntarelle center and tips.

🐟 Puntarelle is a type of chicory, shaped like a fennel head, with a bulb with long leaves. The bulb and the small protruding sprouts that look like the head of an asparagus spear are eaten raw, but the long outside leaves are blanched.

Puntarelle and Anchovy Salad

Insalata di Puntarelle e Acciughe
SERVES 4

1 pound puntarelle
4 ounces dried cannellini or other white beans, soaked in water overnight
2 tablespoons extra-virgin olive oil
2 tablespoons red wine vinegar
Kosher salt and freshly ground black pepper
4 anchovy fillets, coarsely chopped

Clean the puntarelle, separate the outer green leaves from the center, and cook them in boiling water until soft, about 20 minutes. Meanwhile, cut the center and the small asparaguslike tips

Salad of Dandelion Greens with Almond Vinaigrette and Dried Ricotta

Insalata di Cicoria con Vinaigrette di Mandorle e Ricotta Salata
SERVES 6

1 pound tender young dandelion greens (about 10 loosely packed cups)
6 tablespoons extra-virgin olive oil
¼ cup sliced almonds, toasted
2 tablespoons red wine vinegar
1 teaspoon honey
Kosher salt and freshly ground black pepper
¼ pound ricotta salata, shaved into shards with a vegetable peeler

Cut tough stems from the greens, and remove any wilted, yellow, or tough leaves. Wash and dry well. The greens can be prepared up to several hours in advance and kept, loosely covered with a clean towel, in the refrigerator.

To make the dressing: Combine the olive oil, 2 tablespoons of the toasted almonds, the vinegar, and honey in a blender, and blend until smooth. Add salt and pepper to taste. Place the greens in a large bowl, season them with salt and pepper, and pour the dressing over them. Toss well, and divide the dressed greens among six plates, mounding them in the center of the plates. Sprinkle with the remaining 2 tablespoons of toasted almonds, and top with shavings of ricotta salata. Serve immediately.

Pickled Carrots

Carote in Agro
SERVES 6 TO 8

1 cup white wine vinegar
½ cup dry white wine
1 tablespoon sugar
3 garlic cloves, crushed and peeled
2 fresh bay leaves
3 sprigs fresh mint, plus 1 tablespoon chopped
3 sprigs fresh Italian parsley, plus 1 tablespoon chopped
1 teaspoon kosher salt, plus more for seasoning
8 bunches baby carrots with tops, peeled and trimmed, with ½ inch of the greens remaining (about 35 to 40 tiny carrots)
1 tablespoon extra-virgin olive oil

In a wide saucepan just big enough to hold the carrots in a few layers, combine the vinegar, white wine, sugar, garlic, bay leaves, mint sprigs, parsley sprigs, and 1 teaspoon salt. Bring to a simmer, and add the carrots and enough water just to cover the carrots, about 1 cup. Simmer until

carrots are tender—about 15 minutes, depending on their size. Remove carrots with tongs to a serving dish that will fit them snugly in several layers, strain the cooking liquid over top, and cool to room temperature. Cover, and refrigerate overnight.

When ready to serve, bring carrots back to room temperature. Remove from the liquid, and add to a large bowl. Toss with the olive oil, chopped parsley, chopped mint, and salt to taste. Drizzle with a few tablespoons of the marinade, just to moisten, and serve.

Radicchio Salad with Orange

Insalata di Radicchio e Arancia
SERVES 4 TO 6

2 navel oranges
Juice of 1 lemon, freshly squeezed
2 teaspoons Dijon mustard
1 teaspoon kosher salt
Freshly ground black pepper
¼ cup extra-virgin olive oil
2 heads radicchio, coarsely chopped (about 8 cups)
1 cup thinly sliced radishes
¼ cup pitted oil-cured black olives, coarsely chopped

Cut the top and bottom from an orange, so it sits upright on your cutting board. Cut down, following the shape of the orange, to remove the peel and white pith, leaving only the flesh of the orange. To section the oranges: hold the orange in your hand and cut out the segments, leaving the membrane behind. Put the segments in a large serving bowl, and squeeze any juice from the membrane into a medium bowl. Repeat with the remaining orange.

To the medium bowl with the orange juice, add the lemon juice, mustard, salt, and pepper.

Whisk to combine. Whisk in the olive oil in a slow, steady stream to make a smooth, somewhat thick dressing.

To the bowl with the orange segments, add the radicchio, radishes, and olives. Drizzle with the dressing, and toss well. Serve.

oregano. Season with the remaining ½ teaspoon salt and more black pepper. Toss to coat the vegetables well in the dressing. Add the tuna, and toss once more—lightly, so as not to break up the tuna too much. Serve.

Condiggion Salad with Tuna

Condiggion con il Tonno
SERVES 6

4 cups 1-inch crustless day-old country-bread cubes
7 tablespoons red wine vinegar
7 tablespoons extra-virgin olive oil
2 small garlic cloves, crushed and peeled
6 anchovy fillets
½ cup fresh basil leaves
1 teaspoon kosher salt
Freshly ground black pepper
2 ripe medium tomatoes, cut into 1-inch chunks
1 red bell pepper, cut into strips
1 small English cucumber, sliced into ¼-inch-thick rounds
¼ cup pitted, chopped oil-cured black olives
¼ cup chopped fresh Italian parsley
2 teaspoons dried oregano, preferably Sicilian on the branch
Two 5-ounce cans Italian tuna in olive oil, drained

In a large bowl, drizzle the bread with ¼ cup of the vinegar and 2 tablespoons olive oil. Add enough water (up to ½ cup, depending on how dry the bread is) just to moisten it, and let sit 5 minutes.

In a mini–food processor, combine the garlic, anchovies, basil, and remaining 3 tablespoons vinegar and 5 tablespoons olive oil. Season with ½ teaspoon of the salt and some black pepper, and process to make a smooth dressing.

To the soaked bread, add the tomatoes, bell pepper, English cucumber, olives, parsley, and

Raw and Cooked Salad

Insalata Cotta e Cruda
SERVES 6

1 pound sweet onions, such as Vidalia or Walla Walla
½ cup extra-virgin olive oil, plus more as needed
½ teaspoon kosher salt, plus more as needed
12 ounces red-bliss potatoes, medium in size
8 ounces green beans, trimmed
½ cup pitted black olives
3 tablespoons drained tiny capers in brine
1 or 2 fresh ripe tomatoes (about 8 ounces), cored and cut into wedges
1 or 2 heads Bibb lettuce (about 12 ounces), leaves torn, washed, and dried
Freshly ground black pepper to taste
3 tablespoons red wine vinegar

For the *verdura cotta* (cooked vegetables): Preheat the oven to 375 degrees. Peel and trim the onions and slice into rounds about ¾ inch thick. Brush with some of the olive oil, and sprinkle salt lightly on both sides. Lay the onions on a baking sheet, and roast for 20 minutes or longer, until slightly softened and nicely caramelized. Cool, then separate the rounds into rings.

Meanwhile, drop the potatoes—whole, with skin on—into a pot with plenty of water. Bring to a gentle boil, and cook just until a sharp knife blade slides through the potatoes. Remove with a spider, and cut the potatoes into wedges about 1½ inches thick.

When the potatoes are out of the boiling water, drop the green beans in and cook until al dente, 4 minutes or so. Drain, and drop the beans into ice water, to set the color. Once they're chilled, drain and dry the beans, and cut into 2-inch lengths.

Combine the cooked vegetables in a large serving bowl with the olives, capers, and tomatoes. Sprinkle with the remaining salt and some freshly ground pepper, drizzle the rest of the olive oil and the red wine vinegar over vegetables, and tumble them to coat with dressing. Scatter the lettuce on top, then toss to distribute the dressing evenly. Serve immediately.

Roasted Beet and Beet Greens Salad with Apples and Goat Cheese

Insalata di Barbabietole con Mele e Formaggio di Capra
SERVES 6

10 to 12 small yellow and red beets with greens attached (about 3 pounds total)
½ teaspoon kosher salt
⅓ cup extra-virgin olive oil
⅓ cup good-quality balsamic vinegar
Freshly ground black pepper
1 medium tart, crisp apple (such as Granny Smith), cut into matchsticks (peel on)
4 ounces or so slightly aged goat cheese

Preheat the oven to 400 degrees. Remove the beet greens, leaving about an inch of stem on the beets, and poke each beet with a fork a few times. Put the beets in a shallow roasting pan with about an inch of water, uncovered. Roast until tender all the way through, about 45 minutes to 1 hour. Let cool. (The beets can also be boiled whole and unpeeled, if you don't want to heat your oven, but they taste better when baked.)

Bring a large saucepan of salted water to a boil. Rinse the greens, and trim off any very tough parts of the stems or blemishes on the leaves. Trim the softer stems, and keep separate from the leaves. Add the stems to the boiling water and

cook 10 minutes. Add the leaves and cook until all is very tender, about 15 to 20 minutes. Drain well, and season with ¼ teaspoon salt. Let cool.

Peel the beets, and cut into 2-inch wedges. Cut the greens and stems into 2-inch pieces. Put all in a large bowl.

In a small bowl, whisk together the olive oil and vinegar, and season with the remaining salt and some pepper. Toss the dressing with the beets and greens. Add the apples at the last minute, so as not to discolor them too much, and toss all again. Spread on serving plates or a platter, and crumble the goat cheese over all.

Roasted Eggplant and Tomato Salad

Insalata di Melanzane e Pomodori Arrostiti
SERVES 6

2 medium eggplants (about 1¼ pounds)
4 tablespoons extra-virgin olive oil
½ teaspoon kosher salt, plus more to taste
3 cups ripe grape or small cherry tomatoes
¼ teaspoon freshly ground black pepper
¼ cup red wine vinegar
12 small fresh basil leaves, or 2 tablespoons shredded large fresh basil leaves
⅓ cup shredded fresh mozzarella or ricotta salata

Preheat the oven to 450 degrees. Trim the ends of the eggplants and slice crosswise into 1-inch-thick rounds; cut each round into halves or quarters, to make roughly equal pieces no bigger than 2 inches on a side. Put the chunks on a baking sheet lined with parchment, and sprinkle over them 1 tablespoon oil and ¼ teaspoon salt. Toss well.

Put the tomatoes on another parchment-lined sheet pan, sprinkle over them 1 tablespoon oil and a pinch of salt, roll them around, and spread them out. Put both sheets in the oven, and roast until both the eggplant and the tomatoes are soft, shriveled, and nicely caramelized on the edges,

30 minutes or more. Turn the eggplant chunks a couple of times while roasting, roll the tomatoes over, and shift the sheets around in the oven for even heating.

Let the vegetables cool completely on the sheets, then transfer to a large mixing bowl. Toss gently with the remaining 2 tablespoons olive oil, ¼ teaspoon salt, some ground pepper, the vinegar, and basil. Taste, and adjust the seasonings. Arrange the salad on a serving platter or portion on salad plates, and sprinkle the shredded cheese on top.

Cucumber, Potato, and Green Bean Salad

Insalata di Cetrioli, Patate e Fagioli Verdi
SERVES 4 TO 6

1 teaspoon kosher salt, plus more for the pot
3 large red potatoes, cut into 1½-inch chunks (about 1¼ pounds)
1 pound green beans, trimmed
3 tablespoons red wine vinegar
⅓ cup extra-virgin olive oil
Freshly ground black pepper
1 English cucumber, sliced into ¼-inch-thick half-moons
½ medium red onion, thinly sliced

Bring a large pot of salted water to a boil. Add the potatoes, and simmer until about halfway cooked, about 10 minutes. Add the green beans and cook until potatoes and beans are tender, about 5 minutes more. Drain in a colander.

When the beans are just cool enough to handle (you want them still to be warm for the dressing), "French" each bean by pulling it apart at the seam into two long pieces, with the seeds exposed.

In a large bowl, whisk together the vinegar and oil and season with the salt and pepper. Add the potatoes, green beans, cucumber, and red onion. Toss well to coat the vegetables in the dressing, and serve.

Celery Root, Apple, Arugula, and Walnut Salad

Insalata di Sedano Rapa, Mele, Rucola e Noci
SERVES 4 TO 6

4 anchovy fillets, finely chopped
Juice of 1 large lemon, freshly squeezed
½ teaspoon kosher salt
Freshly ground black pepper
¼ cup extra-virgin olive oil
1 medium celery root, peeled and julienned
1 large Granny Smith apple, julienned (skin on)
One 5-ounce package baby arugula
½ cup walnuts, toasted and coarsely chopped

In a large bowl, whisk together the anchovies and lemon juice to dissolve the anchovies. Whisk in the salt, and season with pepper. Whisk in the olive oil to make a smooth dressing.

Add the celery root and apple, and toss to coat well in the dressing. Add the arugula and walnuts, and toss lightly just to combine. Serve immediately.

Celery, Artichoke, and Mortadella Salad

Insalata di Sedano, Carciofi e Mortadella
SERVES 4 TO 6

Juice of 2 lemons, freshly squeezed (save the halves of squeezed lemons)
8 baby artichokes (about 1 pound)
4 inner celery stalks, with leaves, thinly sliced on the bias
One 4-ounce chunk Grana Padano
3 tablespoons extra-virgin olive oil
½ teaspoon kosher salt
One 6-ounce piece mortadella, cut into matchsticks

Fill a bowl with cold water, add the juice of 1 lemon and the squeezed-out lemon halves, so you can store the artichokes as you work. Peel and trim the stems from the artichokes. Pull off any tough outer leaves and discard. With a paring knife, trim away any tough parts around the base of each artichoke. With a serrated knife, cut off the top third of each artichoke and discard. Halve the artichokes and slice lengthwise very thin, either by hand or on a mandoline. (The artichokes can be sliced crosswise if you prefer.) As you are cutting, add the sliced artichokes to the acidulated water. When finished, drain well, set artichokes in a dry bowl, and toss with the remaining juice of one lemon.

Add celery to the bowl. On the coarse holes of a box grater, grate most of the chunk of cheese into the bowl, reserving a small piece for garnish. Drizzle with the olive oil, and season with the salt. Toss well. Add the mortadella and toss gently, so as not to break the pieces. Grate remaining cheese over the top and serve.

Farro Salad with Grilled Eggplant and Peppers

Insalata di Farro e Verdure alla Griglia
SERVES 6

2 teaspoons kosher salt, plus more for cooking the farro
1½ cups farro
2 fresh bay leaves
1 large red onion, cut into ½-inch rings
2 small Italian eggplants, sliced lengthwise into ½-inch-thick strips (about 1 pound)
2 red, yellow, or orange bell peppers, sliced into 1-inch-thick strips
½ cup extra-virgin olive oil
1 cup pitted large green olives, quartered
½ cup chopped fresh Italian parsley
2 tablespoons pine nuts, toasted
3 tablespoons white wine vinegar

Preheat a grill or grill pan over medium-high heat. Bring a large pot of salted water to a boil. Add the farro and bay leaves. Simmer until farro is tender, about 20 to 25 minutes. Drain well, and spread on a sheet pan to cool and dry out while you cook the vegetables. Remove bay leaves from farro.

In a large bowl, combine the onion, eggplants, and bell peppers. Toss with 5 tablespoons of the olive oil and 1 teaspoon salt.

Grill vegetables, turning occasionally, until lightly charred and tender, about 5 to 7 minutes.

When all the vegetables are grilled, cut the onion and eggplant into 1-inch pieces; leave the peppers in strips.

In a bowl, combine the farro, grilled vegetables, olives, parsley, and pine nuts. Drizzle with the remaining 3 tablespoons olive oil, the vinegar, and the remaining teaspoon of salt. Toss well to combine. Serve.

Steamed Broccoli and Egg Salad

Insalata di Broccoli al Vapore con Uova Sode
SERVES 4 TO 6

1 large head broccoli (about 1½ pounds)
½ teaspoon kosher salt, plus more for the pot
2 tablespoons extra-virgin olive oil
2 tablespoons red wine vinegar
2 hard-boiled eggs, cut into wedges

Peel the lower stem and the head of the broccoli and cut in ¼-inch rounds. Bring a large pot of salted water to a boil. Add the broccoli, bring back to a boil, and cook until tender but al dente, about 8 to 10 minutes. Drain and let cool.

In a large bowl, whisk together the olive oil, vinegar, and salt. Add the broccoli, and toss to coat with the dressing. Mound into a serving bowl, and top with the egg wedges. Drizzle with any remaining dressing left in the bowl. Serve immediately. (For a more homogeneous salad, cut the eggs into eighths and toss with the broccoli and dressing.)

Shaved Fennel, Celery, and Red Onion Salad with Salami

Insalata di Finocchio, Sedano, Cipolla e Salame
SERVES 4 TO 6

1 large fennel bulb, trimmed and thinly sliced crosswise (about 4 cups), plus ½ cup chopped fronds (use a mandoline, if you have one, to shave the fennel)
3 large celery stalks, trimmed, peeled, and thinly sliced on the bias
½ medium red onion, thinly sliced
4 ounces salami, thickly sliced and julienned
4 ounces caciocavallo or smoked mozzarella cheese, julienned
Juice of 1 large lemon, freshly squeezed
¼ cup extra-virgin olive oil
½ teaspoon kosher salt
Freshly ground black pepper

In a large bowl, combine the fennel (but not the fronds), celery, red onion, salami, and cheese.

Drizzle with the lemon juice and olive oil, and season with the salt and some pepper. Toss well to coat all of the ingredients with the dressing. Sprinkle with the chopped fennel fronds and toss lightly. Let sit about 10 minutes before serving, to combine the flavors.

Red Cabbage and Bacon Salad

Insalata di Cappuccio Rosso e Pancetta
SERVES 4 TO 6

1 small head red cabbage
¼ cup extra-virgin olive oil
1 pound sliced bacon, cut into 1-inch pieces
5 tablespoons balsamic vinegar
Kosher salt

Clean and remove the tough outer leaves of the cabbage, cut in half, and cut out the core. Thinly shred the red cabbage, by hand or on a mandoline (preferred), into a large bowl.

Heat 1 tablespoon olive oil in a large skillet over medium heat. Cook the bacon until crisp, about 5 or 6 minutes, then remove to a paper-towel-lined plate. Pour off most of the fat, and return the pan to the heat.

Add the remaining olive oil and the vinegar to the skillet. Bring the liquid to an energetic simmer, and pour the hot sauce over the cabbage in the bowl. Mop out the skillet with a handful of the cabbage to get the crusty bits from the bottom of the pan, and add to the bowl. Add the cooked bacon, season with the salt, and toss well so the cabbage doesn't stick together. Serve warm.

Warm Mushroom Salad

Insalata di Funghi Tiepida
SERVES 4 TO 6

5 tablespoons extra-virgin olive oil
4 ounces pancetta, diced
2 pounds mixed fresh wild mushrooms, thickly sliced (cremini, shiitake, porcini, oyster, chanterelle)
1 teaspoon chopped fresh thyme
1¼ teaspoons kosher salt
1 bunch scallions, trimmed and chopped (about 1 cup)

3 medium heads frisée, trimmed into bite-sized pieces, or 8 ounces baby kale or spinach
3 tablespoons red wine vinegar
One 2-ounce chunk Grana Padano

To a large skillet over medium-high heat, add 3 tablespoons of the olive oil and the pancetta. Cook until the pancetta is crisp, about 4 minutes, then remove it to drain on paper towels.

Add the mushrooms to the fat left in the pan. Season with the thyme and 1 teaspoon of the salt. Cover and cook, letting the mushrooms release their juices, about 3 minutes. Uncover, increase the heat to high, and cook until the liquid in the pan is gone and the mushrooms are browned all over, about 6 minutes. Add the scallions, and cook until wilted, about 3 minutes. Scrape the contents of the pan into a large serving bowl, and let cool 5 minutes.

Once the mushrooms are slightly cool, add the frisée and the reserved pancetta, and drizzle with the vinegar and remaining 2 tablespoons olive oil. Season with the remaining ¼ teaspoon salt, and toss well. Mound on serving plates and, using a vegetable peeler, shave some Grana Padano over each serving. Serve immediately.

Place the octopus and bay leaves in a large pot with cold water. Cover, and bring to a boil. Reduce the heat, and cook the octopus at a vigorous simmer until tender but slightly al dente, about 45 minutes. (Test periodically by inserting the tines of a fork into the thickest part of the octopus. It is done when the fork penetrates easily and is removed with a little resistance.)

Meanwhile, cover the whole unpeeled potatoes with cold water in a second pot, and bring to a boil. Cook until tender, about 25 to 30 minutes, then cool, peel, and cut into 1-inch cubes.

Drain the octopus, discarding the bay leaves, and let it cool to room temperature. Cut the tentacles away where they join the head, and, if desired, strip away the skin and suction cups from the tentacles. (I like to leave the skin and suction cups on.) Clean the inside of the octopus head, which looks like a pouch the size of your fist, by cutting it in half; then cut the head meat into thin slices. Cut the tentacles into 1-inch pieces, and set the octopus pieces in a bowl with the warm potatoes. Toss well with the olive oil, red wine vinegar, onion, and parsley. Season with salt and pepper. Place on a serving platter, garnish with lemon wedges, and serve.

Octopus and Potato Salad

Insalata di Polpo e Patate
SERVES 6

One 2-to-3-pound octopus, head cleaned
2 fresh bay leaves
2 medium russet potatoes
5 tablespoons extra-virgin olive oil
3 tablespoons red wine vinegar
1 small red onion, thinly sliced
2 tablespoons chopped fresh Italian parsley
Kosher salt to taste
Freshly ground black pepper to taste

Shrimp and Mixed Bean Salad

Insalata di Gamberetti e Fagioli Misti
SERVES 6

¼ teaspoon kosher salt, plus more for the pot
1 pound freshly shelled borlotti beans
1 pound fresh or frozen fava beans, shelled
½ small onion
2 fresh bay leaves
1 small carrot, peeled and sliced
1 celery stalk, diced
1 pound large shrimp, peeled and deveined
3 tablespoons extra-virgin olive oil
3 tablespoons red wine vinegar
Freshly ground black pepper to taste

Bring a large saucepan of salted water to a boil. Cook the borlotti beans until tender, about 8 minutes, and then cook the fava beans for 4 minutes. Drain, refresh the beans under cold running water as they finish cooking, and remove the outer skins from the favas.

In a medium saucepan, boil the onion, bay leaves, carrot, and celery in 6 cups water for 20 minutes. Add the shrimp, and cook just until opaque throughout, about 2 minutes. Remove and drain the shrimp, and allow them to cool. In a serving bowl, whisk together the olive oil, vinegar, and salt and pepper. Add the beans and shrimp, and toss to coat thoroughly with the dressing. Serve warm.

🦐 You can find frozen favas in Italian specialty stores. To substitute, just cook according to package directions.

Lobster Salad with Fresh Tomatoes

Insalata di Aragosta con Pomodori
SERVES 6 AS AN APPETIZER OR 4 AS A MAIN COURSE

1 teaspoon kosher salt, plus 6 tablespoons for the lobster pot
2 live lobsters, 1¼ pounds each
4 ripe tomatoes (about 1½ pounds), or 1 pound sweet, ripe cherry tomatoes
3 tender celery stalks with a nice amount of leaves
Juice of 2 large lemons, freshly squeezed
2 large hard-boiled eggs, chopped
¼ teaspoon peperoncino, or to taste
¾ cup extra-virgin olive oil
2 tablespoons chopped fresh Italian parsley

Fill a large stockpot with 6 quarts water, add 6 tablespoons salt, and bring to a rolling boil. When the water is at a rolling boil, drop in the lobsters and cook them, uncovered, for exactly 10 minutes after the water returns to the boiling point (and then keep it boiling). At the end of 10 minutes (or a couple of minutes longer if the lobsters are larger than 1¼ pounds), lift the lobsters from the pot, rinse with cold water, drain, and let them cool.

Core and cut the tomatoes into wedges, about 1 inch thick (if you have cherry tomatoes, cut them in half). Chop the celery stalks crosswise into ½-inch pieces, and roughly chop the leaves. Toss the tomatoes and celery together in a large bowl with ½ teaspoon of the salt.

When the lobsters are cool enough to handle, twist and pull off the claws and knuckle segments where the knuckles attach to the front of the body. Lay the lobsters flat on a cutting board, and split them in half lengthwise with a heavy chef's knife. Remove the digestive sac, found right behind the eyes, and pull out the vein running along the back of the body and the tail. Separate the meaty tail piece from the carcass of the four split halves. Remove the shell from the upper half of the lobsters, pluck the feathered attachments and any extra skin, and cut the lobster body with small legs attached into three pieces, putting the pieces in a large mixing bowl as you work. I like to leave the tomalley and roe in the body pieces, as a special treat while eating the salad. Or you can remove them and discard, if not to your liking.

Separate the knuckles from the claws, and crack open the shells of both knuckles and hard claw pincers with the thick edge of the knife blade, or kitchen shears; pull the meat out. Get the meat out of the knuckles as well. Cut the tail sections, shell on, crosswise into three pieces each.

To make the dressing, whisk together the lemon juice, chopped eggs, peperoncino, and remaining ½ teaspoon salt. Pour in the olive oil in a slow stream, whisking steadily to incorporate it into a smooth dressing.

To serve: Add the tomatoes and celery to the bowl of lobster pieces. Pour in the dressing, and tumble everything together until evenly coated. Scatter the parsley on top. Arrange the salad on a large platter, or compose individual servings on salad plates.

Crab and Celery Salad

Insalata di Granchio e Sedano
SERVES 4

1½ cups thin bias-cut inner celery stalks and
leaves
2 large hard-boiled eggs, coarsely chopped
2 ripe medium tomatoes, seeded, cut into
½-inch pieces
3 tablespoons chopped fresh Italian parsley
3 tablespoons freshly squeezed lemon juice
3 tablespoons extra-virgin olive oil
¾ teaspoon kosher salt
1 pound jumbo lump crabmeat, picked through
for shells

In a large bowl, combine celery, eggs, tomatoes,
and parsley. Drizzle with lemon juice and oil, season with salt, and toss well to coat the salad with
the dressing. Add the crabmeat and toss gently to
combine, without breaking up the lumps of crab.

Serve right away, or chill for up to an hour
or two.

Seafood and Rice Salad

Insalata di Riso e Frutti di Mare
SERVES 6

FOR THE RICE
2 fresh bay leaves
2 tablespoons extra-virgin olive oil
1 teaspoon kosher salt
1½ cups long-grain rice

FOR THE SEAFOOD
2 tablespoons extra-virgin olive oil
3 garlic cloves, peeled and sliced
Peel of 1 large lemon, removed with a vegetable
peeler (reserve the lemon)
½ teaspoon kosher salt
¼ teaspoon crushed red pepper flakes
1 cup dry white wine

12 littleneck clams, scrubbed
2 pounds mussels, scrubbed and debearded
8 ounces medium calamari, cleaned (see
page 54), tubes cut into ½-inch rings, head
with tentacles cut in half
8 ounces large shrimp, peeled and deveined

FOR THE SALAD
3 tablespoons extra-virgin olive oil
Juice of 1 lemon (peel used in cooking seafood)
3 tablespoons chopped fresh Italian parsley
1 medium fennel bulb, halved, cored, and thinly
sliced, plus ½ cup chopped fronds
1 teaspoon kosher salt
2 celery stalks, thinly sliced on the bias
½ medium red onion, sliced

For the rice: In a medium saucepan, combine
3 cups water, the bay leaves, olive oil, and salt.
Bring to a boil. Add the rice, reduce the heat to
a simmer, cover the pot, and simmer 15 minutes
without opening the lid. Remove from the heat,
let stand 5 minutes, and fluff the rice with a fork.
Spread rice onto a sheet pan to cool, and discard
the bay leaves.

For the seafood: In a large Dutch oven, heat
the olive oil over medium-high heat. When the
oil is hot, add the garlic and lemon peel, and let
sizzle a minute. Season with the salt and red pepper flakes, and add the wine. Bring to a simmer,
add the clams, and cover the pot. Let steam 2
minutes; then add the mussels. Cover, and simmer until most of the clams and mussels open,
about 4 minutes more. Remove open clams and
mussels to a bowl with tongs. Cover, and give the
last few another couple of minutes to steam. Add
any more open ones to the bowl, and discard any
that refuse to open.

Return the cooking liquid to a simmer, and
add the calamari. Simmer just until the calamari
curls and turns white (don't overcook!), about 2
minutes, and remove with tongs to a large serving
bowl. Add the shrimp to the pot, and simmer just
until they turn pink, about 4 minutes. Add to the
bowl with the calamari.

Pluck the clams and mussels from the shells,

and add to the serving bowl with the calamari and shrimp. Strain the cooking juices, and reserve.

For the salad: In a medium bowl, whisk together ½ cup cooking juices, the olive oil, lemon juice, chopped parsley, and fennel fronds. Season with the salt.

To the serving bowl with the seafood, add the celery, sliced fennel, and red onion along with the rice. Drizzle all with the dressing, and toss well to combine, adding a little more of the cooking juices if the salad seems dry. Serve.

Poached Seafood Salad

Insalata di Frutti di Mare
SERVES 6

FOR THE COURT BOUILLON
½ cup dry white wine
2 celery stalks, trimmed and cut into 1-inch lengths
2 medium carrots, peeled and cut into 1-inch lengths
4 fresh bay leaves
1 teaspoon black peppercorns
1 tablespoon kosher salt

FOR THE SALAD
12 ounces large shrimp, shells and tails removed, deveined
1 pound medium (bodies 4 to 6 inches long) calamari, cleaned (see page 54), bodies cut into ½-inch rings, tentacles cut in half
1½ pound mussels, scrubbed and debearded
4 inner celery stalks with leaves, sliced thin (about 1½ cups)
2 tablespoons coarsely chopped fresh Italian parsley
1 teaspoon chopped garlic
½ cup extra-virgin olive oil
2 tablespoons red wine vinegar
Kosher salt to taste
Peperoncino to taste

For the court bouillon: Bring 2 quarts water, the wine, celery, carrots, bay leaves, peppercorns, and salt to a boil in a wide casserole or skillet. Adjust the heat to simmering, cover, and cook 10 minutes.

Add the shrimp to the court bouillon, and cook them until they are barely opaque in the center, about 4 minutes. Fish the shrimp out with a spider, and spread them out on a baking sheet. Don't worry if they aren't completely drained— you'll use some of the liquid to finish the salad. Add the calamari, and poach just until they are firm and tender, about 2 to 3 minutes. Fish out the calamari, and add them to the shrimp.

Return the court bouillon to a boil. Stir in the mussels, cover the pot, and cook until the shells open and the mussels are firm but not tough, about 4 minutes. Remove with a skimmer and add to the other poached seafood. Reserve half a cup of the cooking liquid. When the mussels are cool enough, pluck the meat from the shells directly into a large serving bowl.

For the salad, transfer the cooled shrimp and calamari to the bowl with the mussels, shaking off peppercorns as you do. Add the celery, parsley, and garlic, then pour in the olive oil and vinegar. Toss until mixed, drizzling in the reserved cooking liquid. Season the salad to taste with salt and peperoncino. The salad should be very moist and glisten with dressing. If not, add a dash of olive oil and vinegar. Let the salad stand at room temperature about 30 minutes, tossing once or twice. Check the seasoning, and toss well just before serving.

Striped Bass Salad

Insalata di Branzino
SERVES 4

2 fresh bay leaves
1 small onion, sliced
1 medium carrot, peeled and sliced
2 tablespoons white wine vinegar

1½ teaspoons kosher salt

2 pounds skinless striped-bass (or other firm fish) fillet

1 English cucumber, sliced into ½-inch-thick half-moons

½ medium red onion, thinly sliced

2 tablespoons chopped fresh Italian parsley

3 tablespoons red wine vinegar

¼ cup extra-virgin olive oil

Freshly ground black pepper

In a large pot, bring 3 quarts water to a boil with the bay leaves, onion, carrot, white wine vinegar, and 1 teaspoon salt. Simmer 15 minutes. Tie the fish fillets so they lie flat in cheesecloth. Add the fish to the liquid, and adjust the heat so it is barely simmering. Cook until fish is just cooked through, about 10 minutes, depending on the thickness of the fillet. Remove the fish to a plate, cool to room temperature, still in the cheesecloth, then refrigerate until chilled.

Remove the fish from the cheesecloth and flake in large pieces into a serving bowl. Add the cucumber, red onion, and parsley. Drizzle with the red wine vinegar and oil, and season with the remaining ½ teaspoon salt and some black pepper. Gently toss just to combine. Serve.

Place the tripe in a large pot. Add cold water to cover by 2 inches and the bay leaves, onion, peppercorns, and a generous pinch of salt. Bring to a simmer, and cook until the tripe is tender all the way through when pierced with a fork in the thickest part, about 1 to 1½ hours. Drain and cool the tripe.

Cut the tripe into 2-by-2-inch pieces. Turn the pieces honeycomb side down, and scrape away any fat or membranes. Cut tripe pieces into julienne strips, and add to a large serving bowl.

In a small bowl, whisk together the vinegar, garlic, salt, and some pepper. Whisk in the olive oil. Drizzle the dressing over the salad, sprinkle with the parsley, and toss well. Serve.

Tripe Salad

Insalata di Trippa

SERVES 4

2 pounds honeycomb tripe

2 fresh bay leaves

1 small onion, halved

6 black peppercorns

1 teaspoon kosher salt, plus more for the pot

3 tablespoons white wine vinegar

1 garlic clove, finely chopped

Freshly ground black pepper

5 tablespoons extra-virgin olive oil

2 tablespoons chopped fresh Italian parsley

SOUPS

Una piccola cucina può far diventare grande una casa.
—Italian proverb

A small kitchen can make the house big.

Chicken Stock

Brodo di Pollo
MAKES ABOUT 4 QUARTS

3 pounds chicken and/or turkey wings, backs,
    necks, and giblets (not including the liver),
    preferably from free-range or organically
    raised birds
1 large onion, halved
3 cups 1-inch-sliced, peeled carrots
3 celery stalks, cut crosswise into 4 pieces
1 leek, white and green parts, washed well
6 garlic cloves
6 sprigs fresh Italian parsley
6 black peppercorns
Rind of Grana Padano cheese, washed (optional)
Kosher salt

Wash the chicken or turkey parts thoroughly
under cold running water, and drain them well.
Put them with 8 quarts water in a large stockpot,
and bring to a boil over high heat. Lower heat to
medium, and boil for 1 hour. Skim off the surface
foam and fat occasionally.

Meanwhile, place the onion, cut sides down,
on an open flame, and cook until the cut surfaces are well browned, about 3 minutes. Move
the onion halves with a pair of tongs as necessary
to brown all over, evenly. (You may also brown
the onion, cut sides down, in a heavy skillet over
medium heat.)

Add the onion, carrots, celery, leek, garlic,
parsley, peppercorns, and Grana Padano rind (if
using) to the stockpot. Bring the pot to a boil
again, occasionally skimming the fat and foam
off the top. Lower the heat until the liquid is
"perking"—one or two large bubbles rising to
the surface at a time. Partially cover, and cook for
3 hours, adding salt to taste.

Strain the broth through a colander lined
with a dampened kitchen towel or cheesecloth.
If you want to use the stock immediately, you
can remove much of the liquid fat floating on the
surface by lightly dragging a folded paper towel
over the surface, or use a fat-separating measuring
cup with a spout. It will be easier to degrease the
stock if you have time to chill it completely in the
refrigerator; the fat will then rise to the surface
and solidify, and can simply be lifted off. The
stock can be refrigerated up to 4 days, or frozen
up to 3 months.

Vegetable Stock

Brodo di Verdure
MAKES ABOUT 2 QUARTS

4 celery stalks with leaves, cut into large dice
4 carrots, peeled and cut into quarters
2 leeks, white and green parts, trimmed, sliced,
    and washed
8 ounces mushrooms or mushroom stems,
    coarsely chopped
2 large ripe tomatoes, quartered, or 1 tablespoon
    tomato paste
6 sprigs fresh Italian parsley
4 sprigs fresh thyme
2 fresh bay leaves
12 black peppercorns
Kosher salt

Put 4 quarts cold water and all ingredients except the salt in a large (about 8-quart) stockpot.
Bring to a boil over medium heat, skimming any
foam that rises to the surface. Adjust the heat
to a strong simmer, and cook, partially covered,
1 hour. Skim the foam that rises to the surface
once or twice as the stock cooks.

Strain the stock through a fine sieve, and cool
to room temperature. The stock can be refrigerated up to 4 days or frozen up to 3 months.

Fish Stock

Brodo di Pesce
MAKES ABOUT 2½ QUARTS

2 pounds fish heads and trimmings from nonoily
    fish, such as red snapper and sea bass (fresh-
    ness is paramount, but frozen when fresh is
    fine)
4 medium carrots, peeled and cut into large
    chunks
2 celery stalks, cut into large chunks
2 small onions, halved
4 garlic cloves
6 sprigs fresh Italian parsley
1 teaspoon black peppercorns
1 tablespoon extra-virgin olive oil
Kosher salt to taste

Rinse the fish heads and trimmings well under
cold running water. Combine all of the ingredients except the salt in a large pot. Add 4 quarts
cold water. Bring to a boil, then simmer gently
for 1 hour, skimming off and discarding the foam
that rises to the surface.

Strain the stock through a double thickness of
moistened cheesecloth. Season lightly with salt.
This stock can be used immediately or refrigerated for up to 2 days or frozen for up to a month.

Mixed Meat Stock

Brodo di Carne
MAKES ABOUT 2½ QUARTS

1 pound chicken backs and wings
1 pound veal bones
1 pound beef short ribs
Extra-virgin olive oil
Kosher salt
2 celery stalks
2 large carrots, peeled and halved
4 whole garlic cloves

1 medium onion
1 bunch Italian parsley, washed
4 peppercorns

Preheat oven to 425 degrees. Trim the meats of
excess fat, and rinse. In a large roasting pan toss
the meat and bones with olive oil. Roast until
lightly browned, about 25 minutes.

Place the meat and bones in a large stockpot.
Cover generously with cold water (about 5 quarts),
salt very lightly, and slowly bring to a boil.

In the same roasting pan, toss the vegetables
with olive oil and roast until lightly browned,
about 20 minutes. Add them to the stockpot with
the parsley and peppercorns.

Simmer until dark and flavorful, about 3 to 4
hours, skimming froth and fat as they accumulate on the surface. Remove from the stove, add
salt if needed, strain through a very fine sieve,
and refrigerate overnight. The next day, skim off
the solid surface fat. The stock then can be kept
under refrigeration for up to 3 days or frozen for
several months.

Tomato and Bread Soup

Pappa al Pomodoro
SERVES 8

3 tablespoons extra-virgin olive oil, plus more for
    finishing
1 small onion, finely diced
6 garlic cloves, crushed and peeled
Three 28-ounce cans whole San Marzano toma-
    toes, crushed by hand
Five ½-inch slices stale Italian bread, crusts
    removed, cut into 1-inch cubes
Kosher salt and freshly ground black pepper to
    taste
10 fresh basil leaves, plus more for garnish
Freshly grated Grana Padano, for serving

Heat the olive oil over medium heat in a large Dutch oven. Add the onion and cook until wilted, about 3 minutes. Add the garlic and cook until golden, about 6 minutes.

Add the tomatoes and their juices plus 2 cups water to the pot, and bring all to a boil, stirring occasionally. Once the tomatoes have boiled for 10 minutes, add the bread to the pot and return to a boil. Season with salt and pepper. Add the basil leaves, and adjust the level of heat to a simmer. Cook, uncovered, whisking occasionally to break up the pieces of bread, until the mixture is dense and silky, about 40 minutes.

Fish out the garlic cloves and basil leaves. Season the soup to taste with additional salt and pepper if needed. Serve in warm bowls, drizzled with extra-virgin olive oil and shreds of fresh basil leaves, and sprinkled with the grated cheese.

Roman "Egg Drop" Soup

Stracciatella alla Romana
SERVES 6

8 cups defatted homemade Chicken Stock
 (page 143)
1¼ teaspoons kosher salt
4 cups packed spinach leaves, shredded
4 large eggs
⅓ cup freshly grated Grana Padano, plus more
 for serving
Freshly ground black pepper

In a medium pot, bring the stock to a simmer. Once it is simmering, add 1 teaspoon salt and the spinach and cook until tender, about 3 minutes.

Meanwhile, in a medium bowl, whisk together eggs, grated cheese, remaining ¼ teaspoon salt, and some freshly ground black pepper to taste.

Once the spinach is tender, add about a third of the egg mixture to the soup, while continuously whisking the soup where the egg is fall-

ing, to make shreds of the eggs. Add and whisk remaining eggs in two more batches, letting the soup return to a boil between additions. Once all of the eggs have been added, bring soup to a final boil, and use the whisk to break up any large clusters of eggs. Serve soup with additional grated cheese.

Soup with Bread and Fontina Pasticciata

Zuppa con Pasticciata di Fontina
SERVES 6

18 ½-inch slices Italian bread from a long oval
 loaf, left out to dry overnight (see procedure)
8 cups homemade Chicken Stock (page 143)
Kosher salt to taste
1 tablespoon butter, softened, for the baking
 dish
8 ounces Italian Fontina, grated on the coarse
 holes of a box grater
1 cup freshly grated Grana Padano, plus more
 for serving

Leave the bread sitting out on the counter on a sheet pan to dry overnight.

Preheat the oven to 400 degrees with a rack in the middle. In a medium saucepan, heat the broth almost to a simmer, and season with salt to taste. Butter the sides and bottom of a 3-quart shallow oval baking dish. In a medium bowl, toss the Fontina with the Grana Padano.

Arrange half of the bread slices in one layer in the baking dish. Ladle out 1 cup of broth, and drizzle it on the bread slices, slightly moistening them all. Sprinkle half of the cheese on top of the bread in an even layer. Cover the cheese with the remaining bread slices, filling the entire surface of the dish. Moisten these slices with another cup or so of stock; top the bread with all the remaining cheese, scattered evenly. Tent the pasticciata with a sheet of heavy aluminum foil, arching it so it doesn't touch the cheese topping, and pressing it against the sides of the baking dish. Set the dish in the oven, and bake until heated through, about 25 minutes. Remove the foil, and continue baking for 10 minutes or more, until the top is golden brown and bubbly. Take the dish from the oven, and let it cool and set for 5 minutes or so. Rewarm the remaining broth in the saucepan.

To serve: Cut out large squares of pasticciata and, with a spatula, transfer them to warm shallow soup or pasta bowls. Ladle a cup of hot broth over each portion, and serve immediately, passing more grated cheese at the table.

❧ Country Italian bread is best for this pasticciata. The width of the bread may vary, since it is layered snugly in the baking dish and then cut into squares when served.

Rice and Potato Soup

Minestra di Riso e Patate
MAKES ABOUT 2 QUARTS, SERVING 8

3 tablespoons extra-virgin olive oil
2 large russet potatoes, peeled and cut into 1-inch cubes
2 medium carrots, trimmed, peeled, and coarsely shredded
2 center celery stalks, trimmed and diced
Kosher salt
2 teaspoons tomato paste
2 fresh bay leaves
Leftover rind of Grana Padano cheese, washed
Freshly ground black pepper
1 cup long-grain rice
½ cup chopped fresh Italian parsley
¼ cup freshly grated Grana Padano

In a large soup pot, heat the olive oil over medium heat. Add the potatoes, and cook, stirring occa-

sionally, until lightly browned, about 5 minutes. (It's fine if the potatoes stick; just adjust the level of heat to prevent the bits of potato that stick from getting too dark.)

Stir in the carrots and celery, and cook, stirring with a wooden spoon, until the carrots are softened, about 2 to 3 minutes. Season lightly with salt, then stir in the tomato paste to coat the vegetables. Pour in 10 cups water and add the bay leaves, then bring to a boil, scraping up the bits of stuck potato.

Add the cheese rind, adjust the level of heat to keep soup at a simmer, and season the soup lightly with salt and pepper. Cover the pot, and simmer until the potatoes begin to fall apart, about 40 minutes.

Stir the rice into the hot soup and let simmer, stirring well, until the rice is tender but still firm, about 12 minutes.

Remove the bay leaves and the cheese rind. Sprinkle the parsley into the soup, and season with the grated cheese and salt and pepper to taste.

Zucchini and Egg Soup

Zuppa di Zucchine con Uova
MAKES ABOUT 2 QUARTS

2 tablespoons unsalted butter
2 tablespoons extra-virgin olive oil
4 large zucchini, sliced into ½-inch-thick half-moons (about 2½ to 3 pounds)
1 teaspoon kosher salt
2½ quarts Chicken Stock, preferably homemade (page 143)
3 large eggs
⅓ cup freshly grated Grana Padano
¼ cup chopped fresh Italian parsley

In a medium Dutch oven, melt the butter in the olive oil over medium heat. When the butter is melted, add the zucchini and season with the salt. Cook until zucchini begins to wilt but is not brown, about 7 minutes.

Add the stock, bring to a simmer, and cook until zucchini begins to fall apart and thicken the soup, about 45 minutes. (Help this along by periodically mashing and stirring the zucchini with a potato masher.)

In a small bowl, beat the eggs with the grated cheese. While stirring the soup in a circular motion, drizzle the eggs into the simmering soup to create "rags" of cooked egg. Stir in the parsley and simmer gently 1 minute, just to cook the eggs. Serve immediately.

Cauliflower and Tomato Soup

Minestra di Pomodori e Cavolfiore
MAKES ABOUT 2½ QUARTS

¼ cup extra-virgin olive oil, plus more for drizzling
1 medium onion, chopped
1 large carrot, peeled and chopped
4 celery stalks, chopped
¼ cup tomato paste
2 fresh bay leaves
1 tablespoon chopped fresh thyme
½ teaspoon crushed red pepper flakes
4 teaspoons kosher salt
1 large head cauliflower, cut into 1-inch pieces, including the tender leaves
1½ cups long-grain rice
½ cup chopped fresh Italian parsley
Freshly grated Grana Padano, for serving

To a large Dutch oven over medium heat, add the olive oil. When the oil is hot, add the onion, carrot, and celery. Cook until the vegetables begin to soften, about 5 minutes. Clear a space in the pan and add the tomato paste. Cook and stir the tomato paste in that spot until it is toasted and

darkens a shade or two, about 2 to 3 minutes. Add 5 quarts cold water, the bay leaves, thyme, crushed red pepper, and salt. Bring to a boil, and simmer rapidly, uncovered, until vegetables are tender, about 30 minutes.

Add the cauliflower, cover, and cook until the cauliflower is very tender, about 30 minutes.

Add the rice. Uncover and simmer rapidly until the soup is thickened and the rice is just tender, about 15 minutes. (If you are not going to serve all of the soup at once, just cook the rice in the amount of soup you want to serve, and cut the rice proportionally.)

Remove bay leaves. Add the parsley, and serve soup with a drizzle of olive oil and a sprinkle of grated cheese.

Vegetable Soup with Poached Egg

Aquacotta
SERVES 6

1 medium onion, cut into chunks
1 large carrot, peeled and cut into chunks
1 celery stalk, cut into chunks
1 cup loosely packed fresh basil leaves
1 cup loosely packed fresh Italian parsley leaves
2 garlic cloves, crushed and peeled
¼ cup extra-virgin olive oil, plus more for drizzling
1 tablespoon tomato paste
¼ to ½ teaspoon crushed red pepper flakes (depending on how spicy you want the soup to be)
2 teaspoons kosher salt, plus more for seasoning
1 large bunch white-stemmed Swiss chard, washed, tough parts of stems discarded, tender stems cut into 1-inch pieces, leaves coarsely shredded (about 2 pounds)
6 large eggs
6 thick slices country bread, toasted

In a food processor, combine the onion, carrot, celery, basil, parsley, and garlic. Process to make a smooth paste or pestata.

In a medium Dutch oven, heat the olive oil over medium-high heat. Add the pestata and cook, stirring occasionally, until it dries out and begins to stick to the bottom of the pan, about 6 minutes. Make a space in the pan and add the tomato paste. Cook and stir the tomato paste in that spot until it toasts and darkens a shade or two, about 2 minutes. Stir the tomato paste into the vegetables, and season with the red pepper flakes and salt. Add 3 quarts cold water and bring to a boil. Add the chard stems, and simmer rapidly until the soup has reduced by about a third and the stems are tender, about 30 minutes.

Add the shredded chard leaves and cook until tender, about 15 minutes more.

Transfer the soup to a wide skillet, and return to a simmer. (If you don't want to serve all of the soup at once, heat up only enough for the number of eggs you want to cook, one egg per portion.)

Break the eggs into a ramekin one at a time, and slide gently onto the top of the soup. The eggs should sit on the vegetables without breaking the yolks. Season the tops of the eggs with salt. Cover, and simmer until eggs are cooked to your liking, about 4 minutes for a set white with a still-runny yolk.

To serve: Put a slice of toasted country bread in each soup bowl. With a wide kitchen spoon, gently transfer an egg, including the vegetables underneath, to each bowl, and ladle remaining soup over. Drizzle each portion with a little olive oil, and serve.

Broccoli Soup

Minestra di Broccoli
MAKES ABOUT 2 QUARTS

¼ cup extra-virgin olive oil
2 ounces pancetta, finely diced
2 garlic cloves, chopped
2 medium potatoes, peeled and chopped into
    1-inch pieces (about 1¼ pounds)
2 tablespoons tomato paste
1 large head broccoli, florets chopped, stems
    peeled and chopped
2 bunches scallions, trimmed and chopped
    (about 2 cups)
2 teaspoons kosher salt
Grated Pecorino Romano, for serving

In a medium Dutch oven, heat the olive oil over medium heat. When the oil is hot, add the pancetta, and cook until the fat is rendered, about 3 minutes. Add the garlic and potatoes, and cook, stirring occasionally, until potatoes begin to stick to the bottom of the pan, about 5 minutes.

Make a spot in the bottom of the pan, and add the tomato paste. Cook and stir the tomato paste in that spot until it toasts and darkens a shade or two, about 2 minutes. Add 3 quarts water, and bring to a boil. Simmer, covered, until potatoes are tender, about 15 minutes.

Add the broccoli florets and stems, scallions, and salt. Simmer, uncovered, until the broccoli is tender, the florets have broken down, and the soup is thick and flavorful, about 35 minutes. Serve the soup with a sprinkle of Pecorino Romano.

Pasta and Peas in Broth

Pasta e Piselli in Brodo
MAKES 4 QUARTS BROTH, 2 QUARTS SOUP

Zest of 1 lemon, removed with a vegetable peeler
8 sprigs fresh Italian parsley
8 sprigs fresh thyme
3 fresh bay leaves
3 garlic cloves
1 medium onion
1 large carrot, peeled and cut into ½-inch pieces
2 celery stalks, cut into ½-inch pieces
1 large stewing hen (about 6 or 7 pounds)
1 tablespoon kosher salt, plus more for seasoning
1½ cups fresh peas (about 1½ pounds before shelling) or frozen peas
2 cups small pasta shells or other small pasta shapes
Freshly grated Grana Padano, for serving

Lay out a double thickness of cheesecloth, and place the lemon zest, parsley, thyme, bay leaves, and garlic in the center. Tie with kitchen string to make a sachet. In a large soup pot, combine the sachet, onion, carrot, celery, and the hen. Add 6 quarts cold water and the salt. Bring to a simmer, cover, and cook until the hen is tender, about 1½ hours.

Remove the hen, strain and defat the broth, and return it to the pot. Reduce it to yield 4 quarts. When the hen is cool, remove the meat, discarding the skin and bones. Shred the meat. You can add some back to the soup if you'd like, or save for another use.

Save 2 quarts of broth and make the soup from the remaining 2 quarts. Add the peas and pasta, and bring to a simmer. Cook until the pasta is just al dente and the peas are tender. Check the seasoning, and add salt if you like. Serve the soup with a sprinkle of grated cheese.

🍀 A large, mature stewing hen will yield about 4 quarts of flavorful broth. I only use 2 quarts to finish the soup, but the remainder can be frozen and used to make this soup again, or as a flavorful base for many of the other soups (and stews) in this book; just substitute it for some of the water in a recipe and adjust the salt accordingly. You can add some of the meat from the hen to the soup, or just reserve it for a salad or another dish. It will keep up to 3 days tightly covered in the refrigerator.

Lettuce Soup with Fontina Gratin

Zuppa di Lattuga Gratinata con Fontina
SERVES 6

2 tablespoons unsalted butter
2 tablespoons extra-virgin olive oil
2 medium leeks, white and light green parts, halved and thinly sliced
2 garlic cloves, sliced
2 medium russet potatoes, peeled and cut into ½-inch cubes (about 1 pound)
2 quarts Chicken Stock, preferably homemade (page 143), or water
2 fresh bay leaves
1 teaspoon kosher salt
1 small head romaine, coarsely chopped (about 6 cups)
1 small head escarole, coarsely chopped (about 6 cups)
Three ½-inch-thick slices country bread, lightly toasted
6 ounces Italian Fontina, shredded

In a medium Dutch oven over medium heat, melt the butter in the olive oil. When the butter is melted, add the leeks and garlic, and cook, without browning, until the leeks are wilted, about 5 minutes. Add the potatoes, and cook, stirring occasionally, until they stick to the bottom of the pan, about 5 minutes.

Add the stock, bay leaves, and salt. Bring this to a boil, and adjust the heat so the soup is simmering rapidly. Simmer until potatoes are almost cooked, about 10 minutes.

Add the romaine and escarole, and simmer until greens are very tender and the potatoes have begun to fall apart and thicken the soup, about 30 minutes more. Remove bay leaves.

Meanwhile, preheat the oven to 450 degrees. Ladle the soup into six ovenproof bowls. Top each with a slice of the toasted bread, and sprinkle the Fontina evenly among the slices. Put the bowls on a baking sheet, and bake until the cheese topping is browned and bubbly, about 8 to 10 minutes.

Toasted Soup

Brodo Brostula
SERVES 6

1½ cups small crustless bread cubes, from a 1- or 2-day-old country loaf
3 tablespoons extra-virgin olive oil
3 garlic cloves, crushed and peeled
1 cup all-purpose flour
8 cups hot Chicken Stock (page 143)
4 large eggs, beaten
Kosher salt
Freshly ground black pepper

Preheat the oven to 325 degrees. Spread the bread cubes on a sheet pan, and bake until crisp and toasted, about 10 to 12 minutes. Set aside.

In a large saucepan, heat the oil over medium-low heat. Add the garlic and flour, and stir to combine and smooth out the flour into a paste. Stir constantly until the flour is lightly toasted, about 3 to 5 minutes. Whisk in the chicken stock, making sure to get the lumps from the corners of the pan. Simmer 20 minutes, until thickened, skimming any foam that rises to the surface. Strain the mixture through a fine sieve, discarding the garlic and any lumps of flour.

In a clean saucepan, return the soup to a sim-

mer, adding a little hot water if it has thickened too much. In a small bowl, beat the eggs with a pinch of salt. Slowly add the eggs to the simmering soup, beating with a fork the whole time. Return just to a boil. Remove from the heat. Season with salt and pepper, and serve topped with the croutons.

Oatmeal Soup

Zuppa di Avena
MAKES ABOUT 2 QUARTS

¼ cup extra-virgin olive oil, plus more for drizzling
2 ounces pancetta, finely chopped
2 garlic cloves, finely chopped
2 medium russet potatoes, peeled and chopped into ¼-inch pieces (about 1¼ pounds)
1 medium onion, chopped into ¼-inch pieces
1 medium carrot, peeled and chopped into ¼-inch pieces
2 celery stalks, chopped into ¼-inch pieces
2 quarts Chicken Stock, preferably homemade (page 143)
2 fresh bay leaves
1 teaspoon kosher salt
Pinch of crushed red pepper flakes
1 cup old-fashioned (not instant) oats

In a medium Dutch oven, heat the olive oil over medium heat. When the oil is hot, add the pancetta and garlic. Cook until the pancetta has rendered its fat and the garlic is fragrant, about 3 minutes.

Increase heat to medium high, and add the potatoes, onion, carrot, and celery. Cook, stirring occasionally, until potatoes begin to stick to the bottom of the pan, about 6 minutes.

Add the chicken stock, bay leaves, salt, and crushed red pepper. Bring to a simmer, and cook until vegetables are very tender and potatoes have begun to dissolve and thicken the soup, about 45 minutes.

Sprinkle the oats into the simmering soup. Simmer until the oats are tender and the soup is thick, about 10 minutes more. Remove the bay leaves and serve immediately, with a drizzle of olive oil.

Kale Soup

Zuppa di Cavolo Nero
MAKES ABOUT 4 QUARTS

⅓ cup extra-virgin olive oil
4 sweet Italian sausages without fennel seeds (about 1¼ pounds)
2 pounds country-style pork ribs
4 teaspoons kosher salt
1 medium onion, chopped into ½-inch pieces
1 medium carrot, peeled and chopped into ½-inch pieces
2 celery stalks, chopped into ½-inch pieces
4 medium russet potatoes, peeled and chopped into ½-inch pieces (about 2 pounds)
One 28-ounce can whole San Marzano tomatoes, crushed by hand
2 fresh bay leaves
½ teaspoon crushed red pepper flakes
2 bunches kale, tough stems discarded, leaves and tender stems chopped (about 12 cups)
1 cup chopped fresh Italian parsley leaves

In a large Dutch oven, heat the olive oil over medium-high heat. Add the sausages, and brown on all sides, about 4 minutes, then remove to a plate. Season the ribs with 1 teaspoon salt, and brown on all sides, about 6 minutes. Remove to the plate with the sausages. When the sausages are cool, slice into ½-inch-thick rounds.

Add the onion, carrot, and celery to the pot, and cook until just beginning to soften, about 6 minutes. Add the potatoes, and cook, stirring occasionally, until the potatoes begin to stick to the bottom of the pot, 5 minutes. Add the tomatoes, and slosh out the can with water, adding that as well. Add 6 quarts cold water, the bay leaves, crushed red pepper flakes, and the remaining 3 teaspoons salt. Bring to a boil, add the ribs to the pot, and adjust the heat so it is simmering rapidly. Simmer, uncovered, until ribs are almost tender, about 1 hour.

Add the kale and sliced sausages, and continue to simmer and reduce the soup until it is thick and flavorful and the rib meat is almost falling from the bone, about 45 minutes to 1 hour more. Remove bay leaves. Mix in chopped parsley. Serve each portion of soup with a rib and some sausage rounds.

Rice and Lentil Soup

Zuppa con Lenticchie e Riso
MAKES ABOUT 2½ TO 3 QUARTS

4 ounces pancetta, cut into small chunks
4 garlic cloves, crushed and peeled
¼ cup extra-virgin olive oil, plus more for drizzling
2 medium carrots, peeled and cut into chunks
2 celery stalks, cut into chunks
1 small onion, cut into chunks
2 cups loosely packed fresh Italian parsley leaves (from about 1 bunch)
One 28-ounce can whole San Marzano tomatoes, crushed by hand
2 fresh bay leaves
1 pound brown lentils, rinsed
1 tablespoon kosher salt
1 cup long-grain rice
Freshly grated Grana Padano, for serving

In a food processor, combine the pancetta and garlic and process to make a smooth pestata. Heat a large Dutch oven over medium-high heat, and add the olive oil. When the oil is hot, add the pancetta pestata. Cook and stir until it renders its fat, about 5 minutes.

Meanwhile, in the same food processor, combine the carrots, celery, onion, and parsley. Process to make a slightly chunky vegetable pestata. When the pancetta is rendered, scrape the second pestata into the pot and cook, stirring occasionally, until it dries out, about 5 minutes.

Add the tomatoes, slosh out the can with water, and add that. Add the bay leaves and 4 quarts cold water. Bring to a boil and simmer rapidly, uncovered, to reduce the soup by about a quarter and concentrate the flavors, about 1 hour.

Add the lentils, cover, and cook about 15 to 20 minutes.

Add the salt and the rice, and stir. Simmer until rice is just al dente (don't overcook—it will cook more in the soup as you are serving) and the soup is thick and flavorful. Remove bay leaves. Serve the soup with a drizzle of olive oil and a sprinkle of grated cheese.

🌱 If you want to make this soup ahead, make it up to the point where you add the rice, then cool and refrigerate it. To serve: return the soup to a boil with a cup or so of extra water, add the rice, and cook as directed in the recipe.

Minestrone Soup with Pesto

Minestrone con Pesto
MAKES ABOUT 2½ TO 3 QUARTS

½ cup extra-virgin olive oil
2 medium leeks, white and light green parts, halved lengthwise and sliced
1 medium onion, chopped
1 tablespoon kosher salt
½ teaspoon crushed red pepper flakes
2 medium carrots, peeled and chopped into ½-inch pieces
2 celery stalks, chopped into ½-inch pieces
2 medium russet potatoes, peeled and cut into ½-inch dice (about 1¼ pounds)
2 tablespoons tomato paste
2 fresh bay leaves
4 cups shelled fresh borlotti beans
2 medium zucchini, chopped into ½-inch pieces (about ¾ pound)
1 medium head escarole, coarsely shredded (about 8 cups)
4 cups loosely packed fresh basil leaves
¼ cup pine nuts, toasted
Freshly grated Grana Padano, for serving

Heat a large Dutch oven over medium heat. Add ¼ cup of the olive oil. When the oil is hot, add the leeks and onion. Season with 1 teaspoon of the salt and the crushed red pepper flakes. Cook until leeks and onion have wilted but not colored, about 6 minutes.

Increase the heat to medium high and add the carrots, celery, and potatoes. Cook, stirring occasionally, until the potatoes begin to stick to the bottom of the pot, about 5 minutes. Make a space in the pan and add the tomato paste. Cook and stir in that spot until the tomato paste is toasted and darkens a shade or two. Increase heat to high. Add 5 quarts cold water and the bay leaves. Bring to a boil, uncovered. Let it cook vigorously to reduce and homogenize the flavors of the soup base, about 30 minutes.

Add the beans and zucchini, and cook until beans are almost tender, about 30 minutes more.

Add the escarole, and cook until it is tender and the soup is thick and flavorful, about 30 minutes more. Season with the remaining 2 teaspoons salt once the beans are cooked through. Remove bay leaves.

When ready to serve the soup, combine the basil and pine nuts with a pinch of salt in a food processor. With the processor running, add the remaining ¼ cup olive oil in a slow, steady stream to make a smooth pesto. Just before serving, swirl the pesto into the soup, and serve with a sprinkling of grated cheese.

❧ Fresh borlotti beans (also known as cranberry beans) are available seasonally and worth the little extra effort it takes to shell them. Depending on how full the pods are, buy about 2 to 2½ pounds of beans to yield the 4 cups needed here. If you can't find fresh borlotti beans, use one pound dried kidney beans, soak overnight, drain, and add with the carrots, celery, and potatoes.

Escarole and White Bean Soup

Zuppa di Scarola e Cannellini
SERVES 6

1½ cups dried cannellini, Great Northern, baby lima, or other small white beans
2 fresh bay leaves
½ cup extra-virgin olive oil
Kosher salt to taste
6 cups (approximately 1 head) coarsely shred-ded escarole leaves (preferably the tough outer leaves), washed and drained
8 garlic cloves, cut in half
4 to 6 whole dried peperoncini (hot red peppers)
Garlic bread or plain grilled country bread, for serving

The day before you want to make the soup, put the beans in a 2-to-3-quart container and pour in enough cold water to cover them by at least 4 inches. Let soak in a cool place at least 8 hours, or up to 24 hours.

Drain the beans thoroughly, and transfer to a large stockpot. Pour in 2 quarts of water, toss in the bay leaves, and bring to a boil. Adjust the heat to simmering, pour in half of the olive oil, and cook until the beans are tender and only an inch of liquid remains, 1 to 1½ hours.

Season the beans to taste with salt, then stir in the escarole and cook, stirring occasionally, until the escarole is quite tender, about 15 minutes. Remove bay leaves.

Heat the remaining olive oil in a small skillet over medium heat. Add the garlic and peppers and cook, shaking the pan, until the peppers change color, about 1 minute or less. Remove from the heat, and carefully—it will sputter quite a bit—pour one ladleful of soup into the skillet. Swirl the pan to blend the two, and then stir the panful of seasoned soup back into the large pot. Give it a boil, check the seasoning, and let the soup rest off the heat, covered, 10 to 15 minutes. Serve with garlic bread if you like, or grilled country bread.

Wedding Soup

Minestra Maritata
MAKES ABOUT 5 QUARTS, SERVING 12

FOR THE VEGETABLE SOUP
1 medium onion, cut into chunks
2 medium celery stalks with leaves, cut into chunks
1 small carrot, peeled and cut into chunks
4 garlic cloves
½ cup loosely packed fresh basil leaves
⅓ cup extra-virgin olive oil
1 head escarole (about 1 pound), cut into ½-inch shreds
1 bunch Swiss chard (about 1 pound), cut into ½-inch shreds
1 large fennel bulb (about 1 pound), trimmed and sliced ¼ inch thick
1 pound zucchini, cut into ½-inch pieces (about 3 small zucchini)
2 tablespoons kosher salt

FOR THE MEATBALLS
4 ounces stale country bread, crusts removed (about 3 or 4 slices)
½ cup milk, or more as needed
1 pound sweet Italian sausage without fennel seeds, removed from casings
1 large egg, beaten

½ teaspoon kosher salt, plus more for the pot
Freshly ground black pepper to taste
2 tablespoons chopped fresh Italian parsley

TO SERVE

Freshly grated pecorino (or half pecorino and
    half Grana Padano), plus more for passing
Extra-virgin olive oil, best quality, for drizzling

Using the food processor, pulse the onion, celery, carrot, garlic, and basil until they form a smooth paste or pestata. Heat the olive oil in a large soup pot over high heat, and scrape in the pestata. Cook, stirring, until the pestata has dried out and just begins to stick to the bottom of the pan, about 5 minutes.

Pour 7 quarts cold water into the pot, stir well, then cover and bring to a boil. Lower the heat, and simmer the broth for about 15 minutes, blending the flavors. Stir in the greens, fennel, zucchini, and salt. Return to a simmer, and cook, covered, for 30 minutes or so, until the greens are tender.

Remove the cover, and cook at an active simmer for another 30 minutes or longer, until the soup has reduced a bit in volume and the flavors are concentrated.

While the soup simmers, prepare the meatballs: Tear the bread into chunks, put them in a small bowl, and pour in just enough milk to cover them. Let soak until completely saturated, then lift the bread out of the bowl and squeeze out the milk with your fists. Tear the moistened bread into shreds, and toss them into a large bowl.

Crumble the sausage into the shredded bread, breaking up any clumps with your fingers. Pour the beaten egg over the meat, and sprinkle the salt, freshly ground black pepper, and parsley on top. Fold and toss and squeeze all the ingredients through your fingers to distribute them evenly. Scoop up a small amount of the meat mixture— about a heaping teaspoon—and roll it in your palms to form a 1-inch ball (the size of a large grape). Continue to form balls until all the meat is used up.

Meanwhile, fill a 4-quart saucepan with 3 quarts of lightly salted water to poach the meat-balls, and bring it to a boil. Drop in the meatballs, cover the pot, and return the water to a boil quickly. Adjust the heat to keep the water simmering gently, and poach the meatballs, uncovered, about 5 minutes, until cooked through. Lift them out with a spider or strainer, let drain briefly, and drop them into the finished soup. Bring the soup to a simmer, and cook meatballs and soup together for about 5 minutes.

Ladle the soup into warm bowls. Sprinkle each serving with some of the grated cheese, and give it a drizzle of your best olive oil. Serve right away, passing more cheese at the table.

Mushroom Soup

Zuppa di Funghi Misti
MAKES ABOUT 2½ TO 3 QUARTS

1 cup loosely packed dried porcini mushrooms
¼ cup extra-virgin olive oil, plus more for driz-
    zling
2 large shallots, chopped
1 large carrot, peeled, shredded on the coarse
    holes of a box grater or in a food processor
1½ pounds russet potatoes, peeled, shredded on
    the coarse holes of a box grater or in a food
    processor
2 tablespoons chopped fresh sage
1 tablespoon kosher salt
One 3-inch piece Grana Padano rind, rinsed
2 pounds mixed mushrooms, thickly sliced
    (button, cremini, shiitake, oyster, chanterelle,
    porcini)
½ cup chopped fresh Italian parsley
Freshly grated Grana Padano, for serving

Put porcini in a spouted measuring cup, and add 1 cup very hot water. Let soak until softened, about 10 minutes. Squeeze the porcini dry, reserving the soaking liquid. Chop the porcini and strain the soaking liquid through cheesecloth.

To a large Dutch oven over medium heat, add

the olive oil. When the oil is hot, add the shallots and sweat until wilted, about 5 minutes. Add the carrot and potatoes, and increase the heat to medium high. Cook until the potatoes begin to stick to the bottom of the pan, about 5 minutes, stirring occasionally. Add 5 quarts cold water, the porcini-soaking liquid, sage, salt, and cheese rind. Bring to a boil, and simmer to blend the flavors, about 20 minutes.

Add the sliced mushrooms and chopped soaked dried porcini. Return the soup to a boil. Simmer rapidly until the potatoes have dissolved to thicken the soup and the mushrooms are very tender, about 40 minutes. Stir in the parsley, and remove and discard the cheese rind. Serve the soup with a drizzle of olive oil and a sprinkle of grated cheese.

❧ For a heartier version of this soup, you can add ½ to 1 cup of rinsed barley when you add the mushrooms.

Farro and Chickpea Soup

Zuppa di Ceci e Farro
MAKES ABOUT 3½ QUARTS

1 pound dried chickpeas
2 ounces pancetta, cut into chunks
4 garlic cloves, crushed and peeled
1 tablespoon fresh rosemary leaves
1 tablespoon fresh sage leaves
5 tablespoons extra-virgin olive oil, plus more for drizzling
1 large onion, cut into chunks
2 large carrots, peeled and cut into chunks
2 celery stalks, cut into chunks
One 28-ounce can whole San Marzano tomatoes, crushed by hand
2 fresh bay leaves
1 tablespoon kosher salt
¼ teaspoon crushed red pepper flakes
1½ cups farro

Put the chickpeas in a bowl with water to cover by several inches. Refrigerate and soak overnight. Rinse and drain.

In a food processor, combine the pancetta, garlic, rosemary, and sage. Process to make a smooth paste or pestata.

Heat a large Dutch oven over medium-high heat. Add the olive oil. When the oil is hot, add the pestata and cook to render the fat from the pancetta, about 5 minutes.

Meanwhile, in the same food-processor work bowl, combine the onion, carrots, and celery, and process to make a second smooth pestata. Add to the pot and cook, stirring occasionally, until mixture dries out and begins to stick to the bottom of the pot, about 10 minutes.

Add the tomatoes, slosh out the can with water, and add that as well. Add 5 quarts water, the drained chickpeas, and the bay leaves. Bring to a boil, uncovered, and simmer rapidly until chickpeas are tender but not falling apart and soup has reduced by about a third and thickened, about 1 hour to 1 hour and 15 minutes, depending on the age of your chickpeas.

Add the salt, red pepper flakes, and farro, and simmer until just tender, about 20 to 25 minutes. Remove bay leaves. Serve soup drizzled with olive oil.

Fresh Chestnut and Winter Squash Soup

Zuppa di Castagne e Zucca
SERVES 6

8 cups Rice and Potato Soup (page 146)
½ teaspoon kosher salt, plus more to taste
Freshly ground black pepper to taste
1½ cups peeled chestnuts, cut into bits and chunks (about 8 ounces)
1½ cups ⅓-inch pieces peeled winter squash
1 cup sliced, finely chopped leek, white and light green parts

Freshly grated Grana Padano, for serving
Extra-virgin olive oil, for drizzling

Heat the broth to a boil. Stir in the ½ teaspoon salt, or more if the broth is bland, and a few grinds of black pepper. Stir in all the chestnut, squash, and leek pieces; return to a steady, perking boil. Cover, and cook for 45 minutes to an hour, until the vegetables have softened, melted, and thickened the soup. Stir frequently, and lower the heat as the soup thickens. Cook uncovered if you want a thicker soup; add water to thin it.

Taste, and adjust the seasonings. Serve hot in warm bowls, with freshly grated cheese and a drizzle of olive oil.

Pasta and Beans

Pasta e Fagioli
MAKES 5½ QUARTS, SERVING 12

1½ pounds dried cannellini beans
4 large potatoes (about 2½ pounds), peeled
3 sprigs fresh rosemary
2 fresh bay leaves
12 slices bacon, cut crosswise into ½-inch strips (about 1 cup)
4 garlic cloves
¼ cup extra-virgin olive oil, plus more for drizzling
1 medium onion, chopped (about 1 cup)
2 medium carrots, peeled and coarsely shredded (about 1 cup)
2 cups canned Italian plum tomatoes, preferably San Marzano, crushed by hand
Kosher salt and freshly ground black pepper
3 cups ditalini or elbow pasta
Freshly grated Grana Padano

The day before you want to make the soup, put the beans into a 3- or 4-quart container and pour in enough cold water to cover them by at least 4 inches. Let soak in a cool place at least 8 hours or up to 24 hours. Drain well.

Pour 8 quarts water into a tall, large (at least 10-quart) pot. Add the drained beans, potatoes, rosemary, and bay leaves. Bring to a rolling boil over high heat, then adjust the heat to a gentle boil. Let cook while preparing the sautéed vegetables.

Process the bacon and garlic to a paste in a food processor, stopping once or twice to scrape down the sides of the bowl. Heat the oil in a large skillet over medium heat, then scrape in the bacon-garlic paste and cook, stirring, until golden, about 5 minutes. Stir in the onion and cook, stirring, until translucent, about 4 minutes. Stir in the carrots and cook until the onions begin to brown, about 5 minutes. Add the crushed tomatoes, bring to a boil, then lower the heat and simmer for 5 minutes.

Pour two ladlefuls of the bean-cooking water into the skillet, and bring to a boil; then pour the contents of the skillet back into the soup pot. Season lightly with salt and pepper, and bring to a slow boil. Cook until the beans are tender, about 45 minutes to 1 hour.

Ladle about a third of the beans, along with enough cooking liquid to cover them, into a baking dish or other shallow container where they will cool quickly. Once the beans are just warm, process them and the liquid in a food processor or blender until creamy. Return the puréed beans to the pot.

Remove bay leaves and rosemary. Fish out the potatoes to a plate, mash them coarsely with a fork, and return them to the pot. Cook the soup another 10 minutes to give the flavors a chance to blend. Let the soup rest off the heat, covered, 10 to 15 minutes.

While the soup is resting, cook the ditalini or elbow pasta in salted water until very al dente. Drain thoroughly, and stir into the soup. Let all rest for 5 minutes, then serve in warm soup bowls, with a drizzle of extra-virgin olive oil and a sprinkle of Grana Padano.

🦋 If you plan to serve all of the soup at once, an alternative is to cook the pasta directly in the soup. The soup will be a bit denser.

Pork, Sauerkraut, and Bean Soup

Jota
SERVES 8 OR MORE

2 cups dried red kidney beans
1-pound chunk fresh pork butt, rinsed before
    cooking
3 fresh bay leaves
2 tablespoons chopped garlic
2 pounds potatoes, peeled and cut into 3-inch
    chunks
2 pounds sauerkraut (preferably the bagged,
    refrigerated variety)
1 tablespoon kosher salt, plus more to taste
½ pound smoked pork sausage, such as kielbasa
½ pound fresh pork sausage, Eastern European
    style or sweet Italian
Freshly ground black pepper to taste
Extra-virgin olive oil, for serving

The day before you want to make the soup, rinse the beans and soak in 8 cups cold water overnight. Drain and put them in a large Dutch oven with 5 quarts cold water, the pork butt, bay leaves, chopped garlic, and potato chunks. Cover the pot and bring to a boil, set the cover slightly ajar, and adjust the heat to maintain a steady, gentle perk; cook until beans and pork are tender, about 1½ hours.

Meanwhile, drain the liquid from the packaged sauerkraut, rinse it in a big bowl filled with fresh water, and drain through a colander. Repeat the rinsing and draining.

When the beans, pork, and potatoes are soft, add 1 tablespoon salt to the broth. Push the pork butt aside, and roughly mash the potato chunks in the bottom of the pot. Dump in the rinsed sauerkraut, stir well, cover the pot, and return to a moderate boil. Uncover and cook for about 30 minutes, stirring occasionally, gradually reducing the soup.

Rinse the sausages, drop them into the pot, and cook for another 30 minutes. If the soup seems thin, boil it uncovered and mash the potatoes more, if they're still chunky, to provide thicken-ing. When the sausages are cooked and the soup has the consistency you like, turn off the heat. Remove the bay leaves and season generously with black pepper and salt to taste. You may serve the soup right away, but for the best flavor, serve the next day. Reheat slowly, stirring frequently to prevent scorching. When it is very hot, remove the sausages and the remainder of the pork butt (most of it will have broken up) to serve later as a separate course. Drizzle extra-virgin olive oil over the jota and stir in. Serve portions of broth with beans and sauerkraut in warm soup bowls.

SAUCES

A pancia piena si consulta meglia.
—Italian proverb

You think better with a full belly.

Marinara Sauce

Marinara

**MAKES ABOUT I QUART, ENOUGH TO DRESS
6 SERVINGS OF PASTA**

¼ cup extra-virgin olive oil
8 garlic cloves
3 pounds ripe fresh plum tomatoes, peeled and
    seeded, or one 35-ounce can Italian plum
    tomatoes, preferably San Marzano, crushed
    by hand
Kosher salt to taste
Crushed red pepper flakes to taste
10 fresh basil leaves, torn into small pieces

Heat the oil in a 2-to-3-quart saucepan over
medium heat. Whack the peeled garlic with the
flat side of a knife, add it to the oil, and cook
until lightly browned, about 2 minutes. Carefully slide the tomatoes and their juices into the
oil. Add 1 cup water (use it to slosh out the can,
if using canned tomatoes). Bring to a boil, and
season lightly with salt and crushed red pepper.
Lower the heat so the sauce is at a lively simmer, and cook, breaking up the tomatoes with
a whisk or spoon, until the sauce is chunky and
thick—about 30 minutes for fresh tomatoes, 20
for canned.

Stir in the basil about 5 minutes before the
sauce is finished. Taste the sauce, and season with
more salt and red pepper flakes if necessary.

Tomato Sauce

Salsa di Pomodoro

**MAKES ABOUT I GENEROUS QUART, ENOUGH TO
DRESS 6 TO 8 SERVINGS OF PASTA**

¼ cup extra-virgin olive oil
1 small onion, chopped (about ½ cup)
¼ cup peeled and finely shredded carrot
¼ cup finely chopped celery, including leaves

Two 35-ounce cans whole San Marzano toma-
    toes, crushed by hand
4 fresh bay leaves
Kosher salt to taste
Crushed red pepper flakes to taste

Heat the oil in a medium Dutch oven over
medium heat. Stir in the onion and cook, stirring
occasionally, until wilted, about 3 minutes. Add
the carrot and celery and cook, stirring occasionally, until golden, about 10 minutes.

Add the tomatoes and bay leaves. Slosh out the
tomato cans with 2 cups of water and add that
as well. Bring everything to a boil. Season lightly
with salt and crushed red pepper. Lower the heat
so the sauce is at a lively simmer, and cook, stirring occasionally, until thickened, about 45 minutes. Remove the bay leaves. Taste, and season
with more salt and red pepper if necessary.

Raw Summer Tomato Sauce for Pasta

Salsa di Pomodoro Crudo

**MAKES 3 TO 4 CUPS, ENOUGH TO DRESS I POUND
COOKED DRIED PASTA**

2 pounds ripe summer tomatoes
2 to 3 garlic cloves
½ teaspoon kosher salt
6 large basil leaves
¼ teaspoon crushed red pepper flakes, or to taste
½ cup extra-virgin olive oil
1 cup or more freshly grated Grana Padano or
    cubed fresh mozzarella (optional)

Rinse the tomatoes, drain, and wipe dry. Cut
out the core and any other tough parts. Working
over a big mixing bowl to catch all the juices, cut
the tomatoes—cherry tomatoes in half, regular
tomatoes into 1-inch chunks—and drop them in
the bowl.

Smash the garlic cloves with a chef's knife, peel, and chop into a fine paste (easier if you add some of the salt as you chop; mash the garlic bits and salt with the flat side of the knife, too). Scatter the garlic paste and the rest of the salt (½ teaspoon in all) over the tomatoes, and stir gently. Pile up the basil leaves and cut into thin strips. Scatter these over the tomatoes, then sprinkle in the crushed red pepper. Pour in the oil; stir and fold to coat the tomatoes and distribute the seasonings.

Cover the bowl with plastic wrap, and let the sauce marinate at room temperature for 1 to 2 hours. Toss the marinated sauce with freshly cooked and drained pasta. Serve as is, or toss in 1 cup grated Grana Padano, or for extra richness, add 1 cup or more cubed fresh mozzarella.

❧ This recipe requires ripe and juicy homegrown tomatoes or heirloom tomatoes from the farmers' market. Be sure to have them at room temperature, because the sauce actually develops in the hour or two it marinates: salt draws the juices from the tomatoes, and they become infused with the flavors of basil and garlic. Then all you do is toss piping-hot pasta with the tomatoes and enjoy one of the rare treats of summer.

Meat Sauce Bolognese

Sugo alla Bolognese
MAKES 6 CUPS, ENOUGH TO DRESS ABOUT
1½ POUNDS COOKED DRIED PASTA

3 tablespoons extra-virgin olive oil
1 medium yellow onion, minced (about 1 cup)
1 medium carrot, peeled and finely shredded (about ½ cup)
½ cup minced celery, with leaves
1 pound ground beef
1 pound ground pork
½ cup dry red wine

1 tablespoon tomato paste
3 cups canned Italian plum tomatoes, preferably San Marzano, crushed by hand or passed through a food mill
3 fresh bay leaves
2 teaspoons kosher salt
Freshly ground black pepper to taste

Bring 4 cups water to a simmer in a small saucepan, and keep hot. Heat the olive oil in a large Dutch oven over medium heat. When the oil is hot, add the onion, carrot, and celery, and cook, stirring, until the onion is translucent, about 7 minutes.

Crumble in the ground beef and pork, and continue cooking, stirring to break up the meat, until all the liquid the meat has given off has evaporated and the meat is lightly browned, about 10 minutes.

Pour in the wine, and cook, scraping the bottom of the pan, until the wine is evaporated, 3 to 4 minutes. Add in the tomato paste into a bare spot in the pan and cook a few minutes, then pour in the tomatoes, toss in the bay leaves, and season with the salt and some pepper. Bring to a boil, then lower the heat so the sauce is at a lively simmer. Cook, stirring occasionally, until the sauce is dense but juicy and a rich dark red color. This will take about 2 to 3 hours—the longer you cook it, the better it will become. While the sauce is cooking, add hot water as necessary to keep the meats and vegetables covered. (Most likely, a noticeable layer of oil will float to the top toward the end of cooking. When you are done, the oil can be removed with a spoon or reincorporated in the sauce, which is what is traditionally done.)

Traditional Bolognese Sauce

Ricetta Tradizionale, Ragù alla Bolognese
MAKES ABOUT 3 QUARTS, ENOUGH TO DRESS
6 POUNDS COOKED PASTA

2 pounds ground beef
2 pounds ground pork
2 cups dry white wine
6 ounces bacon or pancetta
⅓ cup garlic cloves (about 6 fat cloves)
2 tablespoons extra-virgin olive oil
2 medium onions, minced in a food processor or
    finely chopped
2 large celery stalks, minced in a food processor
    or finely chopped
1 carrot, peeled and shredded
½ teaspoon kosher salt, plus more to taste
8 to 12 cups (or more) hot Chicken Stock
    (page 143), Vegetable Stock (page 143), or
    plain hot water
2 cups dry red wine
2 tablespoons tomato paste
2 cups canned Italian plum tomatoes, preferably
    San Marzano, and juices, passed through a
    food mill or crushed by hand
Freshly ground black pepper to taste

Put all 4 pounds of ground meat in a large mixing bowl. With your fingers, crumble and loosen it all up; then toss and crumble the beef and pork together. Pour the white wine over it, and work all the meat through your fingers again so it's evenly moistened.

To make the pestata: Cut the bacon or pancetta into 1-inch pieces, and put them in the bowl of a food processor with the peeled garlic. Process them into a fine paste.

Pour the olive oil into a large Dutch oven, and scrape in all of the pestata. Set the pan over medium-high heat, break up the pestata, and stir it around the pan bottom to start rendering the fat. Cook until the fat is rendered, about 3 or 4 minutes.

Stir the minced onions into the fat, and cook for a couple of minutes, until sizzling and starting to sweat. Stir in the celery and carrot, and cook until the vegetables are wilted and golden, stirring frequently and thoroughly, over medium-high heat, about 5 minutes or more.

Turn the heat up a notch, push the vegetables off to the side, and plop all the meat into the pan; sprinkle the salt on. Give the meat on the pan bottom a few moments to brown, then stir, spread, and toss with a sturdy spoon, mixing the meat into the vegetables and making sure every bit of meat browns and begins releasing fat and juices. Soon the meat liquid will almost cover the meat itself. Cook at high heat, stirring often, until all that liquid has disappeared, even in the bottom of the pan, about 30 to 45 minutes, depending on the heat and the width of the pan. Stir occasionally, and as the liquid level diminishes, lower the heat so the meat doesn't burn.

Warm the broth in a medium saucepan.

When all the meat liquid has been cooked off, pour in the red wine. Cook until the wine has almost completely evaporated, about 5 minutes. Add the tomato paste into a clear space on the pan bottom. Toast a minute in the hot spot, then stir to blend it with the meat, and let it caramelize for 2 or 3 minutes. Stir in the crushed tomatoes; slosh the tomato container out with a cup of hot broth and add that. Bring the liquid to a boil, stirring the meat, and let the liquid almost boil off, 5 minutes more.

Pour in 2 cups of hot broth, stir well, and add more if needed to cover the meat. Bring it to an active simmer, cover the pan, and adjust the heat to maintain slow, steady cooking, with small bubbles perking all over the surface of the sauce. From this point, the Bolognese should cook for 3 more hours. Check the pot every 20 minutes and add hot broth as needed to cover the meat. The liquid level should be reducing by 1½ to 2 cups between additions. Adjust the heat if the sauce is reducing faster than that or not as fast. Stir often to make sure the bottom doesn't burn.

During the final interval of cooking, you want to reduce the level of the liquid—once broth, but now a highly developed sauce. At the end, the meat should no longer be covered but appear suspended in a thick, flowing medium. If the meat is still submerged in a lot of liquid, remove the cover completely to cook off moisture quickly. A few minutes before the end of cooking, taste a bit of meat and sauce, and add salt if you want. Grind 1 teaspoon of black pepper right into the sauce, stir it in, and cook about 5 minutes before removing the pan from the heat. If you'll be using the sauce right away, spoon off the fat from the surface, or stir it in, as is done traditionally. Otherwise, let the sauce cool, then chill it thoroughly and lift off the solidified fat. Store the sauce for several days in the refrigerator, or freeze it (in measured amounts for different dishes) for use within a few months.

Traditional Recipe for Bolognese Sauce with Milk

Ragù alla Bolognese, Ricetta Antica con Latte
MAKES ABOUT 3 QUARTS, ENOUGH TO DRESS
6 POUNDS COOKED PASTA

2 pounds ground beef
2 pounds ground pork
2 cups dry white wine
6 ounces bacon or pancetta
⅓ cup garlic cloves (about 6 fat cloves)
2 tablespoons extra-virgin olive oil
2 medium onions, minced in a food processor or finely chopped
2 large celery stalks, minced in a food processor or finely chopped
1 carrot, peeled and shredded
½ teaspoon kosher salt, plus more to taste
8 cups very hot milk
2 cups or more hot Chicken Broth (page 143) or Vegetable Stock (page 143)
6 tablespoons tomato paste
Nutmeg for grating (to make ½ teaspoon, or more to taste)
Freshly ground black pepper

Put all 4 pounds of ground meat in a large mixing bowl. With your fingers, crumble and loosen it all up; then toss and crumble the beef and pork together. Pour the white wine over it, and work all the meat through your fingers again so it's evenly moistened.

To make the pestata: Cut the bacon or pancetta into 1-inch pieces, and put them in the bowl of a food processor with the peeled garlic. Process them into a fine paste.

Pour the olive oil into a large Dutch oven, and scrape in all of the pestata. Set the pan over medium-high heat, break up the pestata, and stir it around the pan bottom to start rendering the fat. Cook until the fat is rendered, about 3 or 4 minutes.

Stir the minced onions into the fat, and cook for a couple of minutes, until sizzling and starting to sweat. Stir in the celery and carrot, and cook until the vegetables are wilted and golden, stirring frequently and thoroughly, over medium-high heat, about 5 minutes or more.

Turn the heat up a notch, push the vegetables off to the side, and plop all the meat into the pan; sprinkle the salt on. Give the meat on the pan bottom a few moments to brown, then stir, spread, and toss with a sturdy spoon, mixing the meat into the vegetables and making sure every bit of meat browns and begins releasing fat and juices. Soon the meat liquid will almost cover the meat itself. Cook at high heat, stirring often, until all that liquid has disappeared, even in the bottom of the pan, about 30 to 45 minutes, depending on the heat and the width of the pan. Stir occasionally, and as the liquid level diminishes, lower the heat so the meat doesn't burn.

Warm the milk and broth together in a medium saucepan.

When all the meat liquid has been cooked off, drop tomato paste into a clear space on the pan bottom. Toast it for a minute in the hot spot, then stir to blend it with the meat and cook for another 2 or 3 minutes.

Pour in 2 cups of the hot milk and broth, and stir into the meat; add more milk and broth if needed to bring the level just over the top of the meat. Add the grated nutmeg. Bring the sauce liquid to an active simmer, cover the pan, and adjust the heat to maintain slow, steady cooking, with small bubbles perking all over the surface of the sauce.

From this point, the Bolognese should cook for 3 more hours. Check the pot every 20 minutes, and add hot milk and broth as needed to cover the meat. The liquid level should be reducing by 1½ to 2 cups between additions, so you'll need to have warm water ready to replenish the sauce after all the milk and broth have been added. Adjust the heat if the sauce is reducing faster than that or not as fast. Stir often to make sure the bottom doesn't burn.

During the final interval of cooking, you want to reduce the level of the liquid—once milk and broth, but now a highly developed sauce. At the end, the meat should no longer be covered but appear suspended in a thick, flowing medium. If the meat is still submerged in a lot of liquid, remove the cover completely to cook off moisture quickly. A few minutes before the end of cooking, taste a bit of meat and sauce, and add salt if you want. Grind 1 teaspoon of black pepper right into the sauce, stir it in, and cook about 5 minutes before removing the pan from the heat. If you'll be using the sauce right away, spoon off the fat from the surface, or stir it in, as is done traditionally. Otherwise, let the sauce cool, then chill it thoroughly and lift off the solidified fat. Store the sauce for several days in the refrigerator, or freeze it (in measured amounts for different dishes) for use within a few months.

Italian American Meat Sauce

Sugo di Carne Italo-Americano
MAKES ABOUT 8 CUPS, ENOUGH TO FILL AND
SAUCE LASAGNA OR TO DRESS ABOUT 2 POUNDS
COOKED PASTA

Two 35-ounce cans Italian plum tomatoes,
    preferably San Marzano
¼ cup extra-virgin olive oil
2 medium onions, diced (about 2 cups)
6 to 8 garlic cloves, finely chopped
5 or 6 meaty pork neck bones (about
    ¾ pound—ask your butcher to set them
    aside for you)
1 pound ground beef
1 pound ground pork
2 teaspoons kosher salt
4 fresh bay leaves
1½ teaspoons dried oregano, preferably Sicilian
    on the branch
¾ cup dry white wine
⅓ cup tomato paste

Bring 4 cups water just to a simmer in a saucepan, and keep hot. Pass the tomatoes and their liquid through a food mill, or crush by hand. Set aside.

Heat the olive oil in a large Dutch oven over medium heat. Add the onions and cook, stirring occasionally, until golden, about 8 minutes. Make a little room in the center of the pot to dump in the garlic, and cook until the garlic is lightly browned. Add the pork bones and cook, turning, until the bones are lightly browned on all sides, about 5 minutes. Add the ground beef and pork, and season lightly with salt. Cook, stirring to break up the meat, until the meat turns from pink to pale brown and the liquid it gives off is boiled away, about 10 minutes. Continue cooking until the meat is browned, about 5 minutes. Add the bay leaves, remaining salt, and oregano, then pour in the wine. Bring to a boil, and cook, scraping up the brown bits that cling to the pot, until the wine is almost completely evaporated.

Pour the tomatoes into the pot, then stir in the tomato paste until it is dissolved. Bring to a boil, adjust the heat to a lively simmer, and cook, uncovered, stirring often, until the sauce is very thick and takes on a deep brick-red color, 2 to 3 hours. Add the hot water, about ½ cup at a time, to maintain the level of liquid for the length of time the sauce cooks. Skim off any fat floating on top, and adjust the seasoning as necessary. Remove the bones, and bay leaves and serve to dress your favorite pasta. The sauce can be prepared entirely in advance and refrigerated for up to 5 days, or frozen for up to 3 months, so any extra sauce will keep well.

Mushroom Ragù

Ragù di Funghi Misti

MAKES ABOUT 6 CUPS, ENOUGH TO DRESS 3 POUNDS COOKED PASTA

½ ounce dried porcini (about ½ cup loosely packed pieces)
4 cups Chicken Stock (page 143) or Vegetable Stock (page 143)
3 sprigs fresh thyme
1 sprig fresh rosemary
1 sprig fresh sage
¼ cup extra-virgin olive oil
4 tablespoons unsalted butter
1 cup finely chopped shallots
1 medium onion, finely chopped (about 1 cup)
½ teaspoon kosher salt, plus more to taste
2½ pounds small, firm fresh mixed mushrooms (button, cremini, shiitake, oyster, chanterelle, porcini, etc.), sliced ¼ inch thick
⅓ cup tomato paste
1 cup dry Marsala
Freshly ground black pepper

Put the dried porcini in a spouted measuring cup, and cover with 1½ cups very hot water. Let soak until softened, about 15 minutes. Squeeze out the soaked porcini and slice them into pieces

about ¼ inch wide. Strain the soaking water, and reserve. Heat the stock to just a simmer in a small saucepan and keep hot. Tie the sprigs of fresh herbs together with a piece of kitchen twine.

Put the oil and butter in a large skillet or shallow Dutch oven, and place over medium heat. When the butter melts, add the shallots and onion and half the salt, and stir well. Heat to a slow sizzle, and cook until the onions are soft but not brown, about 6 minutes.

Add all the mushrooms, including the soaked porcini, to the pan, and spread them out. Sprinkle in the remaining salt, drop in the herb bouquet, then toss briefly and cover the pan. Raise the heat a bit, and cook, covered, for about 3 minutes, shaking the pan now and then, to sweat the mushrooms.

Uncover, and continue to cook over fairly high heat, stirring frequently, as the mushrooms shrink and the liquid evaporates, 5 minutes or more. When the pan is dry and the mushrooms begin to brown, clear a hot spot, drop in the tomato paste, and toast it, stirring, for a minute or so, then stir it into the mushrooms.

When everything is browning again and just starting to stick, pour in the Marsala. Stir constantly as the wine thickens and evaporates. When the mushrooms again start sticking to the bottom, pour in the warm porcini-soaking water and 2 cups of the hot stock. Bring to an active boil, stirring up any caramelization on the pan bottom. Lower the heat to a simmer, and cover. Cook for about 20 minutes, occasionally stirring and adding stock to keep the mushrooms nearly covered in liquid.

Uncover the pan, and cook for another 20 minutes, maintaining the simmer and adding stock as needed. When the mushrooms are thoroughly tender and the sauce has just thickened, remove and discard the sprigs of herbs. Taste, and add salt, if needed, and freshly ground black pepper to taste. This sauce freezes well, so you can store whatever extra you may have.

Classic Pesto

Pesto alla Genovese
MAKES ABOUT ¾ CUP, ENOUGH TO DRESS
I POUND COOKED PASTA

4 cups loosely packed fresh basil leaves, gently
  washed and dried
¼ teaspoon kosher salt
2 garlic cloves
3 tablespoons pine nuts, toasted
2 tablespoons freshly grated Pecorino Romano
2 tablespoons freshly grated Grana Padano
3 to 4 tablespoons extra-virgin olive oil

To make the pesto in a mortar: Place a few basil
leaves in the bottom of a mortar, and sprinkle the
salt over them. Crush the leaves coarsely with the
pestle, add a few more leaves, and continue crushing, adding new leaves each time those in the
mortar are crushed, until all the leaves are coarsely
ground. Toss in the garlic, and pound until the
mixture forms a smooth paste. Add the pine nuts,
and grind them to a paste. Stir in the cheese, then
enough of the olive oil to give the pesto a creamy
consistency.

To make the pesto in a food processor: Combine the basil, salt, and garlic in the work bowl,
add 2 tablespoons of the oil, and blend at low
speed, stopping frequently to press the basil
down around the blades, until the basil forms a
coarse paste. Toss in the pine nuts, and pour in
the remaining 2 tablespoons olive oil. Blend until
the pine nuts are finely ground. Stir in the grated
cheeses.

Pesto is at its best when used immediately
after it is made, though it can be refrigerated
for up to a few weeks if it's spooned into a container, topped with olive oil, and sealed tightly to
minimize oxidation. If you find yourself with an
abundance of basil in the summer, make some
pesto and store it in jars or containers, in portions, in the freezer, where it will last for several
months.

To serve: Toss the pesto with the cooked
drained pasta, adding a few spoons of the pasta-
cooking water. Pesto should not be heated or
cooked, because it loses its fragrance.

Basil, Parsley, and Walnut Pesto

Pesto di Basilico, Prezzemolo e Noci
MAKES ABOUT I½ CUPS, ENOUGH TO DRESS
I POUND COOKED PASTA

1½ cups loosely packed fresh basil leaves
1 cup loosely packed fresh Italian parsley leaves
4 garlic cloves
2 cups walnut halves or pieces, toasted
1 teaspoon kosher salt
½ cup extra-virgin olive oil
1 cup freshly grated Pecorino Romano (or half
  pecorino and half Grana Padano, for a milder
  flavor), plus more for passing

Combine the basil, parsley, garlic, walnuts,
and salt in the work bowl of a food processor.
Pulse several times, to chop everything together
coarsely; then, with the machine running, pour
in the ½ cup olive oil in a slow, steady stream.
Stop and scrape down the sides of the work bowl,
and process to a uniformly fine bright green pesto.

To store and use the pesto later: Scrape it from
the food processor into a small jar or container.
Smooth the top surface, and cover it with a thin
layer of olive oil or a piece of plastic wrap to prevent discoloration. Refrigerate up to a week, or
freeze for several months; warm to room temperature before using. Combine with the cheese only
when you sauce the pasta.

To serve: Toss the hot drained pasta with the
pesto, adding a few spoons of pasta-cooking water.
Do not heat the pesto—it loses its fragrance.

Butter and Sage Sauce

Salsa al Burro e Salvia

**MAKES ABOUT I CUP, ENOUGH TO DRESS
I POUND COOKED PASTA**

1½ sticks unsalted butter
10 fresh sage leaves
1 cup very hot water from the cooking pot of
    your pasta of choice
¼ teaspoon freshly ground black pepper, or to
    taste
1 cup freshly grated Grana Padano

Heat the butter in a large skillet over medium heat until melted and just foaming. Gently lay the sage leaves in the pan, and heat until they crisp up, about a minute.

Ladle in 1 cup boiling pasta water; stir the sauce, and simmer for about 2 minutes, to reduce liquid by half. Grind the black pepper directly into the sauce.

Keep the sauce hot over very low heat; then return sauce to a simmer just before adding the drained pasta. Toss the pasta in the sauce until well coated. Remove from heat and toss in the cheese just before serving.

Béchamel Sauce

Salsa Besciamella

MAKES ABOUT I QUART

1 quart milk
Kosher salt
Freshly ground white pepper
¼ teaspoon freshly grated nutmeg
1 fresh bay leaf
3 tablespoons unsalted butter
¼ cup all-purpose flour
⅓ cup freshly grated Grana Padano

Pour the milk into a medium saucepan, season lightly with salt and pepper, and add the nutmeg and bay leaf. Heat over medium-low heat until bubbles form around the edge. Remove and keep hot.

Melt the butter in a separate medium saucepan over medium heat. When it starts to foam, dump in the flour and whisk until smooth. Continue cooking, whisking constantly, until the flour mixture just changes color, about 3 to 4 minutes.

Pour the seasoned hot milk into the flour mixture in a steady stream, whisking constantly. Cook the sauce, whisking constantly and paying special attention to the bottom and corners of the pan, until the sauce comes to a simmer. Adjust the heat to a slow boil and cook, whisking constantly, until the sauce is thickened, about 3 minutes.

Strain the sauce through a fine sieve into a clean bowl, and stir in the grated cheese. The sauce will keep at room temperature for up to a few hours.

VEGETABLES AND SIDES

Ogni frutto ha la sua stagione.
—Italian proverb

Every fruit has its season.

Garlic Braised Asparagus

Asparagi all'Aglio
SERVES 4 TO 6 AS A SIDE

2 small bunches asparagus, medium thickness
    (about 1½ pounds)
3 tablespoons extra-virgin olive oil
6 garlic cloves, crushed and peeled
Zest of 1 lemon, peeled in strips with a zester
Kosher salt to taste

Snap off and discard woody stems from the asparagus, and peel about halfway up from the bottom. Wash well and drain.

To a large skillet over medium-high heat, add the olive oil. When the oil is hot, add the garlic. Once the garlic is sizzling and golden on the edges, about 1 to 2 minutes, add the asparagus, ½ cup hot water, lemon zest, and salt. Cover, and let simmer until the asparagus is almost tender, about 5 minutes.

Uncover and increase the heat so the pan sauce reduces to glaze the asparagus, about 2 to 3 minutes. Remove the garlic and lemon zest, and serve.

Roasted Cheese Asparagus

Asparagi al Forno con Formaggio Grattugiato
SERVES 4 TO 6 AS A SIDE

4 tablespoons extra-virgin olive oil
2 bunches asparagus, medium thickness (about
    1½ pounds)
½ teaspoon kosher salt
½ cup freshly grated Grana Padano

Preheat the oven to 450 degrees. Brush a rimmed sheet pan large enough to hold all the asparagus flat, without overlapping, with a tablespoon of the olive oil. (Or use two pans.)

Snap off and discard the woody stems from the asparagus, and peel about halfway up from the bottom. In a large bowl, toss the asparagus with the remaining oil and the salt. Spread the asparagus in the oiled roasting pan(s). Roast on the bottom rack until the asparagus is almost tender, about 8 to 10 minutes, then sprinkle the cheese evenly to cover all asparagus, transfer to the top rack, and roast until the cheese is browned and the asparagus is tender, about 5 minutes more. Serve hot.

Marinated Artichokes

Carciofi Marinati
SERVES 6 AS A SIDE

2 lemons
24 baby artichokes (about 3 pounds)
¼ cup extra-virgin olive oil
8 garlic cloves, crushed and peeled
2 tablespoons chopped fresh Italian parsley
1 tablespoon chopped fresh mint
2 teaspoons kosher salt
¼ teaspoon crushed red pepper flakes

Remove the peel from the lemons with a vegetable peeler. Juice the lemons. Pour half of the juice into a large bowl filled with cold water, and add the squeezed-out lemon halves. Reserve the remaining lemon juice.

Peel and trim the stems from the artichokes. Pull off any tough outer leaves and discard. With a paring knife, trim away any tough parts around the base of the artichoke. With a serrated knife, cut off the top third of the artichoke and discard. Add the artichokes to the bowl of lemon water as you clean them.

Drain the cleaned artichokes thoroughly. Arrange them snugly, cut side down, in a large Dutch oven. Pour the olive oil and remaining lemon juice into the pot. Scatter the garlic, parsley, mint, and lemon strips over the artichokes, up to but not over the base of the stems. Add

1½ cups water, the salt, and crushed red pepper flakes, cover the pot loosely with the aluminum foil, and bring to a boil over high heat. Adjust the heat to a simmer, and cook about 20 minutes; uncover, and cook 15 additional minutes, until the artichokes are tender and about a third of the liquid is left. Let the artichokes cool to room temperature in the cooking liquid. Serve at room temperature with some of the cooking liquid as a sauce.

Artichokes, Fresh Fava Beans, and Potatoes

Ciaudedda

SERVES 6 OR MORE AS A SIDE

1½ pounds russet potatoes
3 pounds fresh fava beans, shelled (about 1 pound cleaned)
6 medium artichokes (about 3 pounds)
1 lemon
6 tablespoons extra-virgin olive oil
4 ounces pancetta or bacon, cut into ½-inch pieces
2 small onions, thinly sliced
½ teaspoon crushed red pepper flakes, or to taste
2 teaspoons kosher salt

Put the potatoes in a pot with water to cover them by about 2 inches, and bring to a boil. Cook just until the potatoes are easily pierced with a knife blade, then drain and cool. Peel, and cut the potatoes crosswise into round slices about ½ inch thick.

For the favas: Bring a large pot of water to a boil, and add the shelled favas. Blanch about 2 minutes, until they turn bright green. Drain, and plunge into a large bowl of ice water. When they are chilled, drain the favas again, and peel off (and discard) the skins. You should have about 2 cups peeled favas.

For the artichokes: Fill a large bowl with cold water, and squeeze in the juice of the lemon, dropping in the cut lemon halves, too. Snap off the thick outside artichoke leaves; cut off the top third of the remaining leaf tips, and trim the stem tip. With a paring knife from the globe of the artichoke, remove the stubs of the snapped leaves and the skin covering the stem, to expose the lighter-colored tender flesh. Slice the artichoke in half lengthwise, and scrape out the choke with a paring knife or the edge of a teaspoon. Slice the artichoke halves into ½-inch-thick wedges, and drop them into the bowl of water.

Pour 4 tablespoons of the olive oil into a big skillet, set it over medium heat, and scatter in the pancetta pieces. Cook for 5 minutes, stirring occasionally, as the pancetta renders its fat, then stir in the onion slices, sprinkle in the red pepper flakes, and cook until the onions are sizzling and wilted, about 5 minutes. Drain the artichokes, and add them to the pan; stir, and toss gently to coat with oil. Cover the skillet, and cook for about 15 minutes, until the artichokes are tender, stirring now and then. Spread the sliced potato rounds in the pan, scatter the favas on top, and turn them over with a stiff spatula, mixing them with the hot vegetables. Cover, and cook for 10 minutes or so, stirring and turning the vegetables over gently so the potatoes don't break apart too much. If they're sticking to the bottom of the skillet, loosen with a few tablespoons of water, scrape them up, and turn them over. If there's liquid in the pan, remove the cover and cook it away over slightly higher heat. When the potatoes start to brown, sprinkle on the salt, and drizzle the remaining 2 tablespoons olive oil all over. Cook, uncovered, for another 5 to 10 minutes, occasionally lifting and tumbling the vegetables over with the spatula. As you do, scrape up the crusty glaze that forms on the skillet bottom—that is the best part—and turn it with the vegetables, to incorporate the crustiness throughout. When everything is golden and lightly crusted, turn off the heat. Serve hot.

Borlotti Bean Pizzaiola

Borlotti Freschi alla Pizzaiola
SERVES 6 AS A SIDE

4 pounds fresh borlotti beans, shelled (about
    4 cups shelled)
2 fresh bay leaves
2 garlic cloves, crushed and peeled
¼ cup extra-virgin olive oil
1 large onion, sliced
1 large carrot, peeled and finely chopped
2 celery stalks, finely chopped
1 tablespoon chopped fresh sage
One 28-ounce can San Marzano tomatoes,
    crushed by hand or passed through a
    food mill
1 teaspoon kosher salt
3 tablespoons chopped fresh Italian parsley

In a medium saucepan, combine beans, bay leaves, garlic, and 6 cups water. Bring to a simmer, cover, and cook until the beans are just shy of tender, about 30 minutes. Discard the garlic and bay leaves. Drain.

Meanwhile, in a large straight-sided skillet, heat the olive oil over medium-high heat, add the onion, carrot, celery, and sage, and cook, stirring occasionally, until softened, about 10 minutes.

Add the tomatoes, slosh the can out with 1 cup hot water, and add that as well. Season with the salt. Bring to a simmer, and cook until thickened, about 20 minutes.

Add the drained beans to the sauce, cover, and simmer until the sauce is thick and flavorful and the beans are tender, about 35 to 40 minutes more, adding a little more water if necessary—if the beans start to stick to the bottom of the pot. Stir in the parsley, and serve hot.

Braised Cannellini Beans

Cannellini Stufati
SERVES 4 TO 6 AS A SIDE

½ pound (about 1¼ cups) cannellini or other
    small white beans, such as Great Northern or
    baby limas
4 sprigs fresh rosemary
2 tablespoons extra-virgin olive oil
Kosher salt

Put the beans in a deep bowl, and pour in enough cold water to cover them by 4 inches. Let soak in a cool place or the refrigerator at least 8 hours or overnight.

Drain the beans, and transfer them to a 2-quart saucepan. Pour in enough water to cover by two fingers, and drop in two of the rosemary sprigs. Bring the water to a boil, and lower the heat so it is at a bare simmer. Cook until the beans are tender but not mushy, with just enough liquid to cover them, 30 to 40 minutes. (If necessary, add more water, a tablespoon at a time, to keep the beans covered as they simmer.)

Remove the beans from the heat, and gently stir in the oil, salt to taste, and the remaining 2 rosemary sprigs. Let stand to cool and absorb the cooking liquid. The end result should be tender beans with a creamy consistency in just enough liquid to coat them. Taste the beans occasionally as they cool, and stir in more salt if necessary. Just before serving, remove the rosemary sprigs.

Braised Broccoli with Oil and Garlic

Broccoli all'Aglio e Olio
SERVES 6 AS A SIDE

Kosher salt to taste
4 stalks broccoli (about 1½ pounds)
3 tablespoons extra-virgin olive oil
4 garlic cloves
¼ teaspoon crushed red pepper flakes, or to taste
¼ cup Chicken Stock (page 143) or water

Bring a large pot of salted water to a boil. Cut the tough ends off the broccoli stalks. Peel the stalks with a vegetable peeler or paring knife up to the florets. Cut each head of broccoli lengthwise into two or three spears, depending on the thickness of the stalk. The cut stalks should be no more than ½ inch thick at their widest point.

Blanch the broccoli spears in the boiling water until they are bright green, about 3 minutes. Drain in a colander.

Heat the olive oil in a large skillet over medium heat. Whack the garlic cloves with the flat side of the knife, peel them, and toss them into the oil. Cook, shaking the pan occasionally, until lightly browned, about 2 minutes. Add the broccoli, and season lightly with salt and the red pepper flakes. Turn in the oil until the broccoli is coated. Pour in the stock or water, cover the skillet tightly, and cook until tender, about 5 minutes. Check the broccoli once or twice as it cooks, adding a tablespoon or two of stock if the liquid evaporates. Taste the broccoli, and season with additional salt and red pepper if you like. Remove garlic and serve immediately.

VARIATION: *Other Blanched Stalk Vegetables*
CAULIFLOWER: Cut out the thick center stems, and pull off the leaves. Cut the cauliflower into large florets, each with some of the stalk attached. Blanch the cauliflower stalks in abundant boiling salted water 3 to 4 minutes, depending on the thickness of the stalk. Drain, reserve ½ cup of the cooking water, and proceed as in the broccoli recipe.

ASPARAGUS: Snap off the tough ends of the stems, and peel the remaining part of the stalks. Blanch the asparagus in abundant boiling salted water 3 minutes. Drain, reserve ½ cup of the cooking water, and proceed as in the broccoli recipe.

Broccoli Rabe Braised with Olive Oil and Garlic

Cime di Rapa all'Aglio e Olio
SERVES 4 AS A SIDE

1 pound broccoli rabe
3 tablespoons extra-virgin olive oil
2 garlic cloves, thinly sliced
Kosher salt
¼ teaspoon crushed red pepper flakes, or to taste

Cut off the tough ends of the stems of the broccoli rabe. Then, holding a stem with the florets in hand, nick a little piece of the end of the stem with a paring knife, and pull the little piece of the stem toward you, peeling the stem partially. Continue working your way around the stem until it is peeled. As you peel the stem, some of the large tough outer leaves will also be removed; discard those as well. Repeat with the remaining stems. Wash and drain in a colander.

Heat the olive oil in a large skillet over medium heat. Scatter the garlic over the oil, and cook, shaking the pan, until golden brown, about 1 minute. Add the broccoli rabe, and season lightly with salt and ¼ teaspoon crushed red pepper. Stir and toss to distribute the seasonings.

Pour ¼ cup water into the skillet, and bring to a boil. Cover the skillet tightly, and cook, lifting the lid to turn the stalks occasionally, until the broccoli rabe is tender, about 13 minutes. Taste, and season with additional salt and crushed red pepper if necessary. Serve hot.

Broccoli Rabe and Sausage

Cime di Rapa con Salsicce
SERVES 4 TO 6 AS A SIDE

3 sweet Italian sausages without fennel seeds
    (about 12 ounces)
3 tablespoons extra-virgin olive oil
6 garlic cloves, crushed and peeled
1 bunch broccoli rabe (about 1 pound),
    trimmed, tough stalks peeled (see preceding
    recipe)
½ teaspoon kosher salt
¼ teaspoon crushed red pepper flakes

Preheat the oven to 500 degrees. Prick the sausages with a fork, set them in an ovenproof skillet, and roast until they are cooked through, about 15 minutes. (Alternatively, cook the sausages in a skillet on the stovetop with some olive oil over medium heat until they are thoroughly cooked.) Remove to a plate until they are cool enough to handle; then slice into ½-inch rounds.

To a large skillet over medium-high heat, add the olive oil and garlic, and let sizzle until the garlic is light golden, about 3 minutes. Add the broccoli rabe, and toss to coat in the oil. Season with the salt and red pepper flakes, and drizzle with ½ cup water. Toss to coat the broccoli rabe in the oil, cover, and cook until it is almost tender, about 8 minutes.

Uncover, add the sliced sausage, and increase the heat to reduce away any excess liquid in the pan. Cook until the sausage is heated through, just a minute two. Remove garlic and serve.

Sautéed Brussels Sprouts with Walnuts

Cavoletti di Bruxelles alle Noci
SERVES 6 AS A SIDE

¼ cup extra-virgin olive oil
1 large red onion, sliced
4 garlic cloves, crushed and peeled
2 pounds Brussels sprouts, trimmed, outer leaves
    removed, halved
½ teaspoon kosher salt
¼ teaspoon crushed red pepper flakes
2 tablespoons white wine vinegar
½ cup whole walnut halves, toasted and then
    coarsely chopped

In a large straight-sided skillet, heat the olive oil over medium-high heat, add the onion, and cook until almost tender, about 5 minutes.

Add the garlic. Once it is sizzling, add the Brussels sprouts and season with the salt and red pepper flakes. Sprinkle with the vinegar, reduce heat to medium, and cook, covered, until golden and tender, about 18 minutes, stirring occasionally. Add a couple of tablespoons of water at any point if it seems they're sticking to the pan.

Add the walnuts, and cook, stirring just until combined, about 1 minute. Remove garlic and serve hot.

Red Cabbage Braised with Wine and Speck

Cavolo Cappuccio Rosso allo Speck
SERVES 6 AS A SIDE

2 tablespoons extra-virgin olive oil
4 ounces thickly sliced speck, julienned
1 medium red onion, thinly sliced
1 small head red cabbage, thinly sliced
1 cup dry red wine
½ cup red wine vinegar
2 teaspoons kosher salt

To a large Dutch oven over medium heat, add the olive oil. When the oil is hot, add the speck. Cook until the speck has rendered but is not quite crisp, about 4 minutes. Add the red onion, and cook until wilted, about 3 minutes. Add the red cabbage, and toss to coat in the oil.

Increase the heat to high, add the wine and vinegar, and bring to a boil. Season with the salt, reduce the heat to a vigorous simmer, and cover. Cook until the cabbage is wilted, about 15 minutes. Uncover, and simmer until the cabbage is very tender and most of the cooking juices have evaporated, about 10 minutes more.

Whole Braised Cauliflower

Cavolfiore Brasato
SERVES 4 TO 6 AS A SIDE

2 tablespoons extra-virgin olive oil
4 ounces thick-sliced bacon, cut into ½-inch pieces
1 large onion, sliced
1 large head cauliflower, cored, but tender leaves left attached (about 2 pounds)
One 28-ounce can Italian plum tomatoes, preferably San Marzano, crushed by hand
1 teaspoon kosher salt
¼ teaspoon crushed red pepper flakes

In a pot just large enough to hold the cauliflower with a few inches to spare around the edges, heat the olive oil over medium heat, add the bacon, and cook until the fat is rendered and the bacon is almost crispy, about 4 minutes. Add the onion, and cook until it is wilted, about 6 minutes.

Set the cauliflower, bottom side down, on top of the onion. Pour the tomatoes over it, along with 1 cup water sloshed from the tomato can to clean it out. Season with the salt and crushed red pepper flakes. Bring to a simmer, and cover. Simmer until the cauliflower is tender but not falling apart, about 25 minutes.

Remove the cauliflower with a spatula to a cutting board, and cut into ½-inch wedges. Serve in a deep bowl with the sauce. Or serve whole with the sauce, and let everyone fish out a portion with a serving spoon.

Skillet Cauliflower with Lemon and Mint

Cavolfiore Brasato con Limone e Mentuccia
SERVES 4 TO 6 AS A SIDE

3 tablespoons extra-virgin olive oil
1 large head cauliflower, broken into florets, washed but not dried
½ teaspoon kosher salt
¼ teaspoon crushed red pepper flakes
Juice of ½ lemon, freshly squeezed
2 tablespoons chopped fresh mint

To a large skillet over medium heat, add the olive oil. When the oil is hot, add the cauliflower and toss to coat it in the oil. Season with the salt, cover, and let steam until the cauliflower is almost tender, about 7 minutes. The water clinging to the florets should be enough to steam the cauliflower, but if it begins to burn, add a tablespoon or two of water and cover again.

Uncover, increase heat to medium high, and let the cauliflower caramelize all over, tossing every minute or so, until it is well browned, about 5 minutes.

If the cauliflower is caramelized but not tender, reduce the heat and cook until it is tender, up to 5 minutes more, sprinkling with the crushed red pepper flakes during the last minute of cooking.

Dump the hot cauliflower into a serving bowl and toss with the lemon juice and mint. Serve hot.

Braised Celery and Mushrooms

Sedano e Funghi Brasati
SERVES 4 TO 6 AS A SIDE

3 tablespoons extra-virgin olive oil
6 garlic cloves, sliced
1 celery heart, cut into ½-inch pieces (about
    4 cups), using the celery leaves as well
2 teaspoons kosher salt
1 pound mixed mushrooms, wiped clean and
    thickly sliced (button, cremini, shiitake,
    oyster, chanterelle)
4 sprigs fresh thyme

In a large straight-sided skillet, heat the olive oil over medium-high heat, and add the garlic. Once the garlic is sizzling, add the celery, and season with 1 teaspoon salt. Toss to coat the celery in the oil, cover, and let it cook until the celery begins to soften around the edges, about 4 minutes.

Uncover, and stir in the mushrooms, thyme, and the remaining teaspoon of salt. Increase the heat to high. Cook, stirring occasionally, until the mushrooms are lightly browned on all sides, about 7 to 8 minutes. Reduce the heat, cover, and cook until the celery is very tender, about 6 to 8 minutes more. Remove the thyme stems, and serve hot.

Eggplant Parmigiana

Melanzane alla Parmigiana
SERVES 6 TO 8 AS A MAIN COURSE

3 medium eggplants, or 5 or 6 smaller eggplants
    (about 2½ to 3 pounds total)
1 tablespoon kosher salt, plus more to taste
3 large eggs
All-purpose flour, for dredging
Freshly ground black pepper
½ cup vegetable oil, or as needed
½ cup extra-virgin olive oil, or as needed
4 cups Tomato Sauce (page 161)

12 fresh basil leaves, shredded
2 cups freshly grated Grana Padano
1 pound fresh mozzarella or Italian Fontina, cut
    into ⅓-inch-thick slices

Preheat the oven to 375 degrees. Trim the stems and ends from the eggplants. Remove strips of peel about 1 inch wide from the eggplants, leaving about half the peel intact. Cut the eggplant lengthwise into ½-inch-thick slices, and place in a colander. Sprinkle with the 1 tablespoon salt, and let drain for 1 hour. Rinse under cool running water, drain thoroughly, and pat dry.

Whisk the eggs in a wide, shallow bowl, and season with salt and pepper. Spread the flour out evenly in a wide, shallow bowl. Dredge the eggplant slices in flour, shaking off the excess. Dip the floured eggplant into the eggs, and set in a colander to drain until ready to fry.

Meanwhile, pour ½ cup each of the vegetable and olive oils into a large skillet. Heat over medium-high heat until a corner of one of the eggplant slices gives off a lively sizzle when dipped into the oil. Add as many of the eggplant slices as fit without touching, and cook, turning once, until browned on both sides, about 4 to 6 minutes total. Remove the eggplant to a baking pan lined with paper towels and repeat with the remaining eggplant slices. Add oil to the pan as necessary during frying to keep the level the same.

Bring the tomato sauce to a simmer in a saucepan. Add shredded basil. Ladle enough sauce into a 9-by-13-inch baking dish to cover the bottom. Sprinkle with an even layer of grated cheese and top with a layer of fried eggplant, pressing it down gently. Ladle about 1 cup of the sauce over the the eggplant to coat the top evenly. Sprinkle a third of the grated cheese over the sauce, and top with a third of the mozzarella or Fontina, spreading it evenly over the eggplant. Repeat the layering as described above two more times, ending with a top layer of mozzarella or Fontina cheese. Drizzle sauce around the border of the baking dish, and sprinkle the top with the remaining grated cheese. Drizzle any remaining sauce on top, cover with foil, and bake until it is bubbling and golden in places, about 30 to 35 minutes.

Uncover, and continue baking until golden brown all over, about 15 minutes. Let it rest 10 to 20 minutes, then cut it into squares and serve.

Baked Eggplant in Tomato Sauce

Melanzane in Teglia
SERVES 6 AS A SIDE

2 pounds small firm eggplants (about 6 to 8 ounces each)
1 tablespoon kosher salt
2 cups Marinara Sauce (page 161)
⅓ cup pitted oil-cured black olives
4 Tuscan-style pickled peperoncini, drained, stemmed, seeded, and thinly sliced (about ¼ cup)
2 tablespoons drained tiny capers in brine
2 tablespoons chopped fresh basil leaves
1 cup freshly grated pecorino (or half pecorino and half Grana Padano for milder flavor)

Trim the stem and bottom ends of each eggplant, and, with a vegetable peeler, shave off ribbons of skin lengthwise, creating a zebra-striped pattern all around. Slice the eggplants crosswise into ½-inch-thick rounds. Lightly salt the slices on both sides, using about a tablespoon in all, and layer them in the colander set in a bowl or the sink. Let the eggplant sweat and drain for 30 minutes to an hour, then rinse and pat dry with paper towels.

Preheat the oven to 400 degrees. Put the marinara sauce in a bowl, and stir in the olives, sliced peperoncini, capers, and basil. Spread about ½ cup of the sauce over the bottom of a 9-by-13-inch baking dish. Lay half the eggplant slices in a single layer in the dish. Drop spoonfuls of sauce, another ½ cup total, on top of the eggplant layer, and sprinkle over it half the grated cheese.

Lay down the remaining eggplant rounds in an even layer, spoon and spread the remaining sauce over them, and scatter the rest of the cheese all over the top.

Tent the baking dish with a sheet of aluminum foil, arching it so it doesn't touch the top and pressing it against the sides. Set the dish on a baking sheet, and bake until the juices are bubbling actively, about 40 minutes. Remove the foil, and bake until the cheese topping is golden brown and the eggplant is caramelized on the edges yet tender and easily pierced with the tip of a knife, about 20 minutes. Let the eggplant rest for 20 minutes (to absorb the sauce). Cut into squares, and serve.

Baked Meat-Stuffed Eggplant

Melanzane Ripiene al Forno
SERVES 6 AS A MAIN COURSE

6 small eggplants (about 2 pounds total)
½ cup extra-virgin olive oil
1 small onion, finely chopped
1 pound ground beef
⅓ cup dry white wine
1 red bell pepper, cleaned, seeded, and finely chopped
2 teaspoons kosher salt
1 cup milk
2 cups day-old country-bread cubes
1 cup freshly grated Grana Padano
½ cup chopped fresh Italian parsley
1 hard-boiled egg, chopped
2 plum tomatoes, seeded and chopped

Preheat the oven to 400 degrees. Cut the eggplants in half lengthwise. Scoop out the flesh to make a shell about ½ to 1 inch thick. Finely chop the eggplant flesh and set aside. Heat 4 tablespoons of the olive oil in a large skillet over medium-high heat. Add the onion, and cook until it begins to soften, about 3 to 4 minutes. Crumble in the ground beef, and pour the wine over the meat. Cook, breaking up the beef with the back of a wooden spoon, until the meat releases its juices and they then cook away, about 6 or 7 minutes.

Add the bell pepper and chopped eggplant, and season with 1 teaspoon of the salt. Cover, and cook until the vegetables are tender, about 10 minutes. Scrape into a bowl to cool. Pour the milk over the bread cubes in a small bowl. Once the bread has softened, squeeze out the excess milk, and crumble the drained bread with your hands in the bowl with the cooled meat filling. Add the grated cheese, parsley, egg, and tomatoes, and mix well. Put the eggplant halves in a large baking dish, and drizzle with the remaining 4 tablespoons oil. Sprinkle with the remaining teaspoon salt, and toss well to coat all of the eggplant with the oil. Fill the eggplant halves with the filling, and arrange snugly in a baking dish just large enough to hold the eggplants. Cover the dish with foil, and bake until the eggplant is tender all the way through, about 40 to 45 minutes. Uncover, and bake until the top of the filling is browned and crispy, about 10 minutes more.

Baked Fennel with Prosciutto

Finocchi al Forno con Prosciutto
SERVES 6 AS A SIDE

½ teaspoon kosher salt, plus more for the pot
2½ pounds fresh fennel bulbs, trimmed and cut into ¾-inch wedges
3 ounces thinly sliced Prosciutto di Parma or Prosciutto di San Daniele
⅓ cup unsalted butter, melted
Freshly ground black pepper
1 cup freshly grated Grana Padano

Preheat the oven to 375 degrees. Bring a large pot of salted water to a boil. Add the fennel wedges,

and cook them at a gentle boil for 10 to 15 minutes, just until you can pierce them easily with a sharp knife tip. Lift out the wedges, and drain well.

Cut the prosciutto slices crosswise into strips about ¼ inch wide. Coat the bottom of a 9-by-13-inch baking dish with a spoonful or two of the melted butter. Lay the fennel wedges in it in one layer, filling the dish, season with black pepper, and scatter the prosciutto strips over and in between the wedges. Drizzle the remaining butter all over. Finally, sprinkle the grated cheese, to cover the whole dish evenly.

Bake until the top is crusty and golden and the edges of the prosciutto and fennel are colored and crisp, about 25 to 30 minutes.

Fennel Parmigiana

Finocchi alla Parmigiana
SERVES 4 TO 6 AS A SIDE

1 teaspoon kosher salt, plus more for the pot
4 medium fennel bulbs, trimmed
One 28-ounce can whole San Marzano tomatoes, crushed by hand or passed through a food mill
3 garlic cloves, crushed and peeled
2 tablespoons extra-virgin olive oil
2 cups shredded low-moisture mozzarella
1 cup freshly grated Grana Padano

Preheat the oven to 400 degrees. Bring a large pot of salted water to a boil. Add the whole fennel bulbs, and boil until just tender, about 15 to 20 minutes. Drain, cool, and slice 1 inch thick. Pat very dry on kitchen towels.

In a large bowl, stir together the crushed tomatoes, garlic, olive oil, salt, and ½ cup water. In another large bowl, toss together the cheeses.

Spread a thin layer of the sauce in the bottom of a 9-by-13-inch baking dish. Layer in the sliced fennel, and top with the remaining sauce. Sprinkle with the grated cheese. Cover with foil, and bake until bubbly, about 20 minutes. Uncover, and bake until the sauce is thickened and the cheese is browned, about 20 minutes more.

Smothered Escarole

Scarola Affogata
SERVES 4 AS A SIDE

3 tablespoons extra-virgin olive oil
6 garlic cloves, crushed and peeled
1 pound (approximately 2 small heads) escarole, trimmed, washed, and coarsely chopped
½ teaspoon kosher salt
¼ teaspoon crushed red pepper flakes

Heat the olive oil in a large Dutch oven over medium-high heat. Add the garlic, and cook until golden, about 3 minutes.

Add the escarole, and season with the salt and red pepper flakes. Reduce the heat to medium low, cover, and cook, stirring occasionally, until the leaves are wilted and tender, about 8 to 10 minutes. Remove and discard the garlic, and serve.

Stuffed Escarole

Scarola Imbottita
SERVES 4 TO 6 AS A SIDE

2 large heads escarole, about 1 pound each
¼ cup pine nuts, toasted
½ cup dried bread crumbs
½ cup freshly grated Grana Padano
9 tablespoons extra-virgin olive oil
3 garlic cloves, thinly sliced
¼ cup black oil-cured olives, pitted then roughly chopped

2 tablespoons golden raisins, plumped in warm water, drained, and roughly chopped
3 tablespoons drained tiny capers in brine
½ teaspoon kosher salt

Preheat the oven to 375 degrees. Bring a large pot of water to a boil. Remove any damaged outer leaves from the escarole heads, but otherwise keep them whole and attached at the base. To wash them, spread the leaves open and dunk the heads, leaves first, into a sink filled with cold water, several times.

Push the heads, leaves first, into the boiling water, then submerge the whole escarole head. Return the water to a boil, and cook for 2 to 3 minutes to soften the leaves. Place the heads, leaves still attached, in a colander to drain and cool.

In a medium bowl, toss together the toasted pine nuts, bread crumbs, and ¼ cup of the grated cheese. Remove about a third of the mixture, and set aside for topping the rolls; leave the larger amount in the bowl for the filling.

Pour 5 tablespoons of the olive oil into a medium skillet, and set over medium heat. Stir the sliced garlic in the oil, and cook for a minute or so, until sizzling. Stir in the olives, toast them for a minute, then toss in the raisins and capers and cook for just a minute more. Scrape all the savories and oil from the skillet into the larger bread-crumb filling mixture, and toss together.

Pour 2 tablespoons of the olive oil into a 9-by-13-inch baking dish. Lay the blanched heads of escarole on a large cutting board. Divide each head in half, lengthwise through the core; now slice each half in two lengthwise through the core: you should have eight clusters of escarole leaves, still attached at the base. Spread the leaves of each cluster open like a fan, and flatten it so it resembles a single large leaf to enclose the filling—just like a cabbage leaf.

When all the clusters are open, cut off and discard the tough bases holding the leaves together. If necessary, move leaves from one cluster to another so the escarole fans are of equal size and shape.

Divide the filling equally among the fans (2 to 3 tablespoons each), laying it near the base of the leaves. Roll up the escarole just enough to cover the filling, fold in the sides, then continue rolling to form fairly compact oval rolls.

Arrange the rolls in the oiled pan, leaving space between them. Sprinkle salt all over the rolls, then the reserved mixture of bread crumbs and pine nuts and the remaining grated cheese. Finally, drizzle with the remaining 2 tablespoons of olive oil.

Cover the baking dish with a sheet of aluminum foil, arched so it doesn't touch the rolls, and press it against the sides. Bake for about 30 minutes, remove the foil, and bake another 10 minutes, until the escarole rolls are lightly caramelized and the topping is crisp and golden brown. Serve hot.

Braised Swiss Chard and Cannellini Beans

Zimino di Bietole e Fagioli
SERVES 6 AS A SIDE

8 ounces dried cannellini beans, or 3 cups canned cannellini, drained and rinsed

1 teaspoon kosher salt, or to taste

2 pounds or more big unblemished Swiss-chard leaves

6 tablespoons extra-virgin olive oil, plus more to taste

4 garlic cloves, thinly sliced

1 tablespoon tomato paste

½ teaspoon crushed red pepper flakes, or to taste

1 cup canned Italian plum tomatoes, preferably San Marzano, crushed by hand or passed through a food mill

Rinse the dried beans, and put them in a bowl with cold water to cover by at least 4 inches. Let them soak in a cool place for 8 hours or overnight. Drain the beans, and transfer them to a large saucepan with fresh cold water to cover by a few inches. Bring them to a boil, partially covered, and cook the beans about 40 minutes, until they are tender but not mushy. Turn off the heat, and stir in ½ teaspoon salt, then let the beans cool to absorb the seasonings. Taste, and adjust the salt if needed. (If you are using canned beans, omit this step; just drain and rinse them.)

Bring 6 quarts of water to a boil in a large pot. Meanwhile, clean the Swiss-chard leaves, and cut off the stems at the base of the leafy part. Slice the leaves crosswise every 2 inches or so, into strips. When the water is boiling, drop in all the sliced chard at once. Bring the water back to a boil, and cook the chard, covered, for about 15 minutes, until thoroughly tender. Drain well in a colander. Drain the cooked cannellini.

Heat ¼ cup of the olive oil and the sliced garlic in a large skillet over medium-high heat, stirring frequently, until the garlic is sizzling, about 2 minutes. Drop the tomato paste into a clear spot in the pan; stir and toast it for a minute. Toast the red pepper flakes in a hot spot, too, then pour in the crushed tomatoes, and stir everything together. Bring the tomatoes to a boil, and add the beans. Season with salt, and add the chard. Cook rapidly for a couple of minutes to reduce the liquid, tossing the beans and greens over and over. As the juices thicken, drizzle the remaining 2 tablespoons olive oil all over, toss it in with the vegetables, and simmer for another 2 or 3 minutes, until most of the liquid has evaporated.

Baked Radicchio

Radicchio Trevisano al Forno
SERVES 6 AS A SIDE

1½ pounds long heads radicchio trevisano (or radicchio di Chioggia) (2 or 3 firm heads)

4 tablespoons unsalted butter

4 tablespoons extra-virgin olive oil

3 garlic cloves, smashed and peeled

1 medium onion, sliced

1 teaspoon kosher salt, or to taste

1 tablespoon red wine vinegar
Freshly ground black pepper to taste
1 cup freshly grated Grana Padano

Preheat the oven to 375 degrees. Trim the radicchio heads, and cut them into quarters (the trevisano) or sixths (the Chioggia), leaving each section attached at the core.

Melt the butter and 2 tablespoons of the olive oil in a large skillet over medium heat. When the butter is melted and foaming, stir in the onion and garlic and cook for a minute, then lay in all the radicchio wedges in one layer. Sprinkle on the salt, cover the pan, and cook slowly, turning the wedges over and stirring the onion every couple of minutes, until everything is slightly softened, about 10 minutes.

Stir the vinegar and ¼ cup water together, and pour into the pan. Raise the heat a bit and bring the liquid to a boil, turning the wedges gently. Cook for a couple more minutes, until the pan juices are reduced and syrupy and the wedges are lightly caramelized.

Remove the skillet from the heat, and arrange the radicchio wedges in a 2-quart shallow baking dish, in one layer. Remove garlic and spoon the onion all around, and pour any skillet liquid over it. Drizzle on the remaining 2 tablespoons olive oil, season with freshly ground black pepper, and sprinkle the grated cheese in an even layer over the radicchio. Tent the dish with aluminum foil, and press it against the sides. Bake covered for about 20 minutes; remove the foil, and bake another 5 minutes or more, until the radicchio wedges are tender and moist and glazed golden on top.

Braised Radicchio Trevisano

Radicchio Trevisano al Tegame
SERVES 4 AS A SIDE

2 tablespoons extra-virgin olive oil
8 garlic cloves garlic, crushed and peeled
4 heads radicchio trevisano, trimmed at the base,
  halved lengthwise through the stem
4 anchovy fillets, chopped
½ teaspoon kosher salt
¼ cup dry white wine

To a medium skillet over medium-high heat, add the olive oil. When the oil is hot, add the garlic and cook, tossing occasionally, until it is golden, about 2 minutes. Add the radicchio, and turn to coat in the oil. Add the anchovies, season with the salt, and stir to dissolve the anchovies in the oil. Add ¼ cup water. Bring to a simmer, and cook, turning the radicchio occasionally, until tender, about 7 minutes. Transfer the radicchio to a warmed serving bowl.

Add the wine to the skillet, and boil until it is reduced to a glossy sauce, about 2 minutes. Discard the garlic, and pour the sauce over the radicchio.

Braised Kale with Bacon

Cavolo Nero Brasato con Pancetta
SERVES 6 AS A SIDE

1½ pounds kale (about 2 medium heads)
3 tablespoons extra-virgin olive oil
6 garlic cloves, crushed and peeled
½ cup diced bacon or pancetta
Kosher salt
¼ teaspoon crushed red pepper flakes, or to
  taste

Remove the outer kale leaves if damaged or discolored. Cut off the bases of the stems, and cut the leaves crosswise into 1-inch strips. Wash and drain, letting a little water cling to the leaves.

Heat the olive oil in a large skillet over medium heat. Add the garlic, and cook until golden, about 2 minutes. Stir in the bacon or pancetta, and cook, stirring, until the fat is rendered, about 4 minutes.

Stir as many of the kale leaves into the skillet as will fit comfortably. Cook, stirring, until they are wilted enough to make room for more kale. Continue adding the kale, a handful at a time, until all of it is in the skillet. Season lightly with the salt and red pepper flakes. Cover the skillet, lower the heat to low, and cook, stirring occasionally, until tender, about 10 minutes. If all the liquid in the pan evaporates and the greens begin to stick to the pan, sprinkle a tablespoon or two of water over them. Taste the greens and season with additional salt and red pepper if you like. Remove garlic and serve immediately.

Turnip Greens and Pancetta

Talli di Rape Brasati con Pancetta
SERVES 6 TO 8 AS A SIDE

¼ cup extra-virgin olive oil
6-ounce chunk pancetta, cut into matchsticks
1 large onion, sliced
3 pounds turnip greens, trimmed, washed, spun dry, and torn into large chunks
2 teaspoons kosher salt
½ teaspoon crushed red pepper flakes

In a large Dutch oven, heat the olive oil over medium heat. Add the pancetta, and cook until the fat is rendered and the pancetta is almost crisp, about 4 minutes.

Add the onion, and cook, stirring occasionally, until it is wilted, about 5 minutes.

Add the greens, and stir to coat them in the oil. Season with the salt and red pepper flakes. Add

½ cup water, cover, and simmer over medium heat until the greens are wilted, about 15 minutes.

Uncover, adjust heat so the liquid is just simmering, and cook until tender, about 10 to 15 minutes more. Serve hot.

❧ Collard greens can be substituted with good results.

Spinach and Chickpeas in Tomato Sauce

Ceci e Spinaci Brasati al Pomodoro
SERVES 6 AS A SIDE

¼ cup extra-virgin olive oil
6 fresh sage leaves, chopped
3 garlic cloves, crushed and peeled
2 cups canned San Marzano tomatoes, crushed by hand
¼ teaspoon crushed red pepper flakes
¾ teaspoon kosher salt
Two 15½-ounce cans chickpeas, rinsed and drained
2 bunches spinach, stems removed, washed, drained, and coarsely chopped (about 2 pounds)

In a large Dutch oven, heat the olive oil over medium-high heat. When the oil is hot, add the sage and garlic, and let sizzle a minute. Add the tomatoes, crushed red pepper, and ¼ teaspoon salt. Bring to a simmer, and cook until thickened, about 5 minutes.

Stir in the chickpeas, and simmer until the sauce coats them, about 5 minutes more.

Add the spinach and the remaining ½ teaspoon salt. Cover, and cook until spinach is tender, about 8 to 10 minutes. Uncover, and simmer a few minutes more to reduce away any excess liquid, until the sauce is thickened to your liking. Remove garlic and serve hot.

Green Beans in Chunky Tomato Sauce

Fagiolini al Pomodoro
SERVES 6 AS A SIDE

1 teaspoon kosher salt, plus more for the pot
6 ripe plum tomatoes
1½ pounds green beans
5 tablespoons extra-virgin olive oil
1 large onion, sliced
Pinch of crushed red pepper flakes

Bring a large pot of salted water to a boil. Halve the tomatoes through the stem ends. Set a fine strainer over a bowl, and scrape seeds and juice from tomatoes into the strainer. Press the solids with the back of a spoon, reserving the juice. Cut the solid tomatoes into four long strips per each half.

Cook the green beans in the boiling water until tender, about 10 minutes.

Meanwhile, in a large skillet, heat 3 tablespoons of the olive oil over medium-high heat. Add the onion, and cook until almost tender, about 5 minutes. Add the tomato strips and juices, and season with ½ teaspoon salt and the crushed red pepper. Add ½ cup string-bean cooking water, and adjust the heat so the sauce is simmering rapidly. Cook until the sauce thickens and the tomatoes just begin to break down, about 6 to 7 minutes.

Drain the beans, reserving ½ cup cooking water just in case. Add the drained beans directly to the sauce. Bring to a simmer, season with the remaining ½ teaspoon salt, and drizzle with the remaining 2 tablespoons olive oil. Simmer to let the beans absorb the flavors of the sauce, about 5 minutes, adding a little more of the bean-cooking water if the sauce seems too dry. Serve immediately.

Chestnut and Mushroom Ragù

Ragù di Funghi e Castagne
SERVES 4 TO 6 AS A SIDE

¼ cup extra-virgin olive oil
2 garlic cloves, thinly sliced
2 medium shallots, finely chopped
1½ pounds mixed mushrooms (button, cremini, shiitake, oyster, chanterelle), thickly sliced
2 teaspoons chopped fresh thyme
1 teaspoon kosher salt
2 tablespoons tomato paste
2 cups chopped chestnuts, freshly cooked and peeled, canned, or jarred

To a large skillet over medium-high heat, add the olive oil. When the oil is hot, add the garlic. Once the garlic is sizzling, add the shallots. Cook and stir until almost tender, about 2 to 3 minutes.

Add the mushrooms, thyme, and salt. Cover, and cook until the mushrooms release their liquid, about 5 minutes. Uncover, and increase the heat to reduce away the liquid in the pan, cooking about 2 minutes. Make a space in the pan, and add the tomato paste. Cook and stir the paste in that spot until it toasts and darkens a shade or two, about 2 minutes, then stir into the mushrooms.

Add the chestnuts and 2 cups hot water. Cover, and simmer until the chestnuts just begin to fall apart and thicken the sauce, about 15 minutes. Uncover and increase heat to reduce the sauce to your liking, if necessary.

🍃 Although you can use jarred or canned chestnuts, freshly boiled and peeled chestnuts are delicious and worth the time it takes. Just do not overcook them, since they will cook with the sauce as well. This recipe is a delicious side to serve with grilled and roasted meats, especially game meats, but it also makes a good bruschetta topping; or try it as a dressing for whole-wheat pasta.

Onions Stuffed with Lamb and Raisins

Cipolle Farcite con Carne di Agnello e Uva Passa
SERVES 6 AS A SIDE

⅓ cup golden raisins
6 medium yellow onions
6 tablespoons extra-virgin olive oil, plus more for the baking dish
2 teaspoons kosher salt
1 cup dry white wine
1 pound ground lamb
2 teaspoons chopped fresh thyme leaves
½ cup fine dried bread crumbs
½ cup freshly grated Grana Padano
¼ cup chopped fresh Italian parsley
2 tablespoons unsalted butter, cut into pieces
1 cup hot Chicken Stock (page 143)

Preheat the oven to 400 degrees. Put the raisins in a small bowl, cover with hot water, and let soak while you prepare the onions.

Halve the onions through their centers. With a spoon, scoop out the centers, leaving three layers of the onion as a shell. Don't worry if you make a hole in one or two of the bottoms; just patch with pieces of cut-out onion. Brush a 9-by-13-inch baking dish with olive oil, and add the onions, with the cavities facing up. Drizzle with 2 tablespoons of the olive oil, and season with 1 teaspoon salt. Finely chop the scooped-out onion pieces.

In a large skillet, heat the remaining ¼ cup olive oil over medium heat. When the oil is hot, add the onion pieces and stir to coat them in the oil. Add ¼ cup of the white wine, and simmer until the onions are softened and the wine is reduced, about 6 minutes.

Add the lamb and chopped thyme, and season with the remaining teaspoon salt. Cook and stir until the lamb is just cooked through, about 8 minutes. Scrape the mixture into a bowl, and let it cool.

Drain the raisins, and squeeze to remove any excess liquid. Add to the cooled lamb along with the bread crumbs, grated cheese, and parsley. Spoon the filling into the onion shells, and dot the tops with the butter pieces. Pour the hot stock and remaining wine into the bottom of the baking dish, and cover tightly with foil. Bake until the onion shells are almost tender, about 25 minutes. Uncover, and bake until the onions are very tender but not falling apart and the filling is browned, about 25 minutes more. Serve hot or at room temperature.

Olive Oil Mashed Potatoes

Purè di Patate all'Olio
SERVES 4 TO 6 AS A SIDE

2 pounds Idaho or Yukon gold potatoes, scrubbed but not peeled
Kosher salt, to taste
½ cup extra-virgin olive oil
Freshly ground black pepper

Pour enough cold water over the potatoes in a large saucepan to cover them by a few inches. Season the water with salt, and bring to a boil. Cook until the potatoes are tender but still hold their shape, about 30 to 40 minutes, depending on their size. Drain, and let stand until cool enough to handle.

Peel the potatoes, and pass them through a ricer or a food mill with a fine disk. Gently stir in the olive oil, and season them to taste with salt and pepper. Serve hot.

♣ For a variation, toast three garlic cloves in olive oil in a large skillet, then let cool to room temperature before adding to the riced potatoes.

Horseradish Mashed Potatoes

Purè di Patate con Rafano
SERVES 6 AS A SIDE

3 pounds russet potatoes, all about the same size
1 stick unsalted butter
1 cup half-and-half
1 cup milk
2 teaspoons kosher salt
2-inch piece fresh horseradish root, peeled and
    grated (about ½ cup)

Put the unpeeled whole potatoes in a large pot
with cold water to cover by about 2 inches. Bring
to a simmer, and cook until tender, about 30
to 40 minutes. Drain, and let sit until just cool
enough to peel.

While the potatoes cool, combine the butter,
half-and-half, milk, and salt in the cooking pot
over low heat, just until the butter melts.

Use a ricer, and press the still-warm potatoes
through into the butter mixture. Add the horseradish, and stir until smooth. Adjust seasoning,
and serve immediately.

❧ The ½ cup of grated fresh horseradish called
for here will give the mashed potatoes a moderate
heat; for a more intense flavor, add up to 1 cup.
Fresh horseradish is best, but if it is unavailable,
use about ½ cup jarred horseradish. Drain the
liquid from the jarred horseradish, then rinse, pat
it dry with a paper towel, and proceed to use as
fresh.

Baked Potatoes with Pancetta and Oregano

Patate al Forno con Pancetta e Origano
SERVES 6 AS A SIDE

4 ounces pancetta, thinly sliced, or bacon, slices
    cut in half crosswise
6 medium russet potatoes, peeled and quartered
    lengthwise
2 tablespoons extra-virgin olive oil
2 tablespoons chopped fresh oregano
1 teaspoon kosher salt

Preheat the oven to 400 degrees. Line a 9-by-
13-inch glass or ceramic baking dish on the bottom with the pancetta or bacon. It's okay if the
slices overlap a little.

In a large bowl, toss the potatoes with the olive
oil, oregano, and salt. Scatter the potatoes on top
of the pancetta or bacon in one layer, and cover
with foil. Bake until potatoes are just tender,
about 20 minutes.

Increase the temperature to 450 degrees. Uncover, and bake until the potatoes are golden and
the pancetta or bacon is crisp, about 10 minutes
more. Remove the potatoes and pancetta to a
platter with a metal spatula, breaking the pancetta into shards and tossing with the potatoes on
the platter.

Baked Potatoes and Onions

Patate e Cipolle al Forno
SERVES 6 AS A SIDE

2 pounds russet potatoes, peeled and sliced
    ¼ inch thick
4 tablespoons extra-virgin olive oil
2 teaspoons kosher salt
2 medium onions, sliced ¼ inch thick
6 large fresh sage leaves, coarsely chopped
1 cup Chicken Stock (page 143), Vegetable
    Stock (page 143), or water

1½ cups grated Italian Fontina
½ cup freshly grated Grana Padano

Preheat the oven to 450 degrees. In a large bowl, toss the potatoes with 2 tablespoons of the oil and 1 teaspoon of the salt. In another large bowl, toss the onions with the remaining 2 tablespoons oil and the remaining teaspoon salt.

Spread half of the potatoes in a layer in a 9-by-13-inch baking dish, and scatter half of the sage over them. Top with all of the onions and the rest of the sage. Top with the remaining potatoes, and pour the stock over all. Cover with foil, and bake until potatoes and onions are tender, about 20 to 25 minutes.

In a medium bowl, toss the cheeses together. Uncover the pan, sprinkle the cheese on top of the potatoes, and bake until the cheese is browned and bubbly, about 15 minutes more. Serve hot.

Roasted Sweet and Yukon Gold Potatoes

Patate Dolci e Yukon Gold Arroste al Forno
SERVES 8 TO 10 AS A SIDE

2 pounds Yukon gold potatoes, peeled and cut into 1½-inch pieces
2 pounds sweet potatoes, peeled and cut into 2-inch pieces
¼ cup extra-virgin olive oil
6 garlic cloves, crushed and peeled
1 tablespoon fresh thyme leaves, coarsely chopped
2 teaspoons kosher salt
½ cup freshly squeezed lemon juice

Preheat the oven to 425 degrees. In a large bowl, toss together the potatoes, sweet potatoes, olive oil, garlic, thyme, and salt.

Spread the potatoes and sweet potatoes on a rimmed sheet pan (or two if necessary, depending on the size of your pan; you want them in one layer). In a measuring cup, whisk the lemon juice with ½ cup water. Pour this over the potatoes.

Roast on the bottom rack, tossing by scraping with a spatula a few times, until the potatoes are golden on all sides and have soaked up all of the liquid, about 35 to 40 minutes. Remove garlic and serve immediately.

ᣔ This recipe is easy and delicious for those big family meals, but it can easily be cut in half.

Savoy Cabbage and Potatoes

Verza e Patate
SERVES 6 AS A SIDE

2 teaspoons kosher salt, plus more for the pot
3 medium russet potatoes, peeled and quartered (about 1¼ pounds)
1 medium savoy cabbage, cored and chopped into 1-inch pieces
¼ cup extra-virgin olive oil
2 tablespoons unsalted butter
4 garlic cloves, crushed and peeled
Freshly ground black pepper

Bring the potatoes to a boil in a large pot in 4 quarts of salted water. After 5 minutes, add the cabbage. Continue to simmer until the potatoes and cabbage are tender, about 20 minutes in all. Drain well.

To a large skillet over medium heat, add the olive oil and butter. When the butter is melted, add the garlic. Let the garlic sizzle until light golden, about 2 minutes, then add the cabbage and potatoes. Season with the salt and some pepper. Stir with a wooden spoon, and mash coarsely with a potato masher, leaving some lumps. If the mixture is too wet, cook a few more minutes to dry it out, stirring occasionally so it doesn't burn. Remove garlic and serve hot.

Mashed Potatoes and Green Beans

Fagiolini con Patate Schicciate
SERVES 4 TO 6 AS A SIDE

1 teaspoon kosher salt, plus more for the pot
1 pound russet potatoes, peeled and cut into
    2-inch chunks
1½ pounds green beans, trimmed, cut into
    2-inch lengths
¼ cup extra-virgin olive oil
Freshly ground black pepper

Bring a pot with 3 quarts of salted water to a boil. Add the potatoes, and cook until they just begin to become tender, about 8 to 10 minutes.

Add the green beans, and cook until the potatoes and green beans are tender, about 10 to 12 minutes more. Drain well.

Put the green beans and potatoes back in the cooking pot. Season with the salt and the olive oil. Use a potato masher to mash the green beans and potatoes together. Serve immediately, topped with freshly ground black pepper.

Swiss Chard and Potatoes

Bietola e Patate
SERVES 6 AS A SIDE

2 pounds Swiss chard
3 medium Idaho potatoes (about 1¼ pounds),
    peeled and cut crosswise into 4 pieces
¼ cup extra-virgin olive oil
4 garlic cloves, crushed and peeled
Kosher salt, to taste
Freshly ground black pepper, to taste

To prepare the Swiss chard: Trim the ends from the stems. Cut off and discard any wilted or yellow parts of the leaves. Strip the stems from the leaves, and cut the stems into ½-inch lengths. Cut the leaves in half lengthwise, then crosswise into ½-inch strips. Wash the leaf and stem pieces thoroughly; then drain them well.

Bring 4 quarts water to a boil in a large pot. Add the potatoes, and cook until almost tender, about 15 minutes. Add the Swiss chard, and cook until the vegetables are tender, an additional 10 to 15 minutes. Drain all well.

Heat 2 tablespoons of the olive oil in a large skillet over medium heat. Add the garlic, and cook just until it begins to turn golden, about 1 minute. Add the Swiss chard and potatoes, and season them lightly with salt and pepper. Cook, stirring and mashing the potatoes, until the liquid is evaporated and the potatoes are coarsely mashed. If the potatoes begin to brown, adjust the level of heat to medium low and continue stirring. Add the remaining 2 tablespoons olive oil, season to taste with salt and pepper, stir, remove garlic, and serve hot.

Marinated Winter Squash

Zucca Gialla Marinata
SERVES 6 AS AN ANTIPASTO OR A SIDE

1 cup apple-cider vinegar or white vinegar
1 tablespoon sugar
½ teaspoon kosher salt, or more to taste
6 garlic cloves, sliced
1 tablespoon extra-virgin olive oil
1 medium butternut squash (about 2 pounds)
1 cup vegetable oil, or as needed
20 fresh basil leaves

Mix the vinegar, sugar, and ¼ teaspoon salt together in a small saucepan. Let simmer over high heat until the sauce is reduced by half. Remove from the heat, drop in the garlic slices, and let the marinade cool. Stir in the olive oil.

Slice the squash in half lengthwise, and scrape out all the seeds. Peel the halves, place them cut side down, and cut crosswise into ⅓-inch-thick half-rounds.

Pour a thin layer of vegetable oil into a large nonstick skillet, and set it over medium-high heat. When the oil sizzles on contact with the squash, fill the pan with a layer of slices, spaced slightly apart. Fry for about 3 minutes on the first side, then flip the slices over. Fry on the second side another 2 or 3 minutes, until the slices are cooked through (easy to pierce with the tines of a fork), crisped on the surface, and caramelized on the edges. Lift out the slices with a slotted spoon, draining off oil, and lay them on paper towels. Sprinkle salt lightly on the hot slices. Fry up all the squash, in batches, the same way.

Arrange a single layer of fried squash in the bottom of a shallow serving dish, large enough to hold all of the squash. Scatter four or five basil leaves on top. Stir up the marinade, and drizzle over the squash a couple of spoonfuls. Scatter some of the garlic slices on the squash, too. Layer all the squash in the dish this way, topping each layer of fried slices with basil leaves, marinade, and garlic. All the seasonings should be used; drizzle any remaining marinade over the top layer of squash.

Wrap the dish in plastic, and let the squash marinate for at least 3 hours at room temperature or preferably overnight in the refrigerator. If it is chilled, let the squash return to room temperature before removing the garlic and serving.

Zucchini with Anchovies and Capers

Zucchine in Salsa di Acciughe e Capperi
SERVES 6 AS A SIDE

2½ pounds small zucchini
6 tablespoons extra-virgin olive oil
4 garlic cloves, crushed and peeled
6 anchovy fillets, finely chopped

1 teaspoon kosher salt
¼ cup drained tiny capers in brine

Trim the ends of the zucchini, and slice them into ¼-inch-thick sticks, 2 to 3 inches long. Heat the olive oil in a large skillet over medium heat. Add the garlic cloves, cook for a minute or so, until sizzling, then add the chopped anchovies. Cook, stirring, until the anchovies melt in the oil, about 1 to 2 minutes. Scatter the zucchini sticks in the skillet, and toss and stir to coat them in oil. Season with the salt, and cook, stirring occasionally, until the zucchini is cooked through, limp, and lightly caramelized, about 15 minutes.

Add the capers, and cook another minute or two to blend the flavors. Remove garlic and serve hot or at room temperature.

Sweet and Sour Zucchini

Zucchine all'Agrodolce
SERVES 6 AS A SIDE OR AN ANTIPASTO

1 cup red wine vinegar
2 tablespoons sugar
3 fresh bay leaves
2 garlic cloves, crushed and peeled
¼ cup extra-virgin olive oil
2 pounds medium zucchini, cut into ¼-inch rounds
Kosher salt, for sprinkling

In a small saucepan, combine the vinegar, sugar, bay leaves, and garlic with 1 cup water. Bring to a simmer, and cook until reduced to ½ cup, about 7 to 10 minutes. Let cool.

Line a baking sheet with paper towels. Heat a large skillet over medium-high heat. Add 2 tablespoons of the oil and enough zucchini to make one layer in the pan without crowding. Cook until browned on both sides, about 5 to 6 minutes in all. Drain on paper towels, and season with salt. Repeat with the remaining zucchini, in batches, adding the rest of the oil to the pan as necessary until all of the zucchini has been browned, drained, and seasoned with salt.

Layer the zucchini in an 8-by-8-inch glass or ceramic dish. Pour the marinade over it, and let it sit at least 1 hour so the flavors can develop before serving. Remove the bay leaves and garlic before serving at room temperature.

Stuffed Tomatoes

Pomodori Farciti al Forno
SERVES 8 AS A SIDE

1¼ teaspoons kosher salt
2 fresh bay leaves
¾ cup Arborio rice
2 tablespoons extra-virgin olive oil
8 firm, ripe medium tomatoes
¾ cup diced fresh mozzarella
2 ounces ham, cut into small cubes
½ cup plus 2 tablespoons freshly grated Grana
   Padano
10 large basil leaves, chopped
½ teaspoon dried oregano, preferably Sicilian on
   the branch

Preheat the oven to 400 degrees. In a medium saucepan, bring 2 cups water to a boil, with ½ teaspoon salt and the bay leaves. Stir in the rice and 1 tablespoon of the olive oil. Bring to a simmer, and cook, uncovered, until the rice is al dente and the liquid is almost all gone, about 10 minutes. Remove bay leaves. Scrape into a bowl to cool.

Slice the tops off the tomatoes, reserving them for later. Gently scoop out the inner flesh of the tomatoes with a spoon, leaving the shell intact. As you work, put the flesh in a strainer set over a bowl to collect the juices. Once all of the tomatoes are scooped out, season the insides of the tomatoes with ½ teaspoon of the salt.

Chop the collected tomato flesh, leaving the seeds behind, and put it in the bowl with the rice. Add the mozzarella, ham, ½ cup of the grated cheese, the basil, the oregano, and the remaining ¼ teaspoon salt. Toss to combine.

Pour the strained reserved tomato juices into the bottom of a 9-by-13-inch baking dish. Evenly divide the stuffing between the tomatoes. Arrange the cut-off tomato tops in the baking dish, cut side down, and place a stuffed tomato on each top. Depending on the size of your tomatoes, you may have a little leftover stuffing. If so, roll it into "meatballs" and place them between the tomatoes in the baking dish. Drizzle the tomatoes with the remaining tablespoon of olive oil, and sprinkle the tops with the remaining grated cheese. Bake until the tomatoes are soft and juicy and the stuffing is browned on top, about 20 to 25 minutes. Serve hot or at room temperature. This is a great dish for buffet tables.

Stuffed Vegetables

Verdure Farcite
MAKES ABOUT 36 VEGETABLE MORSELS

FOR THE STUFFING
¼ ounce dried porcini (about ¼ cup loosely
   packed pieces)
1 cup milk
4 cups 1-inch-cubes day-old or dried country
   bread, crusts removed (about 4 thick slices)
1 cup finely chopped scallions
10 large fresh basil leaves, finely chopped
½ cup freshly grated Grana Padano
1 teaspoon kosher salt
2 large eggs, lightly beaten

FOR THE VEGETABLE ASSORTMENT
2 medium zucchini (6 inches long)
2 small red, yellow, or orange bell peppers
12 large white mushrooms
3 small ripe tomatoes
2 large Vidalia or other sweet onions

½ cup extra-virgin olive oil, or as needed
1½ teaspoons kosher salt
Unsalted butter, for the baking dishes
½ cup freshly grated Grana Padano

Preheat the oven to 425 degrees. For the stuffing: Put the porcini in a spouted measuring cup, and add 2 cups hot water. Soak until softened, about 15 minutes. Squeeze out the porcini, and finely chop. Strain and reserve the soaking liquid. In a large bowl, pour the milk over the bread cubes; toss well, and let sit for a couple of minutes. When they are softened, press the cubes together, squeezing out any excess milk, and return the moistened bread to the dry bowl, tearing it into shreds with your fingers.

To the bread, add the porcini, scallions, basil, grated cheese, and 1 teaspoon salt, and toss to combine. Stir in the beaten eggs with a wooden spoon (or mix with your hands) to form a well-blended, fairly dense stuffing.

To prepare the zucchini for stuffing: Trim off the ends, and slice the squashes in half lengthwise. Scoop out the central pulp and any seeds with a teaspoon or melon baller, so each half resembles a hollowed boat. Cut the long halves crosswise into serving-sized pieces, about 3 inches long.

To prepare the bell peppers for stuffing: Quarter them lengthwise, starting at the stem; trim away the stem and all seeds and fibers, forming cuplike sections to hold the stuffing.

To prepare the mushrooms, tomatoes, and onions: Pull out the stems of the mushrooms, leaving the hollow caps for stuffing. Cut the tomatoes in half crosswise, and squeeze out the seeds to make concavities for stuffing. Peel the onions, and cut them crosswise into ¾-inch-thick slices.

Put all of the vegetables except the onions in a large bowl, and toss with the olive oil and ½ teaspoon salt. Brush some of the oil on the onion slices, keeping them whole.

Butter two large baking dishes. For the zucchini, peppers, mushrooms, and tomatoes: fill each cavity with about a tablespoon of stuffing, and arrange all the pieces in a baking dish, leaving a bit of space between them. Lay the onion slices flat in the dish, and mound a spoonful of stuffing on top of each slice.

When the dishes are filled (but not crowded), sprinkle all the vegetable pieces evenly with the grated cheese and remaining teaspoon salt. Scrape any olive oil left in the vegetable bowl over the stuffed pieces, and pour the reserved porcini-soaking liquid (leaving behind any gritty residue) into the bottom of each baking dish. Cover each dish with a tent of foil, pressing it against the dish sides; make sure the foil doesn't touch the stuffing or the tops of the vegetables. Bake until the vegetables have started to soften and release juices, about 30 minutes; then remove the foil tents, and bake until the stuffing is crispy and brown, another 30 minutes or so. Switch the position of the dishes in the oven once or twice so all the pieces cook and color evenly. Serve hot from the oven, or let the vegetables cool and serve at room temperature.

Lettuce Roll-Ups

Involtini di Lattuga
SERVES 4 TO 6 AS A SIDE OR AN ANTIPASTO

½ teaspoon kosher salt, plus more for the pot
12 large romaine leaves from the outside of the head
2 tablespoons extra-virgin olive oil
4 tablespoons unsalted butter, plus more for the baking dish
2 medium zucchini, thinly sliced
4 ounces mixed mushrooms (button, cremini, shiitake, oyster, chanterelle), sliced
1 bunch scallions, chopped (about 1 cup)
4 large hard-boiled eggs, chopped
1 cup freshly grated Grana Padano
½ cup Chicken Stock (page 143)

Preheat the oven to 425 degrees. Bring a large pot of salted water to a boil. Add the romaine leaves, and blanch until they just begin to wilt, about

1 minute. Immediately plunge them into a large bowl of ice water to stop the cooking. Drain, pat them dry, and cut out the tough center rib in the bottom of each leaf, to form an upside-down "V."

To a large skillet over medium-high heat, add the olive oil. When the oil is hot, add 2 tablespoons of the butter. When the butter is melted, add the zucchini and sauté until it begins to wilt, about 2 minutes. Add the mushrooms, scallions, and salt, and cook until the mushrooms release their liquid and the scallions are wilted, about 4 minutes. Increase the heat to high to boil away any excess liquid in the pan, about 1 to 2 minutes. Scrape into a bowl, and let it cool.

Once the vegetables are cooled, add the chopped eggs and ½ cup of the grated cheese, and mix well.

Butter a 9-by-13-inch baking dish. Lay the romaine leaves on your work surface, with the bottoms closest to you. Divide the filling among the lower thirds of the leaves, folding the bottom of each, then folding the sides over the filling and rolling up into a cylinder. Put rolls, seam side down, in the buttered baking dish, and dot the tops with the remaining 2 tablespoons butter. Pour the stock in the bottom of the dish. Sprinkle the rolls with the remaining ½ cup grated cheese. Cover the dish with foil, and bake until bubbly, about 20 minutes. Uncover, and bake until the cheese is browned and crispy, about 15 to 20 minutes more. Serve hot or at room temperature.

🍃 The recipe recommends the outer leaves of romaine lettuce, but this recipe will be delicious with the outer leaves of other lettuces, such as escarole.

Lentil Stew

Lenticchie in Umido
SERVES 4 TO 6 AS A SIDE

1½ cups brown lentils, rinsed
2 tablespoons extra-virgin olive oil
1 small onion, chopped
1 large shallot, chopped
2 medium carrots, peeled and chopped
2 celery stalks, chopped
2 fresh bay leaves
½ cup canned Italian plum tomatoes, preferably San Marzano, crushed by hand
2 cups Chicken Stock (page 143)
1½ teaspoons kosher salt
Freshly ground black pepper

In a medium saucepan, combine the lentils with cold water to cover by about an inch. Bring to a simmer, and blanch 10 minutes. Rinse and drain.

In a medium Dutch oven, heat the oil over medium-high heat. When the oil is hot, add the onion and shallot, and sauté until they are golden, about 6 minutes. Add the carrots, celery, and bay leaves. Sauté until just beginning to soften, about 4 minutes. Add the tomatoes, chicken stock, and the drained lentils. Bring to a simmer, and cook until the lentils are tender, about 25 to 30 minutes more. Season with the salt and some pepper. The mixture should be more of a stew than a soup. If it's too soupy, reduce it for a few minutes over high heat. Remove bay leaves and serve hot.

🍃 To keep the cooking time about the same, cut all of the vegetables about the same size—just slightly larger than the lentils.

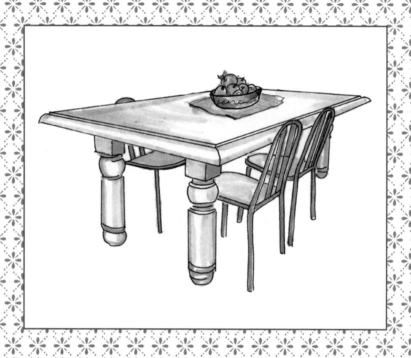

POLENTA, RICE, AND PIZZA

Nessuno sa cosa bolle in pentola meglio di chi la sta mescolando.
—Italian proverb

No one knows what's cooking in the pot better than the one doing the stirring.

Basic Polenta

Polenta
SERVES 6 TO 8

¼ cup extra-virgin olive oil
1 tablespoon kosher salt
4 fresh bay leaves
2 cups medium-grind yellow polenta
1 to 2 cups freshly grated Grana Padano
Up to 1 stick unsalted butter, softened (optional, but nice when you want a richer polenta)

In a medium Dutch oven, combine 10 cups cold water, the olive oil, salt, and bay leaves. Put the polenta in a spouted measuring cup for easy pouring. With the heat still off, whisk the water with one hand and pour in the polenta in a thin stream. Keep whisking until all of the polenta is incorporated and the mixture is smooth. Turn the heat to medium low, and gently bring the polenta to a simmer, whisking frequently, making sure to get the bottom and sides of the pan.

Once the polenta is simmering and thickening, switch to stirring with a wooden spoon. When the polenta is boiling and has become very thick, adjust the heat so just a few bubbles perk to the surface, and cover the pot with the lid ajar. Cook, stirring frequently, making sure to get in the corners and bottom so the polenta doesn't burn, until the polenta is glossy and pulls away from the sides of the pan, about 20 to 25 minutes from the time it began to simmer.

To finish the polenta, remove the pot from the heat and vigorously beat in the grated cheese. Start with 1 cup, and add up to 2, depending on your taste. If using the butter, beat it in a few tablespoons at a time, incorporating it completely before adding more. Discard bay leaves. Polenta will retain its heat for up to 30 minutes. If you want to chill the polenta to fry or grill it, cover it with plastic wrap to keep a crust from forming.

❧ Cold polenta in a piece will keep in the refrigerator sealed in plastic wrap for a week and in the freezer for 2 months.

Fried Polenta

Polenta Fritta
SERVES 6 TO 8

1 recipe Basic Polenta (see previous recipe), prepared without butter or cheese
3 tablespoons extra-virgin olive oil or unsalted butter

Spread the hot polenta on a lightly greased rimmed sheet pan to about ½ inch thick, and smooth with a rubber spatula dipped in cold water. Cover with oiled plastic wrap, and refrigerate until set, at least 2 hours.

Remove plastic, and turn polenta out onto a cutting board. Cut into squares or triangles.

Heat a large nonstick skillet over medium heat, and add the olive oil or butter. When the fat is hot, add the polenta pieces—in batches if necessary, so they don't touch. Fry, turning once, until golden brown on both sides and creamy on the inside, about 8 to 10 minutes. Serve immediately.

Grilled Polenta

Polenta alla Griglia
SERVES 6 TO 8

1 recipe Basic Polenta (see first recipe on this page), still hot, or leftover polenta
Extra-virgin olive oil, for brushing

Spread the hot polenta on a lightly greased rimmed sheet pan to about ½ inch thick, and smooth with a rubber spatula dipped in cold water. Cover with oiled plastic wrap, and refrigerate until set, at least 2 hours.

Preheat a grill or grill pan to medium heat. Remove plastic, and turn polenta out onto a cutting board. Cut into squares or triangles.

Brush polenta with olive oil, and gently place on the grill. Let sit without moving until the polenta develops a nice crust on the underside, about 3 to 4 minutes. Flip the polenta with a metal spatula, and grill until crusted on the second side, 3 to 4 minutes more. Serve immediately.

Baked Polenta with Mushroom Ragù

Polenta Pasticciata ai Funghi
SERVES 12, WITH LEFTOVERS THAT CAN EASILY BE FROZEN

1 batch (about 10 cups) Basic Polenta (page 199), freshly made and hot, with or without grated Grana Padano or Parmigiano-Reggiano (it will be richer if you include it, but is also good without it)
4 to 6 cups Mushroom Ragù (page 166)
2 tablespoons or more butter, softened, for the baking dish
1 cup Béchamel Sauce (page 168) (it will render the pasticciata richer and more complex)
1 to 2 cups shredded Muenster, low-moisture mozzarella, Italian Fontina, cheddar, or other soft cheese
½ to 1 cup freshly grated Grana Padano

Preheat the oven to 400 degrees, and set a rack in the center. Make the polenta, then put plastic wrap over the top, to keep it warm and to prevent a skin from forming on top. Be sure to assemble the pasticciata within ½ hour, while the polenta is still warm and soft with no lumps.

If necessary, heat the filling sauce to quite warm. If it is too dense for spreading, thin it with some hot water.

Thoroughly butter the bottom and sides of a 9-by-13-inch baking dish or 12-inch cast-iron skillet. Use more butter on the bottom, in particular if you want to unmold the pasticciata onto a platter. Put ¼ cup béchamel in the dish or skillet, and spread it around the bottom; it doesn't have to cover every bit.

Pour in half the polenta (about 5 cups) and spread it evenly in the bottom of the pan. Scatter ⅓ cup or more shredded Muenster or other soft cheese all over the top, then sprinkle on 2 to 4 tablespoons of grated Grana Padano. Pour or ladle 2 cups of the warm ragù over the polenta and cheese and spread it all over; use 3 cups sauce if you want a thicker layer.

Pour on a bit more than half of the remaining polenta (about 3 cups) and spread it. Spread another ¼ cup of béchamel on top, top with more shredded soft cheese and grated Grana Padano. Pour in the remaining ragù and spread it evenly.

For the top layer, spread all the rest of the polenta and another ¼ cup béchamel on top of that. Sprinkle on the remaining shredded soft cheese and grated Grana Padano. If you're making a thin pasticciata in a big pan, or want it to have a beautiful deep-gold crust, use enough béchamel and cheese to cover the top completely. Do not compress the cheeses, though.

Set the pan on a baking sheet, and bake for 45 minutes to an hour or more, until the top is deeply colored and crusted. Let the pasticciata cool for 10 minutes before serving. If serving portions from the baking pan, cut into squares (like lasagna), or wedges if you've used a round skillet or pan, and lift them out with a spatula.

If unmolding the pasticciata: Let it cool for at least 10 minutes. Run a knife around the sides of the pan, cutting through the crust sticking to the rim or sides. Lay a big board on top of the baking pan or skillet, hold the two together (with the protection of cloths and the help of other hands if necessary), and flip them over. Rap on the upturned pan bottom to loosen the bottom. Lift the board, and give the pan a good shake. The pasticciata will eventually drop out. Serve on the board, or reflip it onto a serving platter, and serve with a cup or more of warm sauce heaped on the top or served on the side.

❧ This dish also turns out delicious prepared with cold leftover polenta. Make the layers by cutting the cold polenta in sheets to layer the baking dish and filling it as per the rest of the recipe. You can also make this pasticciata using Tomato

Sauce (page 161) or Marinara Sauce (page 161) instead of Mushroom Ragù.

❧ If you want to prepare the pasticciata and bake it later the same or next day, spread the last layer of polenta and coat it well with béchamel, but don't sprinkle on the cheeses. Cover it, wrap it well, and refrigerate overnight. Before baking, sprinkle on the cheeses and make a tent of foil over the baking dish, without touching the cheese. Poke a few small holes in the foil to vent steam. Set the pan on a sheet and bake for ½ hour at 400 degrees, then remove the foil and continue to bake until deeply colored and crusted.

Polenta with Broccoli and Bacon

Polenta con Broccoli e Pancetta
SERVES 4 TO 6

POLENTA
1 tablespoon extra-virgin olive oil
1 fresh bay leaf
1 teaspoon kosher salt
1½ cups instant polenta
2 tablespoons unsalted butter, cut into pieces
½ cup freshly grated Grana Padano

BROCCOLI
¼ cup extra-virgin olive oil
3 garlic cloves, crushed and peeled
4 ounces slab bacon, cut into matchsticks
1 large head broccoli, stems peeled and sliced ¼ inch thick, head cut into 1-inch florets
½ teaspoon kosher salt
¼ teaspoon crushed red pepper flakes
2 ounces aged provola, shredded on the coarse holes of a box grater

For the polenta: In a large saucepan, combine 4 cups cold water with the olive oil, bay leaf, and salt. Set the pot over medium heat, and while it comes to a simmer, whisk in the instant polenta in a thin stream until it is all incorporated.

Once the polenta has come to a boil, reduce the heat so just a few bubbles perk at the surface, and cook until thickened and smooth, about 8 to 10 minutes.

Remove the pot from the heat. Beat in the butter, then the cheese. Cover, and keep warm while you make the broccoli.

To a large skillet over medium-high heat, add 2 tablespoons of the olive oil. When the oil is hot, add the garlic and bacon, and cook until the bacon renders its fat and is crisp on the edges, about 5 minutes.

Push the bacon to the side of the pan, add the broccoli, and season with the salt and red pepper flakes. Drizzle the broccoli with 2 tablespoons water, cover, and let cook, stirring occasionally and adding more water if the pan seems dry, until the broccoli is very tender, about 10 minutes. Uncover and reduce away any excess liquid in the pan. Remove garlic. Drizzle the broccoli with the remaining 2 tablespoons of olive oil, and toss well.

Serve the hot polenta in shallow bowls, with the broccoli mixture on top. Sprinkle with the shredded provola. Serve immediately.

Polenta Dressed as in Friuli

Polenta Condita alla Friuliana
SERVES 6

8 tablespoons (1 stick) unsalted butter
1 recipe hot Basic Polenta (page 199)
1½ cups (about 6 ounces) grated Montasio cheese
2 teaspoons ground cinnamon

Preheat the oven to 375 degrees. Using some of the butter, grease an 8-by-10-inch baking dish. In a small skillet or saucepan, cook the remaining butter over medium heat until the white flecks turn golden brown, about 4 minutes. Remove the skillet from the heat.

Pour about a third of the polenta into the prepared pan, and spread it into an even layer with a rubber spatula dipped in cold water. Pour a third of the browned butter over the polenta in the pan, and sprinkle it with a third of the Montasio cheese and a third of the cinnamon. Repeat this process, using half of the remaining polenta, butter, cheese, and cinnamon each time.

Set baking dish on a baking sheet and bake the polenta until the cheese is lightly browned and the edges are bubbling, about 30 minutes. Remove the polenta from the oven; let it rest for 10 minutes. Cut the polenta into squares, and serve immediately.

Polenta Nest with Truffled Egg

Nido di Polenta con Uova al Tartufo
SERVES 6

2 cups milk
1½ teaspoons kosher salt, plus more for egg yolks
1 fresh bay leaf
¾ cup medium-grind yellow polenta
8 tablespoons unsalted butter
6 egg yolks (or 6 whole eggs, to make a larger serving)
2 ounces fresh white truffle, brushed clean

Preheat the oven to 425 degrees. In a small saucepan, heat the milk. Cover the pan, and keep the milk warm over low heat. In a small heavy cast-iron or enameled cast-iron saucepan, bring 3 cups water, the salt, and bay leaf to a boil over medium heat and add the hot milk. Prepare the polenta according to the directions for Basic Polenta (page 199). Remove the polenta from the heat, and remove bay leaves and stir in 3 tablespoons of the butter.

Use 2 tablespoons of the remaining butter to grease lightly six 8-ounce ceramic ramekins or custard cups. In a small saucepan or skillet, melt the remaining 3 tablespoons of butter over low heat.

Ladle the hot polenta into the ramekins, dividing it evenly and dipping the ladle in water each time. With the back of the ladle dipped in water, make a little indentation in the center of the polenta, large enough for an egg yolk, or a whole egg. Set one egg yolk in each indentation. Sprinkle the yolks lightly with salt, and drizzle them with the melted butter. Place the ramekins on a baking sheet and set it in the oven. Bake until the egg is set outside but still has a runny yolk inside, 4 to 5 minutes—7 to 8 minutes if using a whole egg.

Remove the ramekins to serving plates. With a truffle slicer or the coarse side of a box grater, shave the truffles to cover the egg and polenta. Serve immediately.

❧ This can be a wonderful breakfast or a first course. The truffles make the dish exceptional, but sautéed mushrooms or buttered asparagus also work nicely.

Snails with Polenta

Polenta e Lumache
SERVES 4

2 slices bacon, coarsely chopped
1 small celery stalk
2 garlic cloves, crushed and peeled
3 tablespoons extra-virgin olive oil
1 medium onion, finely chopped
2 cans escargot (about 1 pound total)
2 teaspoons tomato paste
½ cup dry white wine
2 fresh bay leaves
1 cup crushed tomatoes
1 cup Chicken Stock (page 143)
2 tablespoons chopped fresh Italian parsley
½ recipe hot Basic Polenta (page 199)

In a mini–food processor, combine the bacon, celery, and garlic, and process to make a smooth pestata.

To a large skillet over medium-high heat, add the olive oil. When the oil is hot, add the onion and cook until golden, about 5 minutes. Rinse and drain the snails. Add the pestata and the snails, and cook until the bacon renders its fat, about 5 minutes.

Make a space in the pan, and add the tomato paste. Cook and stir in that spot until the tomato paste darkens a shade or two, about 1 minute. Stir the tomato paste into the snail mixture, and add the wine and bay leaves. Let the wine reduce by half, until syrupy, then add the tomatoes and chicken stock. Simmer until a thick sauce coats the snails, about 20 minutes.

Remove the bay leaves, stir in the parsley, and serve over the hot polenta.

🎺 You could buy fresh snails; if you do, you must purge and clean them well before you make this sauce. But I recommend you buy readily available canned escargot. I like the large size, and they usually come about 12 to a can (7.75 ounces). Two cans, six snails per portion, should be enough for this recipe. All you need to do is wash and drain them. If they seem too big you can cut them in half.

Basic Risotto

Risotto

SERVES 6 OR MORE (MAKES ABOUT 8 CUPS)

5 to 7 cups water, Chicken Stock (page 143), or Vegetable Stock (page 143), and an additional 1 to 2 cups of flavorful sauce (optional)
4 tablespoons extra-virgin olive oil, plus 2 tablespoons for finishing
2 cups chopped onions, medium-fine (about 10 ounces); you can substitute leeks, shallots, or scallions
1 teaspoon kosher salt
2 cups short-grain Italian rice, either Arborio or Carnaroli

1 cup white wine
½ to 1½ cups freshly grated Grana Padano or Parmigiano-Reggiano
Freshly ground black pepper, to taste

Pour 7 cups of water or stock into a large pot and bring it almost to a boil. Cover and keep it hot over very low heat, on a burner close to the risotto pan.

Put 4 tablespoons oil, the onions, and ½ teaspoon of the salt in a big pan and set over medium heat. Cook the onions slowly, stirring frequently with a wooden spoon, as they sweat, soften, and gradually take on a golden color, about 8 to 10 minutes. Adjust the heat if the onions are about to get brown.

Ladle ½ cup of water or stock into the onions, stir well, and continue to cook the onions without letting them brown, still over low to medium heat, for another 5 to 10 minutes. The onions should be golden and glistening with oil, but all the liquid must be cooked away. In this stage of cooking, you are softening and caramelizing the onions to form a flavor base for the risotto. You are keeping them from getting brown or crisp, and softening them by cooking in water, so that they will ultimately melt into the risotto. You then cook off the water completely to prepare for the next step, toasting the rice.

Add the rice all at once, raise the heat to medium, and stir constantly with the oily onions. Cook for about 3 minutes, until the rice grains have been toasted, but do not allow them to scorch or color. Have the wine ready to add. In this critical step, every grain of rice becomes coated and cooked in hot fat (the oil). This forms a capsule on the outer layer of each grain that will prevent it from absorbing too much liquid too fast and possibly disintegrating. "Toasting" means that the rice must be cooked on the outside—not brown. Toasted rice will still look white but you can hear a clicking sound when you stir it.

Pour in the wine all at once and cook with the rice for 2 to 3 minutes, over medium or medium-high heat. Stir constantly all around the pan, until the moisture has evaporated. Have the hot water close by and be ready to add it with a ladle or measuring cup. In this quick step, you are balancing the starchy character of the rice with the acidity and taste components of dry white wine. These are quickly absorbed by the rice kernels but the alcohol cooks off. Rice that is not tempered has less flavor and yields a starchy risotto.

Ladle in 1½ to 2 cups of very hot stock or water, enough to barely cover the rice; stir it in continuously, all around the pan. Add the remaining ½ teaspoon of salt, and stir well. Lower the heat, if necessary, to maintain a very gentle perking. You may stop stirring and leave the rice shortly after each addition of liquid, when it is wet and the danger of scorching is minimal—but don't go far. Stir frequently at first and then constantly as the risotto thickens. Make sure the spoon is reaching into all the corners of the pan, on the pan bottom, and around the sides. When all the liquid has been absorbed—the risotto will be harder to stir (the bubbling *sounds* thicker, too) and the pan bottom is visible in the track of the spoon—ladle in another cup of water. (If you are flavoring your risotto with a sauce, stir it in at this point, before the second addition of liquid.) Continue in the same fashion, adding liquid, stirring, and cooking for the next 15 to 20 minutes. Cook, stirring always, and add another 2 cups of liquid when the risotto is ready for it, as just described—anywhere from 3 to 6 minutes between additions. Keep track of how much liquid you have added. The gradual addition of hot liquid (it must be hot!) has two effects on the rice: it draws out the starches stored in the kernels, just a bit at a time, while the kernels are slowly absorbing liquid and cooking. Short-grain Italian rice has an abundance of a particular starch that, when released by the kernel into the warm liquid and fat in the pot, forms a creamy suspension. You must maintain a steady gentle simmering to maintain this process of "amalgamation." While some of the liquid is absorbed by the rice, it is also evaporating and the risotto will thicken and heat up rapidly. You stir continuously to prevent the starches from scorching. And you must add

more liquid in small amounts to continue the process as described, until you have reach optimal softening of the kernels and development of the suspension.

After the addition of at least 5 cups of water, you can taste and gauge the degree of doneness of the rice kernels and the fluidity of the creamy suspension. At any time that you find the rice grains pleasantly al dente and the risotto creamy you can choose to stop cooking. Or you may incorporate more liquid, up to about 7 cups total, if you want a softer, looser risotto.

When you are satisfied, turn off the heat and stir in the olive oil. Stir in grated cheese and freshly ground black pepper to taste. Serve the risotto immediately in heated bowls, with more cheese and pepper at the table. In this final step, you stop the cooking when the risotto reaches the consistency you want. You finish with olive oil, as a flavoring and amalgamating agent, and incorporate grated cheese and fresh pepper as flavor elements, to taste.

❧ You should use a 3-to-4-quart heavy saucepan at least 10 inches wide to allow for steady evaporation of the liquid. Enameled cast-iron or heavy-gauge stainless steel pans with a heat-dispersing bottom layer are particularly well-suited for risotto.

❧ You can substitute 2 tablespoons of butter for the extra-virgin olive oil for finishing the risotto.

Risotto with Vegetables

Risotto alle Verdure
SERVES 6

6½ cups Vegetable Stock (page 143) or Chicken
    Stock (page 143)
8 ounces broccoli (about 1 medium stalk)
1 cup blanched and peeled fava beans (see
    page 13) or frozen baby lima beans

3 tablespoons extra-virgin olive oil
½ cup minced scallions, greens included
1 tablespoon minced shallot
2½ cups Arborio or Carnaroli rice
½ cup dry white wine
½ teaspoon kosher salt, or as needed
2 tablespoons unsalted butter, cut into bits
½ cup freshly grated Grana Padano
Freshly ground black pepper, to taste

Bring the stock to a bare simmer in a medium saucepan. Trim the broccoli florets from the stems, keeping them small enough to fit on a spoon. (You should have about 1¼ cups.) Peel the stems, and cut into 2-inch pieces. Steam the florets just until bright green, about 1 minute. Steam the stems until very tender, about 4 minutes. Reserve the steaming liquid. Transfer the stems to a blender or food processor, and process until smooth. You will probably have to add some of the steaming liquid to make a smooth mixture. Scrape out the purée into a small bowl, and set the florets and purée aside.

If using the baby lima beans, cook them in a small saucepan of boiling salted water for 2 minutes. Drain them thoroughly, and set aside.

Heat the olive oil in a medium Dutch oven or large straight-sided skillet over medium heat. Add the scallions and shallot, and sauté until translucent, stirring often, about 4 minutes. Add the rice and stir to coat with the oil. Toast the rice until the edges become translucent, about 3 minutes. Pour in the wine, and stir well until it is evaporated, 2 to 3 minutes.

Add ½ cup of the hot stock and the salt. Cook, stirring constantly, until all the stock has been absorbed. Continue to add hot stock in small batches—just enough to moisten the rice completely—and cook until each successive batch has been absorbed. After the risotto has cooked for 12 minutes, stir in the broccoli purée and the favas or limas. About 3 minutes after that, stir in the broccoli florets. Stir constantly, and adjust the level of heat so the rice is simmering very gently while you are adding the stock, until the rice mixture is creamy but al dente. This will take about 18 minutes from the first addition of stock.

Remove the casserole from the heat. Beat in the butter; when it has melted, beat in the grated cheese. Adjust the seasoning with salt, if necessary, and pepper. Serve immediately, ladled into warm shallow bowls.

❧ When making this risotto, choose any vegetable that is in season—a wonderful opportunity to create exciting new combinations of flavors that will be yours to pass on. It can become a spring pea risotto, an autumn squash risotto, a winter beet risotto, or a summer corn risotto. This risotto is also a wonderful way to use leftover vegetables you might have in the refrigerator or freezer.

Creamy Rice with Porcini

Risotto ai Funghi Porcini
SERVES 4

6½ cups hot Chicken Stock (page 143) or
    Vegetable Stock (page 143)
5 tablespoons extra-virgin olive oil
1 cup minced onion
2 tablespoons minced shallots
12 ounces fresh porcini mushrooms, thickly
    sliced
2 cups Arborio or Carnaroli rice
½ cup dry white wine
½ teaspoon kosher salt
2 tablespoons unsalted butter, cut into bits
½ cup freshly grated Grana Padano
Freshly ground black pepper to taste

Bring the stock to a bare simmer in a medium saucepan. Heat 3 tablespoons of the olive oil in a medium Dutch oven or large straight-sided skillet, and sauté the onion and shallots until golden. Add the mushrooms, and sauté until tender, about 5 minutes. Remove mushrooms, and set aside.

To the same pan add the remaining olive oil

and the rice. Cook and stir to coat the rice with oil, until toasted but not colored, about 3 minutes. Pour in the wine, and cook until evaporated, about 2 minutes.

Add ½ cup of the hot stock and the salt. Cook, stirring constantly, until all the liquid has been absorbed. Continue to add hot stock in small batches (just enough to moisten the rice completely), stirring constantly to help the liquid absorb, until the rice mixture is creamy and al dente. With the last addition of the stock, return the mushrooms to the pot, and stir and cook for an additional 3 to 4 minutes. Remove the risotto from the heat, beat in the butter and then the cheese, season with pepper to taste, and serve immediately.

❧ Porcini is the ideal mushroom for this recipe, but any mushroom or mixture of mushrooms will yield a delicious risotto.

Risotto with Shavings of White Truffle

Risotto al Tartufo
SERVES 6

2 ounces fresh white truffle
6½ cups Chicken Stock (page 143)
3 tablespoons extra-virgin olive oil
1 cup minced onions
2 tablespoons minced shallots
2½ cups Arborio or Carnaroli rice
½ cup dry white wine
½ teaspoon kosher salt, plus more to taste
2 tablespoons unsalted butter, cut into bits
¼ cup freshly grated Grana Padano
Freshly ground black pepper to taste

Brush the truffles thoroughly with a vegetable brush to remove as much loose dirt as possible. With a damp paper towel, clean them thoroughly.

(You may store the truffles, embedded in the rice to be used in the risotto, in the refrigerator for up to 2 days, to add flavor to the rice.)

In a small saucepan, heat the stock just to a simmer. In a heavy, wide 3-to-4-quart straight-sided skillet or shallow Dutch oven, heat the olive oil over medium heat. Add the onions and shallots, and cook them until golden, stirring often, about 8 minutes. Add the rice, and stir to coat with the oil. Toast the rice until the edges become translucent, about 3 minutes. Pour in the wine, and stir well until evaporated.

Add ½ cup of the hot stock and the salt. Cook, stirring constantly, until all the stock has been absorbed. Continue to add hot stock in small batches—just enough to moisten the rice completely—and cook until each successive batch has been absorbed. Stir constantly, and adjust the level of heat so the rice is simmering very gently while you are adding the stock, until the rice mixture is creamy but al dente. This will take 16 to 18 minutes from the time the wine is added.

Remove the skillet from the heat. Beat in the butter until the butter is melted, then beat in the grated cheese. Adjust the seasoning with salt and pepper. Serve immediately, ladled into warm shallow bowls. Use a truffle slicer or the coarse side of a box grater to shave the truffles over the risotto at the table, and let the sublime aroma rise to delight each guest.

Risotto with Squash Blossoms and Zucchini

Risotto con Fiori di Zucca e Zucchine
SERVES 4 TO 6

6 cups Chicken Stock (page 143) or water
1 pound baby zucchini, blossoms still attached
4 tablespoons extra-virgin olive oil
1 small onion, finely chopped
1 small shallot, finely chopped

¼ teaspoon saffron threads
1½ cups Arborio or Carnaroli rice
½ cup dry white wine
½ teaspoon kosher salt, plus more to taste
6 tablespoons unsalted butter, cut into 6 chunks
1 cup freshly grated Grana Padano

In a medium saucepan, bring the chicken stock or water to a bare simmer. Separate the blossoms from the zucchini. Slice the zucchini into ¼-inch-thick rounds, and the blossoms crosswise into thirds. In a large straight-sided skillet over medium heat, heat 2 tablespoons of the olive oil. When the oil is hot, add the onion and shallot, and cook, stirring occasionally, until golden, about 4 minutes. Add the zucchini and blossoms, and stir until just wilted, about 3 minutes. Remove zucchini and blossoms to a plate, leaving some of the onion bits behind, and add the remaining olive oil to the pot. Soak the saffron threads in ½ cup of the hot stock.

Add the rice, and stir to coat in the oil. Toast the rice, without coloring it, for 3 minutes. Increase the heat to medium high, add the wine, and cook until the wine is reduced away to a glaze, about 2 minutes. Season with the salt. Add 1 cup of the stock and the saffron and its soaking liquid, and adjust the heat so the risotto is simmering. Gradually add more stock as each addition has been absorbed, stirring all the while, until the rice is al dente and the risotto is creamy, about 18 minutes. For the last 5 minutes of cooking, return the zucchini to the risotto. (You may not need to use all of the stock.) Stir so the zucchini cooks and amalgamates with the risotto.

Remove the skillet from the heat, and beat in the butter, incorporating it thoroughly. Stir in the cheese, adjust the seasoning if necessary, and serve.

Seafood Risotto

Risotto al Pesce
SERVES 4 TO 6

¼ teaspoon saffron threads
6 tablespoons extra-virgin olive oil
1 small onion, finely chopped
2 large shallots, finely chopped
1½ cups Arborio or Carnaroli rice
½ cup dry white wine
2 garlic cloves, crushed and peeled
12 littleneck clams, shucked, shucking juices reserved and strained, clams coarsely chopped
1 pound large shrimp, peeled, deveined, and cut into chunks
8 ounces sea scallops, halved through the middle if large
2 tablespoons Cognac or other dry brandy
1 teaspoon kosher salt, plus more to taste
Freshly ground black pepper
¼ cup chopped fresh Italian parsley

In a medium saucepan, bring 6 cups water to a bare simmer. Soak the saffron threads in ½ cup of the hot water.

In a large straight-sided skillet over medium heat, heat 3 tablespoons of the olive oil. When the oil is hot, add the onion and shallots and cook, stirring occasionally, until golden, about 4 minutes.

Add the rice, and stir to coat in the oil. Toast the rice, without coloring it, for 3 minutes. Increase the heat to medium high, add the wine, and cook until the wine is reduced away to a glaze, about 2 minutes. Add 1 cup of the hot water and the saffron and its soaking water, and adjust the heat so the liquid is simmering. Gradually add more water as each addition has been absorbed, stirring all the while, until the rice is still al dente, about 12 to 13 minutes. (You may not use all of the water.)

Heat a second large skillet over medium-high heat. Add 2 tablespoons of the olive oil. When the oil is hot, add the crushed garlic and cook until golden, about 2 minutes. Add the clams, shrimp, and sea scallops, and cook, tossing, until shell-fish just turns opaque. Add the reserved shucking juices, and bring to a boil; pour the mixture directly into the rice (which should still be al dente). Add the brandy, and stir in the remaining tablespoon olive oil. Season with the salt and pepper. Taste—the clam liquor may be salty—and season more if necessary. Cook everything together for 2 to 3 more minutes, adding more hot water if necessary, until the rice and seafood are both cooked. Stir in the parsley, remove garlic, and serve.

Black Cuttlefish Risotto

Risotto Nero di Seppia
SERVES 4 TO 6

6 cups Fish Stock (page 144)
1½ pounds cuttlefish
3 tablespoons extra-virgin olive oil
1 medium onion, finely chopped
1 garlic clove, finely chopped
1 teaspoon kosher salt
Freshly ground black pepper
1 cup dry white wine
1½ cups Arborio rice
1 teaspoon Cognac or other dry brandy
2 tablespoons unsalted butter, cut into pieces

In a medium saucepan, bring the stock to a bare simmer. Clean the cuttlefish by removing the blade-shaped interior cartilage, skin, and innards, reserving two of the ink sacs. (Two ink sacs are enough for this dish; the others can be frozen.) With a mortar and pestle, work the contents of the sac until smooth, discarding the actual sacs, or work in a small chopper with ⅓ cup of water, and reserve. Pull and detach the head and tentacles from the body. Cut off the tentacles, discarding the eyes, and squeeze out the cartilage mouth from the center of the tentacles and discard. Quarter the tentacles lengthwise. Cut the body

into ½-inch strips. Wash the bodies and tentacles and drain.

In a large straight-sided skillet over medium heat, heat the olive oil. When the oil is hot, add the onion, and cook, stirring occasionally, until translucent, about 3 minutes. Add the garlic, and sauté until fragrant but not browned, about 1 minute. Add the cuttlefish, and season with the salt and some black pepper. Sauté until the cuttlefish exudes its liquid, about 5 minutes. Add the wine and 1 cup stock. Simmer, covered, until the cuttlefish is tender, about 30 minutes, adding a little more stock, if necessary, to keep the cuttlefish covered in liquid while cooking.

Add the rice, and adjust the heat so the liquid is simmering. Simmer until the rice absorbs all of the liquid in the pan. Stir in the cuttlefish ink. Gradually add more hot stock as the previous additions have been absorbed, stirring all the while, until the rice is al dente and the risotto is creamy, about 18 minutes from the addition of the rice. (You may not need to use all of the stock.) Add the Cognac and butter during the last minute of cooking, mix well, and serve immediately.

Risotto Milan Style, with Marrow and Saffron

Risotto alla Milanese
SERVES 6

6 to 8 cups hot Mixed Meat Stock (see page 144) (chicken or turkey broth could be substituted)
½ teaspoon loosely packed saffron threads
1½ pounds beef marrow bones, preferably center-cut from the leg bone
2 tablespoons extra-virgin olive oil
2 cups finely chopped onions
1½ teaspoons kosher salt
2 cups Italian short-grain rice, such as Arborio, Carnaroli, or Vialone Nano
1 cup dry white wine

2 tablespoons unsalted butter, cut into pieces
½ cup freshly grated Grana Padano, plus more
  for passing

Heat the stock to a bare simmer in a medium saucepan. Pour about ½ cup of the stock into a heat-proof cup. Toast the saffron: Drop the strands into the bowl of a metal spoon, separating them a bit. Hold the spoon over a low open flame for just a few seconds, until the aroma is released, then add the threads to the stock in the cup. Let them steep while you start the risotto.

Scrape the marrow out of the bones with a sturdy paring knife—don't scrape off any bits of bone. Chop the marrow into little pieces; you should have about ⅓ cup total. Put the olive oil and marrow bits in a medium Dutch oven over medium heat. As the marrow melts, stir in the chopped onions and 1 teaspoon salt. Cook, stirring occasionally, for several minutes, until the onions are wilted and just starting to color; then ladle in ½ cup hot stock from the pot, and let it simmer until completely evaporated.

Add the rice all at once, raise the heat, and stir for 3 minutes, until the grains are toasted but not browned. Pour in the wine, and cook, stirring continuously, until nearly all of the liquid has been absorbed. Ladle in 2 cups of the hot stock, and stir steadily as the rice absorbs the liquid and begins to release its starch. When you can see the bottom of the pan as you stir, after 5 minutes or so, ladle in another couple of cups of stock and the remaining ½ teaspoon salt. Cook, stirring, until the stock is again almost completely absorbed. Now pour in the saffron-infused stock along with a cup or so of hot stock from the pot. Cook, stirring, until the liquid is absorbed and the saffron color has spread. Check the risotto for doneness: it should be creamy but still al dente. Incorporate more stock if necessary. When the risotto is fully cooked, turn off the heat and whip in the butter pieces, until melted. Stir in the ½ cup of grated cheese, and spoon into warm pasta bowls. Serve immediately, passing additional grated cheese at the table.

Risotto with Barolo on a Bed of Carrot Purée

Risotto al Barolo su Purè di Carote

SERVES 6

FOR THE CARROT PURÉE
3 cups chopped carrots (about 1¼ pounds)
3 tablespoons unsalted butter, at room
  temperature
Pinch of freshly grated nutmeg
Kosher salt

FOR THE RISOTTO
5 cups Chicken Stock (page 143) or Mixed Meat
  Stock (page 144)
3 tablespoons extra-virgin olive oil
1 cup minced onions
2 tablespoons minced shallots
2 cups Arborio or Carnaroli rice
1½ to 2 cups good Barolo wine
½ teaspoon kosher salt, or to taste
2 tablespoons unsalted butter, cut into bits
½ cup freshly grated Grana Padano, plus more
  for serving
Freshly ground black pepper

Pour the stock into a small saucepan, and bring to a bare simmer. For the carrot purée: Bring a medium saucepan full of salted water to a boil. Add the carrots, and cook until tender, about 13 minutes. Drain well, and pass through a food mill or purée in a food processor. Stir in the butter, nutmeg, and salt to taste. Cover and keep warm.

In a medium Dutch oven or large straight-sided skillet, heat the olive oil over medium heat. Add the onions and shallots, and cook them until golden, stirring often, about 8 minutes. Add the rice, and stir to coat with the oil. Toast the rice until the edges become translucent, about 3 minutes.

Add ½ cup of the wine, and cook, stirring, until all the wine is absorbed, about 4 minutes. Repeat with the remaining wine in ½-cup batches. Add ½ cup of the hot stock and the salt. Cook, stirring constantly, until all the stock has been absorbed.

Continue to add hot stock in small batches—just enough to moisten the rice completely—and cook until each successive batch has been absorbed. Season with salt. Stir constantly, and adjust the level of heat so the rice is simmering very gently while you are adding the stock, until the rice mixture is creamy but al dente, about 18 minutes from the time the wine was added.

Remove the pot from the heat. Beat in the butter until completely absorbed, then the grated cheese. Adjust the seasoning with salt, if necessary, and pepper.

To serve: Spread the warm carrot purée over the bottom of six warm shallow bowls. Top with some of the hot risotto. Top each serving with additional grated cheese to taste. Serve immediately.

Risotto with Squab

Risotto con Piccione
SERVES 6

FOR THE SQUAB SAUCE
2½ cups Chicken Stock (page 143)
¼ cup dried porcini mushrooms
4 medium squab (about 3½ pounds total)
3 fresh bay leaves
1 teaspoon fresh rosemary leaves
4 whole cloves
¼ cup extra-virgin olive oil
1 medium onion, chopped
2 slices lean bacon, finely diced
½ cup shredded carrots
1 cup dry white wine
1½ tablespoons tomato paste
Kosher salt
Freshly ground black pepper

FOR THE RISOTTO
6½ cups Chicken Stock (page 143)
3 tablespoons extra-virgin olive oil
½ cup minced onion

2 tablespoons minced shallots
2½ cups Arborio or Carnaroli rice
½ cup dry white wine
½ teaspoon kosher salt, or as needed
2 tablespoons unsalted butter, cut into bits
½ cup freshly grated Grana Padano, plus more to taste
Freshly ground black pepper

For the squab sauce: In a small saucepan, heat ½ cup of the chicken stock to boiling. Remove the pan from the heat, and stir in the porcini. Let stand until the porcini are softened, about 20 minutes. Drain the mushrooms, and reserve the liquid. Rinse the porcini briefly under cold water. Drain them well, and finely chop. Strain the soaking liquid through a coffee filter or a sieve lined with damp cheesecloth. Set the soaking liquid and chopped porcini aside separately.

Remove the backbones from the squab by cutting along both sides of the backbones with kitchen shears or a short, sturdy knife. Cut each bird into quarters: two leg and two breast pieces each. Wash the squab pieces, removing any traces of viscera, and pat dry with paper towels. Tie the bay leaves, rosemary, and cloves together in a small square of cheesecloth and set aside.

In a large skillet, heat the olive oil over medium heat. Add the onion and bacon, and cook, stirring, until the onion is wilted, about 3 minutes. Add the squab pieces, and brown, in batches, on both sides, turning as necessary, about 5 minutes each batch. Reduce the heat if necessary to avoid burning the onion. Remove all the squab from the skillet. Add the carrots and chopped porcini. Add the wine, and simmer until evaporated. Stir in the tomato paste, and cook, stirring several times, about 10 minutes. Return all the squab pieces to the pan. Add the reserved porcini-soaking liquid, about ½ cup of the chicken stock, and the cheesecloth bundle. Heat to boiling, then reduce the heat to a simmer over medium-low heat. Cook at a gentle simmer, partially covered, adding the remaining chicken stock about ½ cup at a time when the liquid in the pan is reduced by half, until the squab is tender when pierced with a fork or skewer—30 to 45 minutes, depending on the quality of the birds. At the end of cooking, there should be enough of a syrupy sauce to coat the squab and vegetables lightly.

Remove the bouquet garni and discard. Remove the squab to a platter, and cover with a sheet of aluminum foil. When it is cool, remove the meat from the bones, peel off the skin and any fat, and discard. Shred the meat into small pieces. Skim off as much fat as possible from the sauce. Return the squab meat to the sauce, and simmer over low heat until the sauce is reduced slightly, about 15 minutes. Skim the fat from the surface as it simmers. Season the squab sauce to taste with salt and pepper, and set it aside.

For the risotto: Heat the stock to a bare simmer in a medium saucepan. In a medium Dutch oven or straight-sided skillet, heat the olive oil over medium heat. Add the onion and shallots, and cook them until golden, stirring often, about 4 minutes. Add the rice, and stir to coat with the oil. Toast the rice until the edges become translucent, about 3 minutes.

Pour in the wine, and stir well until evaporated. Add ½ cup of the hot stock and the salt. Cook, stirring constantly, until all the stock has been absorbed. Add the squab and their sauce. Stir constantly until all the liquid is absorbed. Continue to add the hot stock in small batches—just enough to moisten the rice completely—and cook until each successive batch has been absorbed. Stir constantly, and adjust the level of heat so the rice is simmering very gently while you are adding the stock, until the rice mixture is creamy but al dente. This will take about 16 to 18 minutes from the addition of the squab sauce.

Remove the pot from the heat. Beat in the butter until melted, then the grated cheese. Adjust the seasoning with salt, if necessary, and pepper. Serve immediately, ladled into warm shallow bowls. Top each serving with additional grated cheese to taste.

Basic Crespelle

Crespelle
MAKES ABOUT 18

3 large eggs
2 cups milk
½ cup club soda
½ teaspoon kosher salt
3 cups all-purpose flour
6 tablespoons unsalted butter, melted and
    cooled, plus 1 stick unsalted butter, melted,
    for cooking the crêpes
1 teaspoon grated lemon zest

In a large bowl, whisk the eggs until smooth; whisk in the milk, 1 cup cold water, the club soda, and salt. Sift the flour over the top, and whisk just to combine—don't overmix. Whisk in the 6 tablespoons melted butter and the lemon zest. You may add more water, up to 1 cup. The additional water will make the batter looser and the crespelle thinner—they will be a bit harder to fry but will taste better.

Heat a 12-inch nonstick skillet over medium heat. When the skillet is hot, brush with some of the 1 stick melted butter. Remove the skillet from the heat, tilt one side up a bit so the batter will flow, and pour in the batter, rotating the skillet with your wrist as you pour so the batter evenly coats the bottom of the skillet. Cook until golden brown on the underside, about 1 to 1½ minutes, then flip with the help of a large offset spatula and brown the other side, about 30 seconds to a minute. Remove the crêpe to a plate. Repeat the cooking of the crêpes until you have used all of the batter, stacking the crêpes as you go. The crêpes are now ready for filling.

Baked Crespelle with Artichokes, Fava Beans, and Ricotta

Crespelle al Forno con Carciofi, Fave e Ricotta

SERVES 6 TO 8

FILLING

3 pounds fava beans, shelled (frozen is fine)
3 tablespoons extra-virgin olive oil
6 medium artichokes, cleaned (see page 6),
    halved, and thinly sliced
1 teaspoon kosher salt
2 large shallots, chopped (about ½ cup)
1 bunch scallions, trimmed and chopped (about
    1 cup)
1 pound fresh ricotta
2 large eggs, beaten
2 cups freshly grated Grana Padano

BESCIAMELLA

1 quart milk
2 fresh bay leaves
1 stick unsalted butter
½ cup all-purpose flour
1½ teaspoons kosher salt
¼ teaspoon freshly grated nutmeg

HERB PASTE

4 cups loosely packed fresh basil leaves
3 tablespoons extra-virgin olive oil
½ teaspoon kosher salt

ASSEMBLY

1 tablespoon unsalted butter, softened
1 cup freshly grated Grana Padano

12 Basic Crespelle (preceding recipe)

Preheat the oven to 400 degrees. For the filling: Bring a medium saucepan full of salted water to a boil. Add the favas, and blanch until bright green, about 2 minutes. Cool in a bowl with ice water, and peel and discard the outer skins. You should have about 2 cups peeled favas.

To a large skillet over medium-high heat,

add the olive oil. When the oil is hot, add the artichokes, season with the salt, and toss to coat the artichokes in the oil. Cover, and cook until the artichokes begin to wilt, about 6 minutes. Uncover, add the shallots, and stir. Cover the skillet, and cook until the artichokes and shallots are very tender, about 8 minutes more. Add the favas and scallions, stir, and cook until the scallions are just wilted, about 3 minutes. Scrape the vegetables into a large bowl, and cool to room temperature.

Stir the ricotta, eggs, and grated cheese into the cooled vegetables.

For the besciamella: In a medium saucepan, warm the milk with the bay leaves. In another medium saucepan, melt the butter over medium-low heat. When the butter is melted, whisk in the flour to make a smooth paste. Cook, stirring constantly, making sure to get into the corners of the pan, until the paste smells nutty (but don't let it brown), about 6 minutes.

Whisk in the hot milk in a steady stream. Add the salt and nutmeg, bring to a simmer, and cook until thickened, about 8 to 10 minutes, whisking occasionally to remove any lumps and keep the bottom from burning. Set aside.

For the herb paste: In a food processor, combine the basil, olive oil, and salt. Process to make a smooth paste. Scrape the paste into a small bowl, and stir in ½ cup of the besciamella until smooth.

To assemble: Butter a 9-by-13-inch baking dish with the softened butter. Line up the crêpes, herb paste, filling, and besciamella in front of you. Spread a thin layer of besciamella on the bottom of the dish. Arrange four overlapping crêpes on the bottom, so they extend over all four sides of the dish by about 2 inches, and fit one in the middle to fill the gap. Spread with half of the filling, dollop with a third of the herb paste, and spread. Overlap two crêpes on top to cover the filling. Spread with about a quarter of the besciamella, dollop with another third of the herb paste, and spread; then layer with two more overlapping crêpes. Spread with the remaining filling, then spread another quarter of the besciamella on top of that. Top with two more crêpes, then a quarter of the besciamella and the last of the herb paste. Place one final crêpe right in the middle of the dish, and flip the edges of the first crêpes over to enclose the filling. Spread with the remaining besciamella, and sprinkle with the 1 cup grated cheese. Tent with foil, making sure it doesn't touch the top, and bake until bubbly, about 30 to 35 minutes. Uncover, and bake until top is browned and crusty, about 15 to 20 minutes more.

Crespelle "Lasagna" Filled with Spinach and Herbs

Pasticciata alle Erbe con Spinaci
SERVES 6

1½ pounds fresh ricotta
12 Basic Crespelle (page 211)
1 teaspoon kosher salt, plus more for the pot
2 pounds spinach or Swiss chard
3 tablespoons extra-virgin olive oil
3 leeks, white parts only, trimmed, cleaned, and chopped (about 3 cups)
1 bunch scallions, trimmed and chopped (about 1 cup)
2 large eggs
½ teaspoon freshly ground black pepper
8 ounces mascarpone cheese
8 fresh sage leaves, chopped
20 fresh basil leaves, chopped
1 tablespoon chopped fresh thyme
2 tablespoons butter, softened
4 cups Béchamel Sauce (page 168)
3 cups freshly grated Grana Padano

Spoon the ricotta into a large fine-mesh sieve or a colander lined with a double thickness of cheesecloth. Place the sieve over a bowl, and cover the ricotta well with plastic wrap. Let the ricotta drain in the refrigerator at least overnight, or up to 24 hours. Discard the liquid in the bottom of the bowl. Make the crêpes. (This can be done up to 24 hours in advance.)

Preheat the oven to 425 degrees. Bring a large pot of salted water to a boil. Remove the stems from the spinach or chard. (Reserve chard stems for another use, if you like.) Wash and dry the leaves. Add the greens to the boiling water, and cook until just tender, about 2 minutes for the spinach or 5 to 6 minutes for the chard. Drain the greens in a colander, and rinse them under cold water until cool enough to handle. With your hands, squeeze out as much water as you can from the greens. Chop coarsely.

Heat the olive oil in a large skillet over medium heat. Stir in the leeks and scallions, and cook until wilted, about 4 minutes. Stir in the greens, and cook, stirring, 2 minutes. Remove and cool.

Turn the drained ricotta into a large bowl. Add the eggs, salt, and pepper. Stir in the mascarpone, herbs, and greens mixture until blended.

Using the softened butter, grease the bottom and sides of a 9-by-13-inch ceramic or glass baking dish. Arrange four crêpes, side by side and barely overlapping, so they cover the sides of the dish completely and overhang the sides of the dish by about 2 inches. Cover the middle of the dish with another crêpe.

Reserve 2 cups ricotta mixture, 1 cup béchamel, and 2 cups of grated Grana Padano and set aside. Spread ⅓ cup of the béchamel in an even layer over the crêpes lining the bottom of the dish. Spread 1½ cups of the ricotta filling over the béchamel, and top that with another layer of ⅓ cup béchamel. Sprinkle about ⅓ cup of the Grana Padano over the béchamel. Cover this first layer of filling with two crêpes. Make another filling layer, using half the remaining ricotta mixture, béchamel, and grated cheese. Top with a layer of two crêpes. Make the last filling layer using the remaining ricotta mixture, béchamel, and grated cheese. Fold the overhanging edges of the crêpes over the top layer of filling. Top any uncovered filling with additional crêpes. Spread the reserved 1 cup of béchamel in an even layer over the pasticciata, then sprinkle the reserved 2 cups of Grana Padano over the béchamel.

Bake until the top of the pasticciata is well browned and the edges are crispy, about 30 minutes. Remove, and let cool for 15 minutes. Cut the pasticciata into squares and serve.

❧ This pasticciata can be prepared entirely in advance and refrigerated for up to 1 day. Let the refrigerated pasticciata stand at room temperature before baking.

Manicotti

MAKES ABOUT 18 MANICOTTI, SERVING 6 OR MORE

1 pound fresh ricotta, or one 15-ounce container whole-milk ricotta
4 cups Tomato Sauce (page 161)
18 Basic Crespelle (page 211) or 3½-by-3-inch squares of Fresh Pasta (page 221), cooked and cooled
2 large eggs
1 teaspoon kosher salt
1½ cups ¼-inch cubes fresh mozzarella (about 6 ounces), plus 4 ounces fresh mozzarella, grated (about 1¼ cups)
1 cup freshly grated Grana Padano
½ cup chopped fresh Italian parsley
¼ teaspoon freshly ground white pepper
Pinch of freshly grated nutmeg
2 tablespoons unsalted butter, softened, for the baking pans

Spoon the ricotta into a large fine-mesh sieve or a colander lined with a double thickness of cheesecloth. Set the sieve over a bowl, and cover the ricotta well with plastic wrap. Let the ricotta drain in the refrigerator at least overnight, or up to 24 hours. Discard the liquid in the bottom of the bowl. Make the tomato sauce and the crêpes or pasta squares. (The crêpes may be made up to 1 day in advance, the pasta squares up to several hours in advance.)

Preheat the oven to 425 degrees. Whisk the eggs and salt together in a large bowl until foamy. Add the drained ricotta, the mozzarella cubes, ½ cup of the Grana Padano, the parsley, pepper, and nutmeg. Stir well until blended.

Coat the bottom of each of two 9-by-13-inch baking pans with the butter (or any two pans into which the manicotti will fit comfortably), and spread each with ½ cup of the tomato sauce. Working with one crêpe or pasta square at a time, spoon 3 full tablespoons of the ricotta filling about 1 inch from the edge closest to you. Roll loosely into a cylinder, smoothing out the filling along the length of the tube as you roll.

Arrange the manicotti, seam side down and side by side, over the sauce in the baking pans. Spoon the remaining sauce over the manicotti, and sprinkle them with the remaining ½ cup of the Grana Padano. Cover the baking dishes loosely with aluminum foil, and poke the foil several times with a fork. Bake until the edges are bubbly, about 20 minutes. Uncover the dishes, scatter the grated mozzarella over the top of the manicotti, and bake until all is bubbling and the cheese topping is golden brown, about 20 minutes.

❧ If you choose to make the manicotti with pasta squares, fill and roll them on a damp towel—it will make them easier to handle. For a lighter, thinner sauce, add a little stock to the tomato sauce or to the baking dish after you add the sauce, or don't cook the sauce quite so much when you make it. If you have some fresh basil in the kitchen, tear some leaves and scatter them over the manicotti in the dish right before you bake them.

Pizza

MAKES 2 PIZZAS, SERVING 4

DOUGH

1 teaspoon active dry yeast

1 teaspoon sugar

1 tablespoon extra-virgin olive oil, plus more for the bowl

3¼ to 3½ cups all-purpose flour, plus more as needed

1 teaspoon kosher salt

SAUCE

1½ cups drained canned Italian plum tomatoes, preferably San Marzano, crushed by hand or through a food mill

1 tablespoon extra-virgin olive oil

1 teaspoon kosher salt

½ teaspoon dried oregano, preferably Sicilian on the branch

¼ teaspoon crushed red pepper flakes

3 garlic cloves, crushed and peeled

TOPPING

1 pound fresh mozzarella, sliced

Fresh basil leaves

Freshly grated Grana Padano

Extra-virgin olive oil, for drizzling

In a spouted measuring cup, mix the yeast, sugar, and olive oil into 1¼ cups warm water (about 100 degrees, or just warm to the touch), and let sit until bubbly, about 3 minutes.

Put 3 cups flour in a mixer fitted with the dough hook, and add the salt. Pour in the yeast mixture, and mix at medium speed until a rough, sticky ball of dough comes together, about 1 minute, adding a little more flour or water as necessary. Let rest 5 minutes in the mixer, then mix on low until the dough is no longer sticky, about 1 minute. Oil your hands, transfer the dough to the counter, and knead until very smooth, about 30 seconds. Transfer to an oiled bowl, and cover the surface of the bowl with plastic wrap. Refriger-

ate at least 4 hours or overnight. Slowly leavened dough is tastier.

Before making the pizza bring the dough to room temperature. Stir together the sauce ingredients in a bowl, and let the flavors blend at room temperature. Preheat the oven to 500 degrees with a pizza stone on the bottom rack. (If you don't have a pizza stone, use an inverted sheet pan.) Punch the dough down, divide it in half, and let it rest on the counter and come to room temperature.

Stretch one pizza on a sheet of parchment paper on a pizza peel or the back of a sheet pan to approximately a 10-inch round shape (it's okay if it's irregular and more of an oval or a square). Fish the garlic from the sauce, and discard. Spread half of the sauce on the pizza, and top with the mozzarella, a few torn fresh basil leaves, and a light sprinkle of grated cheese. Drizzle lightly with olive oil. Slide the pizza onto the stone (still on the parchment), and bake until the crust is browned on the underside and the cheese is browned and bubbly, about 8 to 10 minutes. Repeat with the remaining ball of dough. (You may have a little bit of sauce left, depending on how wide you've stretched your pizza; you just want a light coating of sauce.)

❧ You can add whatever toppings you like to the pizzas—salumi, grilled vegetables, olives, capers, anchovies, etc. Just go sparingly, because an overloaded pizza will be soggy.

Grilled Pizza

Pizza alla Griglia
MAKES 4 INDIVIDUAL PIZZAS

1 recipe pizza dough, made with only 1 cup
water (preceding recipe)

SAUCE
1½ cups drained canned San Marzano tomatoes,
crushed by hand or through a food mill
1 tablespoon extra-virgin olive oil
1 teaspoon kosher salt
½ teaspoon dried oregano, preferably Sicilian on
the branch
¼ teaspoon crushed red pepper flakes
3 garlic cloves, crushed and peeled

TOPPING
Kosher salt
1 pound fresh mozzarella, sliced
Fresh basil leaves
Freshly grated Grana Padano
Extra-virgin olive oil, for brushing and
drizzling

About an hour before you are ready to make
the pizza, stir together the sauce ingredients in
a medium bowl, and let the flavors blend at room
temperature. Preheat one side of your grill to high
(if your grill has a thermometer, have it between
500 and 600 degrees) and the other side to the
lowest heat possible. Punch the dough down,
divide it into four pieces, and let it rest on the
counter and come to room temperature. Stretch
the dough into four rounds (or ovals) of about
8 inches in diameter. Brush two sheet pans with
olive oil, and lay the rounds on the pans, flipping
once so they are lightly oiled on both sides.

Fish the garlic from the sauce, and discard.
Depending on the size of your grill, you can make
two or four pizzas at a time. Season the rounds
lightly with salt. Slide the dough rounds from the
sheet pans onto the hot side of the grill; it will
stretch a little more as you transfer it, and that's

okay. Cook until the top blisters and bubbles and
the bottom is cooked and charred in places, about
1 to 2 minutes, moving the dough occasionally if
it seems to be cooking unevenly. Flip over to the
cooler side of the grill with the bubbly side down.
(A combination of tongs and a wide metal spatula
are the best tools for this job.)

Quickly cover the pizza with sauce, then a thin
layer of mozzarella. Add a few torn basil leaves, a
dusting of grated Grana Padano, and a drizzle of
olive oil. Cover the grill until the cheese begins to
melt, about 1 minute. Lift the grill cover slightly
to check on it, and lower the temperature if the
dough is getting too charred. Open the grill,
slide the pizza to the hot side, and cook until the
underside is nicely charred, about 30 seconds to
a minute more, moving the pizza around the grill
as necessary to avoid burning. Using tongs, slide
the pizza onto a cutting board, and serve.

❧ The dough for grilled pizza needs to be a little
sturdier to transfer to the grill, so use less water.

Mini Calzone

Calzoni Piccoli
MAKES ABOUT 18 MINI-CALZONES

3 tablespoons extra-virgin olive oil, plus more for
brushing
4 garlic cloves, crushed and peeled
12 ounces sweet Italian sausage without fennel
seeds, removed from casings
12 ounces spinach or escarole, washed, dried,
and chopped
1 pound fresh ricotta, drained
1 batch pizza dough (page 215)

Preheat the oven to 400 degrees. Line two baking
sheets with parchment.

Heat the olive oil in a large skillet. When the
oil is hot, add the garlic and the sausage. Cook

over medium heat, breaking up the sausage with a wooden spoon, until browned, about 4 minutes. Toss in the chopped spinach or escarole, and cook, stirring, until tender and wilted, about 7 minutes. Remove from heat, and scrape into a bowl to cool. When the sausage mixture is cooled, remove garlic and stir in the ricotta.

Roll out the dough on a floured work surface to a rectangle about ¼ inch thick. Using a 4½-inch round, cut out as many circles as you can, rerolling the dough to get more circles. You should have about eighteen.

Fill each circle with about 2 tablespoons of the filling. Brush the edges of the dough with water, then fold over and crimp edges together with a fork. Poke holes in the top of each calzone. Place on the baking sheets, and brush the tops of the calzones with olive oil. Bake in the oven, rotating the pans front to back halfway through, until the calzones are golden brown, about 25 minutes.

PASTA

La vita è una combinazione di magia e pasta.
—Federico Fellini

Life is a combination of magic and pasta.

Fresh Pasta

Here I give you three go-to recipes for fresh pasta that can be used with any of my sauces in this book or with your family favorites. The ingredients in each recipe are basically the same, just in different proportions. What makes the difference in fresh pasta is the number of eggs you use to make the dough. Throughout the book you will encounter many different pasta doughs, made of different flours and flavorings. If you follow each recipe, you will get excellent results, but I especially wanted to share with you these three basic options in pasta dough making.

The most luxurious pasta dough is made only with egg yolks; it is golden in color and rich in taste. This pasta is for Sunday dinners and for special occasions, such as when truffles are in season. It does not need intensely flavored sauces; a dressing as simple as butter and grated Grana Padano turns it into a special dish.

The middle golden pasta dough contains a mixture of egg yolks and whole eggs. It is a good pasta for making stuffed pasta like ravioli, tortellini, lasagna, and manicotti. It is resilient and makes great pappardelle; it is also good with robust tomato-based sauces.

Light egg pasta dough is made with only two eggs, and water is used to bind the dough. It cooks faster than the other two and absorbs sauces more readily. I like it for fish and vegetable sauces, and even more with intense game-based sauces. It is good when shaped like garganelli; I enjoy pappardelle made from this pasta as well.

Fresh Pasta Doughs

Pasta Fresca
MAKES I POUND, SERVING 4 TO 6

RICH GOLDEN PASTA DOUGH
2 cups all-purpose flour, plus more for dusting
9 large egg yolks (⅔ cup)
2 tablespoons extra-virgin olive oil
2 tablespoons water

MIDDLE GOLDEN PASTA DOUGH
2 cups all-purpose flour, plus more for dusting
1 large egg yolk
3 large eggs
1 tablespoon extra-virgin olive oil

LIGHT EGG PASTA DOUGH
2 cups all-purpose flour, plus more for dusting
2 large eggs
¼ cup extra-virgin olive oil
3 tablespoons water

To make the dough by hand: Measure the flour, and shake it through a sieve into a medium mixing bowl. Drop the eggs and/or egg yolks into a small bowl; beat briefly with a fork to break them up. Pour in the measured amounts of oil and water, and mix well with the eggs. Pour the wet ingredients into the flour. Toss and mix everything with a fork until all the flour is moistened and starts to clump together. Lightly flour your hands, then gather the clumps and begin kneading right in the bowl, folding the raggedy mass over, pushing and turning it, then folding again. When you've formed a cohesive clump of dough, turn it out onto a small work surface lightly dusted with ½ teaspoon flour, and continue kneading for 2 to 3 minutes, until the dough is smooth and shiny on the outside, soft throughout (no lumps), and stretchy. If your dough seems too sticky or too hard after it has been kneaded for a minute or two, adjust the consistency with very small amounts of flour or water. Form the dough into a disk, wrap it tightly in plastic wrap, and let it rest at room temperature for ½ hour.

To make the dough in the food processor: Fit the regular steel dough blade in the bowl of the processor. Measure the flour into the bowl; process for a few seconds to blend and aerate. Drop the eggs and/or egg yolks into a small bowl; beat briefly with a fork to break them up. Mix in the measured amounts of oil and water. To minimize the chance of overheating the dough, use eggs right from the refrigerator, and cold water. Start the machine running with the feed tube open. Pour the wet mixture into the bowl quickly; scrape all the egg drippings out of the bowl into the processor, too. Let the machine run for about 30 seconds. A dough should form quickly; most of it should clump or ball up on the blade, where it will twist and knead; some may spread on the sides of the bowl. Let the machine knead the dough for about 10 seconds (no more than 40 seconds total processing). Turn the dough out onto a very lightly floured surface, and knead by hand for another 30 seconds or so, until it's smooth, soft, and stretchy. Wrap and rest the dough, or store it as described for making the dough by hand. If you have a problem in the food processor—if there's no apparent clumping after 30 seconds, or the dough stiffens up very quickly—stop the machine and feel the dough. Adjust for stickiness or dryness by working in either flour or water in small amounts. You can continue to work the dough in the machine, but don't process for more than a total of 40 seconds. Or you can turn the dough out to correct the consistency and finish kneading by hand.

However you have made the dough, you can store it, very well wrapped, in the refrigerator for a day, or for a month or more in the freezer. Defrost frozen dough slowly in the refrigerator, and let it return to room temperature before rolling. Defrosted dough will need a bit more flour.

TO MAKE PAPPARDELLE AND TAGLIATELLE

Cut the dough into four equal pieces. Keep the other pieces covered as you begin to roll. Have two floured baking sheets at the ready. Open the pasta machine to the first widest setting. Press the dough into a rectangle and roll through the pasta machine; fold dough in half, and roll through again. Fold the dough in three like a letter and roll through again. Repeat this folding and rolling several more times, to strengthen and elongate the dough. Repeat this step with the remaining three pieces of dough, keeping the others floured and covered with kitchen towels as you work.

Set to the third setting, which is tighter, on the machine, and roll each piece through twice, with the short end going in first. Set to the fifth setting on the pasta machine, and roll the pieces through. They will get a lot thinner and longer this time, so cut each piece in half crosswise. You should have eight long pieces now, all about the width of the machine. Spread the rolled sheets of pasta layered with kitchen towels or parchment so they do not stick. Roll each piece through once on the sixth setting. You should just be able to see your hand through the back of a strip.

Cut the strips into lengths of about 5 or 6 inches, and trim the sides so they are mostly straight; don't trim too much, because you don't want to waste pasta. Roll a few strips up at a time like a jelly roll, and cut in four equal intervals for pappardelle or in nine equal strips for tagliatelle. Shake the pieces loose, and toss with a little flour, then form it into little nestlike mounds. Rest on floured sheet pans while you cut the rest.

SAUCES RECOMMENDED:
Duck Guazzetto (page 223)
Mushroom Ragù (page 166)
Marinara Sauce (page 161)

TO MAKE MALTAGLIATI (PASUTICE)

Roll the dough in strips, as directed above for pappardelle.

Trim the edges of the strips so they are mostly straight. Roll each strip up like a jelly roll, starting with the short edge, and cut into 1½-inch strips. Unroll and lightly flour the strips. Stack the strips and cut crosswise at a slight angle to make them look like rhombuses, rectangles with angled sides. Toss them in flour, and rest them on floured baking sheets while you make the remaining maltagliati.

SAUCES RECOMMENDED:

Calamari, Scallop, and Shrimp Sauce (page 251)
Lobster Fra Diavolo (page 226)
Classic Pesto (page 167)
Shrimp and Basil Sauce (page 255)

TO MAKE GARGANELLI

Make a batch of maltagliati, being sure not to flour them too much, and keeping the pieces covered as you go; you want the dough to remain soft and pliable to get the ends of the rhombuses to stick together and form the garganelli.

To form the garganelli: Wrap one rhombus piece of pasta around your index finger, or a thick wooden dowel, round pencil, or chopstick so two corners overlap. Press the ends that overlap so they stick together and form a quill shape. Pull the garganelli off your finger or dowel and rest the garganelli in one layer on floured sheet pans as you go.

SAUCES RECOMMENDED:

Meat Sauce Bolognese (page 162)
Duck Guazzetto (page 223)
Chicken Guazzetto (page 303)

Pappardelle with Duck Guazzetto

Pappardelle con Guazzetto d'Anatra
MAKES 5 TO 6 CUPS SAUCE
SERVES 8

5 cups Chicken Stock (page 143)
½ cup dried porcini
3 fresh bay leaves
1 sprig fresh rosemary
5 whole cloves
3½ pounds duck legs (4 or 5 legs), or 1 whole duck, quartered
¼ cup extra-virgin olive oil
¼ teaspoon kosher salt, plus more to taste and for the pasta pot
4 ounces slab bacon, cut into chunks
1 medium onion, cut into chunks
2 tablespoons tomato paste
1 cup dry white wine
Freshly ground black pepper to taste
Double recipe Middle Golden Pasta Dough (page 221), prepared as pappardelle (page 222)
1 cup freshly grated Grana Padano

Heat the chicken stock in a small saucepan until hot. Put the porcini in a spouted measuring cup, add 1 cup hot stock, and let soak until softened, about 15 minutes. Squeeze excess liquid from the porcini and chop them. Drain, strain the soaking liquid, and reserve it. Make a bouquet garni with bay leaves, rosemary, and cloves.

Trim the excess skin and all the visible clods of fat from the duck legs. Shave off the skin and the thick fat layer that covers the thigh, exposing the meat, but leave a strip of skin and fat covering about a third of the thigh (and the skin on the drumstick), to add flavor. Depending on how well the legs were trimmed by the butcher, you may remove up to a pound of fat.

Heat a medium Dutch oven over medium-high heat. Add the olive oil. When it is hot, lay in the duck pieces, skin side down, and let them sear for a couple of minutes in place. When they're slightly crusted, turn them over and brown the other side; turn to brown all the surfaces a bit, 6 to 8 minutes in all. Remove the duck to a plate, and sprinkle ¼ teaspoon salt all over.

In a food processor, combine the bacon and onion and pulse to make a chunky pestata. Add to the pot over medium heat, and cook until the bacon renders its fat, about 5 minutes. Clear a hot spot in the pan bottom, drop in the tomato paste, toast it for a minute, then stir it in with the onion and bacon.

Return the duck legs to the pan, along with any juices they've released. Pour in the wine, raise the heat, and let it boil until almost completely evaporated, turning the duck several times over in the pan. Add the chopped porcini and the soaking water and enough hot broth just to cover the legs. Add the bouquet garni, and bring the liquid to a boil. Cover, and adjust the heat to maintain a steady perking of bubbles all over the surface of the sauce. Cook for about 2½ hours or more, checking every 20 minutes or so and adding just enough more broth to keep the meat covered. When done, the duck meat should be falling off the bone. Remove from the heat, taste the sauce, and adjust the seasonings with salt and pepper. If you'll be using the sauce right away, spoon or pour off the fat from the surface. (Otherwise, wait until you've chilled the sauce and just lift off the solidified layer of fat.)

Let the legs cool completely (or as long as possible) in the sauce. Before refrigerating or serving, lift them onto a large platter or board; also pick out the bouquet garni and discard. Strip and trim all the edible duck meat from the legs; discard bones, skin, and cartilage. Tear the tender meat into rough bite-sized pieces, return to the sauce, and bring all to a boil before serving.

Bring 8 quarts of salted water to a boil. Shake any excess flour from the cut pappardelle, and a handful at a time drop them into the boiling water. Mixing periodically, boil until al dente, about 1 to 2 minutes. Meanwhile, heat the duck sauce to simmering. Taste the sauce, and adjust the seasoning if necessary.

Remove the pappardelle with tongs and a spider and add them directly to the duck guazzetto.

Toss to coat the pasta well with the sauce. Remove from heat, add the grated Grana Padano, toss well, and serve.

Pappardelle with Fresh Porcini Sauce

Pappardelle con Salsa di Porcini Freschi
SERVES 6

½ teaspoon kosher salt, plus more for the pasta pot
1½ cups Chicken Stock (see page 143)
¼ cup extra-virgin olive oil
1½ pounds fresh porcini, trimmed and thickly sliced (you can also use a combination of porcini and morels or other wild mushrooms)
4 garlic cloves, crushed and peeled
Freshly ground black pepper
2 tablespoons unsalted butter, cut into pieces
¼ cup chopped fresh Italian parsley
1 recipe Rich Golden Pasta Dough (page 221), prepared as pappardelle (page 222)
¾ cup freshly grated Grana Padano

Bring a large pot of salted water to a boil for the pasta. Heat the chicken stock to a low simmer in a small saucepan.

Heat a large skillet over medium-high heat. Add 2 tablespoons of the olive oil. When the oil is hot, add half of the mushrooms and half of the garlic. Do not stir the mushrooms; let them brown on one side, about 2 minutes, then gently stir to brown the rest, about 1 to 2 minutes more. Remove to a plate. Repeat with the remaining olive oil, mushrooms, and garlic.

Return all of the mushrooms to the skillet, discarding the garlic, and season with the salt and pepper. Add the butter. When the butter melts, pour in the hot stock and bring to a simmer. Simmer until porcini are tender and the sauce has reduced by about a third, about 5 minutes.

When the sauce is almost done, stir in the

parsley. Cook the pasta: Add the pappardelle to the boiling water and cook until al dente, just 1 to 2 minutes after it all returns to a boil. Carefully remove the pasta with a spider and tongs, and transfer directly to the sauce. Toss to coat the pasta in the sauce, adding a little pasta water if it seems dry. Remove the skillet from the heat, and sprinkle with the grated cheese. Toss, and serve immediately.

Tagliatelle with Mushroom Sauce

Tagliatelle con Salsa di Funghi
SERVES 6

Kosher salt
3 tablespoons extra-virgin olive oil
4 garlic cloves, lightly crushed and peeled
1½ pounds fresh assorted mushrooms, cleaned, trimmed, and sliced
4 fresh sage leaves
3 tablespoons tomato paste
3 tablespoons unsalted butter
1 cup Chicken Stock (page 143)
3 tablespoons chopped fresh Italian parsley
Freshly ground black pepper to taste
1½ recipes Rich Golden Pasta Dough (page 221), prepared as tagliatelle (page 222), or dried egg tagliatelle
½ cup freshly grated Grana Padano

Bring a large pot of salted water to a boil for the pasta. Heat the olive oil in a large skillet over medium heat. Add the garlic and cook until golden, about 2 minutes. Toss the mushrooms with the sage leaves in the skillet to coat them in the hot oil and cook, stirring occasionally, until the mushrooms have given up their liquid and it has evaporated, about 10 minutes. Make a hot spot in the pot by moving some mushrooms. Add the tomato paste and stir, then fold into the mushrooms; cook about 4 minutes. Add the chicken stock and butter to the skillet, and

let simmer over medium heat until the butter is incorporated into the sauce, about 5 minutes. Stir in the parsley, and add salt and pepper to taste. Remove garlic.

Add the tagliatelle to the boiling water and cook until al dente, about 3 minutes after pasta water returns to a boil. Remove the pasta with tongs and add directly to the simmering sauce. Toss to coat the pasta with the sauce, adding a little pasta water if it seems dry. Remove the skillet from the heat, and sprinkle with the grated cheese. Toss and serve.

Pappardelle in Leek Sauce

Pappardelle ai Porri
SERVES 6

½ teaspoon kosher salt, plus more for the pasta pot
2 cups Chicken Stock (page 143)
3 large leeks
3 tablespoons extra-virgin olive oil
3 sweet Italian sausages without fennel seeds, removed from casings (about 12 ounces)
1 medium shallot, chopped
4 tablespoons unsalted butter, cut into 4 pieces
Freshly ground black pepper
1½ recipes Middle Golden Pasta Dough (page 221), prepared as pappardelle (page 222)
¾ cup freshly grated Grana Padano

Bring a large pot of salted water to a boil for the pasta. Heat the chicken stock to a low simmer in a small saucepan.

Trim the leeks, and discard the top third of the tough green portion. Cut the leeks into ½-inch-thick rounds, and wash well. Drain, and dry well on paper towels.

Heat a large skillet over medium-high heat. Add the olive oil. When the oil is hot, add the sausage. Cook and crumble the sausage with a wooden spoon until no longer pink, about 5 minutes. Add the leeks and shallot, and cook until the leeks begin to wilt, about 6 minutes.

Add 2 tablespoons of the butter, and stir to melt and incorporate. Season with the salt and some pepper. Add the stock, and bring to a brisk simmer. Simmer until reduced by about a third, about 4 minutes.

Meanwhile, cook the pappardelle in the boiling water until al dente, just about 3 minutes after it returns to a boil. Carefully remove the pasta with a spider and tongs, and transfer directly to the sauce. Add the remaining 2 tablespoons butter, and toss to coat the pasta in the sauce, adding a little pasta water if it seems dry. Remove the skillet from the heat, and sprinkle with the grated cheese. Toss, and serve immediately.

Lobster Fra Diavolo

Aragosta Fra Diavolo
SERVES 4 TO 6

Two 1½-pound lobsters
All-purpose flour, for dredging the lobster
½ cup vegetable oil
¼ cup extra-virgin olive oil
2 medium onions
3 garlic cloves, crushed and peeled
3 tablespoons tomato paste
One 28-ounce can Italian plum tomatoes, preferably San Marzano, crushed by hand
½ to 1 teaspoon peperoncino flakes
1½ teaspoons kosher salt, plus more for pasta pot
1 recipe Light Egg Dough Pasta (page 221), prepared as maltagliati (page 223), or 4 pounds dried linguine
¼ cup chopped Italian parsley

To prepare the lobsters: Use a large chef's knife. If you wish, stun the lobsters a bit by putting them in the freezer for 15 minutes. Put the tip of your

chef's knife on each lobster's head, about 2 inches or so back from the eyes. Push the knife straight down, then through to split between the eyes. Hold the lobster with a towel where the claws meet the body, and twist to remove the claws. Twist or break the claws from the knuckles, and crack both with the back of the knife to make it easier to open when serving. Twist the walking legs off the body. Split the lobster body and tail in half lengthwise, and clean the body cavity, leaving the tomalley (the green digestive part of the lobster). Cut the tail from the body.

Spread the flour on a rimmed baking sheet. Dredge the cut-side pieces of the lobster body and tail (but not the claw pieces or walking legs) in the flour, tapping off the excess. Pour the vegetable oil into a large Dutch oven, and set over medium-high heat. Slip the body and tail meat into the pot, cut side down, and cook just to seal the meat, about a minute or so. Remove the pieces to a plate. Add the claw pieces, and cook just until they begin to change color, about a minute. Remove the claws to the plate.

Pour off the vegetable oil, return the pot to medium heat, and pour in 3 tablespoons of the olive oil. Add the onions and garlic. Sauté a few minutes, then add ½ cup of the pasta cooking water, and simmer to soften the onions, another 2 to 3 minutes. Increase the heat to let the water boil away, and clear a space in the pan to make a dry spot. Plop in the tomato paste and let sizzle a minute or two, then stir the tomato paste into the onions. Add the crushed tomatoes, and slosh out the can with 4 cups water, adding those to the pot as well. Bring the sauce to a rapid boil, and stir in the peperoncino and salt. Add all of the lobster except for the tail pieces, and let simmer until the sauce is thickened, about 10 minutes. Add the tail pieces, and simmer until the meat is just cooked through, about 2 minutes more.

In the meantime, bring a large pot of salted water to a boil for pasta. After you have simmered the sauce with the lobster for 10 minutes, lightly toss the raw pasta to shake off excess flour and slip the pasta into the salted boiling water, stirring as you add it to the water. Bring water back to a boil and cook an additional minute until al dente.

While the pasta is cooking, transfer about half of the sauce (without the lobster) to a large skillet, and bring to a simmer. When the pasta is al dente, strain with a spider and add directly to the pan with the sauce. Drizzle with the remaining tablespoon of olive oil, and sprinkle with the chopped parsley. Toss to coat the pasta with the sauce. Serve the pasta in shallow bowls, with extra sauce and the lobster tail pieces over top.

Spinach Tortelloni

Tortelloni di Spinaci
SERVES 8

PASTA
4 cups all-purpose flour, plus more as needed
6 large eggs
½ teaspoon extra-virgin olive oil
½ teaspoon kosher salt

FILLING
1 cup frozen spinach, thawed
1 pound fresh ricotta
8 ounces ricotta salata, grated
½ cup freshly grated Grana Padano
1 large egg, whisked
Freshly ground black pepper

SAUCE
1½ sticks unsalted butter
1½ cups heavy cream
Kosher salt
Freshly ground black pepper
½ cup freshly grated Grana Padano

To make the pasta by hand: Make a mound of 3½ cups of the flour on a countertop or large wooden board, and make a well in the center. In a spouted measuring cup, mix the eggs, olive oil, and salt.

Carefully pour the mixture into the well, making sure it doesn't break through the sides. With a fork, flick flour from the inside edges of the well into the egg mixture, mixing as you go. Mix in enough of the flour to make a sticky dough; then, with a bench scraper, mix the rest of the flour into the mixture. Add up to ½ cup of the remaining flour to make a dough that will form a ball without sticking to your hands. (It's okay if you don't use all of the flour.) Knead until smooth and satiny, flouring your hands as you go to keep the dough from sticking. Wrap the dough in plastic wrap, and rest it at room temperature for 1 hour.

To make dough in the food processor: Pulse 3½ cups of the flour and the salt together. Mix the eggs and olive oil together in a spouted measuring cup, and pour into the flour with the machine running. Process until the dough forms a soft ball on the blade, adding up to ½ cup of the remaining flour if necessary. Run the dough in the processor about 20 to 30 seconds to knead it; it should be smooth and shiny but still pliable. Turn the dough onto a lightly floured work surface, and knead just a few times, to bring it together. Wrap it in plastic wrap and let it rest 1 hour at room temperature.

For the filling: Put the thawed spinach in a kitchen towel, and wring out as much liquid as possible. Finely chop the spinach, and put it in a large bowl. Add the ricotta, ricotta salata, Grana Padano, egg, and some pepper, and mix well.

Cut the dough into four equal pieces. Keep the other pieces covered as you begin to roll one. Have two floured baking sheets at the ready. Press the dough into a rectangle, and roll through the pasta machine; fold in half, and roll through again. Fold the dough in three like a letter and roll through again, with the folded ends at the side. Repeat this folding and rolling several more times, each time lowering the setting on the machine until you reach the next-to-last setting, to strengthen and elongate the dough. Repeat this step with the remaining three pieces of dough, keeping the others floured and covered with kitchen towels as you work.

Change to the third setting on the pasta machine, and roll each piece through twice, with the short end going in first. Reset pasta machine to the fifth setting, and roll the pieces through. They will get a lot longer this time, so cut each piece in half crosswise. You should have eight long pieces now, all about the width of the machine. Roll each piece once through the next-to-last setting.

Line rolled sheets of dough between clean kitchen towels. Work with one sheet of rolled dough at a time. Fill a small bowl with water. Using a 3-inch round cutter, cut as many circles as you can from one strip of dough, keeping the other strips covered as you work. Dollop a heaping tea-spoon of filling in each round. Wet the edges with a finger dipped in water, and fold over, making a half-moon; press tightly to seal the edges and press out excess air. Position each piece around your index finger, with the filled part on the fingernail. Bring the two edges to meet on the front of your finger, and press the ends together, forming a ring. Slide it off your finger onto a floured sheet pan. Repeat with the remaining dough circles, keeping all the dough covered as you work.

Bring a large pot of salted water to a boil for the pasta. For the sauce: In a large skillet over medium-high heat, melt the butter. When the butter is melted, pour in the cream and adjust the heat so the sauce is simmering rapidly. Simmer until the sauce is reduced by about a third, about 6 to 7 minutes.

When the sauce is almost done, cook the tor-telloni. Add them to the boiling water and cook until al dente, about 2 to 3 minutes from the time they float. Remove the tortelloni with a spider, and add directly to the simmering sauce. Toss gently to coat the pasta with the sauce, and season with salt and pepper, adding a little pasta water if it seems dry, or reducing it over high heat for a minute if it's too soupy. Remove the skillet from the heat. Sprinkle with the grated cheese, toss, and serve immediately.

🌸 Or dress with 2 cups of Marinara Sauce (page 161) and grated cheese.

Ricotta and Sausage–Filled Ravioli

Ravioli di Salsicce e Ricotta
MAKES ABOUT 24

FILLING
1 small onion, quartered
1 small celery stalk, cut into chunks
1 small carrot, cut into chunks
3 tablespoons extra-virgin olive oil
12 ounces sweet Italian sausage without fennel
   seeds, removed from the casings
¼ cup dry white wine
1 cup fresh ricotta, drained
¼ cup freshly grated Grana Padano
¼ cup chopped fresh Italian parsley

1 recipe Light Egg Pasta Dough
   (page 221)

In a food processor, pulse together the onion, celery, and carrot until finely chopped. Heat a large skillet over medium-high heat, and add the olive oil. Once the oil is hot, add the vegetables, and cook until they begin to soften, about 3 to 4 minutes.

In a medium bowl, pour the white wine over the sausage, and crumble the sausage into small pieces with your fingers. Add the sausage and wine to the skillet with the vegetables, breaking up the sausage as finely as possible with a wooden spoon. Sauté until sausage is completely cooked through, about 4 to 5 minutes. Scrape into a bowl to cool. When sausage is completely cooled, stir in the ricotta, grated cheese, and parsley.

Roll the dough: Cut the dough into four equal pieces. Flatten a piece of dough into a rectangle, about 4 by 5 inches, and roll through the widest setting on the pasta machine. Fold this rectangle of dough like a letter, and roll through again. Repeat the rolling and folding a few more times to knead and smooth the dough. Repeat with the remaining pieces of dough.

Switch to the next setting on the machine. Roll a dough strip through, short end first. Repeat with remaining dough strips. Continue this process, now rolling only once through each setting, until you've gotten to the next-to-last setting and the dough strips are about as wide as the machine (6 to 7 inches).

Lay one strip out on the counter, and dollop the filling at about 4-inch intervals down the center of the strip (you will get about six or seven large ravioli per strip). Brush lightly around the filling with water, fold the strip over, and seal. Using a serrated pastry cutter or pizza cutter, cut the ravioli into rectangles. Repeat with the remaining dough and filling.

In the meantime, bring a large pot of salted water to a boil. Add the ravioli to the boiling water and cook until done, about 3 minutes after they begin to float to the surface. Remove the ravioli with a spider and add them to a pan with a simmering sauce of your choice, and toss gently to coat. When the ravioli are all coated with the sauce, remove from the heat, sprinkle with grated cheese (such as Grana Padano), toss, and serve immediately.

❧ You can serve these with a simple Marinara Sauce (page 161) and some grated Grana Padano, or Butter and Sage Sauce (page 168) again with some grated Grana Padano.

Fresh Pear and Pecorino Ravioli with Cacio e Pepe Sauce

Ravioli Cacio e Pepe
MAKES ABOUT 24 RAVIOLI

RAVIOLI
1 large firm but ripe Bartlett or other pear (or
   2 small pears, 8 to 10 ounces total)
1½ cups freshly grated Grana Padano
2 tablespoons mascarpone, chilled
1 recipe Light Egg Pasta Dough
   (page 221)
Kosher salt

SAUCE
12 tablespoons (1½ sticks) unsalted butter
4 ounces mild 12-month-aged Pecorino
   Romano, grated
Abundant coarsely ground black pepper to taste

For the filling: Peel and core the pear and shred it against the large holes of a box grater. Stir the pear shreds with the Grana Padano in a bowl, and blend in the mascarpone.

Roll the dough: Cut the dough into four equal pieces. Flatten a piece of dough into a 4-by-5-inch rectangle, and roll through the widest setting on the pasta machine. Fold this rectangle of dough in three like a letter, and roll through again. Repeat the rolling and folding a few more times to knead and smooth the dough. Repeat with the remaining pieces of dough.

Switch to the next setting on the machine. Roll a dough strip through, short end first. Repeat with remaining dough strips. Continue this process, now rolling only once through each setting, until you've gotten to the next-to-last setting and the dough strips are about as wide as the machine (6 to 7 inches).

Lay one strip out on the counter and dollop filling at about 4-inch intervals down the center of the strip (you will get about six or seven large ravioli per strip). Brush around the filling with water, fold the strip over, and seal. Using a serrated pastry cutter or pizza cutter, cut ravioli into rectangles. Repeat with remaining dough and filling.

Bring a large pot of salted water to a boil for the pasta. Add the ravioli. At the same time, melt the butter in a skillet over medium heat, and add 1 cup pasta water. Simmer while the pasta cooks, just to reduce the sauce and emulsify it. Cook the ravioli until al dente, about 3 minutes after they begin to float, then remove with a spider, transfer directly to the sauce, and toss gently to coat in the sauce. Remove the pan from the heat and sprinkle over it the grated pecorino, mixing gently so the cheese begins to melt into a sauce, then grind abundant coarse black pepper all around, and serve.

Beet Ravioli in Poppy Seed Sauce

Casunziei

SERVES 6

FILLING

4 medium beets
Extra-virgin olive oil, for rubbing the beets
1¼ teaspoons kosher salt
½ cup fresh ricotta
½ cup freshly grated Grana Padano
¼ cup grated smoked mozzarella
¼ cup dried bread crumbs
Freshly grated black pepper

1 recipe Light Egg Pasta Dough (page 221)

SAUCE

4 tablespoons unsalted butter
2 teaspoons poppy seeds
¼ cup freshly grated Grana Padano
Kosher salt to taste

For the filling: Preheat the oven to 400 degrees. Brush each beet with olive oil, and season with a quarter of the salt total. Wrap each beat in foil, place on a rimmed baking sheet, and roast until tender, about 40 to 45 minutes. Unwrap and let the beets cool, then peel, and shred them on the coarse holes of a box grater. Wrap in a kitchen towel and squeeze as much excess liquid from the beets as possible.

Put the beets in a medium bowl, and mix in the ricotta, Grana Padano, smoked mozzarella, and bread crumbs. Season with the remaining teaspoon of salt and some pepper. Set aside while you roll the pasta.

Bring a large pot of salted water to a boil for the pasta. To roll the pasta: Cut the dough into four equal pieces. Keep the other pieces covered as you begin to roll. Have two floured baking sheets at the ready. Press the dough into a 4-by-5-inch rectangle, and roll through the pasta machine, fold in half, and roll through again. Fold the dough in three like a letter, and roll through again, with the folded ends at the side. Repeat this folding and rolling several more times to strengthen and elongate the dough. Repeat this step with the remaining three pieces of dough, keeping the others floured and covered with kitchen towels as you work.

Change to the third setting on the pasta machine, and roll each piece through twice, with the short end going in first. Skip to the fifth setting, and roll the pieces through. They will get a lot longer this time, so cut each piece in half crosswise. You should have eight long pieces now, all about the width of the machine. Roll each piece through once on the sixth setting. You should just be able to see your hand through the back of a strip.

Fill a small bowl with water. Using a 3½-inch round cutter, cut as many circles as you can from one strip of dough, keeping the other strips covered as you work. Dollop a scant tablespoon of filling in each round. Wet the edges with a finger, and press tightly to seal the edges and press out excess air, making a half-moon shape. Rest the ravioli on floured sheet pans as you go, and repeat with the remaining dough strips and filling.

For the sauce: In a large skillet over medium heat, melt the butter. When the butter is melted, add the poppy seeds and toast until just a few begin to pop in the pan, about 1 to 2 minutes. Add 1 cup pasta cooking water, and simmer while you make the ravioli, letting the sauce reduce by about half.

Cook the ravioli in the boiling water until al dente, about 4 minutes from the time they begin to float (taste one to see). Remove with a spider, and add directly to the sauce. Toss to coat the ravioli in the sauce for a minute, adding a little more pasta water if necessary, then remove the skillet from the heat. Sprinkle with the grated cheese, and season with salt. Toss and serve.

Anolini with Pork Filling in Chicken Broth

Anolini in Brodo
SERVES 8 TO 10

FILLING
½ pound boneless pork shoulder
½ small onion, cut into chunks
½ small carrot, peeled and cut into chunks
½ celery stalk, cut into chunks
2 ounces pancetta, cut into ½-inch pieces
1½ teaspoons crumbled dried porcini mushrooms
1 sprig fresh rosemary
1½ teaspoons tomato paste
¾ cup chicken broth
2 ounces mortadella, diced
1 slice day-old bread
1 large egg
Kosher salt
¾ cup freshly grated Grana Padano
Pinch freshly grated nutmeg
Fine dried bread crumbs, as needed

1 recipe Light Egg Pasta Dough (page 221)
All-purpose flour, for rolling and forming the anolini

FOR COOKING AND SERVING
3 quarts Chicken Stock (page 143)
1 cup freshly grated Grana Padano

For the filling: Preheat the oven to 425 degrees. Cut the pork shoulder into 2-inch pieces, trimming away any excess fat or cartilage as you go. Put the meat in the small roasting pan along with the onion, carrot, celery, pancetta, porcini, and rosemary. Spread the tomato paste on the meat and vegetables, and toss to coat. Pour the broth into the pan.

Roast the meat and vegetables, uncovered, until the meat is brown and tender and the pan juices have reduced to a thick gravy, about 1 hour. (If the meat is tender and the juices are still too thin, remove the pan from the oven and reduce on top of the stove.)

Let the meat, vegetables, and juices cool. Toss in the cubes of mortadella and run the entire mixture through a meat grinder into a large bowl. Run the bread through the grinder to clean out the last bit of meat (and catch it in the bowl). Beat the egg with a pinch of salt, and pour over the meat, along with the grated cheese, nutmeg, and bread crumbs (as needed to make a mixture like a meatloaf). With your hands, work everything together to make a smooth stuffing.

For the anolini: Cut the dough into six equal pieces; work with two pieces of dough at a time, and keep the others covered. Roll one piece of dough through the pasta machine at progressively wider settings, always keeping it lightly floured, until you've created a long strip, as wide as your machine allows and a little less than ⅛ inch thick. Lay it out on the work surface. Roll out the second piece of dough to a strip of the same size.

Lay one strip in front of you. Mark where you will be making the anolini by lightly pressing the 1-inch cutter on the dough—don't cut through it—fitting as many outlined circles on the strip as you can.

Scoop small portions of the filling, ⅓ to ½ teaspoon, and mound them in the center of all the circles. With a pastry brush or your fingertip dipped in water, lightly moisten the rim of the outlined circle around the filling mounds. Lay the second strip of dough over the first, gently stretching and draping it to cover all the mounds. Now center the cutter over each filling mound, and press it firmly, cleanly slicing through both layers of dough and cutting out the anolini. Pull away the excess dough to separate individual pieces, lightly dusting with flour as needed. Press the edges of the pasta circles together if they have gaps. Arrange the anolini in a single layer on a floured and lined tray, and cover them lightly.

Roll out and fill the remaining pieces of pasta dough, in pairs, to make two more batches of anolini in the same way. Anolini that you will cook soon can be left on the tray, lightly covered.

Freeze anolini for future use right on the trays. When they are frozen solid, transfer them to freezer bags, packed airtight and sealed.

To cook: Fill a large pasta pot, preferably with a wide diameter (so the anolini won't be crowded), with at least 6 quarts well-salted water, and bring to the boil. At the same time, heat the chicken stock in another pot, so it is just simmering. Have your soup bowls warm and ready for filling. With the pasta water at a full rolling boil, spill in all the anolini, stir well, cover the pot, and return the water to a boil over high heat. Give the anolini another good stir, and let them cook for a quick minute, just until they're barely al dente. Check one for doneness; the thickest part of the pasta should still be slightly resilient, since the anolini will continue to cook and soften in the brodo.

Turn off the heat and, with a big spider or other strainer, scoop out the hot anolini, let them drain for a second, and put fifteen to twenty into each of the warm soup bowls. Quickly ladle hot broth into each bowl and sprinkle over each a heaping spoonful or two of grated cheese. Serve each bowl of anolini in brodo while piping hot.

Fresh Ricotta Cavatelli with Mussels and Beans

Cavatelli di Ricotta con Cozze e Fagioli
SERVES 6

CAVATELLI
2 cups all-purpose flour, plus more as needed
1½ cups fresh ricotta, drained overnight
1 large egg
Kosher salt

MUSSELS AND BEANS
1 medium carrot, peeled and cut into chunks
1 large celery stalk, cut into chunks
1 medium onion, cut into chunks
2 garlic cloves, crushed and peeled
¼ cup extra-virgin olive oil, plus more for drizzling
6 sprigs fresh thyme
2 cups dry white wine
1 pint grape or cherry tomatoes, halved through the stem
One 15-ounce can cannellini beans, rinsed and drained
1 teaspoon kosher salt
¼ teaspoon crushed red pepper flakes
2 pounds mussels, scrubbed and debearded
¼ cup chopped fresh Italian parsley

For the cavatelli: Put the flour in a food processor, and pulse several times. In a bowl, mix together the ricotta and egg with a pinch of salt. Add to the processor, and process until the dough forms a ball on the blade, a little less than a minute. Add more flour if too soft or a tablespoon or two of water if the dough is too dry, if necessary, to get the right consistency. Knead the dough on the counter a few times, just to bring it together, then wrap it in plastic wrap and let it rest 30 minutes.

Cut the dough into quarters. Working with one quarter of the dough at a time (and keeping the others covered in plastic wrap), pinch off and roll a piece of dough into the thickness of a pencil. Cut into ½-inch lengths. Flour your hands, and roll the pieces into rough ovals. On a lightly floured surface, press a finger (or two) into the center of an oval, roll forward, then back to form a concavity in the dough, then let it flick off your finger. The pressure of your fingers will leave an indentation in the dough as you drag it on the board. Repeat with the remaining dough pieces, placing the cavatelli on well-floured sheet pans as you go.

Bring a large pot of salted water to a boil for the pasta. In a food processor, combine the carrot, celery, onion, and garlic, and process to make a smooth pestata. To a large Dutch oven over medium-high heat, add the olive oil. When the oil is hot, add the pestata. Cook, stirring occasionally, until the pestata has dried out and begins to stick to the bottom of the pan, about 5 minutes. Tie the thyme sprigs with a piece of kitchen twine, and add to the pot with the white wine. Let the wine boil until it's reduced by half, and add the tomatoes and beans. Season with the salt and red pepper flakes, and simmer until the tomatoes begin to give up their juices, about 3 minutes.

When you add the tomatoes, begin cooking the cavatelli. First shake them in a colander to remove excess flour, then cook in the boiling water until tender, about 8 minutes from the time they float to the surface, depending on the size you've made them. Taste one after about 6 minutes just to be sure.

To the tomatoes and beans, add the mussels. Cover, and cook until they open, about 4 minutes, discarding any that don't open. Discard the thyme. When the cavatelli are cooked, remove with a spider and add to the simmering sauce. Add the parsley, drizzle with a tablespoon or so of olive oil, and toss to coat the cavatelli in the sauce, about 1 minute. Serve immediately.

Basic Potato Gnocchi

Gnocchi di Patate
SERVES 6

6 large Idaho or russet potatoes (about
   2¼ pounds)
1 teaspoon kosher salt
Pinch of freshly ground white pepper
2 large eggs, beaten
3 cups unbleached flour, plus more as needed

Boil the potatoes in their skins until easily pierced with a paring knife, about 35 to 40 minutes. When they are cool enough to handle, peel and rice the potatoes, and set them aside to cool completely, spreading them loosely to expose as much surface as possible to air.

On a cool, preferably marble work surface, gather the cold potatoes into a mound, forming a well in the center. Stir the teaspoon of salt and the white pepper into the beaten eggs, and pour the mixture into the well. Work the potatoes and eggs together with both hands, gradually adding 3 cups of the flour and scraping the dough up from the work surface with a bench scraper as often as necessary. (Incorporation of the ingredients should take no longer than 10 minutes—the longer you work it, the more flour it will require and the heavier the gnocchi will become.)

Dust the dough, your hands, and the work surface lightly with flour, and cut the dough into six equal parts. (Continue to dust as long as the dough feels sticky.) Using both hands, roll each piece of dough into a rope ½ inch thick, then slice the ropes at ½-inch intervals. Roll the balls of dough off the tines of a fork, making an indentation with your thumb as you roll, while leaving ridges from the tines of the fork on the other side. Rest them on floured sheet pans as you make the remaining gnocchi.

Bring a pot of salted water to a boil to cook the gnocchi. Shake excess flour from the gnocchi and add to the boiling water (don't crowd them; cook in batches if necessary). Once the gnocchi rise to the surface, cook an additional 2 minutes. Remove the gnocchi with a spider and transfer directly to your choice of sauce.

❧ Gnocchi can be delicious with just butter and cheese, or with Butter and Sage Sauce (page 168) or Tomato Sauce (page 161).

Gnocchi with Peas and Gorgonzola

Gnocchi con Piselli e Gorgonzola
SERVES 6

Kosher salt
1 recipe Basic Potato Gnocchi (preceding recipe)
2 tablespoons unsalted butter
½ cup heavy cream

1 cup Chicken Stock (page 143), Vegetable Stock (page 143), or pasta-cooking water
One 10-ounce package frozen peas, thawed
6 ounces Gorgonzola, crumbled
¼ cup freshly grated Grana Padano

Bring a pot of salted water to a boil to cook the gnocchi. For the sauce: Heat a large skillet over medium-high heat. Melt the butter, then add the cream and stock. Once the mixture is simmering, add the peas. Bring to a rapid simmer, and cook until slightly thickened, about 5 minutes. Stir in the Gorgonzola until it dissolves in the sauce. Keep the sauce warm while you cook the gnocchi.

Meanwhile, shake excess flour from the gnocchi and add to the boiling water (don't crowd the gnocchi; cook in batches if necessary). Once the gnocchi rise to the surface, cook an additional 2 minutes. Remove the gnocchi and transfer directly to the sauce with a spider. Toss the gnocchi in the sauce for a minute (add a little pasta cooking water if it seems too tight), just to coat the gnocchi with the sauce, then remove from the heat. Sprinkle with the grated cheese, toss, and serve.

Butternut Squash Gnocchi

Gnocchi di Zucca
SERVES 4 TO 6

1-pound chunk butternut squash (about half a medium squash)
1 tablespoon extra-virgin olive oil
2 medium russet potatoes (about 12 ounces)
¼ cup freshly grated Grana Padano
1 large egg
1 teaspoon kosher salt
¼ teaspoon freshly grated nutmeg
1½ cups all-purpose flour, plus more as needed

Preheat the oven to 400 degrees. Scoop seeds from the squash, and place in a baking pan, cut

side up. Drizzle with the olive oil. Bake until tender throughout, about 45 minutes to 1 hour. Let cool slightly.

When it is cool, scrape the flesh from the squash, set in cheesecloth, and let hang or set in a strainer in the refrigerator overnight to drain. You should have about ¾ cup squash.

Cook the potatoes in a medium saucepan with water to cover until tender, about 20 to 25 minutes. Drain, let cool until you can peel them, then peel and press through a ricer into an even layer on a sheet pan. Let cool completely. You should have 2 cups potatoes. Pass the drained squash through the ricer as well.

In a large bowl, combine the squash, potatoes, grated cheese, egg, salt, and nutmeg, and mix until smooth. Sprinkle in 1¼ cups of the flour, and mix to combine. Dump the dough onto your work surface, and knead until it comes together. If the dough is still sticky, add the remaining ¼ cup flour, and knead just until smooth. Do not overknead the dough: it will require more flour, and the gnocchi will be heavier.

When you are ready to make the gnocchi, bring a large pot of salted water to a boil. Divide dough into eight equal pieces. Line two large rimmed baking sheets with parchment. Sprinkle parchment lightly with flour. Working with one dough piece at a time, roll dough out on a floured surface to about a ½-inch-thick rope. Cut rope crosswise into ¾-inch pieces. Working with one piece at a time, roll gnocchi along the back of fork tines dipped in flour, making ridges on 1 side and a dimple on the other. Transfer the gnocchi to the floured baking sheets. Repeat with the remaining dough.

Cook the gnocchi in two batches in the boiling water, giving them just a couple minutes more after they all float to the surface. Remove with a spider, and transfer to the awaiting sauce.

❧ Serve with Butter and Sage Sauce (page 168) or Tomato Sauce (Page 161).

Plum Gnocchi

Gnocchi di Susine

MAKES 16 PIECES, SERVING 8

Kosher salt
1 recipe Basic Potato Gnocchi dough, made
    without pepper (page 233)
16 small Italian prune plums
⅓ cup sugar
All-purpose flour, for rolling
6 tablespoons unsalted butter
1¾ cups dried bread crumbs
2 teaspoons ground cinnamon

Bring a large pot of salted water to a boil for the gnocchi. Split the plums open in half and pit them. Fill each plum cavity with ½ teaspoon of the sugar, and re-form the plums by pressing the halves together.

On a floured work surface, use your hands to roll the gnocchi dough into a cylinder that's 2 inches in diameter. Slice evenly into sixteen rounds. Flour your hands well, and flatten a dough round in the palm of one hand. Place a filled plum in the center, and gather the dough around it, pressing the seam to seal. Make sure there are no tears; if there are, press the dough together to patch them. Pat the covered plum in your floured hands to seal and even out the dough. Repeat with the remaining plums and dough rounds.

In a large nonstick skillet, melt the butter. Add the bread crumbs and stir until light golden and toasted, about 7 minutes. Remove from the heat, let cool slightly, and stir in the remaining sugar and the cinnamon.

Add eight gnocchi to the boiling water. Cook until the dough is cooked throughout, about 5 to 6 minutes after the gnocchi rise to the surface and begin to float. Drain well with a slotted spoon, and drop in the bread-crumb mixture. Roll to coat the gnocchi in the flavored crumbs. Repeat the cooking and rolling with the remaining gnocchi.

🐾 Serve these warm, but they are good at room temperature as well.

Eggplant Gnocchi with Fresh Tomato

Gnocchi di Melanzane con Salsa di Pomodoro

SERVES 4 TO 6

FRESH TOMATO SAUCE
½ teaspoon kosher salt, plus more for the pot
2½ pounds ripe plum tomatoes
¼ cup extra-virgin olive oil
1 medium onion, finely chopped
¼ teaspoon crushed red pepper flakes
¼ cup loosely packed fresh basil leaves, chopped

GNOCCHI
2 pounds firm eggplants
1 tablespoon kosher salt
Extra-virgin olive oil, for brushing
1 pound medium russet potatoes
⅔ cup freshly grated Grana Padano
2 large eggs, beaten
Freshly ground black pepper
¼ cup loosely packed fresh basil leaves, finely
    chopped
2 cups all-purpose flour, plus more as needed

For the tomato sauce: Bring a large pot of salted water to a boil. Cut out the stem bases of the tomatoes, and discard. Score an "X" in the opposite ends with a paring knife. Drop the tomatoes in the boiling water, and boil until the skin just begins to pull away at the spot where you made the "X," about 1 minute. Remove the tomatoes with a spider, and put them in a bowl with ice water to stop the cooking. Let them cool for 5 minutes. Drain the tomatoes. Peel the skins off and discard.

In a large skillet, heat the olive oil over medium heat. Add the onion, and season with the salt and red pepper flakes. Cook until the onion is tender, about 8 minutes. Crush the tomatoes with your hands directly into the skillet. Stir in the basil. Simmer the sauce until it is thick and flavorful, about 30 minutes. (The sauce can be made earlier in the day and reheated once you make the gnocchi.)

For the gnocchi: Preheat the oven to 375 degrees. Halve the eggplants, and sprinkle the cut sides with 2 teaspoons of the salt. Set aside for 30 minutes. Rinse the eggplants well, and pat dry. Brush all over with olive oil, and place, cut side down, on a baking sheet. Bake until very tender all the way through, about 40 minutes. When they are cool enough to handle, scoop out the flesh, remove as many of the seeds as possible, and set the flesh in a food processor, discarding the skins. Purée the flesh until very smooth. Scrape into a bowl and let cool completely.

Meanwhile, boil the whole potatoes in salted water to cover until tender, about 25 minutes. When they are cool enough to handle, peel the potatoes and press through a ricer into the bowl with the eggplant. Allow potatoes to cool.

Add ⅓ cup of the grated cheese, the eggs, the remaining teaspoon of salt, some pepper, and the basil. Mix well. Add the flour, and mix to incorporate the ingredients thoroughly but not densely.

Bring a large pot of salted water to a boil for the gnocchi. Fill a pastry bag fitted with a large plain tip with the gnocchi dough. Squeeze the mixture directly over the water, cutting off the gnocchi with a paring knife at ½-inch intervals. Continue rapidly until the dough is used up, stirring the pot occasionally. After the gnocchi rise to the surface, cook for another 2 minutes, then remove the gnocchi from the water with a spider and add directly to the simmering sauce. Toss to coat the pasta with the sauce. Sprinkle with the remaining ⅓ cup of grated cheese, toss, and serve.

🍀 Or use 3 to 4 cups Tomato Sauce (page 161).

Ricotta Gnocchi with Butter and Basil Sauce

Gnocchi di Ricotta al Burro e Basilico
SERVES 4 TO 6

SAUCE
1 stick unsalted butter
¼ cup pine nuts
2 ounces prosciutto, cut into strips
1½ cups heavy cream
½ cup Chicken Stock (page 143)
¼ cup loosely packed fresh basil leaves
½ cup freshly grated Grana Padano

GNOCCHI
1¼ teaspoons kosher salt, plus more for the pot
2 cups all-purpose flour, plus more as needed
1 pound fresh ricotta, drained overnight
2 large eggs, beaten
½ teaspoon freshly ground black pepper
¼ teaspoon freshly grated nutmeg
1 tablespoon chopped fresh Italian parsley

For the sauce: In a large skillet over medium heat, melt the butter. When the butter is melted, add the pine nuts and prosciutto, and cook until the nuts are lightly toasted, about 4 minutes. Add the cream and stock, and simmer until the sauce is reduced by about half, about 8 minutes.

For the gnocchi: Bring a large pot of salted water to a boil. Mound the flour on your work surface, and make a well in the center. In a medium bowl, mix together the drained ricotta, eggs, salt, pepper, nutmeg, and parsley. Add to the well. With a fork, flick inside the well the flour from the sides of the well, and mix with the ricotta, gradually incorporating all the flour until a sticky dough forms. At this point, the dough should be a little sticky but you should be able to form it into a ball; if not, add a little more flour.

Cut the dough into six pieces, and roll each into a rope about ½ inch thick. Cut the ropes at ½-inch intervals. Roll the pieces over the floured tines of a fork, indenting the gnocchi with your thumb as you go. Rest them on floured sheet pans as you make the rest of the gnocchi.

When you are ready to cook the gnocchi, return the sauce to a simmer and tear the basil leaves into the simmering sauce. Add the gnocchi to the boiling water. Simmer until cooked through, about 2 to 3 minutes after they float to the surface, depending on the size of your gnocchi. (Taste one to check.)

Remove the gnocchi with a spider, and add to the simmering sauce. Let sit for a minute to firm up, then toss gently to coat the gnocchi with the sauce, adding a little more pasta water if the sauce seems dry. Remove the skillet from the heat, sprinkle with the grated cheese, toss, and serve.

"Drooling Gnocchi"

Gnocchi alla Bava
SERVES 6

Kosher salt
½ cup Chicken Stock (page 143)
6 tablespoons unsalted butter
¼ cup heavy cream
Freshly ground white pepper
1 recipe Basic Potato Gnocchi (page 233)
1 cup freshly grated Grana Padano
5 ounces Fontina Valdostana cheese, rind removed, shredded (about 1½ cups)

Bring a large pot of salted water to a boil for the pasta. Preheat the oven to 450 degrees. Bring the stock, butter, and cream to a boil in a large skillet over medium heat. Adjust the heat to simmering, season lightly with white pepper, and simmer until lightly thickened, about 3 minutes. Remove from the heat.

Drop the gnocchi into the boiling water a few at a time, stirring gently and continuously with a wooden spoon. Cook just until they rise to the surface and roll over, 2 minutes. Scoop the gnoc-

chi out of the boiling water with a large spider, and add them directly to the sauce in the skillet. Bring the sauce and gnocchi to a boil, stirring gently to coat the gnocchi with sauce. Remove the pan from the heat, and stir in the grated Grana Padano. Check the seasoning, add salt if necessary, and gently spoon the gnocchi into a large (about 10-by-15-inch) baking dish, or two smaller baking dishes into which they fit in a more or less single layer. Scatter the shredded Fontina over the gnocchi, and bake until the sauce is bubbling and the top is golden brown, about 10 minutes. Serve immediately.

Naked Gnocchi

Gnudi
MAKES 25 TO 30 GNUDI, SERVING 6 AS A FIRST COURSE OR 4 AS A MAIN DISH

½ teaspoon kosher salt, plus more for the pot
1 pound fresh ricotta, drained
1 large egg
1 cup dry spinach purée (prepared from 20 ounces frozen or 1 pound fresh spinach)
¼ cup freshly grated Grana Padano
6 tablespoons fine bread crumbs, plus more as needed
¼ cup all-purpose flour, plus more for rolling
Generous amount of freshly ground black pepper

Bring a large pot of salted water to a boil for the pasta. Blend the ricotta and the egg together in a large bowl. Mix in the spinach, cheese, bread crumbs, flour, salt, and pepper, and knead lightly, to make a homogeneous dough.

Test the consistency of the dough by scooping up a heaping tablespoon, forming it into a ball, and flouring it. Drop it into the boiling water; if it does not hold its shape and rise to the surface of the water within a minute, add a bit more bread crumbs and flour to your dough.

When you have the right consistency, shape all of the dough into balls the size of golf balls, roll them lightly in flour, and lay them out on baking sheets covered in parchment paper.

Drop the gnudi gently, one by one, into the boiling water, and cook for about 2 or 3 minutes, until they rise to the top and the water comes back to a rolling boil. To test for doneness, scoop out a ball and press it with your fingers; when cooked, the dumpling should bounce back, leaving no indentation.

❧ To prepare the dry spinach: wring dry two 10-ounce boxes thawed frozen spinach or 1 pound blanched fresh spinach until very dry, and finely chop.

❧ Gnudi would go nicely with Butter and Sage Sauce (page 168). Top with freshly grated cheese before serving.

Bread and Prune Gnocchi

Gnocchi di Pane e Prugne
SERVES 4

1 teaspoon kosher salt, plus more for the skillet
2 cups Chicken Stock (page 143)
5 cups 1- or 2-day-old country bread cubes
1 cup milk
5 tablespoons unsalted butter
¾ cup finely chopped dried prunes
1 bunch finely chopped scallions (about 1 cup)
¼ cup plum brandy
1 large egg, beaten
1 cup freshly grated Grana Padano, plus more as needed
All-purpose flour, as needed (up to 1 cup)
8 fresh sage leaves

Bring a shallow straight-sided skillet with about 3 inches of salted water to a boil for the gnoc-chi. Heat the chicken stock in a small saucepan and keep warm. Put the bread cubes in a medium bowl, and pour the milk over them. Soak them until softened, tossing occasionally to soak evenly.

Meanwhile, heat a medium skillet over medium heat. Add 2 tablespoons of the butter. When the butter is melted, add the prunes and scallions, and cook, stirring occasionally, until the scallions are wilted, about 5 minutes. Add the plum brandy, and simmer until the prunes are softened, about 4 minutes. Increase the heat to boil away any excess liquid in the pan. Scrape onto a plate to cool.

Work the soaked bread into a paste with your hands, and transfer it to a large bowl, leaving the excess milk behind. To the bread, stir in the cooled prune mixture, the egg, ½ cup of the grated cheese, and the salt. Mix with your hands to make a homogeneous dough. Add enough flour, a few tablespoons at a time, to make a dough that is sticky but that your hands can form into a ball that holds its shape. You may only need a few tablespoons of flour, or up to 1 cup—it will depend on the age and density of the bread you are using. Cook one gnoccho as a tester, to make sure they hold together.

Use a small ice-cream scoop or a soup spoon to form the gnocchi into rough balls, and drop into the simmering water, in batches if necessary to keep from crowding. Simmer until cooked through, about 6 to 8 minutes from the time they begin to float. Remove with a slotted spoon, drain, and rest on a sheet pan.

To finish the gnocchi: Melt the remaining 3 tablespoons butter in a large skillet over medium-high heat. When the butter is melted, add the sage leaves. Let the sage leaves sizzle for a minute, then add the hot chicken stock. Bring to a boil, and cook until reduced by about half, about 4 minutes. Slide in the gnocchi, and gently toss to coat in the sauce. Remove the sage leaves, sprinkle with the remaining ½ cup grated cheese, and serve.

Ricotta and Spinach Roll

Roulade di Ricotta e Spinaci

SERVES 8 TO 10

FILLING
½ cup frozen spinach, thawed
4 tablespoons unsalted butter
1 garlic clove, finely chopped
1 pound fresh ricotta, drained overnight
½ teaspoon kosher salt
Freshly ground black pepper

DOUGH
1½ pounds medium russet potatoes
2 large egg yolks
¼ cup freshly grated Grana Padano
¼ teaspoon freshly grated nutmeg
½ teaspoon kosher salt
1½ cups all-purpose flour, plus more as needed

SAUCE
1½ sticks unsalted butter
10 large fresh sage leaves
½ cup freshly grated Grana Padano, plus more
for serving

For the filling: Begin the day before you want to make the roulade. Put the spinach in a kitchen towel, and wring as much liquid from it as possible. Chop and set aside.

In a medium skillet over medium heat, melt the butter. When the butter is melted, add the garlic and spinach, and cook until the garlic is fragrant and the spinach is very dry, about 3 minutes. Scrape into a medium bowl, and let cool. When cool, stir in the drained ricotta, salt, and pepper.

For the dough: Boil the whole unpeeled potatoes in boiling water to cover until tender throughout, about 20 to 30 minutes, depending on their size. Drain and let cool slightly. When the potatoes are cool enough to handle but still warm, peel and press through a ricer into a thin layer on your work surface (don't pile up the riced potatoes), and allow them to cool completely.

When they are cooled, scrape the potatoes into a mound on the counter, and make a well in the center. Add the egg yolks, grated cheese, nutmeg, salt, and flour. With a fork, flick the potatoes into the middle, mixing as you go to form a sticky dough. Once all the flour is incorporated, the dough should come together in a ball. Knead a few times to smooth it out, adding a little more flour if it is sticking to your hands too much.

Bring a large pot of salted water to a boil. (The pot needs to be at least 15 inches in diameter; you can also use a roasting pan set over two burners if necessary.) Roll the dough into a 12-by-15-inch rectangle on a sheet of floured parchment. Spread the filling on the dough, leaving a 1-inch border around the edges. Starting on a long edge, tightly roll up the roulade, using the parchment as a guide (but don't roll it in the parchment). Lay it in a triple thickness of cheesecloth, and roll tight, then tie tightly at both ends. Lower the wrapped roulade gently into the water, and simmer until cooked through and firm, about 45 minutes. Remove the roulade, and let cool 15 minutes, still wrapped.

Meanwhile, for the sauce: Heat a large skillet over medium heat. Add the butter. When the butter is melted, add the sage leaves and cook until the edges begin to sizzle, about 1 minute.

Gently unwrap the roulade, and cut into ½-inch slices. Place each slice on a warmed platter, and spoon the sage butter over the slices. Sprinkle with the grated cheese, and serve immediately, passing more cheese at the table.

Lasagna Napoletana

Lasagne alla Napoletana
SERVES 8

1 recipe Light Egg Pasta Dough (page 221)

SAUCE AND MEATBALLS

1 medium carrot, peeled and cut into chunks
1 celery stalk, cut into chunks
5 garlic cloves, crushed and peeled
3 tablespoons extra-virgin olive oil
Two 28-ounce cans whole Italian plum
    tomatoes, preferably San Marzano, crushed
    by hand
2 teaspoons kosher salt
1¼ pounds ground beef
1 large egg
⅓ cup fine dried bread crumbs
⅓ cup freshly grated Grana Padano
⅓ cup chopped fresh Italian parsley

ASSEMBLY

1 pound low-moisture mozzarella, shredded
1½ cups freshly grated Grana Padano
1 tablespoon unsalted butter, softened
½ cup loosely packed fresh basil leaves,
    chopped
3 large hard-boiled eggs, sliced crosswise ¼ inch
    thick

Make the pasta dough. Wrap it in plastic wrap, and let it rest 30 minutes at room temperature. (The dough can also be made earlier in the day and kept wrapped in the refrigerator, but let it come back to room temperature before rolling.)

For the sauce: In a food processor, combine the carrot, celery, and garlic, and process to make a smooth pestata. Heat a large Dutch oven over medium-high heat. Add the olive oil. When the oil is hot, scrape in the pestata and cook until it dries out and begins to stick to the bottom of the pot, about 4 minutes. Add the tomatoes, fill the can fully with water, and add that as well. Add 1 teaspoon of the salt, and let the sauce simmer gently while you make the meatballs, about 20 minutes.

For the meatballs: In a large bowl, combine the beef, egg, bread crumbs, grated cheese, parsley, and remaining 1 teaspoon salt. Mix well with your hands, and form into 1-inch meatballs on a parchment-lined baking sheet. (You should get about four dozen tiny meatballs.) Once all of the meatballs are formed, drop them into the sauce, add 1 cup water, and simmer until the meatballs are cooked through, about 25 to 30 minutes. (This sauce will be slightly thinner than other tomato sauces, but it shouldn't be watery.)

Bring a large wide pot of salted water to a boil. Preheat the oven to 400 degrees. To roll the pasta: Cut the dough into four equal pieces. Keep the other pieces covered as you begin to roll one of them. Have two floured baking sheets ready. Press the dough into a rectangle, and roll it through the pasta machine, fold in half, and roll through again. Fold the dough in three like a letter and roll through again. Repeat this folding and rolling several more times, to strengthen and elongate the dough. Repeat this step with the remaining three pieces of dough, keeping the others floured and covered with kitchen towels as you work.

Move the dial to the third setting on the pasta machine, and roll each piece through twice, with the short end going in first. Move the dial to the fifth setting on the pasta machine, and roll the pieces through. They will get a lot longer this time, so cut each piece in half crosswise. You should have eight long pieces now, all about the width of the machine. Roll each piece through once on the next-to-last setting of the pasta machine.

Set a large bowl or pan of ice water next to the stove. Dust excess flour from the pasta, and add half of the pasta to the boiling water. Cook until just al dente, about 2 minutes from the time it floats in the water. Transfer immediately to the ice bath to cool, and repeat with the remaining pasta. Drain and keep the pasta between moist kitchen towels, well wrung.

To assemble the lasagna: Mix the shredded mozzarella and 1 cup of the Grana Padano in a medium bowl. Butter a 9-by-13-inch lasagna pan with the softened butter. Spread a little sauce on the bottom of the pan. Lay two or three sheets of pasta side by side in the pan so they spill over the sides of the pan. Add half of the meatballs and a ladle or two of sauce. Sprinkle with a quarter of the grated cheese, and arrange the sliced eggs over the top. Sprinkle with half of the basil.

Layer the pasta over the top; it should *not* come over the sides this time, so cut the pasta to fit to the edges of the pan, and patch with small pieces if needed. Add the rest of the meatballs and another ladle or two of sauce. Sprinkle with another quarter of the cheese and the remaining basil. Make another layer of pasta like the second one, and top with all but 1½ cups of the remaining sauce and another quarter of the cheese. Add the last layer of pasta, fitted to the edges. Spread with ¾ cup sauce and the remaining cheese. Fold the edges from the first pasta layer over the top to seal the sides of the lasagna. Spread with the remaining ¾ cup sauce, and sprinkle with the remaining ½ cup Grana Padano. Tent with foil, making sure it doesn't touch the lasagna. Set on a sheet pan and bake until the edges are bubbly, about 45 minutes to an hour. Uncover, and bake until the top is brown and crusty, about 20 minutes more. Let it rest at least 15 minutes before cutting it into squares to serve.

Dried Pasta

Spaghetti with Garlic and Oil

Spaghetti Aglio e Olio
SERVES 6

Kosher salt to taste
⅓ cup extra-virgin olive oil, plus more as needed
10 garlic cloves, sliced
1 pound spaghetti
½ teaspoon crushed red pepper flakes
½ cup chopped fresh Italian parsley
1 cup packed fresh basil leaves, shredded
    (optional)
½ cup freshly grated Grana Padano

Bring a large pot of salted water to a boil for the pasta. In a large skillet, heat the olive oil over medium heat. Add the garlic, and let sizzle until the garlic begins to turn golden, about 2 minutes. Add the spaghetti to the boiling water once you begin cooking the garlic, and give the spaghetti a stir.

Once the garlic is golden, add the red pepper flakes and let toast for a minute, then ladle in 2 cups pasta water. Bring the sauce to a rapid boil. Season with salt. Once the sauce has reduced by about half and the spaghetti is al dente, scoop the pasta from the water with tongs and add to sauce. Add the parsley. Cook and toss to coat the pasta with the sauce. Off heat, add the basil and grated cheese. Toss, adding a final drizzle of olive oil, and serve immediately.

🦋 This recipe is only one variation. You can transform it into a different sauce without major effort or investment. For instance, you can add four anchovy fillets when you add the sliced garlic, or ½ cup drained capers when you add the pasta water, or you can add both.

Spaghetti with Sheep's Cheese and Black Pepper

Spaghetti Cacio e Pepe
SERVES 6

Kosher salt
2 tablespoons black peppercorns, or more to
    taste
1 pound spaghetti
1½ cups freshly grated Pecorino Romano, or
    more to taste

Bring a big pot of salted water to a boil for the pasta. Grind the peppercorns very coarsely, preferably crushing them in a mortar with a pestle or in a spice grinder. Warm up a big bowl for mixing and serving the pasta; use some of the pasta water to heat the bowl, if you like.

Cook the spaghetti until al dente. Quickly lift it from the pot with tongs, let it drain for an instant, then drop it into the warm bowl. Immediately sprinkle the grated cheese and as you toss, sprinkle on spoonfuls of hot water from the cooking pot to moisten and amalgamate the pasta and cheese; when the pasta is coated with the creaminess of the cheese, toss in the pepper. Serve right away, while the spaghetti is very hot.

Ziti with Roasted Eggplant and Ricotta Cheese

Ziti alla Norma
SERVES 6

2 large firm eggplants (about 2 pounds total)
2 tablespoons kosher salt, plus more to taste
6 tablespoons extra-virgin olive oil
2 garlic cloves, thinly sliced
One 35-ounce can Italian plum tomatoes, preferably San Marzano, crushed by hand
¼ teaspoon crushed red pepper flakes, or to taste
1 pound ziti
1 cup freshly grated Grana Padano
1 cup fresh basil leaves, shredded
8 ounces (1 cup) fresh ricotta cheese or packaged whole-milk ricotta cheese

Trim the stems from the eggplants. Remove strips of peel about 1 inch wide from the eggplants, leaving about half the peel intact. Cut the eggplant into 1-inch cubes, and toss in a large bowl with the 2 tablespoons kosher salt. Dump into a colander, and let drain for 1 hour. Rinse the eggplant under cool running water, drain thoroughly, and pat dry.

Preheat the oven to 400 degrees. Brush a rimmed baking sheet with half the olive oil. Turn the eggplant cubes onto the baking sheet, toss to coat with oil, and spread them out in an even layer. Bake until the eggplant is very tender and browned, about 25 minutes. Turn and stir the eggplant cubes gently once or twice during baking so they cook evenly.

Bring a large pot of salted water to a boil over high heat for the ziti. Heat the remaining olive oil in a large skillet over medium heat. Scatter in the garlic, and cook, shaking the pan, until golden, about 3 minutes. Pour in the crushed tomatoes, add the pepper flakes, and season lightly with salt. Bring to a boil, then reduce the heat and simmer for 10 minutes.

Stir the ziti into the boiling water. Return to a boil, stirring frequently. When it is al dente, drain the pasta and return it to the pot over low heat. Pour in about half of the sauce, tossing lightly to coat the pasta. Remove the pot from the heat, stir in ½ cup of the grated cheese and the basil. Add half of the roasted eggplant and toss, then add the ricotta by heaping teaspoonfuls, stirring it gently into the pasta; you want the ricotta to warm, but you do not want it to blend with the sauce completely.

Plate the pasta, and spoon the reserved sauce over each serving; then divide the remaining baked eggplant on top of each pasta plate. Sprinkle with the remaining grated cheese, and serve.

Shells with Young Peas and Mushrooms

Conchiglie con Piselli e Funghi
SERVES 6

Kosher salt
1½ cups shelled young peas (about 1½ pounds before shelling), or frozen baby peas
2 tablespoons extra-virgin olive oil
2 slices bacon, finely chopped
½ cup chopped spring onions or scallions
2 cups cleaned and sliced mixed mushrooms (such as shiitake, oyster, and cremini)
2 cups Chicken Stock (page 143)
1 tablespoon unsalted butter
Freshly ground black pepper to taste
1 pound pasta shells (conchiglie)
½ cup freshly grated Grana Padano

Bring a large pot of salted water to a boil for the pasta. If using fresh peas, blanch them in a medium saucepan of boiling water 2 minutes. Drain the peas, and rinse them under cold water until cool. Drain them thoroughly. (Frozen peas need to be defrosted and drained, but not blanched.)

Heat the olive oil in a large skillet over medium heat. Add the bacon and onions, and cook, stirring, until the onions are wilted, about 4 minutes. Add the mushrooms and sprinkle them with salt. Continue to cook, stirring occasionally, until the mushrooms have lost their moisture, about 5 minutes.

Add the chicken stock, peas, and butter, and season lightly with salt and pepper. Simmer until the liquid is reduced by half, about 10 minutes. Check the seasoning, and adjust if necessary.

Meanwhile, stir the shells into the boiling water. When the pasta is al dente, remove and transfer directly to the waiting sauce with a spider. Toss to coat the pasta in the sauce. Remove the skillet from the heat, sprinkle with the grated cheese, toss, and serve.

Baked Stuffed Shells

Conchiglie Ripiene al Forno
MAKES ABOUT 30 STUFFED SHELLS, SERVING 6

Kosher salt
¼ cup extra-virgin olive oil
6 garlic cloves, crushed and peeled
One 35-ounce can peeled Italian plum tomatoes, preferably San Marzano, crushed by hand
½ teaspoon crushed red pepper flakes
10 fresh basil leaves
1 pound jumbo pasta shells
1 pound fresh mozzarella cheese
1½ pounds fresh ricotta or packaged whole milk ricotta, drained overnight
1 cup freshly grated Grana Padano

⅓ cup chopped fresh Italian parsley
Freshly ground black pepper to taste
1 large egg

Preheat the oven to 425 degrees. Bring a large pot of salted water to a boil for the pasta. Heat the olive oil in a large skillet over medium heat. Scatter the garlic over the oil, and cook, shaking the pan, until golden brown, about 2 minutes. Pour the tomatoes into the skillet, slosh out the can with 1 cup water, and add that. Add the crushed red pepper, and season lightly with salt. Bring the sauce to a quick boil, then adjust the heat to simmering. Cook until the sauce is slightly thickened, about 30 minutes. Stir the basil into the sauce a few minutes before it is done.

Stir the shells into the salted boiling water, and cook, stirring occasionally, until slightly firmer than al dente, about 7 minutes. Fish the shells out of the water with a spider, and plunge into a large bowl of ice water. Let cool, then drain.

Thinly slice half the mozzarella, and cut the remaining half into ¼-inch cubes. Turn the drained ricotta into a mixing bowl, and stir in the mozzarella cubes, grated cheese, and parsley. Season to taste with salt and pepper. Beat the egg well, and stir it into the ricotta mixture.

Remove the garlic and line the bottom of a 10-by-15-inch baking dish with about ¾ cup of the tomato sauce. Spoon about 2 tablespoons of the ricotta mixture into each shell—the shell should be filled to capacity, but not overstuffed. Nestle the shells next to each other in the baking dish as you fill them, spooning the remaining sauce over the shells, coating each one. Arrange the slices of mozzarella in an even layer over the shells. Bake until the mozzarella is browned and bubbling, about 25 minutes. Remove from the oven, and let stand 5 minutes before serving.

Rigatoni Woodsman Style

Rigatoni alla Boscaiola
SERVES 6

1 teaspoon kosher salt, plus more for the pot
3 tablespoons extra-virgin olive oil
1 medium onion, chopped
1 pound sweet Italian sausage without fennel seeds, removed from casings
1 pound mixed mushrooms (button, cremini, shiitake, oyster), thickly sliced
6 fresh sage leaves
One 28-ounce can Italian plum tomatoes, preferably San Marzano, crushed by hand
1 cup frozen peas, thawed
1 bunch scallions, chopped
½ cup heavy cream
1 pound rigatoni
1 cup freshly grated Grana Padano

Bring a large pot of salted water to a boil for the pasta. In a large skillet, heat the olive oil over medium heat. Add the onion, and cook until it is softened, about 4 minutes. Add the sausage, and cook and crumble with a wooden spoon until sausage is no longer pink, about 4 minutes.

Add the mushrooms, cover, and cook until they release their juices, about 2 minutes. Uncover, and add the sage and tomatoes. Bring to a simmer, slosh out the tomato can with 1 cup pasta-cooking water, and season with the 1 teaspoon salt. Bring the sauce to a simmer, and cook, uncovered, until thickened, about 10 minutes.

Once the sauce is thickened, add the peas and scallions. Cook until the scallions wilt, about 2 minutes. Add ½ cup pasta water and the heavy cream. Bring to a boil, and cook until thickened, about 2 minutes.

Meanwhile, add the rigatoni to the pasta water and cook until al dente. Remove pasta with a spider, and add directly to the sauce, cook, and toss until the pasta is coated with the sauce. Off heat, sprinkle with the grated cheese and toss again. Serve immediately.

Orecchiette with Broccoli Rabe

Orecchiette con Cime di Rapa
SERVES 6

Kosher salt
2 pounds broccoli rabe
3 tablespoons extra-virgin olive oil
8 ounces sweet Italian sausage, removed from casings
3 large garlic cloves, crushed and peeled
¼ teaspoon crushed red pepper flakes
1 to 3 tablespoons unsalted butter
1 cup Chicken Stock (page 143), plus more as needed
1 pound orecchiette
½ cup freshly grated Pecorino Romano cheese

Bring a large pot of salted water to a boil for the pasta. Cut off and discard the tough lower part of the broccoli rabe stems, leaving the broccoli about 8 inches long. Remove the large tough leaves, leaving just the tender leaves and flower buds. Peel the thick, lower part of the stems by lifting strips from the stem end with a paring knife or vegetable peeler and drawing them up toward the bud area. A perfect peel is not necessary, but removing the peel does remove bitterness. Cut into 2-inch lengths. Wash the broccoli thoroughly, and dry it well, preferably in a salad spinner.

Heat the olive oil in a large skillet over medium heat. Add the sausage meat, and cook until the sausage is no longer pink, about 3 minutes. Add the crushed garlic, and cook until the sausage is lightly browned, about 2 to 3 minutes.

Add about half the broccoli rabe to the pan, and toss it until it begins to wilt. Add more of the broccoli as that in the pan begins to wilt. When all the broccoli rabe has been added, cover the pan and steam the broccoli until wilted and bright green, about 4 minutes. Taste, and season lightly with salt and the red pepper flakes. Stir in the butter until it is melted, then add the stock and bring to a boil. Boil gently, uncovered, for several minutes more, to reduce the liquid and concentrate the flavor. Remove the garlic.

Meanwhile, add the orecchiette to the pasta water. When the pasta is al dente and the sauce is ready, transfer the pasta to the sauce with a spider. Toss to coat the pasta with the sauce, adding a splash of pasta water if it seems dry. Remove the skillet from the heat, and sprinkle with the grated cheese. Toss well, and serve.

Capellini with Vegetables

Capellini Primavera
SERVES 6

½ teaspoon kosher salt, plus more to taste
¼ cup extra-virgin olive oil
4 garlic cloves, crushed and peeled
8 ounces green beans, trimmed and cut into 2-inch lengths
8 ounces asparagus, bottoms trimmed and peeled, cut into 2-inch lengths
1 pint grape tomatoes
1 bunch scallions, chopped (about 1 cup)
1 cup frozen peas, thawed
½ cup heavy cream
1 pound capellini
½ cup loosely packed fresh basil leaves, shredded
½ cup freshly grated Grana Padano

Bring a large pot of salted water to a boil for the pasta. Add the olive oil to a large skillet over medium-high heat. When the oil is hot, add the garlic. Once the garlic begins to sizzle, add the green beans, asparagus, and salt. Add ½ cup pasta-cooking water, then cover and let steam until crisp-tender, about 3 minutes.

Add the grape tomatoes, and cook until they begin to wrinkle, about 2 minutes. Add the scallions and peas, the cream, and 1 cup pasta water. Bring to a rapid boil, and cook until reduced by

about half, about 3 to 4 minutes. Remove the garlic.

Once you add the cream to the sauce, add the capellini to the pasta water and cook until just al dente, with still quite a bite to it (it will cook more in the sauce).

When the capellini is ready, remove with tongs and transfer directly to the sauce, and add the basil. Toss to coat the pasta in the sauce, adding a splash of pasta water if it seems dry. Remove the skillet from the heat, sprinkle with the grated cheese, toss, and serve.

Spaghetti and Pesto Trapanese

Pesto alla Trapanese
SERVES 4 TO 6

½ teaspoon kosher salt, plus more to taste
12 ounces cherry tomatoes, very ripe and sweet (about 2½ cups)
12 large fresh basil leaves
⅓ cup whole almonds, lightly toasted
1 garlic clove, crushed and peeled
¼ teaspoon crushed red pepper flakes, or to taste
½ cup extra-virgin olive oil
1 pound spaghetti
½ cup freshly grated Grana Padano

Bring a large pot of salted water to a boil for the pasta. In the work bowl of a food processor, combine the tomatoes, basil, almonds, garlic, red pepper flakes, and salt. Process to make a coarse purée, and scrape down the sides of the bowl. With the machine running, pour in the olive oil in a steady stream, emulsifying the purée into a thick pesto. Taste, and adjust seasoning. (If you're going dress the pasta within a couple of hours, leave the pesto at room temperature. Refrigerate it for longer storage, up to 2 days, but let it return to room temperature before cooking the pasta.)

Scrape the pesto into a large serving bowl.

Cook the spaghetti in the boiling water until al dente, then remove with tongs to the bowl with the pesto. Toss quickly to coat the spaghetti, sprinkle the cheese all over, and toss again, adding a little pasta water if it seems dry. Serve immediately.

to the sauce with a spider. Toss the rigatoni and sausage together, then turn off the heat, and stir in the ricotta and grated cheese. Scatter the basil on top, and toss well to dress the pasta evenly. Serve immediately.

Shepherd's Rigatoni

Rigatoni alla Pastora
SERVES 6

½ teaspoon kosher salt, plus more for the pot
1 pound sweet Italian sausage without fennel
    seeds, removed from casings
¼ cup extra-virgin olive oil
½ teaspoon crushed red pepper flakes, or to taste
1 pound rigatoni
2 cups ricotta, drained overnight (about
    1 pound)
¼ cup freshly grated Grana Padano, plus more
    for the table
½ cup loosely packed fresh basil leaves, shredded

Bring a large pot of salted water to a boil for the pasta. For the sauce: Crumble the sausage meat in a bowl, breaking it into small clumps with your fingers. Pour the olive oil into a large skillet over medium-high heat. Sprinkle in the red pepper flakes, let them toast for a few seconds, then scatter the crumbled sausage in the pan. Cook the sausage, stirring and breaking up any clumps, for 10 minutes or so, as the meat juices are released and cook away, until it is all well browned and crispy.

Meanwhile, when the sausage is sizzling, drop the rigatoni into the boiling water. When the sausage is browned and crisp, ladle about ½ cup of the pasta-cooking water into the skillet, and deglaze the pan bottom, scraping up the browned bits. Season the sauce with the salt.

When the pasta is al dente, transfer directly

Whole Wheat Orecchiette with Cauliflower and Bacon

Orecchiette Integrali con Pancetta e Cavolfiori
SERVES 6

1 teaspoon kosher salt, plus more for the pot
2 tablespoons extra-virgin olive oil, plus more for
    drizzling
4 ounces slab bacon, diced
1 medium onion, sliced
1 small head cauliflower, cut into small florets,
    plus the tender leaves, chopped
10 fresh sage leaves
Pinch of crushed red pepper flakes
1 tablespoon grainy mustard
1 pound whole-wheat orecchiette
¼ cup chopped fresh Italian parsley
¼ cup freshly grated Pecorino Romano

Bring a large pot of salted water to a boil for the pasta. To a large skillet over medium heat, add the olive oil. When the oil is hot, add the bacon, and cook until the fat is rendered, about 5 minutes.

Add the onion, cauliflower leaves and florets, and sage. Season with the salt and red pepper flakes. Toss to coat the vegetables in the oil. Cover, and cook until the onions and cauliflower leaves are wilted, about 4 minutes.

Add 2 cups pasta water, cover, and simmer until the cauliflower is tender, about 6 minutes. Uncover, and simmer rapidly until sauce is reduced by half, about 4 minutes more. Whisk in the mustard.

Meanwhile, cook the orecchiette in the boiling water. When the pasta is al dente, remove with a spider and transfer directly to the simmering sauce. Add the parsley, and toss to coat the pasta with the sauce, adding a little pasta water if it seems dry. Remove the skillet from the heat, sprinkle with the grated cheese, toss, and serve.

to coat the pasta with the sauce, adding a little pasta water if it seems dry. Remove the skillet from the heat, remove the garlic, and sprinkle with the grated cheese. Toss, and serve immediately.

Spaghetti with Fennel and Bitter Greens

Spaghetti con Finocchio e Cicoria
SERVES 6

1 teaspoon kosher salt, plus more for the pot
6 tablespoons extra-virgin olive oil
1 medium onion, sliced
2 garlic cloves, smashed and peeled
1 small fennel bulb, trimmed, halved, cored, and thinly sliced
6 anchovy fillets, chopped
1 medium head escarole, trimmed, leaves coarsely chopped
¼ teaspoon crushed red pepper flakes
1 pound spaghetti
2 tablespoons balsamic vinegar
½ cup freshly grated Grana Padano

Bring a large pot of salted water to a boil for the pasta. In a large skillet over medium-high heat, heat the olive oil, then add the onion and garlic. Cook until the onion is wilted, about 4 minutes. Add the fennel, and cook until it is wilted, about 4 minutes. Add the anchovies, and stir to dissolve them in the oil. Add the escarole, and season with the salt and crushed red pepper. Ladle in ½ cup pasta-cooking water, cover, and cook until the escarole is tender, about 5 minutes.

Meanwhile, add the spaghetti to the boiling water. When the escarole is tender, uncover it, drizzle in the balsamic vinegar, and simmer to combine the flavors, just about 3 minutes.

When the pasta is al dente, remove with tongs and transfer directly to the simmering sauce. Toss

Rigatoni with Cauliflower, Saffron, and Golden Raisins

Rigatoni con Cavolfiori, Zafferano e Uvetta
SERVES 6

1½ teaspoons kosher salt, plus more for the pot
½ cup golden raisins
½ teaspoon saffron threads
One 4-inch-long chunk day-old bread, crust removed
6 tablespoons extra-virgin olive oil
1 medium onion, sliced
1 small head cauliflower, cut into small florets, plus the tender leaves, chopped
¼ teaspoon crushed red pepper flakes
1 tablespoon tomato paste
½ cup dry white wine
1 pound rigatoni
¼ cup chopped fresh Italian parsley
¼ cup pine nuts, toasted
½ cup freshly grated Pecorino Romano

Bring a large pot of salted water to a boil for the pasta. Put the raisins and saffron in a small bowl and cover with 1 cup hot pasta-cooking water. Let the raisins soak while you begin the pasta.

Grate the bread on the coarse holes of a box grater to get about 1 cup crumbs. Heat a medium skillet over medium heat. When the skillet is hot, add 2 tablespoons of the olive oil. Add the crumbs. Cook and stir until the crumbs are crisp and golden all over, about 3 to 4 minutes. Set aside to cool.

To a large skillet over medium heat, add the remaining ¼ cup olive oil. When the oil is hot, add the onion and cook until wilted, about

5 minutes. Add the cauliflower florets and leaves, and season with the salt and red pepper flakes. Cook, tossing occasionally, until the cauliflower is caramelized, about 10 minutes.

Push the cauliflower to the side, and make a hot spot in the middle of the pan. Add the tomato paste, and cook and stir in that spot until it toasts and darkens a shade or two, about 1 minute. Stir the tomato paste into the vegetables. Add the white wine, bring to a simmer, and add the raisins and their soaking liquid. Bring back to a simmer, and cook until the cauliflower is very tender, about 5 minutes.

Meanwhile, cook the pasta in the boiling water. When the sauce is ready and the pasta is al dente, remove the pasta with a spider and transfer directly to the simmering sauce. Sprinkle with the parsley and pine nuts, and toss to coat the pasta with the sauce, adding a little pasta water if it seems dry. Remove the skillet from the heat, sprinkle with the grated cheese, toss, and serve.

to a boil for the favas. Add the fava beans and blanch until bright green, about 2 minutes. Cool in a bowl of ice water, and peel and discard the outer skins of the favas.

To a large skillet over medium heat, add the olive oil. When the oil is hot, add the pancetta. Cook until the pancetta renders its fat, about 3 minutes. Add the leeks, and toss to coat in the oil. Season with the salt and crushed red pepper. Cook until the leeks begin to wilt, about 5 minutes. Add the favas, and toss to coat in the oil. Ladle in 1 cup pasta water, and simmer until the favas and leeks are very tender, about 8 minutes.

Meanwhile, cook the pasta in the boiling water. When the sauce is ready and the pasta is al dente, remove the pasta with a spider and transfer directly to the simmering sauce. Add the mint and a drizzle of olive oil. Toss to coat the pasta with the sauce, adding a splash of pasta water if it seems dry. Remove the skillet from the heat, sprinkle with the grated cheese, toss, and serve immediately.

Mezzi Rigatoni with Fava Beans and Mint

Mezze Maniche con Fave e Mentuccia
SERVES 6

1 teaspoon kosher salt, plus more for the pots
2 cups fresh fava beans, shelled
¼ cup extra-virgin olive oil, plus more for drizzling
2 ounces pancetta, diced
3 medium leeks, white and light green parts, halved, washed, and thinly sliced
Pinch of crushed red pepper flakes
1 pound mezzi rigatoni
¼ cup fresh mint leaves, shredded
½ cup freshly grated Grana Padano

Bring a large pot of salted water to a boil for the pasta. Bring a medium saucepan of salted water

Linguine with Walnuts and Swiss Chard

Linguine con Noci e Bietole
SERVES 6

2 teaspoons kosher salt, plus more for the pot
1 large bunch Swiss chard, including stems (about 2 pounds)
¼ cup extra-virgin olive oil, plus more for drizzling
1 medium red onion, sliced
3 garlic cloves, thinly sliced
¼ teaspoon crushed red pepper flakes
1 pound linguine
2 cups fresh ricotta, drained
½ cup walnuts, toasted and coarsely chopped
½ cup freshly grated Grana Padano

Bring a large pot of salted water to a boil for the pasta. Trim the tough stems at the bottoms of the chard leaves and discard. Separate the tender stems from the leaves, and wash both well. Cut the stems into ¼-inch pieces. Coarsely shred the leaves.

Heat a large skillet over medium-high heat. Add the olive oil. When the oil is hot, add the onion and garlic, and cook until the onion is golden, about 5 minutes. Add the chard stems, and cook until they are almost tender, about 5 minutes. Add 2 cups pasta water, and boil rapidly until reduced by about a third, about 3 minutes. Add the chard leaves, and season with the salt and crushed red pepper. Cover, and simmer until the stems and leaves are both very tender, about 10 minutes.

While the chard cooks, add the pasta to the boiling water. When the sauce is ready and the pasta is al dente, remove the pasta with tongs and transfer directly to the simmering sauce. Add the fresh ricotta and the walnuts, and toss to melt the ricotta into the sauce, just a minute or two. Add a little pasta water if the sauce seems dry. Remove the skillet from the heat, sprinkle with the grated cheese, toss, and serve.

Orzo with Artichokes

Orzo con Carciofi
SERVES 6 AS A SIDE DISH

½ teaspoon kosher salt, plus more for the pot
⅓ cup extra-virgin olive oil
4 garlic cloves, thinly sliced
4 medium artichokes, cleaned (see page 6), halved, and sliced
2 medium russet potatoes, peeled and cut into ½-inch cubes
Pinch of crushed red pepper flakes
8 ounces orzo
2 tablespoons chopped fresh Italian parsley
¼ cup freshly grated Grana Padano

Bring a large saucepan of salted water to a boil for the orzo. Heat a large skillet over medium heat. Add the olive oil. When the oil is hot, add the garlic. Cook until the garlic is light golden, about 2 minutes. Add the artichokes, and toss to coat in the oil. Cover and sweat the artichokes until almost tender, about 10 minutes.

Uncover the artichokes, and add the potatoes. Season with the salt and crushed red pepper. Toss to coat the potatoes in the oil. Cover, and cook until the potatoes are almost tender, about 10 minutes.

Once you cover the potatoes, begin cooking the orzo in the boiling water. After 5 minutes, uncover the potatoes and increase the heat to medium high. Cook the potatoes and artichokes, stirring frequently, until browned all over, like hash, about 5 minutes more.

Drain the orzo, reserving 1 cup pasta water. Add the drained orzo to the skillet, along with the parsley and ½ cup pasta water. Toss to coat the pasta with the sauce, adding a little more of the pasta water if it seems dry. Remove the skillet from the heat, sprinkle with the grated cheese, toss, and serve.

Penne Rigate in a Vodka Sauce

Penne Rigate alla Vodka
SERVES 6

1 teaspoon kosher salt, plus more for the pot and as needed
2 tablespoons unsalted butter
1 tablespoon extra-virgin olive oil
½ cup finely diced onion
2 garlic cloves, crushed and peeled
¼ teaspoon crushed red pepper flakes
One 28-ounce can Italian plum tomatoes, preferably San Marzano, crushed by hand
1 pound penne rigate
½ cup half-and-half
⅓ cup vodka

1 cup freshly grated Grana Padano

½ cup loosely packed fresh basil leaves, shredded

Bring a large pot of salted water to a boil for the pasta. In a large skillet over medium heat, melt the butter in the olive oil. Add the diced onion and crushed garlic. Let the onion and garlic sweat a few minutes, without coloring; then, in a hot spot, add the crushed red pepper. Let it toast for a minute. Ladle in about ½ cup pasta water, and simmer to break down the onion, about 2 to 3 minutes.

Once the onion has softened, add the crushed tomatoes, slosh out the can with about a cup of water, and add that, too. Season with salt. Bring to a simmer, and cook until thickened, about 10 to 12 minutes. When the sauce is almost done, add the pasta to the pot of boiling water and stir.

Once the sauce has thickened, remove the garlic cloves, and add the half-and-half and vodka. Bring to a boil, and cook until the sauce comes together and thickens again, about 3 minutes. When the pasta is al dente, scoop it out of the pot with a strainer or spider and add directly to the sauce. Cook and toss the pasta in the sauce until all of the pasta is coated with the sauce. Off heat, toss with the grated cheese and basil. Serve immediately.

Bucatini with Pancetta, Tomato, and Onion

Bucatini all'Amatriciana
SERVES 6

Kosher salt

5 tablespoons extra-virgin olive oil, or to taste

1 medium onion, thinly sliced

Four ¼-inch-thick slices pancetta or jowl bacon (about 6 ounces), cut into 1½-inch julienne strips

2 whole dried red peperoncini (hot red peppers), or ½ teaspoon crushed red pepper flakes

One 35-ounce can Italian plum tomatoes, preferably San Marzano, crushed by hand

1 pound bucatini

1 cup freshly grated Pecorino Romano cheese, plus more for passing

Bring a large pot of salted water to a boil for the pasta. In a large skillet, heat 2 tablespoons of the olive oil over medium heat. Add the onion, and cook, stirring, until wilted, about 4 minutes. Stir in the pancetta, and cook until rendered but not crisp, about 4 minutes. Add the peperoncini, the tomatoes, and 1 cup water sloshed from the tomato can, and bring to a boil. Adjust the heat to a simmer, and season lightly with salt. Cook, stirring occasionally, until the sauce is thickened, about 20 minutes.

While the sauce cooks, cook the pasta. When the pasta is al dente and the sauce is ready, remove the pasta with tongs and transfer directly to the sauce. Toss to coat the pasta in the sauce, adding a splash of pasta water if it seems dry. Check the seasoning, and add salt if necessary. Remove the pan from the heat, sprinkle with the grated cheese, toss, and serve, passing additional grated cheese separately if you like.

Spaghetti with Calamari, Scallops, and Shrimp

Spaghetti con Calamari, Capesante e Gamberi
SERVES 6

1 teaspoon kosher salt, plus more for the pot

¼ cup extra-virgin olive oil, plus 2 tablespoons for finishing the pasta

6 garlic cloves, sliced

4 cups cherry tomatoes, halved, or 2 cups canned Italian plum tomatoes, preferably San Marzano, crushed

¼ teaspoon crushed red pepper flakes, or to taste

1 pound spaghetti

8 ounces medium calamari, cleaned (see

page 54), tubes cut into ½-inch rings, tentacles halved

8 ounces dry sea scallops (see page 57), side muscle or "foot" removed

1 pound large shrimp, peeled and deveined

¼ cup chopped fresh basil

1 tablespoon chopped fresh Italian parsley

Bring a large pot of salted water to a boil for the pasta. Heat the olive oil in a large skillet over medium-high heat. Scatter in the sliced garlic, and cook, stirring occasionally, until it begins to color, about 1 to 2 minutes. Add the cherry tomatoes, salt, and crushed red pepper, and cook until the tomatoes are softened and sizzling in their juices but still intact, about 5 minutes. Start cooking the pasta first, and the seafood right after, so they are ready at the same time.

Drop the spaghetti into the boiling water, stir, and return the water to a boil.

Scatter the calamari rings and tentacles in the pan with the tomatoes, and get them sizzling over medium-high heat. Let the pieces cook for a minute or two, then toss in the scallops, and spread them out to heat and start sizzling quickly. After they've cooked for a couple of minutes, toss in the shrimp, ladle in a cup of boiling pasta water, stir the seafood and sauce together, bring to a steady simmer, and cook just until the shrimp turn pink and begin to curl, about 3 minutes. Fish out the garlic and discard.

When the sauce is ready and the pasta is al dente, remove the pasta with tongs and transfer directly to the sauce. Toss to coat the pasta with the sauce, adding a little pasta water if it seems dry. Turn off the heat, sprinkle on the basil and parsley, and drizzle on another 2 tablespoons olive oil. Toss well, heap the spaghetti into warm bowls, giving each portion plenty of seafood, and serve immediately.

Calamari Fra Diavolo over Linguine

Linguine ai Calamari Piccanti
SERVES 6

½ teaspoon kosher salt, plus more for the pot

6 tablespoons extra-virgin olive oil

8 garlic cloves, thinly sliced

½ teaspoon crushed red pepper flakes

One 28-ounce can Italian plum tomatoes, preferably San Marzano, crushed by hand

1 teaspoon dried oregano, preferably Sicilian on the branch

1 pound linguine

1 pound calamari, cleaned (see page 54), bodies cut into 1-inch rings, tentacles roughly chopped

Bring a large pot of salted water to a boil for the pasta. To a large skillet over medium-high heat, add 4 tablespoons of the olive oil. When the oil is hot, add the sliced garlic, and cook until it is sizzling, about 1 to 2 minutes. Season with the red pepper flakes, let toast for a minute, then pour in the tomatoes. Rinse out the tomato can with a cup of water, and add that as well. Season with the oregano and salt. Bring to a simmer and cook uncovered, to thicken the sauce and develop the flavors, about 8 to 10 minutes. Fish out garlic.

Meanwhile, add the linguine to the boiling water. When the sauce is ready, stir in the calamari, and simmer until just cooked through, about 2 to 3 minutes. When the pasta is al dente, remove with tongs and add directly to the sauce. Drizzle with remaining 2 tablespoons olive oil, toss, and serve immediately.

Linguine with White Clam Sauce

Linguine alle Vongole
SERVES 6

Kosher salt
6 tablespoons extra-virgin olive oil
6 garlic cloves, thinly sliced
4 anchovies, chopped
36 littleneck clams, scrubbed
¼ teaspoon crushed red pepper flakes
¼ teaspoon dried oregano, preferably Sicilian on the branch
1 pound linguine
¾ cup chopped fresh Italian parsley

Bring a large pot of salted water to a boil for the pasta. In a large straight-sided skillet, heat 4 tablespoons of the olive oil over medium heat. Add sliced garlic, and cook until sizzling, about 1 to 2 minutes. Add anchovies, and cook and stir until they break up and dissolve into the oil, about 2 minutes.

Add the clams to the skillet, along with the red pepper flakes and oregano. Ladle in about 2 cups pasta water. Bring to a simmer, cover, and cook until the clams open, about 5 to 7 minutes, discarding any that do not open. As the clams open, remove them to a bowl.

Meanwhile, add the linguine to the boiling water. When all the clams are out, increase the heat to high and add ½ cup of the parsley. Cook until reduced by half. Meanwhile, remove the clams from their shells.

When the linguine is al dente and the sauce is reduced, remove the pasta with tongs and add it directly to the sauce; drizzle with the remaining 2 tablespoons olive oil. Cook and toss until the pasta is coated with the sauce. Add the shucked clams and remaining ¼ cup chopped parsley. Cook a minute more to blend the flavors, and serve.

Orecchiette with Clams and Zucchini

Orecchiette con Vongole e Zucchine
SERVES 6

1 teaspoon kosher salt, plus more for the pot
¼ cup extra-virgin olive oil, plus more for drizzling
4 garlic cloves, thinly sliced
3 medium zucchini, cut into ¼-inch-thick half-moons (about 1 pound)
¼ teaspoon crushed red pepper flakes
½ cup dry white wine
24 littleneck clams, scrubbed
1 bunch scallions, trimmed and chopped (about 1 cup)
1 pound orecchiette
½ cup chopped fresh Italian parsley

Bring a large pot of salted water to a boil for the pasta. Heat a large Dutch oven over medium-high heat. Add the olive oil. When the oil is hot, add the garlic. Cook until the garlic is light golden, about 2 minutes. Add the zucchini, and season with the salt and crushed red pepper. Cook until the zucchini just begins to wilt, about 4 minutes.

Add the white wine and bring to a simmer. Add the clams and scallions, stir, and cover the pot. Begin cooking the pasta in the boiling water. Cook the clams until they all open, about 5 to 6 minutes, discarding any that do not open. Uncover, and increase the heat to high to reduce and concentrate the sauce while the pasta finishes cooking.

When the sauce is ready and the pasta is al dente, remove the pasta with a spider and transfer directly to the sauce. Add the parsley and a drizzle of olive oil. Toss to coat the pasta in the sauce, adding a splash of pasta water if it seems dry. Serve immediately.

🍀 If you happen to get your hands on some zucchini blossoms, you can chop them coarsely and add along with the scallions.

Spaghetti with Crab Sauce

Spaghetti al Granchio
SERVES 6

1 teaspoon kosher salt, plus more for the pot
½ cup extra-virgin olive oil
8 garlic cloves, thinly sliced
Two 28-ounce cans Italian plum tomatoes, preferably San Marzano, crushed by hand
1 teaspoon dried oregano, preferably Sicilian on the branch
3 pounds snow-crab legs, cut at joints into pieces, nail at end of each leg snipped off
1 pound spaghetti
3 tablespoons chopped fresh Italian parsley

Bring a large pot of salted water to a boil for the pasta. Heat 4 tablespoons of the oil in a large Dutch oven over medium heat. When the oil is hot, add half of the sliced garlic. Once the garlic is sizzling, add the tomatoes. Slosh out the cans with 1 cup water, and add that as well. Bring to a simmer, add the salt and oregano, and simmer until slightly thickened, about 10 minutes.

Meanwhile, heat the remaining 4 tablespoons olive oil in a large skillet over medium-high heat. When the oil is hot, add the remaining sliced garlic. Once the garlic is sizzling, add as many crab-leg pieces as will fit in the pan in one layer (you will need to do this in batches). Sauté the crab legs, turning, until they turn from blue to bright red, about 3 minutes per batch. Remove to a plate, and repeat with the remaining crab legs. Once all of the crab is sautéed, and after the sauce has cooked 10 minutes, add the crab legs to the sauce. Simmer until the crab is cooked through and the sauce is flavorful, another 10 minutes or so.

Once the crab legs are simmering, cook the spaghetti. When the sauce is ready and the pasta is al dente, pour about 3 cups of the sauce into a large skillet, and bring to a simmer. Transfer the pasta with tongs directly to the sauce in the skillet. Sprinkle with the chopped parsley, and toss to coat the pasta with the sauce. Serve the pasta in shallow bowls, with the extra sauce and crab legs piled over the top.

Snow-crab legs are usually sold, like Alaskan king crab legs, frozen and packed individually. They are priced according to size. The larger they are, the more expensive; of course, larger crabs have more meat in each leg. Snow crabs are usually rated from the largest, 3 to 5 legs to a pound, to 5 to 8 legs to a pound and so on. The higher the number of legs per pound, the smaller the legs are. I would recommend 5 to 8 legs to a pound.

Linguine with Shrimp and Zucchini

Linguine con Gamberi e Zucchine
SERVES 6

½ teaspoon kosher salt, plus more for the pot
¼ cup extra-virgin olive oil, plus more for drizzling
1 medium onion, sliced
3 medium zucchini, cut into matchsticks (about 1 pound)
Pinch of crushed red pepper flakes
1 pound linguine
1 pound large shrimp, peeled and deveined
½ cup loosely packed fresh basil leaves, coarsely chopped
½ cup freshly grated Grana Padano

Bring a large pot of salted water to a boil for the pasta. To a large skillet over medium heat, add 3 tablespoons of the olive oil. When the oil is hot, add the onion. Cook until the onion is wilted, about 5 minutes. Add the zucchini, and season with the salt and red pepper flakes. Cover, and cook until the zucchini has wilted a bit, about 3 minutes.

When you uncover the zucchini, add the pasta to the boiling water. Raise the heat under the zucchini to medium high, and add the remaining tablespoon of olive oil. Cook and toss the zucchini until lightly browned, about 5 minutes.

Add the shrimp and basil. Cook and toss until the shrimp are just cooked through, about 3 to 4 minutes. Add ½ cup pasta water, and simmer while the pasta finishes cooking, for a minute or two.

When the pasta is al dente, remove with tongs and transfer directly to the simmering sauce. Drizzle with a little olive oil, and toss to coat the pasta with the sauce. Remove the skillet from the heat, sprinkle with the grated cheese, toss, and serve immediately.

Spaghetti with Shrimp and Basil Sauce

Spaghetti con Salsa di Gamberi e Basilico
SERVES 6

1 teaspoon kosher salt, plus more for the pot
¼ cup extra-virgin olive oil, plus more for drizzling
1 pound large shrimp, peeled, deveined, tails removed, shrimp halved crosswise
1 pound spaghetti
4 garlic cloves, crushed and peeled
1 large shallot, finely chopped
1 hot pickled cherry pepper, chopped (remove seeds for less heat)
1 cup dry white wine
½ cup loosely packed fresh basil leaves
¼ cup loosely packed fresh Italian parsley leaves
2 tablespoons loosely packed fresh mint leaves
Freshly ground black pepper

Bring a large pot of salted water to a boil for the pasta. To a large skillet over medium-high heat, add 2 tablespoons of the olive oil. When the oil is hot, add the shrimp, season with ½ teaspoon salt, and toss until the shrimp curl and turn white, about 3 minutes. Remove to a plate.

Once the shrimp are out of the pan, add the

spaghetti to the boiling water. Add the remaining 2 tablespoons olive oil to the skillet, along with the garlic, shallot, cherry pepper, and remaining salt. Cook until the shallot is almost tender, about 4 minutes. Add the white wine, and boil until reduced by half, about 3 minutes. Coarsely chop the herbs and set aside. Add 1 cup pasta water, and simmer to reduce by half, just while the spaghetti finishes cooking. Remove garlic.

When the spaghetti is al dente, remove with tongs and transfer directly to the sauce. Add the shrimp and any juices collected from the plate, the chopped herbs, a drizzle of olive oil, and black pepper to taste. Toss to coat the pasta in the sauce. Serve immediately.

Capellini with Sea Urchins

Capellini con Ricci di Mare
SERVES 6

Kosher salt to taste
½ cup extra-virgin olive oil
3 garlic cloves, crushed and peeled
½ teaspoon crushed red pepper flakes
Roe of 24 sea urchins, preferably fresh
3 tablespoons chopped fresh Italian parsley
2 medium vine-ripened tomatoes, cored, seeded, and finely chopped
1 pound capellini

Bring a large pot of salted water to a boil for the pasta. In a large skillet, heat 2 tablespoons of the olive oil over medium heat. Add two of the garlic cloves and the crushed red pepper flakes. Cook until the garlic is lightly browned, and remove the skillet from the heat.

Meanwhile, in a bowl, whisk together the sea urchin roe, parsley, the remaining clove of garlic, and salt to taste until blended. Whisk in the remaining 6 tablespoons olive oil. Stir in the tomatoes.

Stir the capellini into the boiling water. Return

the skillet containing the garlic and red pepper flakes to medium heat. When the capellini is still just al dente, remove with tongs and add to the skillet with ½ cup pasta water. Toss until thickened, about 1 to 2 minutes, and remove from the heat. Remove and discard the garlic. Add the sea urchin mixture, toss the capellini well with the sauce, and serve.

🍀 It is possible to purchase fresh sea urchin roe alone. If not, have the fishmonger clean your urchins for you and collect all the roe.

Braised Octopus with Spaghetti

Spaghetti con Polpo in Purgatorio
SERVES 6

½ cup extra-virgin olive oil
2 large onions, thinly sliced (about 4 cups)
2 cleaned octopuses (about 2½ pounds total)
1 cup Gaeta or other black brine-cured olives, pitted
¼ teaspoon kosher salt, plus more for the pot
1 pound spaghetti
2 tablespoons chopped fresh Italian parsley

Heat 6 tablespoons of the olive oil in a medium (4-to-6-quart) saucepan or Dutch oven over low heat. Scatter the onion slices over the bottom of the pan, and lay the octopuses on top. Scatter the olives over the octopuses, cover the pan, and let the octopuses heat slowly, releasing their liquid, and starting to cook in it.

After an hour or so, uncover the pan and check to see that there is plenty of octopus liquid in the pan. If it seems dry, add 1 cup of water at a time. This recipe should yield 2 cups of sauce when the octopuses are done. Continue the covered slow cooking for another hour, until the octopuses are very tender. Start testing for doneness after 1¾ hours: stick the tines of a fork in the thickest part

of each octopus; when the fork slides out easily, the meat is done.

Remove the octopuses from the pot, and let them cool slightly. To make a meaty octopus sauce: cut both octopuses into ¾-inch chunks, skin and all (or you can leave the octopuses whole for serving). Measure the liquid remaining in the saucepan. Again, you should have about 2 cups total. If the volume is greater, return the juices to the saucepan and boil to reduce them. Put the cut octopus meat and the juices in the skillet for dressing the pasta.

Meanwhile, bring a large pot of salted water to a boil for the pasta. Add the spaghetti. As the spaghetti cooks, bring the octopus meat and sauce in the skillet to a rapid simmer; taste, and add ¼ teaspoon salt if needed (octopus is naturally salty). Stir in the parsley. Remove the spaghetti with tongs and transfer directly to the sauce. Toss to coat the pasta with the sauce, adding a splash of pasta water if it seems dry. Turn off the heat, drizzle over the remaining 2 tablespoons olive oil, and toss again. Heap the spaghetti into warm bowls, making sure each portion gets plenty of octopus pieces, and serve immediately.

🍀 You can also serve this—either whole or cut into pieces—over freshly cooked soft polenta or slabs of grilled polenta. Any leftover octopus meat or sauce can be incorporated into a terrific risotto; with so much flavor, just a small amount of leftovers is all you'll need to make a great risotto for two.

🍀 Octopus is usually sold defrosted. In most cases it has been cleaned and is ready to be cooked. If you are lucky enough to get a freshly caught octopus, the only cleaning concern is the round head cavity from which all the tentacles stem. To clean, cut the head off where it meets the tentacles, invert inside out, and clean all of the innards. Cut off the eyes with scissors. The mouth is located under the place where all the tentacles meet; it is a round, pluglike element that will pop out on its own once the octopus is cooked.

Farfalle with Swordfish

Farfalle al Sugo di Pesce Spada
SERVES 6

1 teaspoon kosher salt, plus more for the pot
¼ cup extra-virgin olive oil, plus more for drizzling
1 pound skinless swordfish fillet, about ¾ inch thick, cut into chunks
1 large onion, sliced
4 garlic cloves, thinly sliced
1 teaspoon chopped fresh thyme leaves
One 28-ounce can Italian plum tomatoes, preferably San Marzano, crushed by hand
½ teaspoon crushed red pepper flakes
¼ cup tiny capers in brine, drained
1 pound farfalle
3 tablespoons chopped fresh Italian parsley

Bring a large pot of salted water to a boil for the pasta. To a large skillet over medium-high heat, add 2 tablespoons of the olive oil. Season the swordfish chunks with ½ teaspoon of the salt. Add the swordfish to the skillet, and cook until browned all over but not cooked through, about 3 minutes. Remove to a plate.

Add the remaining 2 tablespoons olive oil to the skillet. When the oil is hot, add the onion. Cook until the onion is golden, about 8 minutes. Add the garlic and thyme, and cook until the garlic is light golden, about 2 minutes. Add the tomatoes, slosh out the can with 1 cup pasta water, and add that, too. Season with the remaining ½ teaspoon salt and the crushed red pepper. Bring to a simmer, and add the capers. Cook until the sauce is thick and flavorful, about 15 minutes.

Meanwhile, cook the pasta in the boiling water. When the pasta is almost done, add the swordfish back to the sauce, and let simmer until just cooked through, about 2 to 3 minutes. When the pasta is al dente, remove with a spider and transfer directly to the simmering sauce. Add the parsley and a drizzle of olive oil, and toss. Serve immediately.

Fusilli with Chicken Ragù

Fusilli al Ragù Bianco di Pollo
SERVES 6

1 teaspoon kosher salt, plus more for the pot
¼ cup extra-virgin olive oil, plus more for drizzling
3 medium leeks, white and light green parts, halved, washed, and thinly sliced
3 medium artichokes, cleaned (see page 6), halved, and sliced
2 celery stalks, diced
¼ teaspoon crushed red pepper flakes
1 pound boneless, skinless chicken thighs, trimmed of fat and sinew, cut into ½-inch chunks
½ cup white wine
2 cups Chicken Stock (page 143)
1 fresh bay leaf
1½ cups frozen peas
1 pound fusilli
¼ cup chopped fresh Italian parsley
Grated zest of 1 lemon
½ cup freshly grated Grana Padano

Bring a large pot of salted water to a boil for the pasta. Heat a medium Dutch oven over medium-high heat. Add the olive oil. When the oil is hot, add the leeks, artichokes, and celery. Season with ½ teaspoon salt and the red pepper flakes. Toss to coat the vegetables in the oil, and cook until they begin to wilt, about 5 minutes.

Push the vegetables to the side of the pan, and add the chicken in the empty space. Season the chicken with the remaining ½ teaspoon salt. Toss the chicken in the empty space until it is no longer raw on the outside, then mix into the vegetables. Add the wine, and cook rapidly until reduced by half, about 2 minutes. Add the chicken stock and bay leaf, and bring to a simmer. Partially cover, and simmer until the chicken and vegetables are very tender, about 20 minutes.

Uncover, add the peas, and simmer, uncovered, to reduce and concentrate the sauce while you cook the pasta. Remove bay leaf and discard.

Add the pasta to the boiling water. When the pasta is al dente, remove with a spider and transfer directly to the simmering sauce. Add the parsley, lemon zest, and a drizzle of olive oil. Toss to coat the pasta in the sauce, adding a little pasta water if it seems dry. Remove the skillet from the heat, sprinkle with the grated cheese, toss, and serve.

Spaghetti and Meatballs

Spaghetti con Polpette di Carne
SERVES 6

FOR THE SAUCE
¼ cup extra-virgin olive oil
1 medium onion, chopped (about 1 cup)
Two 35-ounce cans Italian plum tomatoes, preferably San Marzano, crushed by hand
½ teaspoon crushed red pepper flakes
2 fresh bay leaves
Kosher salt

FOR THE MEATBALLS
8 ounces ground pork
8 ounces ground beef
1 cup fine dried bread crumbs
1 cup freshly grated Grana Padano
¼ cup chopped fresh Italian parsley
2 garlic cloves, finely chopped
1 large egg
1 teaspoon kosher salt
¼ teaspoon freshly ground black pepper
All-purpose flour, for dredging
¼ cup extra-virgin olive oil
¼ cup vegetable oil

1 pound spaghetti

For the sauce: Heat the olive oil in a large Dutch oven over medium heat. Add the onion, and cook, stirring, until it is wilted, about 4 minutes. Pour in the tomatoes, add the crushed red pepper and bay leaves, and season lightly with salt. Slosh out each tomato can with 1 cup water, and add that as well. Bring to a boil, then lower the heat so the sauce is at a lively simmer. Cook, stirring occasionally, for 30 minutes.

For the meatballs: Crumble the pork and beef into a mixing bowl. Sprinkle the bread crumbs, ⅓ cup grated cheese, the parsley, and garlic over the meat. Beat the egg with the salt and pepper in a small bowl until blended, then pour over the meat mixture. Mix the ingredients with clean hands just until evenly blended, and shape the meat mixture into 1½-inch balls. Dredge the meatballs in the flour until lightly but evenly coated. Heat the olive oil and vegetable oil in a large, heavy skillet over medium-high heat. Slip as many meatballs into the skillet as will fit without crowding. Fry, turning as necessary, until they are golden brown on all sides, about 6 minutes. Adjust the heat as the meatballs cook to prevent them from overbrowning. Remove the meatballs, and repeat with the remaining meatballs. Add the browned meatballs to the tomato sauce, and cook, stirring gently with a wooden spoon, until no trace of pink remains at the center of the meatballs, about 30 minutes.

Meanwhile, bring a large pot of salted water to a boil for the pasta. Ladle 2 cups of the tomato sauce (but no meatballs) into a large skillet, and get it simmering. Add pasta to the boiling water. When the pasta is al dente, remove with tongs and transfer directly to the skillet with the sauce. Toss to coat the pasta with the sauce. Remove from the heat, and toss in the remaining ⅔ cup grated cheese. Check the seasoning, and add salt and pepper if necessary.

Serve the pasta in warm bowls, or piled high on a large, warm platter. Spoon a little more of the sauce over the pasta, and pass the remaining sauce separately. Pass the meatballs family-style in a bowl, or top the bowls or platter of spaghetti with them.

Braised Pork Ribs with Rigatoni

Costolette di Maiale Brasate con Rigatoni
SERVES 6

1 full rack pork spare ribs (about 4 pounds)
Kosher salt to taste
Freshly ground black pepper to taste
¼ cup extra-virgin olive oil
2 large yellow onions, sliced (about 3 cups)
8 garlic cloves
6 pickled cherry peppers, stemmed, seeded, and
    quartered
Two 35-ounce cans Italian plum tomatoes, pref-
    erably San Marzano, crushed by hand
2 fresh bay leaves
6 sprigs fresh thyme
1 pound rigatoni
¼ cup chopped fresh Italian parsley
⅔ cup freshly grated Grana Padano, plus more
    for passing

Bring 3 cups water to a bare simmer in a small saucepan, and keep it hot. Cut the rack of spare ribs between the bones into single ribs (or ask your butcher to do this for you). Season the rib pieces with salt and pepper.

Heat the olive oil in a large Dutch oven over medium heat. Add as many of the ribs as will fit without touching. Cook, turning occasionally, until they are browned on all sides, about 10 minutes. Remove the ribs, and drain on a baking sheet lined with paper towels. Repeat with the remaining ribs.

Pour off all but about 4 tablespoons of fat from the casserole. Add the onions, garlic, and cherry peppers, and cook, stirring, until the onions are wilted and caramelized, about 4 minutes. Stir in the tomatoes, bay leaves, and thyme. Bring to a boil, scraping the pan to loosen the brown bits stuck to the bottom. Tuck the spare ribs into the tomato sauce, season lightly with salt and pepper, and bring to a boil. Adjust the heat to simmering, and cook, turning the spare ribs in the sauce occasionally, until the ribs are fork-tender, about

2 hours. Remove the bay leaf. Ladle some of the hot water into the pot from time to time as necessary to keep the ribs covered with liquid.

When the ribs are almost tender, bring a large pot of salted water to a boil. Cook the pasta until al dente. Drain the pasta, return it to the pot, and spoon in enough of the spare-rib sauce to coat the pasta generously. Toss in the parsley, and bring the sauce and pasta to a simmer, tossing to coat the pasta with sauce. Check the seasoning, and add salt and pepper if necessary. Remove the pot from the heat, and stir in the grated cheese. Transfer the pasta to a warm platter or individual plates, and top with the spare ribs. Spoon a little of the remaining sauce over the pasta, and serve immediately, passing additional sauce and grated cheese separately.

Baked Elbows with Pork Ragù

Gomiti al Forno con Ragù di Maiale
SERVES 6

2 teaspoons kosher salt, plus more for
    the pot
1 tablespoon unsalted butter, softened
2 tablespoons fine dried bread crumbs
1½ pounds boneless pork shoulder, trimmed of
    most of the fat and sinews, cut into 1-inch
    chunks
1 medium onion, cut into chunks
1 medium carrot, peeled and cut into chunks
1 celery stalk, cut into chunks
2 garlic cloves, crushed and peeled
¼ cup extra-virgin olive oil
½ teaspoon crushed red pepper flakes
1 cup dry white wine
One 28-ounce can Italian plum tomatoes, pref-
    erably San Marzano, crushed by hand
2 medium zucchini, sliced into ¼-inch-thick
    rounds
1 pound elbow macaroni

2 cups grated low-moisture mozzarella
¾ cup freshly grated Grana Padano

Preheat the oven to 375 degrees. Bring a large pot of salted water to a boil for the pasta. Butter a 9-by-13-inch baking dish. Sprinkle with the bread crumbs, and tap to coat the interior of the dish, tapping out the excess. Run the pork shoulder through the coarse holes of a meat grinder. (You can also use pre-ground pork or sausage, but the coarsely ground texture is preferred.)

In a food processor, combine the onion, carrot, celery, and garlic. Process to make a smooth pestata. To a large Dutch oven over medium-high heat, add the olive oil. When the oil is hot, add the pestata, and cook until it dries out and is light golden, about 5 minutes. Add the ground pork, and season with the salt and crushed red pepper. Reduce the heat to medium, and cook until the pork releases its juices, about 7 minutes. Increase the heat to get the juices boiling, and cook until they're reduced away and the pork is browned, about 5 minutes. Add the white wine, and cook until reduced by half, about 2 minutes. Add the tomatoes, slosh out the can with 1 cup pasta water, and add that, too. Bring to a simmer, and cook until the pork is tender, about 30 minutes.

Add the zucchini, and cook until it is tender and the sauce is thick, about 20 minutes more.

When the zucchini is almost done, cook the elbows in the boiling water until just al dente (they will cook more as they bake). Drain, reserving 1 cup pasta water. In a medium bowl, toss the mozzarella and grated Grana Padano together.

When the sauce is ready, add the elbows and toss to coat the pasta in the sauce, adding a splash of pasta water if it seems dry. Remove the pot from the heat, and fold in half of the cheese mixture. Spread the pasta in the prepared pan, and sprinkle with the remaining cheese mixture. Bake until the sauce is bubbly and the top is brown and crusty, about 25 minutes. Let it sit 5 minutes before serving.

Ziti with Sausage, Fennel, and Onions

Ziti con Salsicce, Finocchio e Cipolla
SERVES 6

½ teaspoon kosher salt, plus more for the pot
1 large fennel bulb, with fronds
⅓ cup extra-virgin olive oil
1 pound sweet Italian sausage without fennel seeds, removed from casings
2 medium onions, sliced
½ teaspoon crushed red pepper flakes
½ cup tomato paste
1 pound ziti
1 cup freshly grated Grana Padano

Bring a large pot of salted water to a boil for the pasta. Trim the fennel bulb: Slice the bulb in half lengthwise, then slice each half into ¼-inch-thick lengthwise slices. Separate the slivers of fennel if they are attached at the bottom; cut the long slivers in half, so you have about 3 cups of 2-inch-long matchsticks of fennel. Chop enough of the tender fronds to yield ⅓ cup.

Heat the olive oil in a large skillet over medium-high heat. Add the sausage meat, and cook, stirring and breaking it up more with a wooden spoon, until it sizzles and begins to brown, about 3 minutes. Push the sausage a bit aside, and drop the onion slices into a clear part of the pan. Cook, stirring, until they sizzle and wilt, another 4 minutes or so, then stir them in with the meat. Clear a new space, and add the fennel. Cook until it begins to wilt, about 3 minute.

Sprinkle on ¼ teaspoon salt; drop the crushed red pepper in a hot spot and toast the flakes for ½ minute, then stir to combine. Clear a good-sized hot spot in the center of the pan, plop in the tomato paste, and cook, stirring it in the spot for a minute or more, until it is sizzling and caramelizing; then stir it in with everything else.

Ladle about 3 cups boiling pasta water into the skillet, stir well, and bring the liquid to a boil. Reduce to a simmer, and let cook until the flavors have developed, the sauce is thickened but not too thick, and the fennel is soft but not mushy, about 8 minutes. (Add more water if the sauce reduces too rapidly.) Season to taste.

Meanwhile, cook the ziti in the boiling water. When the sauce is ready and the ziti is al dente, remove the ziti with a spider and transfer directly to the simmering sauce. Sprinkle in the chopped fronds, and toss to coat the pasta with the sauce. Remove the skillet from the heat, sprinkle the grated cheese over the ziti, toss, and serve.

Ziti with Broccoli Rabe and Sausage

Ziti con Cime di Rapa e Salsicce
SERVES 6

½ teaspoon kosher salt, plus more for the pot
¼ cup extra-virgin olive oil
8 ounces sweet Italian sausage links
3 garlic cloves, crushed and peeled
1 large head broccoli rabe, trimmed, stems peeled (see page 9)
¼ teaspoon crushed red pepper flakes
1 pound ziti
1 tablespoon unsalted butter
½ cup freshly grated Grana Padano

Bring a large pot of salted water to a boil for the pasta. Heat a large skillet over medium-high heat. Add 1 tablespoon of the olive oil. When the oil is hot, add the sausages and brown all over, about 6 minutes. Remove to a plate. (They don't have to be fully cooked at this point; they will cook more in the sauce.)

Add to the skillet the remaining olive oil and the garlic cloves. Cook until the garlic is light golden, about 2 minutes. Add the broccoli rabe, and season with the salt and red pepper flakes. Toss to coat the broccoli rabe in the oil, cover, and let it steam until it is bright green and the leaves are wilted, about 5 minutes.

Meanwhile, slice the sausages into ½-inch

rounds, and add the ziti to the boiling water. Uncover the broccoli rabe and add the sliced sausages, 1 cup pasta water, and the butter. Bring to a simmer, and cook until the broccoli rabe is very tender, about 3 to 4 minutes. Remove garlic.

When the ziti is al dente, remove with a spider and transfer directly to the sauce. Toss to coat the pasta in the sauce, adding a little pasta water if it seems dry. Remove the skillet from the heat, sprinkle with the grated cheese, toss, and serve.

Fregula and Sausage

Fregula e Salsicce
SERVES 6

7 cups Chicken Stock (page 143)
2 tablespoons extra-virgin olive oil, plus more for drizzling
12 ounces sweet Italian sausage without fennel seeds, removed from casings
1 medium onion, chopped
2 fresh bay leaves
8 fresh sage leaves, chopped
1 tablespoon tomato paste
1 pound fregula
¾ cup dry white wine
½ teaspoon kosher salt
Pinch of crushed red pepper flakes
1 bunch scallions, trimmed and chopped
½ cup freshly grated Grana Padano

Bring the chicken stock to a bare simmer in a medium saucepan and keep it hot. Heat a medium Dutch oven over medium heat. Add the olive oil. When the oil is hot, add the sausage. Cook and crumble with a wooden spoon until the sausage is browned all over, about 5 minutes. Add the onion, bay leaves, and sage, and cook until the onion is almost tender, about 5 minutes.

Make a space in the center of the pot, and add the tomato paste. Cook the tomato paste in that spot until it toasts and darkens a shade or two, about 1 minute. Stir the tomato paste into the onion and sausage, and add the fregula. Toss to coat the fregula in the sausage mixture and coat it with oil. Let toast a minute or two, then add the white wine. Bring to a simmer, and cook until the wine is reduced away, about 3 minutes.

Add 4 cups of the simmering stock and the salt and crushed red pepper, partially cover the pan, adjust the heat so the liquid is simmering, and cook, adding the remaining stock in two additions (as for risotto), until the fregula is al dente, about 18 minutes. Remove the bay leaves. Stir in the scallions, cover the pot, and let it sit 5 minutes. Uncover, and fluff the fregula with a fork. Sprinkle with the grated cheese and a final drizzle of olive oil, toss well, and serve immediately.

Spaghetti with Bacon, Eggs, and Grated Cheese

Spaghetti alla Carbonara
SERVES 6

Kosher salt
6 ounces bacon, chopped
Extra-virgin olive oil, as needed
1 medium onion, chopped (about 1 cup)
1 pound spaghetti
2 large egg yolks
1 bunch scallions, trimmed and chopped (about 1 cup)
1 teaspoon freshly ground black pepper
1 cup freshly grated Grana Padano

Bring a large pot of salted water to a boil for the pasta.

Cook the bacon in a large skillet over medium heat until the fat has mostly rendered, about 4 to 5 minutes. (If your bacon is very lean, you can add a drizzle of olive oil to help start the rendering of the fat.) Push the bacon to one side of the pan, and add the onion. Let both cook separately until the onion is tender, about 5 minutes, then mix the two together. (If you like, you can drain off the excess bacon fat here and replace it with olive oil.) Ladle 4 cups pasta water into the skillet with the bacon and onion, bring to a rapid boil, and quickly reduce the sauce.

While the sauce is reducing, add the spaghetti to the boiling water. Meanwhile, whisk the egg yolks with ½ cup hot pasta water in a small bowl. When the sauce has reduced by about half and the spaghetti is al dente, scoop the pasta into the sauce with tongs. Add the scallions, pepper, and salt to taste. Toss the pasta until it is coated in the sauce and the scallions are wilted. Remove the pan from the heat, and quickly mix in the egg yolks, stirring until creamy. Toss the pasta with the grated cheese, and serve immediately.

🍀 There is always concern about uncooked eggs, or, in this case, egg yolks. You can omit the egg yolk altogether and the dish will be a little less complex, or you can buy pasteurized egg yolks. One egg yolk is approximately one and a half liquid ounces if you want to substitute pasteurized egg yolks.

Spaghetti Caruso

Spaghetti alla Caruso
SERVES 6

1 teaspoon kosher salt, plus more for the pot
3 tablespoons extra-virgin olive oil
1 medium onion, sliced
8 ounces mixed mushrooms, sliced (button, cremini, shiitake, chanterelle, oyster)
8 ounces chicken livers, trimmed of fat and sinew, chopped into ½-inch pieces
Pinch of crushed red pepper flakes
1 cup canned whole Italian plum tomatoes, preferably San Marzano, run through a food mill

1 cup frozen peas
1 pound spaghetti
2 tablespoons chopped fresh Italian parsley
1 cup freshly grated Grana Padano

Bring a large pot of salted water to a boil for the pasta. To a large skillet over medium-high heat, add 3 tablespoons of the olive oil. When the oil is hot, add the mushrooms and onion. Cover, and cook until the mushrooms release their liquid, about 4 minutes. Uncover and increase the heat to boil away the liquid and brown the mushrooms, stirring only occasionally so they have a chance to brown.

Add the chicken livers, and season with the salt and crushed red pepper flakes. Cook, stirring occasionally, until the livers are browned all over, about 3 minutes. Add the tomatoes and ½ cup pasta water, bring to a simmer, and add the peas. Cook until the peas are tender, about 5 minutes.

Meanwhile, cook the pasta in the boiling water. When the sauce is ready and the pasta is al dente, remove the pasta with tongs and transfer directly to the simmering sauce. Add the parsley, and toss to coat the pasta with the sauce, adding a splash of pasta water if it seems dry. Remove the skillet from the heat, sprinkle with the grated cheese, toss, and serve.

FISH AND SEAFOOD

Chi dorme non piglia pesci.
—Italian proverb

He who sleeps doesn't catch any fish.

Fried Calamari

Calamari Fritti

SERVES 4 TO 6 AS AN APPETIZER

Vegetable oil, for frying
2 pounds 5-to-6-inch calamari, cleaned (see
    page 54), tubes and tentacles
2 cups all-purpose flour
1 teaspoon kosher salt, plus more to
    taste

In a large straight-sided skillet, heat 2 inches of vegetable oil to 365 degrees. (If you don't have an oil thermometer, the oil is ready when a piece of dry calamari sizzles on contact.)

Cut the calamari tubes into ¼-inch rings. If the tentacles are larger than bite-sized, cut them in half lengthwise. Wash the calamari, and pat very dry on paper towels. In a large bowl, toss the flour and salt together. Add the calamari to the flour in batches as you are ready to fry, and toss well. With your hands, transfer the dredged calamari to a colander set over a rimmed sheet pan, and shake well to remove excess flour.

Add the floured calamari to the skillet, and break apart the pieces if they are stuck together. Let them cook for 2 to 3 minutes, then turn them with a fork. Cook until golden and crispy all over, about 2 to 3 minutes more. Drain on a paper-towel-lined sheet pan in one layer, and season with salt. Repeat with the remaining calamari and flour. Serve immediately.

Oven-Baked Calamari

Calamari al Forno

SERVES 4 AS AN ENTREE

¼ cup extra-virgin olive oil
4 garlic cloves, thinly sliced
½ teaspoon kosher salt
Freshly ground black pepper to taste

Eight 5-to-6-inch calamari, tubes and tentacles
    (cleaned with the skin on is better) (see
    page 54)
½ cup Fish Stock (page 144) or water
¼ cup chopped fresh Italian parsley

Preheat the oven to 375 degrees. In a small bowl, stir together the olive oil, garlic, salt, and some pepper, and toss the calamari well in the mixture. Arrange the calamari in a cast-iron pan in one layer. Cover tightly with foil, and bake 20 minutes.

Remove the foil, turn the calamari, pour in the stock, and continue to bake until very tender, about 20 to 30 minutes more. Put the skillet on the stovetop, and adjust the heat to boil the cooking juices until they thicken and glaze the calamari. Stir in the parsley, and serve.

Grilled Calamari

Calamari alla Griglia

SERVES 6 AS AN ENTREE

Eight 5-to-6-inch calamari, cleaned (see
    page 54) (about 3 pounds)
¼ cup extra-virgin olive oil, plus more for
    drizzling
6 garlic cloves, thinly sliced
1 tablespoon fresh thyme leaves
½ teaspoon kosher salt
½ teaspoon crushed red pepper flakes
Chopped fresh Italian parsley

Clean the calamari, leaving the skin on if you like (as I do).

Toss the cleaned calamari bodies and tentacles together with the olive oil, garlic, thyme, salt, and red pepper flakes in a large bowl until the calamari is coated. Cover the bowl, and marinate in the refrigerator for 1 hour or up to overnight.

Heat a grill or grill pan to high heat. (The calamari can also be done in a hot cast-iron pan or griddle on the stovetop.) When the pan is hot, lay the calamari and calamari heads on the grill, then set a heavy skillet on top of the calamari to weight it down, so as much of the calamari as possible makes contact with the hot grill. (This makes it easier for the calamari to cook evenly and brown well.) Cook, turning once, until they are golden on both sides, about 5 minutes.

Transfer to a warm platter, and drizzle with additional extra-virgin olive oil if you like. Sprinkle with the chopped parsley, and serve immediately.

Stuffed Calamari

Calamari Ripieni
SERVES 4 TO 6 AS AN ENTREE

Twelve 5-to-6-inch calamari with tentacles, cleaned (see page 54) (about 3½ pounds)
6 tablespoons extra-virgin olive oil
1 small onion, finely chopped
1 teaspoon chopped fresh thyme
1¼ teaspoons kosher salt
Pinch of crushed red pepper flakes
½ cup dry white wine
1 bunch scallions, trimmed and finely chopped
¼ cup dried bread crumbs
3 tablespoons chopped fresh Italian parsley

Preheat the oven to 400 degrees.

Chop the calamari tentacles and set aside. In a large skillet over medium-high heat, heat 3 tablespoons of the olive oil. Add the chopped onion, and cook until softened, about 5 minutes. Add the chopped tentacles, thyme, 1 teaspoon of the salt, and the red pepper flakes. Cook and stir until the tentacles are cooked through, about 2 to 3 minutes. Pour in the white wine, and reduce until syrupy. Stir in the scallions, and remove from the heat. Scrape into a large bowl, and stir in the bread crumbs and chopped parsley. Let cool.

When the filling is cool, lay the calamari bodies out on your work surface. Fill each body with about 2 to 3 tablespoons filling. Do not overfill the calamari or they will burst during baking; it is okay if there is a little stuffing left. Pin the calamari closed by sticking a toothpick in a weaving motion through the opening of each body.

Oil a 9-by-13-inch glass or ceramic baking pan with 2 tablespoons olive oil. Lay the calamari in the baking pan in one layer. Sprinkle any remaining stuffing over the calamari. Pour in ½ cup water, drizzle with the remaining tablespoon olive oil, and season with the remaining ¼ teaspoon salt. Cover tightly with foil, and bake until the calamari are cooked through and the liquid is simmering, about 25 minutes. Uncover, and continue to bake until the calamari are golden on top, about 10 minutes. If the calamari are done and there is still too much liquid in the pan, remove the calamari to a platter and continue to reduce the sauce on top of the stove by stirring over high heat until slightly thickened. Serve the calamari with the sauce.

Calamari and Skate in White Wine Sauce

Calamari e Razza in Salsa al Vino Bianco
SERVES 4 TO 6 AS AN ENTREE

¼ cup extra-virgin olive oil
1½ pounds calamari, cleaned (see page 54), tubes cut into ½-inch rings, tentacles halved
1¼ teaspoons kosher salt, plus more to taste
2 tablespoons tomato paste
2 sprigs fresh thyme
2 fresh bay leaves
¾ cup dry white wine
Freshly ground black pepper
1½ pounds boneless, skinless skate wings, cut into serving-size pieces

Vegetable oil, for frying
All-purpose flour, for dredging
¼ cup chopped fresh Italian parsley

1 recipe hot Basic Polenta (page 199), for serving

Bring 2 cups water to a simmer in a small saucepan and keep it hot. Heat a large straight-sided skillet over medium-high heat. Add the olive oil. Pat the calamari very dry, and season with ½ teaspoon of the salt. Add the calamari to the skillet, and cook, stirring, until the calamari turn opaque and curl slightly, about 3 minutes. Make a space in the center of the pan, and add the tomato paste. Cook and stir in that spot until the tomato paste toasts, about 2 minutes. Add the thyme and bay leaves, and let sizzle a few seconds. Pour in the white wine, ¼ teaspoon salt, and a generous grinding of black pepper. Stir to combine with the tomato paste. Bring to a simmer, and add 1 cup of the hot water. Partially cover, and cook until the calamari are very tender, about 45 minutes, adding the remaining water in two or three additions when the liquid level in the pan gets low.

Meanwhile, pat the skate dry with paper towels, and season with the remaining ½ teaspoon kosher salt. Heat a large nonstick skillet over medium-high heat. Spread some flour on a plate, and dredge the skate lightly in the flour, tapping off the excess. Add about ¼ inch vegetable oil to the skillet. Add the skate pieces, and cook, turning once, until they are golden on both sides, about 2 minutes per side. Drain on a paper-towel-lined plate, and season lightly with salt.

When the calamari are tender and the sauce has thickened (if not, give it a rapid boil to thicken it), add the skate and parsley to the sauce. Simmer until the skate is just cooked through and coated with the sauce, about 2 to 3 minutes. Remove the thyme sprigs and bay leaves, and serve over hot polenta.

Razor Clams with Garlic and Parsley

Canolicchi con Aglio e Prezzemolo
SERVES 4 AS AN ENTREE

4 pounds razor clams, mussels, or littleneck clams
¼ cup extra-virgin olive oil
8 garlic cloves, thinly sliced
1 dry cup white wine
¼ teaspoon crushed red pepper flakes, or 1 whole dried red pepper
2 tablespoons chopped fresh Italian parsley
2 tablespoons fine dried bread crumbs
Grilled country bread, for serving

If using razor clams, take care, because they can be very sandy. Place the razor clams under cold running water for 15 minutes. Gently wash, taking care not to break the shells but making sure to get all the sand out. Mussels or clams just need to be washed, scrubbed, and (in the case of mussels) debearded.

In a large Dutch oven, over medium-high heat, heat the olive oil. When the oil is hot, add the garlic. Once the garlic begins to sizzle, pour in the wine. Bring the wine to a rapid simmer, sprinkle in the red pepper flakes, and add the razor clams, mussels, or littlenecks. Cover, and cook until they open, about 6 minutes for razor clams and mussels, about 8 to 10 minutes for littlenecks.

Sprinkle with the parsley and bread crumbs, return to a simmer, stir gently, and serve.

Have plenty of crusty or grilled bread to dunk in the sauce, and if you have any leftovers, pick the clams out of the shells, return them to the sauce, and use it as a dressing for pasta.

🦐 Razor clams might not always be in season and available from your fishmonger, but regular littleneck clams or mussels are a good alternative. Just keep in mind the cooking time of each: mussels cook at about the same speed as razor clams; regular clams will take a few more minutes to open.

Clams with Leeks and Couscous

Vongole e Porri con Cuscús
SERVES 4 AS AN ENTREE

6 tablespoons extra-virgin olive oil
3 large leeks, white and tender light green parts, halved and cut into ½-inch slices
4 garlic cloves, crushed and peeled
1 bunch scallions, coarsely chopped (about 1 cup)
8 sprigs fresh thyme
48 small littleneck clams, rinsed and scrubbed
2 cups dry white wine
½ teaspoon kosher salt
¼ teaspoon crushed red pepper flakes
1 cup couscous
3 tablespoons chopped fresh Italian parsley

To a large Dutch oven over medium-high heat, add the olive oil. When the oil is hot, add the leeks and sauté until almost tender, about 5 minutes. Add the garlic, scallions, and thyme, and cook until the scallions are wilted, about 5 minutes.

Add the clams and wine, and season with the salt and red pepper flakes. Bring the wine to a simmer, cover, and cook until the clams just begin to open, about 4 minutes. What is important in this dish is not to overcook the clams, so the timing of adding the couscous is very important. Uncover, make a well in the center of the pot, pushing the clams to the side, and add the couscous. Cover, reduce the heat to very low, and cook until the couscous is tender and all of the clams are open (discard any that aren't), about 7 to 8 minutes. Stir in the parsley, remove garlic and thyme, and serve.

Soft-Shell Crabs with Fresh Thyme

Moleche al Timo Fresco
SERVES 4 AS AN ENTREE

SAUCE
1 stick unsalted butter
3 garlic cloves, crushed and peeled
1 tablespoon fresh thyme leaves
Juice of ½ lemon, freshly squeezed
½ cup dry white wine
½ cup Fish Stock (page 144) or water
¼ teaspoon kosher salt

CRABS
8 soft-shell crabs
Milk, for dipping the crabs
All-purpose flour, for dredging
Vegetable oil, for frying
Kosher salt and freshly ground black pepper

2 tablespoons chopped fresh Italian parsley

For the sauce: In a medium skillet over medium heat, melt the butter. Add the garlic, and cook until it is light golden, about 2 minutes. Add the thyme leaves, let them sizzle a minute, then add the lemon juice and white wine. Bring to a boil, then add the fish stock and salt. Bring to a simmer, and cook to blend and intensify the flavors by reducing slightly, about 5 minutes. Strain the sauce, and keep it warm while you make the crabs.

To clean the crabs: With scissors, cut off the face and eyes. Turn the crab over, pull back the apron (like a tail) at the base, and pull or cut that off. Pull up the left shell on the top side of the crab, and pull out the spongy gills. Repeat with the right side. Repeat with the remaining crabs.

Put the milk in a bowl deep enough for dipping. Spread some flour on a rimmed sheet pan. Heat ½ inch vegetable oil in a large nonstick skillet. Season the crabs with salt and pepper.

Dip the crabs in milk, and then dredge in flour, tapping off the excess. Cook the crabs (in two batches if necessary) in the hot oil until crisp and brown on both sides and cooked through, about 3 to 4 minutes per side, depending on the size of the crabs. Drain on a paper-towel-lined plate, and season with salt and pepper. Rewarm the sauce, if necessary, and stir in the parsley. Serve the crabs drizzled with the warm butter sauce.

Baked Lobster with Bread Crumb Topping

Aragosta al Forno
SERVES 6 AS AN APPETIZER OR 3 AS AN ENTREE

3 live lobsters, about 2½ pounds each
1½ cups bread crumbs
2 tablespoons chopped fresh Italian parsley
¾ teaspoon kosher salt
½ cup extra-virgin olive oil
2 cups dry white wine
Lemon wedges, for serving

About ½ hour before you plan to cut up the lobsters, put them in the freezer. They will become inactive as their temperature drops (but don't let them freeze). Arrange a rack in the center of the oven, and preheat it to 400 degrees. Split the lobsters in half lengthwise, one at a time: Hold each lobster flat on a cutting board, and place the point of a heavy chef's knife through the shell just behind the head, with the blade lined up between the eyes. Bring the blade down firmly, splitting the head in two. Turn the lobster so you can align the knife blade from behind the head along the tail, and cut down through the entire body and tail in one stroke. When all the lobsters are split, remove and discard the sac and nerve tissue in the head cavity behind each one's eyes, and the thin intestinal tract that runs along the back between shell and tail meat. Arrange the six lobster halves on the baking sheet, cut sides up, claws extended to keep the lobsters in place without rolling.

Toss together the bread crumbs, chopped pars-

ley, and ¼ teaspoon of the salt in a medium bowl. Drizzle in ¼ cup of the olive oil, and toss well, until the crumbs are evenly moistened. Sprinkle the crumbs over the cut surfaces of the lobster halves, covering all the meaty parts; lightly press crumbs into the cavities, too. Pour the wine and the remaining 3 tablespoons olive oil into the pan around the lobsters (not on the crumbs); sprinkle the remaining salt into the wine and oil, and stir. Tent the pan of lobsters loosely with a sheet of foil (don't let it touch the topping). Roast for 10 minutes, remove the foil, and roast another 30 minutes, until the lobsters are cooked through and the crumbs are crisp and golden.

Serve the lobsters immediately, placing a half on each dinner plate, or all the halves on a big platter to share family-style. Spoon any juices in the pan over the lobsters; place lemon wedges on the plates or platters. Make sure the napkins and bowls for the shells are handy, and dig in.

Lobster in Zesty Tomato Sauce

Aragosta in Brodetto
SERVES 6

6 live lobsters, about 1¼ pounds each
½ teaspoon kosher salt, plus more for
    the pot
⅓ cup vegetable oil
1 cup all-purpose flour, for dredging
½ cup extra-virgin olive oil
1½ cups chopped onion
6 tablespoons tomato paste
½ cup red wine vinegar
4 cups canned Italian plum tomatoes, preferably
    San Marzano, crushed
Crushed red pepper flakes to taste
1 pound spaghetti (optional)
1 cup chopped scallions (optional)
½ cup chopped fresh Italian parsley leaves
    (optional)

Cut the live lobsters into serving pieces for sauce according to the directions for the Lobster Fra Diavolo (page 226). If you plan to serve the lobster with pasta, bring a large pot of salted water to a boil. Bring 3 cups of water to a simmer in a small saucepan and keep it hot.

Heat the vegetable oil in a large skillet over medium-high heat. Dredge the exposed meat of the lobster tails with flour, shaking off excess flour. The oil is hot enough when a corner of a lobster tail dipped in it gives off a lively sizzle. Add the lobster tails, meat side down, and cook, shaking the skillet occasionally, until they are golden brown—about 2 minutes, to cook the flour and seal the meat; the lobster will finish cooking in the sauce. Remove the tails from the oil, and set them aside.

Heat ⅓ cup of the olive oil in a large straight-sided skillet over medium heat. Add the onion, and cook until it is translucent, about 3 to 4 minutes. Add the lobster body pieces, and cook, stirring, until they turn bright red, about 5 minutes. Stir the tomato paste into a hot spot, and let it toast about 2 minutes. Blend the vinegar with the 3 cups hot water, and pour this into the pan. Bring to a full boil. Add the tomatoes, salt, and crushed red pepper. Bring to a boil, and simmer just to bring the sauce together, about 3 minutes.

Remove the lobster bodies with tongs, allowing all juices to drain back into the sauce. Keep the bodies warm; they may be served on a communal platter in the center of the table. The most delicate meat is in those bodies and should not be wasted.

Add the claws to the pan, and cook 7 minutes. Add the reserved tails, the lobster legs, and the remaining olive oil. Simmer until the lobster tails are fully cooked, 3 to 5 minutes longer over high heat, skimming off all surface foam. Remove the tails and claws, and keep them warm under aluminum foil. Bring the sauce to a boil, and boil until it is slightly thickened. Arrange the lobster pieces on a warm platter, and spoon the hot sauce over them.

To serve with pasta: Cook and drain the pasta, and return it to the pot. Add half the lobster sauce, add the scallions and parsley, and toss to coat it over low heat. Transfer the pasta to a platter, and flank with the lobster pieces. Spoon the remaining sauce over the lobster.

Scallops in Salmoriglio

Capesante al Salmoriglio
SERVES 4 TO 6

SALMORIGLIO
¼ cup extra-virgin olive oil
Juice of 1 lemon, freshly squeezed
¼ teaspoon kosher salt
3 garlic cloves, crushed and peeled
3 tablespoons chopped fresh Italian parsley

SCALLOPS AND VEGETABLES
¼ cup extra-virgin olive oil
4 garlic cloves, crushed and peeled
4 medium artichokes, cleaned (see page 6), halved, and sliced
1 bunch medium asparagus, halfway peeled and cut into 2-inch lengths
1 teaspoon kosher salt
1½ pounds sea scallops, side muscle or "foot" removed

For the salmoriglio: In a medium bowl, whisk together the olive oil, lemon juice, and salt. Add the garlic cloves, and let sit while you prepare the scallops.

For the vegetables: To a large skillet over medium-high heat, add 2 tablespoons of the olive oil. When the oil is hot, add the crushed garlic. When the garlic starts to sizzle, add the artichokes, and toss to coat in the oil. Cover, and let steam until the artichokes begin to wilt, about 5 minutes. Add the asparagus and ½ teaspoon of the salt. Cover, and cook until the vegetables are tender, about 8 minutes.

Meanwhile, in a large bowl, toss the scallops with the remaining 2 tablespoons olive oil and remaining ½ teaspoon salt. Heat a large non-stick skillet over high heat. Take the scallops out of the oil, and add to the dry skillet. Sear until just cooked through, about 2 minutes per side. Remove to a plate.

Uncover the vegetables, increase the heat to high, and cook just to reduce any excess liquid. Remove the garlic from the vegetables and the salmoriglio. Stir the parsley into the salmoriglio.

To serve: Divide the vegetables among serving plates, top with the scallops, and drizzle with the salmoriglio. Serve immediately.

❧ Salmoriglio is also a delicious simple dressing for poached, grilled, or baked fish.

Shrimp Prepared in the Scampi Style

Gamberi al Vino Bianco, Aglio e Prezzemolo
SERVES 6

2 tablespoons extra-virgin olive oil
3 large garlic cloves, finely chopped
2 tablespoons finely chopped shallots
Kosher salt
Freshly ground pepper to taste
½ cup dry white wine
2 tablespoons freshly squeezed lemon juice
8 tablespoons unsalted butter, at room temperature
2 teaspoons chopped fresh Italian parsley
2 teaspoons chopped fresh tarragon
36 jumbo shrimp (about 3½ pounds)
6 to 8 sprigs fresh thyme

To make the flavored butter: Heat the olive oil in a small skillet over medium heat. Add the garlic, and cook until it is pale golden, about 1 minute. Stir in the shallots, season generously with salt and pepper, and continue cooking, shaking the skillet, until the shallots are wilted, about 2 minutes. Add ¼ cup of the wine, bring to a boil,

and cook until about half of the wine has evaporated. Stir in 1 tablespoon of the lemon juice, and boil until almost all of the liquid has evaporated. Transfer to a small bowl, and cool completely. Add the butter, parsley, and tarragon and beat until blended. To make the butter easier to handle, spoon it onto plastic wrap and roll it into a log shape, completely wrapped in plastic. Chill it thoroughly. (The flavored butter can be made several hours or up to a few days in advance.)

Place an oven rack in the lowest position, and preheat the oven to 475 degrees. Peel the shrimp, leaving the tail and last shell segment attached. Devein the shrimp by making a shallow cut along the curved back of the shrimp and extracting the black or gray vein that runs the length of the shrimp. Lay the shrimp flat on the work surface, and cut the body of the shrimp open three-quarters of the way. Pat the shrimp dry.

Using some of the flavored butter, lightly grease a low-sided baking pan, such as a jelly-roll pan, or an ovenproof skillet into which the shrimp fit comfortably without touching. Place each cut shrimp on the work surface with the tail facing you. Roll each half of the shrimp into the shape of the number six, and join underneath the tail, lifting the tail up. Arrange the shrimp, as is, tails up, on the prepared baking pan as you work, leaving some space between them. Cut the remaining flavored butter into ½-inch cubes, and disperse the cubes among the shrimp. Mix the remaining wine and lemon juice, and pour this into the pan. Scatter the thyme sprigs over and around the shrimp. Season them with salt and pepper, and place the pan on the oven rack. Roast until the shrimp are firm and crunchy and barely opaque in the center, about 5 minutes. Transfer the shrimp to a hot platter, or divide them among warm plates.

Bring the remaining juices in the pan to a boil over high heat until the sauce is slightly thickened, 1 to 2 minutes. Remove the thyme sprigs. Spoon the sauce over the shrimp as it is, or strain it first for a more velvety texture. Serve immediately.

Shrimp Buzara Style

Gamberoni alla Buzara
SERVES 4 TO 6

2 pounds jumbo shrimp (10 to 12 per pound)
1 cup Fish Stock (page 144)
1 tablespoon tomato paste
¼ cup extra-virgin olive oil
½ cup finely chopped onion
2 garlic cloves, crushed and peeled
Kosher salt to taste
Freshly ground black pepper to taste
1 cup dry white wine
1 tablespoon bread crumbs
1 tablespoon chopped fresh Italian parsley

Using poultry shears or a sharp paring knife, cut through the outer curve of the shrimp shells from end to end, but don't remove the shells. Rinse the shrimp under cold running water and devein. Warm the stock in a small saucepan, and stir in the tomato paste till it dissolves.

Heat 2 tablespoons of the olive oil in a medium saucepan over medium-high heat. Add the onion and garlic, and cook until golden, about 5 minutes. Season with salt and pepper, add the wine, and bring to a boil. Add the stock-and-tomato-paste mixture, reduce the heat, and simmer gently for 20 minutes. Remove garlic when done.

Meanwhile, heat the remaining 2 tablespoons of the oil in a large skillet over medium-high heat, add the shrimp, and sear (in two batches) 1 minute on each side. Drain off the oil, return all the shrimp to the skillet, and add the sauce. Cover, and cook over high heat, stirring occasionally, until the shrimp are just cooked through, about 2 to 3 minutes. Sprinkle with the bread crumbs and parsley, mix well, and cook a minute longer, uncovered. Serve immediately.

Shrimp Scampi

Scampi in Umido
SERVES 4 TO 6

½ cup chopped shallots
7 garlic cloves, crushed and peeled
¾ cup extra-virgin olive oil
2 pounds extra-large or jumbo shrimp, peeled and deveined
4 sprigs fresh thyme
1½ teaspoons kosher salt
½ cup white wine
2 tablespoons freshly squeezed lemon juice
6 tablespoons unsalted butter, cut into pieces
½ cup chopped fresh Italian parsley
1 tablespoon dry bread crumbs, or as needed

Combine the shallots, 5 garlic cloves, and 2 tablespoons of the oil in a mini food processor and process to make a smooth paste.

Pour 6 tablespoons olive oil into a large skillet over medium-high heat and add the remaining garlic. Let the garlic sizzle for a minute, then add half of the shrimp and all of the thyme sprigs. Season with ½ teaspoon salt, and cook until the shrimp are seared but not fully cooked, about 1 to 2 minutes. Remove to a plate and repeat with the remaining shrimp and another ½ teaspoon salt. Remove the shrimp, garlic cloves, and thyme from the skillet to the plate.

Add the remaining 4 tablespoons olive oil and the garlic-shallot paste to the same skillet, set over medium heat. Cook, stirring constantly, until the paste has dried out and begins to stick to the bottom of the skillet, about 2 to 3 minutes. Return the thyme to the skillet, and pour in the white wine, lemon juice, and 1 cup water, and add 4 tablespoons of the butter and the remaining ½ teaspoon salt. Bring the sauce to a rapid boil, and cook until reduced by half, about 4 to 5 minutes.

When the sauce has reduced, whisk in the remaining butter and return the shrimp to the pan. Cook and toss until the shrimp are coated with the sauce and just cooked through, about 2 to 3 minutes. Remove the thyme sprigs. Stir in the parsley. If the sauce still seems too thin, stir in the bread crumbs and bring to a boil, just to thicken. Serve immediately.

thyme. Stir in the capers, return to a boil, and add the shrimp back. Simmer until the shrimp are just cooked through, about 2 to 3 minutes. Stir in the parsley, and drizzle with the remaining 2 tablespoons olive oil. Serve immediately.

Shrimp Fra Diavolo

Gamberi in Salsa di Pomodoro Piccante
SERVES 6 AS AN ENTREE

6 tablespoons extra-virgin olive oil
6 garlic cloves, crushed and peeled
2½ pounds extra-large or jumbo shrimp, peeled and deveined
4 sprigs fresh thyme
1½ teaspoons kosher salt
2 cups diced inner celery stalks and leaves
¼ teaspoon crushed red pepper flakes
One 28-ounce can Italian plum tomatoes, preferably San Marzano, crushed by hand
¼ cup drained tiny capers
¼ cup chopped fresh Italian parsley

To a large skillet over medium-high heat, add ¼ cup of the olive oil and the garlic. Once the garlic begins to sizzle, add half of the shrimp and the thyme sprigs. Season the shrimp with ½ teaspoon salt, and toss just until the shrimp are seared but not cooked all the way through, only a minute or two. Remove the shrimp to a plate with tongs, and repeat with the remaining shrimp and another ½ teaspoon salt.

Once all of the shrimp have been seared and removed, add the celery to skillet, and cook until it is wilted, about 2 to 3 minutes. Add the red pepper flakes, let them toast for a minute, then pour in the tomatoes, slosh out the can with 1 cup hot water, and add that, too. Season with the remaining ½ teaspoon salt. Bring the sauce to a simmer, and cook until the celery is tender and the sauce is thickened, about 15 minutes. Remove garlic and

Grilled Shrimp with Arugula Sauce

Gamberoni Scottati con Salsa di Rucola
SERVES 4

32 extra-large shrimp in the shell (about 2 pounds)
8 sprigs fresh thyme
¾ cup extra-virgin olive oil
6 garlic cloves, crushed and peeled
¾ teaspoon kosher salt
¼ teaspoon crushed red pepper flakes
1 large bunch arugula, stems removed, washed and dried well (about 3 cups)

Split the shrimp down the back with a paring knife, and devein. Cut almost all the way through the shrimp to butterfly them open, but leave the shells on.

Toss the shrimp in a large bowl with the thyme, ¼ cup of the olive oil, four of the crushed garlic cloves, ¼ teaspoon of the salt, and the crushed red pepper. Marinate in the refrigerator for 1 hour.

Meanwhile, in a food processor, combine the arugula, remaining two garlic cloves, and remaining ½ teaspoon salt. With the machine running, drizzle in the remaining ½ cup olive oil to make a smooth, thick sauce. Pour into a bowl, and set aside.

When you are ready to cook the shrimp, heat a large nonstick skillet over high heat. Remove the shrimp from marinade, and add in batches, butterflied side down, until they are cooked through and just begin to pull away from the shell, about 2 to 3 minutes per batch. Add the shrimp to a large bowl, and repeat with the remaining shrimp.

When all of the shrimp are cooked, add about half of the sauce to the bowl with the shrimp and toss well. Mound the shrimp on a serving platter, and serve with the remaining sauce on the side for dipping.

Broiled Shrimp

Gamberoni alla Griglia
SERVES 4 TO 6

SHRIMP
2 pounds extra-jumbo shrimp, peeled and
    deveined (about 10 to 12 per pound)
2 tablespoons extra-virgin olive oil
Kosher salt to taste
Freshly ground black pepper to taste
1 cup fine dried bread crumbs

SAUCE
2 tablespoons extra-virgin olive oil
2 large shallots, finely chopped
4 garlic cloves, finely chopped
⅓ cup dry white wine
1½ tablespoons Worcestershire sauce
1 tablespoon freshly squeezed lemon juice
1 tablespoon white wine vinegar
Freshly ground black pepper to taste
2 tablespoons unsalted butter, cold, cut into
    pieces
1 tablespoon chopped fresh Italian parsley

Preheat the oven to 475 degrees. For the shrimp: With a sharp paring knife, butterfly the shrimp about halfway along the back so they fold open. Pour the olive oil into a shallow baking dish large enough to hold the shrimp comfortably. Add the shrimp to the oil, season with salt and pepper, and toss to coat the shrimp in the oil. Spread the bread crumbs on a plate. Toss the shrimp, in batches, to coat them lightly in the bread crumbs, and return them to the baking dish. Arrange the shrimp, butterflied side down, with the tails stick-ing up, pressing lightly to spread the connected halves of the body.

Roast the shrimp until cooked through, about 5 minutes. Transfer them to the broiler, and broil until golden brown, watching carefully to avoid burning, about 1 minute.

Meanwhile, make the sauce: In a medium skillet over medium-high heat, add the olive oil. When the oil is hot, add the shallots and garlic. Cook until the shallots begin to wilt, about 5 minutes. Add the wine, Worcestershire sauce, lemon juice, and vinegar. Season with pepper. Simmer until the shallots are tender, about 3 minutes. Strain into a clean skillet. Over medium heat, whisk in the butter pieces to make a creamy sauce. Stir in the parsley. Spoon the sauce on serving plates and place the shrimp on top, or serve the sauce on the side for dipping.

Salt Cod Fritters

Fritelle di Baccalà
SERVES 4

1 pound boneless baccalà (salt cod) fillets
Vegetable oil, for frying
1 cup all-purpose flour, plus more for dredging
½ teaspoon baking powder
½ teaspoon kosher salt, plus more to taste
1 large egg, lightly beaten
Grated zest of 1 small lemon

Forty-eight hours before you want to prepare the baccalà, place it in a large bowl and cover it with cold water by several inches. Let it soak in the fridge, changing the water completely every 8 to 10 hours. When you are ready to fry, drain the baccalà and pat it dry.

Put the baccalà in a pot with cold water to cover, bring to a simmer, and cook 5 minutes, to reduce the saltiness. Drain, rinse, and let it cool. Cut it into 1-inch chunks.

In a deep pot or Dutch oven, heat several

inches of vegetable oil to 365 degrees. In a large bowl, whisk together the flour, baking powder, and ½ teaspoon salt. Whisk in the egg and ¾ cup water to make a smooth batter. Whisk in the lemon zest just enough to distribute it in the batter.

Spread about a cup of flour on a plate. Pat the baccalà pieces dry once more, then lightly dredge them in the flour on all sides. Dip in the batter, and fry, in batches, until the batter is puffed and dark golden, about 4 to 5 minutes. Drain on fresh paper towels, and season lightly with salt. Serve hot.

Salt Cod with Raisins, Tomatoes, and Pine Nuts

Baccalà con Pomodoro, Pinoli e Uva Passa
SERVES 6

6 pieces skinless, boneless baccalà (salt cod) fillets, about 5 ounces each
⅓ cup golden raisins
All-purpose flour, for dredging
3 tablespoons extra-virgin olive oil
1 medium onion, chopped
½ cup dry white wine
One 28-ounce can Italian plum tomatoes, preferably San Marzano, crushed by hand
¼ teaspoon crushed red pepper flakes
⅓ cup pine nuts, toasted
2 tablespoons chopped fresh Italian parsley

Forty-eight hours before you want to prepare the cod, place it in a large bowl and cover it with cold water by several inches. Let it soak in the fridge, changing the water completely every 8 to 10 hours. When you are ready to cook the cod, drain it and pat it dry.

Put the raisins in a small bowl, and cover them with hot water; let them soak 10 minutes, then drain and squeeze them dry.

Spread the flour on a plate, and lightly dredge

the cod in the flour. To a large skillet over medium heat, add the olive oil. When the oil is hot, add the cod and cook until golden brown on both sides, about 2 minutes per side. Remove the cod to a clean plate.

Add the onion to the skillet, and cook, stirring, until it is almost tender, about 5 minutes. Increase the heat to high, add the wine, and cook until it is reduced, about 4 minutes. Add the tomatoes. Slosh out the tomato can with 1 cup hot water, and add that as well. Bring the liquid to a simmer. Add the soaked raisins and the red pepper flakes. Simmer until it is slightly thickened, about 10 minutes.

Add the cod, and simmer until the cod flakes with a fork—about 10 to 15 minutes, depending on the thickness of your fillets. Stir in the pine nuts and parsley, simmer 1 minute to combine, and serve.

Baked Salt Cod with Potatoes

Baccalà con Patate al Forno
SERVES 6

1 pound boneless, skinless baccalà (salt cod) fillets
1 cup heavy cream
½ cup milk
½ cup Fish Stock (page 144) or water
4 large russet potatoes, peeled, sliced ¼ inch thick
½ teaspoon kosher salt
Freshly ground black pepper
¼ cup extra-virgin olive oil, plus more for the baking dish
1 large onion, thinly sliced
2 tablespoons unsalted butter, cut into pieces

Forty-eight hours before you want to prepare the baccalà, place it in a large bowl and cover it with cold water by several inches. Let it soak in the fridge, changing the water completely every 8 to

10 hours. When you are ready to cook, rinse and drain the baccalà.

To a medium saucepan, add the baccalà with water to cover by about 3 inches. Bring it to a simmer, and cook until the fish begins to fall apart, about 30 minutes. Drain it and set it aside.

Preheat the oven to 450 degrees. In a small saucepan, warm the cream, milk, and fish stock over low heat. In a large bowl, season the potatoes with the salt and some pepper. Drizzle with 2 tablespoons of the olive oil, and toss well. Brush a large baking dish with olive oil, and spread the potatoes to cover the bottom. In the same bowl, toss the onion and baccalà pieces with some pepper and the remaining 2 tablespoons olive oil. Spread them over the potatoes. Dot the top with the butter pieces, and pour the heated cream mixture over all. Cover with foil, and bake until the potatoes are tender, about 30 minutes. Uncover, and bake until the top is brown and bubbly, about 10 minutes more.

Bluefish with Fava Beans

Pesce Azzurro con Fave
SERVES 6

4 pounds fresh fava beans, shelled, blanched, and peeled (see page 13) (about 2 cups)
4 garlic cloves, crushed and peeled
1 teaspoon kosher salt, plus more for seasoning the bluefish
¼ teaspoon crushed red pepper flakes
¼ cup shredded fresh basil leaves
5 tablespoons extra-virgin olive oil
1 lemon, thinly sliced
½ cup dry white wine
Six 6-ounce skinless bluefish or mackarel fillets
12 sprigs fresh thyme

In a medium skillet, combine the peeled favas, garlic, ½ teaspoon salt, the crushed red pepper, and ¼ cup water. Bring this to a simmer, and cook

just until the favas are cooked through, about 5 minutes. Drain and return them to the pot. Off heat, stir in the shredded basil and 3 tablespoons of the olive oil. Keep this warm.

Meanwhile, lay the lemon slices on the bottom of a large nonstick skillet. Add the white wine, ½ cup water, and the remaining ½ teaspoon salt. Lay the bluefish on top, and top each fillet with two sprigs of thyme. Bring the liquid to a simmer, cover, and cook until the bluefish is just cooked through—about 8 to 10 minutes, depending on the thickness of the fillets.

Remove the bluefish to a platter. Remove and discard the thyme sprigs. Whisk the remaining 2 tablespoons olive oil into the fish-cooking juices, add the cooked favas, spoon the lemon slices over the bluefish, and serve immediately.

Grilled Mackerel

Sgombro alla Griglia
SERVES 4

SAUCE
¾ cup extra-virgin olive oil
8 garlic cloves, crushed and peeled
Juice of ½ lemon, freshly squeezed
2 tablespoons chopped fresh Italian parsley
¼ teaspoon kosher salt
Freshly ground black pepper to taste

FISH
8 whole mackerel, cleaned (about 2 pounds)
8 garlic cloves, crushed and peeled
¼ cup extra-virgin olive oil
1 teaspoon kosher salt
Freshly ground black pepper

Preheat a grill to medium-high heat. Put a wire-mesh fish grill basket on the grill to preheat if you have one. For the sauce: Pour the olive oil into a medium bowl. Whisk in the garlic, lemon juice, and parsley. Season with kosher salt and some pepper. Let this blend while you grill the mackerel.

For the fish: Put the mackerel on a rimmed sheet pan. Put a garlic clove in the cavity of each fish. In a small bowl, combine the olive oil, salt, and some pepper. Brush the fish on both sides with the olive-oil mixture. Put the fish in the grill basket, and place it on the grill. If you don't have a grill basket, grill the fish directly on the grates. Either way don't turn it until grill marks form, after about 10 minutes. Then turn and grill on the other side 8 to 10 minutes.

Allow the fish to cool for a few minutes. Remove the skin or not, as desired. With a small serving spatula, open the fish, starting at the belly, and remove and discard the garlic and bones. With a spatula arrange pairs of halved fish, inside up, on serving plates. Discard the garlic from the sauce, and drizzle the sauce over the fish.

Cod with Carrots and Scallions

Merluzzo con Carote e Scalogni
SERVES 6

1 pound baby carrots, with tops (multicolored, if
    available)
5 tablespoons unsalted butter
1¼ teaspoons kosher salt
2 pounds cod fillets, cut into 6 portions
All-purpose flour, for dredging
Vegetable oil, for sautéing
2 tablespoons extra-virgin olive oil
3 garlic cloves, crushed and peeled
1 cup dry white wine
4 sprigs fresh thyme
2 bunches scallions, trimmed and coarsely
    chopped (about 2 cups)

Bring a large pot of water to a boil. Peel or scrape the carrots, and trim the tops to leave about ½ inch of green. Blanch the carrots until tender—about 10 minutes, depending on their thickness. Drain,

return them to the pot, and toss with 1 tablespoon butter and ½ teaspoon salt. Cover, and keep the carrots warm while you make the cod.

Season the cod with ½ teaspoon salt. Spread the flour on a plate, and dredge the cod lightly in it, tapping off the excess. Heat a large skillet over medium-high heat, and add about ¼ inch of vegetable oil. When the oil is hot, brown the cod on all sides, about 2 minutes per side, and remove to a plate.

Carefully pour out the oil, and wipe the skillet clean with a paper towel. Return the skillet to medium-high heat, and add the olive oil and remaining 4 tablespoons butter. When the butter has melted, add the garlic. Once the garlic is sizzling, add the white wine and thyme sprigs. Boil until the wine is reduced by half, about 5 minutes. Season the sauce with the remaining ¼ teaspoon salt. Add the cod and scallions to the skillet, and simmer just until the cod is cooked through, about 3 minutes. Remove the garlic and thyme. Serve the cod and sauce on a bed of baby carrots.

Fried and Marinated Monkfish Medallions

Medaglioni di Rospo in Saor
SERVES 4

1½ pounds monkfish fillet
1 teaspoon kosher salt
Freshly ground black pepper to taste
All-purpose flour, for dredging
Vegetable oil, for frying
¼ cup extra-virgin olive oil
1 large onion, thinly sliced
1 sprig fresh rosemary
4 fresh bay leaves
1 tablespoon white wine vinegar
½ cup dry white wine
½ cup Fish Stock (page 144) or Vegetable Stock
    (page 143)

Remove the membranes and any dark-red portions from the monkfish. Slice it into 1-inch-thick medallions. Season the medallions with ½ teaspoon of the salt and some pepper. Spread some flour on a plate. Lightly dredge the monkfish in the flour, tapping off the excess. Heat a large nonstick skillet over medium-high heat. Add vegetable oil to come ½ inch up the sides of the skillet. Cook the monkfish, in batches if necessary, until it is golden brown on all sides and cooked through, about 4 to 6 minutes. Drain on paper towels.

Pour out the oil, and wipe the skillet clean. Heat the skillet over medium heat, and add the olive oil. When the oil is hot, add the onion. Cook the onion until it is golden, about 10 minutes. Add the rosemary and bay leaves, and cook until fragrant, about 2 minutes. Season with the remaining ½ teaspoon salt and some pepper. Add the vinegar, wine, and stock. Cover, and simmer gently to blend the flavors for 10 minutes. Remove the bay leaves and rosemary.

Put half of the monkfish in a serving dish in one layer. Spread half of the onions from the marinade over it. Layer with the monkfish, then the onion. Now pour the marinade over the monkfish. Let the fish marinate in the refrigerator for 2 hours. Remove bay leaves and rosemary. Let it return to room temperature, or warm it gently, before serving.

Salmon with Mustard Sauce

Salmone alla Senape
SERVES 4

Four 6-ounce skinless salmon fillets
¾ teaspoon kosher salt
Freshly ground black pepper to taste
2 tablespoons vegetable oil
All-purpose flour, for dredging
3 tablespoons unsalted butter

½ cup dry white wine
½ cup Fish Stock (page 144) or Vegetable Stock (page 143)
¼ cup heavy cream
2 tablespoons Dijon mustard

Season the salmon fillets on both sides with ½ teaspoon of the salt and some pepper. Heat a large nonstick skillet over medium-high heat. Add the vegetable oil. While the oil is heating, spread the flour on a plate and lightly dredge the salmon in it, tapping off the excess. Gently add the fillets to the skillet. Cook, turning once, until they are browned on both sides but not cooked through, about 2 minutes per side. Remove them to a plate.

Pour the excess oil from the skillet, and wipe it clean with a paper towel. Melt the butter in the skillet over medium heat. Add the wine, and bring to a simmer. Add the fish stock and cream, and season with the remaining ¼ teaspoon salt. Simmer, whisking occasionally, until the sauce is slightly thickened, about 4 minutes. Whisk in the mustard. Add the salmon, flesh side up, and simmer, occasionally spooning the sauce over the salmon, until the fish is just cooked through—about 3 minutes, depending on the thickness of the salmon. Serve immediately.

Stuffed Smelts

Sperlani Farciti
SERVES 4 AS AN ENTREE, 6 AS AN APPETIZER

4 cups crustless day-old country-bread cubes
¼ cup milk, plus more for soaking the bread
2 tablespoons extra-virgin olive oil
2 garlic cloves, crushed and peeled
4 cups packed spinach leaves
3 large eggs
¼ cup sliced almonds, toasted and then chopped
½ cup freshly grated Grana Padano
¼ cup chopped fresh Italian parsley

½ teaspoon kosher salt, plus more to taste
24 small smelts (about 2 ounces each), head and tail removed, butterflied, backbone removed (by your fishmonger)
1 cup all-purpose flour
2 cups fine dried bread crumbs
Vegetable oil, for frying

Put the bread cubes in a medium bowl, and add milk to cover. Let them soak until softened, about 5 minutes, then squeeze out the excess milk and put the bread in a large bowl, breaking up the chunks with your fingers.

To a medium skillet over medium-high heat, add the olive oil. When the oil is hot, add the garlic. When the garlic is sizzling, add the spinach, and cook until it is wilted and no liquid remains. Scrape the spinach and garlic onto a cutting board, let cool slightly, and chop. Add to the bowl with the bread. Add one egg, the almonds, grated cheese, parsley, and ½ teaspoon salt. Mix well to make a cohesive stuffing that holds together.

Open the smelts like books, and lay them, skin side down, on your work surface. Season them lightly with salt. Divide the stuffing into mounds on twelve of the smelts. Lay the other twelve smelts on top, and press down to make twelve sandwiches.

Spread the flour in a shallow bowl or pie plate. Spread the bread crumbs in a second. In a third, beat the remaining 2 eggs with the ¼ cup milk and a pinch of salt.

Dredge the smelts in flour, then eggs, then bread crumbs, coating all sides well, and rest them on a parchment-lined baking sheet. Refrigerate for 30 minutes, to help the coating set.

In a deep skillet, heat 2 inches of vegetable oil to 360 degrees. Fry the stuffed smelts, in two or three batches, until they are deep golden brown, about 3 minutes per side. Drain on paper towels, and season with salt.

Grilled Red Snapper

Dentice Rosso alla Griglia
SERVES 4

SAUCE
½ cup extra-virgin olive oil
5 garlic cloves, thinly sliced
¼ teaspoon kosher salt
¼ teaspoon crushed red pepper flakes
Juice of 1 lemon, freshly squeezed
¼ cup chopped fresh Italian parsley

FISH
4 garlic cloves, crushed and peeled
¼ cup extra-virgin olive oil
¼ teaspoon kosher salt
Freshly ground black pepper
4 whole red snapper, cleaned (about 1¼ pounds each)
Lemon wedges, for serving

Preheat a grill to medium-high heat. Put a wire-mesh fish grill basket on the grill to preheat if you have one. For the sauce: In a small bowl, combine the olive oil, garlic, salt, and red pepper flakes. Stir in the lemon juice and parsley. Let this marinate while you grill the fish.

For the fish: In a small bowl, combine the garlic, olive oil, salt, and some pepper. Brush the fish on both sides with the olive-oil mixture. Cover the tails with foil. Put the fish in the grill basket, and place it on the grill; if you don't have a basket, place the fish directly on the hot grill. Grill for 12 minutes, or until grill marks form; turn the fish over and let them cook for another 9 to 10 minutes, until cooked through.

Whisk the sauce with a fork, and drizzle a tablespoon of it over each fish, passing the rest at the table. Serve with lemon wedges.

Fillet of Red Snapper with Fresh Thyme

Filetto di Dentice Rosso al Timo

SERVES 4

4 red snapper fillets, with skin (about 2 pounds)
1 teaspoon kosher salt
All-purpose flour, for dredging
¼ cup vegetable oil
4 garlic cloves, crushed and peeled
2 tablespoons extra-virgin olive oil
1 tablespoon fresh thyme leaves
½ cup dry white wine
Juice of 1 small lemon, freshly squeezed
1 cup Fish Stock (page 144) or Vegetable Stock (page 143)
6 tablespoons unsalted butter, cold, cut into pieces

Season the snapper fillets with ½ teaspoon of salt. Spread some flour on a plate. Lightly dredge the fish in the flour. Heat a large nonstick skillet over medium-high heat. Add the vegetable oil. When the oil is hot, add the garlic. Let the garlic sizzle 1 minute, to flavor the oil (but don't let it brown), then add the fillets, skin side down. Brown the fillets on both sides, but don't cook them through at this point—just a minute per side. Drain them on a paper-towel-lined plate.

Push the garlic to the side, and pour the oil from the pan. Wipe the skillet clean. Return the skillet with the garlic to medium-high heat, and add the olive oil. When the oil is hot, add the thyme leaves. Cook the thyme until it is sizzling and fragrant, about 1 minute. Add the white wine and lemon juice, bring it to a simmer, and reduce by half, about 2 minutes. Add the stock, and simmer until the liquid is reduced by half again, about 3 minutes. Season with the remaining salt. Whisk the butter into the simmering sauce a few pieces at a time until the sauce is creamy and slightly thickened. Add the fillets back, skin side down, and simmer until they are just cooked through, about 2 minutes. Discard the garlic, and serve.

Baked Rollatini of Sole

Involtini di Sogliola al Limone

SERVES 6

½ cup dried bread crumbs
½ cup freshly grated Grana Padano
¼ cup chopped fresh Italian parsley
1 large lemon, zest grated, then half of the lemon juiced, the other half thinly sliced
2 teaspoons dried oregano, preferably Sicilian on the branch
6 tablespoons extra-virgin olive oil
2 tablespoons unsalted butter, softened
1 cup dry white wine
6 skinless sole fillets (about 1½ pounds)
2 tablespoons drained tiny capers in brine

Preheat the oven to 350 degrees. Toss together the bread crumbs, grated cheese, parsley, lemon zest, and oregano in a medium bowl. Drizzle this with 4 tablespoons of the olive oil, and toss it until the crumbs are evenly coated with the oil. Coat the bottom of a 9-by-13-inch glass or ceramic baking dish with the softened butter. Arrange the lemon slices in one layer on the bottom of the baking dish. Pour in the lemon juice and white wine. Lay the fish on your work surface, and press the seasoned crumbs into the top of the fish. Starting with the short side, roll all the fillets up with the crumbs on the inside, and secure them closed with toothpicks. Arrange the fish in the baking dish, and scatter the capers in the open spaces between them. Sprinkle any leftover crumbs over the fish, and drizzle with the remaining 2 tablespoons olive oil.

Place the baking dish on the bottom rack of the oven, and bake until the fish is just cooked through, about 20 minutes. Remove the toothpicks, and serve.

Sole Meunière

Filetto di Sogliola al Limone
SERVES 4

5 tablespoons extra-virgin olive oil, plus more for
    finishing the sauce if you like
6 tablespoons unsalted butter
6 fillets of gray or lemon sole (about 2½ pounds)
Kosher salt
Freshly ground black pepper
All-purpose flour, for dredging
5 garlic cloves, crushed and peeled
12 thin lemon slices (about 2 lemons)
3 tablespoons drained tiny capers in brine
¼ cup freshly squeezed lemon juice
¼ cup dry white wine
½ cup Vegetable Stock (page 143) or water
2 tablespoons chopped fresh Italian parsley

Preheat the oven to 250 degrees. Heat 3 table-spoons of the olive oil and 4 tablespoons of the butter in a large heavy skillet over medium-high heat until the butter is foaming. Season the sole with salt and pepper, and dredge the fillets in the flour to coat both sides lightly. Gently lay as many of the fillets into the pan as fit without touch-ing. Cook just until the undersides are lightly browned, about 4 minutes. Flip them gently with a wide metal spatula, and cook until the second side is browned and the fish is opaque in the center, about 2 minutes. Transfer them with the spatula to a baking sheet, and keep them warm in the oven. Repeat, if necessary, with the remain-ing fillets, adjusting the heat under the skillet to prevent the bits of flour in the pan from burning.

When all the sole fillets have been browned, carefully wipe out the skillet with a wad of paper towels. Add the remaining olive oil and the remaining butter and garlic, and return to medium heat. When the butter is foaming, slide in the lemon slices, and cook, stirring gently, until they are sizzling and lightly browned. Stir in the capers, and heat until they are sizzling, about 1 minute. Pour in the lemon juice and wine, bring the liquid to a boil, and cook until it is reduced

by about half. Pour in the vegetable stock, bring it to a boil, and boil until the sauce is slightly thick-ened, about 2 minutes. If you like, drizzle in a tablespoon or two of olive oil to enrich the sauce. Sprinkle in the parsley, taste, and season with salt and pepper if you like, and remove garlic.

Remove the sole from the oven, and set one fillet in the center of each plate. Fish the lemon slices out of the sauce, and top each fillet with two lemon slices. Spoon the sauce around the fillets, dividing it evenly. Serve immediately.

Sweet and Sour Sole

Filetto di Sogliola all'Agrodolce
SERVES 6

¼ cup golden raisins
Six 6-ounce skinless sole fillets, halved the
    long way
1 teaspoon kosher salt
Vegetable oil, for sautéing
All-purpose flour, for dredging
3 tablespoons extra-virgin olive oil
2 medium onions, sliced
4 fresh bay leaves
3 garlic cloves, crushed and peeled
¼ cup pine nuts, toasted
½ cup dry white wine
½ cup white wine vinegar
2 tablespoons chopped fresh Italian parsley

Put the raisins in a small bowl, and cover them with hot water. Let them soak 10 minutes; then drain and pat them dry.

Season the sole on both sides with ½ teaspoon salt. The fillets won't divide into equal halves; one part of each will be larger. Roll them into cylin-ders and secure the edges with toothpicks.

Heat a large nonstick skillet over medium-high heat, and add ½ inch vegetable oil. Spread the flour on a plate, and lightly dredge the rolled sole in flour. Cook the sole in the skillet on all sides until it is golden brown and cooked through, about 2 to 3 minutes per side. As they cook, remove the rolls to a glass or ceramic baking dish in which they will fit snugly.

Safely discard the vegetable oil, and wipe the skillet clean. Over medium-high heat, add the olive oil. When the oil is hot, add the onions, bay leaves, and garlic, and cook until the onions are softened, about 10 minutes.

Add the pine nuts, drained raisins, white wine, vinegar, and the remaining ½ teaspoon salt. Bring the liquid to a simmer, and cook until it is reduced by about half, about 3 minutes. Remove the garlic and bay leaves. Stir in the parsley. Spoon the sauce over the sole in the baking dish. Let it cool to room temperature. Let it sit at least an hour before serving, or overnight in the refrigerator, to let the flavors develop. Return the sole to room temperature before serving.

Lemon Baked Swordfish

Pesce Spada al Forno con Limone
SERVES 6

2 pounds swordfish steak, 1¼ inches thick, with skin
½ cup extra-virgin olive oil
1 lemon, thinly sliced
5 tablespoons drained small capers
¼ teaspoon crushed red pepper flakes
4 garlic cloves, thinly sliced
1 tablespoon dried oregano, preferably Sicilian on the branch
1 teaspoon kosher salt
1½ tablespoons chopped fresh Italian parsley

You will need a 4-quart baking dish, 10 by 15 inches, or similar size; a roasting pan large enough to hold the baking dish inside it (on the rack); a sturdy flat metal baking/roasting rack to fit inside the roasting pan. Preheat the oven to 425 degrees.

Remove skin and cut the swordfish steak into six equal serving pieces. Pour the olive oil into the baking dish, and scatter in the lemon slices, capers, crushed red pepper, and garlic. Crumble the oregano into the pan juices. Turn the lemon slices over, to coat them with oil, and spread them across the bottom of the baking dish. Season the swordfish pieces on both sides with salt, lay them in the baking dish in one layer, and turn each one over several times to coat it with oil on all the surfaces. Distribute some lemon slices on top of the swordfish. Meanwhile, bring a pot of water to a boil. Set the baking rack in the big roasting pan, and pour in boiling water to the depth of an inch, making a water bath. Put the baking dish of swordfish on the rack in the roasting pan, and tent the big pan with a large sheet (or two) of aluminum foil. Arch the sheet so it does not touch the fish, and press it against the sides of the roasting pan. Carefully set the covered pan in the oven, and bake just until the swordfish is cooked through, about 10 to 12 minutes.

Remove the foil, lift the baking dish from the pan and out of the oven, and sprinkle the parsley over all. Serve the fish right away, placing each piece in a warm shallow bowl and spooning over it some of the cooking juices.

Swordfish in Sweet and Sour Sauce

Pesce Spada in Agrodolce
SERVES 4

Four 6-ounce skinless swordfish steaks, about ¾ inch thick
½ teaspoon kosher salt
Freshly ground black pepper
All-purpose flour, for dredging
Vegetable oil, for frying
1 tablespoon extra-virgin olive oil
¾ cup dry white wine

½ cup balsamic vinegar
2 tablespoons drained tiny capers in brine
1 tablespoon chopped fresh Italian parsley
2 tablespoons unsalted butter, cold, cut into
  pieces

Season the swordfish with the salt and some pepper. Spread some flour on a plate. Lightly dredge the swordfish on all sides in the flour, tapping off the excess. Reserve the flour. In a large nonstick skillet, heat ½ inch of vegetable oil over medium-high heat. When the oil is hot, gently lay the swordfish in the skillet, and cook until it is brown on both sides and just cooked through—about 2 minutes per side, depending on the thickness of the fish. Remove it to a platter, cover it with foil, and keep it warm.

Carefully pour out the oil from the skillet, and wipe it clean with a paper towel. Over medium-high heat, add the olive oil. When the oil is hot, sprinkle in a teaspoon of the reserved flour, and stir to make a paste. Let the flour toast for a minute, then add the wine, vinegar, and capers. Bring the liquid to a boil, and cook until the sauce is a light syrup, about 4 minutes. Off heat, stir in the parsley, and whisk in the butter in pieces until the sauce is emulsified. Spoon the sauce over the fish, and serve.

Sautéed Trout with Tomato and Basil

Trota al Pomodoro e Basilico
SERVES 4

Four 12-ounce trout, head and tail removed,
  each deboned, butterflied, and made into
  two fillets
¾ teaspoon kosher salt
All-purpose flour, for dredging
¼ cup extra-virgin olive oil
2 tablespoons unsalted butter

½ cup julienned pancetta
1 pint grape tomatoes, halved
¼ cup coarsely chopped fresh basil
2 tablespoons sliced almonds, toasted

Place a platter for the trout to warm in a 200-degree oven. Season the trout with ½ teaspoon salt. Dredge lightly on both sides in flour, tapping off the excess.

Heat a large nonstick skillet over medium-high heat. Add 2 tablespoons of the olive oil and the butter. When the butter is melted, add the trout, skin side down (in batches, if necessary). Cook, turning once, until the skin is crisp and golden and the trout is cooked through, about 2 to 3 minutes per side. Add the trout to the platter in the oven to keep warm while you make the sauce.

Wipe the skillet clean with a paper towel, and set it over medium heat. Add the remaining 2 tablespoons olive oil and the pancetta. Cook and stir the pancetta until it is crisp, about 3 minutes, then remove it to a paper-towel-lined plate. Increase the heat to medium high, and add the grape tomatoes. Season with the remaining ¼ teaspoon salt. Cook until the tomatoes begin to soften and release their juices, about 3 minutes. Stir in the basil, and remove the sauce from the heat. Remove the trout from the oven. Spoon the sauce over it, sprinkle with the almonds and pancetta, and serve.

Baked Trout with Sage

Trota in Forno alla Salvia
SERVES 4

6 tablespoons unsalted butter, softened
2 tablespoons chopped fresh Italian parsley
2 tablespoons chopped fresh sage
4 rainbow trout (12 ounces each) butterflied and
  deboned, head and tail on

Kosher salt and freshly ground black pepper
2 tablespoons extra-virgin olive oil
1 cup dry white wine

Preheat the oven to 450 degrees. In a small bowl, mash the butter with the parsley and sage.

Open each trout up like a book, skin side down, and season with salt and pepper. Divide the butter mixture into four equal pieces, and spread them on the trout. Close the trout up, and place them in a roasting pan large enough to hold them comfortably. Brush them all over with the olive oil, and season with salt and pepper. Pour in ½ cup of the white wine, and bake the trout until it is just cooked through—about 15 to 20 minutes, depending on the size of your trout—basting and adding more wine as it evaporates.

Remove the trout from the oven. Carefully move the trout to serving plates, and cover to keep them warm. Pour the cooking juices into a small skillet, and reduce over high heat, whisking, until it is emulsified, about 3 minutes. Strain the juices if desired, for a more polished look. Drizzle some of the juices over each fish, and serve.

Pickled Tuna

Tonno Marinato
SERVES 4

1 medium red onion, cut into thin wedges left attached at the root
2 cups celery cut into ½-inch pieces on the bias
2 lemons, thinly sliced, plus zest removed in strips with a zester, and juice of another ½ lemon
½ cup white wine vinegar
1 teaspoon kosher salt, plus more for seasoning
Four 5-ounce fresh tuna steaks, about ¾ inch thick
¼ cup drained tiny capers in brine

2 tablespoons extra-virgin olive oil
4 cups packed baby arugula

In a skillet just large enough to hold the tuna in one layer, combine the red onion, celery, sliced lemon, vinegar, 1 teaspoon salt, and 3 cups cold water. Bring the liquid to a boil, and let it simmer for 10 minutes. Add the tuna, and simmer until it is rare to medium rare, about 2 to 3 minutes (poke into one steak with a paring knife to check). Remove the tuna with a slotted spoon, sprinkle it with salt, and let it cool. Let the poaching liquid and vegetables cool to room temperature.

When you are ready to serve, cut the tuna into thick slices and arrange them on a platter. Remove the onion and celery from the poaching liquid and put them in a medium bowl. Add the capers, olive oil, and lemon juice. Break the onions into slices. Toss well, and mound it on top of the tuna.

In another bowl, toss the arugula with the lemon zest, and arrange this on top of the vegetables. Serve immediately.

Tuna and Bean Salad

Insalata di Tonno e Fagioli
SERVES 4 TO 6

Two 15½-ounce cans cannellini beans, rinsed and drained, or about 3 cups Braised Cannellini Beans (see page 175)
Two 6-ounce cans Italian tuna in olive oil, drained
½ small red onion, thinly sliced
1 head escarole, inner leaves only, coarsely shredded (about 6 cups)
4 tablespoons extra-virgin olive oil
3 tablespoons red wine vinegar
½ teaspoon kosher salt
¼ cup fresh basil leaves, shredded
3 hard-boiled eggs, quartered

In a large bowl, combine the beans, tuna, red onion, and escarole. Drizzle with the oil and vinegar, and season with the salt. Toss well. Add the basil leaves, and toss again.

Mound the salad in a shallow serving bowl or on a platter, and place the egg quarters on top. Or, for a more homogeneous salad, toss the eggs with the salad. Serve.

❧ Use the outer leaves of the escarole for soup, stock, or my Lettuce and Bread Quiches (page 122), and make this salad with the crunchy and tender inner leaves.

Meanwhile, heat another large skillet over medium-high heat. Add ¼ cup of the olive oil. When the oil is hot, add the garlic. Once the garlic is sizzling, add the olives and stir. Once the olives are sizzling, add the wine, lemon juice and zest, oregano, and remaining ¼ teaspoon salt. Bring the sauce to a simmer, and whisk in the ground nuts. Once the sauce has returned to a simmer and thickened slightly, add the tuna, and turn to coat it in the sauce. Simmer until it is heated through and done to your liking—just 1 or 2 minutes if you want the tuna to remain medium rare. Remove the garlic and transfer the tuna to a serving platter or plates. Whisk the parsley into the sauce, and spoon it over the tuna.

Tuna with Olive Sauce

Tonno con Olive
SERVES 4

¼ cup skinned almond slivers, toasted
¼ cup pine nuts, toasted
Four 6-ounce tuna steaks, about 1 inch thick
6 tablespoons extra-virgin olive oil, plus more for oiling the tuna
½ teaspoon kosher salt
3 garlic cloves, crushed and peeled
½ cup pitted black brine-cured olives, such as Gaeta, coarsely chopped
½ cup dry white wine
Freshly squeezed juice and grated zest of 1 lemon
2 tablespoons chopped fresh oregano
2 tablespoons chopped fresh Italian parsley

In a mini–food processor, process the nuts together until they are very finely chopped but not pasty; set them aside. Heat a large cast-iron skillet over high heat. Rub the tuna steaks on both sides with olive oil, and season them with ¼ teaspoon kosher salt. Add the tuna to the hot skillet, and sear until the steaks are browned but not cooked through on both sides, about 1 minute per side. Remove to a plate.

Cold Poached Whiting

Merlano in Bianco
SERVES 4

SAUCE
¼ cup extra-virgin olive oil
1 small shallot, finely chopped
1 tablespoon finely chopped roasted red bell pepper
1 tablespoon chopped fresh fennel fronds or parsley
Juice of ½ lemon, freshly squeezed
¼ teaspoon kosher salt
Freshly ground black pepper

WHITING
1 cup sliced peeled carrots
½ small onion, sliced
4 fresh bay leaves
3 tablespoons white wine vinegar
1 teaspoon kosher salt
1 teaspoon whole black peppercorns
8 whiting, cleaned, heads removed (about 3½ pounds)

For the sauce: In a medium bowl, combine the olive oil, shallot, roasted pepper, and fennel fronds. Whisk in the lemon juice. Season with the salt and a generous grinding of black pepper. Let it marinate while you make the whiting.

For the whiting: In a large straight-sided skillet large enough to hold the whiting in one layer, heat 6 cups cold water, the carrots, onion, bay leaves, white wine vinegar, salt, and peppercorns. Bring to a simmer, and simmer gently for 15 minutes to blend the flavors.

Wrap and tie each whiting in a piece of cheesecloth. Gently lower them into the simmering liquid. Cover, and poach the whiting until just cooked through—about 7 minutes, depending on the size of the whiting. Remove the whiting from the poaching liquid with a long slotted spatula, place them on a rimmed sheet pan, and let them cool completely.

When the fish is cooled completely, carefully unwrap it (whiting is very fragile once cooked). Lay each whiting on a serving plate. Open the fish, belly to back, and remove the bones and any extra skin. Drizzle each serving with some of the sauce, and serve.

Savory Seafood Stew

Zuppa di Pesce
SERVES 6

One 35-ounce can Italian plum tomatoes, preferably San Marzano, crushed by hand
1½ cups dry white wine
4 small leeks, white parts only, trimmed, 2 cleaned and cut into 3-inch lengths, and 2 sliced ½ inch thick
2 medium carrots, peeled and sliced thick
1 large onion, cut into thick slices, and 1 large onion, thinly sliced
10 sprigs fresh thyme
Zest of ½ lemon, removed in wide strips with a vegetable peeler

½ cup extra-virgin olive oil
Kosher salt
8 garlic cloves, crushed and peeled
4 medium 5-inch calamari, cleaned, tentacles left whole, bodies cut crosswise into ½-inch rings (about 1¼ pounds)
18 medium sea scallops (about 8 ounces), side muscle or "foot" removed
8 ounces fresh firm-textured fish fillets, such as salmon, snapper, or swordfish, skin removed, cut into 1-inch pieces
2 cups Braised Cannellini Beans (page 175) (optional)
24 mussels, scrubbed and debearded
12 large shrimp, peeled and deveined (about 8 ounces)
¼ cup chopped fresh Italian parsley
Freshly ground black pepper to taste
Garlic bread or crusty Italian bread, for serving

Make the soup base: Combine 2 quarts water, the tomatoes, wine, 3-inch leeks, carrots, thick-sliced onion, thyme, and lemon zest in a saucepan, and bring to a boil. Lower the heat to a lively simmer, and cook until reduced by about a third, about 45 minutes. Stir in ¼ cup olive oil, season the mixture lightly with salt, and continue to simmer it until the liquid portion of the soup base is reduced to about 8 cups, about 20 minutes. Strain the soup base into a 3-quart saucepan, and keep it warm over low heat. Discard the solids. (The soup base may be prepared up to 3 days in advance and refrigerated.)

If you have prepared the soup base in advance, bring it to a simmer in a medium saucepan. Adjust the heat to very low, and keep it warm. Heat the remaining ¼ cup olive oil in a large Dutch oven over medium heat. Add the thinly sliced onion, the remaining leek, and the garlic, and cook, stirring, until the onion is wilted but still crunchy, about 4 minutes. Add the calamari, and cook, stirring, until they turn opaque, about 2 minutes. Pour in all but 1 cup of the soup base, and bring this to a boil. Stir in the scallops, fish fillets, and beans (if using). Adjust the heat to simmering, and cook until the seafood is barely opaque at the center, about 5 minutes.

Meanwhile, add the mussels to the soup base remaining in the saucepan. Increase the heat to high, cover the saucepan, and steam over medium heat, shaking the pan occasionally, until the mussels open, about 3 minutes. (Discard any mussels that don't open.)

Stir the shrimp, parsley, and steamed mussels into the large pot of soup. Simmer until the shrimp are cooked through, about 2 minutes. Check the seasoning, adding salt if necessary, and pepper. Remove the garlic. Fish is very delicate; ladle it with care into warm soup bowls, passing a basket of the bread of your choice separately.

Istrian Whole Fish Stew

Brodetto all'Istriana
SERVES 6

One 4-pound whole red snapper or sea bass, cleaned
1 teaspoon kosher salt, plus more for seasoning
Freshly ground black pepper to taste
All-purpose flour, for dredging
Vegetable oil, for frying
½ cup extra-virgin olive oil
1 medium onion, finely chopped
1 bunch scallions, trimmed and chopped (about 1 cup)
2 tablespoons tomato paste
½ cup red wine vinegar
Basic Polenta (page 199) or 1 recipe Fresh Pasta Dough (page 221), prepared as maltagliati (page 223)

Bring 3½ cups water to a simmer in a small saucepan, and keep it hot. With a large chef's knife, remove the head and tail from the fish. Cut the body of the fish crosswise into six serving pieces. Season all of the pieces, including the head and tail, with ½ teaspoon salt and some pepper.

Spread some flour on a rimmed sheet pan, and dredge the pieces in flour, tapping off the excess.

Heat a large Dutch oven over high heat. Add vegetable oil to come about ½ inch up the side of the pot. When the oil is hot, add the fish and brown well on all sides, leaving the insides still raw. Drain the pieces on a paper-towel-lined plate, and season lightly with ½ teaspoon salt. Carefully pour the oil out of the pot, and wipe it clean with paper towels.

Heat the pot over medium-high heat. Add the olive oil. When the oil is hot, add the onion, and cook until it is light golden, about 6 minutes. Add the scallions, and cook until they are wilted, about 3 minutes. Make a space in the center of the pan, and add the tomato paste. Cook and stir the paste in that hot spot until it toasts and darkens a shade or two, about 2 minutes. Stir in the tomato paste with the onion, and add the fish in one layer on top, turning to get it sizzling. Add the hot water, vinegar, and remaining ½ teaspoon salt. Bring the liquid to a simmer, and cook until the fish is cooked through, about 10 minutes, occasionally shaking or stirring the pan so the fish does not scorch.

Remove the fish with a slotted spatula, and keep it warm. Set the head and the tail on the side for someone to pick at.

Boil the pan juices until they are thickened, about 10 minutes. Serve the fish over polenta, and spoon the reduced sauce over it, or you can serve the pieces of cooked fish on the side with some of the reduced sauce.

Shellfish Stew with White Wine

Brodetto ai Frutti di Mare
SERVES 4 TO 6

3 tablespoons extra-virgin olive oil
1 small onion, finely chopped
2 large shallots, finely chopped
3 garlic cloves, crushed and peeled

1 pound sea scallops, side muscle or "foot" removed
1 pound large shrimp, peeled and deveined
1 teaspoon kosher salt
Pinch of crushed red pepper flakes
1 cup dry white wine
Juice of ½ lemon, freshly squeezed
24 littleneck clams, scrubbed
36 mussels, scrubbed and debearded
¼ cup chopped fresh Italian parsley
¼ cup fine dried bread crumbs

To a large Dutch oven over medium-high heat, add the olive oil. When the oil is hot, add the onion, shallots, and garlic. Cook until the onion and shallots are softened, about 5 minutes. Add the scallops and shrimp, and season with ½ teaspoon of the salt and the red pepper flakes. Cook until the seafood is opaque, about 2 to 3 minutes. Remove the seafood to a plate.

Increase the heat to high, and add the wine and lemon juice. Bring to a boil, and add the clams; 3 minutes after the clams, add the mussels. Cover the pot, and steam until they opened, about 5 minutes. (Discard any that haven't opened by the end of the cooking time.)

Make a hot spot in the center of the pan by pushing the shellfish to the side. Add the parsley and bread crumbs, and bring the sauce to a rapid simmer until the bread crumbs thicken it, about 1 minute. Season with the remaining ½ teaspoon salt. Return the shrimp and scallops to the pot, and toss to heat them through. Remove the garlic and serve immediately.

MEAT

La troppa carne in pentola non si cuoce.
—Italian proverb

Too much meat in the pot never cooks.

Chicken Parmigiana Light

Pollo alla Parmigiana
SERVES 4

CHICKEN
4 boneless, skinless chicken thighs or breasts
    (about 1½ pounds)
Kosher salt to taste
Freshly ground black pepper to taste
All-purpose flour, for dredging
¾ cup fine bread crumbs
2 large eggs
1 cup vegetable oil
3 ripe plum tomatoes, cored and thinly sliced
6 ounces fresh mozzarella or imported Fontina
    cheese, thinly sliced

SAUCE
3 tablespoons extra-virgin olive oil
6 garlic cloves, crushed and peeled
8 ripe tomatoes, or 12 ripe plum tomatoes,
    peeled, seeded, and chopped
Kosher salt
Freshly ground black pepper
¼ cup shredded fresh basil leaves

Preheat the oven to 400 degrees. Cut off any fat, bone, and gristle remaining on the chicken thighs. Place two thighs between two sheets of plastic wrap. Pound them lightly with the toothed side of a meat mallet to a more or less even thickness. Pound the remaining two thighs the same way.

Season the chicken thighs with salt and pepper. Spread the flour and bread crumbs on two separate plates. Beat the eggs in a wide shallow bowl until blended. Dredge the chicken in flour to coat lightly, and tap off excess flour. Dip the floured thighs in the beaten egg, letting the excess egg drip back into the bowl. Transfer the chicken, one piece at a time, to the plate of bread crumbs, and turn it to coat with bread crumbs, patting gently and making sure that each thigh is well coated.

Heat the vegetable oil in a wide heavy skillet over medium-high heat until a corner of one of the coated thighs gives off a lively sizzle when dipped in the oil. Add to the oil as much of the breaded chicken as fits without touching. Fry, turning once, until the chicken is golden on both sides and cooked through, about 8 minutes. Remove it to a baking sheet lined with paper towels, and drain well. Cook the remaining chicken (if necessary), adding oil and keeping it at the correct temperature.

Remove the paper towels from the baking sheet. Top each chicken thigh with overlapping slices of tomato, dividing the tomatoes evenly. If you like this dish more traditional, top the chicken with some of the tomato sauce as well (see below). Drape the sliced cheese over the tomatoes to cover the chicken completely.

For the sauce: Heat 3 tablespoons of the olive oil in a large skillet over medium heat. When the oil is hot, add the garlic, and cook, shaking the pan, until it is golden brown, about 2 minutes. Carefully slide the chopped tomatoes into the skillet, season with salt and pepper, and cook until the sauce is slightly thickened, about 10 minutes. Remove the pan from the heat, set it aside, and fish out the garlic.

Bake the chicken until the cheese is lightly browned, about 10 minutes. While the chicken is baking, reheat the tomato sauce to simmering, stir in the basil, and taste, seasoning with salt and pepper if necessary. Spoon the sauce onto a heated platter or onto individual plates, and place the baked chicken over the sauce.

Chicken Breast with Eggplant and Mozzarella

Pollo alla Sorrentina
SERVES 4

Four 6-ounce boneless, skinless chicken breasts,
    trimmed
¼ teaspoon kosher salt, plus more to taste
All-purpose flour, for dredging

7 tablespoons unsalted butter

3 tablespoons extra-virgin olive oil

2 small eggplants (about 12 ounces total), sliced lengthwise into 8 slices

1 cup dry white wine

4 thin slices ham (about 2 ounces total)

1 cup Marinara Sauce (page 161)

6 ounces low-moisture mozzarella, thinly sliced

¼ cup freshly grated Grana Padano

Preheat the oven to 400 degrees. Slice open the chicken breasts crosswise to butterfly them. Season the chicken with the ¼ teaspoon salt. Spread the flour on a plate. Lightly dredge chicken in flour, tapping off the excess. Heat a large skillet over medium-low heat. Add 4 tablespoons of the butter and the olive oil. When the butter has melted, add the chicken and lightly brown on both sides, about 2 minutes per side. Remove the chicken to a plate.

Increase the heat to medium, and add the eggplant slices to the skillet. Brown them on both sides, about 3 minutes per side. Remove them to a plate lined with paper towels to drain, and season lightly with salt.

Discard the fat in the skillet, and set it over medium-high heat. Add the remaining 3 tablespoons butter. When the butter is melted, pour in the white wine and bring it to a boil. Adjust the heat so the wine is simmering rapidly, then lay the chicken breasts back in one layer. Lay a slice of ham over each chicken breast. Dollop about 2 tablespoons marinara on top of each piece of ham. Drop the remaining marinara in the spaces between the chicken breasts to make the sauce. Layer the sliced cheese on top of the sauce. Sprinkle the grated cheese over the top. Bake until the chicken is cooked through and the cheese is browned and bubbly, about 20 minutes.

Cheese-Crusted Chicken Tenders

Petto di Pollo al Forno con Crosta di Formaggio
SERVES 4

1 medium carrot, peeled and cut into chunks

1 celery stalk, cut into chunks

¼ cup loosely packed basil leaves

¼ cup loosely packed celery leaves

1½ cups panko

½ cup freshly grated Grana Padano

2 tablespoons extra-virgin olive oil, plus more for drizzling

1 teaspoon kosher salt

1½ pounds boneless, skinless chicken breasts

Lemon wedges, for serving

Preheat the oven to 375 degrees. In a food processor, combine the carrot, celery, basil, and celery leaves. Process to make a smooth pestata. In a medium bowl, toss together the panko, grated cheese, olive oil, and ½ teaspoon salt. Stir in the pestata to incorporate it fully into the crumbs.

Slice the chicken breasts in half crosswise, on the bias. Pound to an even thickness of about ¾ inch. Season the chicken with the remaining ½ teaspoon salt. Line a baking sheet with parchment. Pat the coating on both sides of the chicken pieces, and place them on the sheet pan. Drizzle lightly with olive oil. Bake until the crumbs are golden and the chicken is cooked through, about 20 minutes. Serve with lemon wedges.

Skillet Gratinate of Mushrooms and Chicken

Pollo con Funghi Gratinati in Padella
SERVES 6

3 large skinless, boneless chicken breasts (about 2 pounds)

3 tablespoons extra-virgin olive oil, or more if needed

12 large shiitake mushrooms, stems trimmed

All-purpose flour, for dredging
½ teaspoon salt, or more to taste
3 tablespoons unsalted butter, softened
1 cup Tomato Sauce (page 161)
1 cup dry white wine
6 fresh sage leaves
¾ cup freshly grated Grana Padano
1 cup Chicken Stock (page 143) or Vegetable
    Stock (page 143), if needed

Preheat the oven to 425 degrees. Cut the chicken breasts in half on a bias. Trim off any bits of fat, skin, or tendon. Flatten each breast half with a mallet to an even thickness of about ¾ inch.

Heat 3 tablespoons of the olive oil in a large skillet over medium heat. Toss the mushroom caps in flour to coat well, pat off any excess, and lay them in the pan. Let the pieces caramelize slowly, for about 4 minutes. Turn when the edges are nicely browned on the underside; fry for about 2 minutes on the second side. Remove them to a paper-towel-lined plate, and season with salt.

When the mushrooms are done, add 1 tablespoon of the butter, and reduce the heat to medium low. Salt the chicken pieces, and dredge in flour, tapping off the excess. When the butter is just beginning to sizzle, lay the chicken cutlets in the pan. Cook them gently until very lightly colored, with no browning, about 2 minutes, then flip them and cook the other side, another 2 minutes.

Maintain the gentle cooking while you assemble the gratinate. Spread a heaping tablespoon of tomato sauce on top of each cutlet. Add a third of the Grana Padano. Arrange the mushroom caps on top of the sauced chicken, using two mushroom caps per piece of chicken. Top with another third of the Grana Padano.

Raise the heat a bit, and begin to develop the sauce: Drop the remaining butter, in small pieces, in between the layered cutlets. After a few seconds, pour in ⅔ cup of the wine around the cutlets, and let it heat briefly, 10 to 20 seconds. Spoon the rest of the cup of tomato sauce into the pan (not on the chicken). Bring it to a simmer, and then drop the sage into the sauce, distributing it all around the pan. Give the pan a gentle shake or two, to mix and emulsify the sauce ingredients. Add the remaining wine (or stock, or water, if necessary, so the sauce comes almost to the top of the chicken), plus the last of the cheese, bring it to a simmer, and place the chicken in the oven. Bake, shaking the pan once or twice, until the chicken is cooked through and the top is crusty and golden, about 15 to 20 minutes, adding a little more stock or water if the sauce gets too thick. Remove sage. To serve, place on a plate and spoon sauce around it.

Chicken with Olives and Pine Nuts

Pollo con Olive e Pinoli
SERVES 4

3½ to 4 pounds assorted cut-up chicken pieces
    from 1 chicken (2 legs, 2 thighs, 2 wings,
    2 breasts, optional back and neck)
1 teaspoon kosher salt
2 tablespoons extra-virgin olive oil
2 tablespoons unsalted butter
3 garlic cloves, crushed and peeled
2 fresh bay leaves
1 cup brine-cured green Italian olives, pitted
½ cup dry white wine
¼ cup pine nuts, toasted

Rinse the chicken pieces, and pat them dry with paper towels. Trim off excess skin and fat. Separate the drumsticks from the thighs; cut the breast halves into two pieces each. Season the chicken with the salt. Put the olive oil and butter in a large cast-iron or other heavy skillet, and set it over medium-low heat. When the butter is melted and hot, lay in the chicken pieces, skin side down, in a single layer; drop the garlic cloves and bay leaves in the spaces between them. Cover the pan, and let the chicken cook over gentle heat, browning slowly and releasing its fat and juices. After about 10 minutes, uncover the pan, turn the pieces, and move them around the pan to cook evenly; then replace the cover. Turn again in 10 minutes or so, and continue cooking, covered.

After the chicken has cooked for 20 minutes, scatter the olives onto the pan bottom, around the chicken, and pour in the wine. Raise the heat so the liquid is simmering, cover, and cook, gradually concentrating the juices, for about 10 minutes. Remove the lid, and cook uncovered, evaporating the pan juices, occasionally turning the chicken pieces and olives. If there is a lot of fat in the bottom of the pan, tilt the skillet and spoon off the fat from one side. Scatter the pine nuts around the chicken, and continue cooking uncovered, turning the chicken over gently, until the pan juices thicken and coat the meat like a glaze.

Turn off the heat, remove the garlic, and serve the chicken right from the skillet, or heap the pieces on a platter or in a shallow serving bowl. Spoon out any sauce and pine nuts left in the pan, and drizzle this over the chicken.

Chicken Cacciatore

Pollo alla Cacciatora
SERVES 6

2 broiler chickens (about 3 pounds each)
Kosher salt to taste
Freshly ground black pepper to taste
All-purpose flour, for dredging
¼ cup vegetable oil
¼ cup extra-virgin olive oil
1 small onion, chopped
½ cup dry white wine
One 28-ounce can Italian plum tomatoes, preferably San Marzano, crushed by hand
1 teaspoon dried oregano, preferably Sicilian on the branch, crumbled
8 ounces white or shiitake mushrooms, sliced (about 4 cups)
1 red and 1 yellow bell pepper, cored, seeded, and cut into ½-inch strips (about 2 cups)

Cut each chicken into twelve pieces: With a sturdy knife or kitchen shears, remove the backbone by cutting along both sides of it. Remove the wing tips. (You can save the backbone, wing tips, and giblets—except for the liver—to make chicken stock another time. Or, if you like, cut the backbone in half crosswise, and add it to this dish.) Place the chicken, breast side down, on a cutting board, and cut the chicken into halves by cutting through the breastbone lengthwise. Cut off the wing at the joint that connects it to the breast, then cut each wing in half at the joint. Separate the leg from the breast. Cut each leg in half at the joint. Cut the breast in half crosswise, giving the knife a good whack when you get to the bone to separate the breast cleanly into halves. Repeat with the remaining chicken.

Season the chicken pieces generously with salt and pepper. Dredge the pieces in flour, coating them lightly and tapping off excess flour. Heat the vegetable oil in a wide shallow Dutch oven with 2 tablespoons of the olive oil until a piece of chicken dipped in the oil gives off a very lively sizzle. Add as many pieces of chicken to the pan as will fit without touching (do not crowd the chicken). Remove the chicken from the skillet as it browns.

Once all of the chicken is out of the pot, spoon off all but about 3 tablespoons of the fat. Add the onion, and cook until it begins to soften, about 5 minutes.

Add the wine, bring it to a boil, and reduce it by half, about 2 to 3 minutes. Add the tomatoes and oregano, season with salt and pepper, and bring to a boil. Tuck the chicken into the sauce, and adjust the heat to a gentle boil. Cook, covered, until the chicken is just cooked through, about 20 minutes. Meanwhile, heat the remaining 2 tablespoons olive oil in a large skillet over medium-high heat. Add the mushrooms and peppers, and toss until the peppers are wilted but still quite crunchy, about 8 minutes. Season the vegetables with salt.

Stir the peppers and mushrooms into the chicken. Cook, covered, until the chicken and vegetables are tender, 10 to 15 minutes. (Check the level of the liquid as it cooks; there should be enough barely to cover the chicken. If necessary, add small amounts of water to maintain the level as the chicken cooks.) Serve the chicken pieces nestled between the vegetables on a platter. Delicious with Basic Polenta (page 199).

Chicken Thighs Rolled with Prosciutto

Cosce di Pollo Arrotolate nel Prosciutto
SERVES 6

12 boneless chicken thighs (skin optional) (about 2½ to 3 pounds)
⅓ cup freshly grated Grana Padano
⅓ cup chopped fresh chives
⅓ cup chopped fresh Italian parsley
2 tablespoons chopped fresh sage, plus 1 whole sprig
1 teaspoon kosher salt
Freshly ground black pepper
6 thin slices prosciutto, halved crosswise
All-purpose flour, for dredging
3 tablespoons extra-virgin olive oil
3 tablespoons butter
2 large shallots, finely chopped
1 pound mixed mushrooms, sliced (button, cremini, shiitake, chanterelle, oyster)
½ cup dry white wine
Juice of ½ lemon, freshly squeezed
2 cups Chicken Stock (page 143)

Lay the chicken thighs out, skin side down, and cut shallow slits on both sides of each thigh (do not cut all the way through; just open the meat). Pound them with a mallet to an even ½-inch thickness. The thighs should have a roughly rectangular shape.

In a medium bowl, toss together the grated cheese, chives, parsley, and chopped sage. Lay the thighs flat, skin side down, with the shorter side facing you. Season with ½ teaspoon of the salt and some pepper. Lay half a slice of prosciutto on each, folding to fit within the edges of the thigh. Sprinkle each with some of the herb mixture, tucking the sides in to encase the herbs. Roll each thigh into a bundle. Tie each twice crosswise with kitchen twine.

Spread the flour on a rimmed sheet pan. Dredge the thighs lightly in flour, and tap off the excess. Heat a large Dutch oven over medium-high heat. Add the olive oil. When the oil is hot, add the rolls and brown on all sides, about 8 to 10 minutes in all. Remove to a plate.

Add the butter. When the butter is melted, add the shallots and mushrooms, and cook until they are softened and the mushrooms have released their juices, about 6 minutes. Season with the remaining ½ teaspoon salt, and drop in the sprig of sage. Add the white wine and lemon juice, and bring it to a boil. Add the chicken rolls in one layer on top of the mushrooms, and pour in the stock. Cover, and simmer until the chicken is tender, about about 30 to 40 minutes. Uncover, and bring the sauce to a boil to reduce the consistency and concentrate the flavor. Untie the rolls, and serve them topped with the mushroom sauce.

Chicken Thighs with Potatoes and Olives

Cosce di Pollo con Patate ed Olive
SERVES 6

12 medium chicken thighs (about 4 pounds)
1½ teaspoons kosher salt, plus more for seasoning
All-purpose flour, for dredging
Vegetable oil, for browning
2½ pounds medium Yukon gold potatoes, peeled and cut into 1½-inch chunks
3 tablespoons extra-virgin olive oil
6 garlic cloves, crushed and peeled
1½ cups pitted large green olives, such as Cerignola

4 sprigs fresh rosemary
3 tablespoons red wine vinegar
½ cup dry white wine

Season the chicken thighs with 1 teaspoon salt. Spread the flour on a rimmed plate, and lightly dredge the chicken thighs on all sides, tapping off the excess. Heat a large shallow Dutch oven (or very large skillet) over medium-high heat with ¼ inch of vegetable oil. When the oil is hot, add the chicken, skin side down. Brown well on both sides, about 10 minutes, and remove to a plate.

To the same oil, add the potatoes. Brown them on all sides, about 10 minutes, and remove to the plate with the chicken. Dump the oil out into a safe container, and wipe the pot clean.

Return the pot to medium-high heat, and add the olive oil. Add the garlic. Once the garlic begins to sizzle, add the olives and rosemary. Once they are sizzling nicely in the pot, let them cook for a minute or two to bring the flavors together, then add the vinegar. Boil until the vinegar has reduced away, then add back the chicken and potatoes. Pour in the wine, adjust the heat to a simmer, and cover. Cook until the chicken is almost tender, about 20 to 25 minutes.

Uncover, and simmer rapidly, turning the chicken occasionally, until it is tender and glazed in the sauce, about 15 minutes. Remove the garlic cloves and rosemary sprigs, and serve hot.

4 medium onions, each cut into quarters left attached at the root
4 bell peppers (red and yellow), stemmed, seeded, and quartered
6 garlic cloves, crushed and peeled
1½ cups dry white wine
2 teaspoons sweet paprika

Preheat the oven to 400 degrees. In a large bowl, toss the drumsticks with the olive oil and 1 teaspoon salt. Heat a large skillet over medium-high heat, and brown the drumsticks on all sides, in batches if necessary, about 10 minutes per batch. Transfer to a large shallow roasting pan or rimmed sheet pan.

To the same skillet, add the vegetable oil. When the oil is hot, add the onions, and brown on all sides, about 3 minutes. Add to the roasting pan. Add the peppers and garlic to the skillet, and cook until the peppers are browned on the edges, about 5 minutes. Add the peppers to the roasting pan.

In a spouted measuring cup, stir together the wine, paprika, and remaining teaspoon salt. Pour this into the roasting pan. Roast, uncovered, on the bottom rack of the oven, tossing several times, until the chicken is very tender and glazed with the pan juices, about 40 minutes. Remove the garlic and serve hot.

Chicken Drumsticks with Peppers and Paprika

Cosce di Pollo con Peperoni e Paprika
SERVES 6

12 chicken drumsticks (skin optional) (about 4 pounds)
2 tablespoons extra-virgin olive oil
2 teaspoons kosher salt
2 tablespoons vegetable oil

Chicken Scarpariello

Pollo alla Scarpariello
SERVES 6

2 small broiler chickens (about 3 pounds each)
Kosher salt
Freshly ground black pepper
¼ cup extra-virgin olive oil
8 ounces sweet Italian sausage (without fennel seeds), cut into 1-inch pieces
10 garlic cloves, finely chopped

4 pickled cherry peppers, cut in half, seeded, and
    stemmed
¼ cup red wine vinegar
½ cup dry white wine
1 cup Chicken Stock (page 143)
¼ cup chopped fresh Italian parsley

Preheat the oven to 475 degrees. Cut each chicken into twelve pieces (see page 298). Wash and pat the chicken pieces dry, and season them with salt and pepper. Heat 2 tablespoons of the olive oil in a large skillet over medium heat. Add as many pieces of chicken to the skillet as fit without touching, starting with the leg, thigh, and wing pieces, all skin side down. Cook the chicken, turning as necessary, until the pieces are golden brown on all sides, about 8 minutes. Remove the chicken pieces as they brown, and drain them on paper towels. Place the drained chicken pieces in a roasting pan large enough to hold all of them in a single layer. Repeat with the remaining chicken, adding more oil to the pan as necessary and adjusting the heat to prevent the bits that stick to the pan from overbrowning. As room becomes available in the skillet after all the chicken has been added, tuck in pieces of sausage, and cook, turning, until browned on all sides.

Remove all the chicken and sausage from the pan, add the garlic, and cook until golden, being careful not to burn it. Scatter the cherry peppers into the skillet, season with salt and pepper, and stir for a minute. Pour in the vinegar, and bring it to a boil, scraping the browned bits that stick to the skillet into the liquid; cook until the vinegar is reduced by half. Add the white wine, bring to a boil, and boil until reduced by half, about 3 minutes.

Pour in the stock, and bring it to a boil. Pour the sauce over the chicken in the roasting pan, and stir to coat. Place the chicken in the oven, and roast, stirring occasionally, until the sauce is thick and sticky, like molasses, about 10 minutes. If the sauce is still too thin, place the roasting pan directly over medium-high heat on the stovetop and cook, stirring, until it is reduced enough,

about a minute or two. Once the sauce is thickened, remove the garlic, toss in the parsley, and serve.

❦ Poussins—young chickens that weigh about 1 pound each—are great for this dish. Figure on one half per person, and cut them into pieces at the joints; there's no need to cut them into smaller pieces across the bone. As good as they are, I made this dish using supermarket-bought fryer chickens, because I want to be sure you try this delicious recipe.

Chicken in Beer

Pollo alla Birra
SERVES 6

3½-to-4-pound roasting chicken
2 teaspoons kosher salt
2 medium onions, quartered through the root
1 large carrot, peeled, halved crosswise, and
    quartered lengthwise
2 medium parsnips, peeled, halved crosswise,
    and quartered lengthwise
2 tablespoons fresh sage leaves
4 whole cloves
1 cinnamon stick
1½ cups Chicken Stock (page 143)
12 ounces lager beer or, if you like, a more
    flavorful beer or ale
1 cup nonalcoholic apple cider, preferably
    unfiltered

Preheat the oven to 400 degrees. Trim the excess fat from the chicken, and season it inside and out with half of the salt. Scatter the onions, carrot, parsnips, sage, cloves, and cinnamon in a large Dutch oven big enough to hold the chicken with a little room around the edges; sprinkle over this the rest of the salt, and set the chicken on top of the vegetables. Put the pot on the stove, pour in the stock, beer, and apple cider, and bring to a simmer over medium heat. Cook, uncovered, for about 15 minutes on top of the stove.

Put the pot in the oven, and roast the chicken for about 30 minutes, basting with the pan juices two or three times. Cover the chicken with a sheet of aluminum foil to prevent overbrowning, and roast another 30 minutes. Remove the foil, and roast another 20 to 30 minutes, basting frequently, until the chicken and vegetables are cooked through and tender.

Remove the chicken to a warm platter, and surround it with the vegetables. Bring the pan juices to a boil on top of the stove, skim the fat, and cook until they are reduced by half. Carve the chicken at the table, and spoon some of the pan juices on top.

Chicken in Vinegar Sauce

Pollo all'Aceto
SERVES 4 TO 6

5-pound roasting chicken
2 teaspoons kosher salt
Vegetable oil, for browning the chicken
3 medium onions, quartered, left attached at the root end
1 pound carrots, peeled and cut into 2-inch chunks
2 tablespoons extra-virgin olive oil
2 tablespoons tomato paste
6 garlic cloves, crushed and peeled
1 cup cider vinegar
2 cups dry white wine
2 tablespoons honey
¼ teaspoon crushed red pepper flakes
2 sprigs fresh rosemary

Preheat the oven to 400 degrees. Cut the chicken into pieces as follows: Remove the legs, and separate the thighs and drumsticks. Remove the wings, cut off the tips, then cut into two pieces each. Cut in half down the backbone. Separate the breasts, and cut each into three pieces. You should have sixteen pieces. Season the chicken with 1 teaspoon of the salt.

In a large, shallow Dutch oven, heat ½ inch vegetable oil over medium-high heat. When the oil is hot, brown the chicken all over, in batches, about 4 minutes per batch. As the pieces brown, remove them to a sheet pan. Once all the chicken is out, add the onions and carrots and brown them all over, about 4 minutes; add them to the sheet pan.

Carefully discard the oil, and wipe the pot clean with a paper towel. Return the pot to medium-high heat, and add the olive oil. When the oil is hot, add the tomato paste and garlic, and cook for a minute, until both are sizzling. Add the cider vinegar, and cook until it is reduced by half, about 3 minutes; then add the wine, honey, red pepper flakes, and rosemary. Season with the remaining salt. Add back the chicken and vegetables. Cover, and bake in the oven 20 minutes. Uncover, and cook until it is browned and tender and cooked through, about 20 to 25 minutes more. Remove the chicken and vegetables to a platter. Discard garlic and rosemary sprigs. If the sauce is still too thin, reduce on the stove over high heat for a few minutes. Pour the sauce over the chicken and vegetables, and serve.

Chicken in Guazzetto

Pollo al Guazzetto
SERVES 4

3½-pound chicken, with giblets
1 sprig fresh rosemary
3 fresh bay leaves
½ teaspoon black peppercorns
4 whole cloves
1 teaspoon kosher salt

2 tablespoons extra-virgin olive oil
2 thick slices bacon, chopped
1 large onion, sliced
2 tablespoons tomato paste
1 cup dry white wine
2 cups Chicken Stock (page 143)

Cut the chicken into eight pieces: Cut off the wings. Cut off the legs at the joint, and separate the drumsticks and thighs. Flip the breast skin side down, and cut out the breastbone. Separate the breasts, trim the rib bones, and cut each breast in half crosswise. Freeze the trimmings, giblets, and neck for stock. Trim and chop the liver. Set the rosemary, bay leaves, peppercorns, and cloves in a piece of cheesecloth, and tie with kitchen twine.

Season the chicken all over with ½ teaspoon salt. Heat a medium Dutch oven over medium-high heat. Add the olive oil to the pot. When the oil is hot, add the chicken pieces, skin side down. Cook until they are browned on all sides, about 5 minutes in all. Remove them to a plate.

Add the bacon to the pot, and cook until the fat is rendered, about 3 minutes. Add the onion, and cook until it is wilted, about 5 minutes. Make a space in the center of the pot, and add the tomato paste. Cook and stir the paste in that hot spot until it toasts and darkens a shade or two, about 2 minutes. Mix the tomato paste into the onion, and add the wine. Bring it to a boil, and simmer to reduce by half. Add the stock and the herb bundle. Nestle the chicken pieces back in the pot, skin side up. Simmer, partially covered, until the chicken is tender, about 30 minutes. Remove the chicken to a platter to keep warm. Discard the herb bundle. Increase the heat to reduce and concentrate the sauce. Serve the sauce over the chicken.

This is delicious when served with Basic Polenta (page 199). It is also wonderful with pasta, such as Garganelli (page 223), or with Basic Potato Gnocchi (page 233).

Grandma's Chicken and Potatoes

Pollo e Patate della Nonna
SERVES 4

2½ pounds chicken pieces (use your favorites)
½ cup canola oil
½ teaspoon kosher salt, plus more to taste
1 pound red-skinned potatoes, halved
2 tablespoons extra-virgin olive oil, plus more as needed
2 small onions, peeled and quartered lengthwise through the root end
2 sprigs fresh rosemary

OPTIONAL INGREDIENTS
4 to 6 ounces sliced bacon (5 or 6 slices)
1 or 2 pickled cherry peppers, sweet or hot, cut in half and seeded

Rinse the chicken pieces, and pat them dry with paper towels. Trim off excess skin and fat. Cut the drumsticks from the thighs. If using breast halves, cut each into two small pieces.

Make the bacon roll-ups (if using): Cut the bacon slices in half crosswise, and roll each strip into a neat, tight cylinder. Stick a toothpick through the roll to secure it; cut or break the toothpick so only a tiny bit sticks out (allowing the bacon to roll around and cook evenly).

Pour the canola oil into a deep skillet, and set it over high heat. Sprinkle the chicken on all sides with half the salt. When the oil is very hot, lay the pieces, skin side down, an inch or so apart—watch out for oil spatters. Don't crowd the chicken: if necessary you can fry it in batches, cooking similar pieces together. If using the bacon rolls, drop them into the oil around the chicken, turning and shifting them often. Let the chicken fry in place for several minutes to brown on the underside, then turn and continue frying until the pieces are golden brown on all sides, 7 to 10 minutes or more. Fry the breast pieces for only 5 minutes or so, taking them out of the oil as soon as they are golden. Let the bacon rolls cook and get lightly crisp, but not dark. Remove the chicken to a plate as it browns.

Toss the potatoes in a large bowl with the olive oil and the remaining salt. When all the chicken and bacon are cooked and out of the skillet, pour off the frying oil. Return the skillet to medium heat, and put all the potatoes, cut side down, in a single layer in the hot pan, pouring the olive oil into the skillet, too. Fry and crisp the potatoes for about 4 minutes to form a crust, then move them around the pan, still cut side down, until they're all brown and crisp, 7 minutes or more. Turn them over, and fry another 2 minutes, to cook and crisp on their rounded skin sides.

Add the onion wedges, rosemary, and, if using, peppers. Return the chicken pieces—except the breast pieces—to the pan, along with the bacon rolls; pour in any chicken juices that have accumulated. Raise the heat slightly, and turn the chicken, potatoes, and onion (and bacon and/or pepper pieces) so they are coated with pan juices, taking care not to break the potato pieces. Spread everything out in the pan—potatoes on the bottom as much as possible, so they will keep crisping up—and cover.

Lower the heat to medium, and cook for about 7 minutes, shaking the pan occasionally; then uncover, and tumble everything again. Cover, and cook another 7 minutes or so, adding the breast pieces at this point. Give everything another tumble. Now cook, covered, for 10 minutes more.

Remove the cover, turn the pieces again, and cook in the open skillet for about 10 minutes, to evaporate the moisture and caramelize everything. Turn the pieces now and then; when they are all glistening and golden, and the potatoes are cooked through, remove the skillet from the stove, discard the rosemary sprigs, and—as I do at home—bring it right to the table.

🍀 Grandma's Chicken and Potatoes is a favorite meal at our house, but sometimes I want to add another dimension to this, and who doesn't like crispy bacon? To counter the richness of the

bacon, I add a little acidity and spice, and that comes from the pickled cherry peppers. This classic is delicious either with or without my special touches.

Seared Marinated Breast of Chicken with Mushrooms

Petto di Pollo Scottato con Funghi
SERVES 6

CHICKEN AND MARINADE
6 medium boneless, skinless chicken breasts (about 2 pounds)
½ cup extra-virgin olive oil
1 tablespoon coarsely chopped fresh rosemary
1 tablespoon coarsely chopped fresh sage
4 garlic cloves, crushed and peeled
½ teaspoon kosher salt
Freshly ground black pepper

SHIITAKE MUSHROOM SAUCE
¼ cup extra-virgin olive oil
4 garlic cloves, crushed and peeled
1 pound small shiitake mushrooms, stemmed
½ teaspoon kosher salt
Freshly ground black pepper
1 tablespoon unsalted butter
1 tablespoon brandy
2 tablespoons chopped fresh Italian parsley

For the chicken and marinade: Cut each chicken breast diagonally into thirds. With a meat mallet, lightly pound the pieces to an even thickness of about ½ inch. Put the chicken in a large resealable plastic bag. Pour in the olive oil, rosemary, sage, and garlic, and season with salt and pepper. Massage the bag with your fingers just to distribute the ingredients. Seal and marinate in the refrigerator at least 4 hours, up to overnight.

Heat a large cast-iron skillet over medium-high heat. Remove the chicken from the marinade and place it directly in the skillet (the oil coating the chicken will be enough to brown it). Sear the chicken on both sides until cooked through, about 3 to 4 minutes per side. Remove the chicken to a plate and keep warm.

Return the skillet to medium-high heat. Add the olive oil. When the oil is hot, add the garlic. Let the garlic sizzle for a minute to flavor the oil, then add half of the shiitake caps in one layer. Season with ¼ teaspoon salt and black pepper to taste, and cook, turning once or twice, until golden on both sides, about 2 minutes per side. Remove the mushrooms to a plate, and repeat with the remaining mushrooms and salt and pepper. Push all of the mushrooms back into the skillet, and add the butter, brandy, and parsley. Stir up the pan juices to make a light sauce coating the mushrooms. Remove the garlic. Return the chicken to the skillet, bring to a boil, and serve.

Lemon Roasted Chicken

Pollo Arrosto al Limone
SERVES 4

5-pound roasting chicken
2 lemons, zested and cut into quarters
1½ teaspoons kosher salt
3 tablespoons extra-virgin olive oil
3 medium onions, peeled, cut in sixths but left
    attached at the root end
2 sprigs fresh rosemary
1 cup dry white wine

Preheat the oven to 375 degrees. Gently slide your fingers under the skin of the chicken breast to loosen it. Spread the grated lemon zest under the breast skin. Season the chicken with 1 teaspoon of the salt, and rub it all over with 1 tablespoon of the olive oil.

Set the onions and lemon quarters in a roasting pan, and toss with the remaining ½ teaspoon

salt and 2 tablespoons olive oil. Stuff some of the lemon quarters in the chicken cavity, along with the rosemary. Set the chicken, breast side up, on the onions and lemons. With a paring knife, cut a small slit in the skin at the tip of the breast. Stick the drumsticks in the opposite sides' slits, to keep the chicken together and hold its shape while roasting. Pour the white wine into the pan, and roast the chicken, basting once or twice with the pan juices, until the meat between the thigh and breast reaches 165 on an instant-read thermometer and the skin is crispy and golden, about 1 hour and 20 minutes. Remove the chicken to a cutting board, and let it rest 10 minutes. Fish out the onions from the pan, and set in a sauté pan large enough to hold the chicken as well when it is cut into pieces. Strain the pan juices, pushing on the solids to extract all of the sauce; let the juices rest, then skim off any excess fat.

Carve the chicken into serving pieces, and return to the pan with the onions. Add the strained sauce, bring all to a boil, and serve.

Roast Chicken with Rosemary and Orange

Pollo Arrosto al Rosmarino e Arancia
SERVES 4

4½-pound chicken, with neck (optional)
1 teaspoon kosher salt
Freshly ground black pepper
2 tablespoons extra-virgin olive oil
2 tablespoons unsalted butter
4 sprigs fresh rosemary
2 tablespoons Grand Marnier or other orange
    liqueur
Juice of 1 small orange, freshly squeezed
¾ cup Chicken Stock (page 143)

Preheat the oven to 450 degrees. Put a roasting pan on the middle rack to heat up. Cut the chicken into pieces as follows: two wings, two thighs, two legs, two breasts (each cut in half, to make four pieces), backbone, and neck (if included). Season the chicken all over with the salt and some pepper.

To a large skillet over medium-high heat, add the olive oil. When the oil is hot, brown the chicken on both sides, in batches, about 2 to 3 minutes per side. As they are browned, remove the chicken pieces to a plate. Put all of the dark meat (but not the breast pieces yet) in the roasting pan skin side down, and roast 20 minutes. Turn the dark meat and add the breast pieces skin side up, and roast until the skin is very brown and crisp, about 15 to 20 minutes more. Turn the breast pieces skin side down, and roast 10 minutes more.

Remove the chicken to a serving platter and keep warm. Heat the roasting pan on the stovetop over medium-high heat. Add the butter to the juices in the pan. As soon as it melts, add the rosemary. Once the rosemary is sizzling, add the Grand Marnier and orange juice. Bring to a boil, and add the chicken stock. Boil and whisk to bring the sauce together and thicken it slightly, about 2 minutes. Strain the sauce, spoon over the chicken, and serve.

Quail Stuffed with Mushrooms and Sausage

Quaglie Farcite con Funghi e Salsiccia
SERVES 4

4 cups crustless day-old country-bread cubes
1½ cups milk
6 tablespoons unsalted butter
2 tablespoons extra-virgin olive oil
1 small onion, finely chopped
1 celery stalk, finely chopped
1 pound mixed mushrooms, 4 ounces finely chopped, 12 ounces sliced (button, cremini, shiitake, chanterelle, oyster)

2 links sweet Italian sausage (about 7 ounces), removed from casings
1 bunch scallions, trimmed and chopped (about 1 cup)
1¼ teaspoons kosher salt
Freshly ground black pepper
1½ cups dry white wine
2 tablespoons chopped fresh Italian parsley
⅓ cup freshly grated Grana Padano
8 semi-boneless quail (about 2 pounds)

Preheat the oven to 400 degrees. Put the bread in a large bowl, and pour the milk over it. Let the bread soak while you assemble the stuffing for the quail. In a large skillet over medium heat, melt 2 tablespoons of the butter in the olive oil. When the butter is melted, add the onion and celery. Cook until everything just begins to soften, about 4 minutes.

Increase the heat to medium high, and add the chopped mushrooms and sausage. Cook, breaking up the sausage with a wooden spoon, until the sausage and mushrooms are well browned, about 3 minutes. Add the scallions, season with ½ teaspoon of the salt and some pepper, and cook until the scallions are wilted, about 3 minutes. Add ½ cup of the white wine, and simmer rapidly until the wine is reduced away, about 2 minutes. Scrape the mixture into a bowl to cool.

When the vegetables are cooled, squeeze the bread dry, leaving the milk in the bowl, and add the bread to the vegetables, breaking it up with your fingers. Stir in the parsley and grated cheese, and mix well. Season the quail inside and out with ½ teaspoon salt and some pepper. Divide the stuffing among the body cavities of the quail.

Heat a large roasting pan over medium heat. Add the remaining 4 tablespoons butter. When the butter is melted, add the sliced mushrooms, and season with the remaining ¼ teaspoon salt. Cook and stir until the mushrooms are softened, about 6 minutes. Add the remaining cup of white wine, and bring it to a boil. Set the quail, breast side up, on the mushrooms, and roast them until the skin is golden and the quail are cooked through, about 30 minutes. Adjust the pan sauce for seasoning. Serve the quail with the mushroom pan sauce spooned over the top.

Quail Under a Brick

Quaglie al Mattone
SERVES 4

¼ cup plus 1 tablespoon extra-virgin olive oil
6 garlic cloves, crushed and peeled
4 fresh bay leaves, crumbled
1 tablespoon fresh rosemary leaves
½ teaspoon kosher salt
Freshly ground black pepper
8 semi-boneless quail (about 2 pounds)
2 tablespoons chopped fresh Italian parsley

In a bowl large enough to hold the quail, mix together ¼ cup olive oil, the garlic, bay leaves, rosemary, salt, and some pepper. Add the quail, and toss to coat. Let them marinate in the refrigerator for 4 hours.

Remove the quail from the marinade. Heat a large cast-iron skillet (it must be large enough to fit the quail in one layer; if not, use two skillets at the same time or do in two batches) over medium-high heat. Add the remaining tablespoon of olive oil. Add the quail, breast side down, and weight them with another skillet. Press down, and cook until the underside is browned and crispy, about 5 minutes. Turn the quail, and weight again by pressing on the skillet. Cook until the other side is crispy and brown and the quail are cooked through, about 5 minutes more. Transfer to serving plates, and sprinkle with the parsley and serve.

Duck with Lemon and Honey

Anatra con Limone e Miele
SERVES 4

2 teaspoons kosher salt
2 teaspoons fennel powder
2 tablespoons extra-virgin olive oil
6-pound duck, with gizzards, neck, and liver, trimmed of excess fat
2 sprigs fresh rosemary
1 large onion, quartered
3 cups Chicken Stock (page 143)
1 cup dry red wine
¼ cup dried porcini mushrooms, crumbled
1 to 2 tablespoons honey
Juice of ½ lemon, freshly squeezed

Preheat the oven to 375 degrees. In a small bowl, combine the salt and fennel powder. Drizzle in the olive oil, and stir to make a paste. Rub the salt paste all over the outside and inside of the duck. Stuff the cavity of the duck with the rosemary and the onion.

Chop the gizzards and liver, and put them in the bottom of a roasting pan along with the neck. Set a rack on top, and arrange the duck on the rack in the roasting pan, breast side up. Add the stock, wine, and porcini to the pan. Roast the duck until the skin is crispy, about 1 hour. Increase the oven temperature to 400 degrees, and cook for an additional ½ hour, until the skin is very crisp.

Remove the duck to a cutting board. Remove the rack, and set the roasting pan with the vegetables and sauce on top of the stove, over high heat. Boil until the cooking juices are reduced to about 2 cups. Strain them into a measuring cup (preferably a fat-separating measuring cup), pressing on the solids to get the juices out. Let the juices sit for a minute to separate the fat, and spoon or pour it off. Pour the defatted juices into a skillet, and bring them to a simmer over medium-high heat. Add the honey, to taste, and the lemon juice, and give it a 5-minute boil.

Cut the duck into four portions with kitchen

shears, and place it, skin side up, in the roasting pan. Baste with some of the sauce, and return it to the 400-degree oven to recrisp the duck. Glaze the duck with the sauce, and cook it for about 7 to 10 minutes. Serve the crispy glazed duck with the remaining sauce.

Braised Duck Legs with Cipollini

Anatra alla Romagnola
SERVES 4

4 cups Chicken Stock (page 143)
¼ cup dried porcini mushrooms
4 duck legs (about 3½ pounds)
2 teaspoons kosher salt
2 tablespoons extra-virgin olive oil
2 ounces pancetta, diced
4 medium carrots, peeled and cut into 1-inch chunks
3 celery stalks, cut into 1-inch chunks
2 tablespoons tomato paste
½ cup dry white wine
2 fresh bay leaves
12 cipollini onions, peeled, or 2 medium onions, quartered, left attached at the root end

Put the chicken stock in a medium saucepan, bring it to a simmer, and keep it hot. Put the porcini in a spouted measuring cup, and ladle 1 cup hot stock over them. Soak them until softened, about 10 minutes. Drain and chop the mushrooms. Strain the soaking liquid, and reserve.

Season the duck legs with 1 teaspoon of the salt. Heat a medium Dutch oven over medium heat. Add the olive oil. When the oil is hot, add the duck legs, skin side down. Cook gently to render the fat and crisp the skin, about 6 to 7 minutes, adjusting the heat as you go so it doesn't brown too fast. Flip the legs, and brown the other side, about 3 to 4 minutes more. Remove the duck to a plate.

Pour out all but 2 tablespoons of the fat from the pot. Add the pancetta, and cook until it renders its fat, about 3 minutes. Add the carrots and celery, and stir to coat them in the fat. Make a space in the pan, add the tomato paste, and cook and stir the paste in that hot spot until it toasts and darkens a shade or two, about 2 minutes. Stir the paste into the vegetables. Stir in the remaining teaspoon salt and the chopped porcini. Add the wine, bring it to a boil, and reduce by half, about 2 minutes. Add the bay leaves, 1 cup stock, and the porcini-soaking liquid. Add the duck back to the pot, skin side up. Bring the liquid to a simmer with the lid slightly ajar, and simmer until the duck legs are very tender, about 1½ hours. Add the onions halfway through the cooking time. Add the remaining 2 cups stock in several additions to keep the legs covered in liquid. When they are done, remove the duck legs to a platter (remove the bay leaves). Skim as much fat from the sauce as possible, and bring it to a simmer to reduce it. Return the duck to the sauce, and simmer just to coat the duck in the sauce. You can serve it as is with the vegetables, but it is also delicious served with Basic Polenta (page 199).

Duck Roasted with Sauerkraut

Anatra in Umido con Crauti
SERVES 4

5 fresh bay leaves
1 sprig fresh rosemary
10 black peppercorns
4-pound duck
¼ teaspoon kosher salt
Freshly ground black pepper
½ cup vegetable oil, for browning
2 tablespoons extra-virgin olive oil
5 garlic cloves, crushed and peeled
3 pounds sauerkraut, rinsed well and drained
2 cups Chicken Stock (page 143)

Preheat the oven to 475 degrees. Lay the bay leaves, rosemary, and peppercorns on a piece of cheesecloth, and tie with kitchen twine into a sachet. Season the duck all over with the salt and some pepper. Heat a large straight-sided skillet over medium heat and add the vegetable oil. Brown the duck well on all sides, about 10 minutes in all. Remove the duck, pour out any excess oil and put the duck back, breast side up. Roast in the oven until it is very brown and much of the fat is rendered, about 30 minutes.

Heat a large Dutch oven, big enough to hold the duck and the sauerkraut, over medium heat. Add the olive oil. Add the garlic, and cook until it is golden, about 2 minutes. Add the sauerkraut, and toss to coat it in the oil. Pour in 2 cups chicken stock, and nestle the herb sachet in the sauerkraut. Put the duck on top of the sauerkraut. Pour the juices from the duck skillet into a spouted measuring cup (or a defatting cup, if you have one), and spoon off as much fat as possible. Pour the defatted juices into the sauerkraut, and bring the liquid to a simmer. With the lid ajar, simmer until the duck is tender, about 1 hour.

Discard the herb sachet and remove the duck to a cutting board, and let it rest 5 minutes. Carve into eight serving pieces, and serve with the sauerkraut.

Roasted Pheasant

Fagiano Arrosto
SERVES 4

SAUCE
¼ cup dried porcini mushrooms
Gizzards and neck of the pheasant
8 ounces chicken gizzards or wings
3 tablespoons extra-virgin olive oil
1 small onion, coarsely chopped
1 small carrot, peeled and chopped
1 celery stalk, chopped
1 tablespoon all-purpose flour

2 sprigs fresh rosemary
2 fresh bay leaves
6 juniper berries
1 cup dry white wine
2 cups Chicken Stock (page 143)
½ teaspoon kosher salt

PHEASANT
3-to-4-pound pheasant, dressed
½ teaspoon kosher salt
Freshly ground black pepper
3 tablespoons extra-virgin olive oil
3 sprigs fresh rosemary
3 fresh bay leaves

Preheat the oven to 425 degrees. Put the porcini and 1 cup very hot water in a spouted measuring cup, and soak 10 minutes. Drain and chop the porcini. Strain the soaking liquid, and reserve.

In a medium roasting pan, toss the pheasant gizzards and neck and the chicken gizzards or wings with the olive oil. Roast until they are lightly browned on the underside, about 5 minutes. Stir, and add the onion, carrot, and celery. Roast until the vegetables are just golden, stirring once or twice, about 15 minutes. Sprinkle with the flour, and add the rosemary and bay leaves. Stir well, and roast until everything is well browned, about 10 to 15 minutes more. Remove the rosemary and bay leaves.

While the vegetables are roasting, roast the pheasant: Season it with salt and pepper. Rub it with 2 tablespoons of the olive oil, and stick the rosemary and bay leaves in the cavity. Heat a large cast-iron skillet over medium heat. Add the remaining tablespoon olive oil. When the oil is hot, sear the pheasant on all sides until well browned, about 15 minutes. Tent with foil, and roast for 30 minutes.

Transfer the roasting pan, with the vegetables, to the stovetop over medium heat. Add the porcini, their soaking liquid, the juniper, wine, stock, and salt, and stir to loosen the browned bits on the bottom of the pan. Simmer until the sauce has reduced and the flavors are concentrated, about 30 minutes. Strain through a sieve, pressing on the solids to extract all the liquid. Let the sauce rest, and skim off the fat, or use a fat-separating cup. Keep the sauce warm while the pheasant roasts.

Remove the foil from the pheasant after 30 minutes, and continue roasting until the pheasant is cooked through and tender, an additional 30 minutes. Remove from the oven, and let it rest for 10 minutes; then carve it into serving pieces, removing the rosemary and bay leaves, and serve with the sauce.

Squab with Fried Polenta

Piccione con Polenta Fritta
SERVES 4

4 squab, backbones removed, squab quartered (about 14 ounces each)
1 teaspoon kosher salt
Freshly ground black pepper
2 tablespoons extra-virgin olive oil
2 slices bacon, chopped
1 large onion, chopped
3 fresh bay leaves
1 teaspoon fresh rosemary leaves
4 whole cloves
1½ tablespoons tomato paste
1 cup dry white wine
2 cups Chicken Stock (page 143)
Fried Polenta (page 199), for serving

Season the squab all over with ½ teaspoon of the salt and some pepper. To a large Dutch oven over medium-high heat, add the olive oil. Brown the squab all over, in batches, about 2 minutes per side. Remove the pieces to a plate as they brown.

When all of the squab is out of the pot, add the bacon. Cook until the fat is rendered, about 3 minutes. Add the onion, and cook until it is wilted, about 5 minutes. Season with the remaining ½ teaspoon salt, and add the bay leaves, rosemary, and cloves. Make a space in the pan, and add the tomato paste. Cook and stir the paste in that hot spot until it toasts and darkens a shade or two, about 1 minute. Add the white wine, bring it to a rapid simmer, and cook until it is reduced by about half, about 3 minutes. Add the stock, and return the sauce to a gentle simmer. Add the squab to the pot, cover, and simmer gently until the squab is tender, about 40 to 45 minutes.

Remove the squab to a warm serving platter. Strain the sauce through a fine sieve into a large skillet. Bring the sauce to a simmer. Reduce it until it is thick and coats the spoon, and pour it over the squab and fried polenta.

Sausages with Fennel and Olives

Salsicce con Finocchio e Olive
SERVES 6

4 tablespoons extra-virgin olive oil
12 sweet Italian sausages (about 2½ to 3 pounds)
1 cup dry white wine
6 garlic cloves, crushed and peeled
¼ teaspoon crushed red pepper flakes, or to taste
1 cup large green olives, crushed to open and pit them
3 large fennel bulbs (about 3½ pounds), trimmed, cut into 1-inch chunks
½ teaspoon kosher salt

Heat 2 tablespoons of the olive oil in a large skillet over medium-high heat. Lay in all the sausages, and cook until they are browned all over, about 5 minutes. Pour in the wine, and boil it until it is reduced by half. Remove the sausages to a platter, and pour over them the wine remaining in the pan.

Heat the remaining olive oil in the empty skillet, toss in the garlic cloves, and cook them for a minute or so, over medium heat, until they're sizzling. Drop the crushed red pepper flakes in a hot spot for a few seconds, then scatter the crushed olives in the pan; toss and cook until everything is sizzling, about 2 minutes.

Add the fennel chunks, and stir them in with the garlic and olives. Season with ½ teaspoon salt, cover the skillet, and cook over medium-high heat, tossing and stirring now and then, until the fennel softens, shrinks, and begins to color, about 20 minutes. Add a bit of water to the pan if the fennel remains hard and resistant to the bite; you want it to be wilted but not mushy.

When the fennel is cooked through, return the sausages and the wine to the skillet. Turn and tumble the meat and vegetables together, and cook, uncovered, another 5 minutes or so, until everything is deeply caramelized and glazed. Remove the garlic. Serve piping hot.

and slow cooking until the sausages are cooked through and nicely browned all over, about 25 to 30 minutes.

Remove the pan from the burner, tilt it, and carefully spoon out excess fat. Set the skillet back over the heat, and scatter in the grapes. Stir and tumble them in the pan bottom, moistening them with meat juices. Cover, and cook about 5 to 10 minutes, until the grapes begin to soften but are not overcooked.

Remove the cover, turn the heat to high, and boil the pan juices to concentrate them to a syrupy consistency, stirring and turning the sausages and grapes frequently to glaze them. Remove the garlic. To serve family-style: arrange the sausages on a warm platter, topped with the grapes and pan juices. Or serve them right from the pan (cut in half, if large), spooning grapes and thickened juices over each portion.

Skillet Sausages with Grapes

Salsiccia all'Uva
SERVES 6

¼ cup extra-virgin olive oil
8 garlic cloves, crushed and peeled
2½ pounds sweet Italian sausages, preferably without fennel seeds (about 12 sausages, depending on size)
½ teaspoon crushed red pepper flakes, or to taste
1¼ pounds seedless green or red grapes (or a combination), picked from the stem and washed (about 3 cups)

Heat the olive oil in a large skillet over medium-low heat. Add the garlic. When the garlic is sizzling, lay in all the sausages in one layer, and cover the pan. Cook the sausages slowly, turning and moving them around the skillet occasionally; after 10 minutes or so, sprinkle the red pepper flakes in between the sausages. Continue low

Sausages and Peppers

Salsiccia e Peperoni
SERVES 6 TO 8

2 tablespoons extra-virgin olive oil
12 sweet Italian sausage links (about 2½ pounds)
8 garlic cloves, crushed and peeled
3 small onions, cut into wedges left attached at the root end
1 pound mixed mushrooms, halved (button, cremini, shiitake)
4 hot pickled cherry peppers, stemmed, halved, and seeded (leave some of the seeds in if you like the heat)
3 red, yellow, or orange bell peppers, quartered, or cut in sixths if large
½ teaspoon kosher salt

In a large skillet, heat the olive oil over medium heat. Add the sausages, cover, and cook, turning occasionally, to brown all sides, about 10 minutes in all. Uncover, add the smashed garlic, and cook until the sausages are cooked all the way through, about 10 minutes more. Remove the sausages to a plate.

Add the onion wedges, and cover the skillet. Cook, tossing occasionally, until the onions begin to caramelize on the edges, about 5 minutes. Add the mushrooms, the hot pickled cherry peppers, and the bell peppers, season with the salt, stir, and cover. Cook, stirring occasionally, until all of the vegetables are tender, about 10 minutes more.

Uncover, increase the heat to get the pan juices simmering, and cook until the juices have reduced and glazed the vegetables, about 10 minutes. Remove the garlic.

Add the sausages back to the skillet. Cook and toss to heat the sausages through and combine flavors, about 3 minutes more.

Stuffed Cabbage

Foglie di Verza Farcite
SERVES 6 TO 8

2 teaspoons kosher salt, plus more for the pot
1 large savoy cabbage (about 2 pounds)
8 ounces crustless day-old bread, cut into cubes
    (about 4 cups)
2 medium onions, 1 cut into chunks, 1 sliced
1 medium carrot, peeled and cut into chunks
1 celery stalk, cut into chunks
1 tablespoon fresh rosemary leaves
6 fresh sage leaves
2 garlic cloves, crushed and peeled
2 pounds sweet Italian sausage without fennel
    seeds, removed from casings
1 large egg
½ cup freshly grated Grana Padano
¼ cup chopped fresh Italian parsley
3 tablespoons extra-virgin olive oil
One 28-ounce can Italian plum tomatoes, pref-
    erably San Marzano, crushed by hand

Bring a large pot of salted water (large enough to submerge the entire cabbage) to a boil. With a paring knife, remove the core from the cabbage.

Drop in the cabbage, core side up, and simmer until the leaves become pliable. As the outer leaves become pliable and float away from the head, pluck them off until you have eighteen or so large whole leaves, dropping the leaves in a bowl of ice water as you go. (This process will take about 10 minutes once you add the cabbage to the boiling water.) Remove the leaves from the water, pat them dry, and turn them so the ribbed side is up (the outer side of the leaf). With a paring knife, shave off the rib so the surface of the leaf is flush. Repeat with the remaining of the eighteen leaves. Shred the remaining cabbage.

Put the bread in a medium bowl, and add water to cover. Let it soften while you make the pestata. In a food processor, combine the chunks of onion, carrot, celery, rosemary, sage, and garlic. Process to make a smooth pestata. Scrape half the pestata into a large bowl for the filling. Set aside the other half.

Squeeze all of the excess water out of the bread, and add the squeezed and crumbled bread to the bowl with the pestata. Add the sausage, egg, grated cheese, and parsley. Mix with your hands to make a cohesive stuffing.

Lay the cabbage leaves out, ribbed side down, so they are concave. Form about ¼ cup of filling into a ball, and place it in the middle of a leaf. Fold the sides in and roll the leaf up to make an enclosed bundle. Repeat with the remaining leaves.

For the sauce: Heat a large Dutch oven over medium heat. Add the olive oil. When the oil is hot, add the reserved pestata, and cook until it dries out and begins to stick to the bottom of the pot, about 4 minutes. Add the sliced onion and the remaining shredded cabbage and cook, stirring so nothing burns, until all is wilted, about 7 minutes.

Add the tomatoes, and fill the can and slosh it out into the pot twice with hot water. Stir in the salt, and bring the sauce to a simmer. Add the cabbage rolls, seam side down, in two layers. If necessary, add more water so the rolls are covered. Cover the pot with the lid ajar, and simmer until the cabbage is very tender, about 45 minutes.

🌿 If you don't get the full eighteen leaves from your cabbage to stuff, form any extra stuffing into meatballs and simmer them in the sauce along with the stuffed cabbages.

Oven-Braised Pork Chops with Red Onion and Pears

Costolette di Maiale Brasate al Forno con Pere e Cipolle
SERVES 4

2 cups balsamic vinegar
3 tablespoons extra-virgin olive oil
6 garlic cloves, crushed and peeled
4 center-cut pork rib chops, each about
　　12 ounces and 1¼ inches thick
1 large red onion, cut into 8 wedges
Kosher salt
Freshly ground black pepper
2 ripe but firm Bosc pears, peeled, cored, and cut
　　into 6 wedges each
¼ cup red wine vinegar
2 tablespoons honey

In a small saucepan, bring the balsamic vinegar to a boil over high heat. Adjust the heat to a gentle boil, and boil until the vinegar is syrupy and reduced to about ⅓ cup. Set aside.

Preheat the oven to 425 degrees. Heat the oil in a large ovenproof skillet over medium heat. Whack the garlic cloves with the flat side of a knife, and scatter them over the oil. Cook, shaking the skillet, until the garlic is brown, about 2 minutes. Lay the pork chops in, and cook until the undersides are browned, about 6 minutes. Remove and reserve the garlic cloves if they become darker than deep golden brown before the chops are fully browned. Turn the chops, tuck the onion

wedges into the pan, and continue cooking until the second side of each chop is browned, about 6 minutes. Season with salt and pepper. About halfway through browning the second side, tuck the pear wedges in between the chops.

Stir the red wine vinegar and honey together in a small bowl until the honey is dissolved. Pour this mixture into the skillet, and bring it to a vigorous boil. Return the garlic cloves to the skillet if you have removed them. Place the skillet in the oven, and roast until the onions and pears are tender and the juices from the pork are a rich, syrupy dark brown, about 30 minutes, turning everything once or twice during roasting.

Remove the skillet from the oven. Place a chop in the center of each warmed serving plate. Spoon the pears, onion, and pan juices around the chops. Drizzle the balsamic vinegar reduction around the edge of the plate.

Pork Tenderloin with Balsamic Onions

Filetto di Maiale con Cipolle all'Aceto Balsamico
SERVES 4 TO 6

2 pork tenderloins, trimmed (about 2 pounds)
5 tablespoons extra-virgin olive oil
1½ teaspoons kosher salt
3 cups thickly sliced yellow onions
3 cups thickly sliced red onions
2 cups thickly sliced shallots
3 fresh bay leaves
¼ cup balsamic vinegar

Cut the pork tenderloins in half crosswise. In a large bowl, toss the pork with 2 tablespoons of the olive oil and 1 teaspoon salt. Heat a large skillet over medium-high heat. When the skillet is hot, add the pork (without adding any oil to the skillet) and sear on all sides, about 8 minutes. Reduce the heat to medium, and continue to cook the pork, turning occasionally, until the internal temperature reads 145 degrees on an instant-read thermometer, about 10 to 15 minutes. Let the pork rest 5 minutes on a cutting board before slicing.

Meanwhile, in another large skillet over medium-high heat, heat the remaining 3 tablespoons olive oil. When the oil is hot, add the yellow onions, red onions, and shallots. Season with the remaining ½ teaspoon salt, and toss in the bay leaves. Cook and stir until the onions are completely wilted and golden, about 15 minutes. Reduce the heat to medium, and add the balsamic vinegar and ¼ cup water. Cover, and simmer until the onions are tender, about 10 minutes. Uncover, increase the heat to medium high, and cook, stirring, until the liquid is reduced to a syrupy glaze. Remove the bay leaves and keep the onions warm while you slice the pork.

Slice the pork into 1-inch-thick slices against the grain. Serve the pork on a bed of the balsamic onions.

❧ You can use any combination of onions you like, as long as you have about 8 cups in total.

Prune-Stuffed Roast Loin of Pork

Arrosto di Maiale alle Prugne
SERVES 8

8 ounces dried pitted prunes
½ cup bourbon
3-pound boneless center pork loin roast, trimmed
10 fresh sage leaves
Kosher salt
Freshly ground black pepper
2 tablespoons extra-virgin olive oil
½ cup finely diced carrot
½ cup finely diced celery
½ cup roughly chopped onion
4 garlic cloves, crushed and peeled
2½ cups Chicken Stock (page 143)

In a small bowl, soak the prunes in bourbon 1 hour. Preheat the oven to 450 degrees. Drain the prunes, and set four of them aside along with the soaking liquid.

To stuff the roast: Use a sharp knife to cut a 1-inch pocket along the entire length of the eye, around the top half of the roast, like forming a tunnel. Cut from both sides of the roast until you cut through.

Stuff three quarters of the soaked prunes into the slit in the roast, and tie the roast securely with kitchen twine at 2-inch intervals. Thread the sage leaves underneath the ties on either side of the roast. Season the roast generously with salt and pepper, and rub it with the olive oil.

Put the roast in a large roasting pan, and roast 15 minutes. Reduce the oven temperature to 400 degrees. Tilt the roasting pan, and spoon off excess fat. Scatter the carrot, celery, onion, and garlic around the roast. Roast an additional 15 minutes. Add the reserved prunes and soaking liquid, and roast 10 minutes. Pour the stock into the pan, and continue cooking, basting the roast occasionally with the pan juices, until a meat thermometer inserted into the thickest part of the roast registers 145 degrees, about 30 minutes more.

Remove the roast to a platter. Pass the contents of the pan through a food mill fitted with the fine disk into a small bowl. (Alternatively, strain the liquid through a sieve, pressing on the vegetables to extract as much liquid as possible and to force some of the vegetables through the sieve.) Skim all fat from the surface of the sauce. The sauce should be thick enough to coat a spoon lightly. If not, transfer it to a small saucepan and reduce a bit more. Season the sauce with salt and pepper, if needed. Cut the meat into ¼-inch slices, and serve it with the sauce.

Sauerkraut with Pork

Crauti Guarniti

SERVES 6 TO 8

1 pound smoked pork butt, halved
1 pound kielbasa
1 pound smoked pork ribs
2 tablespoons extra-virgin olive oil
4 pounds sauerkraut, rinsed well and drained
2 garlic cloves, thinly sliced
6 fresh bay leaves
Kosher salt
Freshly ground black pepper
Fresh horseradish (optional)

Put the pork butt, kielbasa, and ribs in a large Dutch oven with water to cover. Bring to a boil. Simmer 10 minutes, drain, reserve the meat, and clean out the pot.

To the Dutch oven, off the heat, add the olive oil. Add a layer of half of the sauerkraut. Sprinkle the garlic and bay leaves over the sauerkraut. Arrange the reserved meat over the seasonings. Cover it with the remaining sauerkraut. Pour in 2 cups water. Bring to a boil, reduce the heat to keep it at a simmer, and cover; cook, occasionally stirring from the bottom up, until the ribs are tender, about 45 minutes.

Remove the ribs and kielbasa and keep them warm in a low oven. Simmer the sauerkraut, stirring occasionally, until the rest of the pork is tender and the liquid in the pot is almost reduced away, about 20 to 30 minutes more. Remove the bay leaves and garlic, and season with salt and pepper.

Return the ribs and kielbasa to the pot, cover, and let sit off the heat 15 minutes. Slice the meats and arrange them on a serving platter, with the sauerkraut at center. Grate some fresh horseradish over the sliced meats, if desired.

Braised Pork Shanks with Fennel

Stinchi di Maiale Brasati con Finocchio

SERVES 6

4 meaty skinless pork shanks (about 7 to 8 pounds total)
1½ teaspoons kosher salt
All-purpose flour, for dredging
¼ cup extra-virgin olive oil
3 small fennel bulbs, trimmed, cored, and quartered, tops reserved
6 medium leeks, trimmed, washed, the white and light green parts cut into 2-inch chunks, the dark green parts reserved
2 cups Chicken Stock (page 143)
3 fresh bay leaves
1½ pounds Yukon gold potatoes, cut into 2-inch chunks

Preheat the oven to 400 degrees. Season the pork shanks with 1 teaspoon of the salt. Spread some flour on a rimmed sheet pan, and dredge the shanks in flour, tapping off the excess. Heat a large skillet over medium-high heat. Add 2 tablespoons of the olive oil. When the oil is hot, sear the shanks, in batches, on all sides until well browned, about 8 minutes per batch. Set the reserved fennel tops and dark green parts of the leeks in the bottom of a large roasting pan. Set the shanks on top. Add the chicken stock, 1 cup water, and the bay leaves. Cover with foil, and roast until the shanks are just tender and beginning to pull away from the bone, about 2 hours, basting periodically.

When the shanks are almost ready, heat the skillet again over medium-high heat. Add the remaining 2 tablespoons olive oil. Add the fennel bulbs and the chunked leeks and potatoes. Season with the remaining ½ teaspoon salt. Toss until the vegetables are light golden on the edges, about 10 minutes.

Remove the pork from the oven, remove the foil, fish out the leek greens and fennel tops, and discard them. Add the sautéed vegetables, and give everything a toss. Roast, uncovered, until the shanks and vegetables are very tender, about 35 to 40 minutes.

Remove the shanks to a cutting board and remove the bay leaves. Make a bed of the vegetables on a warmed platter, and cover them. Pour the pan juices into a spouted measuring cup (or a defatting cup if you have one), and skim off as much fat as possible. Holding the shank upright, carve off the meat and add it to the platter with the vegetables. Spoon the sauce over it, and serve.

Roasted Veal Shanks

Stinchi di Vitello Arrosto
SERVES 4

3 cups Mixed Meat Stock (page 144) or Chicken Stock (page 143)
2 whole veal shanks (about 2½ pounds each)
1 teaspoon kosher salt
Freshly ground black pepper
¼ cup extra-virgin olive oil
1 large carrot, peeled and chopped
1 large celery stalk, chopped
1 small onion, sliced
2 garlic cloves, crushed and peeled
2 tablespoons fresh rosemary leaves
6 fresh sage leaves
1 cup dry white wine

Preheat the oven to 450 degrees. Heat the stock in a small saucepan just to a simmer, and keep it hot. Season the shanks with ½ teaspoon of the salt and some pepper. Heat a large roasting pan over medium-high heat, and add the olive oil. When the oil is hot, add the veal, and brown all over, about 6 minutes. Transfer the pan to the oven, and roast 30 minutes, turning once. Pour off any excess fat from the pan, leaving just a film at the bottom.

To the roasting pan, add the carrot, celery,

onion, garlic, rosemary, sage, remaining salt, and wine, and stir to collect the browned bits from the bottom of the pan. Add 2 cups of the hot stock, and roast—turning and basting the shanks occasionally, and adding more stock as needed to keep the vegetables and veal from burning—until the veal is very tender, about 1½ hours.

Remove the shanks, and scrape the vegetables and pan juices into a sieve. Press through with a wooden spoon to extract as much sauce as possible and some vegetable purée. Skim off any excess fat from the top of the sauce. Return the sauce (and any stock you haven't used) and meat to the roasting pan, baste the meat with the sauce, and return to the oven until the sauce is syrupy and forms a glaze on the meat, about 10 minutes. When it is done, let it rest for 5 to 10 minutes

To serve: Hold the shank by the bone with a kitchen towel on a cutting board, and carve off the meat by slicing it down vertically along the bone. Serve it topped with the sauce left in the pan.

Meatloaf with Ricotta

Polpettone di Manzo con Ricotta
SERVES 8

1 cup milk
3 cups day-old country-bread cubes
3 pounds ground beef
3 large eggs, beaten
1 pound drained fresh ricotta (about 2 cups), plus more for the sauce if you like
1 bunch scallions, trimmed and finely chopped (about 1 cup)
½ cup freshly grated Grana Padano
¼ cup chopped fresh Italian parsley
½ teaspoon freshly grated nutmeg
1 tablespoon kosher salt
Freshly ground black pepper to taste
8 ounces fresh mozzarella, cut into ½-inch cubes (about 2 cups)

¼ cup extra-virgin olive oil
4 to 5 cups Tomato Sauce (page 161)

Preheat the oven to 375 degrees. Pour the milk over the bread cubes in a bowl, and let them soak for a few minutes, until the bread is saturated. Squeeze out as much milk as you can, then crumble the bread into a large bowl. Crumble the ground beef into the bowl, and add the eggs, ricotta, scallions, grated cheese, parsley, nutmeg, salt, and pepper. Mix well with your hands. Add the mozzarella cubes, and mix just to distribute evenly.

Brush a large roasting pan with 2 tablespoons of the olive oil. Gather the meat mixture in the bowl, turn it into the pan, and shape it into a fat oval loaf. Drizzle with the remaining 2 tablespoons olive oil. Cover the pan with foil—tent it so the foil doesn't touch the meat—and bake 45 minutes. Remove the foil, and continue to bake until the meatloaf is browned all over and completely cooked through, another 1 hour and 30 minutes or so. (If you check the loaf with a meat thermometer, it should reach a temperature of 165 degrees.) Remove it from the oven, and let it rest for about 10 minutes.

Heat the tomato sauce to a simmer in a saucepan as the meat rests. Turn off the heat, and, if you like, stir ½ cup or so fresh ricotta into the sauce. Slice the meatloaf, and serve with the sauce.

❧ Most of you have made meatloaf on occasion; you may even have a family-favorite recipe that you make frequently. Well, I want to introduce you to the Marchegiano style of meatloaf, with ricotta added to the mix, which renders the loaf tender and tasty—not heavy and dense, as they so often are. Another textural delight in this loaf is the cubes of mozzarella, oozing and moist when the meatloaf is served hot and fresh from the oven. However, if you plan on having extra meatloaf to enjoy the next day—I think it is almost better that way—omit the mozzarella, because the cubes harden and won't melt again. In this case, use an additional cup of ricotta in the loaf mix.

Meatballs with Eggplant

Polpette con Melanzane
SERVES 10 OR MORE

SAUCE
¼ cup extra-virgin olive oil
2 medium onions, chopped
Four 28-ounce cans Italian plum tomatoes, preferably San Marzano, passed through a food mill
2 teaspoons kosher salt
3 fresh bay leaves
½ teaspoon crushed red pepper flakes

MEATBALLS
¼ cup extra-virgin olive oil
1 medium onion, chopped
2 medium eggplants (about 1¼ pounds), peeled and cut into ½-inch cubes
2 teaspoons kosher salt
2½ pounds ground beef
1 pound sweet Italian sausage, removed from casings
2 cups fine dried bread crumbs
½ cup chopped fresh Italian parsley
½ cup freshly grated Grana Padano
2 large eggs

For the sauce: In a large Dutch oven, heat the olive oil over medium-high heat. Add the chopped onions, and cook until it is slightly softened, about 4 minutes. Add the tomatoes, rinse out the tomato cans with 4 cups water, and add that as well. Add the salt, bay leaves, and red pepper flakes. Bring it to a simmer, and cook, uncovered, until slightly thickened, about 20 minutes.

Meanwhile, for the meatballs: In a large skillet, heat the olive oil over medium-high heat. When the oil is hot, add the onion. Cook until it is almost softened, about 6 minutes, then add the eggplants and season with salt. Cover, and cook until the eggplant and onion are tender, about 10 minutes. Scrape everything onto a sheet pan to cool.

In a large bowl, mix the cooled eggplant with the beef, sausage, bread crumbs, parsley, grated cheese, and eggs until the mixture just holds together. Form into about forty 2-inch meatballs on parchment-lined sheet pans.

Add the meatballs to the simmering sauce, and simmer until the meatballs are cooked through and the sauce is flavorful, about 35 to 40 minutes, stirring occasionally with a wooden spoon, to make sure the meatballs on the bottom don't stick.

❧ This makes a big batch, and it is ideal to keep in the refrigerator or freeze to be used for future meals. If you don't want to make such a big batch, you can easily halve everything.

Stuffed Peppers

Peperoni Farciti con Carne
SERVES 6

3 tablespoons extra-virgin olive oil
1 large onion, chopped
One 28-ounce can whole San Marzano tomatoes, crushed by hand
1 tablespoon dried oregano, preferably Sicilian on the branch
2 teaspoons kosher salt
¼ teaspoon crushed red pepper flakes
5 cups crustless day-old bread cubes
2 pounds ground pork
½ cup freshly grated Grana Padano
2 large eggs, beaten
6 medium bell peppers (red, yellow, or orange)

Heat a Dutch oven large enough to hold the peppers upright in one layer over medium heat. Add the olive oil. When the oil is hot, add the onion, and cook until softened, about 10 minutes. Spoon about half of the onion into a large bowl to cool.

To the onion in the pot, add the tomatoes,

slosh out the can with 2 cups water, and add that, too. Season with 2 teaspoons of the oregano, 1 teaspoon of the salt, and the red pepper flakes. Let this simmer while you stuff the peppers.

Put the bread cubes in a medium bowl with water to cover. Let them soak 5 minutes. Squeeze all of the excess liquid out of the bread, and add the squeezed bread to the cooled onion in the bowl. Add the ground pork, grated cheese, eggs, remaining teaspoon oregano, and remaining teaspoon salt. Mix with your hands to make a cohesive stuffing.

Cut the tops from the peppers, remove the seeds and ribs, and divide the stuffing among them. Nestle the peppers in the sauce, cover, and simmer until the filling is cooked through and the peppers are tender, about 1 hour.

Serve topped with sauce. Mashed potatoes are also traditionally served.

Pan-Seared Steak with Pizzaiola Sauce

Bistecca alla Pizzaiola
SERVES 4

4 tablespoons extra-virgin olive oil
3 garlic cloves, thinly sliced
1 red bell pepper, seeded and cut into 1-inch strips
1 yellow bell pepper, seeded and cut into 1-inch strips
2 cups sliced white button mushrooms
1¼ teaspoons kosher salt
½ teaspoon dried oregano, preferably Sicilian on the branch
One 14-ounce can Italian plum tomatoes, preferably San Marzano, crushed by hand
Four 8-ounce bone-in shell steaks, about 1 inch thick

Heat 3 tablespoons of the olive oil in a large skillet over medium-high heat. When the oil is hot, add the sliced garlic. Let the garlic sizzle a minute, then toss in the bell peppers and mushrooms. Season with 1 teaspoon of the salt and the oregano. Sauté until the mushrooms and peppers are caramelized on the edges, about 5 minutes.

Pour in the tomatoes, slosh out the can with ½ cup hot water, and add that to the skillet as well. Bring it to a simmer, and cook, uncovered, until the sauce is thickened and the peppers break down, about 12 to 15 minutes.

Season the steaks with the remaining tablespoon of olive oil and ¼ teaspoon salt. Sear the steaks in a large cast-iron skillet over high heat until they are done to your liking, about 3 to 4 minutes per side for medium rare, less time for a rare steak (2 minutes). Let the steaks rest for a few minutes while the sauce finishes cooking.

To serve: Put the steaks on plates, and top them with the pepper sauce. Serve immediately.

Seared Beef Fillet with Mushroom Sauce

Filetto di Manzo ai Funghi
SERVES 4

STEAK
Four 6-ounce beef fillets
2 tablespoons extra-virgin olive oil
2 sprigs fresh rosemary, torn into rough pieces
½ teaspoon kosher salt

MUSHROOMS
3 tablespoons extra-virgin olive oil
3 large shallots, sliced (about 1½ cups)
1 pound mixed mushrooms, sliced (cremini, shiitake, button, oyster, chanterelle, porcini)
2 tablespoons tomato paste
2 sprigs fresh rosemary
½ teaspoon kosher salt

½ cup dry Marsala
½ cup dry white wine

For the steaks: In a shallow baking dish, combine the steaks with the olive oil, rosemary pieces, and salt. Let them marinate while you prepare the mushrooms.

For the mushrooms: In a large skillet, heat the olive oil over medium heat. Add the shallots, and cook until they begin to soften, about 4 minutes. Add the mushrooms, and cook until they release their liquid and soften, about 8 to 10 minutes.

Increase the heat to high, and reduce away any excess liquid. Once the skillet is dry, make a space in the pan and drop in the tomato paste. Let it toast in this hot spot for a minute or two, then stir it into the mushrooms. Add the rosemary, and season the mushrooms with the salt. Add the Marsala and white wine, and simmer until the mushrooms are tender and glazed with the cooking juices, about 10 to 12 minutes. Remove the rosemary.

While the mushrooms simmer, cook the steaks. Heat another large skillet over high heat. When the skillet is very hot, remove the steaks from the marinade, picking off any rosemary pieces, and add them to the skillet. Sear until they are well browned on both sides, about 3 to 4 minutes per side for medium rare. Let them rest on a cutting board for 5 minutes.

Divide the mushrooms among four serving plates. Top each serving with a piece of steak, and serve immediately. Or set the steaks on hot plates and top with hot mushroom sauce.

❧ Shell or rib steaks are also delicious prepared this way; just keep in mind the cooking time for the meat temperature you desire and adjust accordingly.

Beef Braised in Barolo

Stufato di Manzo al Barolo
SERVES 6 OR MORE

5-pound boneless beef-roast (flat-iron, chuck, or bottom round), trimmed of fat
2 teaspoons kosher salt, plus more to taste
⅓ cup extra-virgin olive oil
2 medium onions (1 pound total), quartered
3 large carrots, peeled and cut into 2-inch chunks
4 celery stalks, cut into 2-inch chunks
6 plump garlic cloves, crushed and peeled
2 sprigs fresh rosemary
6 large fresh sage leaves
¼ teaspoon freshly grated nutmeg
1 teaspoon black peppercorns
1 cup loosely packed dried porcini mushrooms, rinsed
2 bottles Barolo (750 milliliters each)
2 cups Mixed Meat Stock (page 144), or as needed
Freshly ground black pepper

Preheat the oven to 250 degrees. Season the roast with half the salt. Heat the olive oil in a large Dutch oven set over medium-high heat. Brown the roast on all sides, about 8 minutes in all, then remove it to a platter.

Add the onions, carrots, celery, and garlic, and cook until the onions begin to wilt, about 6 minutes. Add the rosemary, sage leaves, grated nutmeg, peppercorns, dried porcini, and remaining teaspoon salt, and toss all together. Cook for 3 or 4 minutes, just until the vegetables soften, stirring frequently and scraping up the browned meat bits on the pan bottom; then lower the heat.

Push the vegetables to the side, and return the seared roast to the cleared side of the pan. Pour in the bottles of wine and any meat juices that collected on the platter. The roast should be at least half submerged, so add beef stock as needed.

Cover the pot, and heat until the wine is steaming but not boiling. Uncover the pan, and place it in the oven. After 30 minutes, rotate the roast so the exposed meat is submerged in the braising liquid. Braise this way, turning the meat in the pan every 30 minutes, for about 3 hours, until the meat is fork-tender. The liquid should not boil; if it does, pour in some cold water to stop the bubbling, and lower the oven temperature.

After about 2½ hours or so, check the beef. If it is easily pierced with a fork, take the pan from the oven. Remove the meat to a platter, with the carrots and celery. Skim any fat from the braising juices, heat them to a boil, and reduce until the sauce coats the back of a spoon. Pour it through a sieve set over a clean container. Press the juices well from the strained herbs and remaining vegetable pieces. Pour in any juices from the meat platter, and season the sauce to taste with salt and freshly ground black pepper. (If you are not going to serve it right away, put the meat and reserved vegetables in the sauce to rest and cool, for a couple of hours or overnight.)

To serve: Slice the meat crosswise (easiest when it is cool). Pour a shallow layer of sauce into a wide skillet, and lay the slices in, overlapping. Heat the sauce to bubbling, spooning it over the beef, so the slices are lightly coated. Lift them with a broad spatula, and slide them onto a warm platter, fanned out. Heat the carrots and celery in the sauce, too, and arrange them on the platter. Serve, passing more heated sauce at the table.

Braised Beef Rolls

Braciole di Manzo in Sugo
SERVES 6

BRACIOLE
1½ cups milk
2 cups crustless ½-inch day-old Italian-bread cubes
2 hard-boiled eggs, coarsely chopped
¼ cup chopped fresh Italian parsley

¼ cup freshly grated Grana Padano

¼ cup raisins

¼ cup toasted pine nuts

1 garlic clove, finely chopped

2 pounds beef bottom round, cut into 12 slices, each about ½ inch thick

12 slices imported Italian prosciutto (about 6 ounces)

¼ pound imported provola or provolone, cut into ¼-by-2-inch sticks

Kosher salt

Freshly ground black pepper

SAUCE

3 tablespoons extra-virgin olive oil

2 small onions, chopped

2 garlic cloves, finely chopped

½ cup dry red wine

One 35-ounce can Italian plum tomatoes, preferably San Marzano, crushed by hand

3 tablespoons tomato paste

2 fresh bay leaves

Kosher salt to taste

Crushed red pepper flakes to taste

To make the stuffing: Pour the milk into a medium bowl, add the bread cubes, and let them soak until they are very soft, 20 to 30 minutes. Drain the bread, squeeze out excess milk from the cubes with your hands, and return the bread to the bowl. Stir in the chopped eggs, parsley, grated cheese, raisins, pine nuts, and garlic. Mix well, and set aside.

With the toothed side of a heavy meat mallet, pound each slice of beef round to a thickness of about ¼ inch. Arrange one of the pounded meat slices in front of you with one of the short sides closest to you. Top with a slice of prosciutto, and tap the prosciutto with the back side of a knife so it adheres to the beef. Spread 2 tablespoons of the stuffing over the beef slice, leaving a 1-inch border around the edges. Place a stick of provolone crosswise over the edge of the stuffing closest to you. Fold the border over the provolone, then fold the side borders in to overlap the edges of the

stuffing. Roll into a compact roll. Secure the end flap with a toothpick. Repeat with the remaining beef and stuffing, then season the rolls with salt and pepper.

For the sauce: Heat the olive oil in a large Dutch oven over medium heat. Stir in the onions and garlic, and cook until the onions are wilted, about 5 minutes. Add as many of the braciole as will fit in a single layer, and cook, turning the braciole as necessary, until they are golden on all sides, about 7 minutes. If necessary, repeat with any remaining braciole.

Add the wine, and cook until most of it has evaporated. Stir in the tomatoes, and bring to a boil. Add the tomato paste and bay leaves, and stir until the paste is dissolved. Season lightly with salt and crushed red pepper, adjust the heat so the liquid is simmering, and cook, adding water as necessary to keep the braciole completely submerged, until the beef is tender, about 3 hours.

Remove the bay leaves and the toothpicks from the braciole before serving. The braciole can be prepared up to 2 days in advance and stored in their sauce, then reheated over low heat until heated through, adding half a cup of water in the heating process if too dense.

Beef Braised in Beer

Manzo Brasato alla Birra
SERVES 6

4 ounces thick-sliced slab bacon, cut into pieces

3 medium onions, cut into chunks

1 tablespoon kosher salt

4-to-5-pound boneless beef shoulder roast (preferably a top blade or top chuck shoulder)

¼ cup all-purpose flour

4 tablespoons extra-virgin olive oil

5 sprigs fresh thyme, tied in a bundle with kitchen twine

Two 12-ounce bottles flavorful beer or ale
6 cups Chicken Stock (page 143), or as needed
3 tablespoons Dijon mustard

Preheat the oven to 375 degrees. Put the chunks of bacon and onion and a teaspoon of the salt in the food processor, and pulse together to a fine-textured pestata.

Trim the beef of fat, and season with 1 teaspoon salt. Spread the flour on a plate, and dredge the roast thoroughly; shake off any excess. Heat the olive oil in a large Dutch oven over medium-high heat. Brown the beef well, until it is nicely colored all over, about 10 minutes. Push the meat to one side of the pan, drop the pestata into the pan, and stir and cook it on the pan bottom until it has dried out and just begins to stick, about 5 minutes. Move the meat back to the center of the pan, drop in the bundle of thyme sprigs, and pour the beer in around the roast. Bring the beer to a boil, stirring and scraping up any brown bits from the pan bottom. Pour in enough stock so the braising liquid comes halfway up the sides of the roast, and sprinkle the remaining teaspoon salt all over. Cover the pan, bring the liquid quickly to a boil, and then set it into the heated oven.

After 2 hours, lift the cover, drop the 3 tablespoons mustard into the braising liquid, stir carefully, cover again, and braise another hour. Remove the cover, and continue the oven braising, stirring the bottom of the pan occasionally, to thicken and intensify the flavor of the sauce, about 30 minutes more. Remove the bundle of herbs. Lift the meat onto a cutting board, and cut it crosswise into ½-inch-thick slices. Fan the slices on a warm platter, skim off any fat from the surface of the pan sauce, and ladle some of it over the meat. Serve right away, passing more sauce at the table.

❧ Beef chuck, or shoulder, offers excellent cuts for stews and braises, because the meat is extremely tasty and, over long cooking, all the connective tissue adds flavor and body to the dish. For this braise, I especially like the compact chunk of meat cut off the top of the shoulder blade, which is known by many names, including "top blade" or "top chuck shoulder" or "flat-iron." This piece is usually sliced and packaged as steaks, but ask your butcher to give you a whole top blade, as a roast. The more common beef chuck or shoulder roast, which comes from the underside of the shoulder, would be fine in this recipe, too. (It might be called "chuck pot roast" or "underblade chuck.")

Braised Beef with Onions

Manzo Brasato con Cipolle
SERVES 6 OR MORE

6 garlic cloves, crushed and peeled
3 medium onions, cut into chunks
3 celery stalks, cut into chunks
2 carrots, peeled and cut into chunks
½ cup sliced almonds
¼ cup extra-virgin olive oil
5-pound beef rump roast
1 tablespoon kosher salt
6 whole cloves
2 tablespoons tomato paste
3 cups dry white wine
4 fresh bay leaves

In a food processor, combine the garlic and onions, and process to make a smooth paste. Scrape it into a bowl. Without washing the food-processor bowl, add the celery, carrots, and almonds to the processor, and process to a paste.

In a large Dutch oven, heat the olive oil over medium-high heat.

Season the roast with a teaspoon of the salt, and brown on all sides, about 8 minutes. Remove it to a plate, and stud it with the cloves.

Add the onion-garlic mixture to the pot, and cook, stirring occasionally, until the mixture has dried out and begins to stick to the bottom of the pan, about 7 minutes. Add the vegetable-almond mixture, reduce the heat to medium, and cook until the mixture has dried out, stirring often to keep the almonds from burning, about 4 minutes.

Make a space in the bottom of the pan, and add the tomato paste. Cook and stir in this hot spot until it toasts and darkens a shade or two, about 2 minutes, then stir it into the vegetables. Pour in the white wine, bring it to a boil, and boil until it is reduced by about half, about 6 minutes. Add the roast, and pour in 6 cups hot water (or enough just to cover the roast in liquid). Add the bay leaves, and season with the remaining 2 teaspoons salt. Cover, simmer gently, and cook, turning the meat occasionally, until it is very tender and a knife inserted in the center slides out very easily, about 3 to 3½ hours. You may need to add a little more water if it reduces too quickly; you want to keep at least three-quarters of the meat covered in liquid until the end. Let the meat rest in the sauce for 30 minutes, remove the bay leaves, then cut into thin slices, and serve topped with the hot sauce.

Season the short ribs with 1 teaspoon of the salt. Heat a large Dutch oven over medium-high heat. Add the olive oil. When the oil is hot, add the short ribs and the garlic. Cook to brown the ribs on all sides, about 8 to 10 minutes in all. Remove the ribs to a plate, and discard the garlic.

Drain most of the fat from the pot, leaving about 2 tablespoons behind. Put the pot over medium heat, and add the red wine. Bring it to a simmer, and slowly reduce by half, about 15 minutes. Add the remaining ½ teaspoon salt, the oregano, and crushed red pepper flakes. Add the tomatoes, slosh out the can with 2 cups water, and add that, too. Pour in the stock. Bring it to a simmer, and add the short ribs back to the pot. Simmer, uncovered, until the short ribs are almost tender, about 1 hour.

After 1 hour, add the onions, and simmer 15 minutes. Add the bell peppers, and simmer until the ribs and vegetables are very tender, about 15 minutes more, increasing the heat at the end of the cooking time if the sauce is too liquid. Serve with Basic Polenta (page 199).

Short Ribs Pizzaiola

Costolette di Manzo alla Pizzaiola
SERVES 4 TO 6

4 pounds beef short ribs
1½ teaspoons kosher salt
¼ cup extra-virgin olive oil
6 garlic cloves, crushed and peeled
2 cups dry red wine
2 teaspoons dried oregano, preferably Sicilian on the branch
½ teaspoon crushed red pepper flakes
One 28-ounce can Italian plum tomatoes, preferably San Marzano, crushed by hand
2 cups Chicken Stock (page 143)
3 medium onions, quartered but left attached at the root end
3 small bell peppers (red, yellow, or orange), seeded and cut into 2-inch strips

Braised Beef in Guazzetto

Manzo in Guazzetto
SERVES 6 TO 8

½ cup dried porcini mushrooms
4 cups Chicken Stock (page 143)
¼ cup extra-virgin olive oil
3 pounds boneless beef-stew meat, such as chuck, cut into 1-inch cubes
1 teaspoon kosher salt
Freshly ground black pepper
2 large onions, chopped
2 beef marrow bones, about 3 inches long
2 tablespoons tomato paste
3 fresh bay leaves
Pinch of ground cloves
1 cup dry red wine

In a spouted measuring cup, combine the porcini and 1 cup very hot water. Let the mushrooms soak 10 minutes. Drain and chop them. Strain the soaking liquid, and reserve. Heat the chicken stock in a medium saucepan to a bare simmer, and keep it hot.

In a large Dutch oven over medium heat, heat the olive oil. Season the beef with ½ teaspoon salt and some pepper. Brown the beef in batches, removing it to a plate as it is browned, about 4 minutes per batch. Add the onions and bones, and season with the remaining ½ teaspoon salt. Cook and stir until the onions are softened, about 8 minutes.

Make a space in the pan, and add the tomato paste. Cook and stir the paste in that hot spot until it toasts and darkens a shade or two, about 2 minutes. Stir the tomato paste into the onions, and add the chopped porcini, bay leaves, and cloves. Add the wine, and cook until it is reduced by half, about 3 minutes. Add the beef, 2 cups of the hot chicken stock, and the porcini liquid. Cover, and simmer gently, adding the stock in two more additions, until the meat is very tender and falling apart, about 1 hour and 15 minutes. If the meat is tender but the sauce is still soupy, uncover the pan and reduce over medium-high heat, stirring often so it doesn't burn, to get a thick, chunky sauce. Serve with Garganelli (page 223) or Basic Polenta (page 199).

1 pound mixed mushrooms, thickly sliced
2 large shallots, finely chopped (about ½ cup)
½ cup dry Marsala
1 cup Chicken Stock (page 143)
¼ cup chopped fresh Italian parsley

In a large skillet, melt 4 tablespoons of the butter with 2 tablespoons of the oil over medium heat. Spread some flour on a rimmed plate or sheet pan. Season the veal all over with the salt, and dredge it lightly in the flour, tapping off the excess. Add the veal to the skillet, moving it around so it all fits, and cook until it is lightly browned and caramelized on the edges, about 1 to 2 minutes per side. Remove the veal to a plate.

Increase the heat to medium high, and add the remaining 2 tablespoons olive oil and the sage leaves to the skillet. Once the sage is sizzling, add the mushrooms and shallots. Add about 2 tablespoons of the Marsala, to get the mushrooms cooking. Cook and stir until the mushrooms have released their liquid and all the liquid has cooked away, about 3 to 4 minutes. Pour in the rest of the Marsala and the stock. Bring it to a rapid simmer, cook until the sauce has reduced by half, and then whisk in the remaining 2 tablespoons butter in pieces.

Return the veal to the sauce, and simmer until it is just cooked through, about 1 to 2 minutes. Stir in the chopped parsley, and serve.

Veal Scaloppine with Marsala and Mushrooms

Scaloppine di Vitello al Marsala con Funghi
SERVES 4

6 tablespoons unsalted butter
¼ cup extra-virgin olive oil
All-purpose flour, for dredging
8 slices veal scaloppine (about 1½ pounds)
½ teaspoon kosher salt
6 large fresh sage leaves

Scaloppine Saltimbocca with Spinach

Saltimbocca alla Romana
SERVES 4

SPINACH
1 bunch spinach (about 1 pound), stemmed
2 tablespoons extra-virgin olive oil
3 garlic cloves, crushed and peeled
Kosher salt to taste
Freshly ground black pepper to taste

SCALOPPINE

8 slices veal scaloppine (about 1½ pounds)
Kosher salt to taste
Freshly ground black pepper to taste
4 slices imported Italian prosciutto (about
    2 ounces), halved crosswise
8 large fresh sage leaves
All-purpose flour, for dredging
3 tablespoons extra-virgin olive oil, or as needed
6 tablespoons unsalted butter
¼ cup dry white wine
1 cup Chicken Stock (page 143)

For the spinach: Wash the spinach, but don't dry it completely; the water that clings to the leaves will steam the spinach as it cooks. Heat the olive oil in a large skillet over medium heat. Add the garlic, and cook, shaking the pan, until it is golden, about 2 minutes. Scatter the spinach into the pan, a large handful at a time. Season lightly with salt and pepper, and cover the pan. Cook until the spinach begins to release its liquid. Uncover the pan, and cook, stirring, until the spinach is wilted and its water has evaporated, 1 to 3 minutes. Taste, and season it with additional salt and pepper if necessary. Remove it from the heat, cover, and keep it warm while you make the veal.

For the scaloppine: Season them with salt and pepper. Cover each with a half-slice of the prosciutto. Tap the prosciutto with the back of a knife so it adheres well to the meat. Center a sage leaf over the prosciutto, and fasten it in place with a toothpick, weaving the toothpick in and out as if you were taking a stitch.

Spread the flour on a rimmed plate or sheet pan. Dredge the scaloppine in the flour to coat both sides lightly, then shake off excess flour. Heat the olive oil and 2 tablespoons of the butter in a large skillet over medium heat until the butter is foaming. Slip as many of the scaloppine, prosciutto side down, into the pan as fit without touching. Cook just until the prosciutto is light golden, about 2 minutes. Turn, and cook until the second side is slightly browned, about 2 minutes. Remove them, and drain on paper towels.

Repeat with the remaining scaloppine, adding more oil if necessary.

Remove all the scaloppine from the skillet, and pour off the oil. Return the pan to the heat, and pour in the wine. Add the remaining butter, and cook until the wine is reduced by about half. Pour in the chicken stock, and bring it to a vigorous boil. Tuck the scaloppine into the sauce. Simmer until the sauce is reduced and slightly thickened, about 3 to 4 minutes. Taste, and season with salt and pepper if necessary.

To serve: Spoon the hot spinach in a mound in the center of each plate. Arrange two pieces of the saltimbocca over the spinach. Spoon some of the pan sauce over the scaloppine and serve immediately.

Veal Roll-Ups

Involtini di Vitello
SERVES 6

2½ pounds boneless veal shoulder
1½ cups shredded low-moisture mozzarella
½ cup freshly grated Grana Padano
1 teaspoon kosher salt
2 cups baby spinach leaves
All-purpose flour, for dredging
2 tablespoons unsalted butter
2 tablespoons extra-virgin olive oil
8 fresh sage leaves
6 small or 4 medium leeks, white and light green
    parts, trimmed, halved lengthwise, and cut
    into 1-inch pieces
½ cup dry white wine
1 cup Chicken Stock (page 143)

Slice the veal, against the grain of the meat, into twelve slices. Pound these to an even thickness of about ⅛ inch. In a medium bowl, toss together the mozzarella and grated cheese.

Lay the veal slices out flat on your cutting board, and season with ½ teaspoon kosher salt.

Divide the spinach leaves among the veal slices, laying them flat and pressing with the palm of your hand so they adhere. Gently pack the cheese in your hand to form twelve small log shapes, and lay one of them on the lower third of each veal slice. Fold the sides in, then the bottom flap up over the filling. Roll up the log and seal the seam with a toothpick. Repeat with the remaining veal.

Spread the flour on a rimmed sheet pan. In a large Dutch oven, over medium heat, melt the butter in the olive oil. Add the sage leaves. Lightly dredge the rolls in flour, and tap off the excess. Brown the rolls, in batches, on all sides, about 6 minutes per batch. Remove the rolls to a plate as they brown.

Once all of the rolls are out of the pot, add the leeks, and season with the remaining ½ teaspoon salt. Cook until the leeks have wilted, about 8 minutes. Add the wine, and boil until it is reduced by half, about 2 to 3 minutes. Add the stock, and bring to a simmer. Add the rolls, return to a simmer, and cover. Cook until the veal is tender, about 20 minutes.

Remove the rolls to a platter. Bring the sauce to a boil and reduce to thicken and intensify the flavor, about 3 minutes. Spoon the sauce and leeks over the veal, and serve.

Veal Chops Stuffed with Fontina

Costolette di Vitello Farcite con Fontina
SERVES 6

6 bone-in veal rib chops, about 1½ inches thick (about 8 to 10 ounces each)
2 teaspoons kosher salt
8 ounces Italian Fontina, shredded
1 cup freshly grated Grana Padano
4 tablespoons unsalted butter
1 tablespoon extra-virgin olive oil
All-purpose flour, for dredging
12 fresh sage leaves

1 tablespoon tomato paste
2 cups dry white wine
½ cup Chicken Stock (page 143)

Preheat the oven to 400 degrees. Trim the chops, leaving only a thin layer of fat on the edge. With a sharp, thin knife, slice horizontally into the outer edge of each chop, splitting the meaty portion in two almost all the way to the bone, forming a pocket for stuffing. With the mallet, pound each flap of the chop meat to ½ inch thick. Season with 1 teaspoon salt. In a medium bowl, toss together the shredded Fontina and the grated Grana Padano, and divide the cheeses into six equal portions. Lightly compress the cheese portions into oval patties, and slip them into the sliced chop pockets. Fold the bottom meat flap over the top flap, enclosing the cheese, and thread a toothpick through both flaps to keep them together.

Melt 2 tablespoons of the butter in the olive oil in a large skillet over medium-high heat. Spread the flour on a plate, dredge each chop on both sides, shake off excess flour, and lay each chop in the pan. When all the chops are in the pan, drop the sage leaves in between them. Cook the chops until they are well browned on both sides, about 5 minutes. Clear a space in the pan bottom, drop in the tomato paste, and toast it in the hot spot for a minute. Pour the wine over the tomato paste, stir them together, and shake the pan to distribute the liquid. Boil until it is reduced by half, about 3 to 4 minutes.

Add the remaining butter, and whisk it into the pan liquid. Turn the chops over, pour in the chicken stock, sprinkle on the remaining salt, and bring the liquid to a boil. Cover the pan, and place it in the oven. Roast for about 15 minutes, then remove the cover and roast until the chops are cooked through and the sauce has thickened, about 10 minutes more. Remove the pan from the oven, and place the chops on a warm platter. If the sauce is too thin, put the pan over high heat and reduce it until it coats the back of a spoon.

Braised Veal Shanks

Ossobuco
SERVES 6

4 fresh bay leaves
1 large sprig fresh rosemary
3 cups Chicken Stock (page 143), or more as
    needed
¼ cup extra-virgin olive oil
Six 2-to-3-inch-thick veal shanks, tied around
    the circumference
1 teaspoon kosher salt, plus more to taste
1 large onion, cut into 1-inch-thick chunks
2 medium carrots, peeled and cut into 1-inch
    chunks
2 celery stalks cut into 1-inch chunks
3 tablespoons tomato paste
1 cup dry white wine
6 whole cloves
2 small oranges, skin of 1 peeled in thick strips
    with a vegetable peeler, 1 zest grated

Tie the bay leaves and rosemary together with
string. Pour the chicken broth into a small pot,
and keep it warm over low heat.

Heat the olive oil in a large Dutch oven over
medium heat. Season the veal shanks with the
salt. When the oil is hot, add the shanks and
brown on all sides, about 6 to 7 minutes in all.
Remove the browned shanks to a plate.

Add the onion, carrots, and celery to the Dutch
oven. Cook until the onion begins to soften and
all of the vegetables are caramelized, about 5 minutes. Push aside the vegetables to clear a dry spot
in the pan, and add the tomato paste. Let it toast
for a minute or two in this hot spot, then stir it
into the vegetables. Add the wine and the herb
package. Bring the wine to a boil, and cook until
it is reduced by half, about 3 minutes. Drop in the
cloves and the orange peel (reserve the zest from
the other orange for later). Return the veal shanks
to the pot in one layer, and pour the chicken stock
over the top until it is almost but not quite covering the shanks. Adjust the heat so the liquid is

simmering, cover, and cook until the veal shanks
are tender, about 1½ hours.

Once the meat is tender, uncover the pan, and
remove the vegetable chunks to a platter. Put the
veal shanks on top of the vegetables. Discard the
bay-leaf-and-rosemary package. Bring the liquid
in the Dutch oven to a boil, and cook it down
until it is dense and coats the spoon, about 4
to 5 minutes. Remove the strings from the osso
buco. Pour the sauce through a strainer directly
over the osso buco on the platter, pressing on any
remaining vegetable solids with a wooden spoon.
Sprinkle the orange zest over the top, and serve.

Veal Roast with Dried Cherries

Arrosto di Vitello con Ciliegie
SERVES 6 TO 8

2 medium onions, quartered but left attached at
    the root end
6 sprigs fresh sage
6 garlic cloves, crushed and peeled
4-pound boneless veal shoulder roast, tied
2 tablespoons extra-virgin olive oil
2½ teaspoons kosher salt
Freshly ground black pepper
Juice and zest of 1 orange, zest removed in long
    strips with a vegetable peeler
1 cup dry Marsala
1 cup dried cherries
2 cups Chicken Stock (page 143)
2 tablespoons unsalted butter, cut into pieces

Preheat the oven to 450 degrees. In a large roasting pan, make a bed of the onions, sage sprigs,
and garlic. Rub the veal all over with the olive
oil, and season it with 2 teaspoons of the salt and
some pepper. Set the roast on the vegetables, and
roast until everything begins to brown, about 20
minutes.

Reduce the oven temperature to 375 degrees.

Pour in the orange zest and juice, the Marsala, the dried cherries, and 1 cup stock. Tent the pan with foil, not touching the meat, and roast until the veal is tender, about 1 hour and 15 minutes to 1½ hours more.

Remove the meat to a cutting board to rest. Set the roasting pan on the stovetop, and remove and discard the herb sprigs, garlic, and orange zest. Put the onion wedges on a platter, and keep them warm. Bring the sauce to a rapid simmer, and add the remaining 1 cup stock. Simmer the sauce until it is reduced by half, about 5 minutes. Whisk in the butter until the sauce is glossy.

Cut the strings off the meat. Cut the veal into ½-inch-thick slices, and serve on a platter with the onions and sauce.

Country-Style Roast Veal

Arrosto di Vitello Rustico
SERVES 6

2 celery stalks, roughly chopped
2 large carrots, peeled and roughly chopped
1 medium onion, sliced
3 fresh bay leaves
3 sprigs fresh rosemary
1 cup dry white wine
½ cup extra-virgin olive oil
¼ cup balsamic vinegar
3½ pounds veal shoulder with blade bones, hacked into 2 pieces
1½ teaspoons kosher salt
Freshly ground black pepper
2 cups Chicken Stock (page 143)

In a bowl or baking dish large enough to hold the veal, combine the celery, carrots, onion, bay leaves, rosemary, white wine, oil, and vinegar. Add the veal, and turn to coat it. Cover, and refrigerate it overnight, turning occasionally.

Remove the veal from the refrigerator 30 min-utes before you are ready to cook. Preheat the oven to 475 degrees. Pour the veal and marinade into a large roasting pan, and season the veal all over with the salt and some pepper. Pour in the chicken stock. Cover with foil, and roast 30 minutes.

Uncover, and roast, stirring and basting every 15 minutes, until the veal is just tender and browned all over, about 1 hour. With a slotted spoon, remove the veal pieces to a large ovenproof serving dish. Put the roasting pan on the stove, and boil the pan juices, reducing them to about 1 to 1½ cups of sauce. Strain the reduced juices over the veal, and roast, turning frequently, until the veal is glazed and very tender, about 30 minutes more.

Veal with Tuna Sauce

Vitello Tonnato
SERVES 6

VEAL
2-pound piece lean boneless fillet of veal
2 medium carrots, peeled, 1 sliced, 1 julienned
2 celery stalks, 1 sliced, 1 julienned
1 small onion, quartered
2 fresh bay leaves
6 black peppercorns
½ teaspoon kosher salt
1 cup dry white wine

TONNATO SAUCE
One 6½-ounce can white tuna in oil, drained
2 tablespoons extra-virgin olive oil
1 tablespoon drained tiny capers in brine
2 anchovy fillets
3 cornichons
2 hard-boiled egg yolks
1 teaspoon Dijon mustard
1 teaspoon white wine vinegar
Kosher salt
Freshly ground black pepper

Arugula leaves

For the veal: Using a metal skewer, make as many holes in the meat on a bias as you have carrot and celery julienne sticks, distributing evenly around the piece of meat. Insert pieces of carrot and celery until it is "larded" throughout with the julienned vegetables. This will flavor the meat and form a mosaic pattern when it is sliced.

Set the meat in a Dutch oven in which it fits snugly, and add the sliced carrot, celery, onion, bay leaves, peppercorns, salt, white wine, and 1 cup water. Bring it to a simmer over low heat, cover, and cook until the veal is cooked but still slightly pink, about 45 minutes to 1 hour. Uncover, let the veal cool in the poaching liquid, then chill the veal and cooking juices, and chill the vegetables separately.

For the sauce: In a food processor, combine the tuna, olive oil, capers, anchovies, cornichons, egg yolks, mustard, vinegar, and salt and pepper to taste. Chop 1 tablespoon each of the chilled carrot, onion, and celery, and add them to the processor. Measure out ½ cup of the chilled cooking liquid from the veal. Process the tuna mixture, drizzling in the cooking liquid as you go, adding just enough liquid to thin the mixture to the consistency of a thick, spoonable sauce. Scrape this into a serving bowl and chill it thoroughly.

To serve: Thinly slice the chilled veal against the grain, arrange it in overlapping slices on a serving platter, drizzle with a little of the chilled sauce, and serve the rest of the sauce at the table.

Scatter some arugula leaves on top if you wish.

Stuffed Breast of Veal with Salsa Verde

Cima Genovese con Salsa Verde
SERVES 8

VEAL
¼ cup extra-virgin olive oil
2 medium carrots, peeled, 1 cut into 2-by-¼-inch strips, 1 sliced
1 medium zucchini, cut into 2-by-¼-inch julienne strips
1 medium red bell pepper, seeded and cut into 2-by-¼-inch strips
3 ounces fresh spinach, large stems removed
½ cup fresh peas
10 large eggs, 6 raw, 4 hard-boiled
½ cup milk
1½ teaspoons kosher salt
Freshly ground black pepper
4 ounces mortadella, sliced ⅛-inch-thick, julienned
6½-pound boneless breast of veal, butterflied
1 medium onion, sliced
3 fresh bay leaves

SALSA VERDE
¾ cup extra-virgin olive oil
½ cup finely chopped roasted red peppers, freshly prepared or bottled
½ cup chopped fresh Italian parsley leaves
½ cup finely chopped red onion
¼ cup finely chopped cornichons
¼ cup red wine vinegar
1 hard-boiled egg, white and yolk separated and each finely chopped
2 tablespoons drained capers, chopped
Kosher salt
Freshly ground black pepper

For the veal: Heat a large nonstick skillet over medium heat. Add the olive oil. When the oil is hot, add the strips of carrot, zucchini, and pepper, and the spinach and peas. Cook until the vegetables are softened, about 5 minutes. In a medium bowl, beat the six raw eggs, the milk, ½ teaspoon of the salt, and some pepper. Add this to the skillet. Cook and stir until the eggs are just set and scrambled, about 4 minutes. Off heat, stir in the mortadella. Scrape the mixture into a colander over a bowl, to drain and cool.

Cut a length of butcher's twine long enough to fit around the veal three times, keeping in mind that it will be thicker when stuffed. Thread the twine in a trussing needle.

On a flat surface, open the veal like a book, with the longer side facing you. Pound it lightly to spread the meat and even out the thickness; it should look like a rectangle. Season both sides with the remaining teaspoon salt and some pepper. Turn the meat, longer side toward you. Spread the drained frittata on half of the pounded surface closer to you, making a small mound, leaving a 1-inch border on the edges closest to you. Arrange the hard-boiled eggs end to end next to one another, forming a line over the filling. Fold the top half of the veal over the filled side, as you would close a book, and tightly stitch the edges together with the trussing twine, drawing the twine through at 1-inch intervals. Wrap the veal tightly in a double thickness of cheesecloth, and tie crosswise at 2-inch intervals with more twine.

Put the veal in a Dutch oven large enough to fit it comfortably, and scatter in the sliced carrot, onion, and bay leaves. Add enough water just to cover the veal, and bring it to a gentle simmer. Cover, and simmer, adding more water if needed to keep the veal covered, until the veal is tender throughout when poked with a skewer, about 2 hours and 15 minutes. Remove the veal, and transfer it to a roasting pan. Set a smaller roasting pan or casserole large enough to cover the veal on top, and weight it with cans. Allow the veal to cool, still weighted, to room temperature.

For the salsa verde: In a medium bowl, stir together all the ingredients except the salt and pepper. Season it with salt and pepper, and let it sit at room temperature while the veal cools, to allow the flavors to blend.

To serve: Unwrap the veal, remove the stitched twine, and cut the veal into ½-inch-thick slices. Serve the sliced veal on a platter with a bowl of the salsa verde.

Shoulder Lamb Chops with Fennel and Capers

Costolette di Agnello con Finocchi e Capperi
SERVES 4

Four ½-inch-thick bone-in shoulder lamb chops
2 teaspoons kosher salt
All-purpose flour, for dredging
Vegetable oil, for frying
3 tablespoons extra-virgin olive oil
6 garlic cloves, crushed and peeled
4 sprigs fresh rosemary
2 large fennel bulbs, trimmed, cored, and cut into 1-inch chunks
2 medium onions, sliced
¼ teaspoon crushed red pepper flakes
¼ cup red wine vinegar
2 cups Chicken Stock (page 143), plus more as needed
¼ cup drained tiny capers in brine

Season lamb chops with 1 teaspoon of the salt. Spread the flour on a plate, and dredge the chops in the flour, tapping off the excess. Heat a large skillet over medium-high heat, and add ¼ inch of vegetable oil. Cook the chops until they are crisp and browned on both sides, about 3 minutes per side. Remove them to a plate.

Carefully pour out the oil and wipe the skillet clean. Set the skillet over medium heat, and add the olive oil. When the oil is hot, add the garlic and rosemary. Once the garlic and rosemary are sizzling, add the fennel and onions, and season with the remaining salt and the red pepper flakes. Cook, stirring to make sure the vegetables don't burn, until they are wilted and golden, about 10 minutes.

Add the vinegar, and bring it to a boil. Add the stock. Reduce the heat so the sauce is simmering, and add the chops and capers. Simmer, covered, until the chops are tender, about 35 to 40 minutes. Remove the rosemary stems and garlic, and serve.

Lamb Chops with a Pistachio Crust

Costolette di Agnello in Crosta di Pistacchi
SERVES 6

PEA PURÉE
1 pound frozen peas
2 cups Chicken Stock (page 143)
1 small onion, finely chopped
2 tablespoons unsalted butter
2 tablespoons extra-virgin olive oil
¼ cup loosely packed fresh mint leaves
1 teaspoon kosher salt

LAMB CHOPS
¾ cup fine dried bread crumbs
¾ cup finely ground unsalted pistachios
⅓ cup freshly grated Grana Padano
All-purpose flour, for dredging
3 large eggs
Kosher salt
18 single rib lamb chops, bones frenched halfway (about 3 pounds)
Freshly ground black pepper
2 tablespoons unsalted butter
2 tablespoons extra-virgin olive oil

Preheat the oven to 250 degrees. For the pea purée: In a medium saucepan, combine the peas, stock, and onion. Bring it to a simmer, cover, and cook until the peas and onion are very tender, about 15 minutes.

Put the pea mixture in a food processor with the butter, olive oil, mint, and salt. Process until the mixture is smooth. Keep it warm in the saucepan used for cooking while you make the lamb.

On a rimmed sheet pan, toss together the bread crumbs, pistachios, and grated cheese. Spread flour for dredging on a plate. In a shallow bowl, beat the eggs with a pinch of salt.

Season the lamb chops with salt and pepper. Dredge the chops in flour, then egg, then the bread-crumb mixture, patting to make sure the coating adheres to both sides. Coat all the chops, and rest them on a sheet pan.

Heat a large skillet over medium heat. Add the butter and olive oil. When the butter is melted, test the edge of one chop to make sure it sizzles on contact. Add a batch of chops (don't crowd the skillet), and cook them on both sides until the crust is golden, about 2 to 3 minutes per side for medium-rare chops. Keep the finished chops on a parchment-lined sheet pan in the oven while you brown the rest. Season all of the chops lightly with salt.

To serve: place a dollop of the warm pea purée on each plate, and surround it with three chops.

Lamb and Pepper Ragù

Ragù di Agnello e Peperoni
SERVES 4 TO 6

2 ounces pancetta, chopped
4 garlic cloves, crushed and peeled
2 tablespoons extra-virgin olive oil
2 pounds boneless lamb shoulder, cut into 1-inch pieces
2 teaspoons kosher salt
¼ teaspoon crushed red pepper flakes
½ cup dry white wine
One 28-ounce can Italian plum tomatoes, preferably San Marzano, crushed by hand
2 teaspoons dried oregano, preferably Sicilian on the branch
2 teaspoons sweet paprika

2 medium russet potatoes, peeled and quartered

3 small bell peppers (one each red, yellow, and orange), seeded and quartered

In a mini–food processor, combine the pancetta and garlic. Process to make a smooth pestata. Heat a large Dutch oven over medium heat. Add the olive oil. When the oil is hot, add the pestata, and cook until the fat is rendered, about 3 to 4 minutes.

Season the lamb with 1 teaspoon of the salt. Add the lamb to the pot. Cook, stirring occasionally, over medium heat until the lamb releases its juices, about 6 minutes. Once the lamb has let out its juices, increase the heat to concentrate them and brown the meat all over, about 4 minutes more.

Season with the remaining salt and the red pepper flakes. Add the wine, bring it to a boil, and cook until it is almost reduced away, about 4 minutes. Add the tomatoes, slosh out the can with 1½ cups water, and add that, too. Add the oregano and paprika. Bring the liquid to a simmer, cover, and cook 45 minutes.

After 30 minutes, add the potatoes and peppers and 1 cup water. Set the cover ajar, and cook until the vegetables and lamb are tender, about 30 to 45 minutes more. If the lamb is tender but the sauce is still too soupy, bring it to a boil to reduce and thicken it to concentrate the flavor.

Rack of Lamb

Costata di Agnello

SERVES 4

SAUCE

1½ pounds lamb bones and scraps, trimmed of fat

3 tablespoons extra-virgin olive oil

1 tablespoon all-purpose flour

½ cup chopped onion

¼ cup chopped peeled carrot

¼ cup chopped celery

1 tablespoon fresh rosemary leaves

1 tablespoon fresh sage leaves

1 tablespoon fresh thyme leaves

½ teaspoon kosher salt

Freshly ground black pepper

3 cups Chicken Stock (page 143)

½ cup dry white wine

1 cup frozen peas (optional)

LAMB

2 tablespoons extra-virgin olive oil

2 racks of lamb, frenched (about 3½ to 4 pounds)

1½ teaspoons kosher salt

Freshly ground black pepper

½ cup fine dried bread crumbs

2 tablespoons chopped fresh Italian parsley

2 tablespoons freshly grated Grana Padano

2 garlic cloves, finely chopped

¼ teaspoon dried oregano, preferably Sicilian on the branch

1 tablespoon grainy mustard

For the sauce: Preheat the oven to 425 degrees. Place the lamb bones and scraps in a large roasting pan, and toss them with 1 tablespoon of the olive oil. Roast until the bones begin to brown, about 30 minutes. Sprinkle them with the flour, toss, and roast until they are nicely browned, about 15 minutes more.

When the lamb bones are almost done, heat the remaining 2 tablespoons olive oil in a medium Dutch oven over medium heat. When the oil is hot, add the onion, carrot, and celery, and cook, stirring occasionally, until the onion begins to soften, about 5 minutes. Add the rosemary, sage, and thyme, and season with the salt and some pepper.

Transfer the roasted bones to the vegetables, and add a little bit of the stock to loosen the browned bits in the bottom of the pot. Pour all of the fat out of the roasting pan, and set the pan over medium-high heat. Add the wine and

1 cup water, and simmer, scraping the bottom of the pan with a wooden spoon, to loosen the drippings. Pour the contents of the roasting pan into the pot with the bones and vegetables. Add the remaining stock, and bring to a simmer. Simmer, skimming the scum and fat that rise to the top, until the sauce is dark and flavorful, about 1 hour and 15 minutes.

Discard the bones and meat scraps, and pour the rest of the sauce through a sieve into a medium saucepan, pressing on the solids to extract as much liquid as possible. Simmer the sauce to reduce it until it coats the back of a spoon. (It may already be this thick if you pressed out enough of the solids; if so, there is no need to reduce further.) Cover and set the sauce aside while you roast the lamb.

For the lamb: Increase the oven temperature to 475 degrees. Heat a large roasting pan over medium-high heat, and add the olive oil. Season the lamb with 1 teaspoon salt and some pepper. Sear until it is browned on all sides, about 3 minutes. Remove the lamb to a plate, and discard the oil from the roasting pan.

In a medium bowl, combine the bread crumbs, parsley, grated cheese, garlic, oregano, and remaining ½ teaspoon salt, and mix well. Spread the mixture on a plate. Brush the lamb with the mustard, and carefully pat the crust on the chops but not the bone. Roast the lamb, bone side up, until the crust is crisp and brown and the lamb is medium rare (about 125 degrees on a meat thermometer), about 18 to 20 minutes. While the lamb rests, reheat the sauce to a simmer. Add the peas, and simmer until they are tender, about 5 minutes. Carve the rested lamb between the bones into single chops, serving four per person, with the sauce spooned over.

❧ Have the butcher french the racks for you, saving the scraps to make the sauce and leaving a thin layer of fat intact. Purchase lamb bones to make up 1½ pounds with the scraps.

Rabbit Stew

Guazzetto di Coniglio
SERVES 4

4-pound rabbit, cut into 8 pieces
2 teaspoons kosher salt
All-purpose flour, for dredging
3 tablespoons extra-virgin olive oil
8 garlic cloves, crushed and peeled
3 tablespoons tomato paste
2 cups dry white wine
4 sprigs fresh sage, tied together with kitchen twine
¼ teaspoon freshly grated nutmeg
1 pound mixed mushrooms, sliced (cremini, button, shiitake, oyster, chanterelle, porcini)
¼ cup pine nuts, lightly toasted
2 tablespoons chopped fresh Italian parsley

Season the rabbit with 1 teaspoon salt. Spread the flour in a shallow bowl, and dredge the seasoned rabbit in the flour.

Heat a large Dutch oven over medium-high heat, and heat the olive oil. Sear the rabbit pieces on all sides until they are well browned, about 10 minutes, then remove them to a plate.

Add the garlic to the pot. Once it is sizzling, drop the tomato paste into a hot spot and cook until it darkens a shade or two, about 1 minute, then stir to combine it with the garlic. Add the white wine, and boil until it is reduced by half; drop in the sage and nutmeg. Pour in 2 cups hot water, and return the liquid to a rapid simmer.

Once the liquid is simmering, add the mushrooms and rabbit. Season with the remaining 1 teaspoon salt, stir, and cover. Simmer until the rabbit is very tender, about 45 minutes, adding a little more hot water if necessary to keep the rabbit at least halfway covered.

When the rabbit is done, remove the garlic and the sage sprigs, stir in the pine nuts and parsley, and serve.

Rabbit in Gremolata

Coniglio in Gremolata
SERVES 4

4-pound rabbit, cut into 8 pieces
2 teaspoons kosher salt
All-purpose flour, for dredging
2 tablespoons unsalted butter
2 tablespoons extra-virgin olive oil
6 large shallots, halved at the root
Pinch of crushed red pepper flakes
1 cup dry white wine
Freshly squeezed juice and grated zest of 1 lemon
3 sprigs fresh sage
2 medium russet potatoes, peeled and cut into
    2-inch chunks
¼ cup chopped fresh Italian parsley

Season the rabbit with half the salt. Spread the flour on a plate, and dredge the rabbit lightly in the flour, tapping off the excess. Heat a medium Dutch oven over medium-high heat. Melt the butter in the olive oil. When the butter is melted, add the rabbit, and brown it on all sides, about 8 minutes in all. Remove the rabbit to a plate.

To the fat left in the pan, add the shallots and red pepper flakes. Cook and toss the shallots until they are golden on the edges, about 5 minutes. Add the white wine, lemon zest and juice, and sage sprigs. Bring the liquid to a boil. Add the rabbit leg pieces, and reduce the heat to a simmer. Cover, and simmer 20 minutes.

Uncover, and add the rest of the rabbit and the potatoes with the remaining salt, tossing to coat the potatoes in the sauce. Cover, and cook until the rabbit and potatoes are very tender, about 35 to 40 minutes more.

Uncover, and bring the sauce to a boil. Remove sage sprigs, sprinkle with the parsley, and cook, stirring gently, until the sauce coats the rabbit and vegetables, about 2 to 3 minutes. Serve immediately.

Rabbit with Sage

Coniglio alla Salvia
SERVES 4

4 slices bacon, chopped
4 garlic cloves, crushed and peeled
10 large fresh sage leaves
3 tablespoons extra-virgin olive oil
4-pound rabbit, cut into 8 pieces
1½ teaspoons kosher salt
Freshly ground black pepper
All-purpose flour, for dredging
1 cup dry white wine
1 teaspoon balsamic vinegar
2 cups Chicken Stock (page 143)

In a mini–food processor, combine the bacon, garlic, and sage, and process to make a smooth pestata. Heat a medium Dutch oven over medium-high heat. Add the olive oil. Season the rabbit with the salt and some pepper. Lightly dredge it in the flour, tapping off the excess. When the oil is hot, brown the rabbit on all sides, about 3 minutes per side. Remove it to a plate as it browns.

When all of the rabbit is out of the pot, scrape in the pestata. Cook and stir until it renders its fat, about 3 minutes. Add the wine and vinegar, bring the liquid to a simmer, and reduce it by half, about 2 minutes. Add the rabbit back to the pot, along with the stock. Simmer, with the lid ajar, until the rabbit is tender, about 45 minutes.

Remove the rabbit pieces to a warm serving platter, and boil the pan juices to reduce to a glossy, syrupy sauce, about 4 minutes. Strain the sauce over the rabbit, and serve.

Braised Tripe with Potatoes

Trippa Brasata con Patate
SERVES 6 TO 8

4½ pounds honeycomb tripe
6 cups Chicken Stock (page 143)
½ cup extra-virgin olive oil
3 medium onions, chopped
3 fresh bay leaves
1 teaspoon kosher salt
1 cup dry white wine
¼ teaspoon crushed red pepper flakes
3 tablespoons tomato paste
2 cups canned Italian plum tomatoes, preferably
   San Marzano, crushed by hand
3 medium russet potatoes, peeled and cut into
   ¾-inch cubes (about 1½ pounds)
½ cup freshly grated Grana Padano
Freshly ground black pepper

Put the tripe in a large Dutch oven with water to cover by 2 inches. Bring it to a simmer, cover, and cook 2 hours. Drain, cool, scrape off all the fat with the dull side of your kitchen knife from both sides of the tripe pieces, and cut off any tough membranes. Cut the cleaned, cooked tripe into 2½-by-½-inch strips. Wash and drain. Heat the chicken stock to a simmer, and keep it hot.

To a Dutch oven over medium heat add the olive oil. When the oil is hot, add the onions, and cook until they are softened, about 10 minutes. Add the tripe, increase the heat to medium high, and cook, stirring often, until the water from the tripe has evaporated, about 8 minutes.

Add the bay leaves, salt, and wine, and cook until the wine is reduced away, about 4 minutes. Make a space in the center of the pan, and add the red pepper flakes and tomato paste. Cook and stir in that hot spot until the tomato paste toasts and darkens a shade or two, about 2 minutes. Stir the tomato paste into the tripe. Add the tomatoes, and return the liquid to a simmer. Add hot stock to cover the tripe, and cook for 30 minutes, adding more stock as needed to keep the tripe covered. Add the potatoes to the tripe, and enough water to cover the potatoes. Continue to cook until the tripe is tender but still slightly resistant to the tooth, about 30 minutes more. At this point, the sauce should have reduced enough to coat the tripe and potatoes. If not, increase the heat and boil it for a few minutes to reduce it further. Remove the bay leaves.

Serve the tripe sprinkled with the grated cheese and freshly ground black pepper.

Veal Kidneys in Mustard Sauce

Rognoncini Trifolati alla Senape
SERVES 4 TO 6

2 pounds whole veal kidneys
1 cup white wine vinegar
½ teaspoon kosher salt
Freshly ground black pepper
¼ cup extra-virgin olive oil
1 tablespoon plus 1 teaspoon brandy
6 tablespoons unsalted butter
½ cup dry white wine
1 teaspoon freshly squeezed lemon juice
½ cup Chicken Stock (page 143)
½ cup heavy cream
¼ cup Dijon mustard

Remove all exterior fat from the kidneys. Rinse them well, and put them in a bowl with the vinegar and 5 cups water (the kidneys should be covered in the soaking liquid). Refrigerate and soak 2 hours, then wash them well in cold water and pat dry. Cut the kidneys lengthwise into 3 sections, then crosswise into ¼-inch-thick slices, trimming away the interior fat as it becomes exposed. (The kidney fat retains odor, so take care to remove it all.)

Season the kidneys with the salt and some pepper. To a large skillet over medium-high heat, add the olive oil. When the oil is hot, add the kidneys, spreading them out and stirring occasionally, until lightly browned, about 4 minutes. Add the brandy a little at a time as they cook. Transfer the kidneys to a colander to drain.

Pour out the oil, and wipe the skillet clean with a paper towel. Set the skillet over medium heat, and melt the butter. When the butter is bubbling, whisk in the wine and lemon juice. Let the wine simmer for a minute, then whisk in the chicken stock and cream. Bring it to a rapid simmer, and simmer until it is slightly thickened, about 2 minutes. Whisk in the mustard. Add the kidneys, and gently stir to coat them in the sauce. Serve immediately.

Calf's Liver in Balsamic Vinegar

Fegato di Vitello all'Aceto Balsamico
SERVES 6

2 pounds calf's liver
Vegetable oil, for frying
1 teaspoon kosher salt
3 tablespoons extra-virgin olive oil
2 large onions, sliced ¼ inch thick
4 fresh bay leaves
Freshly ground black pepper
½ cup balsamic vinegar
1 tablespoon dry white wine

Trim the liver of its outer covering, blood vessels, and any blemishes. Pat it dry, and cut into 2-by-½-inch strips. Heat a large skillet over medium-high heat. Add a thin film of vegetable oil. Season the liver all over with ½ teaspoon of the salt. When the oil is hot, add the liver, and cook, tossing quickly, until the outside is no longer raw but the inside is still pink, about 3 minutes. Remove the liver to a plate.

Carefully pour the oil out of the skillet, and wipe the skillet clean with a paper towel. Put the skillet back over medium-high heat, and add the olive oil. When the oil is hot, add the onions and

bay leaves, and season with the remaining ½ teaspoon salt and some pepper. Cook, stirring often, until the onions are golden but still have some bite, about 5 minutes. Pour in the vinegar and wine, and simmer just until the sauce thickens, about 5 minutes. Add the liver, and toss to coat it; simmer until the sauce coats the liver like a thin syrup, about 2 minutes. Remove the bay leaves and serve immediately.

Fillet of Venison

Filetto di Capriolo
SERVES 6 TO 8

MARINADE AND VENISON
2-pound piece venison fillet
2 pounds venison bones and scraps (or beef bones, if you can't find venison bones)
2 cups dry red wine
2 cups dry white wine
2 medium carrots, peeled and coarsely chopped
2 celery stalks, coarsely chopped
2 medium onions, coarsely chopped
6 fresh bay leaves
1 sprig fresh rosemary
1 teaspoon black peppercorns
1 teaspoon juniper berries
1 teaspoon kosher salt, plus more to season the venison

SAUCE
4 tablespoons extra-virgin olive oil
½ teaspoon kosher salt
Freshly ground black pepper
3 large shallots, coarsely chopped
4 cups Chicken Stock (page 143) or Mixed Meat Stock (page 144)

For the marinade: Put the venison fillet, surrounded by the bones and scraps, in a large nonreactive pot. Add the red wine, white wine, carrots, celery, onions, bay leaves, rosemary, peppercorns, juniper, and salt. Toss to coat the meat in the marinade. Cover, and marinate in the refrigerator for 2 days, turning the meat occasionally.

When you are ready to make the sauce, preheat the oven to 475 degrees. Remove the venison fillet, bones, and scraps, and pat them dry. Strain the marinade, reserving the solids and the liquids separately.

Put the bones and scraps in a large roasting pan. Toss them with 2 tablespoons of the olive oil, and season with the salt and freshly ground pepper. Roast until everything is browned all over, tossing once halfway through, about 20 minutes. Add the reserved vegetables and the shallots. Roast until the vegetables are caramelized, tossing once, about 15 minutes.

Put the roasting pan on the stovetop over medium heat. Add the reserved marinade liquid, and simmer until it is reduced by half, stirring the bottom with a wooden spoon to loosen any browned bits, about 20 minutes.

Transfer the contents of the roasting pan to a stockpot, and add the stock. Bring it to a boil, skimming any scum that rises to the surface. Reduce to a simmer, and cook until the sauce is dark and flavorful, about 2 hours, skimming scum as it appears on the surface. Strain the sauce through a fine sieve, pressing on the solids. Put the sauce in a wide saucepan or skillet, and bring it to a boil. Reduce to about 1½ cups of dark, flavorful sauce.

When you are ready to serve, slice the venison into ½-inch-thick medallions. Season it lightly with salt. Heat a large skillet over medium-high heat. Add the remaining 2 tablespoons olive oil. When it is hot, sear the venison medallions in batches until they are browned on the outside but still medium rare in the center, about 1 to 2 minutes per side. Arrange the medallions on warmed serving plates, and spoon the sauce over them.

Wild Boar Braised in Barolo

Cinghiale Brasato al Barolo
SERVES 8

6 fresh bay leaves
6 whole cloves
8 cups beef stock, or as needed
1 large onion, cut into chunks
2 ounces pancetta, cut into chunks
1 medium carrot, peeled and cut into chunks
1 tablespoon fresh rosemary leaves
¼ cup extra-virgin olive oil
1 boneless wild boar shoulder roast (about 3½ pounds)
1½ teaspoons kosher salt
Freshly ground black pepper
3 tablespoons tomato paste
1 cup canned whole San Marzano tomatoes, crushed by hand
2 bottles (750 milliliters) Barolo or other hearty red wine

Set the bay leaves and cloves in a piece of cheesecloth, and tie with kitchen twine to make a sachet. Put the stock in a medium saucepan, and warm it over low heat. In a food processor, combine the onion, pancetta, carrot, and rosemary to make a smooth pestata.

Heat a large Dutch oven over medium heat. Add the olive oil. Season the boar with 1 teaspoon salt and some pepper. When the oil is hot, brown the boar on all sides, about 10 minutes. Remove it to a plate.

Make a space in the pan, and add the tomato paste. Cook and stir the paste in that hot spot until it toasts and darkens a shade or two, about 2 minutes. Add the tomatoes and wine and stir into the tomato paste. Bring it to a boil, add the remaining salt, and simmer until reduced by about half, stirring the bottom of the pot to prevent burning, about 8 minutes.

Add the boar to the pot with enough stock just to cover the meat. Adjust the heat so the liquid is just simmering, set the cover ajar, and simmer until the boar is tender all the way through, about

3 hours, adding more stock as necessary to keep the meat covered. Remove the meat to a cutting board, and cover it with foil to keep it warm while you reduce the sauce.

Bring the sauce to a boil over medium-high heat, and cook, stirring often, until it is reduced to about 3 to 4 cups of thick, flavorful sauce, skimming the foam from the surface as you go, about 10 to 15 minutes. Remove the sachet with the herbs. Slice the boar against the grain into thin slices, and slip these back into the sauce. Spoon the sauce to coat the meat, transfer all to a platter, and serve.

DESSERT

Non vendere il miele a chi ha le api.
—Italian proverb

It's no use selling honey to one who has bees.

Baked Semolina Pudding with Cherries

Budino di Semolino con Ciliegie
SERVES 6 TO 8

CHERRIES
2 cups pitted sweet cherries
2 tablespoons honey
Freshly squeezed juice of 1 orange, plus
    2 teaspoons grated zest

PUDDING
2 tablespoons unsalted butter, plus more for the
    baking pan
4 cups milk
1 additional teaspoon grated orange zest
¾ cup plus 2 tablespoons sugar
¼ teaspoon kosher salt
1 teaspoon pure vanilla extract
1 cup fine semolina
4 large eggs, separated

Preheat the oven to 350 degrees. Butter an 8- or 9-inch round soufflé dish. For the cherries: In a medium saucepan, combine the cherries, honey, and orange juice and zest. Bring this to a simmer over medium-low heat, and cook until the cherries break down and the sauce is syrupy, about 15 to 20 minutes

For the pudding: In a medium saucepan, combine the milk, orange zest, ¾ cup of the sugar, and the salt. Bring this to a simmer over medium heat, stirring until the sugar is dissolved. Stir in the vanilla. Whisk the semolina into the simmering milk in a thin stream until all is incorporated and there are no lumps. Simmer until it is thickened, about 3 minutes. Remove it from the heat, and whisk in the butter. Scrape it into a large bowl, and let it cool while you beat the egg whites.

In a large bowl with a handheld mixer, beat the egg whites at medium-high speed until they are frothy. Add the 2 tablespoons sugar, and continue to beat until the egg whites form soft peaks,

about 2 minutes. Whisk the egg yolks into the slightly cooled semolina. Stir in about a quarter of the egg whites to lighten the mixture, then fold in the remaining egg whites. Pour into the prepared baking dish, and bake until the pudding is puffed and set, about 40 to 45 minutes. Serve it immediately with the warm cherries.

❧ You can also make the sauce with a combination of fresh seasonal berries, though the cooking time will be less—just simmer until they begin to break down.

Chestnut Flan

Sformato di Castagne
SERVES 8

1½ cups sugar
4 large eggs
2 cups sweetened chestnut purée (canned is fine)
Zest of 1 orange
⅛ teaspoon kosher salt
1 cup milk
½ cup heavy cream

Preheat the oven to 350 degrees. Put on a kettle of water to heat. For the caramel: In a medium saucepan, combine 1 cup of the sugar and ¼ cup water. Bring it to a simmer, without stirring, over medium heat. Cook, swirling the pan occasionally, until the caramel is a deep amber, about 5 to 6 minutes. Pour the caramel into a 3-quart oval baking dish, coating the bottom and swirling to come a bit up the sides.

In a food processor, combine the eggs, the remaining ½ cup sugar, the chestnut purée, orange zest, and salt. Process until smooth. Add the milk and cream, and process until very smooth, scraping down the sides of the work bowl once or twice.

Pour the mixture into the baking dish. Put the

baking dish in a roasting pan, and pour enough hot water from the kettle into the roasting pan to come halfway up the sides of the baking dish. Bake until the custard is set with just a tiny bit of jiggle left in the center, about 1 hour to 1 hour and 10 minutes. Remove it from the oven, but let the flan cool to room temperature in the roasting pan. Then refrigerate until it is well chilled, preferably overnight.

To serve: Run a knife around the edge of the flan to loosen it. Cover the dish with a platter, and quickly invert it. The flan should plop out. If it doesn't, rap the platter on the counter a few times, holding the baking dish firmly in place.

Butternut Squash Flan

Sformato di Zucca
SERVES 8

½ cup granulated white sugar
1 cup puréed butternut squash (canned or thawed frozen squash purée is fine)
2 large eggs and 2 large egg yolks
¼ cup light brown sugar
½ teaspoon ground cinnamon
¼ teaspoon freshly grated nutmeg
¼ teaspoon kosher salt
1 teaspoon pure vanilla extract
¾ cup milk
½ cup heavy cream

Preheat the oven to 350 degrees. Put on a kettle of water to heat. For the caramel: In a medium saucepan, combine the white sugar and ¼ cup water. Bring it to a simmer, without stirring, over medium heat. Cook, swirling the pan occasionally, until the caramel is a deep amber, about 5 to 6 minutes. Divide the caramel among eight 6-ounce or larger ramekins, coating the bottom and swirling to come a bit up the sides.

In a food processor, combine the squash, whole eggs, brown sugar, cinnamon, nutmeg, salt, and

vanilla, and purée until smooth. Add the egg yolks, milk, and cream, and purée again until very smooth.

Divide the mixture evenly among the ramekins. Place the filled ramekins in a roasting pan large enough so that they aren't touching. Pour enough hot water from the kettle to come halfway up the sides of the ramekins. Bake until the flans are set with just a tiny bit of jiggle in the center, about 30 to 35 minutes. Let them cool completely on a rack, then refrigerate them until cold, at least 4 hours.

To serve: Run a knife around the edge of each ramekin to loosen the custard, and dip the bottom in hot water for a few seconds. Set a plate on top, and invert it. If the custard is stuck, tap the bottom of the ramekin with the spoon, and jiggle the ramekin until it plops loose.

Panna Cotta with Fresh Berries

Panna Cotta al Frutti di Bosco
SERVES 6

1 tablespoon unflavored gelatin
2 cups cream
1 cup milk
½ cup granulated sugar
1 vanilla bean, split lengthwise
1 cup blackberries, gently washed and drained
1 cup raspberries, gently washed and drained
1 cup small strawberries, gently washed, drained, hulled, and halved or quartered
1 teaspoon superfine sugar (optional)

Sprinkle the gelatin over ¼ cup cold water in a small bowl, and let it sit until the gelatin is softened, about 5 minutes.

In a medium saucepan, combine the cream, milk, granulated sugar, and vanilla bean over medium heat. Bring just to a simmer, stirring to dissolve the sugar. Remove it from the heat, and let it steep 5 minutes. Scrape the seeds from the vanilla bean into the mixture, and discard the bean. Whisk the softened gelatin in until dissolved. Strain the mixture through a fine sieve into a spouted measuring cup, and let it cool to room temperature.

Pour the mixture into six 5-ounce or larger ramekins, and refrigerate until they are set, at least 4 hours or overnight.

About ½ hour before you are ready to serve, gently toss the berries together in a medium bowl. Taste a few berries. If they're too tart, sprinkle them with the superfine sugar and toss again. Let them sit at room temperature about ½ hour.

To serve: Run a thin paring knife around the edge of each ramekin, and invert it on a serving plate. Tap the bottom of the ramekin to loosen the panna cotta. It should plop out when you lift the ramekin. If not, hold the ramekin firmly in place and shake the plate a few times to loosen the panna cotta. If one or two are really stuck, you can also dip the base of the ramekin in hot water for a few seconds to melt it a little before inverting. Serve the panna cotta topped with the mixed berries.

Barolo-Flavored Zabaglione

Zabaglione al Barolo
SERVES 6

6 large egg yolks
¾ cup superior Barolo
6 tablespoons sugar

In a large copper or stainless-steel bowl, whisk together the egg yolks, wine, and sugar. Set the bowl over a pan of simmering water, and whisk constantly until the mixture is light and frothy and forms a ribbon figure-8 when you draw your whisk out.

Serve it immediately in parfait glasses.

Sweet Delight of Wheat Berries, Fruit, and Chocolate

Dolce al Grano
MAKES ABOUT 8 CUPS, SERVING 8

1 cup wheat berries (about 6 ounces), soaked overnight
1 fresh bay leaf
2 cups pitted and halved fresh sweet cherries
1 cup dried apricots, cut in thirds
½ cup pitted dried dates, coarsely chopped
4 ounces semisweet chocolate, cut into ¼-inch chunks
1 cup chopped hazelnuts, toasted
½ teaspoon ground cinnamon
½ cup honey
2 tablespoons Saba or Aceto Balsamico Tradizionale
1 cup heavy cream, whipped

Drain the soaked wheat berries, and put them in a saucepan with 3 quarts fresh cold water and the bay leaf. Bring it to a boil, stirring occasionally, cover slightly ajar, and adjust the heat to maintain a steady simmer. Cook until the wheat berries are tender but still slightly firm to the bite, about 40 to 45 minutes. Drain, discard the bay leaf, and let the wheat berries cool.

Put the wheat berries, cherries, apricots, dates, chocolate, and hazelnuts in a large bowl, and fold them together. Sprinkle the cinnamon over them, and drizzle the honey and Saba on top. Mix gently just to combine. To serve: scoop the mixture into wineglasses and top each with a dollop of whipped cream.

Apple Bread Pudding

Budino di Pane con Mele
SERVES 6 TO 8

1 tablespoon unsalted butter, softened
1 cup sugar
¼ teaspoon ground cinnamon
6 large eggs
1 cup heavy cream
1 cup milk
Pinch of kosher salt
½ teaspoon pure almond extract
5 cups ½-inch crustless day-old country-bread cubes
2 small Golden Delicious apples, peeled, cored, and cut into ½-inch cubes
6 tablespoons raspberry preserves
½ cup sliced almonds

Preheat the oven to 325 degrees. Butter a 7-by-11-inch rectangular baking dish, or a similar-sized oval gratin dish, with the soft butter. In a small bowl, stir together 2 tablespoons of the sugar with the cinnamon.

In a large bowl, whisk together the eggs, remaining sugar, the cream, milk, salt, and almond extract until smooth. Add the bread, and let it soak 5 minutes, stirring occasionally.

Stir in the apple chunks, and pour the mixture into the prepared pan. Spoon the raspberry preserves on top, spaced evenly in about twelve additions. Sprinkle the almonds evenly over the top, then sprinkle with the cinnamon sugar.

Put the baking dish on a sheet pan, and bake it until the top of the pudding is golden brown and the custard is just set, about 50 minutes. Let it cool on a rack about 20 to 30 minutes, but serve warm.

Espresso Mousse

Crema di Caffè
SERVES 8

1 tablespoon unflavored gelatin
1 cup milk
1 cup sugar
½ teaspoon freshly squeezed lemon juice
1¾ cups heavy cream
3 large eggs, separated
½ cup brewed espresso, at room temperature
¼ teaspoon pure vanilla extract
Espresso beans and shaved chocolate, for garnish

In a small bowl, sprinkle the gelatin over ½ cup cold water, and allow it to soften. In a small saucepan, warm the milk over low heat to just below a simmer, and keep it warm.

In a medium saucepan over medium heat, combine the sugar with ¼ cup water and the lemon juice. Bring it to a boil, and cook until the sugar turns a deep-golden caramel color, about 7 minutes. Swirl the pan occasionally as it cooks, but don't stir.

When the caramel is ready, carefully pour in ¾ cup of the cream (it will bubble up). Cook and stir over medium heat until it is blended, then stir in the hot milk, whisking until smooth.

In a large bowl, whisk the egg yolks. In a slow stream, whisk in the caramel mixture, whisking constantly so as not to scramble the eggs. Pour it back into the saucepan, and cook over medium-low heat, stirring with a wooden spoon, until the mixture is thick enough to coat the back of the spoon, about 8 minutes.

Off the heat, whisk in the softened gelatin until no lumps remain. Stir in the brewed espresso and vanilla. Cover, and refrigerate until chilled, at least 1 hour, but can be left overnight.

With a handheld mixer, beat the remaining 1 cup heavy cream to stiff peaks. In another bowl, with clean mixer beaters, beat the egg whites to stiff peaks. Gently fold the egg whites, then the whipped cream into the chilled espresso custard.

Pour it into individual serving dishes or a large serving bowl, and chill until it is set, at least 3 hours. Garnish with espresso beans and shaved chocolate.

Coffee-Flavored Pick-Me-Up

Tiramisù al Caffè
SERVES 10 OR MORE

1 pound bittersweet chocolate, chopped
2 cups heavy cream
2 cups mascarpone (1 pound), at room
   temperature
1 cup confectioners' sugar
2 cups freshly brewed espresso
½ cup granulated sugar
½ cup coffee liqueur
48 ladyfingers (preferably imported Italian
   savoiardi)

Melt the chocolate in a double boiler over simmering water, and keep it warm in the double boiler. Meanwhile, whisk the cream in an electric mixer fitted with the whisk attachment until it just holds soft peaks. (Don't overwhip—you will be whisking it again with the mascarpone, and you don't want to make butter!)

Whisk the mascarpone in a separate bowl with the mixer at medium speed until smooth. Sift in the confectioners' sugar, and whisk until it is smooth. Whisk the whipped cream into the mascarpone until they are just combined. Refrigerate if not using it right away.

Combine the espresso and granulated sugar in a medium saucepan set over low heat. Cook until the sugar has dissolved, then stir in the coffee liqueur. Remove it from the heat, and stir in about two-thirds of the melted chocolate. Pour the chocolate-espresso mixture into a large shallow pan, big enough to soak half the savoiardi at one time. Add half of the savoiardi to the liquid,

and soak, turning to coat all sides until they are almost soaked through, about 1 minute.

Arrange the savoiardi in two rows in the bottom of a 9-by-13-inch (3-quart) Pyrex or ceramic dish to make a tight bottom layer, breaking as necessary to patch empty spaces. Drizzle with a third of the remaining warm melted chocolate. Spread half of the mascarpone in an even layer over the top of the cookies.

Soak the remaining twenty-four savoiardi in the remaining soaking liquid. Arrange these soaked savoiardi on top of the mascarpone, just as you did the first layer, and drizzle with another third of the warm melted chocolate.

Spread the remaining mascarpone in an even layer over the top. Pour the remaining melted chocolate on top. Use a toothpick or paring knife to make lines at 2-inch intervals connecting the long sides of the pan. Now make perpendicular lines through the chocolate, also at 2-inch intervals, to create a crosshatch pattern. Chill the tiramisù at least 4 hours, or up to overnight, before cutting into squares to serve.

Limoncello Pick-Me-Up

Tiramisù al Limoncello
SERVES 10

5 or 6 lemons
5 large eggs
1 cup sugar
1½ cups limoncello liqueur
1 pound mascarpone (2 cups), at room
   temperature
40 ladyfingers (preferably imported Italian
   savoiardi), or more as needed

Zest enough of the lemons to get 2 tablespoons of grated zest. Juice all the lemons, to get ¾ cup of lemon juice.

Pour just enough water into a double-boiler

pan so the water level is right below the bottom of the mixing bowl when it is sitting in the pan. Separate the eggs, putting the yolks in the large bowl and the whites into another stainless-steel bowl for whipping with an electric mixer.

To make the base for the tiramisù: Heat the water in the pan to a steady simmer. Beat the egg yolks with ¼ cup of the sugar and ½ cup of the limoncello until well blended. Then set the bowl over the simmering water, and whisk constantly, frequently scraping the whisk around the sides and bottom of the bowl, as the egg mixture expands and heats into a frothy zabaglione, about 5 minutes. When the zabaglione has thickened enough to form a ribbon when it drops on the surface, take the bowl off the double-boiler pan and let it cool.

Meanwhile, pour the remaining cup of limoncello, all of the lemon juice, 1 cup water, and ½ cup of the sugar into a saucepan. Bring it to a boil, stirring to dissolve the sugar, and cook for 5 minutes, evaporating the alcohol. Let the syrup cool completely.

In another large bowl, stir the mascarpone with a wooden spoon to soften it, add the grated lemon zest, and beat it with a whisk until light and creamy. Whip the egg whites with the remaining ¼ cup sugar, by hand or by machine, until they hold moderately firm peaks.

When the cooked limoncello zabaglione is cooled, scrape about a third of it over the mascarpone, and fold it in with a large rubber spatula. Fold in the rest of the zabaglione in two or three additions. Now fold in the whipped egg whites in several additions, until the limoncello-mascarpone cream is light and evenly blended.

Pour some of the cooled syrup into a shallow pan, no deeper than ¼ inch. One at a time, roll a ladyfinger in the syrup briefly—if it soaks up too much syrup, it will fall apart. Arrange the moistened ladyfingers in neat, tight rows in a 9-by-13-inch glass or ceramic pan, filling the bottom of the pan completely. You should be able to fit in about twenty ladyfingers in a single layer.

Scoop half of the limoncello-mascarpone cream

onto the ladyfingers, and smooth it to fill the pan and cover them. Dip and arrange a second layer of ladyfingers in the pan, and cover it completely with the remainder of the cream.

Smooth the cream with a spatula, and seal the tiramisù airtight in plastic wrap. Before serving, refrigerate for 6 hours (or up to 2 days), or put it in the freezer for 2 hours. To serve: cut portions of tiramisù in any size you like, and lift them out of the pan onto dessert plates.

Cappuccino Frozen Pie

Dolce di Gelato al Caffè
SERVES 8 TO 10

CRUST
12 chocolate graham-cracker sheets
3 tablespoons sugar
2 tablespoons instant espresso
Pinch of kosher salt
5 tablespoons butter, melted and cooled

FILLING
1 quart coffee ice cream
2 cups heavy cream
2 tablespoons sugar
1 cup sour cream

Preheat the oven to 350 degrees. In a food processor, grind together the graham crackers, sugar, espresso powder, and salt to make fine crumbs. With the processor running, add the melted butter, and process just to combine. Press the crumbs into the bottom and up the sides of an 8-inch pie plate, making sure the crumbs are evenly distributed. Press well against the bottom and sides of the pie plate. Bake until the crust is crispy, about 10 to 12 minutes, then cool completely before filling.

Remove the ice cream from the freezer to soften it a bit while you make the whipped cream.

In a mixer fitted with the whisk attachment, whip the cream and sugar to soft peaks. Add the sour cream, and whisk until it is just combined.

Spread the ice cream in an even layer over the crust. Dollop the whipped-cream mixture on top, and spread to a dome shape. Freeze overnight, or until the cream is frozen. To serve: cut with a sharp knife dipped in hot water.

Italian Rum Cake

Zuppa Inglese
SERVES 8

2 cups milk
1¾ cups sugar
4 teaspoons cornstarch
Pinch of kosher salt
3 large eggs
2 ounces bittersweet chocolate, finely chopped
⅓ cup diced candied orange peel
¼ cup dark rum
2 cups heavy cream, chilled
⅛ teaspoon ground cinnamon
40 ladyfingers, preferably imported Italian savoiardi

For the pastry cream: Pour the milk into a medium saucepan. Whisk in ½ cup sugar, the cornstarch, and a pinch of salt. Bring the milk to a simmer, just to dissolve the sugar. In a medium bowl, whisk the eggs. While whisking, slowly pour the hot milk into the eggs, to temper them. Pour the mixture back into the saucepan. Return the saucepan to medium-low heat. Cook, stirring and whisking, until the mixture just simmers and thickens. Immediately remove from the heat, and scrape it into a bowl to cool completely.

Once it is cooled, fold in the chopped chocolate and candied orange peel. Refrigerate until this is chilled and thickened, at least 1 hour.

For the sugar syrup: Bring 3 cups water and 1 cup of the sugar to a boil. Boil until the liquid is reduced by about a quarter. Remove from the heat, stir in the rum, and let it cool completely.

When you are ready to assemble the zuppa, whip the cream and remaining ¼ cup sugar to soft peaks. Fold half of the whipped cream, along with the cinnamon, into the chilled pastry cream.

In a 9-by-13-inch Pyrex or other rectangular dish, make a flat layer with half of the savoiardi. Brush with half of the sugar syrup, to moisten all of the savoiardi. Spread half of the pastry cream over the savoiardi. Top with another layer of savoiardi, and brush them with the remaining syrup. Spread the rest of the pastry cream over the top in an even layer, then spread the whipped cream over the top. If you have any savoiardi left, crumble them over this. Chill it several hours, or overnight, to let the flavors come together, before serving.

Sacher Torte

Torta Sacher
SERVES 10

TORTE
6 ounces butter, plus 1 tablespoon for the cake pan
¾ cup sugar
5 large eggs, separated
5 ounces semisweet chocolate, melted and cooled to lukewarm
1 cup all-purpose flour, plus a bit for the cake pan

FILLING AND GLAZE
2 cups apricot preserves
⅔ cup light corn syrup
2 tablespoons dark rum
Pinch of kosher salt
10 ounces semisweet chocolate, chopped into small chunks

Heavy cream, whipped, for serving

Preheat the oven to 375 degrees. Butter the bottom of a 9-inch springform pan, cover it with a circle of parchment cut to fit, then butter the top of the paper and the sides of the pan.

Cream the butter and sugar in the bowl of an electric mixer fitted with the whisk attachment until light and smooth. Incorporate the egg yolks one at a time, and then pour in the chocolate gradually, mixing it in thoroughly and scraping the sides of the bowl as needed. At low speed, incorporate the flour. Whip the egg whites by hand (or by machine, in a clean bowl with a clean whisk) to stiff peaks. Fold the egg whites into the batter with a rubber spatula. Scrape the batter into the prepared cake pan, and spread it in an even layer. Bake it until a cake tester comes out clean—or until the top springs back when lightly pressed—35 minutes or longer. Put the pan on a wire rack, cool it briefly, then remove the side ring of the springform and let the cake cool completely.

Lift the cake off the metal pan bottom, and peel off the parchment. Slice the cake horizontally in thirds, making three thin layers. Return the top layer of the cake to the metal pan bottom, upside down, so the crusty baked top is against the pan. This will be the base of the torta. To prepare for glazing: set the wire rack inside a rimmed baking sheet, and place the base layer on the rack.

Put ⅓ cup of the apricot preserves in a small saucepan with ¼ cup water, and heat, stirring, until the preserves dissolve into a loose syrup. Brush this syrup on all the cut surfaces of the layers, including the base, to moisten the cake.

To fill the layers: Put 1 cup of thick apricot preserves in a bowl, and stir just to loosen them. Spread ½ cup of this filling over the base layer. Now place the center layer of the cake (the layer with two cut surfaces) on top of the base, and spread the rest of this filling over the top. Finally, place the bottom layer of cake over the filling, upside down, so the flat, smooth surface that was originally the very bottom of the cake is now the top. Center the three layers so the sides of the torta are straight, and scrape off any drippings of apricot that have oozed out.

To seal the cake: Put the remaining ⅔ cup of apricot preserves in the small saucepan with ¼ cup water, and heat this to a simmer, stirring. Pour the preserves through a small strainer set in a cup, to remove any solid bits of apricot, and immediately pour the hot strained glaze from the cup over the torta.

Spread the glaze rapidly with an offset spatula, before it cools, coating the top completely, then spilling the glaze over the edges and down the sides. Smooth the glaze against the sides to seal them. Let the apricot glaze set, and scrape up any glaze that has dripped on the rack or into the pan underneath.

Meanwhile, prepare the chocolate glaze: Pour the corn syrup, rum, and 2 tablespoons water into a small saucepan, add a pinch of salt, and bring to a boil, stirring. Put the chopped chocolate in a large heat-proof bowl. Boil the syrup for a couple of minutes, then pour it over the chocolate, and stir until all the chunks have melted and the glaze is smooth and shiny. Let it cool, stirring occasionally, until it is barely warm to the touch but still flowing.

Pour the chocolate glaze over the top of the torta, spreading it with a clean offset spatula so it coats the top evenly and flows over the edge and down the sides. Smooth the sides so they are evenly coated, with no bare spots. Let the glaze solidify at room temperature.

Lift the torta off the rack onto a cake plate, still on the metal disk. Or, if you prefer, slide a broad spatula (or two) under the cake to separate it from the metal disk, then lift and move it. (If you want, warm up the excess glaze and spoon it into a paper piping cone. Write the name "Sacher" across the top—the traditional inscription on a Viennese Sacher torte—or pipe other decorative flourishes.) Cut it in wedges to serve, with mounds of whipped cream.

Ricotta Cheesecake with Prunes

Torta di Ricotta e Prugne
SERVES 8

1 tablespoon unsalted butter, softened
1 cup all-purpose flour, plus more for
    the pan
1¼ cups pitted dried prunes
Juice of 1 grapefruit, freshly squeezed, and
    grated zest of ½ grapefruit
Juice of 1 lemon, freshly squeezed, and grated
    zest of 1 lemon
2 tablespoons honey
3 large eggs, at room temperature
½ cup sugar
1½ pounds fresh ricotta, drained
¾ cup Greek yogurt
Pinch of kosher salt
1 teaspoon pure vanilla extract
¼ teaspoon baking powder

Preheat the oven to 350 degrees. Grease a 9-inch springform pan with the butter, and flour it, tapping out the excess. In a small saucepan, combine the prunes, grapefruit juice, lemon juice, and ½ cup water. Bring this to a simmer, and cook until the prunes are very soft, and the liquid is almost reduced away, about 12 minutes. Purée the prunes and cooking liquid with the honey in a mini–food processor to make a thick jam.

In a mixer fitted with the paddle attachment, beat the eggs and sugar at high speed until the mixture is light, about 2 minutes. At medium speed, beat in the ricotta, yogurt, and salt until smooth, about 2 minutes. Beat in the lemon and grapefruit zest and the vanilla. At low speed, add the flour and baking powder, and mix until just combined.

Spread half the batter in the prepared pan, and dollop half of the prune jam on top of the batter. Spread the remaining batter on top, and dollop it with the remaining prune jam. Lightly swirl the jam around into the batter with a paring knife to make a design. Bake it until a tester inserted in the center of the cake (but not in the jam) comes out clean, about 50 minutes. Let the cake cool for about 10 minutes, then open the spring and remove the side ring. Let the cake cool thoroughly before serving. Slide a broad metal spatula, or two, under the cake to separate it from the metal pan bottom, then lift and set the cake on a serving plate.

Chocolate-Hazelnut Cake

Torta Gianduia
SERVES 8

1 stick (8 tablespoons) unsalted butter, plus
    more for the baking pan
All-purpose flour, for the baking pan
4 ounces bittersweet chocolate, chopped
¾ cup skinned hazelnuts, lightly toasted
6 large eggs, separated
2 tablespoons sugar
One 13-ounce jar chocolate-hazelnut spread,
    such as Nutella, at room temperature
Pinch of kosher salt
1 tablespoon brandy

Preheat the oven to 350 degrees. Butter and flour a 9-inch springform pan. Melt the chocolate in the top of a double boiler or a metal bowl set over a saucepan of simmering water. Let it cool slightly. Grind the hazelnuts in a food processor until they are fine but not pasty.

In a mixer fitted with the whisk attachment, beat the egg whites until they are foamy. Add the sugar, and beat until the whites form stiff peaks, about 2 minutes. In a clean bowl, with the paddle attachment, beat the butter and chocolate-hazelnut spread until light, about 2 minutes. Add the yolks, salt, and brandy, and mix until smooth. Add the melted chocolate and ground hazelnuts, and mix until smooth. Remove the bowl from the mixer.

Stir about a quarter of the egg whites into the chocolate mixture to lighten it, and then gently fold in the remaining egg whites. Don't overmix. Pour the mixture into the prepared pan. Bake until a tester comes out clean, about 45 to 50 minutes. Let the cake cool for about 10 minutes, then open the spring and remove the side ring. Let the cake cool thoroughly before serving. Slide a broad metal spatula, or two, under the cake to separate it from the metal pan bottom, then lift and set the cake on a serving plate.

Walnut and Coffee Cake

Torta di Noci al Caffè
SERVES 8

1½ sticks unsalted butter, softened, plus more for the loaf pan
1½ cups all-purpose flour, plus more for the loaf pan
2 tablespoons dark rum or brandy
4 teaspoons instant espresso
3 large eggs, separated
2 pinches kosher salt
1 cup sugar
½ teaspoon pure vanilla extract
¾ cup coarsely chopped walnuts, toasted

Preheat the oven to 350 degrees. Butter and flour a 4½-by-8½-inch loaf pan. In a small bowl, stir together the rum or brandy and the instant espresso until the espresso dissolves.

In a mixer fitted with the whisk attachment, beat the egg whites with a pinch of salt until they are frothy. Add ¼ cup of the sugar, and beat at high speed until the egg whites form firm peaks, about 1 to 2 minutes. Set aside.

In a clean bowl in the mixer fitted with the paddle attachment, cream the butter and remaining ¾ cup sugar at medium-high speed until light and fluffy, about 2 minutes. Add the yolks, beating well between additions. Beat in the vanilla

and the espresso-rum mixture. Sift the flour directly over the bowl, and mix just to combine.

Remove the bowl from the mixer, and stir in about a quarter of the egg whites to lighten the batter. Gently fold in the remaining egg whites. Fold in the walnuts. Scrape the batter into the prepared pan, and bake until the cake is golden and a tester comes out clean, about 50 minutes. Cool it on a rack before unmolding and slicing.

Quince Cake

Torta di Mele Cotogne
SERVES 8

QUINCE
¾ cup sugar
1 cinnamon stick
Zest of 1 lemon, removed with a vegetable peeler
3 small ripe quince, peeled, cored, and sliced ¼ inch thick

CAKE
1 stick (8 tablespoons) unsalted butter, at room temperature, plus more for the cake pan
1¾ cup all-purpose flour, plus more for the cake pan
1½ teaspoons baking powder
¼ teaspoon ground cinnamon
Pinch of kosher salt
1¼ cups sugar
3 large eggs
1 teaspoon pure vanilla extract
½ cup milk

For the quince: In a medium saucepan, combine the sugar, cinnamon stick, and lemon zest with 2 cups water. Bring this to a simmer over medium heat, stirring to dissolve the sugar. Once the sugar is dissolved, add the quince. Bring it to a gentle simmer, and cook, stirring occasionally, until the quince is tender, about 20 minutes. Strain, and spread the quince on a rimmed sheet pan to cool. Discard the solids and syrup. (Or use the syrup to poach other fruit. You can also cool and keep it to sweeten tea or other cold drinks.)

For the cake: Preheat the oven to 350 degrees. Butter and flour a 9-inch round cake pan, and line the bottom with a circle of parchment. Sift the flour, baking powder, cinnamon, and salt onto a piece of parchment paper. In an electric mixer fitted with the paddle attachment, beat the butter and sugar at medium-high speed until light and fluffy, about 2 minutes. Add the eggs, one at a time, beating well between additions. Beat in the vanilla. Reduce the speed to low, and beat in the flour mixture in batches, alternating with the milk, in several additions beginning and ending with the flour. Beat at high speed for 30 seconds to make a smooth batter.

Gently fold the cooled quince into the batter, and spread this into the prepared pan. Bake until the cake is golden and a tester inserted in the center comes out clean, about 45 minutes. Cool it on a rack before unmolding.

Preheat the oven to 350 degrees. Butter an 8-by-13-inch baking dish, and coat it lightly with panko, tapping out the excess. Put the raisins in a small bowl, and cover them with hot water. Put the bread in a large bowl, and pour over it the milk and 1 cup water. Let the raisins and bread soak until they are softened, about 5 to 10 minutes.

In a food processor, combine the eggs, 1 cup of the sugar, and the salt. Process until smooth and light, about 1 minute. Add the bread (don't squeeze it out), lemon zest, and vanilla. Pulse just to combine. (Don't overmix—you still want the bread to be slightly chunky.)

Scrape the bread mixture into a large bowl, and stir in the peaches. Squeeze out the raisins, and stir them in. Pour the mixture into the prepared baking dish. In a small bowl, combine the panko and remaining ⅓ cup sugar. Sprinkle this evenly over the top of the bread mixture. Bake until it is set and golden brown on top, about 50 minutes. Let it cool on a rack until warm, then cut it into squares. The cake can also be served at room temperature.

Bread and Peach Cake

Dolce di Pane e Pesche
SERVES 8

Unsalted butter, softened, for the baking dish
¾ cup panko, plus more for the baking dish
½ cup golden raisins
6 ounces country bread, tough crusts removed, cut into chunks
1 cup milk
3 large eggs
1⅓ cups sugar
Pinch of kosher salt
Grated zest of 1 lemon
1 teaspoon pure vanilla extract
2 pounds ripe peaches, peeled, pitted, and cut into ½-inch chunks

Chocolate Zucchini Cake

Torta al Cioccolato e Zucchine
SERVES 8 TO 10

1 stick unsalted butter, softened, plus more for the baking pan
2 cups all-purpose flour, plus more for the baking pan
2 medium zucchini
¾ cup unsweetened natural cocoa powder
1 teaspoon baking soda
¼ teaspoon kosher salt
1½ cups sugar
½ cup vegetable oil
2 large eggs
1 teaspoon pure vanilla extract
½ cup buttermilk
1 cup coarsely chopped walnuts, toasted

Preheat the oven to 350 degrees. Butter and flour a 9-by-13-inch baking pan. Grate the zucchini on the coarse holes of a box grater. You should have about 2½ cups of grated zucchini.

On a piece of parchment, sift together the flour, cocoa, baking soda, and salt. In a mixer fitted with the paddle attachment, beat the butter, sugar, and oil at medium-high speed until smooth and light, about 2 minutes. Add the eggs one at a time, beating well after each addition. Beat in the vanilla. Add the flour mixture in several additions, alternating with the buttermilk, beginning and ending with the flour. Beat the batter at high speed about 10 seconds, just to mix thoroughly.

Remove the bowl from the mixer, and stir in the zucchini and walnuts. Pour the batter into the prepared pan. Bake until a tester inserted in the center comes out clean, about 40 minutes. Let it cool completely on a rack before cutting it into squares to serve.

Almond Cake with Chocolate Chips

Torta di Mandorle con Gocce di Cioccolata
SERVES 8 TO 10

2 sticks (16 tablespoons) unsalted butter, at room temperature, plus more for the pan
1½ cups all-purpose flour, plus more for the pan
½ teaspoon baking powder
¼ teaspoon kosher salt
1 cup sugar
4 large eggs
Grated zest of 1 small orange
½ teaspoon pure almond extract
1¾ cups almond meal
½ cup mini–chocolate chips
¼ cup sliced almonds

Preheat the oven to 350 degrees. Butter and flour a 9-inch springform pan. Sift the flour, baking powder, and salt onto a piece of parchment.

In a mixer fitted with the paddle attachment, cream the butter and sugar at medium-high speed until light and fluffy, about 2 minutes. Add the eggs one at a time, beating well between additions and scraping down the sides of the bowl. Beat in the orange zest and almond extract. At low speed, beat in half of the flour mixture, then half of the almond meal. Repeat with the remaining flour and almond meal. Mix at medium speed just to combine all the ingredients well.

Remove the bowl from the mixer, and stir in the chocolate chips. Scrape the batter into the prepared pan, and smooth out the top. Sprinkle the sliced almonds evenly over the batter.

Bake until the torta is golden brown on top and a toothpick inserted in the center comes out clean, about 40 to 45 minutes. Let the cake cool for about 10 minutes, then open the spring and remove the side ring. Let the cake cool thoroughly before serving. Slide a broad metal spatula, or two, under the cake to separate it from the metal pan bottom, then lift and set the cake on a serving plate.

Wine and Grape Cake

Torta di Vino con Uva
SERVES 8

6 tablespoons unsalted butter, at room temperature, plus more for the cake pan and grapes
1½ cups all-purpose flour, plus more for the cake pan
1½ teaspoons baking powder
½ teaspoon baking soda
⅛ teaspoon kosher salt
¾ cup granulated white sugar
2 eggs
1 tablespoon extra-virgin olive oil
1 teaspoon pure vanilla extract
1 tablespoon grated lemon or orange zest, or a combination
¾ cup dry white wine

2 cups small red seedless grapes, stemmed, washed, and dried, or 2 cups blueberries or raspberries

FOR TOPPING THE CAKE DURING BAKING
2 tablespoons unsalted butter, cut into small bits
1 tablespoon cane sugar or granulated white sugar

OPTIONAL GARNISHES
Confectioners' sugar
Whipped cream

Preheat the oven to 375 degrees. Butter and flour a 9-inch springform pan. Sift together the flour, baking powder, baking soda, and salt onto a piece of parchment.

In a mixer fitted with the paddle attachment, at low speed, cream the butter and sugar together; when they are blended, beat at high speed for a couple of minutes, until smooth and light. Scrape down the sides of the bowl, and beat in the eggs, one at a time, at medium speed; then mix in the olive oil, vanilla, and citrus zest. Beat at high speed for 2 minutes or so, to lighten and smooth the batter.

Scrape down the sides, and, at low speed, mix in the dry ingredients, alternating with the wine, beginning and ending with the flour. When everything has been incorporated, scrape the sides (and bottom) of the bowl, and beat at high speed for about 20 seconds, to finish the batter.

Spread the batter in the prepared cake pan in an even layer. Sprinkle a teaspoon of flour over the grapes, and toss so they're all lightly dusted. Scatter the grapes over the surface of the batter. Swirl a spatula or knife around them, folding and stirring them into the top of the batter—don't fold or swirl deeper than an inch. The fruit doesn't need to be completely covered, because it will sink as the cake rises.

Set the pan in the oven, and bake for 25 minutes, or until the top is set, though the batter underneath will still be loose and shaky. Scatter the butter bits and cane sugar on the top.

Return the cake to the oven, and bake until it is set and the top is golden brown and lightly glazed by the final sugar and butter, about 15 minutes more. Test for doneness by inserting a cake tester or toothpick into the middle to see if it comes out clean. Remove the cake from the oven to a cooling rack.

Let the cake cool for about 10 minutes, then open the spring and remove the side ring. Let the cake cool thoroughly before serving. Remove the metal pan bottom, if you want, after an hour or so, when you can handle the cake: lay a piece of parchment or wax paper on the cake top (so the pretty surface doesn't get messed up), then a plate or a wire rack. Flip the cake over, and pry and lift off the pan bottom. Invert the cake again, onto a rack if it needs to cool further, or onto a serving plate.

Serve it at room temperature, sliced into wedges. I love this cake plain, with just a dusting of confectioners' sugar, or you can garnish it with whipped cream.

Polenta Sponge Cake

Pan di Spagna di Polenta
SERVES 8

1 tablespoon unsalted butter at room temperature
All-purpose flour, for the pan
2 tablespoons milk, warmed to around body temperature
⅔ cup sugar
1 teaspoon active dry yeast
4 large eggs, separated
Grated zest of 1 lemon, and freshly squeezed juice of ½ lemon
Grated zest of 1 orange
½ teaspoon pure vanilla extract
3 tablespoons dark rum
⅔ cup instant polenta

Preheat the oven to 350 degrees. Grease an 8-inch cake pan with the butter, and dust it with flour, tapping out the excess.

In a small bowl, stir together the milk, 1 tablespoon of the sugar, and the yeast until the yeast dissolves. In a mixer fitted with the paddle attachment, beat the egg yolks and remaining sugar minus 1 tablespoon at high speed until pale yellow. Add the yeast mixture, lemon zest and juice, orange zest, vanilla, and rum, and blend just to combine. Sift the polenta over the egg mixture, and mix at medium speed until everything is combined.

In a clean mixer bowl with the whisk attachment, beat the egg whites and remaining tablespoon sugar at high speed until they form stiff peaks. Stir about a quarter of the egg whites into the batter to lighten it. Gently fold the remaining egg whites into the batter, just to combine—don't overmix. Pour the batter into the prepared pan, and bake until the cake is golden brown and a tester inserted in the center comes out clean, about 25 to 30 minutes.

Chocolate Zabaglione Cake

Torta di Zabaglione al Cioccolato
SERVES 8 TO 10

SPONGE CAKE
Unsalted butter, softened, for the cake pan
1 cup all-purpose flour, plus more for the cake pan
¼ cup unsweetened natural cocoa powder
⅛ teaspoon baking powder
⅛ teaspoon baking soda
3 large eggs, at room temperature
¾ cup granulated sugar

SYRUP
½ cup dry Marsala
2 tablespoons superfine sugar

FILLING
1 teaspoon unflavored gelatin
8 ounces semisweet chocolate, finely chopped
⅓ cup plus 1 tablespoon granulated sugar
7 large egg yolks, at room temperature
½ cup dry Marsala
1½ cups heavy cream, whipped to soft peaks

CHOCOLATE ZABAGLIONE SAUCE
3 ounces semisweet chocolate, finely chopped
6 large egg yolks, at room temperature
¼ cup dry Marsala
¼ cup granulated sugar

3 tablespoons unsweetened natural cocoa powder, for garnish

For the sponge cake: Preheat the oven to 375 degrees. Butter and flour a 10-inch cake pan with 3-inch sides. Sift the flour, cocoa, baking powder, and baking soda into a bowl or onto a piece of parchment.

In a large bowl set over simmering water, whisk the eggs and sugar together until the mixture is warm to the touch and the sugar is dissolved, about 3 minutes.

Using a handheld electric mixer, beat the egg-sugar mixture, still on the heat, at high speed until it is doubled in volume, about 5 minutes. Off heat, sprinkle in the dry ingredients, and fold gently until just combined. Pour the batter into the prepared pan, and bake until a tester comes out clean and the surface of the cake bounces back when pressed, about 25 minutes. Cool it on a rack for 15 minutes, then unmold and cool completely.

For the syrup: In a small saucepan, warm the Marsala and superfine sugar over low heat, stirring just until the sugar is dissolved. Let it cool completely.

For the filling: In a small saucepan, sprinkle the gelatin over 1½ tablespoons cold water. Melt the chocolate in a small bowl over a pan of simmering water, then let it cool slightly. In a medium saucepan, combine the sugar with ¼ cup water.

Bring to a boil. Cook, without stirring but swirling the pan occasionally, until the syrup reaches 250 degrees on a candy thermometer or forms a ball when a drop is dropped into cold water, about 5 minutes.

Whisk the egg yolks in a large stainless-steel bowl over a pan of simmering water until they are warm to the touch. With a handheld mixer, pour in the simple sugar syrup in a thin stream, beating at medium speed until it is combined. Remove the bowl from the heat.

Warm the gelatin mixture over very low heat, just until the gelatin is melted. Beat the cooled melted chocolate; then beat the gelatin and the Marsala into the egg mixture at low speed until everything is just combined. Fold the whipped cream into the mixture until no traces of white remain.

To assemble the cake: With a serrated knife, cut the sponge cake horizontally into three equal layers. Fit the bottom layer into a 10-inch springform pan. Brush with a third of the Marsala syrup. Spread with a third of the filling. Repeat all steps with the remaining two layers of sponge cake, ending with the filling. Smooth with a spatula, cover, and refrigerate overnight.

When ready to serve, make the sauce: Melt the chocolate in a bowl over a pan of simmering water. Remove the bowl and let the chocolate cool slightly.

Over the same pan of water, whisk the egg yolks, Marsala, and sugar in a large stainless-steel bowl. Whisk constantly until the mixture is light and frothy and forms a ribbon figure-8 when you draw your whisk out.

Remove the bowl from the heat, and gently fold in the melted chocolate in three additions.

Unmold the cake. Dust with the cocoa powder. Slice the cake, and serve it with the hot zabaglione sauce.

🍀 Note that the cake must be made and chilled a day ahead, but the zabaglione sauce should be made at the last minute.

Grain and Ricotta Pie

Pastiera Napoletana
SERVES 12 OR MORE

PASTA FROLLA DOUGH
2 cups granulated sugar
4 large egg yolks
Grated zest of 1 lemon
4 cups all-purpose flour
2 cups (1 pound) unsalted butter or shortening, cut into 1-inch pieces, at room temperature, plus more for the pan

FILLING
1½ cups wheat berries
4 cups milk
2½ cups granulated sugar
5 large eggs, separated
4 cups fresh ricotta, drained overnight
2 teaspoons orange-flower water (optional; if you can't find it, use pure vanilla extract and 2 teaspoons grated orange zest)
½ teaspoon ground cinnamon
½ cup candied lemon or orange peel, cut into ¼-inch dice

Confectioners' sugar, for garnish

For the dough: Process the sugar, egg yolks, and lemon zest in the bowl of a food processor fitted with a metal blade until blended. Add the flour and butter, and process just until you have a smooth dough. Stop once or twice to scrape down the sides of the bowl. Wrap the dough in plastic wrap, and chill it for at least an hour, or up to 1 day.

For the filling: Soak the wheat berries in a bowl with enough water to cover by three fingers until softened, 3 to 4 hours. Drain them well. Bring the milk to a simmer in a medium saucepan. Stir in the drained grain and ¼ cup of the sugar. Return it to a gentle simmer, and cook, stirring occasionally, until the wheat berries are tender but still have some bite, about 45 minutes. Drain, and cool to room temperature.

Preheat the oven to 350 degrees. Butter a 12-inch springform pan. Roll out two-thirds of the dough into a 16-inch circle. Fold the circle in quarters, place one of the points in the center of the buttered pan, and unfold the dough, pressing it gently against the bottom and sides and into the corners of the pan. Refrigerate the dough while continuing with the filling.

Process the remaining 2¼ cups sugar and 5 egg yolks in the bowl of a food processor fitted with the metal blade until the mixture is pale yellow. Spoon in the ricotta, and add the orange water (or vanilla and orange zest) and cinnamon. Mix, using quick on-and-off pulses, just until blended. Scrape the ricotta into the bowl with the grain, scatter the candied fruit peel over all, and fold everything together with a rubber spatula until blended.

Beat the egg whites in a separate bowl until they form stiff peaks. Fold a quarter of the egg whites into the grain mixture, scraping up the filling from the bottom of the bowl and bringing it up through the mixture. When just a few streaks of egg white remain, add the remaining beaten whites and fold them into the filling in the same way. Scrape the filling into the dough-lined pan.

Roll out the remaining piece of dough to a 13-inch circle. Cut it into ½-inch-thick strips. Make a lattice top by alternating the cut strips of the dough in alternating directions. Join the strips of dough to the dough along the sides of the pan by pressing gently.

Bake until the crust is golden brown and the center feels springy, about 1½ hours. Remove it from the oven, and cool it completely before serving. The cake will keep, refrigerated, for up to 1 week. It will be better a day or two after baking. Sprinkle with confectioners' sugar before serving.

VARIATION:

A version of this pastiera that I made in my first restaurants was a bit creamier and lighter. To make that version, which is quite common in Campania, substitute 1 cup pastry cream in the filling for ½ cup of the ricotta, 1 egg, and ½ cup sugar. Add the pastry cream to the filling along with the ricotta mixture.

Ricotta Cheesecake

Torta di Ricotta
SERVES 8

½ cup raisins
3 tablespoons dark rum
Unsalted butter, softened, for the pan
Fine dried bread crumbs, for the pan
5 large eggs, separated
¾ cup sugar
Pinch of kosher salt
3½ cups fresh ricotta cheese, drained overnight
Grated zest of 1 large lemon
Grated zest of 1 large orange
½ cup heavy cream
½ cup pine nuts

Preheat the oven to 375 degrees. Soak the raisins in the rum in a small bowl, tossing occasionally, until they are softened and have absorbed most of the rum.

Brush an 8-inch springform pan lightly with softened unsalted butter. Sprinkle the bread crumbs over the butter to coat the pan generously. Shake out the excess crumbs.

Beat the egg yolks and sugar and salt in a large bowl with a whisk until the mixture is pale yellow. Add the drained ricotta, lemon zest, and orange zest, and beat until blended thoroughly. Beat in the cream. Fold in the pine nuts and the raisins and rum with a rubber spatula, blending well. Beat the egg whites in a separate bowl with a hand mixer or wire whisk until they form firm peaks when a beater is lifted from them. Add about a quarter of the egg whites to the ricotta mixture, and gently stir them in. Add the remaining egg whites and fold them in, using a large rubber spatula to scrape the batter from the bottom of the bowl up and over the whites. Pour the cake mixture into the prepared pan, and bake until the cake is golden brown on top and set in the center, about 1 hour.

Let the cake cool for about 10 minutes, then open the spring and remove the side ring. Let the cake cool thoroughly before serving. Slide a broad metal spatula, or two, under the cake to separate it from the metal pan bottom, then lift and set the cake on a serving plate.

Cherry Jam Tart

Crostata di Marmellata di Ciliege
MAKES A 10-BY-15-INCH TART, SERVING 10 OR MORE

11 ounces unsalted butter (2¾ sticks), plus more for the pan
1 cup sugar
2 cups all-purpose flour, plus more for handling the dough
2 cups almond flour or almond meal
¼ teaspoon kosher salt
½ cup dried cherries
½ cup dark rum or warm water
2 cups chunky cherry preserves (or a bit more: about 24 ounces in jars)
½ cup sliced blanched almonds, lightly toasted

For the tart dough: Cream the butter and sugar in a mixer fitted with the paddle attachment at medium-high speed until light and fluffy, about 2 minutes. Add the flours and salt to the bowl, and beat at low speed just until the dry ingredients are incorporated and a cohesive dough forms. Scrape the dough out of the bowl onto a work surface, and knead a few times, until it comes together in a ball. Divide it into two pieces, a larger piece of two-thirds of the dough, and a small piece of a third of the dough. Press both pieces into flat dough rectangles about 3 by 4 inches, and wrap them well in plastic wrap. Refrigerate for 2 hours (or up to a day) before rolling; freeze for longer keeping.

When you are ready to bake the tart, preheat the oven to 350 degrees. Butter the bottom and sides of a 10-by-15-inch jelly-roll pan. In a small bowl, cover the dried cherries with rum or warm water; let them soak and soften. Place the larger piece of dough between two sheets of parchment, and roll it out to a rectangle a bit larger than the jelly-roll pan. Peel off the top layer of parchment, invert the dough so it lies centered in the pan, then peel off the second parchment sheet. Gently press and push the dough into the pan to form a smooth, intact crust, evenly thick on the bottom, and slightly thicker against the sides of the pan. Scrape off excess dough so the crust is flush with the pan sides, and save all the scraps. (If the crust tears or is too thin in spots, patch these with the extra dough.)

For the tart filling: Scrape the cherry preserves into a bowl, drain the rehydrated cherries, and stir them into the preserves. Spread the filling in the crust, covering the bottom evenly. Roll the smaller piece of dough between the parchment sheets to a round or oblong sheet (about as thick as you rolled the larger piece of dough). Peel off the top layer of parchment; to make a decorative top crust, you can cut out circles or other shapes with floured cookie cutters, or use a pastry wheel to cut diamonds or lattice strips. If you are short on top-crust dough, gather and reroll all the dough scraps to make more shapes, and lay them all over the tart, in any pattern you like, with the cherry filling peeking through. Sprinkle the sliced almonds evenly over the top of the tart. Bake, rotating the pan halfway through the baking time, until the crust is deep golden brown and the filling is bubbling, about 45 to 50 minutes. Let the tart cool completely on a wire rack before cutting it into squares to serve.

Apricot Blueberry Tart

Crostata di Albicocche e Mirtilli
SERVES 6 TO 8

DOUGH
1¼ cups all-purpose flour, plus more for rolling
1 tablespoon sugar
½ teaspoon baking powder
Pinch of kosher salt
1 stick (8 tablespoons) unsalted butter, cold, cut into small pieces
2 large egg yolks

FILLING
8 ounces dried apricots, halved
Juice of 1 lemon, freshly squeezed
½ cup apricot preserves
¼ cup sugar
1 cup blueberries

1 large egg, beaten, for brushing
1 tablespoon sugar

For the dough: In a food processor, combine the flour, sugar, baking powder, and salt, and pulse just to combine. Sprinkle in the butter pieces, and pulse to form small lumps of butter and flour. Beat the egg yolks with 1 tablespoon cold water, and drizzle them into the processor. Pulse in short bursts just until the dough comes together in a few big clumps. Add a little more water if the dough is still lumpy and dry, or a little more flour if it forms a sticky ball on the blade.

Dump the dough onto a floured counter, and knead it a few times, just to bring it together. Flatten it into a disk, wrap it in plastic, and refrigerate for 1 hour (or up to a day).

For the filling: In a medium saucepan, combine the apricots, lemon juice, and 1 cup water. Cover, and simmer gently until the apricots begin to plump, about 5 minutes. Stir in the preserves and sugar, and simmer, uncovered, until the apricots are glazed with a thick syrup, about 10 to 12 minutes. Transfer the filling to a bowl, cool it to room temperature while you roll the dough, then stir in the blueberries.

Preheat the oven to 375 degrees. Remove the dough from the refrigerator 10 minutes before you're ready to roll it. Roll the dough between two floured pieces of parchment to about an 11-inch circle. With a pizza cutter, trim the dough into a circle. Transfer it to a sheet pan, still on the bottom parchment.

Spread the filling on the circle of dough, leaving a 2-inch border. Fold a 2-inch border over the filling, until you have folded the whole tart, leaving the center bare. Bake 20 minutes, or until the dough is set. Brush the crust with the egg, and sprinkle it with the sugar. Bake until the filling is bubbly and the crust is a deep golden brown, about 40 to 45 minutes total. Let it cool on the sheet pan before cutting into wedges.

Peach Cake

Crostata di Pesche
SERVES 8 TO 10

3 tablespoons unsalted butter, softened, plus more for the pan
2 cups all-purpose flour, plus more for the pan
3 large ripe peaches
1 tablespoon freshly squeezed lemon juice
¾ cup plus 1 tablespoon sugar
2½ teaspoons baking powder
¼ teaspoon kosher salt
2 large eggs
2 tablespoons milk
½ teaspoon pure vanilla extract
2 tablespoons smooth apricot jam

Preheat the oven to 350 degrees. Butter and flour a 9-inch springform pan. Core (but don't peel) the peaches, and slice them into eighths. You should have about 2½ cups peaches. In a medium bowl, toss the peaches with the lemon juice and

1 tablespoon of the sugar. Let them marinate 10 minutes at room temperature.

Sift the flour, baking powder, and salt together into a bowl or onto a sheet of parchment. In a mixer fitted with the paddle attachment, beat the remaining sugar, the eggs, milk, and vanilla until smooth. Add the dry ingredients, and mix at low speed until smooth. Increase the speed to medium, and beat in the butter a tablespoon at a time to make a smooth dough.

Spread the dough in the prepared pan, making it an even thickness at the bottom and sides. Arrange the peaches, skin side down, in a radiating pattern, and press them lightly into the dough. Bake until the tart is puffed and golden brown and the peaches are tender, about 40 to 45 minutes. Cool it on a rack until just warm.

Warm the jam in a small saucepan with 1 tablespoon water, and mix to make a smooth glaze. Brush the glaze over the peaches, let it cool for 20 minutes, removing from the pan, and serve the tart warm.

Plum Tart

Crostata di Prugne Fresche
SERVES 8

SWEET TART DOUGH
1½ cups all-purpose flour
½ cup sugar
½ teaspoon baking powder
Pinch of kosher salt
1 stick unsalted butter, cold, cut into pieces
1 large egg
¼ teaspoon pure almond extract

FILLING
6 tablespoons smooth apricot jam
14 Italian prune plums, halved and pitted
2 tablespoons sugar
1 teaspoon freshly squeezed lemon juice

For the dough: In a food processor, combine the flour, sugar, baking powder, and salt. Pulse just to combine. Drop in the butter pieces, and pulse until the dough is lumpy, like coarse oats or meal. Beat the egg and almond extract together in a spouted measuring cup. With the processor running, pour in the egg. Process until the dough just comes together, adding a little more flour or cold water if it is too wet or too dry. Scrape the dough onto your work surface, and knead a few times, just to bring it together. Flatten it into a disk, and wrap it in plastic. Let it rest in the refrigerator for 1 hour.

Preheat the oven to 375 degrees. On a floured work surface, roll the dough into an ⅛-inch-thick round. (If you have trouble rolling, roll the dough between two layers of parchment.) Fit the dough into a 10-inch fluted tart pan with a removable bottom. Trim off any excess or overhang. Put the shell in the freezer to firm up for 10 minutes.

Line the shell with parchment and dried beans to weight it down. Bake until the dough is set and light golden, about 18 minutes. Let it cool.

Brush 4 tablespoons of the jam over the bottom of the cooled tart shell. Starting from the outside edge of the shell, arrange the plums in concentric circles until the shell is filled. Bake the tart 10 minutes, then sprinkle it with the sugar, and return it to the oven until the pastry is nicely browned and the plums are caramelized, about 25 minutes total. Remove it from the oven, and cool it on a rack.

While the tart is still warm, melt the remaining apricot jam in a small saucepan with 1 teaspoon water and the lemon juice. Mix until it is smooth, then brush the glaze over the plums. Let tart cool for 20 minutes, remove from pan, and serve at room temperature.

Strawberry Tart

Crostata di Fragole
SERVES 8 TO 10

SWEET TART DOUGH
1½ cups all-purpose flour
½ cup sugar
½ teaspoon baking powder
Pinch of kosher salt
1 stick unsalted butter, cold, cut into pieces
1 large egg
¼ teaspoon pure almond extract

½ recipe Pastry Cream (page 375), chilled
2 pints ripe strawberries, washed, halved, and
    hulled
¼ cup smooth apricot jam
1 teaspoon freshly squeezed lemon juice

For the dough: In a food processor, combine the flour, sugar, baking powder, and salt. Process just to combine. Drop in the butter pieces, and pulse until the dough is crumbly, like coarse oats or meal. Beat the egg and almond extract together in a spouted measuring cup. With the processor running, pour in the egg. Process until the dough just comes together, adding a little more flour or cold water if it is too wet or too dry. Scrape the dough onto your work surface, and knead a few times, just to bring it together. Flatten it into a disk, and wrap it in plastic. Let it rest in the refrigerator for 1 hour.

Preheat the oven to 375 degrees. On a floured work surface, roll the dough into an ⅛-inch-thick round. (If you have trouble rolling, roll the dough between two layers of parchment.) Fit the dough into a 9- or 10-inch fluted tart pan with a removable bottom. Press the dough lightly into the pan and trim off any excess or overhang. Put the shell in the freezer to firm up for 10 minutes.

Line the shell with parchment and dried beans to weight it down. Bake until the dough is set and light golden, about 18 minutes. Remove the parchment and beans, and continue to bake until the tart shell is crisp and golden, about 12 to 14 minutes more. Cool it completely on a rack before filling.

When you are ready to serve, spread the pastry cream evenly over the bottom of the tart shell. Starting from the outside, arrange the strawberries, cut side down, in tight concentric circles so they mound up toward the center of the tart. In a small saucepan, combine the jam, lemon juice, and 1 teaspoon water. Heat and stir it over low heat until it is smooth and syrupy. Brush the glaze gently over the strawberries. Let the glaze set for 10 minutes, remove tart from the the pan, and serve.

Apple Custard Tart

Crostata di Mele alla Crema
SERVES 8 TO 10

SWEET TART DOUGH
1½ cups all-purpose flour
½ cup sugar
½ teaspoon baking powder
Pinch of kosher salt
1 stick unsalted butter, cold, cut into pieces
1 large egg
¼ teaspoon pure almond extract

FILLING
2 medium Golden Delicious apples
¼ cup smooth apricot preserves
¼ cup sugar
Juice of ½ lemon, freshly squeezed
¼ teaspoon pure vanilla extract
1 large egg
6 tablespoons heavy cream
¼ cup milk

For the dough: In a food processor, combine the flour, sugar, baking powder, and salt. Process just to combine. Drop in the butter pieces, and pulse until lumpy, like coarse oats or meal form. Beat the egg and almond extract together in a spouted measuring cup. With the processor running, pour in the egg. Process until the dough just comes together, adding a little more flour or cold water if it is too wet or too dry. Scrape the dough onto your work surface, and knead a few times, just to bring it together. Flatten it into a disk, and wrap it in plastic. Let it rest in the refrigerator for 1 hour.

Preheat the oven to 375 degrees. On a floured work surface, roll the dough into a ¼-inch-thick round. (If you have trouble rolling, roll the dough between two layers of parchment.) Fit the dough into an 8- or 9-inch fluted tart pan with a removable bottom. Trim off any excess or overhang. Put the shell in the freezer to firm up for 10 minutes.

Line the shell with parchment and dried beans to weight it down. Bake until the dough is set and barely light golden, about 15 minutes. Cool it completely on a rack. Reduce the oven temperature to 350 degrees.

For the filling: Peel and core the apples, and cut them into ½-inch-thick slices. Put the apple slices in a large bowl, and toss them with 2 tablespoons each of the apricot preserves and the sugar and all the lemon juice. Let the filling sit 10 minutes.

In a medium bowl, whisk together the vanilla, the egg, and the remaining 2 tablespoons sugar until pale yellow. Whisk in the cream and milk until smooth.

Spread the remaining 2 tablespoons apricot jam on the bottom of the cooled tart shell. Arrange the apple slices (leaving the juices behind in the bowl) over the jam in two concentric, slightly overlapping circles. Put the tart on a baking sheet, and pour the custard mixture over the apples. Bake until the custard is set and the apples are tender, about 40 minutes. Cool the tart completely on a rack. Remove tart from the pan and serve.

Free-Form Plum Tart

Crostata di Prugne Fresche
SERVES 6

FREE-FORM DOUGH
1½ cups all-purpose flour
3 tablespoons sugar
⅛ teaspoon kosher salt
7 tablespoons unsalted butter, cold, cut into bits

FILLING AND TOPPING
1½ pounds purple or red plums, pitted and
    cut into sixths
Grated zest and freshly squeezed juice of
    1 lemon
¼ cup sugar
2 tablespoons apricot jam
2 tablespoons unsalted butter, cold, cut into
    pieces
¼ cup panko
¼ teaspoon ground cinnamon

For the dough: In a food processor, combine the flour, sugar, and salt. Pulse just to combine ingredients. Drop in the butter pieces, and pulse until mixture is lumpy. With the processor running, pour in 6 tablespoons cold water. Process until the dough just comes together in a lump around the blade, adding a little more flour or cold water if it is too wet or too dry. Scrape the dough onto your work surface, and knead a few times, just to bring it together. Flatten it into a disk, and wrap it in plastic. Let it rest in the refrigerator for 1 hour.

Preheat the oven to 375 degrees. In a large bowl, toss the plums with the grated lemon zest and juice, 2 tablespoons of the sugar, the jam, and butter. In a small bowl, combine the panko, cinnamon, and remaining 2 tablespoons sugar.

On a piece of parchment, roll the dough into a rough circle about 14 to 15 inches in diameter. With a pizza cutter, cut the dough into as perfect a round as you can get, about 12 to 13 inches in diameter. Slide the dough on the parchment onto a flat baking sheet.

Sprinkle all but 1 tablespoon of the crumb mixture in an 8-inch circle in the middle of the dough. Arrange the plums on their sides in concentric circles, finishing in the center. Fold up the edges of the dough to form a crust of about 2 to 3 inches. Sprinkle the exposed fruit with the remaining crumb mixture.

Begin baking on the bottom rack of the oven. Bake about 30 to 40 minutes. Then switch it to the middle rack, and continue baking until the top crust is deep golden brown and the plums are soft and the juices bubbly, about 15 to 20 minutes more—50 minutes to an hour in total.

Slide the crostata and parchment onto a rack to cool. While it is still warm, slide it with the aid of a spatula from the parchment onto a serving plate. Serve it warm or at room temperature.

🍀 This tart would also be delicious with fresh apricots. Use the same weight, but quarter them. The cooking time may be a few minutes less, depending on their ripeness.

Apple Strudel

Strudel di Mele
MAKES 1 STRUDEL, SERVING 10

FOR THE DOUGH
2 cups sifted all-purpose flour, plus more for kneading the dough
3 tablespoons extra-virgin olive oil
½ teaspoon salt

FOR THE FILLING
1 cup golden raisins
2 tablespoons dark rum
½ cup (1 stick) unsalted butter, cut into ½-inch pieces
1 cup dried bread crumbs
1½ cups granulated sugar
½ teaspoon ground cinnamon

3 pounds tart green apples, such as Granny Smith, peeled, cored, and cut into ½-inch wedges
Grated zest and freshly squeezed juice of 1 lemon

Confectioners' sugar, for dusting

To make the dough: Combine the flour, oil, and salt in the work bowl of a food processor. With the motor running, add ½ cup lukewarm water, and process until the mixture forms a smooth, silky dough. (If the mixture is too dry, add more water, 1 tablespoon at a time.) Turn the dough out onto a lightly floured surface, and knead, adding flour as necessary to prevent the dough from sticking, until the dough is very smooth and elastic, about 3 minutes. Wrap the dough in plastic wrap, and let it rest at room temperature 2 to 3 hours, or in the refrigerator for up to 2 days. (Let the refrigerated dough sit at room temperature for at least 1 hour before rolling it.)

For the filling: In a small bowl, toss the raisins with the rum. Let them stand, tossing occasionally, while preparing the strudel. Melt half the butter in a medium skillet over medium heat. Add the bread crumbs and toast, stirring constantly, until they are lightly browned, about 5 minutes. Remove the skillet from the heat, and stir in ½ cup of the sugar and the cinnamon.

Put the remaining cup of granulated sugar, the apples, grated lemon zest and lemon juice, and the rum and raisins in a large bowl. Let the apples stand, tossing them occasionally, until the sugar begins to dissolve and the apples are coated with the syrup, about 15 minutes.

Preheat the oven to 450 degrees, and line a large baking sheet with parchment paper.

On a floured work surface, roll out the dough, from the center to the edges, into a very thin rectangle, approximately 22 by 16 inches. As it gets thinner, you should be able to pull and stretch it gently with your hands to coax it into the shape you want. Don't worry if the dough tears a little in spots—you can patch it later—or if it doesn't form a perfect rectangle. Turn the dough so one of the longer sides is facing you. Place a kitchen towel or length of double-thick cheesecloth under the entire far side of the dough rectangle by about 4 inches. (This will help you move the strudel to the baking sheet once it is formed.) Spread the bread-crumb mixture evenly over the dough, leaving a 1½-inch-wide border on all sides. Dot the bread crumbs with small pieces of the remaining ¼ cup of butter.

Arrange the apple mixture in a long mound along the side closest to you. The mound of apples should measure about 4 inches wide and be as long as the bread-crumb mixture, leaving the 1½-inch-wide border clean. Fold the clean border closest to you over the apples. Begin rolling the strudel into a fairly tight roll, like a jelly roll, starting at one end of the apple mound, giving it a half-roll, and gradually working your way down the roll. Don't worry if the roll is uneven or tears in places, just patch it with your fingers. You should end up with a fairly even, lumpy-looking roll that is centered, seam side down, on the kitchen towel. Cut off any excess dough from the ends. Seal the ends of the strudel by folding them underneath the roll and pressing them firmly with your fingers. Use the towel to transfer the strudel to the prepared baking sheet, bending the strudel into a crescent shape if necessary to fit it on the pan.

Brush the strudel lightly with olive oil, and place it in the oven; immediately reduce the oven temperature to 375 degrees. Bake 30 minutes, until the top of the strudel is a light golden brown. (If it is deeper in color than that, reduce the temperature to 350 degrees.) Rotate the baking pan in the oven, and continue to bake until the strudel crust is deep golden brown and firm, about 30 minutes more.

Remove the strudel from the oven, and let it stand until completely cooled. To serve: cut the strudel with a serrated knife into 2-inch-thick slices, and sprinkle it with confectioners' sugar.

Cannoli Napoleon

Cannolo a Strati
SERVES 6 TO 8

FOR THE PASTRY DOUGH
1½ cups all-purpose flour, plus more for rolling
2 tablespoons granulated sugar
¼ teaspoon kosher salt
2 tablespoons extra-virgin olive oil
1 teaspoon white wine vinegar
½ cup dry red wine, or as needed

FOR THE CANNOLI CREAM
1 pound (2 cups) fresh ricotta, drained overnight
⅔ cup confectioners' sugar, plus more for garnish
1 tablespoon Grand Marnier (optional, but very good!)
1 ounce unsweetened chocolate, coarsely chopped (or 3 tablespoons bittersweet chips)
2 tablespoons candied orange rind, coarsely chopped
2 tablespoons toasted almonds, coarsely chopped

Vegetable oil, for frying

For the dough: Put the flour, granulated sugar, and salt in a food-processor bowl, and process just to mix. Mix the olive oil, vinegar, and wine together in a spouted measuring cup, and, with the machine running, pour all but 2 tablespoons of the liquid in, and process it for 20 seconds or so, until a dough gathers on the blade. If it feels hard and dry, sprinkle in the remaining liquid a little at a time and process briefly, to make it moist and malleable. Turn the dough out of the bowl, and knead it by hand into a soft, smooth ball. Flatten it to a disk, wrap it in plastic, and let it rest for 4 hours or up to 2 days.

To make the cannoli cream: Whip the ricotta with the whisk attachment of an electric mixer until smooth. Whip in the ⅔ cup confectioners' sugar and the Grand Marnier (if using). Fold in the chopped chocolate, orange rind, and almonds, and refrigerate until chilled, at least 30 minutes.

Cut the pastry dough in half. On a lightly floured surface, roll out one piece of dough to a rectangle 11 by 14 inches (or as close as possible). With a sharp knife and a ruler, trim the edges and divide the rectangle into a dozen squares, about 3½ inches on a side. (If you can only get nine squares of that size or slightly larger, that's fine!) Set the squares aside, on a lightly floured tray, to rest for 15 minutes before frying them. Meanwhile, roll out and divide the remaining half of dough the same way.

To fry the pastry: Pour vegetable oil into a large skillet to a depth of ½ inch, and set it over medium heat. Use the point of a small sharp knife to pierce each pastry square about ten times all over its surface. (These tiny holes will prevent the pastry from ballooning when fried.) Heat the oil until the edge of a square sizzles gently when dipped into it, then lay in as many squares as you can without their touching. Raise the heat to keep the oil temperature up (but lower it as soon as the sizzling gets too fast). Fry the squares for about 2 minutes on the first side, pushing them under the oil occasionally to heat the top surface. As the tops begin to bubble, press with tongs to prevent big bubbles from ballooning—small bubbles are okay. When the bottom is golden brown, flip the squares over and fry until they are evenly colored and crisp on both sides, about 2 minutes. Drain them on paper towels. Fry all the squares this way, adding oil as needed and heating it between batches.

To assemble: Set one square on a plate, and drop about 1½ tablespoons of cannoli cream in the center. Lay another square on top of the filling, sides aligned, and press gently to spread the cream. Drop on another layer of cream, cover with a third square, and press. Finally, shower the top of each napoleon with confectioners' sugar, and serve.

Ricotta Cookies

Biscotti di Ricotta
MAKES ABOUT 42

2¼ cups all-purpose flour
1 teaspoon baking powder
Pinch of kosher salt
1 cup granulated sugar
1 stick unsalted butter, at room temperature
2 large eggs
8 ounces fresh ricotta, drained
½ teaspoon pure vanilla extract
Finely grated zest of 1 lemon, plus ¼ cup freshly squeezed juice
2 cups confectioners' sugar, sifted

Preheat the oven to 325 degrees. Sift together the flour, baking powder, and salt into a bowl, and set aside. Line two baking sheets with parchment paper.

Cream the sugar and butter in a mixer fitted with the paddle attachment at high speed until light and fluffy, about 2 minutes. Reduce the speed to medium, and crack in the eggs one at a time, beating well between additions. Add the ricotta, vanilla, and lemon zest, and beat to combine. Add the flour mixture, and beat at low speed until everything is just combined—do not overmix.

Drop the dough in heaping tablespoons onto the sheet pans at 2-inch intervals. Bake, rotating the pans halfway through the baking time, until the cookies are puffed, golden, and cooked all the way through, about 18 to 20 minutes. Remove them, and cool them on wire racks.

When the cookies are completely cool, make the glaze. In a bowl, whisk together the confectioners' sugar and lemon juice to make a smooth glaze. Adjust the consistency if too dense by adding a little water; if too loose add more confectioners' sugar to make a glaze that will adhere to the cookies when dipped. Dip the tops of the cookies in the glaze, and let them dry on racks.

Chocolate Anise Biscotti

Biscotti al Cioccolato con Anice
MAKES ABOUT 36

2½ cups all-purpose flour
3 tablespoons natural unsweetened cocoa
    powder
1 teaspoon baking powder
½ teaspoon baking soda
½ teaspoon ground aniseed
¼ teaspoon kosher salt
½ stick (4 tablespoons) unsalted butter, at room
    temperature
1 cup sugar
3 large eggs, plus 1 egg yolk
½ teaspoon anise extract, or 1 tablespoon
    sambuca or other anise liqueur
Finely grated zest of 1 small orange
½ cup slivered almonds

Preheat the oven to 350 degrees. Line a baking sheet with parchment paper. On another piece of parchment, sift together the flour, cocoa, baking powder, baking soda, aniseed, and salt. In a mixer fitted with the paddle attachment, beat the butter and sugar until smooth. Add the eggs and yolk at medium speed, one at a time, beating well to combine the mixture. Beat in the anise extract or sambuca and the orange zest. Add the dry ingredients, and mix to form a smooth dough. Add the almonds, and mix just to combine. Chill the dough in the refrigerator for 15 minutes.

Divide the dough in half, and form into two flattish 12-inch logs, about 3 inches apart, on the baking sheet. (If the dough is too sticky, dust it and your hands with flour.) Bake until the logs are puffed and cooked through but not colored, about 25 minutes. Remove from the oven, and carefully place the logs on a cooling rack. Decrease the oven temperature to 325 degrees.

Let the logs cool until you can handle them but they are still soft, about 10 minutes. With a serrated knife, cut the logs on a slight bias into ½-inch-thick biscotti. Arrange these on the bak-ing sheet so they aren't touching, and bake them until crisp on the top, about 10 minutes. Flip the biscotti and bake until the other side is crisp, about 10 to 15 minutes more. Cool them completely on baking racks.

Almond Pine Nut Cookies

Amaretti con Pinoli
MAKES ABOUT 30

Two 7-ounce tubes almond paste
1 cup sugar
2 large egg whites
Finely grated zest of 1 orange
1½ cups pine nuts

Preheat the oven to 350 degrees. Line two baking sheets with parchment.

Crumble the almond paste into the work bowl of a food processor, and process until the paste is in fine crumbs. Sprinkle in the sugar with the motor running. Once the sugar is incorporated, add the egg whites and orange zest. Process to make a smooth dough, about 20 to 30 seconds

Spread the pine nuts on a plate. Form the dough into 2-tablespoon-sized balls, roll and press to coat them in pine nuts, then place them on the baking sheets at 2-inch intervals. Bake by rotating the baking sheets from top to bottom halfway through, until the cookies are lightly golden and springy to the touch, about 13 to 15 minutes. Let them cool on the baking sheets for 5 minutes, then transfer them to cooling racks to cool completely.

Sesame Candy

Dolcetti di Sesamo
MAKES ABOUT 60 PIECES

1¼ cups sesame seeds (about 6 ounces)
Scant 1 cup sugar
3 tablespoons honey
2 teaspoons unsalted butter
Extra-virgin olive oil
¾ cup slivered almonds, toasted
Finely grated zest of 1 lemon
Finely grated zest of 1 orange
1 teaspoon ground cinnamon

Preheat the oven to 350 degrees. Spread the sesame seeds on a rimmed baking sheet, and toast them in the oven until light golden, shaking them on the baking sheet occasionally, about 8 minutes. Let the seeds cool on the baking sheet.

Combine the sugar, honey, butter, and 2 teaspoons water in a small saucepan over medium-low heat. Stir with a wooden spoon frequently as the butter melts and the sugar dissolves and the syrup comes to a boil. Simmer until the syrup is a deep caramel color, about 5 minutes. Meanwhile, brush a nonporous work surface (such as granite or stainless steel) with olive oil; coat a metal spatula with olive oil as well. When the caramel is done, turn off the heat, and stir in the sesame seeds, almonds, citrus zests, and cinnamon. Pour (and scrape) the molten candy from the pan onto the work surface, and quickly spread it into an even rectangular layer, about ½ inch thick, with the metal spatula. Allow it to cool and firm up for a minute or two, but not to harden.

With a serrated knife and a straight edge, slice the sheet of candy into 1-inch strips. Then cut diagonal slices 1 inch apart. Divide the strips into diamond-shaped pieces. With a metal spatula, separate the pieces, and arrange them in a single layer, not touching, on trays lined with parchment; let them harden completely. Store them in an airtight container with parchment between the layers.

"Ugly but Good" Nut Cookies

Brutti ma Buoni
MAKES ABOUT 24

8 egg whites
Pinch of kosher salt
2 cups confectioners' sugar, sifted
2 cups skinned hazelnuts, toasted and finely
    chopped

Preheat the oven to 275 degrees. Line two baking sheets with parchment paper. Beat the egg whites and salt in the bowl of an electric mixer with the whisk attachment until foamy. Continue beating, adding the sugar gradually, until all the sugar is incorporated and the egg whites hold stiff and shiny peaks.

Scrape the beaten whites into a wide, heavy saucepan, and set it over medium-low heat. Stir in the hazelnuts, and cook at medium heat, stirring, until the batter comes away from the sides of the pan and is light golden brown.

Remove the pan from the heat. Spoon the batter by rounded teaspoonfuls at 2-inch intervals onto the prepared pans. Bake until the cookies are golden brown and firm to the touch, about 30 minutes. Remove, and cool them completely before serving.

Cornmeal Cookies

Crumiri
MAKES ABOUT 48

2 cups very fine cornmeal
1 cup all-purpose flour
2 large eggs
2 large egg yolks
1 teaspoon pure vanilla extract
¾ cup sugar
2½ sticks (10 ounces) unsalted butter, at room
    temperature, cut into 16 pieces

Preheat the oven to 400 degrees. Line two baking sheets with parchment. Stir the cornmeal and flour together in a small bowl. Beat the eggs, egg yolks, and vanilla together in a separate bowl with a handheld electric mixer until foamy. As you continue beating, pour in the sugar gradually, until the mixture is smooth. Add the butter, and beat until it is incorporated. Spoon in the dry ingredients, and beat at low speed, just until mixed. (The dough can be formed into cookies and baked at this point, or wrapped in plastic and refrigerated up to 1 day.)

Divide the dough into three pieces. Working with one piece at a time, roll it into a thick log, and slide it into a pastry bag fitted with a large star tip. Squeeze the dough out of the pastry bag and onto the prepared baking sheet, cutting each piece into 4-inch lengths as it comes out of the pastry bag. Leave 1 inch between them as you do. When you are finished with the strips go back and, with your fingers, turn one end and shape the strips of dough into crescents. Repeat with the remaining two pieces of dough, filling both baking sheets.

Bake the cookies until golden, about 20 minutes, rotating the baking sheets from top to bottom halfway through. Cool the cookies completely before serving. They can be stored in an airtight container at room temperature for up to a week.

Saint Joseph's Fig Cookies

Biscotti di San Giuseppe
MAKES ABOUT 54

COOKIES
½ cup honey
6 tablespoons grappa or brandy
4 teaspoons freshly squeezed orange juice
2 cups diced dried black figs
3¾ cups all-purpose flour

½ cup granulated sugar
1½ teaspoons baking powder
¼ teaspoon kosher salt
2 large eggs
6 tablespoons milk
2 teaspoons grated lemon zest
¼ teaspoon ground cinnamon
½ cup coarsely chopped walnuts

GLAZE
1½ cups confectioners' sugar
3 tablespoons milk, or as needed

For the cookies: In a medium saucepan, bring the honey, grappa, and orange juice to a boil. Add the figs, and bring the mixture to a simmer. Simmer until the figs are plumped, about 2 to 3 minutes. Remove it from heat, and let it cool thoroughly while you make the dough.

In a food processor, combine the flour, granulated sugar, baking powder, and salt. Pulse to combine. In a small bowl, beat together the eggs and milk. With the processor running, pour the egg-milk mixture into the dry ingredients, and process until the dough forms a ball, about 15 to 20 seconds. Knead the dough on a counter once or twice, then wrap it in plastic wrap and let it rest in the refrigerator at least 1 hour, or until firm.

When the fig filling is cool, scrape it into a food processor and add the lemon zest and cinnamon. Process to make a smooth paste. Add the walnuts, and pulse a few times, leaving the nuts slightly chunky. Transfer the filling to a bowl, and freeze until it is firm, about ½ hour.

Preheat the oven to 350 degrees. Line two baking sheets with parchment. Divide the dough in half, and roll one half, between sheets of parchment, to a rectangle about 7 by 16 inches. Cut this in half to make two long strips. Roll a quarter of the filling into a log that fits down the center of one strip. Wet the edges of the strip with water, and use the parchment as a guide to roll the dough into a log and seal it. Flatten the top slightly with the palm of your hand. Repeat with the remaining dough and filling.

Using a wet knife, cut the logs into 1-inch lengths, and place them, with the cut sides facing up, on parchment-lined baking sheets. Bake until the cookies are golden, about 15 to 20 minutes, rotating the racks from top to bottom halfway through. Transfer the cookies to a wire rack, and cool them completely.

To glaze the cookies: Sift the confectioners' sugar into a bowl, and whisk in the milk to make a smooth glaze. Dip the top of a cookie in the glaze. It should stick to the cookie in a thin layer. If not, adjust its consistency with more milk or confectioners' sugar. Dip all the cookies in the glaze, and let them dry on wire racks.

Cookie Crumble

Fregolotta
MAKES TWO 9-INCH COOKIES FOR CRUMBLING, SERVING 12 TO 14

2 tablespoons butter, softened, for the pans
6 ounces (about 1¼ cups) whole unblanched almonds, toasted
6 ounces all-purpose flour (about 1 cup, plus 3 tablespoons)
1 scant cup sugar
¼ teaspoon salt
3 large egg yolks
6 tablespoons heavy cream, or more if needed

Preheat the oven to 350 degrees. Assemble two 9-inch springform pans and butter the bottom disks and about an inch up the sides.

Set aside two whole almonds and chop all the rest coarsely into chunks the size of chocolate chips. Stir the flour, sugar, and salt together in a mixing bowl and toss in the chopped almonds.

Beat the yolks together briefly and drizzle over the dry ingredients. Toss with a fork to blend. Drizzle the cream over the mixture by tablespoons,

tossing and stirring to moisten the nut mixture evenly. It should be crumbly but not floury; add a small amount more cream if necessary.

Pour half of the crumb mixture into each buttered cake pan. Spread and press the crumbs down lightly in an even, thick layer covering the bottom of the pan.

Bake for about 25 minutes or more, until the cookie rounds are nicely browned and starting to shrink from the side ring of the pan. Let them cool, then remove the springform side rings and bottom disk.

To serve, set a fregolotta in front of your guests on the table, with one of the reserved whole almonds underneath it. Smack the fregolotta in the center with the back of a spoon until it crumbles. Serve with poached fruits or ice cream, or enjoy a crunchy piece all by itself with a cup of espresso.

❧ *Fregola* means "crumb" and *fregolotta* means "one big crumb": for this delightful treat you make and bake lots of little crumbs into two round cookie crumbles.

❧ This is an ideal cake/cookie: It keeps for days in a tin and is delightful after dinner with some ice cream or whipped cream. It is the quintessential cookie to have with your espresso to finish a true Italian meal. The leftovers are great for breakfast with caffè latte.

Fried Sweet Dough

Zeppole
MAKES ABOUT 18

FILLING
2 cups fresh ricotta, drained
1 cup mascarpone (8 ounces), at room temperature
3 tablespoons amaretto

½ cup confectioners' sugar, sifted, plus more for dusting

2 tablespoons finely chopped candied lemon peel

2 tablespoons finely chopped candied citron or orange peel

2 tablespoons finely chopped bittersweet chocolate or mini–chocolate chips

DOUGH

Vegetable oil, for frying

4 tablespoons unsalted butter

1 tablespoon granulated sugar

½ teaspoon kosher salt

1 cup all-purpose flour, sifted

Finely grated zest of 1 lemon

4 large eggs, at room temperature

For the filling: In a bowl, whisk together the ricotta, mascarpone, amaretto, and confectioners' sugar until smooth. Stir in the candied peel and chocolate. Refrigerate the filling while you make the zeppole.

For the dough: Heat the vegetable oil in a wide saucepan to 350 degrees. (The oil should be an inch or two deep.) In a medium saucepan, combine 1 cup water, the butter, granulated sugar, and salt over medium heat. Bring this to a boil, stirring to melt the butter. While stirring, add the flour and zest all at once. Cook, stirring constantly, until the dough dries out and pulls away from the sides of the pan, about 3 or 4 minutes. Off heat, add the eggs one at a time, stirring vigorously to incorporate one before adding the next, until the dough is completely smooth.

Drop the zeppole in 2-tablespoon dollops (a small ice-cream scoop is perfect for this) into the oil, making sure you don't crowd them in the pan, because they will grow in size. Fry the zeppole, turning on all sides, until they are light and golden brown all over, about 5 minutes per batch. Drain them on paper towels, and repeat with the remaining dough.

To serve, split the zeppole. Top one half of each with some filling and place the other half on top. Dust with additional confectioners' sugar.

Fried Sweet Dough Ribbons

Crostoli

MAKES ABOUT 36

6 tablespoons unsalted butter, at room temperature

¼ cup plus 2 tablespoons granulated sugar

¼ cup milk

¼ teaspoon kosher salt

1 large egg, plus 1 large egg yolk

3 tablespoons dark rum

Juice of ½ lemon, freshly squeezed

Zest of 1 lemon, grated

2½ cups all-purpose flour, plus more for rolling

Vegetable oil, for frying

Confectioners' sugar, for dusting

In a food processor, combine the butter, sugar, and milk, and process until smooth. Add the salt, egg and yolk, rum, lemon juice, and lemon zest, and process until smooth, scraping down the sides of the work bowl once or twice to incorporate everything evenly. Add the flour, and process to make a smooth, sticky dough. Scrape the dough out onto a floured work surface, and knead for a minute to make a silky dough, adding a little more flour if the dough sticks to your hands too much. Wrap the dough in plastic wrap, and refrigerate it for 1 hour. (The dough can be made a day ahead and refrigerated, but let it come to room temperature again before rolling.)

In a medium Dutch oven, heat 3 inches of vegetable oil to 350 degrees. Cut the dough in half. Roll one piece out into a 12-to-14-inch square. Using a fluted rolling cutter, cut the dough into strips about 6 inches long by 1 to 1½ inches wide. (You'll get eighteen to twenty strips from each half of the dough.) Tie the strips into loose knots, and rest them on a parchment-lined sheet pan while you roll, cut, and tie the other half of the dough.

Add a dozen or so crostoli to the hot oil. Fry, turning occasionally, until they are deep golden on both sides, about 4 minutes per batch, adjusting the heat to keep the oil at around 350 degrees. (If you don't have an oil thermometer, test one crostolo in the oil to make sure it starts sizzling but not burning, before adding the whole batch.). With a spider or tongs, transfer the fried crostoli to a sheet pan lined with paper towels to drain. Fry the remaining crostoli in the same manner. Put some confectioners' sugar in a small mesh sieve, and dust it generously over the cooled crostoli.

dough out once more, until you get about twenty-four rounds. Fill each round with a scant tablespoon of preserves. Brush the edges with water, and fold them over to make half-moons. Crimp them closed with a fork. Chill them in the refrigerator while the oil heats: heat several inches of vegetable oil in a deep pot to 365 degrees. Fry the pastries, in batches, until golden brown on both sides, about 5 to 6 minutes per batch. Drain on paper towels. To serve: dust lightly with confectioners' sugar.

Fried Half Moons

Mezzelune Fritte
MAKES ABOUT 24

3 cups all-purpose flour, plus more for rolling
1 tablespoon granulated sugar
¼ teaspoon kosher salt
12 tablespoons (1½ sticks) butter, cold, cut into pieces
1 large egg yolk
1½ cups thick, chunky preserves, such as apricot or cherry
Vegetable oil, for frying
Confectioners' sugar, for dusting

In a food processor, combine the flour, sugar, and salt, and pulse to combine. Drop in the butter pieces, and pulse until the mixture resembles coarse crumbs. In a measuring cup, mix together ⅓ cup cold water and the egg yolk. Drizzle this over the flour, and pulse just until the dough comes together in a ball; add a little more flour or water to adjust the consistency as necessary. Dump the dough onto a floured counter, and knead it once or twice to form a disk. Wrap it in plastic, and let it rest in the refrigerator for 30 minutes.

Roll the dough on a floured surface to about ⅛ inch thick. With a floured 2½-inch cutter, cut into rounds; transfer them to parchment-lined baking sheets. Reroll the scraps, and roll this

Small Custard-Filled Doughnuts

Bomboloni
MAKES ABOUT 30 TO 36

FILLING
1¼ cups milk
1 large strip orange zest, removed with a vegetable peeler
3 large egg yolks
¼ cup sugar
2 tablespoons cornstarch
Pinch of kosher salt
½ teaspoon pure vanilla extract

BOMBOLONI
1 packet active dry yeast (about 2¼ teaspoons)
6 tablespoons warm water (about 100 degrees, just warm to the touch)
2 cups all-purpose flour, plus more as needed
¼ cup sugar, plus ½ cup for rolling
2 large eggs, at room temperature
¼ teaspoon kosher salt
6 tablespoons unsalted butter, cut into pieces
Vegetable oil, for coating the bowl and frying

For the filling: In a small saucepan, bring the milk and orange zest to a bare simmer. Remove this from heat and let it steep 10 minutes. Remove and discard the orange peel. In a large bowl, whisk together the egg yolks, sugar, cornstarch, and salt until smooth. Whisk in the warm milk in a slow, steady stream. Return the mixture to the saucepan and cook over medium-low heat until it has thickened and a few bubbles appear at the surface. Strain the mixture through a fine sieve into a clean bowl, stir in the vanilla, and directly cover the surface of the filling with a piece of plastic wrap so it does not form a crust. Refrigerate until it is chilled, at least 4 hours.

For the bomboloni: Dissolve the yeast in the warm water, and let it proof until foamy, about 5 minutes. In a mixer fitted with the paddle attachment, combine the flour, sugar, eggs, and salt, and mix at medium speed until just combined. Add the yeast mixture, and mix to incorporate well, and switch to the dough hook. Add the butter a few pieces at a time, then knead at medium-high speed for 2 minutes. The dough should still be a little sticky; it should not completely clean the sides of the bowl. If the dough is very wet, add a little more flour, a tablespoon at a time, until it comes together in a mass. Gather the dough into a ball, and transfer it to an oiled bowl. Cover it with plastic wrap, and let it rise until doubled in volume, about 1 hour.

Punch the dough down, and, on a floured work surface, roll to about ½ inch thick. Using a 1½-inch round cutter, cut out as many rounds as you can, about thirty to thirty-six (reroll the scraps only once). Line two baking sheets with plastic wrap, and brush them with vegetable oil. Arrange the rounds on the baking sheets so they don't touch, about 2 inches apart. Cover them loosely with plastic wrap, and let them rise until doubled again, about 1 hour.

To fry: Heat about 2 inches of vegetable oil in a deep straight-sided skillet to 360 degrees. Fill a pastry bag fitted with a medium plain tip with the filling cream. Spread about ½ cup of sugar in a shallow bowl, and line a sheet pan with paper towels.

Fry the bomboloni in two batches, about 2 minutes per side. Drain them on the paper towels. While they are still hot, roll them all over in the sugar. Let them cool. With a chopstick, make a hole in the top of each bombolone just large enough to fit the pastry tip, but don't go all the way through with the chopstick. Fill each bombolone with some of the filling cream, until it fills the hole, and serve.

Baked Crêpes with Ricotta and Raisins

Crespelle al Forno con Ricotta e Uva Passa
SERVES 6

FOR THE CRÊPES
2 large eggs
1 tablespoon dark rum
1 teaspoon pure vanilla extract
2 tablespoons sugar
⅓ teaspoon kosher salt
2 cups all-purpose flour
8 tablespoons unsalted butter, melted and cooled slightly
Finely grated zest of 2 lemons

FOR THE FILLING
¼ cup golden raisins
3 tablespoons unsalted butter, softened
1 cup fresh ricotta, drained
2 tablespoons sugar
Grated zest and freshly squeezed juice of ½ orange
½ cup plus 2 tablespoons apricot jam

To make the batter: Whisk together the eggs, 2 cups water, the rum, vanilla, sugar, and salt in a large bowl, until well blended. Sift the flour on top, a bit at a time, whisking each addition until smooth. Drizzle in half the melted butter, whisking until the batter has slightly thickened into the consistency of melted ice cream. Finally, whisk in the lemon zest. Put the remaining butter in a small cup, and keep it warm.

Set a crêpe pan or medium nonstick skillet over medium-high heat until it is quite hot. Brush it with some of the remaining melted butter. Immediately ladle in a scant ⅓ cup of batter, tilt and swirl the pan so the batter coats the bottom, and set the pan on the burner.

Lower the heat to medium, and cook the crêpes for a little less than a minute, until the underside is lightly browned in a lacy pattern. Flip it over with a spatula, and fry for ½ minute or longer, until the second side is lightly browned, then remove it to a warm platter. Heat the empty pan briefly, then brush with butter, fill it with a scant ⅓ cup batter, and cook another crêpe. Repeat the sequence, stacking up the finished crêpes on the platter, until all the batter is used up.

Preheat the oven to 400 degrees. In a small bowl, combine the raisins with hot water to cover, and let them soak until softened, about 10 minutes. Butter an 8-by-8-inch baking dish with 1 tablespoon of the butter.

In a medium bowl, stir together the ricotta, sugar, and orange zest and juice. Squeeze the excess water from the raisins, and stir into the ricotta mixture. Lay the crêpes out flat on your work surface, and spread each with 1 tablespoon of the apricot jam. Spread a line of filling on the center of each crêpe. Roll the crêpes up like cigars, and place them in the baking dish. Spread the tops with the remaining 2 tablespoons softened butter and the remaining ¼ cup apricot jam. Cover with foil, and bake until the jam is melted and bubbly, about 15 minutes. Uncover, and bake until the tops of the crêpes are crisp and golden, about 10 to 15 minutes more.

Crêpes Filled with Chocolate and Walnuts

Crespelle al Cioccolato e Noci
SERVES 6

FOR THE CRÊPES
2 large eggs
1 tablespoon dark rum
1 teaspoon pure vanilla extract
2 tablespoons sugar
⅓ teaspoon salt
2 cups all-purpose flour
8 tablespoons unsalted butter, melted and cooled slightly
Finely grated zest of 2 lemons

FOR THE FILLING
10 ounces excellent bittersweet or semisweet chocolate (12 ounces, or more, for extreme chocolate-lovers), chopped
1 cup heavy cream, chilled
1½ cups walnuts, toasted and coarsely chopped

To make the batter: Whisk together the eggs, 2 cups water, the rum, vanilla, sugar, and salt in a large bowl, until well blended. Sift the flour on top, a bit at a time, whisking each addition until smooth. Drizzle in half the melted butter, whisking until the batter has slightly thickened into the consistency of melted ice cream. Finally, whisk in the lemon zest. Put the remaining butter in a small cup and keep it warm.

Set a crêpe pan or medium nonstick skillet over medium-high heat until it is quite hot. Brush it with some of the remaining melted butter. Immediately ladle in a scant ⅓ cup of batter, tilt and swirl the pan so the batter coats the bottom, and set the pan on the burner.

Lower the heat to medium, and cook the crêpe for a little less than a minute, until the underside is lightly browned in a lacy pattern. Flip it over with a spatula, and fry for ½ minute or longer, until the second side is lightly browned, then remove it to a warm platter. Heat the empty pan briefly, then brush with butter, fill it with a scant ⅓ cup batter, and cook another crêpe. Repeat the sequence, stacking up the finished crêpes on the platter, until all the batter is used up.

Melt the chocolate in a double boiler or a bowl set over a pan of simmering water. When the chocolate has begun to melt, stir until it is completely smooth, and keep it warm, over the water, off the heat.

Fill and serve the crêpes as soon as possible, while they are fresh and warm. Whip the heavy cream to soft peaks. Take one crêpe off the stack, and place it with its lacy-patterned side down. Spoon a generous tablespoon (or more) warm chocolate in the center of the pancake, and spread it over the surface, leaving an inch-wide border uncoated. Scatter a spoonful of chopped walnuts over the chocolate layer, then fold the round in half, hiding the fillings, and fold again into a plump quarter-round. Fill and fold all the crêpes the same way. For each serving, place two filled and folded crêpes, overlapping, on a dessert plate, heap some cream on top, scatter some nuts on top of the cream, and drizzle with warm chocolate.

Pastry Cream

Crema Pasticcera
MAKES ENOUGH FOR TWO 8-TO-10-INCH TARTS

1⅔ cups milk
1 large egg, plus 2 large egg yolks
2 tablespoons plus 1 teaspoon cornstarch
3 tablespoons sugar
1 teaspoon pure vanilla extract

Heat the milk in a medium saucepan to just below simmering. In a large bowl, whisk together the egg, yolks, cornstarch, and sugar until smooth. Gradually pour in the hot milk, whisking constantly to avoid scrambling the eggs.

Pour the mixture back into the saucepan and cook over medium-low heat until it is thickened and coats the back of a spoon, about 5 to 7 minutes, stirring constantly. Make sure you get the spoon in the corners of the pan. Remove from the heat, and stir in the vanilla. Scrape the mixture into a clean bowl. Press plastic wrap directly on the surface to keep a skin from forming. Chill in the refrigerator until it is very cold, at least 2 hours.

❧ Pastry cream is a delicate custard used in fillings of fruit pies, cakes, and fried dough, but it is also delicious served as a dessert topped with some berries, sugar, or honey and whipped cream.

Peaches in White Wine

Pesche al Vino Bianco
SERVES 4

1 cup prosecco
1 cup dry white wine
1 tablespoon peach schnapps
2 tablespoons sugar
2 tablespoons fresh mint leaves, plus 4 mint sprigs for garnish
3 ripe peaches, pitted and sliced ½ inch thick
1 cup pitted sweet cherries

In a deep glass serving bowl, stir together the prosecco, white wine, schnapps, sugar, and mint leaves until the sugar dissolves.

Add the peaches and cherries. Cover, and chill until very cold, about 3 hours. Serve in stemmed glasses, with mint sprigs for garnish.

Strawberries with Balsamic Vinegar

Fragole al Balsamico
SERVES 6 TO 8

3 pints ripe strawberries, washed, hulled, and
  halved or quartered, depending on size
2 tablespoons Aceto Balsamico Tradizionale
2 tablespoons superfine sugar
2 tablespoons freshly squeezed orange juice
Fresh mint sprigs, for garnish

Put the berries in a large bowl. Sprinkle them with
the vinegar, sugar, and orange juice. Toss well to
coat the berries in the vinegar, sugar, and juice.
Cover, and refrigerate them 20 minutes, or more.
   Serve the berries in chilled glasses, each topped
with a mint sprig.

Oranges in Marsala

Arance alla Marsala
SERVES 4 TO 6

6 navel oranges
½ cup sugar
1 cup sweet Marsala
Fresh mint sprigs, for garnish

With a paring knife, cut the peel from the
oranges, removing the white pith as well. Cut the
oranges crosswise into ½-inch slices.
   Layer a third of the orange slices in a glass
serving bowl. Sprinkle with half of the sugar and
a third of the Marsala. Layer another third of the
oranges, then the remaining sugar, and another
third of the Marsala. Top with the remaining
oranges, and pour the remaining Marsala over
them.
   Cover, and refrigerate until the oranges are
well chilled, at least 2 hours. Serve garnished with
mint.

Roasted Pears and Grapes

Pere e Uva al Forno
SERVES 6

2 cups seedless red grapes
1 cup sugar
Juice of 2 lemons, freshly squeezed
⅔ cup Moscato
½ vanilla bean, split lengthwise
2 tablespoons apricot jam
3 firm but ripe Bosc pears, halved and cored

Preheat the oven to 375 degrees. Place the grapes
in a baking dish. Combine the sugar, lemon juice,
Moscato, vanilla bean, and apricot jam in a bowl,
and stir until blended. Pour this over the grapes.
Nestle the pear halves, cut side up, into the grapes.
   Bake until the pears are tender and the liquid
around the grapes is thick and syrupy, about 45
to 50 minutes. Remove the pears, and let them
stand for about 10 minutes. Discard the vanilla
pod. Serve them with some of the grapes and
their liquid spooned around them.

VARIATION:
   Pears and grapes are a great marriage of flavors,
but I also like this preparation with quince and
fresh cranberries. To try this, cut the peeled and
cored quince in quarters (they take longer to bake
than the pears), and substitute fresh cranberries
for the grapes. It will take more sugar since cranberries are not as sweet as grapes.

Vanilla Orange Ice Cream

Gelato di Vanilla ed Arance
MAKES ABOUT I QUART, SERVING 4 TO 6

3 cups milk
1 cup heavy cream
1 long strip of orange peel, removed with a
  vegetable peeler

½ vanilla bean, split lengthwise
1 cup sugar
2 tablespoons cornstarch
⅛ teaspoon kosher salt

In a medium saucepan, bring 2 cups of the milk, the cream, orange peel, and vanilla to a gentle simmer. Remove it from the heat, and let it steep 10 minutes. Scrape the seeds from the vanilla bean into the milk mixture, discarding the pod and the orange peel. Return the milk mixture to medium heat.

In a medium bowl, whisk together the remaining 1 cup cold milk, the sugar, cornstarch, and salt. Pour in the hot milk mixture, whisking constantly, until it is smooth. Pour everything back into the saucepan, and bring it to a simmer over medium heat, stirring, until bubbles pop to the surface and the mixture thickens, about 3 to 4 minutes. Transfer the mixture to a clean bowl or container, cover, and chill completely, at least 2 hours.

Pour the chilled mixture into an ice-cream or gelato maker, and freeze according to the manufacturer's instructions until it is soft-set. Scrape the churned gelato into a freezer container, cover, and freeze until it is firm and scoopable, at least 2 hours.

In a medium bowl, toss together the almonds, chocolate, amaretti, and brandy, and let the mixture soak while you whip the eggs.

In a large bowl, with a handheld mixer, beat the egg whites until foamy. Add ½ cup of the superfine sugar. Beat until the whites hold stiff peaks.

In another bowl, with the mixer, beat the egg yolks and remaining sugar until pale yellow and thick.

In a third large bowl, whip the heavy cream with the mixer to soft peaks.

Gently fold the yolk mixture into the whites, then fold in the whipped cream.

Line a 9-cup loaf pan with plastic wrap, with a 4-inch overhang on all sides. Spoon a third of the egg mixture into the pan, and rap it on the counter a few times to settle it. Sprinkle with half the chocolate-almond mixture, then repeat with another third of the egg mixture, rapping the pan on the counter again. Sprinkle with the remaining chocolate-almond mixture, then the remaining egg mixture, rapping on the counter once more.

Smooth the surface with a spatula, and cover with the plastic overhang. Freeze until it is solid, preferably overnight.

To serve: unwrap and slice it into ¾-inch-thick slices, using a serrated knife warmed in hot water.

Soft Ice Cream with Almonds

Semifreddo alle Mandorle
SERVES 8 TO 10

½ cup whole skinned almonds, toasted and finely chopped
½ cup grated semisweet chocolate
6 amaretti, crumbled
1 tablespoon brandy
5 large eggs, separated
1 cup superfine sugar
2 cups heavy cream

Peach Granita

Granita di Pesche
SERVES 4

1 pound ripe peaches, pitted and quartered
⅓ cup sugar
Juice of 1 lemon, freshly squeezed
1 drop pure vanilla extract
Fresh mint sprigs, for garnish

In a medium saucepan, bring 2 cups water to a boil. Add the peaches and sugar, and simmer gently until the peaches are very tender, about 20 minutes. Let them cool thoroughly.

Purée them with the cooking liquid in a food processor, then pass them through a sieve. Stir in the lemon juice and vanilla extract. Pour the mixture into an 8-by-8-inch nonreactive metal baking pan. Freeze it until crystals begin to form around the edges of the pan, about 45 minutes. Scrape the crystals into the center of the pan with a fork, and return the pan to the freezer. Continue to scrape, every 30 minutes or so, until the entire mixture is lightly fluffy crystals. Serve in chilled glasses with a sprig of mint.

Pomegranate Sorbet

Sorbetto di Melagrano
SERVES 4 TO 6

¾ cup sugar
2 cups pure pomegranate juice
1 tablespoon dark rum
½ cup pomegranate seeds

In a small saucepan, bring 1 cup water and the sugar to a simmer, stirring just until the sugar is dissolved. Stir in the pomegranate juice and rum. Let it cool to room temperature, then transfer it to a covered container and refrigerate until chilled, at least 4 hours.

Process the sorbet in an ice-cream maker according to the manufacturer's instructions until it is soft-set. Transfer it to a covered container, and freeze until it is scoopable, at least 2 hours. To serve: scoop it into chilled serving glasses, and garnish with the pomegranate seeds.

Coffee Granita with Whipped Cream

Granita di Caffè con Panna
SERVES 4 TO 6

2 cups brewed espresso
½ cup sugar
1 tablespoon coffee liqueur
½ teaspoon pure vanilla extract
1 cup heavy cream, cold

In a small saucepan, combine the espresso and sugar. Cook over low heat, stirring, just until the sugar dissolves. Remove from the heat, and stir in the coffee liqueur and vanilla. Let it cool to room temperature.

Pour the mixture into a 9-by-13-inch metal pan. Freeze until crystals begin to form around the edges of the pan, about 1 hour. With a fork, scrape the crystals into the center of the pan. Continue to freeze and scrape every 30 minutes until the granita is a pan of light, fluffy crystals, about 4 hours.

In a mixing bowl, whisk the cream to soft peaks. Serve the granita in chilled glasses with a dollop of the unsweetened cream on top.

ITALIAN CULTURE AND LANGUAGE

BOAR HUNTING: A FAVORITE ITALIAN PASTIME

Autumn is boar-hunting season, and in Italy, the diehard boar hunters reside in the center of Italy, along the Apennine Mountains. The challenge when hunting boar is their acute sense of smell; hunters must remain downwind of their prey so as to not give away their whereabouts. Being charged by a wild boar could be life-threatening (never mind a whole pack of them!), so the benefits of this trick are twofold for hunters. During my own wild-boar-hunting expedition (I was simply an observer, and, fortunately, nothing was caught that evening), I was given a pair of infrared binoculars, the better to see the pack. I was surprised by how close this large pack of boar came to the homes on the outskirts of the Umbrian town of Spoleto. If the hunt is successful, a *festa* is planned, in which everyone gathers together to eat several courses of boar served in different styles. Wild boar is stewed (a long process, because the meat can be tough) or braised, to be served with pasta, and can be made into fresh and aged sausage as well as cured prosciutto. I would hazard a guess that there isn't one hunting lodge in Umbria or Tuscany that does not have a mounted boar's head, but one of my favorites is in San Gimignano, where the boar's head outside the butcher shop is wearing spectacles.

CICCHETTI

Cicchetti are traditional snacks served in little hole-in-the-wall *osterie* (plural of *osteria*) in the city of Venice. These usually include tiny sandwiches, hard-boiled eggs, small servings of seafood and meat, and plates of olives and other goodies. Italians and tourists alike participate in eating cicchetti and washing them down with some wine. Venetians call this tradition the *giro d'ombra*; *giro* means "stroll," and *ombra*—slang for a glass of wine—means "shade." The name dates back to when a portable wine bar would move with the shadow of the Campanile, the bell tower across Saint Mark's Square, in the heat of the warmer months.

ENOTECAS

An *enoteca* is an Italian wine bar, a fast and relatively inexpensive option for a quick and tasty meal. At lunchtime, in cities all over the country, *enoteche* are crowded with local office workers eating fancy salads, panini, or plates of meats and cheeses, and enjoying a glass of fine wine. These "bars" are unlike those in many other countries in that they are open all day long and serve food as well as alcohol. When traveling in Italy, stop into a wine bar for a quick lunch and a glass of whatever wine is featured that day.

EVER WONDER WHY IT'S CALLED WEDDING SOUP?

In the dialect of the Lucani (as natives of Basilicata are known), *maritare* means "to wed," and I have always thought that this wonderful soup was so named because it was customarily served at wedding celebrations. Recently, however, while doing some research, I came upon another explanation: because it weds vegetables (in the soup base) with meat (in the polpette), and with this added protein it becomes a complete and balanced one-course meal. I like both interpretations of the name; they seem to be compatible.

IL PALIO

The Palio is the famous annual horse race in the city of Siena. The town's main square, called the Piazza del Campo (or simply Il Campo), serves as the racetrack for this exciting event. Each of the town's seventeen neighborhoods (*contrade,* as they are called in Italian) has its own colorful flag and is represented by a rider who competes in a race—the first of which occurs on July 2, the second on August 16. Festivities begin days before the actual races, during which the small city floods with locals and travelers alike. If you find yourself in Tuscany during the Palio, be sure to experience this great historic festival. So meaningful are these races to the *contrade* that, on the day of one of the races, the horses and their riders walk into the Duomo to be blessed.

ITALIAN BREAKFAST

Early in the morning all over Italy, bars begin warming their espresso machines and start rolling out their breakfast fare, but Italian breakfast, *la colazione,* is usually eaten between 7:00 and 8:00 a.m. Traditionally, breakfast at home is tea, or hot milk with coffee, always accompanied by something sweet, such as brioche or bread with butter and marmalade; but it is common in Italy to eat breakfast on the way to work at a "bar" or caffè. Like everything else in Italy, however, *colazione* is almost as regional as lunch or dinner. In the mountainous areas of Italy, platters of cheese, ham, and prosciutto can easily be found, served with boiled eggs and hearty breads for breakfast.

ITALIAN EATERIES

The clearly defined lines between the types of sit-down restaurants have been blurred over the past few decades, as food culture has changed. Today you can find many fine chefs at Michelin-starred places with *osteria* in their names.

TRATTORIA The middle ground between a *ristorante* and an *osteria.* A trattoria has tablecloths and service, but the food is usually less elaborate and not as costly as in a *ristorante.*

RISTORANTE The most formal of the three kinds of sit-down restaurants, with tablecloths, refined service, and higher prices.

OSTERIA A very relaxed eatery, with no linen service and often long communal tables.

BAR In Italy, bars have more to do with coffee than with alcohol. At a bar you can grab a quick coffee and pastry in the morning for breakfast, or have a light lunch throughout the day; they usually serve panini (sandwiches) or some simple salads and hot dishes. A bar is also the place to have an apéritif before dinner, more often than not with some pretzels, chips, and nuts set up to go along with your drinks.

ITALIAN FOOD SHOPS

FOCACCERIA In the strictest use of the word, these shops sell only focaccia and pizza items, although the distinction is far less rigid, and often *focaccerie* also produce and sell bread loaves and rolls.

FORMAGGERIA A cheese shop.

GELATERIA An Italian ice-cream shop, although there are clear differences between ice cream and gelato. Gelato has less fat than ice cream, and a smoother, creamier, less dense texture. It contains less cream than ice cream, using more milk and fewer egg yolks—if any are included. Gelato is served at a warmer temperature than ice cream, giving it a silkier feel; ice cream would melt if served at the same temperature. Gelato is churned at a slower pace, making it denser, whereas the faster churning of ice cream adds air, fluffing it up.

LATTERIA A shop that sells only dairy products, ranging from cheese to various types of milk, yogurt, and ice cream.

MERCATO ALL'APERTO An open-air market. In Italy these can be everyday markets, or markets scheduled in an open-air space, such as a piazza, on a specific day of the week. Markets in Italy can be only food-related but more often than not there is a food section and another part of the market dedicated to household items and clothing. The goods are sold from individual booths or stands.

NORCINERIA A shop that sells products made exclusively from pork meat, such as salami, prosciutto, or pancetta. The term *norcineria* comes from the town Norcia in Umbria, and in the Middle Ages it had a negative connotation. A *norcino* was skilled at butchering a pig, and these men often traveled together from village to village, offering their skills. Their adept use of tools to butcher a pig eventually led to their performing surgery on humans, such as tooth extraction and the setting of broken bones.

PANIFICIO A shop that makes and sells dough products, including bread, rolls, pizza, focaccia, buns, and other dough-based items. The term specifically indicates that the whole process, from scratch ingredients, occurs in this one shop. A *forno* (oven) or *panetteria* might buy ready-made dough and simply bake or cook it.

PASTICCERIA A pastry shop selling mostly sweets, although some also produce and sell bread, pizza, and focaccia. These are stores where pastries are purchased and taken away, not eaten on the premises, although some shops might have a small café section, where the sweets could be eaten accompanied by a cup of coffee.

PESCHERIA A fish market where they sell all types of fish and will also clean and cut the fish to the customers specifications.

ROSTICCERIA The Italian version of a fast-food restaurant. This might sound like a contradiction in terms, but *rosticcerie* (plural of *rosticceria*) are common in Italy. In these shops you can pick up simple, hot, ready-to-go meals, such as vegetables and roasted meats. Here you will find a whole roasted chicken or sliced-steak sliders, with arancini (fried rice balls), croquettes (potato fritters), and verdure miste (mixed greens) as popular sides. You can eat in or take the food home.

SALUMERIA The Italian equivalent of an American deli. Different types of cured meats are sliced and sold there. *Salumerie* might also sell cheese, in chunks or sliced, as well as possibly some antipasti, like pickled vegetables and olives. Some *salumerie* also have bread and will make sandwiches to go.

ITALIAN FOR "SHEEP"

Speaking of sheep in Italian can be confusing. *Agnello* is lamb, a young sheep with delicate, tender meat. *Agnellone,* on the other hand, is a slightly older sheep, slaughtered between the ages of six and ten months. To complicate things further, *pecora* is the term for an adult sheep, and the root of the word "pecorino," a hard and peppery (and delicious) cheese made from ewe's milk. Lastly, *ovino* is a more general term, referring not only to sheep, but to lambs and goats as well!

ITALIAN GREETINGS

The list of ways to say "hello" in Italian is long. Here are a few of the most popular: *"Buon giorno!"* means both "hello" and "good morning." Later in the day, you might say *"Buon pomeriggio"* or *"Buona sera,"* "good afternoon" or "good evening." Just before bedtime, the traditional salutation is a dignified *"Buona notte."* *"Ciao"* and *"salve"* will do any time of day. When meeting someone, *"Piacere"* means "pleasure," or "pleased to meet you."

AN ITALIAN SAGRA

A *sagra* is an Italian festival—a local celebration usually honoring whatever is being harvested at that time of year. *Sagre* (the plural of *sagra*) range in size and often feature live music, sporting competitions, and, of course, lots and lots of food. For example, during the Vendemmia (grape harvest) in September, Italians all over the country celebrate the wine and grapes with *sagre* of all sizes. Attending a *sagra* is an excellent and affordable way to get up close and personal with Italian life and locals, so, next time you are traveling through Italy, insert the local *sagre* into your itinerary.

LEARN A LITTLE ITALIAN

Even if your Italian vocabulary is limited to food and profanity, you have probably heard the suffix *"-ino"* or *"-ina"* tacked on to the end of various Italian words. These are the masculine and feminine diminutive word endings. For example, if *sorella* means "sister," *sorellina* means "little sister," and a *biscottino* is a little cookie. On the other hand, the suffix *"-one"* (pronounced "oh-nay") means "big"; so if a *bacio* is a kiss, a *bacione* would be a big kiss!

THE MEDITERRANEAN DIET: A UNESCO WORLD HERITAGE SITE

Just as a cathedral or ancient ruin can be declared a World Heritage Site, so can intangible traditions, such as the Mediterranean diet. The skills, knowledge, and practices that make up the diet concern everything from crops, harvesting, fishing, and conservation to the processing, preparation, and consumption of food. This delicious and healthful diet has remained unchanged for centuries, and is central to social customs in Italy and surrounding Mediterranean countries. To read more: http://www.unesco.org/culture/ich/en/RL/00394

SICILIAN BREAKFAST

As early as 5:00 a.m. in Sicily, bars begin rolling out their breakfast fare. Just to list a few, there are cornetti alla crema, cioccolata, ricotta, marmellata, Nutella, and miele; cornetti integrali, macallè, cannoli, sfoglie, flauti, bocca di leone, ciambelle, pane cioccolato, and fagottini! Sicilians really enjoy their breakfast, which is usually much larger and richer than in other parts of Italy, where breakfast is largely similar to a Continental breakfast. Granita, a typical Sicilian dessert made of frozen sugar, water, and flavoring, is enjoyed for breakfast in Sicily during the warm summer months. The most popular morning granita is coffee-flavored and topped with fresh unsweetened whipped cream, but the famous citruses of Sicily are popular flavors any time of day. The breakfast I enjoy the most when in Sicily is a brioche stuffed with pistachio ice cream.

STUZZICHINO

A *stuzzichino* is a snack or small appetizer often eaten between regular meals, in vernacular referred to as "picking." The verb *stuzzicare* means to poke or pick at, bother or tease someone, and so the *stuzzichino* is often a small snack or something to tease your appetite; *stuzzichini* are mostly served with toothpicks, which are called *stuzzicadenti*.

TOASTING IN ITALIAN

I have been asked about the meaning behind the toast I do on my show, which is pronounced "chin-chin." We are all familiar with *salute* or *cent'anni,* but this slightly less famous toast is believed to have originated with Italian peasants in the countryside; when they drank wine out of wooden cups, they would say "chin-chin" to imitate the sound of wineglasses clinking. Though there are some other theories about the origins of this toast, I think this one is the most fun.

TRULLI

Meet the *trullo.* This quirky little conical dwelling can be found in Puglia, the long and skinny region of Italy that makes up the heel of the boot. *Trulli* are whitewashed stone huts with stacked slate-tile roofs that are often decorated with astrological signs. The heart of *trullo* country is the town of Alberobello in Puglia, where the fifteen hundred *trulli* that make up a large part of the town are filled with little shops and wine bars that attract a large number of tourists. Some *trulli,* however, are still inhabited; if you visit Puglia, be sure to seek out this more authentic representation of the *trulli.* If you really want to see what it was like to live in these ancient structures, book a night or two in a *trullo* instead of a hotel! This is easy to arrange and will make your trip memorable.

GLOSSARY

ABBACCHIO Young unweaned lamb.

ABBINAMENTO Pairing, as in food and wine.

ABBRUSTOLITO Toasted.

ABRUZZO, CUCINA DELL' Food from Abruzzo focuses on primary ingredients. Abruzzo produces wine, olive oil, and cheese, such as scamorza, pecorino, and caciocavallo. The most recognized dish from Abruzzo is maccheroni alla chitarra dressed in a tomato-based sauce with tiny veal meatballs. Along the coast, much fish is used in the cuisine, and a well-known dish of polpo in purgatorio (octopus in purgatory) is made. There is also a traditional soup, minestrone delle virtù, consisting of fava beans, peas, chickpeas, lentils, and pork.

ACCARTOCCIATO Bagged, twisted, or wrapped with something.

ACCIUGATA Ligurian sauce made with anchovies.

ACCIUGHE Anchovies.

ACCIUGHE ALLA CARABINIERA Anchovies with potato salad.

ACCIUGHE CONTADINA Anchovy salad with onions, capers, and olives.

ACCIUGHE IN SALSA VERDE Anchovies in a green sauce of chopped parsley, garlic, peperoncino, and bread soaked in vinegar, placed in a jar in layers with olive oil, refrigerated until needed.

ACCIUGHE MARINATE Filleted fresh anchovies marinated in lemon juice, olive oil, garlic, parsley, and peperoncino.

ACCIUGHE RIPIENE AL FORNO Fresh anchovies, cleaned of head and tail, with the backbone removed, made into a sandwich and stuffed with a filling of herbs, garlic, pinoli, and olive oil, sprinkled with bread crumbs, and baked.

ACCOSTAMENTI Accompaniments, combinations, and variations of food in a meal, from side dishes to main plates and sauces.

ACERBO Bitter, sour; used to describe unripened fruit or vegetables.

ACETINI Pickles.

ACETO Vinegar.

ACETO BALSAMICO Balsamic vinegar, produced in the area of Modena in Emilia-Romagna.

ACETO DOLCE Vinegar sweetened with honey.

ACETOSA Sorrel, a wild green, used in salad.

ACETOSELLA Wood sorrel.

ACHILLEA MOSCATA Yarrow nutmeg, a bitter herb mainly used in soups and in the production of liqueurs.

ACIDO Acidic, sour.

ACIDULARE To render a liquid acidulous.

ACINI Tiny pasta shapes similar to rice, also called acini di pepe.

ACINI DI PEPE See acini.

ACQUAVITE Alcohol distilled from the must of fruit or grain—for example, grappa.

ADDENSARE To thicken.

ADDITIVO Chemical additive to food.

ADRAGANTE, GOMMA Tragacanth, a gum or gelatin extracted from plants in Turkey and Iran and used mainly in desserts.

AFFETTATARTUFI Truffle slicer.

AFFETTATO Sliced.

AFFETTATRICE Slicing machine.

AFFETTAUOVA Egg slicer.

AFFETTAVERDURE Vegetable slicer.

AFFILARE Sharpen.

AFFILATRICE Sharpener.

AFFIORATA The lighter oil that rises to the top during the first cold pressing, containing a maximum of 1 percent free oleic acid.

AFFOGATO Poached, steamed, or smothered.

AFFUMICARE To smoke.

AFFUMICATO Smoked.

AFFUMICATORE Smoker.

AFFUMICATURA The smoking of food, usually meat.

AFRODISIACO Aphrodisiac.

AFROMETRO Aphrometer, used to measure the pressure inside a bottle of champagne or prosecco during fermenting.

AGARICO Agaric, a kind of mushroom.

AGHIOTTA A Sicilian term for cooking fish in a stew.

AGLIACEO Term used to describe a wine that has gone bad, producing a garlicky smell.

AGLIATA Ligurian sauce made of bread and vinegar with a garlic base, used on fish and meat.

AGLIETTO Young garlic.

AGLIO Garlic.

AGLIO DOLCE Garlic that has been mellowed by cooking whole cloves either in milk or in boiling water.

AGLIO E OLIO Sauce or dressing composed of garlic and oil.

AGNELLO Lamb.

AGNELLO AL FORNO Lamb roasted with onions, garlic, salt, and rosemary, and often served with roasted potatoes.

AGNELLO CON CICORIA Boned leg of lamb cut in pieces and baked in the oven with onions, olive oil, tomatoes, and peperoncini, then covered with chicory, endive, or blanched dandelion and cooked further.

AGNELLO CON OLIVE ALL'ABRUZZESE Leg-of-lamb steaks, floured and browned in olive oil, cooked with pitted black olives, oregano, and chopped green peppers, served with lemon juice.

AGNELLO IN FRICASSEA Lamb chops browned with chopped onion, pancetta, and nutmeg, braised in stock and white wine. The pan juices are defatted off heat; whisked egg yolks and lemon juice are poured over the lamb chops, which are then cooked a few minutes more and served.

AGNELLONE Commercial term used for a sheep that has been butchered between 6 and 10 months of age.

AGNOLI, SORBIR D' Traditional soup from Mantova that has agnolini in a broth with red wine.

AGNOLINI Stuffed pasta (like tortellini) from Lombardy.

AGNOLOTTI Half-moon-shaped ravioli stuffed with minced meat and onion, sautéed in butter, and mixed with boiled spinach and cheese.

AGNOSTINELE Tiny red mullet, floured, seasoned, and fried.

AGO DA ASSAGGIO Needle made of horse bone, used to pierce prosciutto to smell the maturation and determine how the curing process is proceeding.

AGO PER CUCIRE Large needle used to sew meat and poultry closed.

AGO PER LARDARE Needle used to insert lard into meats.

AGONI Small, flat, freshwater fish found in Italian lakes, salted and dried.

AGRESTI Sour grapes from which verjuice is made.

AGRESTO Sour grape juice, verjuice.

AGRETTO Watercress (also called crescione).

AGRO Sour.

AGRO, ALL' Dressed with oil and lemon juice, or just lemon juice.

AGRODOLCE Sour and sweet, usually a sugar-and-vinegar sauce.

AGRUME Citrus fruit.

AIDOS Another name for the small gnocchi (malloreddus).

AIOLI Garlic pounded with egg yolk, salt, and olive oil; mayonnaise.

AJULA Striped sea bream, found in northern Italy.

ALACCIA 1. Large sardine. 2. In Naples, a word for "celery."

ALBATRA Fruit of the strawberry tree (arbutus), also known as corbezzola.

ALBERINI, MASSIMO Important food historian, born in Padova in 1909; he researched antique cookery manuals and published thirty-six books of his own.

ALBESE Area in southern Piedmont around the city of Alba.

ALBICOCCA Apricot.

ALBUME White of an egg.

ALCHERMES Sweet red liqueur used in making desserts.

AL DENTE Literally, "to the tooth"; used to describe the stage of doneness of pasta or vegetables that are cooked to be firm to the bite.

ALENOTO Abruzzese preparation of lamb and goat offal.

ALETTA Wing of a bird or fin of a fish.

ALFREDO, ALL' Tossed in cream and butter, such as pasta.

ALICE Fresh anchovy.

ALIMENTARI Groceries, or grocery store.

ALLAPPANTE Astringent, a tannic sensation in the mouth, such as the taste caused by eating a green banana.

ALLODOLA Skylark.

ALLORO Bay leaf tree.

ALLUNGARE To stretch out, as by adding stock or water to a sauce.

ALMAVICA Dessert of semolina pudding.

ALPESTRE Literally, "Alpine"; a digestive liqueur made by distilling thirty-four different plants gathered in the Alpine high plains.

AMALGAMARE To amalgamate.

AMARENA Morello cherry, sour cherry.

AMARETTO Cookie made from almond flour, sugar, and egg white.

AMARETTO Liqueur made from seventeen aromatic ingredients, including almonds, cherries, prunes, and cocoa. The best known is Amaretto di Saronno.

AMARETTUS Bittersweet cookies from Sardinia made with almonds.

AMARO Digestive drink made with medicinal herbs and sometimes citrus.

AMATRICIANA, ALL' Pasta cooked in the manner of the town of Amatrice, in the province of Rieti, traditionally made with guanciale, tomato, and an abundant amount of grated pecorino cheese.

AMBROSIA Dessert traditionally made from layers of sliced oranges, bananas, fresh pineapple, dried coconut, and sugar.

AMERICANO Apéritif made of vermouth, Campari, club soda, and citrus rind.

AMIDO Starch.

AMMIRAGLIA, ALL' Admirals' style, indicating a dish that contains fish or shellfish.

AMMOLLICATO Soaked.

AMMONTATO Topped with another ingredient such as cheese or sauce.

AMMORBIDIRE To soften.

ANANAS Pineapple.

ANATRA Duck, also called anara.

ANATRA ARROSTO Roasted duck, seasoned and rubbed with rosemary, sage, salt, and black pepper, stuffed with the same seasonings along with chopped duck liver, and served with a sauce made from the pan juices.

ANATRA COL PIEN Braised duck stuffed with meat, sausage, nuts, and mushrooms.

ANCONO Soup made with tomatoes, shellfish, and fish.

ANELLINI (ANELLETTI) Small ring-shaped pasta.

ANESONE Aniseed liqueur similar to the French pastis or Greek ouzo.

ANETO Dill.

ANGELICA Herb in the carrot family with tiny white flowers, used to infuse alcohol.

ANGUILLA Eel.

ANGUILLA ALLA FIORENTINA Eels breaded and baked.

ANGUILLA ALLA GRIGLIA Deboned eel cut into pieces, seasoned, oiled, and grilled.

ANGUILLA ALLA MARINARA Eel in a vinegar sauce.

ANGUILLA IN CARPIONE Appetizer of pieces of eel, salted, fried, or grilled, then marinated with oil, vinegar, bay leaves, and garlic.

ANGUILLA ALLA VENEZIANA Eel with tuna and lemon sauce.

ANGURIA Watermelon.

ANICE Anise; semi di anice is anise seed.

ANICINI Dry, hard aniseed cookies.

ANISETTA Anisette.

ANITRA Alternative spelling of anatra (duck).

ANNEGATO Simmered in or drowned in wine.

ANOLINI Small half-circle-shaped stuffed pasta with a braised meat stuffing.

ANTICA, ALL' In an old-fashioned style.

ANTIPASTI ASSORTITI Mixed antipasti containing anchovies, olives, vegetables, cheese, fruit, cured meats, etc.

ANTIPASTO (PLURAL ANTIPASTI) Starter, first course of the meal, usually an assortment of various vegetables, fish, cured meats, cheeses.

ANTIPASTO ALLA GENOVESE Favas with cured sausage.

ANTIPASTO AL MAGRO Antipasto of vegetables and seafood salads, without meat.

AOLE Freshwater fish.

APERITIVO Drink consumed prior to a meal, thought to open up the appetite.

APEROL Apéritif made from bitter orange, gentian, rhubarb, and cinchona, with a bittersweet taste, an orange color, and a low alcohol content.

APICIO (APICIUS) Ancient figure who lived during the time of Tiberius, thought to be the author of the *De re coquinaria,* a cookery manual.

APPASSIRE To wilt.

ARACHIDE Peanut.

ARAGOSTA Rock lobster or spiny lobster.

ARAGOSTA ALLA GRIGLIA CON BURRO Grilled lobster with melted butter.

ARAGOSTA BOLLITA Boiled lobster, usually served as a salad.

ARAGOSTA FRA DIAVOLO Lobster cooked in a spicy tomato sauce.

ARAGOSTA MEDITERRANEA Spiny lobster.

ARANCE CARAMELLATE Dessert of peeled, pithed, and sliced oranges coated with sugar syrup and decorated with caramelized orange peel.

ARANCIA Orange, the fruit.

ARANCIA CARDINALE Peeled and segmented orange dressed with olive oil and salt.

ARANCINI Croquettes made of savory rice cooked with butter and saffron, surrounding a filling such as meat and tomatoes or mozzarella and tomatoes and then breaded and fried.

ARANCIA AMARA Seville orange.

ARGENTINA Argentine, a small fish similar to a sardine.

ARIGUSTA Crawfish, crayfish.

ARINGA (PLURAL ARINGHE) Herring.

ARINGA ALLA CASALINGA Appetizer of sliced pickled herring mixed with sliced onion, cooked apples, and boiled potatoes with cream and parsley.

ARISTA Loin of pork.

ARMELLINE Kernels.

AROMA Aroma; fragrance; flavor.

ARRABBIATA, ALL' Used to describe a spicy preparation of food.

ARRICCHITO Enriched.

ARROSTICINI ALL'ABRUZZESE Grilled skewers of lamb, dressed with olive oil and seasonings, including marjoram and garlic.

ARROSTIRE To roast.

ARROSTITO Roasted.

ARROSTO Roasted, also roast meat or anything baked in the oven: arrosto di bue, roast beef; arrosto di castrato, roast mutton; arrosto d'agnello, roast lamb; anguilla arrosta, grilled eel.

ARROSTO, SUGO D' Roast pan juices.

ARROSTO DI MAIALE Roast leg of pork, salted, oiled, and basted with a mixture of white wine, finely chopped carrots, garlic, and pepper, and cooked until done.

ARROSTO DI MAIALE UBRIACO Tied, boned, larded pork loin, floured and browned in butter with carrots, braised slowly in grappa, red wine, nutmeg, and bay leaves until tender, and served with the cooking liquid. Literally translated as "drunken roast pork."

ARROTOLATO Rolled up.

ARSELLE Tiny clams.

ARSUMA Uncooked custard like zabaglione, made with whole eggs whipped with sugar and dry white wine.

ARTUSI, PELLEGRINO Gastronome and writer born in Forlimpopoli in 1820, author of *La scienza in cucina e l'arte di mangiar bene.*

ARZILLA Skate, the fish.

ASCIUTTO Dry or drained.

ASCOLANA Type of olive cultivated in the area of Ascoli Piceno.

ASCORBICO, ACIDO Ascorbic acid.

ASIAGO D'ALLEVO Hard, granular, semi-fat grating cheese from northwestern Italy, made from skimmed and full-cream milk, curdled and scalded, and cast into large rounds (8 to 12 kilograms). It can be aged up to 2 years and becomes sharper with aging.

ASIAGO GRASSO DI MONTE Semisoft, cooked-curd, mild summer cheese made in northwestern Italy from raw whole cow's milk.

ASIAGO PRESSATO White, scalded-curd, mild-tasting cheese from northwestern Italy, with a white to pale-straw paste containing a few irregular holes and a thin elastic rind; it matures for 20 to 40 days.

ASINO Donkey.

ASPARAGI AL PARMIGIANO Cooked asparagus topped with grated Parmigiano-Reggiano.

ASPARAGI PASTICCIATI CON UOVA Dish of asparagus and eggs. Cut the asparagus stalks into 2-inch pieces, boil, drain, mix with sliced onion, and sauté in butter until the onion is translucent. Add whisked eggs with salt and grated Parmigiano-Reggiano or Grana Padano, and stir until scrambled. Serve immediately.

ASPARAGO (PLURAL ASPARAGI) Asparagus.

ASPERULA Sweet woodruff.

ASPRO Acrid, sour.

ASSO, FORMAGGIO DI Goat cheese made in Valsassina, in the province of Lecco.

ASSONZA Lard with peperoncino and fennel seed.

ASSORTITO Assorted.

ASTACO (PLURAL ASTACI) Crustacean *Astacus fluviatilis,* also known as crayfish.

ASTACO AMERICANO American lobster.

ATENEO Athenaeus of Naucratis, Greek scholar, born in Egypt, author of *Deipnosophalstae* (meaning *Learned Banqueters*), a work with lots of references to food, drink, and customs of ancient Greeks and Romans.

ATTACCARSI To stick together, as pasta will while cooking in water.

ATTERRATO Vermicelli with butter, pine nuts, and chocolate.

AURORA Smooth, creamy sauce used to accompany eggs, kidneys, chicken, or fish; literally "dawn."

AURUM Distilled liqueur made of different wines, with an orange aroma, used often in pastry.

AVANZI Leftovers.

AVELLA Hazelnut, cobnut.

AVE MARIA Small tubular pasta, like rosary beads, used in soup.

AVENA Oats.

BABÀ Usually individual cylindrical soft sponge-cake desserts soaked in rum or cognac syrup.

BACCA (PLURAL BACCHE) Berry.

BACCALÀ Salt cod.

BACCALÀ ALLA BOLOGNESE Salt cod cooked in butter and oil with garlic and pepper.

BACCALÀ ALLA CAPPUCCINA Salt cod cooked with oil, vinegar, parsley, and garlic.

BACCALÀ ALLA GENOVESE Salt cod, boiled, grilled, and served with oil, lemon juice, and boiled potatoes.

BACCALÀ ALLA NAPOLETANA Salt cod fried in oil and stewed in a sauce of tomatoes, garlic, oil, and capers.

BACCALÀ ALLA VENEZIANA Salt cold with oil and onion in a thick anchovy sauce.

BACCELLO Pod.

BACCHE (SINGULAR BACCA) Berries.

BACCI, ANDREA Doctor, born in 1524 near Ascoli Piceno, author of *De naturali vinorum historia,* a comprehensive book on enology and growing wine grapes.

BACI (SINGULAR BACIO) Small chocolate sweets eaten in one bite that put a smile on your face, similar to what a kiss would do; literally, "kisses."

BACI DI DAMA Small almond cookies from Piedmont.

BAGGIANA A soup from Umbria made with beans, tomatoes, and basil.

BAGNA CAUDA Hot sauce made of olive oil, garlic, and anchovies into which vegetable crudités are dipped and then eaten.

BAGNET Sauce for boiled meats from Piedmont.

BAGNOMARIA Bain-marie, a water bath in which food in another pan is cooked.

BAGOZZO (BAGOSS) A hard yellow grana-type cheese with a sharp flavor and red rind.

BAICOLI Small Venetian cookies used during long trips taken by Venetian merchants. The name comes from their shape, similar to fish, also called baicoli, in the Venetian lagoon; flat and oval in shape, they also look like toasted pieces of bread.

BALDONAZZO (BALDONE) Typical sausage of Trentino, made with pork blood, chestnuts, lard, raisins, and spices. It is boiled in a casing, allowed to cool, then sliced and fried in lard.

BALLOTTA Whole chestnut poached in salted water seasoned with a bay leaf.

BALSAMELLA Besciamella, béchamel sauce, white sauce made from milk cooked with rue until creamy, seasoned with nutmeg.

BARBABIETOLA Beet.

BARBA DI BECCO Salsify.

BARBA DI FRATE (AGRETTO) Summer vegetable that looks like thick grass, similar to samphire but without the saltiness and gritty texture.

BARBAJADA (BARBAGLIATA) Chocolate drink invented by Domenico Barbaja.

BARBOTTA Corn-flour focaccia typical of the Lunigiana.

BARDARE To cover meat or fish with bacon or prosciutto so it does not dry out during the roasting process.

BARZOTTO Way of cooking boiled eggs that allows them to remain tender.

BASE English term used to indicate the fundamental part of a sauce, which can then be developed into many different sauces.

BASILICATA, CUCINA DELLA The cuisine of this region is known for its peppers from Senise. It uses a lot of peperoncino and cured pork meat (sausage, prosciutto, lard), as well as fresh pork meat and lamb. An area in Basilicata, Lucania, is where the thin sausages called lucaniche come from. The areas near the coast use fish, particularly in a well-done stew. The local Easter dessert scarcedda resembles the pastiera napoletana.

BASILICO Basil.

BASTARDA, SALSA Sauce used for fish and beans made of butter, flour, hot salted water, and egg yolks.

BASTARDELLA Metal bowl with two handles, usually used for whisking something over a flame or bain-marie.

BASTONE Long bread loaf similar to a baguette.

BATTERE To beat or pound, as dried cod or meat.

BATTICARNE Meat tenderizer.

BATTUTO Chopped onion, garlic, celery, and herbs, used as a cooking base.

BATÙ D'OCA Duck confit.

BAULETTI Little packages of veal.

BAVETTE (BAVETTINE) Long thin pasta, often used in soup.

BAVOSO Soft, runny in the center, as an omelette or a frittata.

BAZZOFFIA Minestrone from Lazio, usually made with fava beans, escarole, and artichoke, with a fresh egg placed in the center of each bowl of hot soup.

BECCACCIA Woodcock.

BECCACCINO Snipe.

BECCAFICO Game bird.

BECCUTA (BECCIATA) Rustic panino from near Ancona.

BELLAVISTA, IN Method of cooking and presenting food, in particular in gelatin with vegetable garnish and boiled eggs, most often used with fish.

BEL PAESE Industrial-made spreadable cheese made with cow's milk, with a soft paste.

BELTRAME, ALFREDO Innovator of Italian cuisine; in the 1960s, he was the chef to King Farouk in Cairo. He was born in Treviso in 1924 and founded the famous restaurant El Toula in Cortina.

BEN COTTA Well done, as steak may be cooked.

BENSONE Focaccia and sweet bread from the area of Modena or the Tuscan coast, usually served at breakfast or lunch or with wine. It is made of flour, eggs, lemon zest, and milk, sometimes including local fruits.

BERGAMOTTO Large aromatic citrus fruit grown almost exclusively in Italy, in the region of Reggio Calabria. Not eaten, but the oil of the zest is used to make liqueur and candied fruit. There are also bergamotto candies and a type of cookie called pazientino.

BERGESE, NINO Born in Piedmont in 1904, he was one of the biggest proponents of modern Italian cuisine, cooking for the house of the kings of Italy, among others, and ultimately opening his own place, La Santa, in the city of Genova. In 1969, he published the book *Mangiare da re* (*Eating Like a King*), which includes traditional regional recipes.

BERLINGOZZO A sweet eaten in Tuscany during Carnevale, derived from the Tuscan word for Fat Thursday, "berlingaccio." Usually they would be cookies made of flour, egg, sugar, and finely chopped aniseed. Also, cream cake.

BERNI, FRANCESCO Poet (1497–1535) who parodied Petrarch's poetry by writing about everyday happenings, especially about gastronomic subjects, which had become popular.

BIANCHETTI (SINGULAR BIANCHETTO) Tiny, transparent immature white fish. They are fried, or mixed with egg and made into an omelette.

BIANCO, IN "In white," a description of boiled fish served with oil, melted butter, and lemon juice.

BIANCO E NERO D'AGNELLO Lamb dish made in Liguria, in which dark parts (liver, heart) are cooked with white parts (lungs).

BIANCOMANGIARE Preparation that can be sweet, savory, or a mix, in which milk and almond flour are used to create a gelatinous consistency and other ingredients are added. In old recipes, biancomangiare might contain chicken breast, rice flour, sheep's milk, melted sugar, or melted lard.

BIANCONE Early-season type of truffle.

BICARBONATO Sodium bicarbonate, a salt formed by the combination of carbonic acid and salts, used to soften dried beans and to keep vegetables green during cooking.

BIETE Swiss chard.

BIETOLA Swiss chard or beetroot.

BIETOLINA See erbetta.

BIGA Starter for bread made of flour, water, and yeast mixed into a dough and left to rest for 12 hours.

BIGOLI Thick homemade extruded spaghetti from the Veneto region.

BIRBANTI Dry Umbrian sweets made of flour, sugar, and pinoli.

BIROLDO Blood pudding from Tuscany containing pine nuts and raisins or cheese.

BISCOTTARE To toast, literally meaning to toast or bake twice.

BISCOTTO Originally this term referred to bread cooked or toasted twice, but it has become synonymous with a dry cookie.

BISCOTTO, PAN Type of bread with very little rising that was cooked once and then placed in the oven for a second baking. This bread would dry out and could be stored for a long time, and used only after having been wet with water. It was most often used on ships and in port towns. Some recipes derive from it, such as the recipe for cappone magro from Genova.

BISMALVA Marshmallow (the plant).

BISMARCK, ALLA Term to describe a steak served with a fried egg. The recipe became prevalent in Italy in the nineteenth century. Bismarck at the time represented the strong German power, and the recipe was probably so named because it provides quite a bit of protein power.

BISTECCA Beefsteak.

BISTECCHINA Thin steak.

BITTER English word used in Italy to signify a drink that has a bitter taste.

BITTO Hard round cheese weighing 15 to 25 kilograms, repeatedly dried and salted for anywhere from 2 months to 3 years, which becomes denser and more crumbly with age. Often served with polenta.

BLU, AL Method of cooking fish or shellfish by plunging them alive, and whole, into boiling water or stock.

BOCCONCINO Term used to signify a mouthful of items put together, or a small bite.

BOERO Candy with a chocolate shell and cherry and liqueur inside.

BOLDONE Sweet blood sausage typical of the Veneto, made with pork blood, rice, boiled chestnuts, pinoli, raisins, chocolate, and spices. It is cased in the intestines, boiled, sliced, and fried in butter or grilled.

BOLLIRE To boil, cooking in water.

BOLLITO Boiled.

BOLLITO MISTO Diverse meats—such as veal's head, flank of beef, beef shin, capon, tongue, and cotechino—with vegetables—carrots, onions, and celery—and seasonings, cooked for 4 hours. Usually served from a special trolley, the meats are carved at the table and presented with various sauces.

BOLOGNESE, ALLA In a method typical of Emilia-Romagna and in particular Bologna, usually referring to a long-cooking meat-sauce ragù.

BOMBA Generic term to indicate sweet or salty fried dough. Also a type of ice-cream dessert with layers of different-flavored ice cream.

BOMBA DI RISO Dish of cooked rice molded around a filling of cooked minced meat, herbs, seasonings, chopped mushrooms, and diced cheese or ham.

BOMBOLOTTI Short, slightly curved pasta with a hole in the center (or running through it), usually used to prepare first-course pasta dishes such as a typical Sicilian dish of pasta with broccoli.

BONET Typical Piedmontese dessert, a rich chocolate pudding with amaretto.

BONITA Bonito tuna.

BORDATINO Tuscan soup with yellow corn flour as the base, along with beans and local vegetables.

BORLENGHI Specialty from Emilia-Romagna made of salt, flour, and water, fried and eaten with a paste of chopped lard, rosemary, and garlic.

BORLOTTO Bean variety, meaty, with a yellowish green skin and some red markings, about 2 to 3 inches long, containing about four seeds inside.

BORRAGINE Borage.

BOSCAIOLA, ALLA Sauce used to dress pasta "woodman style," usually containing tomato, mushroom, sausage, and ricotta.

BOTTARGA Mediterranean caviar, silver-mullet roe, cured and dried using sea salt.

BOUQUET French term used in Italy when describing the aroma of wine.

BOVINO Bovine.

BRA Piedmontese cheese that originated in the town of Bra, made using mainly cow's milk, though goat's or sheep's milk may be added in small quantities. It can be eaten hard or soft, and is aged for varying lengths of time.

BRACCIATELLA (BRACCIATELLO) Yeast-raised round cake served in Emilia-Romagna, particularly during the Easter season.

BRACHETTO Sweetish, aromatic sparkling red wine from Piedmont, often served as a dessert wine.

BRACE Embers.

BRACIOLA Chop.

BRACIOLETTA Lamb chop cut on the side of the bone toward the shoulder, with a small piece of meat attached.

BRACIOLETTINE Pure Italian-language translation of the Sicilian term "braciulittini arrustiti," which are small veal cutlets rolled and cooked on embers.

BRANZINO Sea bass.

BRASARE To braise.

BRASATO Braised.

BRESAOLA Cured, air-dried beef matured for several months, cut in thin slices, and served as an antipasto.

BRICIOLA Crumb, as of bread.

BRIGATA Team of professional cooks or chefs, under the direction of the executive chef.

BRIGIDINI Aniseed-flavored biscuits.

BRILLANTINA Method of finishing a dessert that usually implies giving it a shine with gelatin.

BRIOSCIA Brioche.

BROCCOLETTI Broccoli rabe, or broccoli florets.

BROCCOLI DI RAPA Broccoli rabe.

BROCCOLO Broccoli.

BRODETTATO Finished with egg yolks and lemon juice, as, for example, a lamb stew.

BRODETTO 1. Soupy sauce made of broth with whisked eggs and lemon juice. 2. Saffron-flavored fish stew similar to bouillabaisse. Also known as boretto and broeto.

BRODETTO ALLA ROMANA Easter stew of beef and lamb finished with egg yolks, lemon juice, and grated Grana Padano or Parmigiano-Reggiano.

BRODO Broth, stock.

BRODO DI MANZO Clear beef broth.

BRODO RISTRETTO Consommé.

BROETO See brodetto.

BRONZINO Sea bass.

BROVADE OR BROADE (SINGULAR BROVADA) Specialty from Friuli–Venezia Giulia of thinly sliced turnips macerated in vinegar, often eaten with museto.

BRUCIO Piedmontese word for a very dark sauce usually used to dress the local egg pasta, tajarin.

BRUSCANDOLI Terminology from the Veneto used for two types of wild shoots: hop shoots in the province of Padova, and holly shoots in the province of Verona.

BRUSCHETTA Lightly toasted thick slices of bread rubbed with cut garlic cloves and cut ripe tomatoes, sprinkled with olive oil and salt, and eaten as an accompaniment to a meal or as a snack. Also called fettunta, fett'unta, fregolatta.

BRUSCO Sharp, sour.

BRUTTI MA BUONI Cookies originally from Piedmont; literally "ugly but good."

BUCATI Type of maccheroni, from "bucare," to pierce.

BUCATINI Smaller version of bucati, also called perciatelli or perciatelloni.

BUCCELLATO Aniseed-flavored cake typical of Lucca, containing currants. Also another name for the Sicilian cucciddato cake stuffed with figs.

BUCCINO Whelk, sea snail.

BUDELLA Intestines, entrails, guts, casings.

BUDELLINE Giblets.

BUDINO DI RICOTTA Ricotta cheese pudding.

BUDINO TORINESE Chestnut pudding.

BUE Mature ox.

BURRATA Cheese made in Andria, Puglia, from cow's milk; the outside of the cheese is stretched and elastic like mozzarella, but the center is softer and contains more cream.

BURRIDA Seafood soup made in Sardinia.

BURRINO Small cheese from the Salerno area with an outside similar to provolone and an inside like butter. Cured for a week; if cured longer, the cheese becomes sharper. Pear-shaped and eaten young.

BURRO Butter.

BURRO, AL With butter only, usually referring to pasta.

BURRO AROMATIZZATO O COMPOSTO Originally used in France and now in many Italian restaurant kitchens, butter emulsified while hot with vinegar and shallots, often used with freshwater fish.

BURRO E FORMAGGIO Sauce of melted butter and grated cheese.

BURRO FUSO Melted butter.

BURRO MANEGGIATO Butter and flour mixed together and solidified, used as an emulsifier in sauces.

BURRO NERO Beurre noisette (brown butter).

BUSECCA Thick tripe soup made with onions and usually with beans.

BUTAREGA (BUTTARIGA) Bottarga, the salted and pressed dried roe of a female tuna or grey mullet.

BUZARA Cooking method in Istria and the Veneto, used to cook shrimp, crab, lobster, and mollusks.

CACAO Cocoa.

CACCIAGIONE Wild game.

CACCIATORA, ALLA Cooked in hunter's style, a northern-Italian style, usually signifying meat with onions, tomato, mushrooms, and pancetta. In central Italy, it usually means meat cooked with rosemary, garlic, and vinegar.

CACCIATORE Pure pork salami, originally from Piedmont and Lombardy; the name derives from its small size, ideal for the hunters to bring along as a snack on their hunt.

CACCIATORINO Small salami.

CACCIUCCO Fish-and-shellfish stew originally from coastal Tuscany and Liguria, the name derives from the Turkish word *kačukli*, meaning a mix of small fish. It is a highly seasoned fish soup served with pieces of garlic-flavored toast.

CACHI Persimmon.

CACIETTO Smaller version of caciocavallo.

CACIO Cheese.

CACIO BACCELLONE Tuscan cheese often eaten with fava beans.

CACIOCAVALLO Semihard, mild pear-shaped cheese from Sicily with a yellow rind, similar to provolone. It is ripened for 2 to 3 months for slicing, and 6 to 12 months for grating.

CACIOFIORE Hard ewe's-milk cheese with a high fat content and no rind; good for eating and for cooking.

CACIORICOTTA Ewe's-milk cheese from central and southern Italy and Sardinia. The soft version can be eaten fresh or salted and ripened for 2 to 3 months; the hard version is coagulated with rennet or fig juice, and the curd is molded, salted, and ripened for 3 to 4 months.

CACIOTTA Small, soft, mild cheese for slicing, made from a variety of pasteurized milk with a lactic starter.

CACIOTTA DI PECORA Soft ewe's-milk cheese shaped like a small drum, with a mild, soft paste and smooth rind.

CAGLIO Rennet.

CALABRIA, CUCINA DELLA Cuisine influenced by the Normans, Arabs, French, and Spanish. From its Greek origins come large tagliatelle (Greek word *laganon*) and makaria, which are cylindrical gnocchi, apparently the original macaroni. Nnuglia, Calabrian salami made of meat, lard, liver, and lung, seems to be quite similar to the French andouille. The coastal diet is fish-based and quite similar to that of Sicily.

CALAMARETTI Small squid.

CALAMARI (SINGULAR CALAMARO) Squid.

CALCIONE DI RICOTTA Savory pastry made in Abruzzo. The dough is made with flour, egg, lard, lemon juice, and salt and stuffed with ricotta, provola, egg, chopped prosciutto, and parsley. Fried in oil.

CALCIONETTI Apple-and-almond fritters.

CALCIONI Also called caciuni, cheese ravioli typical of the province of Ascoli Piceno in Marche. Prepared with pastry dough and stuffed with pecorino, ricotta, egg, sugar, and lemon rind, and baked in the oven.

CALENDOLA (CALENDULA) Marigold.

CALZONCELLI Small stuffed dough pockets typical of Puglia and Campania, made just like a calzone, but smaller in size.

CALZONE Yeasted dough rolled out, formed into a pocket, and filled with cheese or salami and cheese (Naples) or with onions, olives, anchovies, capers, and cheese (Sicily). Baked in the oven or fried. Also called calzengliede or calzuncieddi.

CAMICIA, IN Of poached eggs, in their jackets, where the albumen cooks, but the yolk remains runny; literally, in a shirt.

CAMOMILLA Dried chamomile flowers that are steeped in hot water and consumed as tea.

CAMOSCIO Small goatlike wild mammal, the meat of which is eaten in Italy, usually marinated and stewed as game meat.

CAMPANIA, CUCINA DELLA Cuisine of Naples, a bit different from that of the rest of its region, influenced by Greek, Roman, Byzantine, Arab, Norman, French, and Spanish elements. Seafood is an important component, and the symbol of Neapolitan cuisine is the invention of pizza. The regional food also uses the many cheeses produced in the area, such as mozzarella di bufala, mozzarella, provolone, and scamorza. There are many minestre, such as minestra maritata. Other typical dishes include spaghetti alle vongole and parmigiana di melanzane.

CAMPARI Named after its inventor, Gaspare Campari, a bitter alcoholic liqueur served on ice with soda, or mixed in drinks such as the Negroni and the Americano.

CAMPO, DI Wild, as mushrooms or asparagus; literally, "from the field."

CANARINI Small artichokes typical of the Venetian lagoon area with a bright yellowish green color, usually cut in half, battered, and fried.

CANARINO A beverage made of lemon rind steeped in hot water, yellow in color (hence named literally "canary"), and used as an after-dinner digestif.

CANDIRE To soak fruit in a sugar solution until

the fruit is saturated with sugar, which takes the place of the liquid in the fruit and hardens.

CANDITO Candied.

CANEDERLI Large gnocchi from the Trentino area, made of bread; they can be savory or sweet, and are often served in broth.

CANESTRATO Cow's or sheep's milk cheese with a hard or semisoft paste and a yellow-brownish color. It is usually aged in a canestro, a woven basket.

CANESTRELLI 1. Small scallops. 2. Scallop-shaped pastries from northwestern Italy.

CANNELLA Cinnamon.

CANNELLINI Generic name for various types of white beans.

CANNELLONI Large squares of pasta boiled, then rolled around a stuffing (usually meat) to form tubes, then placed in a baking dish, covered with sauce and grated cheese, and baked in the oven.

CANNOLI Fried pastries filled with ricotta, whipped cream, chocolate cream, or something similar.

CANNOLICCHI Short, fairly thick tubes of pasta used in soups.

CANNOLICCHIO Razor clam.

CANNOLO, STAMPO PER Cone- or cylinder-shaped metal around which the round dough for cannoli is wrapped; the dough is then fried to retain its hollow tubular form.

CANOCCHIA Mantis shrimp, also called pannocchia; a long crustacean, gray in color with two black spots and lots of teeth and spines, often used in caciucco (Tuscan seafood stew).

CANTUCCI Small, hard biscuits containing almond pieces. Often dunked in Vin Santo; also called biscotti di Prato or cantuccini.

CANTUCCINI See cantucci.

CAPA LONGA Venetian dialect for cannolicchio.

CAPASANTA Scallop.

CAPELLI D'ANGELO Angel's hair, a very fine, thin pasta noodle, sometimes dried in a shape similar to a bird's nest.

CAPELLINI Very thin spaghetti—hair-thin (hence the name).

CAPELVENERE Maidenhead fern.

CAPITONE Conger eel.

CAPOCOLLO Salami made from cured pork-shoulder chunks, mixed with finely minced pork fat, sweet and hot red peppers, seasonings, and spices, then air-dried. Served in thin slices. Also called coppa.

CAPONATA (CAPPORATA) Mélange of fried eggplant with onions, tomatoes, celery, capers, and olives, flavored with an agrodolce sauce.

CAPOZZELLA Roasted lamb's head.

CAPPA General term for shellfish like mussels or clams.

CAPPELLACCI Stuffed pasta from Ferrara, in Emilia-Romagna.

CAPPELLA DI FUNGO Mushroom cap.

CAPPELLO Literally, "hat"; used for foods shaped like a hat.

CAPPELLO DI PRETE Cut of beef often used in boiled meat, for goulash, or in long-cooking sauces such as spezzatino.

CAPPELLO DI PRETE (CAPPEL DI PRETE) Traditional name for a salami or cotechino made near Parma, in Emilia-Romagna, originally produced from what was left over from the pig's thigh when producing culatello. The extra pieces were chopped, sealed in the skin of the last part of the hoof, and sewn in a triangle.

CAPPERI Capers.

CAPPON MAGRO An elaborate salad of cooked vegetables, anchovies, lobster, and/or other fishes seasoned with oil, vinegar, and garlic.

CAPPONE Capon, castrated male domestic fowl, larger and more tender.

CAPPONE Small red mullet.

CAPPONE IN GALERA Salad of anchovies and capers.

CAPPUCCINA Lettuce.

CAPPUCCINO Espresso coffee mixed with milk that has been heated and foamed by steam, sometimes served garnished with powdered cocoa or cinnamon.

CAPPUCCIO Round, as in a round lettuce; literally, like a hood or cap.

CAPRA Goat. Also, a freshwater lake fish similar to trout.

CAPRA, FORMAGGIO DI Goat cheese; the most common in Italy is caprino or tomino.

CAPRA, PROSCIUTTO DI Salted and air-cured goat leg, goat prosciutto.

CAPRA DI MARE Spider crab.

CAPRINI (SINGULAR CAPRINO) Small goat's-milk cheeses. See Montevecchia.

CAPRIOLO Deer, roebuck.

CARABACCIA Traditional Florentine soup with an onion base.

CARAMELLA Caramel or hard candy.

CARAMELLARE Action of transforming sugar into caramel by heating over a low flame.

CARAMELLATO Caramelized, candied, or glazed.

CARAMELLIZZAZIONE Process in cooking by which food takes on a warm golden or caramel hue.

CARBONARA Coal miner's sauce or dressing, usually used with spaghetti alla carbonara; contains egg, onions, and bacon or pancetta.

CARBONATA Dish from the northwest of Italy, beef or salt beef stewed in red wine.

CARCIOFI (SINGULAR CARCIOFO) Artichokes.

CARCIOFI ALLA GIUDIA Small-to-medium artichokes fried whole until the leaves become crisp, a preparation from the old Jewish ghetto of Rome.

CARCIOFINI Small artichokes, usually refering to artichoke hearts.

CARDAMOMO Cardamom.

CARDI (SINGULAR CARDO) Cardoon.

CARDINALE, ALLA Term used to describe certain preparations of food that are red in color, such as a passata di gamberi alla cardinale, red shrimp soup. Sweets that are red in color can also be called alla cardinale.

CARDONE Cardoon.

CARNE Meat.

CARNE DI MAIALE Pork.

CARNE IN UMIDO Stewed beef.

CARNE LESSA Boiled beef.

CARNE SECCA Cured meats; dried meats.

CARNE TRITATA Minced meat.

CARPA Carp.

CARPACCIO Finely sliced, high-quality beef, usually the fillet, served raw; the preparation was first executed by Giuseppe Cipriani, the founder of Harry's Bar in Venice.

CARPIONE Freshwater fish, like white fish.

CARRELLO Trolley with food (sweets or hors d'oeuvres) brought to the table in a restaurant.

CARRETTIERA, ALLA Sauce for pasta named after a carrettiere, the cart driver who used to transport things, and therefore often a customer in an osteria, because he was on the road. The ingredients include olive oil, garlic, peperoncino, salt, peeled tomatoes, and parsley.

CARROZZA, IN In a carriage—a way to prepare mozzarella.

CARRUBA Carob.

CARTA CINESE Rice paper.

CARTA DI MUSICA (CARTA DA MUSICA) Paper-thin crispbread made in Sardinia. Also called pane carasau.

CARTELLATE Traditional Pugliese dessert made during the Christmas season that look like pinwheels. They are fried, then topped with honey or reduced must.

CARTOCCIO, AL In a paper bag, describing a cooking method of sealing food in wax paper, aluminum foil, or a brown bag, and baking it in the oven.

CASA, DI Homemade.

CASALINGA A housewife.

CASALINGO Homemade.

CASONSEI Stuffed pasta typical of Brescia in the shape of a tube, stuffed with bread, egg, and salami.

CASSATA Ice cream cake made of layers of at least three different flavors and colors, containing nuts and candied fruits.

CASSATA, STAMPO PER Aluminum or stainless-steel form used to make the Sicilian ice cream of the same name, cassata.

CASSATA ALLA SICILIANA Layered cake from Sicily, soaked in liqueur, filled with ricotta, and decorated with marzipan, almond paste, nuts, and candied fruit.

CASSATEDDE DI RICOTTA Deep-fried crescent-shaped pastry filled with chocolate and sweetened ricotta cheese.

CASSERUOLA Casserole.

CASSOEULA Typical Milanese dish with various types of meat and savoy cabbage, baked or braised together.

CASSOLA Fish soup with peperoncino and tomatoes, from Sardinia.

CASSONI Fried pastries filled with green vegetables.

CASTAGNA Chestnut.

CASTAGNACCI Fritters made with chestnut flour.

CASTAGNACCIO Cake made with chestnut flour and water mixed with pine nuts, fennel seeds, and raisins, baked.

CASTAGNE ALL'UBRIACO Peeled roasted chestnuts soaked in red wine and kept warm for 30 minutes, sometimes eaten with honey.

CASTAGNOLE Fritters made in the Emilia-Romagna region during Carnevale, shaped a little like chestnuts.

CASTELMAGNO DOP cheese made in Castelmagno, in the province of Cuneo, Piedmont. Made with cow's milk and sometimes a small portion of sheep's milk. The cheese is crumbly and smells earthy and can sometimes have blue veins.

CASTELVETRO, GIACOMO Born in 1546 in Modena, he wrote of all the herbs, roots, and fruits that were comestible raw in Italy.

CASTRATO Mutton.

CATALOGNA Puntarelle, a variety of chicory with a bulb base, long, thin leaves, and asparagus-like heads.

CAVALLO Horse.

CAVALLO, A On horseback, designating a dish of meat such as steak, hamburger, or a cutlet topped with one or more fried eggs, on top, such as in alla Bismarck or alla Holstein.

CAVATIDDI Sicilian name for pasta made with durum wheat in a cylindrical shape with the ends turning upward.

CAVATIEDDI (CECATELLI) Pasta curls, also called mignule.

CAVIALE Caviar.

CAVIGLIONE Small gurnard (fish).

CAVOLATA Sardinian pork, cabbage, and potato soup.

CAVOLFIORE Cauliflower.

CAVOLFIORE ALLA ROMANA Browned cauliflower served with tomato sauce and cheese.

CAVOLFIORE ALLA VILLEROY Cauliflower with lemon sauce.

CAVOLFIORE A VASTEDDA Cauliflower dipped in anchovy butter and deep-fried.

CAVOLFIORE INDORATO E FRITTO Breaded and fried cauliflower.

CAVOLINI DI BRUSSEL (CAVOLINI DI BRUXELLES) Brussels sprouts.

CAVOLO Cabbage.

CAVOLO BROCCOLUTO A leafy green that tastes like broccoli.

CAVOLO MARINO Sea kale.

CAVOLO NERO Kale.

CAVOLO RAPA Kohlrabi.

CAVOLO RICCIO Collard greens.

CAVOLO VERZA Savoy cabbage.

CAVOUR, ALLA Indicating two preparations named after a political figure of Piedmont, inspired by Piedmontese cuisine. The first is thin slices of yellow polenta topped by slices of meat, either veal or kidney, served with braised mushrooms. The second is croquettes of fried semolina served with large cuts of roasted meat.

CECE (CECIO) Chickpea.

CEDIOLI Tiny eels.

CEDRATA Thirst-quenching drink made of cedro (citron).

CEDRINA Verbena.

CEDRO Citron, the fruit.

CEDRONE Wood grouse.

CEFALO Grey mullet, also called galupe.

CELLENTANI Short pieces of ridged pasta in a swirl shape.

CENCI Venetian snack of crisp, wafer-thin, deep-fried strips of pastry, dusted with powdered sugar. Also called galani or frappe.

CENERE Ashes.

CENTERBE Liqueur typical of Abruzzo, made by infusing various herbs in alcohol; literally, "one hundred herbs."

CEREALI Cereal, grains.

CERFOGLIO Chervil.

CERNIA Mediterranean grouper.

CERVELLO Brains.

CERVO Venison.

CETRIOLINI Gherkins.

CETRIOLO Cucumber.

CHECCA, SPAGHETTI ALLA Roman name for spaghetti sauced with raw tomato and basil.

CHENELLINE Tiny dumplings used for soup.

CHIACCHIERE Name used in Lombardy for the fried dough sweets topped with powdered sugar that are served during Carnevale.

CHIARIFICARE To clarify.

CHINA Evergreen tree, the bark of which is used in the production of digestifs and medicinal remedies and in alcohol, such as china rosso; it has a bitter taste.

CHINOTTO Citrus grown in Liguria, Calabria, and Sicily, like a small orange, used to make syrup, candies, and a drink also named chinotto.

CHIOCCIOLE Snails—the animal, or small pasta shells used for soup.

CHIODI DI GAROFANO Cloves.

CHIODINO Mushroom that looks like a nail (chiodo).

CHITARRA Wood-and-string-tool used in Abruzzo to cut pasta to make a square spaghetti, maccheroni alla chitarra.

CHIZZE Stuffed, fried pasta made in Reggio Emilia.

CIABATTA Oval bread made from a dough of flour, water, and olive oil with yeast or sourdough; literally, "slipper."

CIACCI Borlenghi typical of the Appenine areas, near Reggio Emilia, thin crêpes made with chestnut flour, stuffed with ricotta or other cheeses, and cooked on a flat top, soft and sweet.

CIACCI DI RICOTTA Similar to ciacci, but in this case the ricotta is mixed with milk, salt, yeast, and flour. The mixture is then cooked on a flat-top grill and pressed with slices of prosciutto and coppa.

CIALDA Wafer, waffle.

CIALZONS Half-moon-shaped pasta from the Carnia area of Friuli stuffed with a mixture of savory and sweet, most commonly spinach, raisins, unsweetened cocoa, candied citron, egg, and sugar, boiled, then dressed with browned butter and a sprinkling of cinnamon, sugar, and shaved smoked ricotta.

CIAMBELLA Baked ring-shaped dough usually made of flour, yeast, and eggs, with either sweet or savory elements added.

CIAMBELLE Ring-shaped cakes or pastries with nuts and candied fruit, also (in Tuscany) called panafracchi (bread loaves).

CIAMBOTTA Omelette made with potatoes, sweet green peppers, tomatoes, and eggplant cooked in olive oil, also called ciamotta or cianfrotta.

CIAN Fritters, crêpes made with chestnut flour, salt, and water, eaten stuffed with ricotta or fresh cheese.

CIAUDEDDA Braised vegetables typical of the Basilicata region.

CIBREO Cockscombs, chicken liver, testicles, and sweetbreads braised with wine, served with a vegetable timbale.

CICALE DI MARE Mantis shrimp, also called stomatopods.

CICCIOLI Pork or duck cracklings.

CICERCHIA Antique yellow pebble-shaped legume used by the Etruscans and the Romans, the size of a pea.

CICERCHIATA Typical Umbrian dessert made during Carnevale, also known in other areas as pignolata, struffoli, or corona di Santa Rita.

CICORIA Chicory leaf.

CICORIA SELVATICA Wild chicory, dandelion.

CICORIA SPADONA Sword-shaped green chicory.

CICORIELLA Cicoria catalogna, chicory.

CICORINO Salad greens in the chicory family, such as radicchio, frisée, crumolo.

CILIEGIA (PLURAL CILIEGE) Cherry or cherries.

CIMA ALLA GENOVESE Typical dish of Genova, veal breast stuffed with an egg-and-vegetable frittata, rolled, sewn, and boiled, served sliced with salsa verde.

CIMA DI VITELLO Veal in aspic.

CIMBOPOGONE Lemongrass.

CIME DI RAPA Broccoli rabe.

CINGHIALE Wild boar.

CIOCCOLATINO Small chocolate treat with a chocolate base that can include, nuts, liqueurs, fruits, or jams.

CIOCCOLATO Chocolate sweet created by blending sugar and cocoa to which milk, cocoa butter, spices, honey, and fruits can also be added.

CIOPPINO See ciuppin.

CIPOLLA Onion. There are many different types in Italy, such as the red onion from Tropea, the golden onion from Parma, the Vernina from Florence, and the Ramata from Milano.

CIPOLLATA Onion soup with pork meat, typical of the area around Siena.

CIPOLLINA, ERBA Chive.

CIPOLLOTTO Young onion plant, not completely matured, spring onion.

CITRONETTE Salad condiment prepared with lemon and oil, often also with finely chopped onion or chives.

CIUPPIN Generic Ligurian term for a fish soup. Originally a dish prepared by Ligurian fishermen on their boats with the fish they did not consider worth selling. Also called cioppino.

COCOMERO (ANGURIA) Watermelon.

COCOZELLE Small summer squash resembling a zucchini.

COCUZZA (CUCUZZA) Name used in southern Italy to indicate squash, sometimes referring to the long green squash.

CODA DI ROSPO (RANA PESCATRICE) Monkfish.

COLAZIONE Breakfast.

COLLA DI PESCE Fish gelatin, usually used in making pastry.

COLLO Neck.

COLLO D'OCA Neck skin of a duck, stuffed and made into a sausage.

COLOMBA Dove-shaped Easter cake.

COLOMBANI, FRANCO Restaurateur born in Milan in 1929 who focused on revitalizing and conserving regional Italian cuisine. After 1958, he ran the Albergo del Sole (Maleo), a place dating back to the sixteenth century.

COLOMBO Wood pigeon.

COLTELLO Knife.

COMPOSTA Compote of stewed fruit.

COMPOSTO Composed, put together.

CONCHIGLIA DI SAN GIACOMO Coquille Saint-Jacques, scallop.

CONCHIGLIE Shells, pasta shaped like a half-shell, or small, shell-shaped, citron-flavored cakes from Sicily.

CONCHIGLIETTE Small pasta shells used in soup.

CONDIGGION (CONDIJUN) Ligurian salad of fresh leafy greens, vegetables, such as peppers, cucumber, tomatoes, and bread, and tuna; the name derives from a local aromatic green, condiglione.

CONDITO Seasoned or dressed.

CONFETTO Small sweet, usually a sugar-coated almond, which can be soft or hard. The inner fruit or nut is called the anima (soul), and it is covered by a candy coating. They are often used in party favors to celebrate important events in Italy. The most famous ones are made in Sulmona, Abruzzo.

CONFETTURA Jam.

CONGELATO Frozen.

CONIGLIO DOMESTICO Rabbit.

CONIGLIO ALLA REGGIANA Rabbit in pieces, sautéed in oil and bacon fat with onion, garlic, celery, and tomato, then simmered in dry white wine. Finished with parsley.

CONIGLIO SELVATICO Wild rabbit, bigger than a domestic rabbit but smaller than a hare.

CONSERVA Preserve made from fruit or vegetable.

CONSERVA DI FRUTTA Jam.

CONSOMMÉ French word often used to indicate a dense meat broth used in cooking.

CONTORNO Side dish or vegetable dish.

COPATA (CUPATA) Tuscan dessert, from Siena, made of honey, nuts, and anise pressed between two wafers; also produced in Sicily (cubbaita), Basilicata (copete), Puglia (copeta or cupeta), and Lombardy (copett).

COPERTO Cover charge in a restaurant. Also means covered—for example, a slice of cheese.

COPOLLOTTO Bulbs of the wild hyacinth, boiled, then braised in a sweet-and-sour sauce; also called labascione.

COPPA Pork sausage, dried and smoked with herbs. Or a large sausage containing distinct pieces of pork shoulder and pork fat.

COPPA COTTA The meat of pig's heads and tongues, pressed until set into a solid mass.

COPPA DI GELATO Mixed ice creams.

COPPO Heavy cream cooked in the oven and then eaten.

COQUE French term for a soft-boiled egg in its shell.

CORALLO Lobster coral.

CORATA Interior organs that include the lungs, kidneys, heart, and liver. Also called frattaglio.

CORATELLA Offal. Also a stew of lamb's lungs, liver, and heart.

CORBEZZOLO Arbutus, a small tree or shrub with red bark and edible red berries often used in making jam. Also known as the strawberry tree. The honey of the bees that pollinate the corbezzolo flower is distinct and slightly bitter in taste.

CORIANDOLO Coriander.

CORNETTI (SINGULAR CORNETTO) Sweet breakfast croissants.

CORREZIONE Italian habit of adding a small amount of liqueur to coffee or tea, literally translated as a "correction."

CORZETTI Traditional pasta from the Polcevera Valley in Liguria, most often cooked with a sauce of melted butter, fresh marjoram, pinoli, and Grana Padano or Parmigiano-Reggiano.

COSCETTA Thigh portion of a leg of a small lamb or poultry.

COSCIA Haunch or leg of venison, a small veal, lamb or ox.

COSCIOTTO Leg of lamb.

COSTA Popular name for Swiss chard.

COSTALAME DI BUE Ribs of beef.

COSTATA Rib chop.

COSTOLE Ribs.

COSTOLETTA Cutlet or boned chop.

COTECHINO Filled large sausage made with pork, lard, and pork rind, originally from Emilia-Romagna, boiled and sliced, and served with mustard. In Friuli–Venezia Giulia it is called musetto.

COTENNA DI MAIALE (COTICA) Pig skin or rind, rich in gelatinous substance, thick and fatty. For use in the kitchen, it is boiled and the fatty substance is scraped off as well as the bristles.

COTICHE Pork rinds.

COTOGNA Term to indicate fruit from the East. Mela cotogna is quince; there are also pere cotogne, more oblong in shape than the apple. Astringent with tannins unless very ripe, these fruits are used in the preparation of jams, or often baked with sugar.

COTOGNATA Sweet paste made by cooking quince and sugar, mostly made in Puglia and Sicily.

COTOGNO Quince.

COTOLETTE (SINGULAR COTOLETTA) Chops, cutlets.

COTURNICE Partridge.

COZZE (SINGULAR COZZA) Mussels.

CRAUTI Sauerkraut.

CREMA Cream, custard.

CREMA DI CASTAGNE Chestnut cream used in making desserts or served with ice cream.

CREMA DI LATTE Heavy cream.

CREMA FRITTA Fried egg custard, savory or sweet, chilled, then cut in diamond shapes and fried.

CREMA PASTICCERIA Confectioners' custard, a cake filling.

CREMA ROVESCIATA Baked egg custard.

CREMOLATA Typical Milanese topping made of finely chopped garlic, parsley, lemon rinds; it is added to meats during braising and often sprinkled on osso buco before serving it.

CREMOLATO Roman term for a granita usually flavored with lemon or coffee.

CREMONESE Small dessert, typical of Cremona, made with sugar, flour, and butter; a shiny and golden baked sweet.

CRÊPE Thin pancake.

CRESCENTE (SINGULAR CRESCENTA) Dough made with flour, baking soda, salt, and milk, rested, then rolled into thin disks and fried, and served hot with savory cabbage.

CRESCENTINA Flatbread made with dough containing pieces of bacon.

CRESCENZA Soft cow's-milk cheese with a buttery texture from northern Italy.

CRESCIONE Watercress. Also called agresto.

CRESPELLA Thin stuffed crêpe.

CRESTA Cockscomb.

CRITMO Type of wild fennel that grows near the

sea, also called "marine fennel," usually served in a salad or conserved in vinegar and served along with other antipasti.

CROCCANTE Praline; as adjective, crunchy.

CROCCHETTA Croquette.

CROSTA Crust—of bread, cheese, cake, etc.

CROSTA, PASTA PER PREPARAZIONI IN Dough used to wrap meat, chicken, fish, or vegetables that are baked; the dough retains the flavor of the items inside, and vice versa.

CROSTACEI Crustaceans.

CROSTATA Pie.

CROSTATA DI FRAGOLE Strawberry pie.

CROSTATINA Tart.

CROSTATO Browned, with a crust.

CROSTINI ALLA FIORENTINA Crostini topped with chicken-liver pâté.

CROSTINI ALLA NAPOLETANA Crostini topped with tomatoes and anchovies.

CROSTINI ALLA PARMIGIANA Crostini topped with melted cheese and anchovies.

CROSTINI AL MARE Crostini topped with minced shellfish.

CROSTINO (PLURAL CROSTINI) Toasted sliced bread served with toppings.

CROSTONCINO See crostino.

CROSTONE (PLURAL CROSTONI) A thick crust or a thick slice of bread, toasted and served with toppings.

CROSTONE, SU On toasted bread.

CRUDITÀ Crudité.

CRUDO Raw.

CRUMIRO Dry, crumbly cookie typical of Casale Monferrato in Piedmont.

CUBAITA Soft nougat with honey, almond, and sesame seeds; a Sicilian specialty, but also made in Calabria.

CUCCHIAINO Teaspoon.

CUCCHIAIO, AL Referring to a soft dessert that needs to be eaten with a spoon.

CUCCIDDATO Typical Sicilian dessert similar to buccellato; also a fig-stuffed cookie.

CUCUZZA Term used in southern Italy for squash.

CUCUZZELLA Term used in southern Italy for zucchini.

CUGNÀ Piedmontese chutney made by cooking quince, pears, hazelnuts, and wine.

CULACCIO Rump of beef.

CULATELLO Large, air-cured, salamilike ham, made near Parma; it uses the upper hind part of the pig leg, seasoned and air-cured in a casing.

CUMINO Cumin.

CUMINO DEI PRATI Wild cumin.

CUOCERE ALLA GRATICOLA To cook on a grill.

CUOCERE A VAPORE To cook by steaming.

CUOCERE IN UMIDO To braise, stew.

CUORE Heart.

DADOLATA Mirepoix with large cubed pieces.

DATTERO DI MARE Date mussel—a bivalve mollusk with an oblong brown shell, similar-looking to the fruit.

DENTE, AL Indicating something cooked to have a slight bite—literally, "to the tooth"—often used to indicate pasta cooked properly.

DENTE DI LEONE Dandelion.

DENTICE Dentex, toothed bass.

DENTI DI CAVALLO Pasta similar-looking to rigatoni but smaller in size.

DIAVOLA, ALLA Cooked in "the devil's style," spicy.

DIAVOLILLO Peperoncino, small spicy red pepper, chili pepper.

DIAVOLO DI MARE Venetian and Sicilian term for monkfish.

DI CENTRO Term for Parmigiano-Reggiano produced in July or August.

DI CODA Term for Parmigiano-Reggiano produced from September 1 to November 11.

DIGESTIVO Digestif, an after-dinner drink that aids digestion, usually a bitter, but could also be a Cognac or grappa.

DIPLOMATICO Layered chocolate cake flavored with rum and coffee, usually cut into rectangular portions.

DISOSSATO Deboned; without bones.

DISSALARE To remove salt from food products that have been cured in salt, usually involving several baths in water.

DITALI Thimble-sized tubes of pasta.

DITALINI Small version of ditali, used in soup.

DI TESTA Term for Parmigiano-Reggiano produced from April to June.

DOLCE LATTE Soft, creamy, mild blue cheese made from cow's milk.

DOPPIO Strong, concentrated, double.

DORARE To give a golden color in cooking, or to brown in the oven.

DORATO Method by which food is floured, dipped in egg, and fried.

DOTTATO Prized type of fig.

DRAGONCELLO Tarragon.

DURELLO (DURONE) Term used to indicate poultry gizzard.

EMILIA-ROMAGNA, CUCINA DELL' Cooking from this region is rich in food traditions, from fresh pasta and stuffed pasta made in Bologna, to Prosciutto di Parma from Langhiranno, to Aceto Balsamico Tradizionale from Modena, Lambrusco wine, Grana Padano, and Parmigiano-Reggiano. The area near Piacenza is well-known for coppa, pancetta, and prosciutto, Parma for culatello, and Felino for salami.

ERBA ACCIUGA Santoreggia, an herb in the rosemary family with aphrodisiac qualities.

ERBA CIPOLLINA Chive.

ERBAGGI Pot herbs, green vegetables, salads—a general term.

ERBAZZONE Traditional specialty in Emilia-Romagna, a dough pie stuffed with vegetables such as Swiss chard and spinach bound with cheese and eggs.

ERBE AROMATICHE Aromatic herbs.

ERBE FINI Derived from the French *fines herbes,* delicate herbs, such as a mix of parsley, chervil, chives, and tarragon, used mainly in frittate.

ERBE SELVATICHE Wild herbs.

ERBETTA Swiss chard, also called bietolina.

ERBORINATO Term to describe cheeses that develop mold in the paste, usually characterized by dark flecks or veins in the cheese.

ESSENZA Meat or fish essence, flavor.

ESTRATTO Extract, concentrate of meat or vegetables, such as a bouillon cube.

EXTRAVERGINE Extra-virgin olive oil, in the grading of olive oils.

FAGIANO Pheasant, also called fagianella.

FAGIOLI Dried beans.

FAGIOLI ASCIABOLI Butter beans.

FAGIOLI ASSOLUTI Cooked beans sautéed with garlic in oil.

FAGIOLI DI LIMA Lima beans.

FAGIOLINI French green beans.

FAGOTTINO Bundle, as in wrapped pastry.

FARAONA Guinea fowl.

FARCITO Stuffed.

FARE BOLLIRE To boil.

FARFALLE Small pasta pieces made in the shape of a bow tie or butterfly.

FARINA DI GRANTURCO Corn flour.

FAVATA Stew of dried fava beans, pork, fennel, cabbage, and tomatoes.

FAVE Fava beans, broad beans.

FEDELINI Very thin pasta noodles used in soup.

FEGATINI Chicken livers.

FEGATO Liver.

FEGATO ALLA VENEZIANA Liver and onions Venetian-style.

FERRI, AI Grilled over a barbecue or an open fire.

FESA Leg of veal.

FETTUCCINE Flat, narrow ribbon pasta made from an egg-based dough, either dried or fresh.

FETTUCCINE AL BURRO Fettuccine with butter and best-quality Grana Padano or Parmigiano-Reggiano.

FETTUCCINE ALLA PAPALINA Fettuccine with ham and butter.

FETTUNTA See bruschetta; literally, "oily slice."

FIAMMA, ALLA Flamed, flambéed.

FIASCO, AL Cooked in a flask, particularly beans.

FICHI Figs.

FICHI SECCHI Dried figs.

FICO D'INDIA Prickly pear.

FINANZIERE See cibreo.

FINOCCHIO Fennel.

FINOCCHIONA Salami flavored with fennel, typically Tuscan.

FIOCCHETTI Small bow-shaped pasta.

FIOR D'ARANCIO Flower of the plant that renders bitter oranges. These flowers are distilled and made into orange-flower water, which is used in pastry.

FIOR DI LATTE Soft cow's-milk cheese made like mozzarella.

FIORE DI SAMBUCO Small pasta stars used in soup; literally, "elderflowers." Also used in the making of the liqueur sambuca.

FIORE SARDO Sometimes referred to as Pecorino Sardo, a hard ewe's-milk cheese from Sardinia with a cylindrical or wheel shape. It is salted in brine, dry-salted, and ripened for 3 to 4 months. It has a sharp-tasting paste with a brown rind.

FIORE DI ZUCCA Often used to mean "zucchini blossom," although zucca is actually squash or pumpkin. Only the male, non-fruit-producing flowers are picked; the insides are removed, then the flowers are stuffed, dipped in batter, and fried. Most commonly stuffed with ricotta and an anchovy.

FIORE DI ZUCCHINI RIPIENE Stuffed zucchini blossoms.

FIORENTINA Large grilled T-bone steak.

FIORENTINA, ALLA Grilled in the Florentine style of steak, usually served very rare, carved off the bone, then sliced and served around the bone.

FIORENTINA, BISTECCA ALLA Tuscan steak, porterhouse cut, bone in, with the loin and fillet, usually about 2 to 3 pounds.

FOCACCIA Bread made of flour, salt, and water, a yeast-raised dough rolled out thinly and formed into a square, flat loaf. Dimpled, and seasoned with salt, olive oil, and rosemary.

FOCACCIA DEL VENERDÌ SANTO Savory tart usually made on Holy Friday, filled with a mixture of fennel, endive, anchovies, olives, and capers; also known as scalcione.

FOCACCIA LIGURE Baked round of bread with with topping such as herbs, sea salt, diced ham, onions, artichokes, and cheese.

FODERARE To line a dish or pan with dough or cake.

FONDENTI Small savory croquettes.

FONDERE To melt.

FONDUTA Fontina cheese soaked in milk for 30 minutes, heated while stirring, then embellished with a beaten egg and butter and whisked until thick. Served with toasted bread.

FONDUTA AL CIOCCOLATO Chocolate melted in a double boiler in which pieces of fruit are dipped for dessert.

FONTINA Semihard, mild-flavored, dark yellow cheese with small holes and a tough brown rind, made from fresh unpasteurized cow's milk in the Valle d'Aosta. Rich in taste, it is used for fondue, eaten fresh, and used in desserts.

FORMAGELLE Small farmhouse cheeses from northern Italy, made with any type of milk.

FORMAGGINI Small cheeses.

FORMAGGIO Cheese.

FORMAGGIO BIANCO General term for soft, unripened, lightly salted cow's-milk cheese.

FORMAGGIO DI CREMA Cream cheese.

FORNO, AL Cooked in the oven.

FRAGOLE Strawberries.

FRAGOLINI (FRAGOLE DI BOSCO) Wild strawberries.

FRANGELICO A sweet hazelnut liqueur from Canale, Italy, that comes in a bottle shaped like a Franciscan friar.

FRANTOIANA Variety of olive oil cultivated and produced in Tuscany.

FRAPPE Fried stripe of pastry; knotted.

FRATTAGLIA See corata.

FRATTAU, PANE Sardinian dish made of the thin crispbread carta di musica; it is soaked in hot water, then placed on a plate and topped with smashed tomatoes, grated pecorino, and a poached egg.

FREGOLOTTA Giant crumbly cookie from the Veneto and Treviso area. Also fregolatta.

FREGULA Typical Sardinian semolina dumplings, varying in size, but close to peppercorn size, similar to couscous. Usually cooked in flavored broth. Also called succu tundu.

FRIARIELLI Neapolitan name for broccoli rabe.

FRICASSEA Fricassee of meat, a dish usually finished with eggs and lemon juice.

FRICO Dish typical of the Carnia area in Friuli–

Venezia Giulia. Montasio cheese and potatoes are baked together, and served hot in squares with polenta.

FRITTATA Egg omelette incorporating a variety of ingredients with the eggs, such as cheese, prosciutto, cooked vegetables, and pasta.

FRITTATINE Pancakes.

FRITTELLA Fritter, pancake.

FRITTELLA Thick yeast-raised flour-and-water batter mixture with chopped vegetables or fruits, deep-fried.

FRITTELLI DI VENEZIA Balls of yeast dough, flavored with white wine, grated lemon zest, and raisins, deep-fried in oil and dusted with confectioners' sugar.

FRITTO Fried.

FRITTOLE Fried raised dough balls with raisins and pinoli, usually prepared during Carnevale.

FRITTO MISTO Various pieces of boned meat, poultry, offal, and vegetables, breaded or coated in batter and deep-fried.

FRITTO MISTO DI MARE Like fritto misto, but with fish or shellfish. Served with lemon wedges.

FRITTURA Fried food.

FRIULI–VENEZIA GIULIA, CUCINA DEL Friuli–Venezia Giulia is the northeastern region of Italy, bordering Slovenia, Austria, and the Veneto region. It has been occupied by various countries and its borders have shifted many times, so the cuisine reflects its neighbors', from Austro-Hungarian flavors, to Slavic flavors, to the flavors of the spice trades of the Serenissima, the Venetian Republic (Friuli–Venezia Giulia was part of the republic for several hundred years). The Carnia area to the north is known for its cialzon, a type of agnolotti, and its use of lots of legumes in cooking, and cheeses such as Montasio. Frico is a specialty made with Montasio cheese, and the crispy fried frico is often stuffed with apples or potatoes and onions. Also commonly eaten in the area is musetto con brovada, a type of pork sausage like cotechino served with pickled turnips. Iota or jota is a typical soup of sauerkraut and beans cooked with smoked-pork products. The area is also well-known for the famous Prosciutto di San Daniele and excellent sweets, such as strudel and struccolo. Friuli–Venezia Giulia produces some of the best Italian white wines.

FRIULANO Semihard scalded-curd cheese from Friuli–Venezia Giulia rather like a young Montasio, with a yellow-brown rind enclosing a firm paste that contains a few small holes. Also, the delicious, fruity, and dry white wine made from the Tocai varietal.

FROLLATURA Tenderizing, as meat.

FRULLARE To whip or mince, as in a blender.

FRULLATO Whisked, whipped, or minced in a blender.

FRUMENTO Wheat.

FRUTTA Fruit; in cooking, used in sweets and also in savory dishes, such as long-braised meats.

FRUTTA CANDITA Candied fruit.

FRUTTA SECCA Dried fruit, such as apricots, raisins, or prunes.

FRUTTI DI MARE Shellfish, often including sea urchin and some types of shrimp.

FUGAZZA Old Venetian dessert, usually made during Easter season, of leavened dough with lots of dried fruit and nuts; a similar dessert is made in the Trentino region, called brazadel.

FUMETTO Concentrated stock.

FUMO, AROMA DI Aroma of something smoked. Also, a light preservative, such as for smoked salmon.

FUNGHI PORCINI Porcini mushrooms.

FUNGHI SECCHI Dried mushrooms, often porcini, that need to be reconstituted prior to use.

FUNGO Generic name for a mushroom, either wild or farm-cultivated.

FUSILLI Pasta made into the shape of a corkscrew.

FUSO Melted or clarified.

GALANI Venetian snack of crisp, wafer-thin, deep-fried strips of pastry, dusted with powdered sugar.

GALLETTA Wafer, biscuit.

GALLETTI Typical Ligurian fried sweets, also called cuculli.

GALLETTO Cockerel, young male chicken.

GALLINA Hen.

GALLINACCIO Turkey-cock, or chanterelle mushroom.

GALLINA DI FARAONE Guinea fowl.

GALLINELLA Hen.

GALLO Rooster, male chicken.

GALUPE Grey mullet, also called cefalo.

GAMBERETTI Small shrimps.

GAMBERO Shrimp, prawn.

GAMBERO DI ACQUA DOLCE Freshwater crayfish.

GAMBERO IMPERIALE Caramote prawn. See also mazzancolla.

GAMBERONE Large shrimp, usually 20 to 30 centimeters, usually the red Mediterranean kind, mostly used in soups and sauces, and also often grilled.

GAMBERO ROSA Crevette rose (in French), pink shrimp.

GAMBERO ROSSO Crevette rouge (in French), red shrimp.

GARGANELLI Typical pasta from Emilia-Romagna, similar to penne in shape. Usually served with ragù, but can also be served in soup.

GARMUGIA Beef stewed with peas and artichokes.

GAROFOLATO With cloves.

GATTO DI PATATE Mashed potatoes with eggs, milk, and grated cheese, spread in an ovenproof dish, covered with mozzarella or grated cheese, sprinkled with bread crumbs, and baked.

GELATINA DI FRUTTA Pectin gel with sugar and some fruit juice, often used with fruit in pastry and fruit tarts.

GELATO Ice cream made of milk, cream, sugar, egg yolk, and fruit or other flavorings.

GELO Ice.

GELSOMINO Jasmine.

GEMELLI Short strands of spaghetti twisted together.

GENOVESE, ALLA In the Genoese style, usually with olive oil and garlic.

GENOVESE, CARNE ALLA Neapolitan meat-and-onion dish cooked slowly, like a stew; its sauce is also used to dress pasta.

GENOVESE, PASTA Baked sweet made with flour, starch, sugar, butter, and eggs, often used as a base for cakes. The recipe is attributed to the Parisian pastry chef Chiboust, from the nineteenth century.

GENOVESE, SALSA Cold or room-temperature sauce served with fish, made of eggs, olive oil, lemon, pistacchio, and pinoli nuts.

GERMANO REALE Mallard, the wild duck.

GHERIGLI Kernels of nuts.

GIAMBONETTO Boned leg of chicken shaped and tied to resemble a ham.

GIANCHETTI See bianchetti.

GIANDUIA (GIANDUJA) A hazelnut-and-chocolate spread from Piedmont, the name of which is derived from that of a popular Piedmontese hat worn by Commedia dell'Arte military characters.

GIANDUIOTTO (GIANDUJOTTO) Chocolates made in Torino, based on gianduia and shaped like a boat. They were first created in 1852 by Caffarel Prochet, which made them in the shape of the hat of the Gianduia costume.

GIARDINIERA, ALLA In the gardener's style, with assorted freshly pickled vegetables.

GINEPRO Juniper.

GINESTRATA Light soup from Tuscany made with chicken stock, egg yolks, butter, and white wine.

GIORNO, DEL The dish of the day.

GIRASOLE Sunflower.

GIUGGIOLA Jujube, a fruit from an Asian tree that is common in the Mediterranean area as well, similar in size to an olive, red in color, with a bittersweet taste. Often used dried to make syrups.

GLASSATO Glazed, iced.

GNOCCHETTI Tiny gnocchi used in soup.

GNOCCHETTI SARDI See malloreddus.

GNOCCHI Small dumplings made of boiled potatoes and flour, shaped in the form of little balls, boiled, and dressed with sauce and cheese.

GNOCCHI ALLA BAVA Gnocchi usually made with buckwheat flour, then topped with fresh cheese and cream—"drooling gnocchi."

GNOCCHI ALLA ROMANA Gnocchi made from a semolina porridge, cooled, then cut into cylinders or circular slices that are served with a sauce, or baked with cheese.

GNOCCHI DOLCI Sweet-potato dumplings stuffed with jam or fresh prunes, boiled, then rolled in toasted bread crumbs with sugar and cinnamon.

GNOCCO DI VERDURE Large roll of gnocchi dough stuffed with vegetables, wrapped in cloth, boiled, and served sliced, topped with melted butter and cheese or with tomato sauce.

GNOCCO FRITTO Fried dough square, often served in Emilia-Romagna, with prosciutto.

GNOCCULI Potato gnocchi from Sicily served with cheese and broth or meat sauce.

GORGONZOLA Soft blue-veined DOP cheese with creamy texture and sharp flavor from pasteurized cow's milk, made in the Lombardy region since the eleventh century. Eaten as a semisoft cheese, also used in cooking and in desserts.

GRAMOLATA Finely chopped ice infused with fruit pulp. Different from a granita, or slushy, in which the ice is in larger grains and syrups are used to flavor it.

GRAMUGIA Artichoke, asparagus, bean, and bacon soup from Tuscany.

GRANA Delicious granular cheese made from partially skimmed 100 percent cow's milk. The curd is molded and drained for 2 days, brined for 28 days, and ripened for up to 18 months. The wheel can weigh anywhere from 25 to 40 kilograms. It is used in cooking and soups, grated on pastas and stuffing, or eaten as a snack or dessert.

GRANA PADANO Grana from specific regions in Italy, a cheese that dissolves in the mouth with mellow but complex flavors, which increases with aging.

GRANA PARMIGIANO See Parmigiano-Reggiano.

GRANATINE DI RISO Small fried-rice balls from Liguria.

GRANA TRENTINO Grana Padano cheese produced in the Trentino region.

GRANCEOLA Large spiny crab, whose meat is usually served in the shell.

GRANCEVOLA Spider crab. Also granseola.

GRANCHIO Crab.

GRANCHIO COMUNE Shore crab.

GRANCHIO DI SABBIA Sand crab, small with a dark body and pink claws and legs.

GRANCIPORRO (GRANCHIO PORO) Common crab.

GRANELLI Grains or seeds, or lamb's testicles.

GRANELLI ALLA MAREMMANA Lamb's testicles floured, egged, and fried.

GRANITA A dessert made of frozen flavored sugar syrup of mushy ice crystals.

GRANO Wheat, corn, grain.

GRANO SARACENO Buckwheat.

GRANOTURCO Maize, corn.

GRANOTURCO DOLCE Sweet corn.

GRANSEOLA See grancevola.

GRAPPA Clear alcoholic drink distilled from the fermented remains of the grapes after they have been pressed for wine making.

GRASSO D'ARROSTO Drippings.

GRATINARE To brown, or to create a crispy crust topping, usually in the oven.

GRECA, ALLA Method of cooking vegetables (artichokes, cauliflower, celery, leeks) for use as a cold hors d'oeuvre in a liquid consisting of water, olive oil, lemon juice, bay leaf, thyme, coriander seeds, and other seasonings. Also means "in the Greek style," with olive oil, lemon, dried oregano, herbs, and spices.

GREMOLATA Mixture of chopped parsley, chopped garlic, and grated lemon zest, usually used on braised meats, especially osso buco; also called gremolada.

GRICIA, PASTA ALLA Typical way of dressing pasta, usually spaghetti or bucatini, in Rome and the Lazio area, using guanciale (cured pork cheek) or bacon, and cheese.

GRIFFONE Highly prized type of mushroom, also called griffo or grifolo.

GRIFOLE Type of fungus that grows on trees in a cluster, like a coral.

GRIGLIA, ALLA Cooked on the grill.

GRIGLIATA MISTA Mixed grill, usually containing lamb, veal liver, and sausage; can also be mixed fish.

GRIGLIATO Grilled.

GRISSINI (SINGULAR GRISSINO) Long, thin dried bread sticks, also called torinese.

GRONGO Conger eel.

GROSSETANA, ALLA In the style of Grosseto, Tuscany, usually with mushrooms and tomato sauce.

GROSSO ROMBO Halibut.

GUANCIALE Cured pork cheek, used like pancetta or bacon.

GUARNITO Garnished.

GUAZZETTO Stew, usually stewed meats.

GUBANA Typical Friulian Easter dessert—chopped nuts, dried fruits, and chocolate, doused with grappa, rolled in a yeast dough shaped like a snail, and baked.

GUSCIO Shell, husk, pod.

GUSCIO, AL Boiled in the shell.

IMBIANCARE To blanche.

IMBOTTITO Stuffed.

IMBRECCIATA Chickpea, bean, and lentil soup from Umbria.

IMPANATA (IMPANATIGGHIA) Sicilian dialect term for food preparations cooked inside focaccia or bread dough.

IMPANATO Breaded, coated with bread crumbs.

IMPASTARE To knead.

INCANESTRATO (CANESTRATO) Semihard cheese made from ewe's milk and matured in a wicker basket (called canestro) to give it a distinctive surface pattern.

INCASSETTATO Encased, as in pastry or paté.

INDIVIA BELGA Belgian endive.

INFIAMMATO Flambéed.

INFUSO Infusion, usually herbs and flowers in boiling water.

INSACCATI (SINGULAR INSACCATO) Sausages; literally, "encased in a bag."

INSALATA Salad.

INSALATA COTTA E CRUDA Salad of mixed cooked vegetables and raw salad greens.

INSALATA DI MARE Seafood salad.

INSALATA MISTA Mixed salad.

INSALATA PAESANA Peasant salad of potatoes, eggs, and vegetables, all cooked and cooled.

INSALATA RUSSA Russian salad of cooked peas, carrots, and potatoes, diced and dressed with mayonnaise.

INSALATA VERDE Green salad, usually of only one type of leaf.

INSALATINE Small salad greens.

INSALATONA Mixed salad of cooked vegetables, which could also contain ham, cheese, and other proteins.

INTEGRALE Wholemeal, whole-wheat, of bread, flour, etc.

INTERCOSTA Cut of steak from between the ribs.

INTERIORA Offal, innards.

INTINGOLO Sauce, gravy; also, tasty dish, sometimes a stew.

IN UMIDO Braised, stewed, in a sauce.

INVOLTINI (SINGULAR INVOLTINO) Slices of meat such as ham, cheese, and sometimes vegetables, rolled together.

INVOLTINI DI VITELLO Little bundles of veal stuffed and cooked.

INVOLTINO Roll or roulade.

IOTA (JOTA) Slowly cooked soup from northeastern Italy with beans, potatoes, sauerkraut, and sometimes pickled turnips, with bacon or some smoked-pork products.

IPPOGLOSSO Halibut.

JOTA See iota.

KAKI (CACHI) Persimmon.

LACERTO Mackerel.

LACIADA Typical dessert from Lombardy, made with small disks of fried dough placed one on top of another alternating with layers of marmalade.

LAMELLA Extremely thin slice, almost transparent, usually of truffle, mushroom, or cheese.

LAMPASCIONE (LAMPAGIONE, LAMPASCIUOLO) Small, usually wild onion plant, the bulbs of which are eaten.

LAMPONE Raspberry.

LAMPREDA Eel.

LANGUSTA Venetian name for the spiny lobster.

LARDO Lard, bacon, salt pork.

LARDONCINI Fried cubes or strips of salt pork, lardons.

LASAGNE Wide flat pasta in a strip. Poached in salted water before being used.

LASAGNE ALLA BOLOGNESE Cooked lasagna pasta layered with a meat sauce and topped with béchamel sauce and grated Grana Padano or Parmigiano-Reggiano, then baked.

LASAGNE ALLA FIORENTINA Cooked lasagna pasta with meat sauce and cheese, then baked.

LASAGNE VERDE Lasagna made of a green pasta made with spinach purée.

LATTE Milk.

LATTE ACIDO Sour milk.

LATTE DI MANDORLA Almond milk.

LATTE DI PESCE Soft fish roe.

LATTUGA Lettuce.

LATTUGA A CAPPUCCIO Round head of lettuce.

LATTUGA ROMANA Long-shaped head of lettuce.

LAURO Laurel, bay leaf.

LAVERELLO Lake trout.

LAZIO, CUCINA DEL There are three main currents in the cuisine of Lazio. One is dishes from the Jewish tradition, such as carciofi alla giudia and small whiting with raisins and pinoli. The second current is called burina, or "from the countryside," which includes dishes such as bucatini all'amatriciana and pasta alla carbonara, or pork and lamb dishes. The third is often dubbed la macellara, or dishes prevalent from a butcher, using cuts and pieces of animal that were basically left over, such as rigatoni alla pajata (a sauce made from intestines of a milk-fed calf) and coda alla vaccinara, braised oxtails with celery and tomato.

LECCIA Pompano, the fish.

LEGUMI Vegetables, legumes.

LENTICCHIE Lentils.

LENTISCHIO Mastic.

LEPRE Hare.

LEPRE IN SALMÌ Hare marinated in vinegar and cooked in red wine.

LEPUDRIDA Rich Sardinian meat-and-vegetable stew.

LESSATO Boiled; as a noun, boiled meat, boiled beef, also known as lesso.

LETTERATO Small tuna.

LIEVITARE To leaven, or raise with yeast.

LIEVITO Yeast.

LIEVITO CHIMICO Baking powder.

LIEVITO NATURALE Sourdough starter.

LIGURIA, CUCINA DELLA The cuisine of Liguria has been shaped by the scarcity of local produce because of the difficult agricultural landscape, and is based mainly on olive oil and food products derived from a large mercantile business. The cuisine uses a lot of herbs and is simple but not poor.

LIMONCELLO Very popular lemon-flavored liqueur made by soaking lemon zest in alcohol until it releases its oils, then mixing the alcohol with simple syrup for sweetness. Originating in southern Italy, it is usually served very cold as an after-dinner drink, but in the United States it is also often used in cocktails.

LIMONE Lemon.

LINGUA Tongue. In Italy, the tongue eaten most often is veal. Older beef tongue requires a longer preparation: It needs to be soaked in cold water for 4 to 5 hours, changing the water every hour, then cooked for 45 minutes. Only then can one begin the preferred cooking preparation. Younger veal tongue has a similar prep, but requires only 2 hours of soaking.

LINGUA DI BUE Mushroom that looks like a meaty tongue, orange-colored with red and reddish-brown flecks. It can be eaten raw—thinly sliced, washed with lemon and water, and dressed like a salad. Usually grows like a fan high on the trunk of trees.

LINGUE DI GATTO Flat tea biscuits made with butter and egg whites; literally, "cat's tongue."

LINGUINE Long flat spaghetti-like pasta.

LIQUIRIZIA Licorice, either the candy or the plant.

LIQUORE In English, liqueur; alcoholic beverage obtained through distillation that can be infused with fruit and herbs, often used as an after-dinner drink or digestif. The first modern liqueur in Italy was produced in the fifteenth century by Girolamo Savonarola, who combined acquavite, similar to grappa, with vegetal herbs. The production of alcoholic beverages continued in Italy, in particular after the eighteenth century, with the discovery of a low-cost process of distilling alcohol.

LISCIO Smooth.

LIVORNESE, ALLA In the style of Livorno, Italy—accompanied by shallots, tomatoes, and poached fish, and sometimes olives.

LOMBARDIA, CUCINA DELLA Because of its geographic diversity, with plains and Pre-Alps, the cuisine of Lombardy has a great variety of indigenous products. Butter is used more often than oil, and rice more often than pasta, and there is a large production of dairy and cheeses. Classic dishes include risotto alla milanese, osso buco with gremolata, and breaded veal milanese. The cuisine closer to the mountains uses lots of polenta, cheeses, and cured meats such as bresaola. Toward the lakes there are many dishes using freshwater fish. Mantova is highly prized for its food, with influences from Emilia-Romagna and the Veneto, which it borders, and it is well known for its tortelli di zucca. Some other well-known dishes of Lombardy are: risotto alla certosina, zuppa pavese, riso alla pitocca, casonsei, and polenta con anitra in guazzetto.

LOMBATA Loin of meat.

LOMBATINA Entrecôte steak of beef, loin chop.

LOMBO Loin of meat.

LOMBO DI MAIALE AL LATTE Pork loin studded with cloves, braised in milk with cinnamon bark.

LONZA Loin of pork, salted and air-dried. Eaten raw in very thin slices.

LUCANICA (PLURAL LUCANICHE) Small, pure pork-based sausage flavored with Parmigiano-Reggiano cheese, also called luganega (plural, luganeghe), luganiga.

LUCCIO Pike, the fish.

LUCCIO MARINO Barracuda.

LUCCIOPERCA Pike-perch.

LUMACA DI MARE (CHIOCCIOLA DI MARE) Gastropod that lives along the Italian coast, adhering to the rocks, usually smaller than 3 centimeters, with a brownish or grayish shell. The most common is called caragolo in the Veneto, and is served as an antipasto.

LUMACA DI TERRA Land-based snail.

LUMACHE Snail-shaped pasta.

LUMACHE Snails.

LUPINO Herbaceous plant cultivated for its seeds. Due to the toxic nature of the seeds, they need to be soaked in running water for 24 hours, with several water changes, and then boiled for about 2 to 3 hours in salted water. Much used by the Romans.

LUPPOLI (SINGULAR LUPPOLO) Hops.

MACCARELLO Mackerel.

MACCHERONCINI (MACCHERONCELLI) Thinner version of macceroni.

MACCHERONI Macaroni, often used as a general description for types of dried pasta.

MACCO Mashed boiled beans mixed with oil and fennel, from Sicily, also called maccù.

MACEDONIA DI FRUTTA Fruit salad, often with a liqueur.

MACELLERIA Butcher shop.

MACH Northern Italian soup made of milk with chestnuts and rice.

MACINARE To grind.

MACINATO Ground, pounded, or minced.

MADRE "The mother," or a group of yeasts used in making vinegar.

MAFALDI Long flat pasta with curly edges.

MAGGIORANA Marjoram.

MAGNONESE Warm mayonnaise.

MAGNOSA Flat Mediterranean lobsterlike creature very similar to the slipper lobster, with small claws; also called cicala grande del mare.

MAGRO Used to describe a dish without meat. Also lean meat.

MAIALE Pig or pork.

MAIALE UBRIACO Pork chops cooked in red wine.

MAIALINO Suckling pig.

MAIONESE Mayonnaise.

MALFATTA Homemade ball of pasta dough; literally, "badly made."

MALFATTINA Mix of finely and coarsely chopped sheets of pasta dough.

MALLOREDDUS Sardinian name for small gnocchi made with semolina flour, water, and saffron. Also called gnocchetti sardi. Often served with butter and pecorino or with a tomato sauce.

MALTAGLIATI Roughly cut elongated diamonds of pasta; literally, "badly cut."

MALTO Malt.

MAMMELLA Udder.

MANDARINO Mandarin.

MANDORLA Almond.

MANDORLATO Type of torrone cooked in the oven, made with caramelized sugar and almonds.

MANICOTTI Tubelike pasta stuffed with a ricotta-cheese mixture and baked in a sauce; literally, "muffs" or "sleeves."

MANIERA DI In the style of. Also "alla maniera."

MANINA FERRARESE Crisp bread roll in the shape of a double horseshoe.

MANTECARE To whip or whisk.

MANTECATO 1. Softened, pounded while incorporating olive oil or butter. 2. Soft ice cream made by adding whipped cream to ice cream.

MANTOVANA Antique yeast-raised sweet typical of Prato in Tuscany.

MANTOVANO Bread with a crisp crust and light interior, typical of the lower Padania region, often used to accompany heavier dishes.

MANZO Beef from cattle.

MANZO ALLA CERTOSINA Beef stewed with bacon, anchovies, and herbs.

MANZO ARROSTO Roast beef.

MANZO BRASATO Braised beef.

MANZO LESSO Boiled beef.

MANZO SALATO Corned beef.

MANZO STUFATO Stewed beef.

MARANTA Arrowroot.

MARASCA Sour cherry often used to make a sweet syrup, maraschino cherry.

MARASCHINO Liqueur obtained by taking whole marasca cherries, including the pits, crushing them, and allowing them to ferment in wine. First made in the nineteenth century by Girolamo Luxardo in Zara, Dalmatia. The liqueur is light and fragrant and often used in making fruit salad.

MARCHE, CUCINA DEL Marche geographically has coastline, hills, and mountains, and dishes from each reflect the topography. At the coast they often make fish stew. A dish that seems common throughout the region is vincisgrassi, a lasagna with ragù, of layers made of cockscomb, mushrooms, brain, beef, and besciamella, with truffle if in season. Near Pesaro, ravioli with fish-fillet stuffing are very prized. There is also the cotechino from San Leo, the prosciutto from Montefeltro, and the soppressata from Fabbriano.

MARCHESI, GUALTIERO Born in Milan in 1930, he was a foremost proponent of the renewal of European cuisine during the Nouvelle Cuisine movement. His restaurant was one of the first Italian restaurants to win coveted Michelin stars. He is the author of the book *La mia nuova grande cucina italiana*.

MAREMMANO, BOVINO White longhorn cattle raised in southern Tuscany, in the Maremma region.

MARINARA Tomato sauce prepared very quickly from ripe tomatoes.

MARINARA, ALLA In the sailor's style—with seafood.

MARINARE To marinate.

MARINATO Pickled, marinated.

MARMELLATA Marmalade, jam.

MARMORA Striped sea bream.

MARO Pounded and sieved cooked beans mixed with chopped mint, garlic, cheese, and oil; also called pestun de fave.

MARRONE Term used for a chestnut that is larger and therefore prized.

MARRONI Chestnuts.

MARSALA Sweet fortified wine from Sicily used to make zabaglione.

MARUBINI Ravioli typical from the Cremona area, cooked in soup.

MARZAPANE Marzipan, particularly that made in Sicily, in a tradition that began in the thirteenth century.

MASCARPONE Thick double or triple cream cheese from Lombardy.

MASCULINI Tiny anchovies from Sicily.

MASTICE Mastic.

MATTARELLO Rolling pin.

MAZZAFEGATI Pork-liver-and-pine-nut sausage from Umbria flavored with fennel and garlic.

MAZZANCOLLA Term often used in the Lazio region for a transverse-striped king prawn from the Mediterranean. It is brown with reddish tints, becoming pink when cooked, and up to 22 centimeters long.

MEDAGLIONI (SINGULAR MEDAGLIONE) Small slices of fillet steak or of veal; medallions.

MELA Apple.

MELA COTOGNA Quince.

MELAGRANA Pomegranate.

MELANZANA (PLURAL MELANZANE) Eggplant.

MELASSA Molasses.

MELE ALLA CERTOSA Baked stuffed apples.

MELE IN GABBIA Apple dumplings; literally, "apples in a cage."

MELICA (MELIGA) Term used in southern Italy for corn.

MELISSA Aromatic plant also known as cedronella (citronella) that smells like a lemon and is used in liqueurs and perfume making, also as a digestif.

MELONE (POPONE) Melon.

MENTA Mint, the herb.

MENTUCCIA Plant in the mint family with smaller leaves, often used in carciofi alla romana.

MERCA Grey mullet boiled in broth and rolled with a coating of herbs.

MERENDA Snack, light meal.

MERINGATO With meringue.

MERLANO Whiting.

MERLUZZO Cod, hake.

MESCOLARE To mix, stir, or blend.

MESTICANZA Mixture of tender salad leaves.

MESTOLO Ladle.

MEZZALUNA Type of knife shaped like a crescent moon with two handles, usually used in finely chopping meat or vegetables.

MEZZEFEGATI See mazzafegati.

MEZZE PENNE Short pasta quills.

MEZZI RIGATONI Ridged pasta tubes, smaller than regular rigatoni in size.

MEZZI ZITI Short ziti.

MEZZO Half.

MICHETTA (MICCA) Small round bread typical of Lombardy, also called rosetta because of its roselike shape. First produced during the Austro-Hungarian Empire, a combination of the micca lombarda roll and kaiser roll.

MIDOLLA Inner part of a loaf of bread, or flesh of a fruit.

MIDOLLO Bone marrow.

MIELE Honey.

MIGLIO Millet.

MIGNUIC (MIGNULE) Pasta curls served with sauces or cheese.

MILLEFOGLIE Puff pastry.

MINESTRA (PLURAL MINESTRE) First course of soup or pasta, but often refers to a vegetable soup. Word comes from the verb minestrare, "to administer," since the minestra was usually administered by the head of the family.

MINESTRA STRAPPATA Tuscan soup in which pasta is ripped directly from the sheet of dough and thrown into the boiling soup.

MINESTRA STRASCINATA Another name for the stracinati, or dragged pasta, in soup.

MINESTRINA Diminutive form generally used for a lighter minestra, usually including small-format pasta.

MINESTRONE Term indicating a larger or heavier minestra with more vegetables, usually thicker, including potatoes, beans, and squash, and often including cured pork products.

MINNICH Maccheroni typical of Basilicata.

MIRTILLI (SINGULAR MIRTILLO) Bilberries, blueberries.

MIRTO Myrtle.

MISCHIARE To mix or blend.

MISSOLTITTI (MISTOLINI) Salted and dried needlefish, a specialty from the lake region of Lombardy.

MISTICANZA Mixed salad.

MISTO Mixed.

MISTO MARE Mixed fried seafood.

MITILI (SINGULAR MITILO) Mussels.

MOCETTA (MOTZETTA) Cured salami made with the leg of an Alpine ibex.

MOLISE, CUCINA DEL Simple and genuine cuisine; inland dishes are mainly meat and pasta, and coastal dishes fish. Often tomato that has been dried in the sun in a special wooden container is used in local dishes. Homemade pasta is prevalent, such as crejoli (similar to maccheroni alla chitarra), cavatelli, fusilli prepared by winding pasta around a metal stick, laganelle (similar to pappardelle), and teccozze (a diamond-shaped pasta). Most pasta is served in a sauce of pork or lamb with peperoncino and pecorino. Pasta e fagioli can be found infrequently everywhere within the region. Mutton and lamb are often eaten, as are offal.

MOLLE (MOLLETTO) Soft, soft-boiled.

MOLLECA Venetian term for a male crab that has just shed its hard shell, a small soft-shelled crab, usually floured and fried.

MOLLECHE Small soft-shell crabs cultivated on the shores of the Venetian lagoon, eaten just after they have shed their shells and before the new shells have hardened; also called granchio comune.

MOLLECHE ALLA MURANESE Molleche floured, dipped in beaten egg batter, and fried.

MOLLECHE RIPIENE Molleche left in beaten egg for 2 hours, so they are impregnated with the egg batter, then floured and fried.

MOLLICA Crumb, or the white soft interior of a loaf of bread.

MOLLUSCHI (SINGULAR MOLLUSCO) Mollusks.

MOLTO COTTO Well done, cooked through.

MONTASIO Hard, wheel-shaped cow's-milk cheese, pressed, salted 10 days, brined for 7 days, ripened for 6 to 12 months.

MONTATA Whipped.

MONTEVECCHIA Small cheeses, often called caprini or robiolini, made from cow's or sheep's milk, served fresh or aged, often covered with some mold to give a picquant taste. When first made, they were a specialty of Montevecchia in Brianza, but now they are made almost everywhere on the Italian peninsula.

MONTONE Mutton.

MONZITTE Snails.

MORA (PLURAL MORE) Blackberry.

MORA DI GELSO Mulberry.

MORCHELLA Morel. See spugnola.

MORMORA Striped bream.

MORTADELLA Cold cut originally from Bologna, made from 60 percent lean pork meat (shoulder or hind leg) and 40 percent fat pork meat (cheek), made into a paste with lard cubes throughout. The long cooking process is very carefully executed by indirect steam. It is served thinly sliced as an antipasto, or often used in stuffings for pasta, potato pies, and meatballs or meatloaf.

MORTAIO Mortar.

MORTELLA Myrtle.

MOSCARDINO Dormouse. Also, a small mollusk cepholapod, in the octopus family but smaller, which is prepared in any way that one would prepare octopus or cuttlefish.

MOSCATO D'ASTI Sweet, sparkling dessert wine produced in the province of Asti, in Piedmont.

MOSCOVITA Rich dessert mousse.

MOSTACCIOLO Rich fruitcake with almonds, chocolate, and candied fruit.

MOSTARDA Spicy candied fruit.

MOSTO Unfermented grape juice, must.

MOZZARELLA Soft, pale cheese, worked like toffee, made from buffalo or cow's milk, eaten very fresh. Formed into round balls or pear-shaped, and often stored in the whey.

MOZZARELLA AFFUMICATA Smoked mozzarella cheese.

MOZZARELLA IN CARROZZA Fried sandwich filled with mozzarella cheese.

MUCCA Cow.

MUGNAIA, ALLA Italian translation of the French "à la meuniere," a method of preparing white fish, but also kidneys and brain, in which thin slices are floured, browned in butter, salted, peppered, and garnished with lemon and chopped parsley.

MURENA Moray eel.

MURICE Murex, the shellfish.

MUS Polenta, wheat flour, and milk boiled to a gruel with poppy seeds and sweetened.

MUSCOLETTI (MUSCOLO) Muscle of beef or veal shank.

MUSCOLI Mussels.

MUSETTO Traditional pork sausage used in Friuli–Venezia Giulia made of the skin and face of the pig, stuffed into a casing of pork intestine. In Friuli, it is boiled, and usually accompanied by brovada.

NASELLO Hake, the fish.

NEPITELLA Calamint. A cross between oregano and mint.

NERO DI SEPPIA Cuttlefish ink, often used in risotto.

NERVETTI (GNERVITT) Term used to indicate the cartilage in the knee and shank of veal, which is usually boiled and served as an antipasto.

NESPOLA Medlar, loquat.

NESPOLA DEL GIAPPONE Loquat, Japanese medlar.

NIDI (SINGULAR NIDO) Tangles of thin pasta; literally, "nests."

NIDO, AL In a nest, or one ingredient inside another.

NIZZARDO Italian translation of the French "niçoise."

NOCCIOLA 1. Hazelnut. 2. Noisette of meat.

NOCCIOLINA Peanut.

NOCCIOLATO Sweet made with dark or milk chocolate and whole toasted hazelnuts.

NOCE 1. Nut, walnut. 2. Rump of meat. 3. Knob of butter.

NOCE DEL BRASILE Brazil nut.

NOCE DI ACAGIÙ Cashew nut.

NOCE DI COCCO Coconut.

NOCE MOSCATA Nutmeg.

NOCINO Liqueur made from unripe walnuts (green walnuts).

NODINO Meat chop cutlet. Also a mozzarella knot.

NOSTRANO Local; a word used to indicate the opposite of something sophisticated. Usually, it indicates a country-style cheese.

NOVELLO Of wine, made with nonpressed whole grapes in vats with carbon dioxide, which transforms the sugars into alcohol without the help of yeast. Novello wine is usually very fresh and intense in flavor. Of olive oil, newly pressed.

OCA Goose.

OCA FARCITA ALLA BORGHESE Roast goose stuffed with chopped pork, apples, chestnuts, and the goose liver.

OCCHI DI LUPO Short dried pasta tubes.

OCCHIALONE Bream.

OCCHIATURA Holes in salami and cheeses.

ODORI Herbs that impart aroma, such as parsley, thyme, and sage.

OFFELLA Sweets made using a barley focaccia, derived from sweets from ancient Roman times. In the fifteenth century, the term indicated sweets made with a pastry shell, egg white, saffron, and cinnamon. Today there are many regional varieties.

OLIO Oil.

OLIO, ALL' Cooked in oil.

OLIO, SOTT' Preserved in oil.

OLIVA (ALSO ULIVA) Olive, the fruit of a tree that has been cultivated since ancient times in the Mediterranean Basin and other countries. Olives begin to grow green and then, depending on the species, can remain green or turn purplish black. The olives are harvested, sometimes by hand and sometimes by machine, in the late fall, usually November. Some varieties include Leccino, Frantoio, Lavagnina, Cerignola, and Coratina.

OMELETTE Omelette.

ORATA Gilt-head bream.

ORECCHIA DI SAN PIETRO Abalone.

ORECCHIA MARINA Abalone.

ORECCHIETTE Small ear-shaped pasta.

ORECCHIO Ear, as of a pig.

ORIGANATO With oregano.

ORIGANO Oregano.

ORTAGGI (SINGULAR ORTAGGIO) Vegetables, greens, things grown in an orto, or garden.

ORTICHE (SINGULAR ORTICA) Nettles.

ORZATA Refreshing beverage of water, germinated orzo, barley, and crushed almonds, with some added sugar to taste. It can be made with either still or sparkling water.

ORZO Barley.

ORZO PERLATO Pearl barley.

OSSO Bone.

OSSO BUCO 1. Braised veal shank with marrow and bone. 2. Veal shank cut across the bone, simmered with garlic, oil, carrots, celery, and tomatoes, sprinkled with chopped parsley and grated lemon zest, often served with barley or risotto.

OSTIA Wafer.

OSTRICHE Oysters.

O'TEANO Neapolitan vegetable pie with steamed potatoes, zucchini, eggplant, and oregano. Literally, "saucepan" in the Neapolitan dialect.

OTTARDA Bustard, the bird.

OVINI Sheep.

OVOLO Egg-shaped mushroom praised in ancient Greece and Rome and called the eye of the gods by Nero. It has a white body with an orange-red cap. Highly prized, they are often served raw, thinly shaved to make a salad.

OVULO Mozzarella, the size and shape of an egg.

PADELLA Frying pan.

PAESANA, ALLA In the country style, usually with bacon, mushroom, and tomatoes.

PAGLIA E FIENO Strips of green and yellow fresh or dried pasta; literally, "straw and hay."

PAGNOTTA Round loaf of bread.

PAGURO Hermit crab.

PAILLARD More correctly written as paillarde, a thin slice of veal or beef cooked on a grill or seared in a pan and served simply with salt, pepper, and lemon juice.

PAIOLO Pot most often used for cooking polenta, with a concave bottom and no rim, so the mixing spatula can reach all corners to mix the polenta properly.

PALOMBACCIO Wood pigeon.

PANADA (PANEDA) Name used in Emilia-Romagna for soup made with bread cooked in it; also called pancotto.

PANAFRACCHI (CIAMBELLE) Ring-shaped cakes or pastries with nuts and candied fruit.

PANARDA Celebratory feast of twenty or more dishes in the Abruzzo region.

PANCETTA Belly of pork cured with salt and spices, rolled up, and eaten either in thin slices raw, or cooked in thicker slices (pancetta or panchetta). Used like bacon in cooking.

PAN DI NATALE Soft yeast-raised dough mixed with candied fruit, nuts, and raisins; literally, "Christmas bread."

PAN DI SPAGNA Light sponge cake, usually liqueur-soaked, filled with cream or jam.

PAN PEPATO A nutmeg-and-pepper flavored cake with raisins, almonds, hazelnuts, and chocolate.

PANDOLCE Christmas holiday dessert bread made in Genova, similar to panettone made in Milan, except with more raisins and candied fruit.

PANDORATO French toast, egg-dipped fried bread.

PANDORO Traditional Christmas holiday dessert from Verona, which has its origin in pan d'oro, a sweet bread covered in gold leaf served at the end of a meal for the Patriarchs of Venice. It is cone-shaped and forms a star at the top. It is made with flour, sugar, eggs, butter, beer, and yeast, and baked.

PANE Bread.

PANE BIANCO White bread.

PANE BIGIO Brown bread.

PANE BOLOGNESE Sweet bread made from cornmeal with candied fruit and nuts.

PANE CARASAU Very thin crispbread from Sardinia.

PANE DI SEGALE Rye bread.

PANE DI FRUMENTO Whole-wheat bread.

PANE GRATTUGIATO (PANGRATTATO) Bread crumbs.

PANE SCURO Dark bread.

PANE TOSTATO Toast.

PANELLE Fritters made in Sicily with chickpea flour.

PANETTONE Yeast-raised sweet dough with raisins and candied fruit served mainly at Christmas.

PANFORTE Rich cake from Siena with glacéed fruits and nuts.

PANGRATTATO Bread crumbs.

PANICCIA (PANISSA) Flat, round pizza-shaped loaf, the dough made from boiled chickpea flour and finely chopped sweated onions, baked, then sliced, and sometimes fried.

PANICIA Barley soup from the Dolomite region.

PANINI IMBOTTITI Stuffed sandwiches.

PANINO Bread roll or sandwich.

PANISCIA Rice, beans, and sausage cooked in broth.

PANNA Cream.

PANNA COTTA 1. Crème caramel. 2. Custard

cream, thickened with some gelatin; literally, "cooked cream."

PANNA FERMENTATA Sour cream.

PANNA MONTATA Whipped cream, usually sweetened.

PANNARONE Soft cheese from southern Lombardy, made from whole milk. Not salted; the curds are gathered in cheesecloth, drained, and kept for about 25 days. With a thick yellow rind, it has a mild and slightly bitter paste with lots of small holes.

PANNOCCHIA Mantis shrimp. Also, corn on the cob.

PANSOTI (PANSOTTI) Triangular-shaped ravioli filled with meat, offal, or cheese; also called panzerotti.

PANTOSTA Toast.

PANUNTA Also called fett'unta, a toasted piece of bread upon which oil, usually new or novello oil, is drizzled. Often the toasted bread is scraped with a garlic clove and sprinkled with salt.

PANUNTO Nickname of Domenico Romoli, who wrote *La singolar dottrina* in Venice in 1560.

PANZANELLA Bread salad from Tuscany made with chunks of old bread mixed with chopped tomatoes, basil, and other salad vegetables, dressed with oil and vinegar, and allowed to sit for a few hours before serving.

PANZAROTTE Also called chinulille. Sweet flour-and-egg ravioli filled with ricotta, candied fruit, chocolate, rum, and sugar, then fried in lard and oil. A specialty of Calabria, and often made around Easter.

PANZEAROTTI (PANZEROTTI) Deep-fried pastry turnovers filled with chopped ham, cheese, parsley, and egg, or with mozzarella and tomato. The term was originally Neapolitan.

PAPAIA Papaya.

PAPALINA, ALLA In the style of the Pope; usually pasta with ham, eggs, cream, and Parmigiano-Reggiano.

PAPALINO (PAPALINA) Sprat (also called spratto), small fish in the herring family.

PAPAROT Typical Friulian soup made with yellow and white cornmeal and spinach.

PAPASSINO Small fried sweet typical of Sardinia made with dried fruit, flour, egg, sugar, lard, orange, and spices. Also called pabassino and papassinu. Tradionally made during the feast of All Saints' Day.

PAPAVERI, AI With poppy seeds.

PAPERINA Gosling.

PAPPA (PANCOTTO) Soup thickened with stale bread, containing seasonal vegetables, a drizzle of oil, and a sprinkle of cheese.

PAPPA AL POMODORO Tuscan bread-and-tomato soup with oil, garlic, and basil.

PAPPARDELLE Wide egg noodles with either flat or crinkly edges.

PAPRICA DOLCE Sweet paprika.

PARDULAS (CASADINAS) Sweets made in Sardinia in the shape of a basket, with fresh cheese or ricotta, egg, saffron, citrus zest, and sugar. They are baked in the oven or fried, and drizzled with honey.

PARMIGIANA, ALLA Describing vegetables or meat cooked with butter and then topped with grated Parmigiano-Reggiano and baked crisp.

PARMIGIANO-REGGIANO Cheese of 100 percent cow's milk. Large, barrel-shaped, about 70 pounds, salted in brine, brushed and turned regularly, and aged until it matures with a hard rind. Made all year long, but there are special names tied to the time of manufacturing; like Maggiano from spring, for example. It is used as an appetizer, grated and served in soups, over pasta, in stuffings, and in baking. High in calcium and granular in texture.

PARROZZO Derived from pane rozzo, a type of sweet bread from the Pescara area in Abruzzo, made with flour, toasted almonds, sugar, and egg, and covered with chocolate.

PASQUALINA, TORTA Typical torte prepared around Genova at Easter time with thirty-three layers of puff-pastry dough (Christ's age when he was crucified). It is made in a simpler form throughout the year and sold in shops and "tavole calde," literally meaning "hot tables," but more like self-service restaurants. Usually the dough is filled with ricotta, spinach, artichokes, and other vegetables.

PASSAPATATE (SCHIACCIAPATATE) Potato ricer.

PASSATA Purée.

PASSATELLI Pasta usually used in soup, typical of Emilia-Romagna. A short thick spaghetti, made with bread crumbs, eggs, and grated parmigiano.

PASSATO 1. Puréed soup, or skinned, seeded tomatoes, simmered with chopped onions, garlic, basil, bay leaf, and celery until reduced by half, then seasoned and passed through a food mill.

PASSAVERDURE Sieve or foodmill through which vegetables are passed.

PASSERA Plaice, a flat fish (like sole).

PASSERA PIANUZZA Flounder.

PASTA 1. Dough, paste. 2. A variety of extruded or cut dough shapes, fresh or dried, made basically from flour, water, and sometimes eggs and salt (also possibly oil). 3. Pastry.

PASTA ALLE ACCIUGHE Pasta with tomato sauce, anchovies, and clams.

PASTA ALLE SARDE Layers of macaroni, fennel, and fresh sardines, cooked in a pie plate and served cold.

PASTA ALL'UOVO Fresh or dried pasta made from flour and eggs.

PASTA ASCIUTTA (PASTASCIUTTA) Generic term for dried or fresh pasta that is boiled, drained, and served with a sauce. Different from pasta in brodo, which is served with liquid.

PASTA CON LE SARDE Typical Sicilian dish of dried pasta, such as spaghetti, dressed with wild fennel, fresh sardines, raisins, and pine nuts.

PASTA CRESCIUTA Fritters whose batter is made with yeast-raised flour, water, and salt.

PASTA D'ACCIUGHE Anchovy paste.

PASTA E FAGIOLI Traditional soup made with pasta, white beans, and salt pork.

PASTA FATTA IN CASA Fresh pasta, usually made in the place where it is cooked.

PASTA FILATA Term for scalded-milk curds that are kneaded until they become an elastic paste easy to shape, such as mozzarella.

PASTA FROLLA (PASTA A FONCER) Short-crust pastry.

PASTA IN BRODO Pasta cooked and served in a broth.

PASTA LISCIA Smooth pasta.

PASTA REALE Small pasta grains for soup.

PASTA REALE Another name for marzipan.

PASTA RIGATA Ridged pasta, which has more mouth feel and to which sauce clings better than smooth pasta.

PASTA ROSSA Red or pink pasta, colored with tomatoes.

PASTA SECCA Dried pasta.

PASTA SFOGLIA Puff pastry.

PASTA VERDE Green pasta, colored with spinach.

PASTELLA Batter.

PASTICCERIA Pastry, pastry making, cakes, or cake shop.

PASTICCIATA Baked pasta, such as lasagna, but can also refer to a soup.

PASTICCINO Pastry.

PASTICCIO Savory meat pie with pasta, vegetables, or cheese.

PASTICCIO DI MACCHERONI Large double-crust deep pie made in a cake tin with a removable base, lined with a sweet egg-and-butter enriched pastry, filled with a mixture of cooked pasta, meatballs, peas, tomato sauce, and mozzarella, and filled with sweetened egg custard, covered with a pastry lid, and cooked.

PASTIERA Tart filled with ricotta.

PASTIERA NAPOLETANA A festive cheesecake baked in a shortbread crust, filled with ricotta, pine nuts, candied citron, and fruit, then baked. Usually made for Easter.

PASTINE Tiny pasta shapes for soup.

PASTISSADA Venetian term for stewed meat, typically horse or donkey.

PATATA (PLURAL PATATE) Potato.

PATATE ALLA BORGHESE Potatoes with butter and lemon.

PATATE ALLA VENEZIANA Diced potatoes fried with onion and herbs.

PATATE ARROSTITE Roasted potatoes.

PATATE ASADE Boiled potatoes.

PATATE DOLCI Sweet potatoes.

PATATE FRITTE Fried potatoes.

PATATE LESSE Boiled potatoes.

PATATE TENERE New potatoes.

PATELLA Limpet (barnacle, like a flat snail).

PATERNOSTRI Small pasta used in soup with a cylindrical shape and a hole in the middle.

PAVESE, ALLA Describing a classic mixed-meat broth topped with a slice of toasted bread and poached egg; attributed to the region of Lombardy, but eaten throughout Italy.

PAZLACHE See agnoletti.

PEARÀ Typical condiment from Verona that accompanies bollito misto. Its name derives from pepe, the pepper in the sauce. It consists of toasted bread, crumbled and mixed with bone marrow and plenty of ground black pepper. An antique recipe with medieval roots.

PECORA Sheep, ewe, mutton.

PECORINO See canestrato.

PECORINO CANESTRATO See canestrato.

PECORINO ROMANO Hard, cooked-curd sheep's-milk cheese made around Rome and in Sardinia, shaped into 4-to-6 pound cylinders. It has a pronounced, sharp sheep's-milk flavor, and a dense paste.

PECORINO SICILIANO Hard sheep's-milk cheese made in Sicily between October and June, formed in a basket mold. Has a pale yellow rind and pale paste, with a few peppercorns and a few holes.

PELATO Peeled, skinned.

PELLE DI PORCO Pork skin, cracklings.

PENNE Short tubes of pasta cut on the diagonal to resemble quill pens.

PENNE RIGATE Finely ribbed penne.

PENNETTE Thin penne.

PENNONI Large penne.

PEOCI Mussels, in Venetian dialect.

PEPATELLI Dry cookies that last a long time, made near Teramo around Christmas, and used to dunk into hot wine.

PEPATO Pecorino-type cheese containing crushed peppercorns.

PEPE Pepper.

PEPE DI CAIENNA Cayenne pepper.

PEPE FORTE Chili pepper.

PEPE NERO Black pepper.

PEPERATA Peppery sauce made with bone marrow and bread crumbs and served with roasts (also called peverada).

PEPERONATA Type of ratatouille made with sweet onion, red and yellow sweet peppers, tomatoes, and some garlic, often served as a cold antipasto.

PEPERONCINO Red pepper flakes.

PEPERONE Sweet pepper.

PEPERONI GIALLI Sweet yellow peppers.

PERCIATELLI See bucatini.

PERA (PLURAL PERE) Pear.

PERSICATA Paste made from peaches, dried and cut into squares.

PESCA 1. Peach (plural pesche). 2. Fishing; *andare a pesca* is "to go fishing."

PESCA NETTARINA Nectarine.

PESCATORA, ALLA Describing a preparation of pasta or rice with seafood, usually shellfish and mollusks.

PESCE (PLURAL PESCI) Fish.

PESCE AL CARTOCCIO Fish baked in parchment paper.

PESCE AZZURRO Blue fish (literally), usually used to describe fish that lives in deep water, such as anchovies, tuna, and swordfish.

PESCECANE Dogfish, shark.

PESCE DA TAGLIO Large cuts of fish that can be portioned, like halibut.

PESCE SAN PIETRO John Dory.

PESCE SPADA Swordfish.

PESCE STOCCO Stockfish, dried cod.

PESCE VOLANTE Flying fish.

PESCHE NOCI Nectarines.

PESTATA Mashing together ingredients, often using a mortar and pestle, to create a flavorful base for a recipe.

PESTO Traditional Ligurian condiment. Basil, pine nuts, grated cheese, olive oil, and garlic pounded or processed together, making a green paste used to dress pasta, particularly in the region of Liguria.

PESTO ALLA SICILIANA Also called mataroccu. Typical of the Marsala area, similar to pesto genovese.

PESTO GENOVESE Basil, parsley, pine nuts, and olive oil, pounded or processed together, making a green paste used to dress pasta, with the addition of cooked potato cubes and string beans particularly in the region of Liguria.

PETTI DI POLLO Chicken breasts.

PETTINE Small scallops.

PETTO Breast of an animal, brisket.

PEVERADA Sauce in which black pepper is prevalent, often used in the fourteenth century on bread and used to conserve meat.

PIACERE, A Consumer's choice.

PIADA (PIADINA) Soft flatbread, slightly leavened, usually split open when cooked and served warm, filled with sausage, ham, or spinach, and ricotta.

PIATTI Dishes, plates of food.

PIATTO DEL GIORNO Dish of the day.

PICCANTE Hot, spicy.

PICCATA Small medallions of meat, usually veal, served in lemon sauce.

PICCIONCELLO Pigeon.

PICCIONE Pigeon.

PICCOLO Small.

PIEDINI Feet, trotters.

PIEMONTE, CUCINA DEL The region is composed of a rice-producing plain, borders with Lombardy, and has territory in the Alps. Each area has a different cuisine. That of the plains around Novara and Vercelli is very similar to Lombardy's. Typical dishes are panissa from Vercelli and paniscia from Novara, both made with rice, beans, vegetables, and pork. Also well known is the salami cured in lard known as salamin d'la duja. The area around Alba, the Langhe, and Roero produces some wonderful wines, such as Barolo and Barbaresco, and offers some great meat dishes, such as fassone and sanato. There is also a prolific use of peppers. The prized white truffle hails from this area, and is shaved on risotto and the long, thin fresh egg pasta known as tajarin in dialect. Other dishes include bagna cauda, fondue, and finanziera.

PIGNATTA Earthenware cooking pot.

PIMPINELLA Salad burnet, herb that tastes like cucumber.

PINAROLI Small fungus found in pine woods.

PINOLI (SINGULAR PINOLO) Pine nuts (often pignoli in English).

PINZA Sweet or savory bread made with different grains, raisins, and other dried fruit, usually round; a very rustic bread, usually made in the Veneto and Emilia-Romagna.

PINZIMONIO Mixture of olive oil, salt, and pepper used as a dressing for raw vegetables.

PISELLI Peas.

PISELLI ALLA ROMANA Peas cooked in butter with chopped onions and ham.

PISELLI SECCHI Dried split peas.

PISTACCHIO Pistachio nuts, often used in stuffings and desserts. In Italy, the most famous are from Bronte, Sicily.

PISTOCCO Paper-thin crispbread; also called carta di musica.

PITTA Flatbread pizza from Calabria with various toppings.

PITTA MANIATA Sandwich of pitta filled with eggs, cheese, sausages, and peppers.

PITTA 'NCHIUSA Sandwich of pitta filled with nuts and raisins moistened with grape juice.

PITULLE Yeast-raised plain flour dough mixed with a selection of chopped onions, sun-dried tomatoes, olive, capers, anchovies, and mushrooms, allowed to rise again, and then fried in small teaspoonfuls until golden and puffed up.

PIZZA Yeast-raised dough rolled out into thin circles covered with tomato sauce, oregano, and pieces of mozzarella, with various additional toppings such as anchovies or sausages, then cooked quickly in the oven until the cheese melts and bubbles.

PIZZA DI RICOTTA Cheesecake.

PIZZA DOUGH Yeast dough made of flour, warm water, and olive oil. Allowed to rise, and then punched down several times.

PIZZAIOLA Sauce made from peeled and seeded tomatoes with garlic, parsley, oregano, and other seasonings. Sometimes with peppers and mushrooms.

PIZZA NAPOLETANA Best-known of all pizza types, an individual round pie, in its simplest form with mozzarella, tomato, olive oil, and basil, cooked in a wood-burning oven. The center of the finished pie is wet and juicy while the "cornicione" border is puffy and very crisp.

PIZZELLE 1. Deep-fried dough served with tomato sauce and fillings. 2. Thin circular cookies baked on a hot patterned griddle and bent while still hot to form a cone for filling with various creams.

PIZZETTE Dough made from flour, eggs, Gorgonzola or similar cheese, and butter, plus seasonings. The dough is rolled out, cut into shapes, glazed with egg white, and baked.

PIZZOCCHERI Short, oddly cut flat pasta made from buckwheat flour.

POLENTA Fine yellow cornmeal. Used as a thick porridge, and also used to make bread or gnocchi. The cornmeal is cooked in salted water. It is often left to cool, and then sliced and fried.

POLENTA AL FORNO Baked polenta with sausage in a meat sauce and covered with cheese.

POLENTA ALLA BERGAMASCA Polenta baked with tomatoes, sausage, and cheese.

POLENTA TARAGNA Polenta flour with some added buckwheat flour. Traditionally from the Valtellina area in Lombardy.

POLLAME Poultry.

POLLANCA Young chicken or turkey.

POLLASTRO Young chicken.

POLLO Chicken.

POLLO ALLA CONTADINA Chicken fried in oil, mixed with potatoes, then stewed with chopped, seeded, and peeled tomatoes with seasonings and a little wine until tender. Literally translated as "peasant woman's chicken."

POLLO ALLA MARENGO Chicken stewed in stock and white wine with tomatoes, mushrooms, parsley, black olives, and seasonings.

POLPA Piece of meat with no bones. Also, flesh of fruits.

POLPESSA Warm-water octopus.

POLPETTA Meatball; a round ball that can be prepared with meat, vegetables, or fish, then fried, baked, or cooked in a sauce.

POLPETIELLO See polpo.

POLPETT Milanese dialect for involtini or small meat rolls.

POLPETTINE Small meatballs.

POLPETTINE DI SPINACI Spinach-flavored-and-colored dumplings.

POLPETTONE 1. Meat or fish loaf. 2. Mixture of meat and/or vegetables bound with egg and baked.

POLPO Octopus.

POMODORI DI MAGRO ALLA SARDA Tomatoes stuffed with anchovies, tuna, and eggplant, then baked.

POMODORINI Small tomatoes.

POMODORO Tomato.

POMPELMO Grapefruit.

PORCHETTA Suckling pig.

PORCINI Mushroom that gets it name from being shaped like a little piglet.

PORRO Leek.

PRAIO Sea bream.

PRANZO Lunch.

PREBOGGION Collection of wild herbs used in the cooking of fritatte or soups in Liguria, usually consisting of parsley, wild chard, sow thistle, burnet, dogtooth, and borage, all boiled first.

PREZZEMOLO Parsley.

PRIMA COLAZIONE Breakfast.

PRIMAVERA Spring. Also, a garnish of raw or blanched spring vegetables.

PRIMIZIA Word used to describe herbs, fruits, and vegetables that are the first of the season, usually indicating something special.

PRIMO SALE First salt; indicates the first stage of aging and salting process.

PROFUMATO Flavored with (herbs, spices, seasonings).

PROSCIUTTO Fresh ham preserved by salt curing and air drying. Served in thin slices, usually as an antipasto, also used in cooking.

PROSCIUTTO COTTO Cooked ham, boned and pressed into a typical ham shape.

PROSCIUTTO CRUDO See prosciutto.

PROSCIUTTO DI MONTAGNA Type of prosciutto, usually cured in the mountains, with a more rustic flavor and darker color.

PROSCIUTTO DI PARMA Prosciutto produced around the town of Parma, salt-cured, then air-dried for at least 6 months. It is branded on the skin with a crown; only the prosciutto from this area has this brand.

PROSECCO Sparkling white wine used as an aperitif or as a base for cocktails (such as the Bellini, combining prosecco and peach purée). It is made mostly in the Veneto and Friuli–Venezia Giulia.

PROVOLA Soft spun-curd cheese made with buffalo or cow's milk made like mozzarella but firmer. Formed into pear shapes, string-tied on top, and left to air-dry for 2 to 3 months or more.

PROVOLONE Hard, smooth-textured yellow cheese made from unpasteurized cow's milk. Started from fermented whey, to which the rennet is added; the forming curd is warmed, then drained. It is molded into a variety of shapes, brined for some time, then strung and ripened at high humidity; it is brushed and washed before sale.

PROVOLONE AFFUMICATO Provolone cheese that is lightly smoked.

PROVOLONE PICCANTE Provolone used for grating, left to mature for up to 2 years. As it ages, it darkens and intensifies in flavor.

PUGLIA, CUCINA DELLA Pugliese food is mainly characterized by the local production of olive oil, pasta, and vegetables, as well as the fish from the region, which has such a long coastline. There is a minestra with fava beans and artichokes, or pasta with chickpeas (cicero e tria). There is frequent use of eggplants, and a well-known soup of fava beans and chicory. The soft-centered cheese burrata is produced in Andria, Puglia.

PUNTA DI VITELLO Breast of veal.

PUNTARELLE Winter chicory, a green that develops a head with thin, long leaves and short shoots, like an asparagus head; particularly eaten in Rome.

PUNTINA Pinch—for example, of salt.

PUNTINE Tiny pasta.

PUNTINO, A Medium well done, as meat.

PUREA (PURÈ) Purée.

PUREA DI PATATE Mashed potatoes.

QUADRETTI (QUADRUCCI) Small egg-pasta squares, best suited for soup.

QUAGLIA Quail.

QUAGLIE RINCARTATE Dish of quail wrapped in bread dough and baked. Native to Umbria.

QUATTRO SPEZIE Spice mix of pepper, nutmeg, juniper, and cloves; literally, "four spices."

QUATTRO STAGIONI Type of pizza in which the four quarters have four different kinds of cheese.

RABARBARO Rhubarb.

RADICI Roots.

RADISSER Radishes.

RAFANO Radish, also horseradish.

RAFANO TEDESCO Horseradish.

RAFFREDDATO Chilled.

RAGÙ Sauce made of olive oil, cooked meat, and garlic, sometimes also with tomato.

RAGUSANO Hard cheese with a sharp flavor from Sicily, made in rectangular blocks, matured for 3 months for dessert, and for up to 12 months for grating.

RAMARINO Rosemary.

RAMOLACCIO Horseradish, spicy root.

RANA PESCATRICE Monkfish.

RANE FRITTE Fried frog's legs.

RANOCCHIO Edible frog.

RAPA Turnip.

RAPATA Rice-and-turnip soup from Lombardy.

RAPE ROSSE Beet.

RAPINI Broccoli rabe.

RASCHERA Semihard cow's-milk cheese, made in a square with a soft yellow paste and a few holes.

RATATOUILLE Vegetable ragout made of stewed vegetables.

RAVANELLO Radish root.

RAVIOLI Egg pasta that is cut round and made with a filling of cheese, spinach, ground meat, or other items. The filling is placed in small portions on a sheet of egg pasta, which is egg-washed around each portion of filling. A second layer of pasta is placed on top, and the layers are cut out in circles with the filling in the middle of each. Boiled, and served with a sauce.

RAVIOLI DOLCI Raviloi from Liguria, stuffed with beef marrow and candied fruit, fried, and dredged in sugar.

RAZZA Common skate, the fish.

RAZZA CHIODATA Thornback ray.

RETE Pig's caul (fat covering the intestines).

RETICELLA Pig's caul.

RIBES Red currant.

RIBES NERO Black currant.

RIBOLLITA Typical Tuscan soup, with beans and kale, cooked twice—literally, "boiled twice." Sometimes bread is added to it.

RICCIARELLI Almond biscuits, particularly in Siena.

RICCIO DI MARE Sea urchin.

RICCIOLA Amberjack fish.

RICCIOLINA Curly endive.

RICCIOLINI Pasta curls.

RICCO Rich.

RICOTTA Soft cow's- or sheep's-milk cheese made from whey enriched with milk or cream. Used in Italian cooking; also eaten as dessert with fruit or nuts. It can be matured for grating, and also smoked.

RICOTTA ROMANA Ricotta made with the whey left over from making Pecorino Romano.

RICOTTA SALATA MOLITERNA Semihard cooked-curd cheese made from the whey of sheep's milk. The filtered curd is salted and formed into cylinders.

RIGATO Ridged, as the surface of pasta.

RIGATONI Tube-shaped pasta with ridges on the outside.

RIMESTATO Stirred or scrambled.

RIPIENO Stuffed with, or stuffing.

RISETTI Croquettes made with tiny anchovies and sardines.

RISI E BISI Classic Venetian soup prepared with rice and peas.

RISO Rice.

RISO AL FORNO Meat sauce with rice baked in the oven.

RISO ALLA MILANESE Rice boiled in meat broth with saffron and served with butter and cheese.

RISO ALLA PIEMONTESE Rice with a chicken or meat sauce.

RISO ALLA RISTORI Rice with cabbage, bacon, and sausage.

RISO ALLA SICILIANA Rice with eggplant, tomato, parsley, and basil, au gratin with cheese, and baked.

RISO COMMUNE Cheapest rice, common rice.

RISO RICCO Boiled rice with a cream-and-cheese sauce.

RISOTTO Rice dish made with Arborio or Carnaroli rice sautéed in butter or oil with chopped onion (other flavoring elements can be added as well); a splash of white wine is added over the heat; when it is absorbed, hot stock is progressively added while constantly stirring. The dish is creamy and moist.

RISOTTO ALLA MILANESE Risotto made with chopped onions, flavored with saffron, marrow, and Parmigiano-Reggiano. Served by itself or as an accompaniment to osso buco.

RISOTTO AL SALTO Milanese preparation in which leftover risotto is made into a small patty and fried.

RISOTTO AI CALAMARI Risotto flavored with chopped squid, colored with ink from the squid.

RISOTTO POLESANO Risotto with eel, mullet, and sea bass.

RISTRETTO Reduced, concentrated.

ROBIOLA Soft surface-ripened cow's-milk cheese from Lombardy and Piedmont. The curd is cast into square molds to drain and then removed and cut into four pieces, dry-salted or brined, and ripened at high humidity.

ROBIOLINI Very small, soft, raw cow's-milk cheese curdled with acid whey and rennet and ripened for 10 to 15 days at high humidity.

ROGNONE Kidney.

ROMBO Turbot.

ROMBO CHIODATO Turbot.

ROSMARINO Rosemary.

ROSOLARE To brown in a pan on the stovetop.

ROSPO Monkfish.

ROSTICCERIA Rotisserie, or delicatessen.

ROSTICINI Small kebabs of sheep meat roasted on an open fire in Abruzzo.

ROTINI Small corkscrew-shaped pasta.

ROTOLO Roll.

RUCOLA (RUGOLA) Rocket. Rucola, arugula.

RUGHETTA (RUCHETTA) Small rocket. Rucola, arugula.

RUOTI Small wagon-shaped pasta.

RUOTINI Small ruoti.

RUTA Rue; herb with small greenish-blue leaves that is bitter and often used, soaked in grappa, as a digestif.

SALAME Type of cased sausage named after Salamis, which was a city of the Roman Empire in Cyprus. Salame is variable in composition and texture, although, with few exceptions, it is 100 percent meat with flavorings, and is usually known by a regional name in Italy.

SALAME CASALINGO Homemade salami.

SALAME COTTO Type of salami containing pork and peppercorns with herbs, cooked in the casing and then cured.

SALAME DI PORCO Pork salame.

SALAME FELINO Salami of pure pork mixed with white wine, flavored with garlic and whole peppercorns, made in the town of Felino.

SALAME FINOCCHIONA Large salami of pure pork flavored with fennel.

SALAME FIORENTINO Tuscan salami made of pork.

SALAME GENOVESE Salami made of roughly equal parts veal and fatty pork.

SALAMELLA DI CINGHIALE Wild-boar sausage.

SALAME MILANESE Salami made with 50 percent lean pork, 20 percent fat pork, and 30 percent beef or veal, flavored with garlic and white peppercorns, air-dried and matured for 2 to 3 months.

SALAME NAPOLETANO Long thin salami from Naples made of pork and beef, seasoned with ground pepper.

SALAME SARDO Salami from Sardinia flavored with red pepper.

SALAME UNGHERESE Hungarian-style salami made in Italy from finely chopped pork, pork fat, beef, and garlic, moistened with white wine, and flavored with paprika and other seasonings.

SALAMIN D'LA DUJA Soft, mild salami preserved in fat in a special pot called a duja.

SALAMINI Small salami.

SALAMINI DI CINGHIALE Strong-flavored sausage made of wild-boar meat and preserved in brine or oil.

SALAMOIA Salted pickling liquid or brine.

SALATINA Fresh salad leaves.

SALATO Salted, savory.

SALATURA Ancient tradition of salting meats to conserve them. The salt dehydrates and penetrates the meat it is placed on, and is antibacterial.

SALE Salt.

SALE GROSSO Coarse salt.

SALE MARINO Sea salt.

SALMI, IN In a rich wine sauce, usually used for game.

SALMISTRATO Pickled, cured in brine.

SALMONE Salmon.

SALMONE AFFUMICATO Smoked salmon.

SALSA Sauce, gravy, ketchup.

SALSA ALLA PIZZAIOLA Tomato sauce with garlic, basil, oregano, and chopped parsley, sometimes with added mushrooms and peppers, served with meat poultry and pasta.

SALSA COMUN Spice mixture of cinnamon, cloves, pepper, and ginger with a little coriander seed and saffron.

SALSA DI NOCI Skinned walnuts processed with moistened bread, parsley, salt, oil, and a little garlic, mixed into cream, and served with ravioli.

SALSA ROSSA Sauce made from sautéed shallots in butter and oil, tomato, chopped carrots, roasted and skinned chopped red peppers, and some peperoncino, simmered until amalgamated.

SALSA VERDE Oil-and-vinegar mixture flavored with crushed garlic, anchovy essence or chopped salted anchovies, chopped parsley, and capers. Served with salads, cold meats, and hard-boiled eggs.

SALSICCE E FAGIOLI Tuscan dish of cannellini beans and sausage with garlic, tomatoes, and sage.

SALSICCIA BOLOGNESE Sausage containing minced heart and lungs.

SALSICCIA DI FEGATO Sausage made with liver and flavored with pepper and fennel seeds.

SALSICCIA FRESCA (LUGANEGA) Small pure pork sausage flavored with Parmigiano-Reggiano, from northern Italy.

SALSICCIA NAPOLETANA A pork-and-beef sausage flavored with ground red pepper.

SALSICCIA SALAMELLA Thicker fresh sausage divided into links and looped with string.

SALSICCIA SECCA Dried sausage.

SALSICCIA TOSCANA Sausage flavored with garlic, pepper, and aniseed.

SALTATO Sautéed.

SALTIMBOCCA Meat dish of thin slices of veal and ham together with sage and seasonings, rolled, and sautéed in butter and wine.

SALTO Turned over and fried, sautéed.

SALUME Salt pork.

SALUMERIA Delicatessen, shop selling mostly cured meat products.

SALUMI Salted meats, cured meats.

SALVIA Sage.

SAMBUCA Liqueur produced from anise and sambuco flower. The liqueur is white and clear, and smells a bit like licorice.

SAMBUCO Elder, a small tree with white flowers which can be used in gelatins and syrups. The dark purple berries are used in jams and liqueurs.

SANGUE Blood.

SANGUE, AL Rare, as meat.

SANGUINACCIO Blood pudding.

SAN MARZANO Plum tomato typically grown in San Marzano, near Naples, in soil that is heavily concentrated in volcanic ash. The tomato has a lot of pulp and few seeds.

SAOR, IN Pickled.

SAPORE Flavor.

SAPOROSO Flavorful. Complexly flavored.

SAPOTA Sapodilla.

SARACENO Buckwheat.

SARAGO Sea bream.

SARDA Sardine.

SARDEGNA, CUCINA DELLA Typically a shepherd's cuisine, Sardinian cuisine reflects the many cultures that have passed through the island throughout the centuries. The bread in Sardinia is often flat and crispy, pane carasau or carta di musica. Pasta—maccarones and malloredus, semolina pastas—are dressed with sheep's-cheese and meat sauces, and, in the case of malloredus, also flavored with saffron, which grows in Sardinia. Fregula—crumblike, small saffron-semolina balls—are used in soups. Meat, especially lamb, is often cooked on the grill over coals, including such dishes as lamb-and-lard kebabs with sheep intestines, and lamb stew with wild fennel. Because it is an island, the cuisine also includes fish, soups such as buridda, made near Cagliari, or lobster Catalana.

SARDELLE Sardines, salted and preserved in tin cans or wooden buckets.

SARDINA Sardine.

SARGO Sea bream.

SASSEFRICA (SALSEFICCA) Salsify.

SATUREIA Savory, the herb.

SAURO Sorrel.

SAURSUPPE Tripe soup.

SAVOIARDI (SINGULAR SAVOIARDO) Sponge finger cookies.

SBATTERE To whip or whisk.

SBIRA Substantial soup of meat and tripe typical of Genova. The name probably comes from "sbirro," an undercover cop, who would or could eat such a substantive soup to keep himself full during stakeouts.

SBOLLENTARE Process of placing vegetables or meat in boiling salted water, or water with vinegar, before actually beginning their true cooking process. This is often done to eliminate a bitter taste or excess salt in cured meats.

SBRISOLONA Flat, crumbly, crisp cake made with a mixture of wheat flour and cornmeal and chopped almonds.

SCACCIATA Stuffed focaccia typical of Catania.

SCALCIONE (FOCACCIA DEL VENERDÌ SANTO) Tart filled with a mixture of fennel, endive, anchovies, olives, and capers, usually made on Good Friday.

SCALOGNI Shallots.

SCALOPPINE Thin cut of veal or pork fillet, either breaded and fried or floured and fried.

SCALOPPINA ALLA MILANESE Veal cutlet, breaded and fried.

SCAMORZA Cow's-milk cheese similar to but firmer than mozzarella.

SCAMPO (PLURAL SCAMPI) White, yellow, and red small shrimp with ten legs.

SCAPECE Spanish name for a marinade for cooked fish made of onions, vinegar, olive oil, pine nuts, and raisins, similar to saor.

SCAROLA Escarole, endive.

SCARPAZZONE Dough-and-vegetable tart from Emilia-Romagna, similar to erbazzone but with less dough.

SCHIACCIATA Very thin yeast-raised bread with olive oil and sometimes herbs.

SCHIACCIATO Crushed, flattened.

SCHIAFFONI Macaroni made by hand in Campania.

SCHIDIONATA Spit-roasted.

SCHIUMARE To skim.

SCIATTI Pancakes filled with cheese and grappa, served hot.

SCIROPPATO Sweetened in syrup.

SCIROPPO Syrup.

SCIROPPO D'ACERA Maple syrup.

SCIROPPO DI ZUCCHERO Sugar syrup.

SCORZA Skin, rind, peel.

SCORZABIANCA Herbaceous root plant, long in form, with yellow skin and soft, white interior pulp.

SCORZONE Black truffle about the size of an egg; though it has a good taste, it is less prized than the white truffle.

SCORZONERA Long black root of a member of the daisy family, used in salads.

SCOTTADITO Small cutlets eaten with the fingers while hot; literally, "burning fingers."

SCOTTARE To scald.

SCRIGNI DI VENERE Large stuffed pasta shells.

SCRIPELLE 'MBUSSE O'NFUSSE Traditional Abruzzese soup from near Teramo, made with thin crêpes rolled and stuffed with pecorino or parmigiano, placed in a bowl, and covered with chicken soup.

SCUNGILLI Small conch, gastropod mollusk.

SEADAS Traditional Sardinian fried, stuffed pasta rounds (like ravioli) that can be served as an appetizer or as a dessert. They are usually large (about 4 inches in diameter), but smaller sizes can be made to be hors d'oeuvres. Seadas are stuffed with provolone cheese and drizzled with honey while still hot. Cheese always goes well with honey, and this combination yields a salty and sweet fritter.

SECCHIELLI Dried chestnuts.

SECCO Dry, dried.

SECONDA PORTATA Main dish or course of a meal.

SECONDO Main course of a meal.

SECONDO GRANDEZZA According to size.

SEDANI Ridged macaroni; literally, "celery stalks."

SEDANI CORTI Short sedani, the classic pasta for minestrone.

SEDANO Celery.

SEDANO DI VERONA Celeriac.

SEDANO RAPA Celeriac.

SEGALE Rye, rye bread.

SELLA Saddle of lamb or veal.

SELVAGGINA Game, venison.

SELVATICO Wild, uncultivated.

SEMI 1. Seeds. 2. Half.

SEMIDURE Soft-boiled, as eggs.

SEMIFREDDO Semisoft ice cream on a crushed cookie base.

SEMINI Small seed-shaped pasta.

SEMOLINO Semolina, flour made from durum wheat.

SEMPLICE, ALLA Cooked simply.

SENAPE Mustard.

SEPPIA Cuttlefish.

SERVIZIO Service charge in a restaurant.

SESAMO Sesame.

SFILATINO Bread from Tuscany.

SFINCIONE Sicilian pizza with a thick, soft base topped with tomato, cheese, anchovies, and olives.

SFINGI Sweet biscuits. Also, fried dough pieces.

SFOGLIA Sheet of pasta dough.

SFOGLIATA Flaky pastry.

SFOGLIATELLE Neapolitan specialty cake, individual triangle-shaped cakes with many crispy layers stuffed with ricotta and candied fruit.

SFORMATO Molded, as food timbales.

SGOMBRO Mackerel.

SICILIA, CUCINA DELLA Sicilian cuisine is influenced by the many cultures that inhabited the island, from ancient Greek to ancient Roman, Arab, and Norman. In particular, the Arabs integrated couscous and the dessert cassata, and developed tuna and swordfish fishing around Sicily. Common dishes are pasta con le sarde (pasta with fresh sardines), riso con le melanzane palermitana (rice with eggplant), and pasta alla norma (pasta with ricotta and eggplant). Marzipan is a large part of the Sicilian pastry tradition.

SIERO DI LATTE Buttermilk or whey.

SILVANO Chocolate-meringue tart.

SMACAFAM Focaccia made in Trentino with buckwheat flour, chopped onion, and sliced sausage. A similar focaccia is made near Vicenza, known as macafam.

SOBBOLLIRE To simmer.

SODO Hard-boiled, as eggs.

SOFFIATO Soufflé.

SOFFRITTO Base made by slowly simmering chopped onions, carrots, and celery in oil; it can also include herbs, tomatoes, pepper, and pork products.

SOGLIOLA Sole fish, such as Dover sole.

SOIA Soy.

SOPPRESSATA Large sausage made from large ovals.

SOPRAFFINO Superfine olive oil.

SOPRESSA (COPA) Salt-cured pork sausage, air-dried, flavored with herbs, and sometimes smoked.

SORBETTO Sorbet.

SORPRESINE Tiny pasta shapes used in soups.

SOSPIRI Small custards with a cheese-and-egg filling; literally, "sighs."

SOTÈ Also written as "sauté," a French term used to describe cooking something over medium heat in a pan.

SOTTACETI Pickles or pickled vegetables; literally, "under vinegar."

SOTTO Under, or cured in, as in vinegar.

SOTTOACETO Pickled.

SOTTOBOSCO Describing a dessert made using strawberries, raspberries, and blueberries.

SOTT'OLIO Method of conserving foods, usually vegetables and fish, by submerging them in olive oil.

SPAGHETTI Thin strands of dried pasta, about 1 to 2 millimeters in diameter.

SPAGHETTI AGLIO E OLIO Spaghetti with garlic and olive oil.

SPAGHETTI AL BURRO Spaghetti with butter.

SPAGHETTI AL PESTO Spaghetti with a pesto sauce.

SPAGHETTI ALLA CARBONARA Spaghetti, bacon, cream, and sometimes beaten egg yolk added to it. Served with grated cheese.

SPAGHETTI ALL'AMATRICIANA Spaghetti with tomato sauce with sliced onions and bacon, sprinkled with grated pecorino cheese.

SPAGHETTI ALLA BOLOGNESE Spaghetti with a long-cooked tomato-and-ground-meat sauce.

SPAGHETTI ALLA CARRETTIERA Spaghetti with canned tuna, mushrooms, and tomatoes; literally, "cart driver's spaghetti."

SPAGHETTI ALLA MARINARA Spaghetti with garlicky tomato sauce, sometimes also with clams and mussels.

SPAGHETTI ALLA POMMAROLA Spaghetti with tomatoes, garlic, and sometimes capers, black olives, and parsley.

SPAGHETTI ALLE VONGOLE Spaghetti with a sauce of chopped clams, garlic, parsley, and olive oil.

SPAGHETTINI Thin version of spaghetti.

SPALLA 1. Shoulder of veal, pork, etc. 2. Cured and pressed shoulder of pork forced into a rectangular mold.

SPANOCCHI Large prawns.

SPEZIE Spices.

SPEZZATINO Light stew, usually of sautéed pieces of meat.

SPICCHI, IN In segments or sections.

SPICCHIO Clove, as of garlic.

SPIEDINO Skewered meat or shrimp.

SPIEDO, ALLO Grilled over charcoal.

SPIGOLA Sea bass.

SPINACI Spinach.

SPONGADA Sherbet made with stiffly beaten egg whites.

SPOSI Soft, small cream cheese.

SPRATTO Sprat. (See also papalino.)

SPREMUTO Squeezed, as orange juice.

SPRUZZARE To baste or sprinkle with a liquid.

SPUGNOLA Family of mushrooms with a very high cap, varying in color from brown to gray. These mushrooms are most often used in a cream sauce and used to dress pasta. Also known as morchella or morel.

SPUMA Mousse.

SPUMONI Light sweet cream made with mascarpone, typical of Piedmont. It can also be a type of gelato, such as a semifreddo.

STAGIONATO Aged, ripe, or mature.

STAGIONE Season of the year.

STALLINA, ALLA In the style of the stable, as with bacon and garlic.

STAMBECCO Wild goat.

STARNA DI MONTAGNA Grouse.

STECCO, ALLA On a skewer.

STELLINA ODOROSA Sweet woodruff.

STELLINE (STELLETTE) Very small pasta stars used in soup.

STINCO Shank of veal.

STIVALETTI Small varied pasta shapes; literally, "small boots."

STOCCAFISSO Stockfish, dried cod.

STORIONE Sturgeon.

STORTINI Small pasta crescents used in soup.

STOVIGLIE Earthenware.

STRACCETTI Thin slices, shreds.

STRACCHINO Soft cow's-milk cheese placed in square molds, and salted in brine.

STRACCHINO DI GORGONZOLA Cheese made in the town of Gorgonzola from the evening's and the following morning's cow's milk, brought down from pasture. The evening curd is cooled and mixed with the warm curd of the next morning.

STRACCIATA 1. Chiffonade. 2. Shredded.

STRACCIATE Flat cake.

STRACCIATELLA 1. Clear meat stock into which egg and grated Parmigiano-Reggiano or Grana Padano cheese are whisked. 2. Vanilla ice cream with chocolate chips.

STRACCIATO Scrambled, as eggs.

STRACOTTO Very slowly cooked pot roast or meat stew; literally, "overcooked."

STRANGOLAPRETI (STROZZAPRETI) Small dumplings; literally, "priest chokers."

STRAPAZZATO Whisked or scrambled eggs.

STRASCINARE (STRASCICARE) Verb used in southern Italy for a method of cooking in which the food, particularly vegetables like broccoli or chicory, is literally dragged in the pan.

STRASCINATI Pasta made in Basilicata of flour, lard, and water; strands of pasta are dragged along a wooden board, leaving an imprint on them.

STRASCINATI Baked ravioli with sauce.

STRAVECCHIO Very old, mature; used of cheese or other foods that improve with age.

STREGA Herbal liqueur (the name means "witch"), served as a digestif, which is a combination of many ingredients, including mint, fennel, and saffron.

STRINGOZZI Another name for Umbrian cariole, typical rustic tagliatelle.

STROZZAPRETI See strangolapreti.

STRUCCOLI Sweet pastry rolls filled with fruit or cream cheese.

STRUDEL Pastry with savory or sweet fillings, most commonly with apples and spices.

STRUFFOLI Small balls of fried dough rolled in hot honey, usually topped with sprinkles.

STRUTTO Lard.

STUCOLO (STRUCCOLO) Strudel that is layered rather than rolled.

STUFARE To braise.

STUFATINO (STUFATO) Beef braised in red wine with onions, tomatoes, celery, garlic, and ham.

SUCCO Juice.

SUCCU TUNDU See fregula.

SUFFRITTE Neapolitan dish made with pig's heart, lung, trachea, and spleen, also including tomato and peppers. It can be served on toasted bread, like a soup, or on pasta.

SUGO Gravy, juice, sauce.

SUGO, AL Served in a sauce.

SUGO DI CARNE Meat gravy.

SUINO Pork.

SULTANINA Raisins from white grape without seeds.

SUPERFINO Finest grade of rice, with large, long grains; Arborio is the best-known example.

SUPPLÌ Fried balls made from flavored cooked rice mixed with butter, Parmigiano-Reggiano, egg, and pepper, with a center filling of ham and cheese or tomato and chicken liver. Usually eaten as a snack or an antipasto.

SURGELATO Deep-frozen.

SUSINE Plums.

SUSINO SELVATICO Bullace, the fruit, a wild plum.

SVARIATI Assorted, varied.

TACCHINA Turkey hen.

TAGLIARINE (TAGLIATELLE) Flat noodles made with egg pasta, available fresh or dried.

TAGLIATA Piece of meat either grilled or cooked in a pan.

TAGLIATELLE Flat noodle pasta.

TAGLIATELLE VERDI Green tagliatelle made from egg-based pasta dough with spinach purée added.

TAGLIATO Cut or sliced.

TAGLIERINI Also known as tajarin, a handmade egg pasta from Piedmont, cut like medium-thick spaghetti, often served with truffle.

TAGLIOLINI Thinner tagliatelle.

TAJARIN See taglierini.

TALEGGIO Semisoft cow's-milk cheese from Lombardy. It is produced in squares and has a white paste with a few small holes. Very flavorful, and used frequently in Italian cooking.

TANNINO Tannin.

TARAGNA Type of polenta.

TARALLO (TARALLUCCIO) Typical of the Campania region, a round, twice-baked, bagel-shaped cracker often with fennel seeds.

TARASSACO Dandelion.

TARGONE Tarragon.

TAROCCO Type of orange.

TARTELETTA Tartlet.

TARTINA Canapé, tartine.

TARTUFATO With truffles.

TARTUFI DI CIOCCOLATO Chocolate truffles.

TARTUFO Truffle.

TARTUFO DI MARE Warty venus clam.

TAZZA Cup or small bowl.

TAZZINA Small cup, coffee cup.

TAZZINA, NELLA In the cup; coddled, as eggs.

TEGAME Heavy frying pan or casserole.

TEGAME, AL Fried or pot-roasted.

TEGAMINO, AL In a small pan; coddled, as eggs.

TEGLIA Wide, shallow baking dish or pie plate.

TELLINA Wedge shell clam.

TENERO Tender, fresh, soft.

TERRINA Terrine.

TESTA (TESTINA) Head of an animal, or cap of a mushroom.

TESTICOLI Testicles.

TIELLA Round baking dish. Pies of meat or seafood mixed with vegetables are usually baked in a tiella.

TIGLIO Lime.

TIMBALLO Hot pie or mold.

TIMO Thyme.

TIRAMISÙ Dessert made with mascarpone and coffee, probably originally from Venice.

TONNATO With tuna or a tuna sauce.

TONNETTO Little tunny, the fish.

TONNINO Smaller tuna.

TONNO Canned tuna.

TOPINAMBUR Jerusalem artichoke.

TORLO (TUORLO) Egg yolk.

TORRONE Nougat.

TORTA MARGHERITA Sponge cake dusted with cocoa powder.

TORTA PASQUALINA Easter pie with boiled eggs, beets, and cottage cheese layered with pastry crust and baked.

TORTELLATA ALLA CREMA Cream tart.

TORTELLI Variously shaped ravioli.

TORTELLI DI ZUCCA Tortelli filled with squash flavored with a mixture of fruit, mustard, and cheese.

TORTELLINI Small hat-shaped pasta filled with braised meat or cheese.

TORTELLINI IN BRODO Tortellini cooked in a meat broth.

TORTELLO Doughnut or sweet fritter.

TORTELLONI Large version of tortellini.

TORTIERA Cake tin.

TORTIGLIONE Tube pasta with a ridged turning line on the outside.

TORTINA Tartlet.

TORTINO Pie.

TORTONI Ice cream made with cream and sugar, flavored with maraschino cherries, chopped almonds, and rum.

TOSCANA, CUCINA DELLA Tuscan cuisine uses very little pasta and has a characteristically salt-less bread. Game sauce is often used, and there are many hearty vegetable soups, such as ribollita, which literally translates as "reboiled" or "twice boiled." The region produces much olive oil and also has a culture of cured meats, such as finocchiona, a salami laced with fennel seeds. Lesser parts of the animal are often used, such as offal and cockscomb; however, there is also a very important prime meat, the chianina, a large T-bone steak from white Maremma longhorn cattle. Beans are a staple of the cuisine, so much so that the Tuscans are called "mangia-fagioli," bean eaters.

TOSCANELLO Semihard sheep's-milk cheese from Tuscany and Sardinia made in cylinders, drained, molded, brined, and ripened. Yellow to white rind, and a dense white paste with a few small holes.

TOSTATO Toast; as adjective, toasted.

TOTANO Flying squid.

TOURNEDOS Fillet of beef.

TOVAGLIA Tablecloth.

TRANCIA Slice.

TRATTORIA Family-run restaurant, or one maintaining that style, usually serving local fare.

TRENETTE Ligurian name for a long, flat pasta similar to linguine.

TRENTINO–ALTO ADIGE, CUCINA DEL Trentino offers simple, local peasant food: the food of Alto Adige has German and Slavic influences. In Trentino, large gnocchi or dumplings made out of stale bread called canederli are served in soups, as a pasta course, or with roasted meats. There are many minestre, a lot of them using orzo or barley. In Alto Adige, cured meats, especially cured game meats, are popular. Dishes in this region with Austrian influence include goulash, strudel, and spaetzle.

TRIA Term used in Puglia and Sicily for tagliatelle made with durum wheat.

TRIFOLARE To cook chopped vegetables or other foods by sautéing in olive oil, garlic, and chopped parsley.

TRIGLIA Red mullet.

TRIGLIA DI FANGO Red mullet caught specifically near a delta with a muddy bottom.

TRIPPA Tripe.

TRIPPA ALLA FIORENTINA Thinly sliced tripe stewed with onions, tomatoes, and stock, served with white beans and grated cheese.

TRIPPA ALLA ROMANA Braised tripe with a cheese sauce.

TRITATO Finely chopped or minced.

TRITICALE Hybrid grain, cross between rye and wheat with a higher protein content than wheat.

TROFIE Long twisted gnocchi-shaped pasta typical of Recco in Liguria.

TROTA Trout.

TUBETTI (TUBETTINI) Very small pasta tubes used in soup, especially in bean and vegetable soups.

TUMA Sicilian cheese typical of the area near Messina and Catania, made with sheep's milk.

TUONI E LAMPI Bits of cooked pasta with cooked chickpeas; literally, "thunder and lightning."

TUORLO D'UOVO Egg yolk.

TURBANTE Ring mold for food; literally, "turban."

TUTTI FRUTTI Ice cream containing chopped dried or candied fruits; literally, "all fruits."

UBRIACO Drunk; cooked in wine, soaked in wine or liqueur.

UCCELLETTI Small birds.

UCCELLETTI SCAPPATI Small pieces of veal with bacon cooked on a skewer.

UCCELLI Birds.

ULIVA See oliva.

UMBRIA, CUCINA DELL' This region produces much olive oil and cures quite a bit of pork and game products. In Umbria one can find the black truffle Norcino, named after the Umbrian city Norcia, which is used with pasta. Main courses are usually braised or grilled meats, such as lamb, game, and pork. Crescia is a typical local flatbread cooked in ash, then stuffed with local cheeses, cold cuts, and salad greens.

UMIDO Stew.

UMIDO, IN Braised, stewed.

UOVA ALLA BELLA ROSINA Eggs served with mayonnaise.

UOVA CON PANCETTA Bacon and eggs.

UOVA DI BUFALA Small buffalo-milk mozzarella balls.

UOVA DI PESCE Fish roe; when dry-cured, called bottarga.

UOVA STRAPAZZATE Scrambled eggs.

UOVO (PLURAL UOVA) Egg.

UOVO AFFOGATO Poached egg.

UOVO AL BURRO Fried egg (in butter).

UOVO AL TEGAMINO Shirred egg.

UOVO SODO Hard-boiled egg.

UVA Grape.

UVA FRAGOLA Strawberry grape.

UVA PASSA Raisins and currants.

UVA SECCA Raisins and currants.

UVA SPINA Gooseberry.

UVA SULTANINA Raisins and currants.

UVETTA Smaller raisin.

VALERIANELLA Small-leafed lettuce in the valerian family.

VALLE D'AOSTA, CUCINA DELLA Mountain cuisine with lots of cheeses and fondues, as well as cabbage and pasta made with buckwheat or rye wheat. Lots of bacon and cured meats. Well known also for hearty soups, such as onion soup and almond soup. Costoletta alla valdostana, a veal chop stuffed with savory cheese and prosciutto, is a well-known and well-liked dish from the region.

VANIGLIA Vanilla.

VANIGLIATO Vanilla-flavored.

VASSOIO Tray or cheese board.

VECCHIA MANIERA, ALLA Prepared in the old-fashioned way.

VECCHIO Old, aged.

VEGETALE Vegetable.

VENETO, CUCINA DEL The geographic diversity of the region is reflected in its food. The cuisine from near Venice has fish as its main component, shellfish and whole fish, and many variations on seafood risotto. On the plains, many animals are raised, and a lot of beef, rabbits, and chicken are eaten. Some wonderful cheese comes from the region as well, such as Montasio and Asiago.

VENTAGLIO Scallop, the shellfish.

VENTAGLIO, A Scallop- or fan-shaped.

VENTRESCA 1. Belly of tuna. 2. Pork belly; pancetta.

VENTRESCA BOLLITA Boiled belly of tuna, considered to be the tastiest part.

VERACE Authentic, fresh, not canned, wild, local.

VERDE Green.

VERDE, SALSA Sauce made of parsley, anchovies, onion, and garlic, served with boiled meats.

VERDURE Vegetables, greens.

VERGINE High-quality, as in olive oil; literally, "virgin."

VERMICELLI Very fine, thin pasta, usually bundled up like a bird's nest and used in soups.

VERMUT Vermouth.

VERO Real, authentic.

VERZA Savoy cabbage.

VERZELATA Grey mullet.

VERZINI Small cooking sausages.

VERZOTTO Small stuffed balls of cabbage.

VESCICA Bladder, used as a sausage casing.

VIALONE NANO RICE Fine-grade short-grain rice. Used for soups as well as risotto.

VINCISGRASSI Typical lasagna from Le Marche, made with innards.

VIN SANTO Traditional Tuscan dessert wine (the name means "holy wine").

VIOLETTA, ALLA With crystallized violets.

VIRTÙ Typical Abruzzese minestrone; literally, "virtue."

VISCIOLA Sour cherry.

VITELLO Veal from milk-fed calves.

VITELLO ALLA GENOVESE Thin slices of veal cooked with wine and artichokes.

VITELLO DI LATTE Suckling calf.

VITELLONE Meat from up to 3-year-old beef cattle, darker than normal veal but lighter than beef.

VITELLO ALLA PARMIGIANA Veal Parmesan, veal cutlet breaded and fried, then baked with tomato sauce and cheese.

VITELLO TONNATO Cold roast veal thinly sliced, coated with a sauce made from canned tuna, capers, mayonnaise, and lemon juice.

VONGOLA VERACE Carpet-shell clam.

ZABAGLIONE (ZABAIONE) Warm dessert made of Marsala whipped with egg yolk and sugar.

ZABAGLIONE SAUCE Sauce made of Marsala, whipped eggs, and sugar, served warm on fruit desserts.

ZAFFERANO Saffron.

ZAMPE Feet, trotters.

ZAMPETTO Pig's leg.

ZAMPONE DI MODENA Sausage made of pork meat, cartilage, and skin from the pig's head, seasoned with spices and white wine, and packed into the emptied skin of the foot with trotters left on. It is aged for a week or two, then simmered for an hour or more and served with potatoes and a fruit-mustard sauce.

ZEPPOLE Fried raised dough balls sprinkled with powdered sugar.

ZIA, ALLA In the aunt's style, home-cooked.

ZIMINO Soup or stew of fish with white wine, tomatoes, mushrooms, and herbs.

ZITI Long lengths of thick macaroni.

ZITONI Thicker version of ziti.

ZITONI RIGATI Fluted or ridged ziti.

ZOCCOLO Dish where the base is a toasted piece of bread or rice; literally, "slipper."

ZUCCA Squash dish.

ZUCCA GIALLA Pumpkin.

ZUCCHERO Sugar.

ZUCCHETTI Small yellow squash.

ZUCCHINA (PLURAL ZUCCHINE) Zucchini.

ZUCCOTTO Molded dome-shaped, chocolate-covered dessert of ice cream and sponge cake.

ZUPPA Substantial soup, thickened with either bread or another farinaceous food.

ZUPPA ALLA CANAVESANA Cabbage, bread, and cheese layered in a deep casserole dish, soaked in broth, and browned in the oven.

ZUPPA DI PESCE Fish soup.

ZUPPA INGLESE English-style trifle, with a base of sponge cake or ladyfingers moistened in Marsala, covered with custard, and topped with whipped cream and glacéed fruit.

ZUPPA PAVESE Dish consisting of a slice of toast topped with a poached egg, sprinkled with grated Parmigiano-Reggiano or Grana Padano, and floated on beef broth.

ZUPPA RUSTICA Country-style soup containing potatoes, beans, and sausages.

INDEX

A Note About the Authors

Lidia Bastianich, Emmy award–winning public television host, best-selling cookbook author, restaurateur, and owner of a flourishing food and entertainment business has married her two passions in life—her family and food—to create multiple culinary endeavors.

Lidia's cookbooks, coauthored with her daughter Tanya, include *Lidia's Commonsense Italian Cooking, Lidia's Favorite Recipes, Lidia's Italy in America, Lidia Cooks from the Heart of Italy,* and *Lidia's Italy*—all companion books to the Emmy-winning and three-time-nominated television series *Lidia's Kitchen, Lidia's Italy in America,* and *Lidia's Italy,* which have aired internationally, in Mexico, Canada, Middle East, Croatia, and the UK. Lidia has also published *Lidia's Family Table, Lidia's Italian-American Kitchen, Lidia's Italian Table,* and *La Cucina di Lidia,* and three children's books: *Nonna Tell Me a Story: Lidia's Christmas Kitchen, Lidia's Family Kitchen: Nonna's Birthday Surprise,* and *Lidia's Egg-citing Farm Adventure.*

Lidia is the chef/owner of four acclaimed New York City restaurants—Felidia, Becco, Esca, and Del Posto, as well as Lidia's Pittsburgh and Lidia's Kansas City with her daughter Tanya. She is also the founder of Tavola Productions, an entertainment company that produces high-quality broadcast productions. Lidia also has a line of pastas and all natural sauces called LIDIA'S. Along with her son, Joe Bastianich, and Mario Batali and Oscar Farinetti, she opened Eataly, the largest artisanal Italian food and wine marketplaces in New York City, Chicago, and São Paulo, Brazil.

Tanya Bastianich Manuali's visits to Italy as a child sparked her passion for the country's art and culture. She dedicated herself to the study of Italian Renaissance art during her college years at Georgetown University, and earned a master's degree from Syracuse University and a doctorate from Oxford University. Living and studying in many regions of Italy for several years, she taught art history to American students in Florence, although she met her husband, Corrado Manuali, who is from Rome, in New York.

In 1996, Tanya created Esperienze Italiane, a custom-tour company devoted to the discovery of Italian food, wine, and art. Currently, Tanya is integrally involved in the production of Lidia's public television series as an owner and executive producer of Tavola Productions, and is active daily in the family restaurant business. She has also led the development of the website, lidiasitaly.com, and related publications and merchandise lines of tabletop items and cookware.

Together with her husband, Corrado, Tanya oversees the production and expansion of the LIDIA'S food line, which includes ten cuts of pasta, seven sauces, and fresh meals for nationwide distribution. Tanya has coauthored five cookbooks with her mother: *Lidia's Commonsense Italian Cooking, Lidia's Favorite Recipes, Lidia's Italy, Lidia Cooks from the Heart of Italy,* and *Lidia's Italy in America.* In 2010, Tanya coauthored *Reflections of the Breast: Breast Cancer in Art Through the Ages,* a social history/art history look at breast cancer in art from ancient Egypt to today. In 2014 Tanya coauthored a book with her brother, Joe, *Healthy Pasta.* Tanya and Corrado live in New York City with their children, Lorenzo and Julia.

A NOTE ON THE TYPE

This book was set in Adobe Garamond. Designed for the Adobe Corporation by Robert Slimbach, the fonts are based on types first cut by Claude Garamond (ca. 1480–1561). Garamond was a pupil of Geoffroy Tory and is believed to have followed the Venetian models, although he introduced a number of important differences, and it is to him that we owe the letter we now know as "old style." He gave to his letters a certain elegance and feeling of movement that won their creator an immediate reputation and the patronage of Francis I of France.

Composed by North Market Street Graphics
Lancaster, Pennsylvania

Printed and bound by RR Donnelley
Willard, Ohio

Designed by M. Kristen Bearse